Special thanks to Charles Merullo, Jennifer Jeffrey, and Franziska Payer at Endeavour.

The Oxford Illustrated Companion to the Bible was created by Black Dog and Leventhal in conjunction with Endeavour London Limited.

PHOTO CREDITS

Art Resource: Bildarchiv Preussischer Kulturbesitz/Art Resource, NY: 270; Cameraphoto Arte, Venice/Art Resource, NY: 58; Erich Lessing/Art Resource: 46, 72, 174, 271, 272; NYFinsiel/Alinari/Art Resource,NY: 38; Réunion des Musées Nationaux/Art Resource, NY: 269; The Jewish Museum, NY/Art Resource, NY: 214

Shutterstock: 9, 10, 29, 33, 36, 44, 70, 90, 131, 132, 136, 148, 154, 165, 187, 198, 202, 203, 209, 213, 216, 227, 246

All other images courtesy of **Getty Images,** including the following which have additional attributions:

Agence France Presse: 121,285; **Bridgeman Art Library:** front cover(1L)/Tretyakov Gallery,Moscow, (2L)/ Rafael Valls Gallery, London,(2R)/ Louvre,Paris, bottom/Private Collection; back cover (1L)/ Hotel Dieu, Beaune, France, (1R)/ Vatican Museums & Galleries, Vatican City, (2R)/Kunsthistorisches Museum, Vienna, Austria; title page (1L)/ Tretyakov Gallery,Moscow, (2L)/ Rafael Valls Gallery, London, (2R)/ Louvre, Paris; contents page/Universitatsbibliothek, Gottingen, Germany; iv/St. Bavo Cathedral, Ghent, Belgium; 1/Southampton City Art Gallery, UK; 3/Musee des Beaux-Arts,Valenciennes,France; 8/Hotel Dieu, Beaune, France; 12/Sanctuary of Santa Casa, Loretto,Italy; 15/Sant'Apollinare Nuovo,Ravenna,italy; 16/Duomo,Orvieto,Italy; 17/Private Collection,Bonhams; 18/Musee des Beaux-Arts, Strasbourg; 23/Hermitage,St Petersburg; 24/National Museums & Galleries of Wales,Cardiff; 27/Louvre,Paris; 28/Kunsthistorisches Museum,Vienna; 35/Kunsthistorisches Museum,Vienna; 48/ Kunsthistorisches Museum,Vienna ; 51/Musee d;Orsay,Paris; 53/Musee des Beaux-Arts,Caen; 54/Prado, Madrid; 57/Bibliotheque Sainte-Genevieve, Paris; 62/Galleria Borghese, Rome; 63/Musee National de la Renaissance,Ecouen,France; 65/Kremlin Museums, Moscow; 66/ Musee des Beaux-Arts,Tours, France; 71/Musee de Tesse, Le Mans, France; 74/Universitatsbibliothek, Gottingen, Germany;77/ Musee des Beaux-Arts, Quimper; 82/Private Collection; 83/Vatican Museums & Galleries, Vatican City; 84/Dahesh Museum of Art, New York; 85/Vatican Museums & Galleries, Vatican City; 88/Louvre,Paris;89/Vatican Museums & Galleries, Vatican City; 91/Alliance Israelite Universelle,Paris; 92/British Museum,London; 95/Private Collection, Archives Charmet; 98/Musee des Beaux-Arts, Angiers,France; 101/Vatican Museums & Galleries, Vatican City;102/Deir el-Medina, Thebes; 103/San Francesco della Vigna, Venice; 109/Musee des Beaux-Arts, Arras; 111/Koninklijk Museum voor Schone Kunsten, Antwerp, Belgium; 113/Bibliotheque de l'Ecole des Beaux-Arts,Paris; 115/Musee des Beaux-Arts,Rouen; 118/Private Collection; 119/Private Collection;124/Yale Center for British Art, Paul Mellon Collection; 125/Private Collection, Richard & Kailas Icons,London; 126/Burrell Collection,Glasgow; 129/Private Collection, The Stapleton Collection; 130/Bibliotheque Nationale, Paris; 135/National Gallery, London; 137/University of Liverpool Art Gallery and Collections,UK; 138/Santa Maria della Grazie,Milan; 141/Private Collection, Christie's; 145/Collegiata, San Gimignano,Italy; 147/Louvre, Paris; 150/Museo Regionale,Messina,Sicily; 153/Bibliotheque Municipale,Moulins, France; 157/Church of Saint George, Madaba,Jordan; 159/Biblioteca Marciana,Venice;166/Private Collection; 167/Musee des Beaux-Arts, Dunkirk; 169/Tretyakov Gallery,Moscow; 182/Louvre,Paris; 188/Galleria Sabauda,Turin; 189/Museo Lazaro Galdiano, Madrid; 190/Musee des Beaux-Arts,Arras; 193/Alte Pinakothek,Munich; 194/Musee de la Chartreuse, Douai,France; 196/Victoria and Albert Museum,London; 197/Narodni Galerie, Prague; 172/Tretyakov Gallery, Moscow; 207/Galleria Sabauda, Turin; 211/Musee Atger, Faculte de Medecine, Montpellier; 219/St.Peter's, Louvain, Belgium; 223/Musee d'Art et d'Archeologie, Moulins, France; 225/Musee National de la Renaissance, Ecouen,France; 237/Whitworth Art Gallery, University of Manchester,UK; 238/Cathedral of St James,Santiago da Compostela, Spain; 241/Victoria and Albert Museum, London; 245/Private Collection; 248/Hamburger Kunsthalle, Hamburg; 247/ Whitworth Art Gallery, University of Manchester,UK; 248/Musee des Beaux-Arts,Rennes; 250/Wallraf Richartz Museum, Cologne; 253/Museo della Civilta Romana,Rome; 259/Civica Raccolta Stampe Bertarelli, Milan; 263/Private Collection; 267/Rafael Valls Gallery, London; 273/Musee des Beaux-Arts, Dijon; 283/National Library of Jerusalem, Israel; 286/ Baptistry of Ariani, Ravenna, Italy; 289/Duomo, Monreale,Sicily; 294/Kunsthistorisches Museum, Vienna; 298/Vatican Museums & Galleries,Vatican City; 300/Lambeth Palace Library, London; **de Agostini Picture Library:** 13,40,230; **Imagno:** 45, 79,261,264; **Fred Mayer:** 258; **National Geographic Society:** 25,277; **Robert Harding Picture Library:** back cover(3L), 67; **Time & Life Pictures:** 34,60, 68,116,122,162,177,232,257,279,282,288

Published by Tess Press, an imprint of
Black Dog & Leventhal Publishers, Inc.
151 West 19th Street
New York, NY 10011

Jacket Design by Lindsay Wolff
Interior Design by Red Herring Design

ISBN: 978-1-60376-042-3

Printed in China

h g f e d c b a

CONTENTS

Introduction iv

Abbreviations vii

The Oxford Companion to the Bible 1

Acknowledgements 302

Directory of Contributors 302

Bibliography 307

Index 310

Maps 314

INTRODUCTION

For nearly two millennia, the Bible has been the cardinal text for Judaism and Christianity. Its stories and characters are part of both the repertoire of Western literature and the vocabulary of educated women and men. It is, however, more than a collection of ancient tales. Even before a canonical list of books considered sacred scripture or holy writ was established, the writings we now call the Bible were considered normative: they laid down the essential principles of how human beings should deal with God and with each other. The practice of quoting from, and alluding to, earlier texts as authoritative is found within the Bible itself and has continued unabated in subsequent Jewish and Christian writings. At the same time, the Bible has also been formative; subsequent generations of believers have seen themselves as descended from, and in continuity with, those to whom God had spoken and for whom he had acted definitively in the past, and the recital of those words and events has been instrumental in shaping the religious communities of succeeding generations. The Bible has thus had an immeasurable influence on Judaism and Christianity, on the cultures of which they have formed a part, and on all those traditions in some ways derived from them, such as Islam.

Although the word "Bible" means "book," and the Bible has been treated as a single book for much of its history, it is in fact many books, an anthology of the literatures of ancient Israel, and, for Christians, also of earliest Christianity. The Bible thus speaks with many voices, and, from the time of its emergence as an authoritative sacred text, readers and interpreters have noted its many repetitions, inconsistencies, and contradictions. Since the Enlightenment especially, critical consideration of the Bible—that is, study of it insofar as possible without presuppositions—has irreversibly affected what may be called the "precritical" understanding of the Bible as simply a unified text, God's eternal, infallible, and complete word. Discoveries of ancient manuscripts (such as the Dead Sea Scrolls) and of literatures contemporaneous with, or earlier than, those preserved in the Bible (such as stories of creation and the Flood from ancient Babylonia and the gospels of Thomas and Philip from Nag Hammadi in Egypt), as well as innumerable archaeological finds, have deepened our understanding of the Bible and the historical and cultural contexts in which its constituent parts were written. This new understanding of the Bible has resulted in continuous scholarly attention and popular interest.

The Oxford Illustrated Companion to the Bible is an authoritative reference for key persons, places, events, concepts, institutions, and realities of biblical times. In addition, the *Companion* provides up-to-date discussions of the interpretation of these topics by modern scholars, bringing to bear the most recent findings of archaeologists and current research methods from such disciplines as anthropology, sociology, and literary criticism. Interpretation of the Bible has of course not been consistent, and throughout history the Bible has been used to support contradictory positions on such issues as slavery, the role of women, war and peace, forms of government, and finance. The *Companion* reflects this diversity: it is consciously pluralistic, and its more than 100 contributors, as well as its editors and editorial advisory board, encompass a wide spectrum of intellectual and confessional perspectives. They represent the international community of scholars, coming from some twenty countries, on five continents. No attempt has been made by the editors to produce any dogmatic unanimity; readers should not be surprised to find differing interpretations in different entries. Contributors have been urged to present their own scholarly views while noting diverse perspectives. In general, the articles aim to present the consensus of interpretation, or its lack, attained by the most recent scholarship, and to avoid partisanship and polemic.

Recognizing that different communities of faith have different understandings of which books form their Bibles, the *Companion* has deliberately adopted a maximalist position: any book or part of a book that is recognized as canonical by any religious community is treated in this volume. A similarly inclusive and ecumenical view has led to the use of neutral terminology whenever possible; thus, following increasingly frequent scholarly practice, the term "Hebrew Bible" is used in preference to "Old Testament," and the abbreviations BCE (Before the Common Era) and CE (Common Era) are in place of BC and AD.

The *Companion* is more comprehensive than the usual Bible dictionary, and provides in alphabetical sequence a broad range of more than two hundred articles, each signed by the contributor. Articles vary in length from short summaries of what the Bible says about a topic and how biblical traditions have been interpreted and used, to major interpretive essays. The latter often take the form of composite entries, consisting of two or more articles by specialists on various periods and regions: Afterlife and Immortality;

LEFT: The Virgin Mary from The Ghent Altarpiece (Hubert van Eyck & Jan van Eyck, 1432)

Chronology; Interpretation, History of; Literature and the Bible; Translations; and Women are just a few examples. In planning the volume, the editors used the following categories; they illustrate how the development, understanding, and influence of the Bible receive comprehensive coverage in the *Companion:*

- **The Formation of the Bible**

The Bible is the final product of a series of stages, including orally transmitted traditions, shorter and longer written units, collections edited and in some cases translated in ancient times, and final selection by various religious communities as canonical scriptures. There is treatment of all of these processes, and detailed discussion of how the various parts of books and the books themselves were collected, passed on, edited, selected, and arranged, as well as articles on all the books of the Bible.

- **The Biblical World**

Under this heading are included key individuals, events, dates, institutions, and realities of daily life in ancient Israel and the earliest Christian communities, understood within the larger contexts of the ancient Near East, Hellenistic Judaism, and Greco-Roman culture. There are, in addition, articles on broader topics, such as the brothers and sisters of Jesus, circumcision, and geography; and synthetic interpretive essays on subjects such as the history of ancient Israel and Judah, feasts and festivals, kingship and monarchy, and letter-writing in antiquity.

- **Biblical Concepts**

The Bible has been both the basis for and stimulus to reflection on a wide range of theological topics and human concerns. Under this rubric the *Companion* examines biblical theology as such, as well as biblical views of such perennial issues as afterlife and immortality, creation, death, faith, hope, love, monotheism, and Satan.

- **The Uses and Influence of the Bible**

Since its formation, the Bible has been a primary resource for Western culture. Its immense influence on British, North American, European, and other literatures is traced in an extensive composite entry on Literature and the Bible. There are also major interpretive surveys of the use of the Bible in art, dance, law, and music, and on the complex interplay between the Bible and such areas as feminism, medicine, politics, and science.

The *Companion* is thus an authoritative and comprehensive reference for a wide audience, including general readers; students and teachers in high schools, colleges, seminaries, and divinity schools; rabbis, ministers, and religious educators; participants in religious education and Bible study programs; and scholars in the variety of disciplines for which the Bible is in some way pertinent.

The *Companion* does not aim to be an encyclopedia or encyclopedic dictionary, and is not intended as a substitute either for the Bible itself or for a concordance to the Bible. Quotations from the Bible have deliberately been kept to a minimum, and biblical references are illustrative, not exhaustive. Nor has it been thought necessary to include every name found in the Bible, but only those judged important within the biblical traditions or by later readers. This is especially true of persons and places about whom little if anything is known other than what appears in the Bible. Within the scope of one volume, then, the *Companion* is a reliable guide, from Aaron or Zion, to what the Bible says about a topic and how scholars have interpreted biblical traditions. It explores as well how those traditions have been used since the books of the Bible became scripture.

USE OF THE COMPANION

The *Companion* is arranged alphabetically. Further investigation of particular topics is made possible by a detailed index, which provides page references for pertinent subjects and for ancient and modern proper names. Very few volumes comparable to the *Companion* have such an index; its use will enable readers to locate topics throughout the book.

When appropriate, references are made within entries to the maps found at the end of the *Companion,* so that readers may locate places named in the text more precisely.

At the end of the volume, there is an extensive annotated bibliography, which will enable readers to explore in more detail topics covered in the *Companion.* The bibliography is divided into categories for easier use, such as the history, geography, and archaeology of biblical times; anthologies of nonbiblical texts; critical and popular introductions to the Bible; reference works; surveys of the history of interpretation; and methodologies used in biblical scholarship.

The translation used in the *Companion* is *The New Revised Standard Version* (NRSV), the most recent authoritative translation of the Bible into English, produced by an interfaith committee of scholars and published in 1990. The renderings of the NRSV are the basis for entry titles. Within individual entries, contributors have on occasion used other published translations or their own; in these cases, differences from the NRSV are noted.

ABBREVIATIONS

Biblical Citations

Chapter (chap.) and verse (v.) are separated by a period, and when a verse is subdivided, letters are used following the verse number; thus, Gen. 3.4a = the book of Genesis, chap. 3 v. 4, the first part. Biblical books are abbreviated in parenthetical references as follows:

Acts	Acts of the Apostles	Lam.	Lamentations
Amos	Amos	Lev.	Leviticus
Bar.	Baruch	Luke	Luke
Beland the Dragon	Beland the Dragon	1 Macc.	1 Maccabees
1 Chron.	1 Chronicles	2 Macc.	2 Maccabees
2 Chron.	2 Chronicles	3 Macc.	3 Maccabees
Col.	Colossians	4 Macc.	4 Maccabees
1 Cor.	1 Cornithians	Mal.	Malachi
2 Cor.	2 Corinthians	Mark	Mark
Dan.	Daniel	Matt.	Matthew
Deut.	Deuteronomy	Mic.	Micah
Eccles.	Ecclesiastes	Nah.	Nahum
Eph.	Ephesians	Neh.	Nehemiah
1 Esd.	1 Esdras	Num.	Numbers
2 Esd.	2 Esdras	Obad.	Obadiah
Esther	Esther	1 Pet.	1 Peter
Exod.	Exodus	2 Pet.	2 Peter.
Ezek.	Ezekiel	Phil.	Philippians
Ezra	Ezra	Philem.	Philemon
Gal.	Galatians	Pr. of Man.	Prayer of Manasseh
Hab.	Habakkuk	Prov.	Proverbs
Hag.	Haggai	Ps(s).	Psalm(s)
Heb.	Hebrews	Rev.	Revelation
Hos.	Hosea	Rom.	Romans
Isa.	Isaiah	Ruth	Ruth
James	James	1 Sam.	1 Samuel
Jer.	Jeremiah	2 Sam.	2 Samuel
Job	Job	Sir.	Sirach
Joel	Joel	Song of Sol.	Song of Solomon
John	Gospel of John	Sus.	Susanna
1 John	1 John	1 Thess.	1 Thessalonians
2 John	2 John	2 Thess.	2 Thessalonians
3 John	3 John	1 Tim.	1 Timothy
Jon.	Jonah	2 Tim.	2 Timothy
Josh.	Joshua	Titus	Titus
Jude.	Jude	Tob.	Tobit
Judg.	Judges	Wisd. of Solomon	Wisdom of Solomon
Jth.	Judith	Zech.	Zechariah
1 Kings	1 Kings	Zeph.	Zephaniah
2 Kings	2 Kings		

Rabbinic Literature

To distinguish tractates with the same name, the letters m. (Mishnah), t. (Tosepta), b. (Babylonian Talmud), and y. (Jerusalem Talmud) are used before the name of the tractate.

'Abod. Zar.	*'Aboda Zara*	*Ketub.*	*Ketubot*	*Qph. Rab. Sabb.*	*Qohelet Rabbah*
'Abot R. Nat.	*'Abot de Rabbi Nathan*	*Mek.*	*Mekilta*	*Šabbat*	*Šabbat*
B. Bat.	*Baba Batra*	*Mid.*	*Middot*	*Sanh.*	*Sanhedrin*
Ber.	*Berakot*	*Midr.*	*Midrash*	*Sukk.*	*Sukkot*
'Erub	*'Erubin*	*Nez.*	*Niddah*	*Ta'an.*	*Ta'anit*
Gen. Rab.	*Genesis Rabbah*	*Nid.*	*Neziqin*	*Yad.*	*Yadayim*
Ḥag.	*Ḥagiga*	*Pesaḥ.*	*Pesaḥim*	*Zebaḥ.*	*Zebaḥim*

Other Ancient Literature

Adv. haer.	Irenaeus, *Adversus haeresis*
Ag. Ap.	Josephus, *Against Apion*
Ant.	Josephus, *Antiquities*
Apol.	Justin, *Apology*
Bapt.	Tertullian, *De baptismo*
CD	Cairo Geniza, Damascus Document
1 Clem.	1 Clement
De Dec.	Philo, *De Decalogo*
De spec. leg.	Philo, *De specialibus legibus*
Did.	Didache
Ep.	Cyprian, *Epistles*
Exhort. Chast.	Tertullian, *De exhortatione castitatis*
Geog.	Strabo, *Geographica*
GT	Gospel of Thomas
Haer.	Epiphanius, *Haereses*
Hist.	Polybius, *Histories*
Hist. eccl.	Eusebius, *Historia ecclesiastica*
Instit. Rhetor.	Quintilian, *Institution of Rhetoric*
Jov.	Jerome, *Against Jovianum*
Leg. ad Gaium	Philo, *Legatio ad Gaium*
1 Q34	Qumran Cave 1, No. 34
1 QH	Qumran Cave 1, *Hôbdāyôt (Thanksgiving Hymns)*
1 QIsab	Qumran Cave 1, Isaiah, second copy
1 QM	Qumran Cave 1, *Milḥāmdāh (War Scroll)*
1 QpHab	Qumran Cave 1, *Pesher on Habakkuk*
1 QS	Qumran Cave 1, *Serek hayyaḥad (Rule of the Community, Manual of Discipline*
4Q246	Qumran Cave 4, No. 246
4Q503-509	Qumran Cave 4, Nos. 503-509
4QDeuta	Qumran Cave 4, Deuteronomy, first copy
4QMMT	Qumran Cave 4, *Miqsat Ma'aseh Torah*
4QpNah	Qumran Cave 4, *Pesher on Nahum*
11QMelch	Qumran Cave 11, Melchizedek text
11QTemple	Qumran Cave 11, *Temple Scroll*
Praescr	Tertullian, *De praescriptione haereticorum*
Test. Abr.	Testament of Abraham
T. Naph.	Testament of Naphtali
War	Josephus, *Jewish War*

Other Abbreviations

ABS	American Bible Society
AV	Authorized Version
BCE	Before the Common Era (the equivalent of BC)
BCP	Book of Common Prayer
BFBS	British and Foreign Bible Society
ca.	circa
CE	Common Era (the equivalent of AD)
chap(s).	chapter(s)
D	Deuteronomist source in the Pentateuch
E	Elohist source in the Pentateuch
EB	Early Bronze
GNB	Good News Bible
Grk.	Greek
H	Holiness Code
Hebr.	Hebrew
J	Yahwist source in the Pentateuch
KJV	King James Version
L	Special Lucan material
Lat.	Latin
LB	Late Bronze
LXX	Septuagint
M	Special Matthean material
MB	Middle Bronze
MSS	Manuscripts
MT	Masoretic Text
NBSS	National Bible Society of Scotland
NEB	New English Bible
NJV	New Jewish Version
NRSV	New Revised Standard Version
P	Priestly source in the Pentateuch
par.	parallel(s), used when two or more passages have essentially the same material, especially in the synoptic Gospels
Q	from German *Quelle*, "source," designating the hypothetical common source used by Matthew and Luke
REB	Revised English Bible
RSV	Revised Standard Version
RV	Revised Version
TDH	Two Document Hypothesis
UBS	United Bible Societies
v(v).	verse(s)

AARON. A major figure in Israel's origins and the first of its high priests. In very ancient narratives, he appears without specifically priestly features, as a leader with Hur (Exod. 17.9–16; 24.14), or as Miriam's brother with no mention of their being related to Moses (Exod. 15.20), to whom they even appear opposed (Num. 12). Later, but still in fairly early stages of the Pentateuch's formation, Aaron is said to be Moses' brother and a Levite (Exod. 4.14), and he begins to appear with features that implicitly suggest a tie with priesthood. He is with Moses when Pharaoh asks for intercession with Israel's God (Exod. 8.25; 9.27–28; 10.16–17); in Exodus 18.12, he may have been added to the account of the covenant between Midian and Israel because a later editor may have felt that the covenant sacrifice required a priest; his presence with his sons Nadab and Abihu, reckoned elsewhere as priestly sons, seems also to have been added to the covenant-making scene at Sinai (Exod. 24.1, 9). The important question of Aaron's role in the episode of the golden calf (Exod. 32) is problematic. The incident is almost certainly told with the sanctuaries in mind established by Jeroboam I at Bethel and Dan in the northern kingdom of Israel (1 Kings 12.26–32), but in the story Aaron is not presented as a priest or as a Levite; his guilt is brought out mainly in Exodus 32.25b, 35b, evident additions to a text in which the behavior of the people, looking to Aaron for leadership, was already contrasted negatively with the religiously correct zeal of Levites (32.25–29). In the Priestly components of the Pentateuch (P), Aaron's role as Moses' companion in Egypt and in the wilderness is heightened, but in P he is above all Israel's first high priest, and the other priests inaugurated with him are called his sons (Exod. 28–29; 39; Lev. 8–10; Num. 3.5–4.49; 16–18). The historical background of this development in the figure of Aaron is not clear. Although legitimate priests are called sons of Zadok in Ezekiel (40.46; 43.19; 44.15; 48.11), with Aaron's name quite unused in that exilic book, some suspect that the preexilic priesthood of Jerusalem itself claimed an Aaronite origin; others believe that the first group to do so was the priesthood of Bethel, or a Levitical group in Judah not originally identical with the priesthood of Jerusalem. In any case, the postexilic priests of Jerusalem settled peacefully into their own claim to be the sons of Aaron.

AELRED CODY, O.S.B.

ABRAHAM. Abraham is the earliest biblical character who is delineated clearly enough to be correlated, to a limited extent, within world history. His homeland on the Fertile Crescent (possibly at Haran, at least in Gen. 12.1–5) and movements southeast toward Chaldean Ur (Gen. 11.31), then west to Canaan and Egypt, correspond to known Amorite migratory and commercial routes. He may have been a caravan merchant, though the Bible presents him only as a pastoralist. This vague relation of Abraham to history does not exclude debate as to how much of his biography might have been worked up for vividness or as retrojection of a later tribal unity. More insistent claims of historicity presume contemporaneity with Hammurapi (despite the discredited equation of the latter with Amraphel [Gen 14.1]). An even earlier date was put forward on the basis of some premature interpretations of Sodom at Ebla. The name Abram (= Abiram, as Abner = Abiner), used in Genesis from 11.27 to 17.5, is there ritually changed to Abraham, a normal dialectal variant, though explained in relation to 'ab-hāmôn, "father of many."

A certain unity in the whole Abraham saga (Gen. 11.27–25.11) involves a rich variety of peoples and individuals conditioning his activity; twenty-two separate episodes are discernible (see L. Hicks, *Interpreter's Dictionary of the Bible* 1.16). Eleven are attributed to the Yahwist (J): base around Haran, Genesis 11.28–30; call westward, 12.1–3; Canaan pause, 12.4–9; separation from Lot, 13.1–13;

Aaron with the Scroll of Law

1

promise involving Mamre, 13.14–18; progeny like stars, covenant-incubation, 15.1–6, 7–24; Hagar, 16; the three at Mamre, 18.1–15; vain plea for Sodom, 18.16–33; birth of Isaac, 21.1–7; and old age, 24.1–25.11. Five other episodes suggest the Elohist (E): parts of the narrative of the covenant in chapter 15, especially verses 13–16; Gerar, 20; Ishmael expelled, 21.6–21; Abimelech 21.22–34; and the call to sacrifice Isaac, 22. The Priestly (P) additions include: journey to Canaan, parts of Genesis 11–12; birth of Ishmael, 16.1–16; covenant of El-Shaddai and circumcision, 17; birth of Isaac, 21.1–3; Machpelah, 23; death, 25.7–11; and, less clearly, the unique episode concerning Melchizedek (chap. 14).

The three strands respectively see Abraham as "father of all nations" (J); "model of faith" (E; see Rom. 4.9; Heb. 11.8); and "guarantor of Israel's survival" (P, in the context of exile). The covenant with Abraham is also a blessing for all the peoples of the earth (Gen. 12.3; 18.18) and especially a bond of religious unity with his other descendants, the Ishmaelites (Arabs: Gen. 21.21; 25.12). Abraham's progress from (Ur or) Haran through Canaan into Egypt involves numerous theophanies (Gen. 12.6, Shechem; 12.8, Bethel; 13.18, Hebron; 21.33, Be-ersheba; 22.14, Moriah), justifying his eventual takeover of the whole area (Gen. 13.14–17) or, more sweepingly, the takeover by "his god" (El) of the cult of the local El, not clearly seen as either identical or different.

In Deuteronomy, Abraham is associated with Isaac and Jacob (Deut. 1.8; 6.10); the three are often generalized as "your fathers" (9.18; 11.9; NRSV: "your ancestors"), especially as those with whom God made a covenant (7.12; 8.18), a covenant still in force (5.3). The Deuteronomic history recalls Abraham in Joshua 24.2–3; 1 Kings 18.36; 2 Kings 13.23; but it is surprising how seldom he is mentioned there, as well as in the Psalms (only 47.9; 105.6, 9, 42) and the preexilic prophets (only Mic. 7.20, probably a late addition). The poorer classes of Judah who never were sent into exile justified their inheritance as the promise to Abraham (Ezek. 33.24), but the stronger group of returnees attributed their own liberation to God's faithfulness to Abraham "my friend" (Isa. 41.8, prominent in James 2.23 and in Muslim tradition, notably as the name of Hebron, al-Halil). Abraham is often mentioned in the book of Jubilees and sometimes in other pseudepigrapha.

Abraham is second only to Moses among New Testament mentions of biblical heroes. Sometimes this is in a slightly belittling sense, when he is claimed as father of the impious (Matt. 3.9; John 8.39). More often the truly Abrahamic descent of the Jews is acknowledged as a stimulus for them to live up to their heritage (Luke 19.9; 16.24; Heb. 6.13). This true but qualified descent from Abraham forms a key factor in Paul's anguished efforts to determine how and in what sense Christianity can claim the promises made to Israel (Rom. 4.1, 13; Gal. 3.7; 4.22). Ultimately, as father of all believers (Gal. 3.7), Abraham is to be looked to as a source of unity and harmony rather than dissent among Jews, Christians, and Muslims.

ROBERT NORTH

ACTS OF THE APOSTLES. The fifth book of the New Testament in the common arrangement, Acts records certain phases of the progress of Christianity for a period of some thirty years after Jesus' death and resurrection. Acts was originally written as a sequel to the gospel of Luke; both are clearly from the same author, who apparently planned the complete work from the outset.

Structure. Seven main divisions may be discerned in Acts: the formation and development of the church of Jerusalem (1.1–5.42); the rise and activity of the Hellenists in the church, which led to their persecution and expulsion from Jerusalem (6.1–8.3); the dissemination of the gospel by these Hellenists, culminating in the evangelizing of gentiles in the Syrian city of Antioch (8.4–12.25); the extension of gentile Christianity from Antioch into Cyprus and Asia Minor (13.1–14.28); the decision reached by the Jerusalem church on problems raised by the influx of gentile converts (15.1–16.5); the carrying of the gospel by Paul and his colleagues to the provinces bordering on the Aegean Sea (16.6–19.20); Paul's last journey to Jerusalem, his arrest there, and his journey to Rome under armed guard to have his case heard before the emperor (19.21–28.31).

Acts, in short, is concerned with the advance of the gospel from Jerusalem to Rome; its simultaneous advance in other directions is ignored. The narrative reaches its goal when Paul arrives in Rome and, while under house arrest, preaches the gospel there without interference to all who came to visit him (28.30–31).

Authorship and Sources. For Acts, as for the gospel of Luke, the author was dependent on the information handed down by others (see Luke 1.2). But he probably made further inquiry on his own account (Luke 1.3), and he may have been present at some of the events recorded in the later part of the book of Acts. This is the *prima facie* inference to be drawn from the "we" sections—those sections in which the third-person pronouns "they" and "them" give way to the first person "we" and "us." There are three such sections: Acts 16.10–17; 20.5–21.18; 27.1–28.16. All three are largely devoted to journeys by sea—from Troas to Neapolis, and then by road to Philippi; from Philippi (Neapolis) to Caesarea, and then by road to Jerusalem; from Caesarea to Puteoli, and then by road to Rome—and may have been extracted from a travel diary. The traditional view, which still has much to commend it, is that the "we" of those sections includes the "I" of Acts 1.1—that the transition from "they" to "we" is the author's unobtrusive way of indicating that he himself was a participant in the events he narrates.

Ever since the second century CE the author has been traditionally identified with the Luke mentioned in Colossians 4.14 as "Luke the beloved physician." The attribution of the twofold work to such an obscure New Testament character has been thought to speak for the genuineness of the tradition. The only question of consequence to be considered is the degree of likelihood that the author of Acts was personally acquainted with Paul, whose missionary activity forms the main subject of the second half of the book. The critical judgment of several scholars is that such personal acquaintance is highly unlikely—that the "Paulinism" of Acts is too dissimilar to the teaching of Paul's letters for the idea to be entertained that the author of Acts knew Paul or spent any time in his company. On the other hand, many authorities maintain that, when account is taken of the difference between the picture of him as seen through the eyes of an admirer and, indeed, hero-worshiper, the Paul of Acts is identical with the real Paul.

The identification of other sources than the "we" narrative is precarious. A new source is sometimes indicated by such transitional formulas as "now during these days" (6.1), "after some days" (15.36), "about that time" (19.23), or by the sudden introduction of terms or names for which no advance explanation has been given, such as Hellenists and Hebrews in 6.1 or King Herod in 12.1. The abruptness of a transition from one source to another may be made smoother by an editorial paragraph, for example, 15.1–5. Occasionally the author follows one source for some time, then breaks off to follow another, and turns back later to resume the earlier one. Thus a source relating the early Hellenistic mission is followed by 8.4–40, a section beginning: "Now those who were scattered went from place to place preaching the word." The author then leaves it to relate the conversion of Paul and Peter's evangelistic ministry (9.1–11.18); he returns to it in 11.19, "Now those who were scattered because of the persecution that took place over Stephen," and goes on to tell of the founding of the church of Antioch.

From 15.35 on there is a continuous narrative of Paul's missionary work, broken only by occasional speeches (notably, to the Athenians, 17.22–31, and to the elders of the Ephesian church, 20.18–35). A new departure is marked in 19.21, at which Paul's plan to visit Rome is first announced; the remainder of the work tells how that plan was fulfilled in unforeseen ways.

Speeches and Letters. Luke does not appear to have been dependent on written sources for the speeches that play an important part in his work. These conform to the policy inherited by Greek historians from Thucydides (ca. 400 BCE), who explains that he has "put into the mouth of each speaker the sentiments appropriate for the occasion, expressed as I thought he would be likely to express them, while at the same time I endeavored, as nearly as I could, to give the general purport of what was actually said" (*History,* 1.20.1). Following this principle, Luke introduces speeches with proper regard for the speakers and the setting. Stephen's defense in Acts 7.2–53, for example, presents a wholly negative appraisal of the Jerusalem Temple, whereas Luke himself, for the greater part of his narrative, treats it with respect. It is not by accident that Paul is the only speaker in Acts to call Jesus "the Son of God" (Acts 9.20) or to mention justification by faith (13.38, 39) or redemption by the blood of Christ (20.28). It is widely maintained that Paul's speech to the court of the Areopagus at Athens (Acts 17.22–31) cannot in any sense be credited to Paul. But, if the author of Romans 1–3 were brought to Athens and invited to expound the basis of the gospel to its cultured and sophisticated members in terms that they might in some degree understand, it can be argued that he was bound to say something not wholly different from what Luke represents Paul as saying on that occasion. Both here and elsewhere in Acts the speeches are appropriate to the occasion, to the speaker, and to the audience.

What is true of speeches is true also of the letters cited by Luke—the letter from the leaders of the Jerusalem church to the gentile Christians of Antioch and other places in Syria and Cilicia (Acts 15.23–29) and the letter from the commanding officer of the Roman garrison in Jerusalem to the procurator of Judea explaining the circumstances of Paul's arrest (23.26–30). Even if Luke is the composer of those letters as we have them, their contents fit the settings in which they are placed.

Date. The latest event to be recorded in Acts is Paul's spending two years under house arrest in Rome (28.30). This period begins with his arrival in the city, probably in the early spring of 60 CE. Most of the book deals with the twenty years preceding that date, and the book as a whole is true to its "dramatic" date, that is, it reflects the situation of the middle of the first century CE, especially with regard to the administration of the Roman empire. But the date of writing is not the same as the "dramatic" date. Some scholars have

argued that it was written very shortly after that event, possibly even before Paul's appeal came up for hearing in the imperial court. Paul's death is not recorded: would it not have been mentioned (it is asked) if in fact it had taken place?

But the goal of Luke's narrative is not the outcome of Paul's appeal, whether favorable or otherwise, or the end of Paul's life; it is Paul's unmolested preaching of the gospel at the heart of the empire (Acts 28.30–31). In fact Paul's death is alluded to, by implication, in his speech to the elders of the Ephesian church (Acts 20.24, 25), in a manner that suggests that Luke knew of it. And in general Luke appears to record the apostolic history from a perspective of one or two decades after the events. By the time he wrote, Paul, Peter, and James had all died; and the controversies in which they were involved, while important enough at the time (as Paul's letters bear witness), had lost much of their relevance for Luke's purpose, so he ignored them.

The date of Acts cannot be considered in isolation from that of the gospel of Luke. A date later rather than earlier than 70 CE is probable for the gospel. If we date the composition of the twofold work toward the end of Vespasian's rule (69–79 CE), most of the evidence will be satisfied.

Recipients. The one recipient of Acts named explicitly is Theophilus, to whom Luke's gospel also was dedicated (Luke 1.3). We know virtually nothing about him. His designation "most excellent" may mark him as a member of the equestrian order (the second-highest order in Roman society), or it may simply be a courtesy title.

The Stoning of St. Stephen (Acts 7.58) (Peter Paul Rubens, 17th century)

One could regard him as a representative of the intelligent middle-class public of Rome, to whom Luke wished to present a reliable account of the rise and progress of Christianity. As late as the time when Tacitus, Suetonius, and Pliny were writing (ca. 110 CE), Christians enjoyed no good repute in Roman society; writing some decades earlier, Luke hoped to bring his readers to a less prejudiced judgment. There is much to be said for the view of Martin Dibelius that, unlike the other New Testament books, Luke and Acts were written for the book market. Perhaps there was already a positive interest in Christianity in the class of readers Luke had in mind; this could account for the substantial theological content of the work, especially its emphasis on the Holy Spirit.

Rome is the most likely place for the first publication of the work. Not only is Rome the goal toward which it moves, but with Paul's arrival there, Rome implicitly replaces Jerusalem as the center from which the faith is to spread.

Historical Significance. Whereas the gospel of Luke has at least partial parallels in the other Gospels, all of which are concerned with Jesus' activity from his baptism to his death and resurrection, Acts is unparalleled as a record of events. Its only parallels are occasional passages in the letters of Paul (notably Gal. 1.13–2.14), in which the apostle reviews phases of his career or mentions his travel plans. Apart from Acts, we have no other continuous record of the expansion of Christianity during the thirty years after Jesus' death and resurrection. It is necessary to wait two and a half centuries for the next Christian historian—Eusebius, bishop of Caesarea in Palestine.

Even in his gospel, Luke indicates his interest in relating the gospel to world history when he introduces the ministry of John the Baptist with an elaborate synchronism (Luke 3.1, 2). This interest becomes more evident in Acts, when the gospel moves into the gentile world. Luke is the only New Testament writer who so much as names a Roman emperor; in addition to emperors, he introduces provincial governors, client kings, civic magistrates, and other local officials. Scholars have drawn attention to the accuracy with which these officials are designated by their correct titles—an accuracy the more noteworthy because some of those titles changed from time to time. Provinces under the nominal control of the Roman senate, for example, are governed by proconsuls, like Sergius Paulus in Cyprus and Gallio in Achaia; Philippi has praetors or duumvirs as its chief magistrates because it is a Roman colony; Thessalonica is administered by politarchs, a title attested on a number of inscriptions as borne by the chief magistrates of Macedonian cities.

The record of Acts is interrelated with contemporary world history in a way that entitles it to be cited as an authority in its own right. Its authority has also been acknowledged in the matter of travel conditions, on land and sea, in the Roman empire in the period that it covers. Its reports of Paul's journeys in Asia Minor provide unrivaled evidence for lines of communication in that area and for the comparative ease with which they could be used. The "ease" was enjoyed more along the main roads, which were well policed; travel along other roads exposed one to hazards from robbers and others. As for travel by sea, the account of Paul's stormy voyage to Italy and shipwreck at Malta has long been recognized as a valuable document for our knowledge of seafaring in the Greco-Roman world.

Theological Significance. Luke is no mere chronicler: he envisages a pattern in the events he records. His interest is concentrated on the advance of the gospel; it has been launched into the world by the resurrection of Jesus and the coming of the Spirit, and nothing can stop it. Paul and others may plan their journeys, but they would achieve little without the guidance of the Spirit of God, directing the course of events by occasionally diverting the missionaries from the path they intend to take and leading them into another (e.g., 16.6–10). Luke has been called the theologian of "salvation history"; Peter and Paul are the principal human agents, but the dominant part is played by the Spirit.

Apologetic Emphasis. In commending Christianity to the good will of his readers, Luke insists that it presents no threat to imperial law and order. He adduces in evidence the judgments expressed by officials of higher and lower degree throughout the empire. Already in the Third Gospel Pontius Pilate, the Roman governor who hears the charges against Jesus, finds him not guilty of any capital offense (Luke 23.13–17); he sentences him to death because he gives in weakly to the chief priests and their colleagues. In the early chapters of Acts the apostles are flogged by order of the supreme court of Israel (5.40), a body dominated by the chief-priestly families; and Stephen, leader of the Hellenists, is stoned to death after their rejection of his defense (Acts 7.58). But when the heralds of Christianity move out into the gentile world, they receive fairer treatment.

Sergius Paulus, proconsul of Cyprus, gives Paul and Barnabas a courteous hearing and is impressed by their teaching (Acts 13.7, 12). The praetors of Philippi sentence Paul and Silas to be beaten and locked up overnight, but on learning that the two men are Roman citizens, they apologize for their illegal conduct (16.22–24, 35–39). The politarchs of Thessalonica respond to the serious charge of high treason brought against Paul and his companions by making Paul's friends in the city guarantee his peaceful departure (17.6–9). At Corinth Paul is accused before Gallio, proconsul of Achaia, of propagating an illegal form of religion, but Gallio, seeing the issue as a dispute between the local Jews and a Jewish visitor, refuses to take up the matter; so far as he is concerned, Paul must be tolerated as long as no breach of law or public morals is committed (18.12–16). In Ephesus, some leading citizens of the province of Asia befriend Paul, and when an unruly assembly demonstrates against him, the town clerk, the chief executive officer of the city, absolves him of any offense against the cult of Ephesian Artemis (19.23–41).

All this builds up a case in favor of Paul, who at the end of Acts, charged with offenses against public order, is about to have his appeal heard by the emperor; it also builds up a case for Christians throughout the empire, who will still be around when Paul is no longer alive.

Canonical Significance. Early in the second century CE, when the four Gospels began to circulate as one collection, Acts was detached from Luke's gospel. But when, about the middle of that century, decisions were made about the New Testament canon, Acts came into its own as the "hinge" that joined the gospel collection to the collection of Pauline letters. Those like Marcion, who ascribed apostolic authority to Paul alone, had no use for Acts. Acts, while not giving Paul the title apostle in a distinctive sense, provided ample evidence that he was all that his letters claimed him to be; at the same time, it gave Peter and his colleagues full apostolic status. There is an impressive series of parallels in Acts between Paul and Peter, as though Luke planned to show that the status and ministry of both had equal divine attestation. James of Jerusalem, whose claims were exalted above those of Peter and Paul in at least one branch of second-century Christianity, plays a minor part in Acts (15.13–21).

Acts, in short, is a thoroughly catholic work, catering to all legitimate viewpoints in the church. Perhaps it was this aspect of Acts that stimulated the inclusion in the canon, alongside the Pauline collection, of another collection of letters, the catholic letters as they are traditionally called, bearing the names of James, Peter, John, and Jude. It is a matter of further interest that Acts was closely associated with these catholic letters in the copying and transmission of the New Testament, regularly sharing one codex with them or, in a more comprehensive codex, being followed immediately by them.

F. F. BRUCE

AFRICA.

Names and Words for Africa. Africa appears throughout the Bible from Genesis 2.11–13, where the sources of the Nile River are located in the garden of Eden, to the apostle Philip's baptism of the African official in Acts 8.26–39. To recover these numerous references in the original Hebrew and Greek of the Bible, sometimes lost or obscured in English translation, one must first identify the key biblical names for Africa and its people.

"Cush" in Hebrew and "Ethiopia" in Greek designate the land and people of the upper Nile River from modern southern Egypt into Sudan (Map 7:F6). The more indigenous term for this region is Nubia. "Ham" is another Hebrew term for the darker hued people of antiquity. In Genesis 10, Ham is son of Noah who populates Africa, Canaan, and Arabia after the Flood. In poetry, the name Ham is a synonym for Egypt (e.g., Ps. 78.51).

"Niger," the Latin word for "black," is used in Acts 13.1 to identify an African named Simeon. Simeon's companion Lucius was also African as is indicated by his place of origin, Cyrene, in Libya (Map 14:04; see Acts 2.10). Jesus' cross is carried by Simon, also from Cyrene (Matt. 27.32).

In addition to Hebrew, Greek, and Latin terms for Africa, the Bible also uses Egyptian and Nubian names for the land and its people. The references to Africa encompass the length of the Nile Valley from the deep southern origins of the Nile down to the delta where it empties into the Mediterranean Sea. From the Lower Nile in the north to the Upper Nile in the south, the African skin color varied from brown to copperbrown to black. For the Egyptians used to these color variations, the term for their southern neighbors was *Neḥesi*, "southerner," which eventually also came to mean "the black" or "the Nubian." This Egyptian root (*Nḥsj*, with the preformative *p'* as a definite article) appears in Exodus 6.25 as the personal name of Aaron's grandson Phinehas (= *pa-neḥas*). In Acts 8.27, the first non-Jewish convert to Christianity is an African official of the Nubian queen, whose title, Candace, meaning "queen mother," is mistaken for her personal name.

Africa and Egypt. Egypt is in Africa, and both the Bible and the early Greek and Roman explorers and historians viewed this great civilization of the Nile as African. Before the modern idea of color prejudice, the distinctions noted in antiquity between the brown Egyptians and their darker-hued neighbors to the south did not contain the racial and cultural connotations that exist today. The Bible therefore

The Queen of Sheba (1 Kings 10.1–13)

classified Egypt, along with Canaan and Arabia, as African in the Genesis account of the restored family of peoples after the Flood (Gen. 10).

This linkage between Egypt and its southern neighbor Nubia/Cush is reinforced by the presence of these darker southerners in Canaan during the ancestral period and afterward as major elements in the Egyptian army garrisoned there. The early-fourteenth-century BCE Amarna Letters, correspondence from Canaanite kings to Pharaoh Akhnaton, testify to the early African presence there. One letter, from Abdu-heba, king of pre-Israelite Jerusalem, complains of the rebellious Nubian troops stationed there. One can speculate that an African presence remained in the area, and that maintaining their tradition of military prowess, later generations of Nubians/Cushites either became part of David's forces, which captured Jerusalem, or remained part of Jerusalem's militia, which David incorporated as his own, as he did with the older Jebusite priesthood.

Still later in Israelite history, during the reign of Hezekiah of Judah (727–698 BCE), Nubia ruled Egypt as its Twenty-fifth Dynasty (751–656 BCE) and forged a close alliance with Judah in a common effort to ward off capture by the Assyrians. Even as the prophet Isaiah protested that the king should trust in God rather than in the Egyptians for the defense of Jerusalem, his oracle on the Cushite emissaries (Isa. 18.1–2) fixed in biblical tradition the Egypt/African common identity. This same equation is expressed in Nahum's lament over the fall of the Egyptian capital Thebes (Nah. 3.8–9), even as he exults over the destruction of Assyria's capital Nineveh.

Africa at the Royal Court and in the Wisdom Tradition. The Africans who are named in the Hebrew Bible are closely aligned with the royal court and wisdom traditions of ancient Israel. One of David's Cushite soldiers brought news of the death of his son Absalom (2 Sam. 18.21–32), and Solomon, already married to an Egyptian princess (1 Kings 3.1), entertained the Queen of Sheba who had come to visit him on a trade mission (1 Kings 10.1–13). Jeremiah was saved from death under King Zedekiah by an African court official Ebed-melek ("servant of the king"; Jer. 38–39), while in an earlier incident under King Jehoiakim a messenger of African heritage named Jehudi communicated with the prophet (Jer. 36.14). The prophet Zephaniah is called "son of Cushi" (Zeph. 1.1) in his genealogy, which extends back to Hezekiah.

Solomon as patron of wisdom opened the door to Egyptian proverbs and poetry as evidenced in segments of the book of Proverbs modeled upon the Egyptian "Instructions of Amen-em-ope" (Prov. 22.17–24.34), and in Psalm 104, which echoes an Egyptian hymn to Aton. Hezekiah, who aligned himself with the Cushite Dynasty, is also listed as a royal patron of Israel's proverbial wisdom (Prov. 25.1). The maiden in Song of Solomon 1.5 proclaims, "I am black and beautiful, O daughters of Jerusalem, like the tents of Kedar, like the curtains of Solomon." The dual imagery is clear; dark hue is paralleled by the black goatskin tents, and beauty is matched by the sumptuous royal curtains. (The Hebrew connector *wĕ* is taken in its normal sense as a conjunctive "and" rather than the less usual disjunctive "but").

Africa in Israelite Worship and Messianic Thought. Among those known to God under the imagery of Zion as mother of nations is Cush (Ps. 87.4), who also brings tribute to the Temple (Ps. 68.31). This concern for Cush and the other nations may extend from the formative experience of the Exodus and wilderness sojourn, where Hebrews

were accompanied by a "mixed multitude" (Exod. 12.38), including Phinehas (Exod. 6.25) and Moses' Cushite wife (Num. 12.1).

In prophetic literature, after God's wrath is vindicated on the nations of the earth, God will change their speech so all can worship God, and "from beyond the rivers of Ethiopia my suppliants, the daughter of my dispersed ones, shall bring my offering" (Zeph. 3.10). This refers to the African diaspora, to Israelite exiles in Africa returning with gifts of thanksgiving to God. Africa then with its people seen as converts shall come to worship God in Zion, along with dispersed Israelite exiles. It is in this context of God's universal reign that the prophet Amos proclaims, "Are you not like the Ethiopians to me, O people of Israel? says the Lord" (Amos 9.7). God is judge and ultimately redeemer of all nations.

The New Testament proclamation of Jesus as Messiah continues in the early mission of the apostle Philip who baptizes the African official in Acts 8.26–39. It is significant that in this incident the term "messiah" is interpreted in light of Isaiah 53.7–8 as God's suffering servant. That the African was reading Isaiah suggests that the emissary was a recent convert or a proselyte.

In the light of the Psalms and the prophets, then, Africans can be viewed both as diaspora and as proselytes among Israel's dispersed people, and also as forerunners of the conversion of all the nations of the earth.

ROBERT A. BENNETT

AFTERLIFE AND IMMORTALITY. *This entry consists of two articles on views of life after death within the historical communities of* Ancient Israel *and* Second Temple Judaism and Early Christianity.

Ancient Israel

Israelite views of the afterlife underwent substantial changes during the first millennium BCE, as concepts popular during the preexilic period eventually came to be rejected by the religious leadership of the exilic and postexilic communities, and new theological stances replaced them. Because many elements of preexilic beliefs and practices concerning the dead were eventually repudiated, the Hebrew Bible hardly discusses preexilic concepts at all; only scant and disconnected references to afterlife and the condition of the dead appear in the texts. A few passages from late-eighth through sixth-century sources are illuminating, however, because they attack various aspects of the popular notions about the dead during that period. With these data, a general though sketchy picture of Israelite views can be proposed.

Like all cultures in the ancient Near East, the Israelites believed that persons continued to exist after death. It was thought that following death, one's spirit went down to a land below the earth, most often called Sheol, but sometimes merely "Earth," or "the Pit." In the preexilic period, there was no notion of a judgment of the dead based on their actions during life, nor is there any evidence for a belief that the righteous dead go to live in God's presence. The two persons in the Hebrew Bible who are taken to heaven to live with God, Enoch (Gen. 5.24) and Elijah (2 Kings 2.11), do not die. All who die, righteous or wicked, go to Sheol (see Gen. 42:38; Num. 16.30–33).

The exact relationship between the body of a dead person and the spirit that lived on in Sheol is unclear, since the Bible does not discuss this issue. Many scholars assume that the Israelites did not fully distinguish between the body and the spirit, and thus believed that the deceased continued to have many of the same basic needs they had when they were alive, especially for food and drink. Unless these needs were met, the dead would find existence in Sheol to be unending misery. Such a close connection between feeding the dead through funerary offerings and their happiness in the afterlife is well attested in Mesopotamia and Egypt. It is assumed that Israelite funerary practices were similar and included long-term, regular provision of food and drink offerings for the dead.

Other scholars have pointed out the lack of evidence in the Bible for such funerary offerings. Two passages often quoted in reference to such offerings, Deuteronomy 26.14 and Psalm 106.28, are ambiguous and can be interpreted in different ways. Archaeological evidence from Iron Age tombs suggests that food and drink were provided at the tomb only when the burial took place. There is no evidence for regular post-funeral offerings of food at tombs in Israel. It is possible that the Israelites assumed that Sheol had its own food supply, and that the food placed in the tomb was conceived as provisions for the journey of the deceased to Sheol, but this is speculative.

Virtually no discussion of what existence in Sheol was thought to be like is preserved in preexilic literature. The few datable texts in the Bible that describe Sheol tend to be late and belong to authors who opposed important aspects of the popular view. They present Sheol in negative terms, as a place of darkness and gloom, where the dead exist without thought, strength, or even consciousness (Ps. 88.3–12; Isa. 38.18–19; Job 10.21–22; Eccles. 9.10).

These texts appear to be reactions against a considerably more positive view of existence in Sheol that was held in the preexilic period. There is evidence that many Israelites thought that the dead continued to play an active role in the world of the living, possessing the power to grant blessings to their relatives and to reveal the future. This was done through the process of necromancy, the consultation of the dead by a medium, and related practices, which appear to have been quite popular in Israel. Evidence for this is found in the substantial number of vehement denunciations of necromancy in the prophetic and legal literature of the eighth through sixth centuries BCE (e.g., Lev. 19.31; 20.6, 27; Deut. 18.10–14; Isa 8.19–20). Only one narrative account of a necromantic session has been preserved in the Bible—the story of Samuel's ghostly consultation with Saul at Endor (1 Sam. 28), and Saul is roundly criticized by the seventh-century editor of the books of Samuel for having resorted to this practice.

Necromancy was particularly opposed by the religious group that supported the worship of Yahweh alone. This group argued that blessings and the telling of the future were prerogatives of Yahweh, not of the dead, and that consultation with the dead for such purposes was an abomination against Yahweh. The popular views of afterlife and the dead came under increasing attack during the late eighth and seventh centuries. The laws against necromancy date to this period, and a number of outright attacks and satires on the older ideas about the nature of existence in Sheol appear in the literature of the time (e.g., Isa. 8.19–22; 14:9–11). It is interesting to note, however, that the laws against necromancy in Deuteronomy and Leviticus still assume not that it was impossible to summon the dead from Sheol but that it was inappropriate.

These laws apparently did not have the desired effect on the Judean population. During the exile, when the "Yahweh alone" party finally came to control the religious leadership of Judah, a further step was taken. Several texts appearing to date from the exilic and postexilic periods suggest that it is not only improper to consult the dead but actually impos-

sible to do so. A new theology developed that argued there is no conscious existence in Sheol at all. At death all contact with the world, and even with God, comes to an end. This notion explicitly appears in several late Psalms (6.5; 30.8–10; 88.3–12; etc.), Job (3.11–19; 14.10–14; 21.19–21), and Ecclesiastes (9.3–10). This startling idea was not new in the Near East. Skepticism about the afterlife is found in some Egyptian texts as early as the Middle Kingdom (ca. 2000–1750 BCE), but such notions were never adopted as an official doctrine there. In postexilic judah, however, this became the authoritative stance of the religious leadership, though it was probably not widely held by most Judeans.

WAYNE T. PITARD

Second Temple Judaism and Early Christianity

In the postexilic period, and particularly in the Hellenistic period following the conquest of Alexander the Great in 332 BCE, Jewish thought concerning death and afterlife underwent a major change, owing to the widespread influence of the Platonic idea of the immortality of the soul. Whereas prior to the period of the Hellenistic empires the official religious stance of Israel acknowledged some form of shadowy existence in Sheol for the person after death, beginning in the third century we find a flowering of literature describing the fate of the human soul after death, often in vivid and moving terms. This change is best illustrated by two passages from the wisdom literature. The book of Ecclesiastes (ca. third century BCE) illustrates the dominant view at the end of the exile: "Whoever is joined with all the living has hope, for a living dog is better than a dead lion. The living know that they will die, but the dead know nothing; they have no more reward, and even the memory of them is lost. . . . Whatever your hand finds to do, do with your might; for there is no work or thought or knowledge or wisdom in Sheol, to which you are going" (Eccles. 9.4–5, 10). The Wisdom of Solomon, written during the Hellenistic period, shows strong influence of Greek, especially Stoic, thought: "God created us for incorruption, and made us in the image of his own eternity, but through the devil's envy death entered the world, and those who belong to his company experience it. But the souls of the righteous are in the hand of God, and no torment will ever touch them. In the sight of the foolish they seemed to have died, and their departure was thought to be a disaster, and their going from us to be their destruction; but they are at peace. For though in the sight of others they were punished, their hope is full of immortality" (Wisd. of Sol. 2.23–3.4).

Two ideas concerning the fate of the soul after death were held in tension during the Hellenistic and Roman periods. The first was that of resurrection, that is, that at the end of time the soul would be rejoined with the body and each person would then receive reward or punishment. The concept is found in the Hebrew Bible only at Daniel 12.2: "And many of those who sleep in the dust of the earth shall awake, some to everlasting life, and some to shame and everlasting contempt." A modification of this idea was that only the righteous dead would be resurrected to share in the messianic age.

The second idea was that the immortal soul lived on after the death of the body, and immediately received its reward or punishment. This idea is vividly illustrated in the Testament of Abraham (ca. 100 CE), which depicts the judgment of souls after death. Each soul is brought before Abel, son of Adam, for judgment. The deeds of the soul are weighed in the balance; the righteous receive salvation, but the wicked are given over to fiery torments (Test. Abr. 12–13).

A

St. Michael weighing the souls, from The Last Judgment

The tension between these two ideas continued in rabbinic Judaism and early Christianity. References to the rabbis' views of the afterlife are scattered, but may be summarized thus: at death, the soul leaves the body, but may return from time to time until the body disintegrates. The righteous souls go to paradise, but the wicked to hell. Finally, in the messianic age there will be a bodily resurrection.

In early Christianity, the tension of the "already" of immortality and the "not yet" of resurrection continued to exist, but was transformed by the death and resurrection of Jesus. This is best illustrated by the teaching of Paul: "But if Christ is in you, though the body is dead because of sin, the spirit is life because of righteousness. If the Spirit of him who raised Jesus from the dead dwells in you, he who raised Christ from the dead will give life to your mortal bodies also through his Spirit that dwells in you" (Rom. 8.10–12). In certain groups, such as the community of John, the notion of the bodily resurrection was overridden by the spiritual life of the believer in Christ: "Very truly, I tell you, anyone who hears my word and believes him who sent me has eternal life, and does not come under judgment, but has passed from death to life" (John 5.24). Neither view has become dominant, and both continue to exist in tension in Judaism and Christianity until the present.

SIDNIE ANN WHITE

AGRICULTURE. In the Bible, agriculture and religion are intimately connected. Of the three major festivals two were clearly connected with the agricultural year. The Feast of Weeks was associated with the first fruits and the end of the grain harvest. The Feast of Booths was an occasion of joy at the completion of the harvesting of fruits. Some have connected the Passover with the beginning of the grain harvest. Furthermore, the poetic imagery of the Bible is heavily freighted with agricultural metaphors. The blessing of God was perceived in agricultural abundance and his cursing in drought. The golden age was described in terms of agricultural productivity. The singer in the Song of Solomon uses agricultural images to portray his beloved. Renewal for the author of the later part of Isaiah (chaps. 40–66) was expressed visually in miraculous agricultural phenomena. Jesus' teachings include many agricultural metaphors. The New Testament often uses agricultural images for the church.

Water. Palestine has almost no rain for six months of the year (15 April to 15 October). In late October and November the "early rain" begins. Precipitation then slackens in December and January only to intensify again in March (the "later rain"). The Mishnah prescribes a series of fasts if the rain fails to appear in October and November (m. Ta'an. 1.4–7). The dew in May and June triggers the final ripening process of the grain and renders the stalks soft enough to facilitate reaping.

Snow usually falls each winter on the hill country. The snow is seen as a special blessing and is called in Arabic "the salt of the earth." It kills the insects and is absorbed rather than running off. From ancient times there has been some irrigation from the Jordan River, from its tributaries, and from the great spring of En-gedi.

Land Preparation. The soil is rich and deep in the valleys, but most of the land is rocky hills that must be terraced to be used for agriculture. Solid rock is but a few inches below the surface. A wall is built on the slope, then stones are removed and earth carried in to level the ground (see Isa. 5.1–2). Thus the rocky ground in the parable of the sower indicates an area where the soil covering is too thin to support a mature plant (Luke 8.6). Plowing is done with a light one-handled plow. The farmer's other hand holds a thin pole with a small spade on one end used for cleaning the plow point and a spike on the other end used for driving the oxen. The point of the plow is covered with iron. This metal sleeve is held together with strips of iron about the shape of a sword (cf. Isa. 2.4). After plowing, the large clods are generally broken up with heavy hoes. The land is plowed in preparation for the rain. After the first rains the seed is scattered by hand, and then the seed is covered by a second plowing. If this second plowing is done carelessly the birds will eat the seeds (see Luke 8.5). Grain is cut by hand and transported to threshing floors near the villages.

The Farmer's Enemies. Drought was an ever present threat. A locust plague was rare (Joel 1.2–4) but devastating. There were no sprays for blight (see Amos 4.9). Fire could destroy a crop at harvest time. The hot southeast desert winds of May and June can critically damage a number of crops. Thus, remembering past losses, the farmer would "sow in tears" (Ps. 126.5–6).

Crops. Among the food-producing trees, the hardy olive bears fruit each year after six months of drought. The oil was used for food, medicine, soap, and light. Figs were a major source of sugar. The tree's deep shade was a convenient place to study (John 1.48); it symbolized peace (Mic. 4.4). The sycamore fig is small and tasteless; only the poor dress and gather them (see Amos 7.14). The tasty red pomegranate grows on a large shrub; this fruit is referred to metaphorically in love poetry (Song of Sol. 4.3). The almond blooms first in the spring (see Jer. 1.11–12). The word apple (quince?) figures prominently in the Song of Solomon. A tasty molasses is boiled out of carob pods, and the remaining husks become animal feed (Luke 15.16). Date palms flourished in the Jordan valley.

The common grains were wheat, barley, and spelt (KJV: rye). The wheat was cut and transported to the threshing floor where it was systematically trodden by animals and flailed with sticks or crushed with a threshing sledge. The latter is made of two wide boards joined on the top with two cross arms. The bottom is embedded with rows of sharp-edged flint nodules. The sledge is dragged by animals in a circle over the wheat with the driver standing on the sledge to add weight. Occasionally pieces of iron were used rather than flint (Amos 1.3). The wheat was then winnowed by throwing it into the air on a windy day (Ps. 1.4; Luke 3.17). Finally the wheat was put through a sieve to remove the remaining impurities (see Luke 22.31). Flax was grown for clothing and rope. Sesame produced cooking oil. Lentils and chickpeas supplemented the protein available. Onions, garlic, cucumbers, and melons were among the vegetables cultivated. Herbs included mint and cumin. The Mishnah lists the bitter herbs to be eaten at Passover as lettuce, chicory, pepperwort, snakeroot, and dandelion (*m. Pesaḥ*. 2.6).

KENNETH E. BAILEY

ALEXANDER III ("THE GREAT"). Macedonian, born in 356 BCE. After the assassination of his father, Philip II, at Aegae in 336, Alexander ascended to the throne and took over his father's plan of a crusade to punish the Persians for Xerxes' invasion of Greece almost a century and a half ear-

lier. Alexander crossed the Hellespont with a total force of about fifty thousand in 334 and defeated the Persian army in three major battles, the last in 331.

These victories opened the heart of the Persian empire to Alexander. Persepolis was sacked and the palace of Xerxes burned. From Persepolis and Media, Alexander conquered Bactria and Sogdiana (330–329) and then extended his eastern frontier to the Hyphasis (Beas) and the lower Indus River (327–325). At the Hyphasis, the Macedonian army refused to march farther east. From the Indus Delta, Alexander marched west with part of his army across the Gedrosian desert, where his army suffered great losses during the fall of 325. He reached Susa in March of 324, where he and ninety-one members of his court married wives from the Persian nobility. During the final year of his life, Alexander discharged ten thousand Macedonian veterans at Opis, and then at Babylon, in 323, made plans for future conquests (especially Arabia). He died, probably of a fever following a drinking party, on 10 June 323.

Alexander undoubtedly was the greatest general in Greek history; he made the army forged by his father into an irresistible force by a combination of uncanny strategic insight, versatility, and courage beyond reason. The cities he founded (reportedly over seventy) planted pockets of Hellenism throughout the Near East. He also made monarchy central to the politics of the Greek world; his kin and generals fought to establish themselves as his heir until about 275, when there emerged the three kingdoms that dominated the eastern Mediterranean until the advance of Rome: Macedon, ruled by the Antigonids until 168 BCE; Egypt, ruled by the Ptolemies until 31 BCE; and Syria, ruled by the Seleucids until 64 BCE. It is against the background of the origins of the Seleucid dynasty that the author of 1 Macca-

Olive grove in Galilee, Israel

Alexander the Great

bees presents a sketch of Alexander's conquests (1.1–7) and the character of Antiochus Epiphanes (1.10–64).

GUY MACLEAN ROGERS

ALIEN. Also translated "sojourner," "resident alien," and "stranger," an alien (Hebr. *gēr*) is technically a person in a community who is not part of its traditional lineages. In the Hebrew Bible, "aliens" usually are non-Israelites living ("sojourning") in Israel (Exod. 12.19; Isa. 16.4; Jer. 42.15), but they can also be Israelites of one tribe "sojourning" in the territory of another tribe (Judg. 19.16; 2 Sam. 4.3; 2 Chron. 15.9). Such persons were often financially distressed, forced to be dependents of "native" residents (but see Lev. 25.45, 47). Thus, aliens are often mentioned alongside widows, orphans, and die poor as typically in need of assistance (Deut. 24.17–21; Jer. 7.6; Zech. 7.10). Aliens could be subjected to manual labor (Deut 29.11); yet, special attention is given to accord them equal status with native Israelites (Num. 15.14–16; Ezek. 47.21–23), making them corecipients of God's blessings (Deut. 10.18) and curses (Num. 15.26; Deut. 31.12; Josh. 8.35). The Israelites are commanded to treat aliens well, because they were once aliens in Egypt (Exod. 22.21; 23.9; Deut. 10.19). In fact, they are to view themselves as aliens "sojourning" on God's land (Lev. 25.23; 1 Chron. 29.15; Ps. 39.12), thereby furthering their sense of dependence on God.

New Testament writers describe their Israelite ancestors as aliens in Egypt (Acts 7.6; 13.17) and the exile in Babylon as the time of "sojourning" (Matt. 1.11, 12, 17). In dealing with the problem of incorporating gentiles into an all-Jewish community, Paul says that they are "no longer strangers and aliens, but. . . citizens. . . of the household of God" (Eph. 2.19). Any hint of separation is thereby eliminated. On the other hand, all who have become members of God's "peo-

ple" must disavow allegiance to other groups, considering themselves aliens in the world around them (1 Pet. 2.11). In this regard, Abraham is held up as an ancient model (Heb. 11.9; cf. Gen. 23.4).

TIMOTHY M. WILLIS

ALTARS. References to altars appear in the Bible some four hundred times, including their construction, materials (e.g., unhewn stone, wood, earth, brass/bronze, gold), types (especially for burnt offerings in the majority of cases, with a smaller number of references to incense altars), ritual acts (especially the slaughter and burning of animal sacrifices, and the sprinkling of blood), associated fixtures and paraphernalia (e.g., staves, rings, grates, horns, and vessels used), as well as more casual aspects.

The ordinary Hebrew word for altar is *mizbēaḥ*, meaning "slaughtering place"; the Greek word *thusiastērion* has a similar meaning. In biblical and nonbiblical traditions, an altar is not a natural object but rather a built structure. It is not inhabited by a supernatural force, though it attracts that force; thus, the altar is not the same as a sacred stone.

In biblical narrative, altars are built at a location where divine-human contact has been, or presumably could be, encountered. They are not habitation places; rather, they provide cultic access to the deity. They may be overturned, displaced, or rebuilt without any impact upon their use or meaning. Profaning them does not, therefore, affect the deity; instead, it precludes their use for proper ritual access, at least temporarily.

The altar in the Bible is a constructed platform, initially intended for slaughtering sacrifices for the God of Israel next to or upon its surface, who would visit the site regardless of its location (see Exod. 20.24). An altar, then, could be located anywhere needful or appropriate, and its installation and purpose would be accepted by the deity. Thus, the early proliferation of such installations posed no theological problem. It was only when, due to sociopolitical necessity, the cult was centralized at the Temple in Jerusalem and exclusive access to the deity was located there, that, theoretically at least, other altars were no longer permitted.

Other aspects of altars were similarly rather loosely conceived. How an altar was to be constructed—its materials, its permanency of location, and even its precise use—seem not to have been uniformly fixed. In all probability, the occasional demand for simplicity (e.g., unhewn stone for construction) can be explained only on the basis of real or fictive practice acquiring the weight of tradition, and therefore becoming proper, or on the basis of anachronistic insistence on purity.

The variation in types of altars, and the precise ritual involved for each, is perfectly explicable on both developmental and institutional grounds, as the cult developed in sophistication. However, the generic altar continued to be a point of access to the deity, regardless of the specific sacrifice made upon it to attract divine attention.

Other uses of the altar, such as a place of sanctuary or asylum place (see 1 Kings 1.50–53; 2.28–34), or for the declaration of binding oaths (Josh. 22.26–28, 34), are secondary. Since the deity could be met at altars, divine protection or divine witness could be sought at the same location.

Certain altars, especially those constructed or repaired by important people, are specifically mentioned in the Bible, either to enhance the concept, or because of the prominence of their builders. The idea of altar construction is thus carried back to Noah (Gen. 8.20), with subsequent reinforcement of the tradition attributed to Abraham and others of the ancestral family. Several kings, likewise, are singled out for having performed the same pious act: Saul, David, Solomon, and other monarchs are specifically noted.

Just as construction and use varied through time, the correct rituals for offering sacrifices varied. Various references deal with sprinkling or pouring the blood of slaughtered animals upon the altar, upon its "horns" or sides, and to burning the entire sacrifice or only the fat upon it. Uniformity developed principally with the centralization of the cult, and was read back into the time of Moses and Aaron in order to authenticate the practice.

The appearance of altars is complicated by references to "horns" (e.g., Exod. 29.12; 1 Kings 1.50; Amos 3.14). When these appurtenances first appear is difficult to judge, as is their precise use. On the basis of archaeological finds from somewhat later periods, these corner uprights may have served to support vessels containing the sacrifices, beneath which the coals of the altar were placed on grates. Such a utilitarian construction would have facilitated cleaning, as well as the actual placement of various kinds of offerings on separate occasions. This view is supported to some extent by references to the vessels of the altars as separate items.

PHILIP C. HAMMOND

AMMON. A tribal state located to the east of the Jordan River (Map 1:Y-Z4) that played a marginally significant role in the history of Palestine during the Iron Age. Relatively little is known about Ammon, its history, and its culture. Our main sources of information about it are the Bible and Assyrian inscriptions, both of which deal almost exclusively with Ammon's external affairs. Only a few substantive Ammonite inscriptions have been discovered so far, and excavations are just beginning to illuminate Ammonite culture.

The origins of the tribe of Ammon are obscure. Genesis 19:30–38 presents an artificial and satiric legend that portrays the eponymous ancestor of the Ammonites, Ben-ammi, as the offspring of the incestuous union of Lot and his daughter. But this provides no insight into the initial development of Ammon. The region that became the land of Ammon was occupied fairly densely during the Middle and Late Bronze Ages, but there is no evidence whether the tribe of Ammon was already a distinct ethnic group during that time.

By the early part of the Iron Age (ca. 1200–1000 BCE), however, both archaeological and literary evidence indicates that a somewhat centralized state began to form around the capital city of Rabbat-bene-ammon ("Rabbah of the sons of Ammon"; modern Amman, Jordan). Conflict arose during this period between the Ammonites and the Israelites who lived to the east of the Jordan River (Judg. 11 and 1 Sam. 11). The earliest Ammonite king whose name is preserved is Nahash, who besieged the Israelite town of Jabesh-gilead and was defeated by Israelite troops rallied by the young Saul (1 Sam. 11). Nahash's son, Hanun, provoked a war with Israel during the reign of David, which led to Ammon's defeat and incorporation into David's empire as a vassal (2 Sam. 10; 12.26–31).

After the death of Solomon and the breakup of the united kingdom of Israel, Ammon presumably became independent again. Little is known of the kingdom during the ninth century, but it likely came under the domination of Aram-Damascus, especially during the reign of Hazael (ca. 842–800 BCE), as did most of Palestine. During the eighth century, Damascus declined, and Israel and Judah experienced a resurgence of political power. Ammon appears to have come under the control of Judah during the reigns

Nineteenth-century engraving of Cain and Abel offering their sacrifices on an altar (Genesis 4: 3–5)

of Uzziah and Jotham (2 Chron. 26.8; 27.5), but with the arrival of the Assyrian king Tiglathpileser III, Ammon, like the other small kingdoms, became an Assyrian vassal.

The Assyrian period (late eighth to late seventh century) was a prosperous period for Ammon. The Assyrians guaranteed its position on the international trade routes and helped protect its flanks from the various nomadic groups that threatened the security of the routes. Excavations and Assyrian texts indicate that Ammon extended its boundaries during this period, westward to the Jordan River, northward into Gilead, and southward toward Heshbon. The most substantial ruins of the Iron Age date to this period, and seals, inscriptions, and statuary indicate the kingdom's wealth. A number of stone towers found in several regions of Amnion appear to date to this period. Once thought to be a system of Ammonite fortresses, recent studies now identify most of them as agricultural towers such as the one described in Isaiah 5.2.

There is uncertainty about the situation of Ammon during the Neo-Babylonian period. It is probable that Ammon was involved in the great rebellion against Nebuchadrezzar in 589–586 BCE, and that, as a result, it was annexed into the Babylonian provincial system. By the succeeding Persian period only the name of the kingdom of Ammon survived, largely as a geographical rather than as a political term (Map 10:Y5). Recent excavations and surveys indicate that a modest population continued to inhabit the region through this period.

Ammonite religion and culture remain little known. Even the characteristics of its patron deity, Milcom, are uncertain.

WAYNE T. PITARD

Amos the prophet, with an angel above.

AMOS, THE BOOK OF. The early prophets of Israel—Samuel, Elijah, Elisha, and many others—are known from stories included in the historical books of Samuel and Kings. Amos was the first of the prophets whose name goes with a book entirely concerned with his life and message; nothing is known about him from any other source. The composition of his prophecy represented the creation of a new kind of literature. It was followed by other books that carry the names of a succession of prophets: three large books ("major" prophets) and twelve small ones ("minor").

The authors behind these shorter books were by no means "minor" in stature. Amos himself is one of the giants of the ancient world, one of the most powerful of the biblical prophets. He brought the prophetic word against social injustice and international terrorism and he preached repentance—and, when that failed, he denounced the impenitents. As a visionary ("seer": 1.1; 7.12) he located the domestic wrongs within Israel, and the crimes within the community of nations in a global, indeed cosmic setting. He held the rulers responsible for the evils in the world (1.3–2.16) and addressed his messages primarily to them. He placed Israel, the chosen people of Yahweh, on the same footing as other nations (3.9; 4.11; 6.2; 9.7). God expects the same morality from them all, but the words of reproach, condemnation, and judgment are addressed most directly to Israel because of its domestic wrongs.

Amos was not only a prophet of doom; he also called the people to reform, and when they failed and disaster became inescapable, he pointed to the hope of future restoration (9.11–15).

Amos's career is set in the time of two kings, Uzziah of Judah and Jeroboam II of Israel. Both monarchs had exceptionally long reigns, covering most of the first half of the eighth century BCE. Many scholars date Amos toward the end of that period (about 750 BCE), or even later; but recent research into the political situation disclosed by the book suggests that it could be earlier than that. Assyria is nowhere recognized as a factor (except in the Septuagint text of 3.9), and the six nations surrounding Israel are addressed in 1.3–2.3 as if they are all still independent; this more accurately describes the early decades of the eighth century.

On first reading, the literary materials in the book of Amos seem to be diverse and poorly coordinated. There is some narrative in chaps. 7–9, but the main ingredients are prophetic oracles of many different kinds. In addition, the book contains a considerable number of wisdom sayings as well as several liturgical hymns.

The vocabulary and grammar are closer to standard Hebrew prose than to the lyrical poetry of Psalms, or even to the prophecy in Hosea. It is, nevertheless, highly rhythmic in form and rhetorical in artistry, a distinctive medium that may be identified as "prophetic oratory." The originally oral message has been transformed into literature by skillful editing that has integrated the variegated material into a coherent composition. The result is a real book. Each constituent oracle may have had a limited application when it was originally delivered, but their arrangement brings these pieces together into a comprehensive statement about Amos's lifework, and one that is of enduring value and significance.

Scholars who expect Amos's message to be consistent, almost uniform, have doubted his authorship of some portions because they differ from the rest. Several of the oracles against the nations (Tyre, Edom, Judah) have been bracketed out by some scholars because they seem more appropriate to later times; but all eight are needed, not only for complete geographical coverage, but also to secure the intricate and remarkably symmetrical design that unifies the great speech of chaps. 1–2 and secures its total impact on ancient hearer and modern reader alike.

The three short poems that celebrate the power of Yahweh in creation and history (4.13; 5.8–9; 9.5–6) are distinct hymnal-credal statements, possibly fragments of earlier epic recitals. They have been skillfully used in the final composition of Amos's message so as to secure a vital theological component. Their scope is cosmic; God's claims on the whole world—all nations, not just Israel—are grounded in his relationship and interest as creator, owner, and judge of the universe.

The historical perspective is likewise vast. God's dealings with Israel are reviewed in the light of events that have taken place over centuries, with the Exodus as a major point of reference (2.10; 3.1; 5.25; 9.7).

The book falls into three distinct sections, each with its own message and mood. The last, the Book of Visions (7.1–9.8) contains the only narrative material. The autobiographical report of five visions (7.1–9; 8.1–3; 9.1) provides a framework that carries the dramatic report of Amos's confrontation with Amaziah, priest of Bethel (7.10–17), as well as prophetic oracles.

In the first pair of visions (7.1–6), Amos is able to secure a reprieve for Israel by his intercession. This situation, in which there is still some hope, corresponds to the central message of the Book of Woes (5.1–6.14), which is built around the exhortation (at 5.24):

Let justice roll down like waters, and righteousness like an everflowing stream.

There is still time for repentance. The plagues reported in chap. 4 were intended as chastisements that would lead to contrition and reparation, but they failed to achieve this, and turned into destructive judgments.

In the second pair of visions (7.7–9; 8.1–3) the situation has completely changed. There is no intercession; rather, the Lord says twice that he will never pass by them again. This new attitude corresponds to the message of certain doom that pervades the first four chapters, and especially the opening speech, with its note of finality. The situation has become hopeless. Amos's early messages, corresponding to the intercessions of the first two visions, have been presented in the middle of the final book (chaps. 5–6); his final message comes first (chaps. 1–2), with the following material analyzing the causes and justifying the decision.

The major cause of the change in attitude between the first and second pairs of visions, the final proof that repentance will never be forthcoming, is the refusal to listen to the prophets, and worse, the attempt to silence them altogether (2.12; 3.8; 7.10–17). Amaziah's ban is the turning point: when the highest religious leader rejects the word of God and his messenger, judgment is inevitable (4.12). The fifth vision and the oracles that go with it (9.1–10) predict the total destruction of "all the sinners of my people" (9.10).

That is not the end of everything, however. As elsewhere in the Bible, death can be overcome by the miracle of resurrection, and Amos promises the recovery of Israel's life and institutions in a new age of prosperity and bliss (9.11–15).

FRANCIS I. ANDERSE

ANDREW. A disciple of Jesus and brother of Simon Peter. The two are pictured as fishermen working beside the sea when Jesus summons them to follow him and become "fish-

Close-up of a mural of an angel, Church of St, Catherine of Alexandria, Galatina, Apulia

ers of people" (Mark 1.16–18; Matt. 4.18–20). In John's gospel (1.35–42) Andrew first appears as a disciple of John the Baptist.

Although less prominent than his brother, Andrew is present for Jesus' bread miracle (John 6) and the apocalyptic speech on the Mount of Olives (Mark 13.3–37). Lists of the Twelve name Andrew second (Matt. 10.2; Luke 6.14) or fourth (Mark 3.18; Acts 1.13). According to late medieval tradition, Andrew was martyred by being crucified on an ✕-shaped cross, which later appears on the flag of Great Britain representing Scotland, whose patron is Andrew.

PHILIP SELLEW

ANGELS. In Israel's early traditions, God was perceived as administering the cosmos with a retinue of divine assistants. The members of this divine council were identified generally as "sons of God" and "morning stars" (Job 1.6; 38.7), "gods" (Ps. 82) or the "host of heaven" (Neh. 9.6; cf. Rev. 1.20), and they functioned as God's vicegerents and administrators in a hierarchical bureaucracy over the world (Deut. 32.8 [LXX]; cf. 4.19; 29.26). Where Israel's polytheistic neighbors perceived these beings as simply a part of the pantheon, the Bible depicts them as subordinate and in no way comparable to the God of Israel.

The most ancient Israelites would probably have felt uncomfortable in describing all these beings as "angels," for the English word "angel" comes from the Greek *aggelos,* which at first simply meant "messenger" (as does the Hebrew term for angel, *mal'āk*). God's divine assistants were often more than mere messengers. Cherubim and seraphim, for example, never function as God's messengers, for their bizarre appearance would unnecessarily frighten humans. On the contrary, God is frequently depicted in early narratives as dispensing with divine messengers, for he deals directly with humans without intermediaries.

A

As time passed, however, an increasing emphasis on God's transcendence correlated with an increasing need for divine mediators. These beings who brought God's messages to humans are typically portrayed as anthropomorphic in form, and such a being may often be called a "man" (Gen. 18.2; Josh. 5.13; Ezek. 9.2, 11; Dan. 9.21; 12.6–7; Zech. 1.8; Luke 24.4). The members of God's council are the envoys who relay God's messages and perform tasks appropriate to their status as messengers (1 Kings 22.19–22; Job 1.6–12). In some narratives of encounters with supernatural beings, there is reluctance to identify them by name (Gen. 32.29; Judg. 13.17–18). But as these messengers become more and more frequent, they eventually are provided with individual names and assigned increasingly specific tasks that go beyond that of a messenger. The only two angels named in the Hebrew Bible are in the book of Daniel: Gabriel reveals the future (Dan. 8–9; cf. Luke 1) while Michael has a more combative role, opposing the forces of evil (Dan. 10, 12; Jude 9; Rev. 12.7). The angelic hierarchy becomes more and more explicit and elaborate (Dan. 10.13; Eph. 6.12; Jude 9; 1 Pet. 3.22;), and each human being has his or her own protecting angel (Matt. 18.10; Acts 12.15). The term "messenger" (Grk. *aggelos;* Hebr. *mal'āk*) is used so frequently to depict these beings in their encounters with humans that it becomes a generic term to describe all supernatural beings apart from God, whether or not they actually functioned as messengers.

Angels are depicted as having the freedom to make moral choices, for they require judicial supervision (1 Cor. 6.3; Jude 6) and God himself is reluctant to trust them (Job 4.18). The Bible records a number of angelic rebellions or perversions (Gen. 6.1–4; Ps. 82; Isa. 14.12–15; Ezek. 28; 2 Pet. 2.4; Rev. 12.4–9), as a result of which some rebel angels are already incarcerated (Jude 6).

"The Angel [or Messenger] of the Lord" is a problematic figure. The ambiguous Hebrew phrase is best translated without the definite article, that is, "an angel [messenger] of Yahweh" (as do the Septuagint and NJV; cf. Matt. 1.20; 2.13, 19; 28.2; Acts 8.26). Later Christian theology tended to see the preincarnate Christ in this figure (hence the definite article), but the phrase probably referred vaguely to any mediator sent by God. He may be human (Hag. 1.13; Mal. 2.7). When the figure is clearly referred to as superhuman, he does not always function as a messenger but instead talks and behaves as if he were God, even failing to introduce his words as the message of another who sent him. Since early stories are internally inconsistent, identifying the figure as both God and God's messenger (Gen. 16.7–13; 22.11–12; 31.11–13; Exod. 3.2–4; Judg. 6.11–23), it is probable that some of these stories originally described God at work but were modified through time to accommodate God's increasing transcendence as one who no longer casually confronted humankind.

The increasing role played by angels in the later stages of the Hebrew Bible is found everywhere in the New Testament. The voice of God (the Father) is only exceptionally heard in the New Testament, unlike earlier biblical traditions. Instead, angels bring God's message to humans (Matt. 1.20; Luke 1.11, 26; 2.9; Acts 8.26; 10.3) and assist Jesus (Matt. 4.1; Luke 22.43) and his followers (Acts 5.19; 12.7). Angels have limited knowledge (Matt. 24.36; 1 Pet. 1.12), and when they appear to human beings, they may be described as descending from heaven (Matt. 28.2; John 1.51; cf. Gen. 28.12). Although Jesus alludes to the absence of the institution of marriage among angels (Matt. 22.30), angels are sexual beings (Gen. 6.4; Zech. 5.9). Some Jews, particularly the most conservative, denied their existence (Acts 23.8). But among Jews and Christians in general, angelology continued to develop so that not only was Satan provided with his own retinue of angels as a counterpart to God (Matt. 25.41; 2 Cor. 12.7), but hundreds of names and functions are also applied to angels in extrabiblical texts such as the books of Enoch.

SAMUEL A. MEIER

ANIMALS. As a modern general designation for all living creatures other than plants, "animal" does not always have a simple equivalent in the Bible. The closest equivalents in the Hebrew Bible include *ḥayyâ* ("living [creature]," Lev. 11.2), and *bĕhēmâ*, which usually refers to all quadrupeds (Gen. 6.7), or more specifically to domesticated animals (Exod. 22.9–10). Yet even these Hebrew terms do not usually include birds or fish. The Septuagint and the New Testament frequently use *tetrapous* ("quadruped") or *thērion* to translate both Hebrew terms.

Classification Systems. Aside from problems in basic terminology, the differences between biblical and modern Linnaean systems of animal classification sometimes create uncertainties in translation. For example, the Hebrew *dîšōn* (Deut. 14.5) has been translated by different versions or scholars as "ibex," "white-rumped deer," "pygarg," or "Arabian oryx," all representing completely different genera in most modern classifications. More than one species of predatory birds (e.g., eagles and vultures) may be subsumed under the Hebrew term *nešer*.

Dietary laws in Leviticus 11 and Deuteronomy 14.3–20, as well as the sacrificial system, depended on a system of classification which distinguished clean and unclean animals. In general, a clean land animal had cloven hoofs and chewed its cud (a ruminant artiodactyl in modern zoology), thus eliminating reptiles, amphibians, rodents and carnivorous animals from the diet. Animals that only chewed their cud (e.g., the hare) or only had cloven hoofs (e.g., the pig) also were eliminated. Most insects are unclean (the locust being one exception), and only those aquatic animals with fins and scales are fit to eat (Lev. 11.9–10). The logic underlying the clean/unclean dichotomy in Leviticus remains unclear. Other ancient Near Eastern cultures had views similar to those found in Leviticus and Deuteronomy regarding unclean animals, including the pig. Not surprisingly, for the Jewish sect that became known as Christianity, Levitical animal classification was a major issue in the debate about observance of dietary laws (Acts 11.5–9).

Origin, Use, and Relationship with Humans. Biblical views concerning animals are linked closely with the two principal myths of creation. In the first account, generally ascribed to P, all the animals were created before both man and woman (Gen. 1.20–30). In the other account (Gen. 2.7–22), usually ascribed to J, the creation of all the animals follows that of the first man, and God creates the first woman only after none of the animals was found helpful to the man. In both accounts animals were created to serve the needs of human beings, though Genesis 9.3 (cf. Gen. 1.30) indicates that humans were not expected to use animals for food before the Flood. Psalm 104.10–30 depicts Yahweh, not human beings, as responsible for the general welfare of the animal kingdom.

Sheep, goats, cattle, and pigs are the most extensively attested domestic animals from the Neolithic period onward in ancient Palestine. The camel may have been domesticated by the early third millennium BCE in some portions of Asia,

Jesus as the shepherd separating the sheep from the goats (Matt. 25.32)

but the geographical extent of domestication by the second millennium remains undetermined.

Aside from providing a ready reserve of fresh meat and milk, most domestic animals could provide hides, bone implements, transportation, and other commodities. Wealth and status were often measured by the number of animals that a person owned (Job 1.3). The raising and trading of horses played an important role in achieving and maintaining military power in the Near East (1 Kings 4.26; 10.28–29).

Although offering animals to appease a deity has a strong magico-religious basis, animal sacrifice formed an important part of the economy in ancient Israel. Ordinances that required that only the best of the flock be brought to the Temple for sacrifice (Lev. 1.2; Deut. 15.21) in effect demanded the allocation of the best animal resources (especially cattle, sheep, and goats) for the priesthood. Smaller animals such as pigeons were acceptable if the worshipper was too poor to offer larger animals (Lev. 5.7). Christian writers argued that Jesus' death nullified the need for animal sacrifice altogether (Heb. 10.1–18).

The Bible also mentions various animals that were considered harmful. Some of the plagues sent upon Egypt (Exod. 7–11) included the uncontrolled multiplication of frogs, gnats, flies, and locusts. Locusts were particularly feared because they could destroy agriculture and so cause a famine (Joel 1.4). Rituals sometimes were devised for protection from poisonous animals (e.g., snakes in Num. 21.1–4).

Animal Imagery. Biblical authors often use animal imagery to express aspects of their culture. Sheep imagery is used to depict a future messianic Utopia (Isa. 11.6–7), as well as the Israelite community (Pss. 44.11; 79.13; 80.1). In the New Testament Jesus was portrayed as a lamb (John 1.29), and he warned his disciples about wolves dressed in sheep's clothing (Matt. 7.15).

Lions and other ferocious animals are often used to speak of hostile armies or personal enemies (Ps. 22.21; 1 Pet. 5.8), though lions may also symbolize positive figures (e.g., Judah in Gen. 49.9). Certain birds are associated with desolation (Ps. 102.6). Dogs usually are represented negatively in the Bible (Prov. 26.11; Matt. 7.6), though a recently discovered dog cemetery from the Persian period at Ashkelon may suggest the existence of non-Israelite cults that viewed the dog positively.

The Bible is also stocked with a variety of mythological creatures such as the cherubim (1 Kings 8.6–7) and seraphim (Isa. 6.2), which combine human and animal traits. Leviathan (Isa. 27.1) and Rahab (Isa. 51.9) are primordial beasts that were believed to threaten God's creation. As was the case with El, Baal, and other Canaanite deities, Yahweh may have been depicted as a bull (Exod. 32.4–6). Bull figurines from the second and first millennia BCE have been found at, among other places, Hazor and Ashkelon, though it is difficult to determine which deity, if any, is represented by the figurines.

Aside from biblical scholars and archaeologists, ecologists and ethicists have recently become interested in the extent to which the biblical view of animals has influenced the relationship of modern civilizations with nature (see A. Linzey, *Christianity and the Rights of Animals*, 1987; and

E. J. Schochet, *Animal Life in the Jewish Tradition: Attitudes and Relationships,* 1984).

HECTOR IGNACIO AVALOS

ANTICHRIST. The word "antichrist" occurs in the Bible only in 1 and 2 John. The prefix *ánti-* in Greek means "over against," "instead of," and so may imply usurpation as well as substitution. In 1 John, the coming of Antichrist is referred to as a standard sign of the "last hour," which has already happened in people who deny that Jesus is the Christ who has come in the flesh and have seceded from the community; they are "false prophets" who embody the "spirit of antichrist" (1 John 2.18–22; 4.1–3; 2 John 7).

On the other hand, 2 Thessalonians warns, again as standard teaching, that the day of the Lord cannot come until the "lawless one," "the one destined for destruction," has appeared. He will usurp God's place in his Temple, and deceive people with Satan-inspired signs and wonders, until the Lord Jesus appears and destroys him (2 Thess. 2.1–12). There are links with the prophecies of a desolating sacrilege in the holy place (Dan. 9.27; 12.11; Matt. 24.15; Mark 13.14), and of false messiahs and false prophets, which must precede the coming of the Son of Man (Mark 13.21–22; Matt. 24.23–24). Luke has historicized the picture in terms of the fall of Jerusalem in 70 CE (21.20); and John sees the "one destined for destruction" not as a future figure but as Judas Iscariot (17.12).

The marks of the figure of Thessalonians recur in the two beasts of Revelation 13: the beast from the sea, which in its death and resurrection is a parody of Christ and claims divine honors; and the beast from the earth, which deceives people into worshiping the first beast, and with its lamblike

The preaching of the antichrist, from the chapel of the Madonna di San Brizio, 1499–1504

voice and signs and wonders is a parody of the Holy Spirit. But there is also here an element of political coercion, and the sea beast's healed wound and his number identify him as Nero, returned from the dead, the persecuting emperor who was worshiped as a god.

The antecedents of this figure lie in Daniel 7, which was immensely important for New Testament writers. This vision relates that before the coming of God's kingdom there would be a time of disasters, persecution, and apostasy, and that opposition to God and his people would be summed up in a nation or person, human or superhuman, whom God or his agent would destroy. The vision is related to the Near Eastern myth of God's conflict with the dragon of the chaos waters, out of which this world was created. The myth celebrated the victory of order over chaos in nature; in some biblical passages the powers of chaos were historicized as nations opposed to God and his people—Egypt (Ezek. 29.3) and Babylon (Jer. 51.34)—and in Daniel 7 the four beasts arising out of the sea (on which the sea beast of Rev. 13 is modeled) represent persecuting empires. They culminate in the "little horn" on the fourth beast, which represents the Greek king Antiochus Epiphanes, who tried to hellenize Judaism, and set up his statue in the Temple (the desolating sacrilege referred to at Mark 13.14 and Matt. 24.15). The book of Revelation updates this picture in terms of the Roman empire, the emperor cult, and collaborating Christians (Rev. 2.14–29; 13.1–18).

On the other hand, those who accepted the state as God's ordinance (Rom. 13.1–7) saw the expected Antichrist as the embodiment of a specious spirit of lawlessness, which the state was keeping in check (2 Thess. 2.6, 7, according to one interpretation). After the Christianization of the Roman empire, this understanding became popular and even Revelation was read in this light, but corruptions in church and state led people back to Revelation's original sense.

The Antichrist expectation, with its attendant disasters, apostasy, and martyrdom of the faithful, dominated the Middle Ages and the sixteenth and seventeenth centuries. The myth expresses both the speciousness of evil and its apparent omnipotence, while asserting the imminence of God's final victory and the value of faithful witness in its achievement. From another point of view, it has provided a forceful way of characterizing opponents in church or state, and dignifying resistance to them.

JOHN SWEET

APOCALYPTIC LITERATURE. The words "apocalyptic" and "apocalypse" (from a Greek root meaning "to uncover," "to reveal") are terms that came to be used from the second century CE onward to indicate a type of Jewish and Christian literature akin to the New Testament Apocalypse (an alternative title of the book of Revelation), which gave its name to this style of writing.

The term "apocalyptic literature" is taken to refer to a body of revelatory writing produced in Jewish circles between 250 BCE and 200 CE and subsequently taken up and perpetuated by Christianity. It includes not only the genre "apocalypse" but may also include other related types of literature, such as testaments, hymns, and prayers, which share some of its more important characteristics and motifs; that is, it does not have a common literary form but is diverse and even hybrid in its literary expression. The apocalypse type of writing, which forms the core of this literature, is a record of divine disclosures made known through the agency of angels, dreams, and visions. These

The last judgment

may take different forms: an otherworldly journey in which the "secrets" of the cosmos are made known (the so-called vertical apocalypses), or a survey of history often leading to an eschatological crisis in which the cosmic powers of evil are destroyed, the cosmos is restored, and Israel (or "the righteous") is redeemed (the so-called horizontal or historical apocalypses).

Biblical Apocalypses. The scholarly consensus sees a strong link between the apocalypse and biblical prophecy, and regards such writings as Ezekiel 38–39, Isaiah 24–27, Zechariah 12–14, and Joel 3 if not as apocalypses per se then as forerunners of them. The wisdom tradition undoubtedly also influenced the apocalyptic in its growth and development, but arguments that its origins lie there rather than in prophecy remain unconvincing. However closely related prophecy and apocalyptic may be, they are to be distinguished from each other in at least two respects: whereas the prophets for the most part declare God's word to his or her own generation, the apocalyptists record revelations said to have been made known by God to some great hero in earlier times and now to be revealed in a "secret" book at the end of the days; and whereas the prophets see the realization of God's purpose within the historical process, the apocalyptists see that purpose reaching its culmination not just within history but above and beyond history in that supramundane realm where God dwells.

Within the Bible itself there are two great apocalypses: Daniel and Revelation. In the first of these, five stories are told of a wise man, Daniel, who remained faithful to his Jewish religion during the Babylonian exile in the sixth century BCE, and was enabled by God to interpret dreams and visions. In the second half of the book, four of Daniel's visions are recorded, along with their interpretations, which give a survey of history from the exile (when the writer is reckoned to have lived) to its denouement in the second century BCE in the time of Antiochus IV, when the book in its present form was actually written. In this sense, the book of Daniel is addressed to the writer's own contemporaries, but the method and approach are altogether different from those of the prophets. So too with his hope for the coming kingdom; in keeping with the prophets, he sees it established here on earth as the climax of history, but in no way is it to be separated from that transcendent, heavenly realm where God dwells with his holy angels.

The book of Revelation follows a somewhat similar form, for it too reveals the future course of events by means of visions and declares the triumph of God's purpose. In the course of time other Christian apocalypses appeared, some as independent works, such as the Apocalypses of Peter and Paul, and others as interpolations in or additions to existing Jewish apocalyptic books.

Extrabiblical Apocalyptic Books. A number of extrabiblical Jewish apocalypses appeared during the Greco-Roman period which, for the most part, have survived only in translation, having been preserved within the Christian tradition. They are of considerable value for the light they throw on the four hundred and fifty or so years between 250 BCE and 200 CE and not least on our understanding of the background of the New Testament. There is no agreed list of such books, but the following works are generally so regarded: 1 Enoch (Ethiopic Apocalypse of Enoch), third century BCE to first century CE; Apocalypse of Zephaniah, first century BCE to first century CE; Apocalypse of Abraham, first to second century CE; 2 Enoch (Slavonic Apocalypse of Enoch), late first century CE; 2 Esdras (= 4 Ezra) 3–14, ca. 100 CE; 2 Baruch (Syriac Apocalypse of Baruch), early sec-

A

Hell, right-hand panel from the Triptych of Earthly Vanity and Divine Salvation

Revelation through visionary experience. This is a stock-in-trade of these writings, though visions may be replaced by dreams, trances, auditions, and visual/physical transference to the ends of the earth or to heaven itself. The ancient seer (in whose name the author writes) is confronted with the heavenly mysteries, either directly or as mediated by an angel, and is bidden to record what he has seen and heard.

In so doing, the writer often makes use of two literary devices that, though not confined to the apocalyptic writings, are a common feature. The first is that of secret books, in which the seer is bidden to conceal these mysteries until the end time, when he will reveal them to the wise as a sign that the end is now at hand. The second is that of pseudonymity, whereby the author writes in the name of some honored person of antiquity, such as Adam, Enoch, Abraham, Moses, or Ezra. The intention is not to deceive but rather to strengthen the conviction that the apocalyptist is transmitting a long and authoritative tradition. The same device is followed in Christian apocalypses, such as those of Peter and Paul, but not in the book of Revelation, where it is enough that the writer should declare in his own name the revelations he himself has received directly from his risen Lord.

Symbolic imagery. Symbolism, it has been said, is the language of the apocalyptic style of writing, a code language rich in imagery culled both from biblical and from Canaanite and Babylonian traditions. Generally speaking, the code is fairly easily recognizable: wild beasts represent the gentile nations, animal horns are gentile rulers, people are angels, and so on. Elsewhere it is less easily broken, particularly where vestiges of early myths have no obvious relation to the content of the book itself.

Tracts for the times. The apocalyptic books, particularly those "historical" apocalypses of Palestinian origin, were in many cases the product of their age and its political and economic climate. As tracts for the times, they were written to encourage those who were oppressed and saw little or no hope in terms of either politics or armed might. Their message was that God himself would intervene and reverse the situation in which they found themselves, delivering the godly from the hands of the wicked and establishing his rule for all to see. Sometimes such encouragement is given in the form of discourse in which the revelation of God's sovereignty is disclosed; at other times, as in the book of Daniel, it takes the form of a story or legend concerning the ancient worthy in whose name the book is written.

Such features are not peculiar to the apocalyptic books, but their form of presentation, together with their recurring theme of revealed secrets and divine intervention, indicates an identifiable and distinct body of literature within Judaism that, though sharing the ideals of prophecy, is nevertheless markedly different from it.

Common Themes. Certain well-marked themes run through the apocalyptic writings:

History and "the end." The whole of history is a unity under the overarching purpose of God. It is divided, however, into great epochs that must run their predetermined course; only then will the end come, and with it the dawning of the messianic kingdom and the age to come when evil will be routed and righteousness established forever.

Present troubles are in fact birth pangs heralding the end. Calculations, involving the use of numerology, demonstrate that soon, very soon, earth's invincible empires will disappear and be replaced by God's eternal rule: "The coming of the times is very near. . . . The pitcher is near the well and the ship to the harbor, and the journey to the city, and life

ond century CE; 3 Baruch (Greek Apocalypse of Baruch), first to third century CE.

Besides these, there are from this period certain other Jewish writings that, though not themselves apocalypses, belong to the same milieu and are generally recognized as part of the apocalyptic literature. They are as follows: Jubilees, second century BCE; Testaments of the Twelve Patriarchs, second century BCE; Jewish Sibylline Oracles, second century BCE to seventh century CE; Treatise of Shem, first century BCE; Testament (Assumption) of Moses, first century CE; Testament of Abraham, first to second century CE.

To this list may be added material found among the Dead Sea Scrolls: fragments of a Testament of Levi (related to a late and redacted Greek Testament of that name) and a Testament of Naphtali, and likewise fragments of the (composite) first book of Enoch and the book of Jubilees. Other writings and fragments belonging to the Qumran community indicate a close relationship between the religious outlook of the apocalyptic writers and that expressed in the scrolls, such as certain passages in the Manual of Discipline, the War Scroll, the Hymns, and such works as the book of Mysteries, the Genesis Apocryphon, and the Description of the New Jerusalem.

Literary Features. The apocalypse is recognized by many scholars as a distinct literary genre expressing itself, as we have seen, in terms of divine disclosure, transcendent reality, and final redemption. As such, it shares with other related apocalyptic books certain literary features that are worthy of note:

to its end" (2 Bar. 85.10). The writer of Daniel tries to be more precise, interpreting Jeremiah's seventy years' captivity as seventy weeks of years, ending in the writer's own day (9.21–27; cf. Jer. 25.11–12; 29.10). The Christian expectation is no less eager, though less precise: " 'Surely, I am coming soon.' Amen. Come, Lord Jesus!" (Rev. 22.20).

Cosmic cataclysm. The coming end will be "a time of anguish, such as has never occurred since nations first came into existence" (Dan. 12.1). Sometimes this is described in terms of political action and military struggle; at other times the conflict assumes cosmic proportions involving mysterious happenings on earth and in the heavens—earthquakes, famine, fearful celestial portents, and destruction by fire. Such things find an echo in the New Testament, where it is said that in the last days there will be an eclipse of the sun, and the stars will fall from heaven (Mark 13.24–25).

This cosmic upheaval is closely related to the concept of cosmic powers in the form of angels and demons. The angel hosts are drawn up in battle array against the demon hosts under the command of Satan. In the final battle the powers of evil, together with the evil nations they represent, will be utterly destroyed.

The consummation. The coming kingdom is, generally speaking, to be established here on this earth; in some instances it has a temporary duration, and is followed by the age to come for, as 2 Esdras puts it, "The Most High has made not one world but two" (7.50). In this new divine order, the end will be as the beginning and paradise will be restored. "Dualism" is sometimes used to describe the discontinuity between this age and the age to come, but continuity remains: generally speaking, this earth (albeit renewed or restored) is the scene of God's deliverance.

In some of these writings the figures of Messiah and Son of man, among others, are introduced as agents of the coming kingdom. These probably represent two originally distinct strands of eschatological expectation which, in the course of time, became intertwined.

One significant development is the prevailing belief in a resurrection, a coming judgment, and the life to come (see Dan. 12.2 for an early reference). It is by this means that the gap, as it were, between the eschatology of the nation and the eschatology of the individual is finally bridged. Both together find their fulfillment in God's final redemption when all wrongs are to be righted and justice and peace are established forever.

D. S. RUSSELL

APOCRYPHA. *This entry consists of two articles dealing with books or parts of books not considered canonical by every community of faith,* Jewish Apocrypha *and* Christian Apocrypha. *The first article,* Jewish Apocrypha, *surveys Jewish religious writings not recognized as part of the Bible in Jewish tradition or by some Christian churches. Among the latter these are commonly referred to as the Apocrypha of the Old Testament; those churches that do include some or all of these writings in their canon frequently refer to them as "deuterocanonical." Each of these books has a separate entry devoted to it. The second article,* Christian Apocrypha, *deals with early Christian writings not included in the canon of the New Testament but which contain similar types of literature often attributed to figures of the apostolic age.*

Jewish Apocrypha

The word *apocrypha,* a Greek neuter plural (singular, *apocryphon),* is used to designate a group of important religious writings from antiquity that are not universally regarded as belonging to the authentic canon of Scripture, though many of them have been so regarded by particular communities. The word is applied primarily to the fifteen (or fourteen) books that are included in many editions of the English Bible as a supplement, usually printed between the Hebrew scriptures and the New Testament. The name, which means "things hidden away," is inappropriate, since none of these books (with the possible exception of 2 Esdras) was ever regarded as hidden or secret. For the most part, they are simply those books found only in manuscripts of the Septuagint (LXX), the ancient Greek translation of the Hebrew scriptures, and therefore possibly regarded as "canonical" by Greek-speaking Alexandrian Jews, though ultimately rejected by the Jewish community of Palestine and rabbinic authorities of later times (2 Esdras and the Prayer of Manasseh are not covered by this definition). Their preservation is largely due to the Christian community, which, for most of the first four centuries CE, accepted the Greek Old Testament as normative for its life and thought. In modern times the term "apocrypha" has been extended more loosely to other books from the later Hellenistic and early Roman periods but which, so far as we know, never attained even quasi-canonical status (these books are more commonly designated as pseudepigrapha), and has also been extended by analogy to a large group of early Christian writings excluded from the New Testament canon in its final form. In this article we shall be concerned principally with the fifteen books described at the beginning of the paragraph; for the analogous early Christian writings, see the second article in this entry.

Until recently it was commonly assumed that Jews of the period immediately before and after the beginning of the common era had two canons, one that was current in Palestine and another in Alexandria, the greatest center of Jewish life in the Hellenistic world. But newer evidence, including that from Qumran, suggests a more complex reconstruction, and indeed the use of the word "canon" may be somewhat inappropriate, since the list of included books was not explicitly fixed until the second century CE. The contents of the first two parts (Law and Prophets) of what would ultimately be called the canon had been accepted as sacred and authoritative since at least 200 BCE, but the works that constitute the third part of the Hebrew Bible (the Writings) have a less authoritative status and have been individually evaluated in quite different ways. It is to this last class that the books of the Apocrypha belong. Their one common denominator is the fact that all are contained, in Greek, in some manuscript of the Septuagint (with the exception, once again, of 2 Esdras and Prayer of Manasseh, to which we shall return).

The definition and final closing of the Jewish canon was in large measure due to the inner restructuring of Jewish society and the tightening of standards that resulted both from the destruction of the Temple in 70 CE and from the need for self-definition in the face of the threat presented by the rise of an aggressive Christian church. Christians, increasingly of gentile origin, naturally accepted the scriptures in the form most accessible to them, the Greek Septuagint. Jews, quite as naturally, reacted by emphatically rejecting the Septuagint and insisting that only those ancient books that were written in Hebrew could be regarded as authoritative. Even such books as Sirach and 1 Maccabees, which had clearly been written originally in Hebrew, were rejected, since internal evidence showed that they had been composed long after the time of Ezra, when, it was believed, prophecy had ceased.

The archangel Raphael appears to the family of Tobit
(Tob. 12.6–22)

Among Christians, the Old Testament continued for a long time to be tacitly accepted in its Greek form, even though objections were occasionally voiced by theologians and other scholars who were familiar with the Jewish position. The question of the canonicity of the "extra books" became acute only with Pope Damasus's choice of Jerome, in 382 CE, to make an authoritative translation of the Bible into Latin. As he worked on the Old Testament, Jerome became convinced that the Hebrew text alone was definitive and he therefore felt obliged to reject those books found only in Greek; these books he called "apocrypha." Whatever precise meaning he attached to that word, it was certainly intended to be pejorative. Strangely, his views were not accepted, and to the present the books he designated as "apocryphal" are incorporated in the canon of the Roman Catholic church and distributed, according to their type, among the other books of the Old Testament. The formal designation for these books among Roman Catholics is "deuterocanonical," meaning books that belong to a second layer of the canon, but with no implication that they are of less worth than the others. The view of the Orthodox churches, for most of which the Septuagint continues to be the authoritative form of scripture, is substantially the same, though the list of books they regard as at least liturgically useful tends to be somewhat longer and can include such works as 1 Esdras, 3 and 4 Maccabees, and Psalm 151.

It was only with the Reformation and its emphasis upon the sole authority of scripture that Jerome's view came into its own. Protestants were unanimous in accepting the Jewish definition of the Old Testament canon. They were agreed that the extra books of the Greek canon, which was also that of the Latin Vulgate, should be gathered together and removed from among the books of the Hebrew canon; if included in the Bible at all, they should be placed in a separate section between the Testaments clearly labeled "Apocrypha." But they were not of one opinion with regard to the

value of these books. Calvinists took the most extreme view, asserting in the Westminster Confession that they were of no more value than any other human writings, and their use was discouraged. Lutherans were inclined to value them more highly and to encourage their study, though not with any sense that they were of equal value with the authoritative books of the Hebrew canon. The Church of England requires the books of the Apocrypha to be included in any edition of the Bible authorized for use in public worship, and provides for considerable use of them in its lectionary while also insisting (in Art. 3 of the Thirty-Nine Articles) that they cannot be used to prove any point of doctrine. In the early seventeenth century, some Protestant editions of the Bible were published without the Apocrypha and, since 1827, when the British and Foreign Bible Society, followed shortly by the American Bible Society, under pressure from the Calvinist (Presbyterian) churches, decided to omit the apocryphal books from all its editions, omitting them has become the common practice. In the middle of the twentieth century, however, there began a considerable revival of interest in these books among both Protestants and Jews, based partly upon a more relaxed view of the nature of the canon, but even more upon a realization of the importance of the apocryphal literature for biblical research and interpretation. As a result, numerous editions of the Apocrypha have become available and a number of significant new commentaries on the apocryphal books have been published. Newer translations (e.g., GNB, NRSV) often include them in at least some editions.

Briefly described, the books of the standard Apocrypha are as follows: 1 Esdras is an alternative version of the Hebrew book of Ezra that includes a short extract from 2 Chronicles at the beginning and from Nehemiah at the end. It is found in manuscripts of the Septuagint, but is not considered one of the deuterocanonical books by the Latin church; in the Vulgate it is called 3 Esdras and is printed, for purely historical reasons, in an appendix after the New Testament. The apocalyptic work traditionally called 2 Esdras is of Jewish origin, with some Christian additions, and was never part of the Septuagint. Except for a tiny fragment, the Greek text is lost, so it is best known in the Latin version that (like 1 Esdras) is printed in an appendix to the Vulgate, where it is called 4 Esdras; it is not considered deuterocanonical. Tobit is a romantic oriental tale, best known for its very human characters, its high ethical teaching, and its use of magic and demonology. Judith is the fictitious story of a heroic Jewish woman who delivers her people by using feminine wiles to accomplish the assassination of the general of a pagan army that was besieging them. The Additions to the Book of Esther consists of a series of discontinuous passages that appear only in the Greek version of that book, apparently added, for the most part, to give a religious tone to that embarrassingly secular work. Two of the apocryphal books fall into the category of wisdom literature: there is, first of all, the Wisdom of Solomon, a patently pseudonymous work that deals with such basic themes as immortality and the nature of divine wisdom in language that is a mixture of Jewish theology and Greek philosophy; and, second, Sirach (or Ecclesiasticus), a much more traditional work, originally composed in Hebrew, that has its closest analogue in the book of Proverbs. The second part of the confused composition called Baruch (3.9–4.4) also belongs to wisdom literature, being a poem in praise of wisdom as God's special gift to Israel, while the preceding prose section consists of a brief narrative introducing a lengthy confession of Israel's sins as the cause of the Babylonian exile; the concluding poem (4:5–5.9) deals with the theme of Israel's restoration. If the Letter of Jeremiah is counted as chap. 6 of Baruch, as is often done, there are fourteen rather than fifteen apocryphal books, but it is clearly a separate work having for its theme the foolishness of idolatry. The Prayer of Azariah and the Song of the Three Young Men, Susanna, and Bel and the Dragon are additions that appear in the Greek version of Daniel, the first containing two widely used liturgical hymns, while the other two are popular tales in which Daniel is the hero. A Greek form of the Prayer of Manasseh exists, but was not part of the original Septuagint, and it is deuterocanonical for only some eastern churches. The books called 1 and 2 Maccabees are two entirely independent and disparate historical narratives that record the heroic struggles that led to a brief period of independence for Jews in the second and first centuries BCE.

The importance of these books arises first of all from the fact that they were composed later than the canonical books of the Hebrew Bible and, apart from 2 Esdras, before the books of the New Testament. They therefore shed a welcome light on political, religious, and cultural developments in the later Hellenistic and early Roman periods and thus on the background of the New Testament. Furthermore, when regarded for their own sake, the Wisdom of Solomon is an important theological treatise, representing the first attempt to fuse two different intellectual strains, the Israelite and the Greek; and, for most readers, Sirach is at least as interesting as Proverbs and perhaps more accessible; Tobit, Judith, and Susanna are splendid examples of narrative art; and 1 Maccabees is a fine specimen of sober historical writing.

Among other ancient works sometimes classified as "apocrypha" are 3 and 4 Maccabees, the Psalms of Solomon, the several books of Enoch, the Baruch apocalypse (2 Baruch), the Book of Jubilees, and the Testaments of the Twelve Patriarchs.

ROBERT C. DENTAN

Christian Apocrypha

Beyond the twenty-seven books collected in the New Testament canon, many other examples were produced of each of the four types of New Testament literature: gospels, acts, letters, and apocalypses. The intentions of the authors of these books, which are now known as New Testament Apocrypha, were diverse; some sought to supplement works already in circulation, while others sought to supplant them. In some cases, these books simply served as light entertainment for Christian believers; in others, the authors wanted to promulgate practices and ideas condemned by the church.

Apocryphal Gospels. Of the roughly two dozen gospels produced during the early centuries of Christianity, those concerning on the one hand Jesus' infancy and childhood, and on the other his descent into hell between his death and his resurrection clearly augment the canonical Gospels, which pass over these matters in almost total silence (Luke 2.42–51 relates one incident when Jesus was a boy of twelve). Naturally, however, early Christians were curious about both of these periods; not surprisingly, traditions grew up around each and were recorded. The Protevangelium of James and the Infancy Gospel of Thomas, two second-century infancy gospels, were developed over the following centuries into the History of Joseph the Carpenter and the Arabic Gospel of the Infancy, as well as other similar writings describing Jesus' early years and the miracles surrounding contact with the infant, his clothing, and even his bathwater.

In these works, the young Jesus is portrayed as possessing miraculous powers. The uses to which such powers are put, though, is often incompatible with the character found in the canonical Gospels. For example, while playing with other children on the Sabbath, Jesus molded twelve clay birds. When an elder reported Jesus' desecration of the Sabbath to Joseph, Jesus clapped his hands and the birds came to life. Another time, when Jesus was walking through a crowd, someone bumped him, whereupon Jesus turned and said, "You will never get to where you are going," and the person fell down dead.

Apocryphal accounts of Christ's descent into the underworld and his victory over its powers are more rare. One of the earliest can be found in the fourth-century Gospel of Nicodemus (also called the Acts of Pilate); another, from the next century, is the Gospel of Bartholomew.

With the discovery in 1945 of the Nag Hammadi library, several previously unknown (or known only by name) gnostic gospels have come to light. These and related works (e.g., the Epistle of the Apostles) commonly present the risen Christ's revelations to the disciples during the period between his resurrection and ascension (a period that the gnostics expanded from 40 days [Acts 1.3] to 550 days). Often these accounts are related as a dialogue in which the disciples question Jesus about subjects that remained obscure in his earlier teaching. Most often, however, the discussion goes beyond the Gospel traditions to speculations about cosmology, gnostic interpretations of the creation accounts of Genesis, and the fate of the different classes of humanity. Notable examples preserved at Nag Hammadi are the Apocryphon of James, the Sophia of Jesus Christ, the Book of Thomas, and the Dialogue of the Savior. Among the most significant of the Nag Hammadi documents, and very different in character, is a Coptic version of the Gospel of Thomas, a collection of 114 sayings (*logia*) of Jesus, many similar to logia in the synoptic Gospels and in a late second-century CE papyrus.

Still other gospels are known only by name or from brief patristic quotations. Some of these originated among early Jewish-Christian sects, as is clear from their titles (Gospel of the Hebrews; Gospel of the Ebionites; Gospel of the Nazarenes).

Apocryphal Acts. Since the canonical Acts of the Apostles record in detail the activities of only a few of the apostles, second- and third-century Christian authors drew up narratives of the other apostles' activities. Even apostles portrayed in Acts had further exploits recounted, sometimes in minute detail. The most notable are five works from the second and third centuries, attributed to Leucius Charinus, alleged to have been a disciple of John; scholars agree, however, that the actual authors of these and all other apocryphal acts remain unknown.

The Acts of Peter (ca. 180–190 CE) describes the rivalry between Simon Peter and Simon Magus. Among Peter's miracles are a speaking dog, a dried fish restored to life, and resurrections from the dead. The comical climax of the contest takes place in the Roman forum, when the magician attempts to fly to heaven. The document closes with an account of Peter's martyrdom by crucifixion.

The Acts of John (ca. 150–180) purports to be an eyewitness account of John's missionary travels in Asia Minor. The sermons attributed to him evince docetic tendencies: Jesus had no proper shape or body, only an appearance, so to one person he appeared in one shape, and to another in a totally different shape; when he walked, he left no footprints. Besides a droll tale about bedbugs, the work has a Hymn of Christ as well as the apostles dancing in a circle.

The Acts of Andrew (early third century?) is known chiefly through a long epitome prepared by Gregory of Tours (sixth century). To judge by the extant portions, the Acts are in essence a narrative of Andrew's journey from Pontus to Achaia, during which he performed many miracles and delivered many lengthy, severely ascetic exhortations. The Martyrdom of St. Andrew, a variant text of part of the work, describes the apostle's death by crucifixion.

The Acts of Thomas (first half of the third century), is the only apocryphal Acts preserved in its entirety, surviving in Greek, Syriac, Ethiopic, Armenian, and Latin versions. It tells of Thomas's missionary work in India, his healing miracles, and martyrdom. It also contains several fine liturgical hymns; the best-known is the "Hymn of the Soul" (also called the "Hymn of the Pearl"), which has suggestive allegorical overtones.

The Acts of Paul, according to Tertullian, was written by a presbyter of Asia Minor with the purpose of honoring the apostle. Despite ecclesiastical disapproval, his book become quite popular with the laity. Among the surviving episodes is one that tells of Paul and Thecla, a noble-woman and follower of Paul who preached and administered baptism; in this section we find the famous description of Paul: "little in stature, with a bald head and crooked legs . . . with eyebrows meeting, and a nose somewhat hooked." Another episode, discovered in 1936, gives a detailed account of Paul's encounter in the amphitheater at Ephesus with a lion to which he had earlier preached the gospel and had baptized.

These works are generally sectarian in character, whether orthodox or theologically deviant (Docetic, Gnostic, Manichean). Sectarian influence can especially be seen in emphasis on sexual asceticism and martyrdom. Other legendary Acts dating from the fourth to the sixth century are the Acts of Andrew and Matthias among the Cannibals, Acts of Andrew and Paul, Acts of Barnabas, Acts of James the Great, Acts of John by Prochorus, Acts of the Apostles Peter and Andrew, Slavonic Acts of Peter, Acts of Philip, Acts of Pilate, and Acts of Thaddaeus. This type of literature may be seen as paralleling the novels of antiquity.

Apocryphal Letters. The apocryphal epistles are relatively few in number. The spurious Third Letter of Paul to the Corinthians, with an introductory note to Paul from presbyters at Corinth, is part of the Acts of Paul, and came to be highly regarded in the Armenian and Syrian churches. It addresses doctrinal issues such as prophecy, creation, the human nature of Christ, and the resurrection of the body.

In the west, Paul's Letter to the Laodiceans was disseminated widely and is actually included in the all eighteen printed German Bibles prior to Luther's translation. The Correspondence between Paul and Seneca, consisting of fourteen letters between the Stoic philosopher Seneca and Paul, has come down to us in more than three hundred manuscripts; the banal content and colorless style of the letters show that they cannot come from the hands of either the moralist or the apostle. Other apocryphal letters are the Epistle of Titus and the Epistles of Christ and Abgar.

Apocryphal Apocalypses. In addition to the Revelation of John, there are several apocalypses attributed to other apostles. The earliest is the Apocalypse of Peter (ca. 125–150 CE), preserved in part in Greek and fully in Ethiopic. Making use of beliefs about the afterlife from the *Odyssey* and the *Aeneid,* it tells of the delights of the redeemed in heaven and (at much greater length) the torments of the damned in hell. These ideas were elaborated extensively in the following century by the author of the Apocalypse of Paul, who describes how Paul is caught up to paradise (see 2 Cor. 12.1–4) and witnesses the judgment of two souls, one righteous and the other wicked. He is then led through hell, where he sees the tortures of the wicked and intercedes on their behalf, obtaining for them relief every Lord's day. A visit to paradise ensues, during which Paul meets the patriarchs, the major prophets, Enoch, and finally Adam. Some of these themes became part of medieval beliefs given wider dissemination through Dante's *Divine Comedy.* With the discovery in 1946 of the Nag Hammadi library, the number of apocryphal apocalypses increased: another Apocalypse of Peter, another of Paul, the First and Second Apocalypses of James, and others.

Modern Apocrypha. The urge to supplement the Bible has continued down through the ages. In modern times, fraudulent productions continue to excite the hopes of naive readers that priceless treasures have been uncovered. Despite repeated claims of authenticity, such productions invariably lack historical or literary value. Among the most often published are The Aquarian Gospel, The Archko Volume, The Letter of Benan, The Description of Christ, The Confessions of Pontius Pilate, The Gospel of Josephus, The Book of Jasher, The Lost Books of the Bible, The Nazarene Gospel, The Letter from Heaven, Cahspe, and The Twenty-ninth Chapter of Acts.

BRUCE M. METZGER

AQEDAH. The Hebrew word for "binding," and the common designation for Genesis 22.1–19, in which God tests Abraham by commanding that he sacrifice his son Isaac. Abraham binds Isaac (v. 9). When he is about to slaughter him, an angel calls to him to desist, whereupon Abraham offers a ram instead. Although the Aqedah is the climax of the Genesis narratives about Abraham, a final testimony to his faith in, obedience to, and fear of God, it is not mentioned elsewhere in the Hebrew Bible. Isaac's role in Genesis 22 is passive, but postbiblical Jewish interpretations of the first to the eighth centuries CE transform him into an adult, voluntary sacrificial offering. Some texts give reasons for the episode, including Satan's questioning of Abraham's devotion to God (*b. Sank.* 89b; cf. Job 1–2) and Isaac's and Ishmael's arguments concerning who was the more righteous (*Gen. Rab.* 55.4). During this period, the Aqedah became associated with the Ro'sh ha-shanah liturgy, with the shofar recalling the substituted ram. Mount Moriah, where the Aqedah took place, was identified with the site of the Temple. Isaac emerges both as the paradigm of the martyr and as the perfect sacrifice whose act brings merit to and has redemptive value for his own descendants. Some rabbinic traditions maintain that Isaac, as a sacrificial victim, shed blood, and others conclude that he also died and was resurrected; thus wrote the twelfth-century rabbi Ephraim of Bonn, in the context of the martyrdom of many Rhineland Jews and the destruction of their communities.

The New Testament refers to the Aqedah not as an example of a redemptive sacrificial death but rather as an example of faith (James 2.21; Heb. 11.17–19; possibly Rom. 4.16–18). Echoes of the former may however be found in Paul's understanding of the significance of the death and resurrection of Jesus, and the Septuagint of Genesis 22 may be alluded to in Romans 8.32, Mark 1.11, and Matthew 3.17. Early church fathers such as Clement and Tertullian understood Isaac's sacrifice as a prototype of the sacrifice of Jesus. The divine testing of Abraham and the subsequent near sacrifice of his son also appear in the Qur'ān (37.101–113). Early Muslim exegetes disagreed as to whether the son, unnamed in the Qur'ānic passage, is Isaac or Ishmael. Some of the earliest traditions declare him to be Isaac, but by the ninth or tenth century the consensus was that Ishmael, increasingly associated with Mecca and identified as the ancestor of the northern Arabs, was the voluntary sacrificial offering.

From antiquity to the present, the Aqedah has been portrayed in the arts. For example, it appears on a wall painting of the third-century CE synagogue at Dura-Europos and on a floor mosaic of the sixth-century synagogue at Beth Alpha. During the Renaissance, such sculptors and painters as Ghiberti, Donatello, Titian, Caravaggio, and Rembrandt included the Aqedah among their depictions of biblical subjects. Among notable modern literary treatments of the Aqedah is Søren Kierkegaard's *Fear and Trembling* (1843).

BARBARA GELLER NATHANSON

ARABIA. Arabia is a large, predominately arid peninsula bounded on the east by Mesopotamia and the Persian Gulf, on the north by the Mediterranean coastal highlands of Syria and Palestine, and on the west and south by the Red Sea and Indian Ocean (Maps 1,2: G–K 4–6). Northwest Arabia is mountainous, stony desert. Like the neighboring Negeb, it is desolate but habitable for sheep/goat nomads. The sandy deserts of interior Arabia remained impenetrable until domestication of the camel allowed its scattered oases to be linked by means of caravan routes in the first millennium BCE. Southern Arabia (Yemen) is, by contrast, a well-watered highland where terraced agriculture has supported permanent settlement from at least the second millennium BCE.

The Bible reflects close familiarity with the desert places and nomadic peoples of northwestern Arabia, and southern Arabia (Sheba, 1 Kings 10.1; Job 6.19; or Seba, Gen. 10.7; Ps. 72.10; Isa. 43.3) was also known as a source of camels, gold, frankincense, and myrrh. Some places, like Dumah (Josh. 15.52; Isa. 21.11; modern Jawf) and Tema (Gen. 25.15; Job 6.19; Isa. 21.14; Jer. 25.23; modern Tayma), can be identified with sites in northern Arabia; however, recent attempts to relocate the ancestral narratives wholesale from Palestine to northern Arabia must be rejected. The Hebrew word *ʿărābâ* means "desert," but in one form it also means "nomad" (Isa. 13.20; Jer. 3.2). The phrase "all the kings of Arabia" (1 Kings 10.15; 2 Chron. 9.14; Jer. 25.24) can mean "all the kings of the Arabs" or "all the kings of the nomads." Few of the numerous nomadic peoples mentioned in the Bible are called "Arabs," and only rarely is their territory called "Arabia." Rather, they are identified by their geographic or ethnic origin: Amalekites (1 Sam. 15.6–8; 30.1; Judg. 6.5; 7.12), Ishmaelites (Gen. 37.25), Midianites (Judg. 6.5; 7.12).

In the New Testament, "Arabians" (denoting probably Arabic speakers) were among the polyglot crowd gathered in Jerusalem at Pentecost (Acts 2.5–11). For a time after his call, Paul "went away into Arabia," perhaps to eastern Syria or Transjordan (Gal. 1.17).

JOSEPH A. GREENE

ARARAT. A mountainous country surrounding Lake Van in Armenia (Map 6:H3). It is commonly referred to as Urartu in Assyrian texts, in which it first appears as a conglomeration of kingdoms in the thirteenth century BCE. A unified kingdom reached its zenith in the late ninth century

Abraham and Isaac (Gen. 22.10–11) (Rembrandt van Rijn, 1634)

under the dynasty founded by Sarduri I; its decline began when Sarduri II was defeated by Tiglath-pileser III in 743 BCE. The end came in the early sixth century, when Urartu was conquered by the Medes. In the Bible, Ararat can be an enemy of Assyria (2 Kings 19.37; Isa. 37.38) or Babylon (Jer. 51.27). It is best known, however, as the region ("the mountains of Ararat," not "Mount Ararat"; Gen. 8.4) in which Noah's ark came to rest after the Flood. In spite of later Jewish, Christian, and Muslim traditions that sought to identify the mountain on which Noah landed, all attempts to do so have ended in failure.

CARL S. EHRLICH

ARK. The English word "ark" translates two Hebrew words that differ from each other both in form and in usage, though the Septuagint employs one Greek word (*kibōtos*) for both.

Tēbâ means "box" or "chest." Apart from its use to designate the papyrus basket in which Moses, as an infant, was left to float among the bulrushes of the Nile (Exod. 2.3, 5), this word is used in the Bible solely as the designation of the vessel that God commanded Noah to construct of gopher wood (Gen. 6.14), a wood not mentioned elsewhere. It was to be large enough to contain one representative human family along with one pair of every species of animals (Gen. 6.18–21). Another form of the story speaks of seven pairs of clean animals, sufficient quantity for the sacrifice after the Flood, and one pair of unclean animals (Gen. 7.2–3). These would

The finding of Moses (Exod. 2.5)

ride out the rainstorm of the wrath of God. The description of Noah's ark (Gen. 6.14–16) is rather hard to understand. Its dimensions, roughly 140 m (450 ft) long, 22 m (75 ft) wide, and 12 m (45 ft) high, make it literally a very large "box." The ark had three decks (Gen. 6.16), and also naturally a door. An opening, about .5 m (18 in) high, apparently ran all around the ark just below the roof and gave light and air to the vessel. There are certain points of resemblance, but more of dissimilarity, between Noah's ark and Utnapishtim's gigantic boat of the Gilgamesh flood story.

In 1 Peter 3.20–21, Noah's ark prefigures baptism.

'Ărôn, apart from its use in the sense of "coffin" (Gen. 50.26) and in the sense of "chest" for receiving money offerings (2 Kings 12.9–10; 2 Chron. 24.8, 10–11), is employed as the name of the sacred box that is variously called the ark of God, the ark of the Lord, the ark of the covenant, and so on. Data concerning this ark come from different sources and periods. It was in form a rectangular box or chest, measuring about 1 by .7 by .7 m (45 by 27 by 27 in), and made of acacia or shittim wood.

As the years went by this object became evermore venerated. It symbolized the presence of the living God at one particular spot on earth; for the God who dwelled "in the high and holy place" was also present at the ark in the midst of his people. As a result, later generations embellished descriptions of it in their traditions, seeing it as overlaid with gold both within and without (Exod. 25.10–16). The ark was transportable; it could be carried on poles overlaid with gold, which passed through rings on its side. It was considered to be of such sanctity that were an unauthorized person to touch it, even accidentally, this infraction would be punishable by death (2 Sam. 6.6).

The ark seems at one time to have contained only the two tablets of the law (1 Kings 8.9), but according to other traditions (Heb. 9.4) it contained also Aaron's rod that budded (Num. 17.1–10) and a golden urn holding manna (Exod. 16.32–34).

The history of the ark parallels many of the vicissitudes of Israel. It was carried by the sons of Levi on the wilderness wanderings (Deut. 31.9); borne over the Jordan by the priests (Josh. 8.1); captured by the Philistines (1 Sam. 4); brought to Jerusalem by David (2 Sam 6; 1 Chron. 13.3–14; 15.1–18). After being kept in a tentlike sanctuary, it was finally installed in the holiest chamber of Solomon's Temple.

The ark had a cover or lid. Its name (Hebr. *kappōret*) is actually a theological term (cf. *kippēr*, "to purify, atone"), so we do not know what this cover looked like (Lev. 16.2, 13–15). Martin Luther described it in his German Bible as the "mercy seat" because the Lord "sat" enthroned over it in mercy, invisibly present where the wingtips of two cherubim met above it, guarding the divine presence. So the ark represented for Israel the localized presence of God in judgment, mercy, forgiveness, and love; and because it contained the Ten Commandments, it was a visible reminder that their life was to be lived in obedience to the expressed will of God. Since the Ten Commandments were incised on stone so as to last for all time, Israel carried in her midst God's demands for total loyalty and obedience to himself and for social justice and love of neighbor.

The ark is thought to have been captured when Jerusalem fell in 587/586 BCE, and nothing is known of its later history. Later legend reports that Jeremiah rescued it and hid it on Mount Nebo (2 Macc. 2.4–8; but cf. Jer. 3.16).

GEORGE A. F. KNIGHT

ARMAGEDDON. A place name found only in Revelation 16.16, where it is identified as the "Hebrew" name for the location where the kings of the earth will assemble to fight against God. Scholars generally explain Armageddon (NRSV: "Harmagedon") as a Greek transliteration of the Hebrew phrase *har mĕgiddô* ("the mountain of Megiddo"). The city of Megiddo, strategically located in the western part of the Esdraelon valley at the crossroads of two trade routes (Map 1:X3), was the site of several important battles in ancient times. The reference to the "mountain" of Megiddo is, however, more problematic, corresponding to no evident geographical feature in the area. Although Armageddon appears only once in the Bible, it has become a familiar designation for the future final battle between the forces of good and evil.

WILLIAM H. BARNES

ASIA. In the Hellenistic period, Asia is a term for the Seleucid Empire (Map 11; e.g., 1 Macc. 11.13; 13.32). In the Roman period, Asia means the province of that name, in the western part of what is now Turkey (Map 14:E3; see, e.g., 2 Esd. 16.1; Acts 19.6; 1 Cor. 16.19; 1 Pet. 1.1). It was an important province, containing within its boundaries a number of wealthy cities, including Ephesus, its capital. The seven churches of the opening chapters of the book of Revelation are all in the province of Asia (Rev. 1.4), as is Colossae, to whose church the letter to the Colossians was sent.

MICHAEL D. COOGAN

ASSYRIA. The ancient land of Assyria (Map 6: H3–4), located in what is now northeastern Iraq, drew its name from the small settlement of Assur (or Ashur) built on a sandstone cliff on the west bank of the Tigris about 35 km (24 mi) north of its confluence with the lower Zab River. Situated at a major river crossing but outside the zone for reliable annual rainfall, Assur early attracted settlements by pastoralists, since it was easily defensible and had ready access to water. Early levels of a small shrine there dating to ca. 2800–2200 BCE show affinities with Sumerian culture to the south in furnishings and statuary.

The earliest independent ruler of the city-state of Assur attested in a contemporary inscription is Shalim-ahum, who reigned about 1900 BCE. At this time, firms of merchants in Assur established branches in several Anatolian cities and traded textiles and tin from Assur for silver.

About 1813 BCE, Shamshi-Adad I, an Amorite prince from the middle Euphrates, took possession of Assur and subsequently founded an empire with its capital at Shubat-Enlil (modern Tell Leilan in northeast Syria), with two sons reigning as subkings in Mari and in Ekallate (just north of Assur). Under Shamshi-Adad's son Ishme-Dagan I, the empire was quickly lost, and the dynasty of Shamshi-Adad was replaced within a few decades by native Assyrians, who ruled—in relative obscurity—during the next four centuries, at times as vassals of Mitanni.

Under the dynamic Ashur-uballit I (1364–1328 BCE), Assyria reemerged as a major power, and in the next century conquered and gradually annexed much of the old heartland of Mitanni to the west, setting up an extensive provincial system and then briefly taking over much of Babylonia to the south. Its imperialist ethic was embodied in the Middle Assyrian coronation ritual, in which the officiating priest solemnly charged the king: "Expand your land!" After 1200 BCE, amid widespread upheavals and population movements in Western Asia, the Middle Assyrian empire declined both politically and territorially. An extensive if short-lived revival in the time of Tiglath-pileser I (1115–1076 BCE) dissipated under the pressure of invading Arameans, who confined Assyrian political power to a narrow strip along the Tigris until the late tenth century.

After 935 BCE, Assyrians kings reclaimed lost sections of the Assyrian heartland from the Arameans and began to expand militarily, especially to the west. Over the next three centuries, these monarchs created an extensive Neo-Assyrian empire, which at its height (ca. 660 BCE) embraced a substantial part of the ancient Near East from southern Egypt, Cyprus, and western Anatolia through Palestine-Syria and Mesopotamia to Elam and the Iranian plateau (see Map 6). The foundations of Assyrian imperial power were effectively laid by Ashurnasirpal II (884–859 BCE), who built a splendid new capital at Calah (Nimrud), restructured the Assyrian army into a fighting force without peer in southwestern Asia, reorganized the Assyrian provincial system, and earned a reputation for ruthless treatment of rebels and prisoners. His massive deportations from conquered lands, continued by his successors, brought large numbers of western Arame-

Excavations at the ancient biblical city of Megiddo, Israel, called Armageddon in Revelation 16.16, the site of the final battle between the forces of good and evil.

King Ashurnasirpal II (885–860 BCE) of Assyria

marched across Syria and Palestine (once in response to a request from Ahaz of Judah for intervention [2 Kings 16:7–9]) as far as Gaza. His son, Shalmaneser V (727–722 BCE), besieged Tyre and captured Samaria, bringing the kingdom of Israel to an end. Sargon II (722–705 BCE), a usurper, deported the population of Israel to various parts of the empire, campaigned as far as the border of Egypt, brought Babylonia under his control, and built a magnificent capital at Dur-Sharrukin (Khorsabad) in the north of the country. His son, Sennacherib (705–681 BCE), expanded further into Anatolia. Faced with perennial unrest in Babylonia (fomented for the most part by Merodach-baladan and his fellow Chaldeans) and smarting from the murder of his crown prince, Ashur-nadinshumi, who had been king there from 700 to 694 BCE, Sennacherib eventually sacked and depopulated Babylon. In Palestine, he received the submission of Hezekiah, who had rebelled in collusion with Merodach-baladan, and, after a siege, extracted tribute from Jerusalem (2 Kings 18:13–16). Assassinated by one of his sons, Sennacherib was succeeded by another son, Esarhaddon (681–669 BCE), who invaded the Iranian plateau and Egypt, but died prematurely of illness while on campaign. His empire was inherited principally by his son Ashurbanipal (669–627 BCE), who reigned in Assyria; but another son, Shamash-shumukin (668–648 BCE), was installed as king in Babylon. Ashurbanipal campaigned extensively in Egypt, reaching as far as Thebes, and brought the empire to its territorial apogee in about 660 BCE. In 652 BCE, Shamash-shumukin launched a massive revolt, which won support from Elamites, Arabs, and other disaffected Assyrian subjects. Ashurbanipal spent more than ten years defeating and wreaking reprisals on the dissidents, exhausting the empire in the process.

After Ashurbanipal's death in 627 BCE, civil war broke out in Assyria between three contenders for the throne; it took several years before Sin-shar-ishkun (623?–612 BCE) emerged as the victor. Within a decade he was faced with a coalition of Medes and Babylonians, who invaded and destroyed the central provinces of Assyria. A final king, Ashur-uballit II (612–609 BCE), ruled briefly in the western provincial capital of Haran with the support of Egyptian armies; but he was driven out by the Babylonians. The fledgling empires of Babylon and Media divided the territories of the Assyrian empire, which disappeared with barely a trace even in its former heartland.

Assyria in the first millennium BCE, though renowned primarily as a massive military power that overwhelmed and intimidated much of southwestern Asia, had a vigorous cultural and economic life. In the decorative arts, its craftsmen displayed creative sensitivity in such diverse media as ivories, seals, and palace wall reliefs; the latter depict an astonishing variety of subjects, including formal protective deities, scenes of battlefield and siege, daily life at court, and the botanical zoological parks created in and around the Assyrian capitals. Literature also flourished, its most notable monument being the large library amassed by Ashurbanipal (669–627 BCE) at Nineveh, whose excavation in the mid-nineteenth century led to the rediscovery of Mesopotamian literature. On the economic side, trade prospered throughout the empire as new markets were opened to entrepreneurs even from the conquered territories. Booty, tribute, and trade goods poured into the Assyrian heartland, financing the erection and renovation of resplendent urban capitals as well as the maintenance of the military machine that made the empire possible.

ans into the heartland of Assyria, swelling the ranks of the court and army, influencing artistic and architectural styles, and, by the early seventh century, replacing the Assyrian language with Aramaic as the vernacular. Ashurnasirpal's campaigns consolidated Assyrian territorial gains as far west as the Upper Euphrates and extracted tribute from these areas; his trading ventures, with military escort, succeeded in reaching the Mediterranean. His son, Shalmaneser II (859–824 BCE), began to extend Assyrian control into northern Syria; but his advance was checked temporarily at the battle of Qarqar (853 BCE) by a broad coalition of states led by Damascus and Hamath and including Arab tribes and Israel (under Ahab). Shalmaneser's subsequent campaigns, which reached into Cilicia, secured north Syria and brought the Phoenician cities Tyre and Sidon into the Assyrian orbit. Despite a revolt of the major cities in Assyria (827–821 BCE) and an ensuing weakness in monarchic power, Assyria continued to be active in the west until about 785 BCE.

Meanwhile, in the late ninth and early eighth centuries in the mountains to the north of Assyria, the rival power of Urartu had risen to prominence. As the fortunes of Assyria declined after 783 BCE under weak kings and strong provincial governors, the Urartians pushed south into Iran and west across the Euphrates into northern Syria. By 745 BCE, Urartu had conquered or concluded alliances with most of the important states in south-central Anatolia and northern Syria and had assumed hegemony over the region. A revolt in Calah brought to the Assyrian throne Tiglath-pileser III (745–727 BCE), a vigorous monarch who checked encroaching Aramean and Chaldean tribesmen in Babylonia, restricted Urartu to its homeland, and

JOHN A. BRINKMAN

BAAL. A common Semitic word meaning "owner, lord, husband." As "lord" it is applied to various Canaanite gods, such as the Baal of Peor (Num. 25.3) and the Baals (Judg. 2.11), which were largely local manifestations of the storm god Baal. Although the head of the Canaanite pantheon was El, Baal was the most important god because of his association with the storms that annually brought revival of vegetation and fertility. Baal is prominent in the great complex of fifteenth century BCE Ugaritic epics, where he is called son of Dagon and is named some 250 times, sometimes interchangeably with Hadad, the widely known Semitic storm god whose symbol, like Baal's, was the bull.

In art, Baal is depicted as the storm god Aliyan ("triumphant") Baal, who holds a thunderbolt in one hand and swings a mace with the other. Baal is the champion of divine order over earthly chaos—over deadly drought, represented by the deity Mot ("death"), and the unruly forces of the sea (the god Yamm). The Ugaritic epics tell how Baal defeats these powers and wins the title "rider on the clouds" (the same title ascribed to the God of Israel in Ps. 68.4).

The theme of opposition to Baal worship runs throughout the Deuteronomic literature and the prophets. By the ninth century BCE, Baalism had deeply pervaded Israelite life. Personal names formed with Baal appear already in the time of the Judges (6.25–32). Even Saul and David had sons with Baal names (1 Chron. 8.33; 14.7). Intense conflict appeared with the introduction of the Baal of Tyre into Israel by Ahab's queen, Jezebel, daughter of Ethbaal of Sidon (1 Kings 16.31–32; 18.17–19). Even as late as the time of Manasseh, altars to Baal were still among the appointments in the Jerusalem Temple (2 Kings 21.2–4).

Opposition to Baalism was led by Israel's prophets. The fertility rites associated with Baal worship corrupted the faith in Yahweh, and the myths undergirding them wrongly deified aspects of nature. The prophets endeavored to show Yahweh as a transcendent, universal God who provides rains and fertility yet who is no "nature god" trapped in unvarying seasonal cycles. Because agriculture was so vital and so precariously dependent on the weather, it became important to show that Yahweh, not Baal, was the one who rode the clouds, controlled the storms, and brought freshening rains (Pss. 29; 68.4, 9; 104.3). That the struggle against Baalism was finally successful is signalled by the replacement of the Baal element in some proper names by the word *bōšet* ("shame"; 2 Sam. 2.8; cf. Hos. 9.10).

DAVID G. BURKE

BABEL, TOWER OF. Babel is the Hebrew word for Babylon, which the Babylonians themselves explained as meaning "gate of God." This etymology is probably not original, but the meaning is significant for a famous city whose central temple tower was said to reach the heavens (Gen. 11.4). In Genesis 11.9 the meaning of Babel is explained by the Hebrew verb *bālal,* "to confuse, mix," and the confusion of speech.

The brief narrative in Genesis 11.1–9 also explains how there could exist such a variety of languages among the earth's people. The understanding that the earliest humans shared a common language is found in the Sumerian *Enmerkar Epic* (141–46). Genesis 11.1–9 tells how Noah's descendants wandered to the plain of Shinar (Babylonia), where they perfected the techniques for monumental brick architecture and built the renowned tower of Babel. Building the tower is interpreted as an act of arrogance, and human history is here understood to take a decisive turn from a common thread to many strands as God descends to confuse human speech and scatter the people all over the earth.

The enormous ziggurats of Mesopotamia could easily have symbolized the presumptuousness of the urban elite, and their ruin the judgment of God. Even as ruins their massive dimensions would have been striking. The Sumerian temple tower of the moon god Nanna at Ur could have been the

The storm-god Baal with a thunderbolt (Syria, ca. 13th century BCE)

B

Tower of Babel (Gen. 11.4)

model for the tower of Babel. This huge terraced mountain of brick, with the god's temple on top, at least 21 m (70 ft) above ground level, was built ca. 2100 BCE. Of similar construction, the great temple of Marduk in Babylon, the E-sagila, is possibly the referent of the Genesis narrative; according to the Babylonian epic *Enuma Elish* (6.60–62), it took a year just to make the bricks for this colossally high structure.

DAVID G. BURKE

BABYLON (Map 2:H4). Babylon is the rendering of Akkadian Babilum (Babilim), the city that for centuries served as capital of the "land of Babylon" (Jer. 50.28). Cuneiform sources interpret its name as *bāb-ilim*, "gate of the deity." The Bible rejected this popular etymology in favor of a more scurrilous one that linked the name to the confusion of tongues (Gen. 11.9, Hebr. *bālal*, "[God] confused"), and so the city is called Babel.

Not until around 1900 BCE did an independent dynasty establish itself at Babylon. Like most of their contemporaries, its rulers bore Amorite (Northwest Semitic) names, but unlike some of them, they enjoyed lengthy reigns, passing the succession from father to son without a break; this may have helped Babylon survive its rivals in the period of warring states (ca. 1860–1760 BCE). Under the adroit Hammurapi (ca. 1792–1750 BCE), Babylon succeeded in restoring the unity of Mesopotamia under its own hegemony.

Babylon's triumph was short-lived, though; under its next king, Samsu-iluna (ca. 1749–1712 BCE), the extreme south was lost to the new Sealand Dynasty and the north to the Kassites at Hana. About 1600 BCE, the city itself was sacked by an invading army of Hittites from distant Anatolia (modern Turkey), and these rivals took it over, the Sealanders only briefly, but the Kassites for almost half a millennium (ca. 1590–1160 BCE).

It remained for the Second Dynasty of Isin (ca. 1156–1025 BCE) to restore Babylon to its earlier prominence. The recapture of the cult statue of Marduk from Elamite captivity by Nebuchadrezzar I (ca. 1124–1103 BCE) probably capped this development. Babylon was henceforth regarded as the heir to the millennial traditions of the ancient Sumerian centers of cult and culture. Marduk, the local patron deity of Babylon, was endowed with the attributes of the ancient Sumerian deities of those centers—notably Enki of Eridu and Enlil of Nippur—and exalted to the head of the pantheon. This exaltation was celebrated in new compositions such as *enūma elish* ("when above"; conventionally known as the "Babylonian Epic of Creation") and can be compared in certain respects with the exaltation of the God of Israel as celebrated in the roughly contemporary Song of the Sea (Exod. 15).

In the early first millennium, Babylon could not sustain a military and political posture to match these cultural and religious pretensions, and it gradually declined into the status of a vassal state to Assyria, the powerful neighbor to the north. Occasional alliances with Elam in the east or, notably under Marduk-apal-iddina II (the biblical Merodach-baladan), with Judah in the west (2 Kings 20.12–19; cf. Isa. 39), provided brief periods of precarious independence. The city was devastated by the Assyrian king Sennacherib (704–681 BCE) not long after his abortive siege of Jerusalem in 701 BCE (2 Kings 18.13–19.37; cf. Isa. 36–37). It was restored by that king's son and successor Esarhaddon (680–669 BCE), only to be caught up again in the violent civil war (652–648 BCE) between the two sons of Esarhaddon that pitted Shamash-shumukin of Babylonia against Assurbanipal of Assyria. The resultant weakening of the Assyrian empire no doubt helped clear the path for the accession of the last and in some ways greatest Babylonian dynasty, that of the Chaldeans, sometimes referred to as the Tenth Babylonian Dynasty (625–539 BCE).

With this restoration, Babylon ranked as one of the major cities, indeed, in Greek eyes, as one or even two of the seven wonders of the ancient world, by virtue of its walls in some accounts and invariably for its famous "hanging gardens." The gardens were more likely the work of Marduk-apal-iddina II than of Nebuchadrezzar II (as claimed by Berossos in one Hellenistic tradition), but the latter certainly rebuilt the city most grandly during his forty-four-year reign (605–562 BCE). He is remembered in biblical historiography as the conqueror of Jerusalem in 597 and 587/586 BCE (2 Kings 24–25; cf. 2 Chron. 36). The biblical record is supported and supplemented by the Babylonian Chronicle and other cuneiform documents. But the stories told in the book of Daniel about Nebuchadrezzar (especially chap. 4), as well as about Belshazzar (chap. 5), should rather be referred to Nabonidus, who proved to be not only the last king of the dynasty (555–539 BCE) but the last ruler of any independent polity in Babylon. The city surrendered to Cyrus the Persian in a bloodless takeover and thereafter, while continuing as a metropolis of the successive Achaemenid, Seleucid, and Parthian empires, ceased to play an independent role in ancient politics.

In the Bible, Babylon plays a dual role, positively as the setting for a potentially creative diaspora, negatively as a metaphor for certain forms of degeneracy. The "Babylonian exile" imposed by Nebuchadrezzar on the Judeans removed the center of Jewish life to Babylon for fifty or sixty years, if not the seventy predicted by the prophet Jeremiah (Jer. 29.10, cf. 2 Chron. 36.21). The exiled king Jehoiachin was released from prison by Nebuchadrezzar's son and successor Amel-Marduk, the Evil-merodach of 2 Kings 25.27 (cf. Jer. 52.31), and provided for from the royal stores, as indicated also by cuneiform sources. Jeremiah wrote to the exiles in God's name, advising them to enjoy the positive aspects of life in Babylon and to pray for its welfare (Jer. 29.4–7; contrast Ps. 122.6). Ezekiel lived among the exiles and prepared them for the restoration, while Second Isaiah welcomed the arrival of Cyrus (Isa. 44.28–45.1), which paved the way for the return of those exiles who chose to accept his proclamation (2 Chron. 36.22f.; Ezra 1.1–3).

Under Persian rule, Babylon continued to flourish as the seat of one of the most important satrapies of the Persian empire (cf. Ezra 7.16; Dan. 2.49; etc.), and the Achaemenid Artaxerxes I could still be called "king of Babylon" (Neh. 13.6). The Jews who chose to remain there enjoyed considerable prosperity, as indicated by business documents from nearby Nippur in which individuals identified as Judeans or bearing Jewish names (in Hebrew or Aramaic) engage in various agricultural and commercial activities. The foundations were thus laid for the creative role that Babylonia was to play in the Jewish life of the postbiblical period.

The Bible also reflects a negative view of Babylon. Already in the primeval history, the tower of Babel (Gen. 11.1–9) uses the traditional ziggurat present in each city of Sumer as a metaphor for the excesses of human ambition that led to, and accounted for, the confusion of tongues and dispersion of peoples. The Psalmists emphasized the negative aspects of exile (Ps. 137), and the fall of the "arrogant" city (Jer. 50.31) and "its sinners" (Isa. 13.9) was predicted confidently, even gleefully, by the prophets. In the New Testament, Babylon became the epitome of wickedness (Rev. 17.5) and a symbolic name for Rome (Rev. 17–18; cf. 1 Pet. 5.13).

WILLIAM W. HALLO

BAPTISM. A term first appearing in the New Testament as a purification ritual used by an unorthodox Jewish figure named John (the Baptist). All four Gospels and the book of Acts describe him "preaching a baptism of repentance for the forgiveness of sins" (Mark 1.4; Luke 3.3).

Scholars have speculated how John's mission might be related to other Jewish separatist groups such as the Qumran community, but exact origins remain unclear. There is abundant evidence that lustral bathing was an important aspect of Greco-Roman religions, especially related to healing divinities such as Asklepius. In the Hebrew Bible, cleansing with water is an important part of purification rites, especially after sexual activity or contact with a corpse (Lev. 15.18, Num. 19.13). John the Baptist calls for a more general repentance symbolized by baptism.

The report that Jesus himself was baptized in the Jordan by John (Mark 1.9–11) raises the possibility that Jesus was a disciple of John who broke off and started his own movement. It is clear that later followers of Jesus were concerned about this perception. Matthew's gospel includes a dialogue in which John recognizes Jesus' spiritual superiority and baptizes him reluctantly only after Jesus insists (Matt. 3.13–17). Luke goes a step further by excluding John from the account of Jesus' baptism (Luke 3.21) and telling the story of John's imprisonment immediately before the event takes place (Luke 3.19–20). Thus, in Luke, Jesus is baptized, but the story line indicates that the baptism could not have been performed by John.

In the Gospels, John is of interest only as he is related to the ministry of Jesus (Mark 1.2–3, 7–9; Matt. 3.11–12; Luke 3.15–17), but the baptism symbol used by John

John baptizing Jesus (Mark 1.9–11)

becomes a central image for the developing churches. Matthew's gospel concludes with the charge to "make disciples of all nations, baptizing them in the name of the Father and of the Son and of the Holy Spirit" (Matt. 28.19). The book of Acts elaborates further when Peter says to the crowd gathered on Pentecost, "Repent, and be baptized every one of you in the name of Jesus Christ so that your sins may be forgiven" (Acts 2.38).

Baptism in Acts takes place immediately after someone comes to believe in Christ, and it is usually followed by receiving the Holy Spirit. This two-stage process is founded on the contrast between John's water baptism and "being baptized by the Holy Spirit" (Acts 1.5; cf. Mark 1.8; Matt. 3.11; Luke 3.16; John 1.33). It is so important that the leaders of the Jerusalem church send Peter and John to lay hands on believers in Samaria who had "only been baptized in the name of the Lord Jesus," after which they receive the Holy Spirit (Acts 8.14–17). The situation is reversed when the gentiles of Cornelius's house come to believe. They receive the Holy Spirit and speak in tongues as a sign of God's acceptance of gentile converts, so Peter asks, "Can anyone withhold the water for baptizing these people who have received the Holy Spirit just as we have?" (Acts 10.44–48).

Paul's letters provide the earliest evidence about baptism among the Jesus followers. It is striking, therefore, that Paul makes no mention of John the Baptist or of baptism and receiving the Holy Spirit as a dual process. Paul sees that the person who has been baptized is "in Christ," no longer subject to the divisions of human society (Gal. 3.27), and part of a unified body (1 Cor. 12.13; cf. Eph. 4.5). Emphasis is on the state that has been achieved, not the way in which it has been accomplished. In fact, Paul is concerned that the Corinthians are putting too much stake in the person by whom they were baptized, and he is grateful that he baptized only a few of them: "For Christ did not send me to baptize but to proclaim the gospel" (1 Cor. 1.17).

In 1 Corinthians 15, Paul is using every possible argument to convince his readers that a resurrection of the dead will take place. In doing so he asks why people are baptized on behalf of the dead if there will be no resurrection (15.29). This brief allusion indicates that within the early churches it was possible to receive baptism in order to include in the body of Christ a friend or relative who was already dead. Paul does not specifically condemn the practice here, but it did not become an accepted part of Christian ritual.

Paul equates baptism symbolically with the death of Jesus (Rom. 6.3–4, cf. Col. 2.12), and he insists that rituals such as baptism are not spiritual guarantees, since God was not pleased with the Hebrews even though they went through a proto-baptism with Moses at the Red Sea (1 Cor. 10.1–5). This latter point is also made in the letter to the Hebrews (9.9–10), while 1 Peter contends that the story of Noah's ark prefigures the saving value of baptism (1 Pet. 3.21).

The New Testament evidence is used in debating later Christian baptismal practice, but it is rarely definitive. Certainly the majority of people who are baptized in the New Testament are adults who are entering the community. The exception might be children included in some of the households baptized in Acts (11.14; 16.15, 33). The baptism of infants became a more routine practice within the church as the doctrine of original sin became more widely accepted.

Another controversy concerns baptism by immersion or by the sprinkling of water on the participant. The descriptions of specific New Testament baptisms indicate that the person being baptized was dipped under the water. Jesus is said to come out of the water (Mark 1.10; Matt. 3.16), while Philip and the Ethiopian eunuch go down into the water (Acts 8.38). Going under the water also fits best with the image of being buried with Christ in baptism (Col. 2.12). At the same time baptisms in the New Testament are not described in specific terms, so diverse interpretations and practices develop.

DANIEL N. SCHOWALTER

BARABBAS. Outside the Gospels nothing is known of Barabbas. His name is Aramaic and means "son of the father" (Abba), ironically denoting the status given exclusively to Jesus. Barabbas was imprisoned for robbery (John 18.40) or for insurrection and murder (Mark 15.7; Luke 23.19), crimes not uncommon in the turbulent Palestine of the first century CE. In the account of the trial of Jesus, the Roman prefect Pontius Pilate is portrayed sympathetically, finding no fault in Jesus and recognizing that Jewish priests plotted his arrest. Following a Passover custom unknown outside the Gospels, Pilate offered to free a Jewish prisoner and suggested Jesus, but the crowd (in John, "the Jews") demanded that Pilate release Barabbas and crucify Jesus. This helped establish a negative attitude toward Jews in Christian tradition.

GREGORY SHAW

BEHEMOTH. A mythical beast described in Job 40.15–24 as the first of God's creations, an animal of enormous strength that inhabits the river valleys. Although frequently identified with the hippopotamus (as Leviathan is with the crocodile), not all the details of the creature's physiology fit that well-known mammal. In view of the references to Behemoth in the apocrypha and pseudepigrapha, it is more likely that it is a form of the primeval monster of chaos, defeated by Yahweh at the beginning of the process of creation; in fact, according to Job 40.24, the monster is represented as tamed by him and with a ring through his lip, so that like Leviathan he has become a divine pet. According to later Jewish tradition, at the end time Behemoth and Leviathan will become food for the righteous (see 2 Esd. 6.52).

MICHAEL D. COOGAN

BETHLEHEM (Map 1:X5). Village in Judah, ca. 10 km (6 mi) south of Jerusalem. The site was settled in the Paleolithic era, but is first mentioned in the Amarna letters (fourteenth century BCE); the meaning of its name is probably "house of (the deity) Lahmu" rather than the traditional "house of bread." It appears first in the Bible as home of a Levite who became a household priest in the hill country of Ephraim and was carried off by the Danites to their new city Dan (Judg. 17–18). Ruth came to Bethlehem with her mother Naomi, married Boaz, and became the ancestor of David (Ruth 4.13–22).

One account of how David's career began says that he was brought to play the lyre for Saul (1 Sam. 16.14–23), the other that he was a shepherd whom Samuel anointed as king (1 Sam. 16.1–13). Hope for a king like David persisted in the postexilic period, and Micah 5.2–4 prophesies a shepherd king from Bethlehem. According to Matthew 2 and Luke 2, Jesus was born in Bethlehem, and Matthew interpreted this as the fulfillment of Micah's prophecy.

Christian tradition, perhaps as early as the second century CE, identified a cave as the site of Jesus' birth. About 338 CE, Constantine had a church built over the grotto (and Justinian reconstructed it in the early sixth century). Jerome settled in Bethlehem in 386; here he made the Latin Vulgate translation of the Bible.

Among other traditional sites in or near Bethlehem are the shepherds' field, the tomb of Rachel (Gen. 35.19), and the well from which David's warriors brought him water (2 Sam. 23.13–17; 1 Chron. 11.15–19).

SHERMAN ELBRIDGE JOHNSON

BIBLE. The English word "Bible" is derived from the Greek word *biblia* (neuter plural), which means simply "books." As the collections of Jewish and Christian texts came increasingly to be considered as one unit, the same plural term in medieval Latin began to be understood in popular usage as feminine singular, no longer denoting "The Books" but "The Book." By the second century BCE the adjective "holy" had come to be used to designate some of these books (see 1 Macc. 12.9), and so now "Holy Bible" means a collection of sacred books.

Contents. The number of these sacred and/or authoritative books varies in different religious traditions. The Samaritans recognize only five books (Genesis, Exodus, Leviticus, Numbers, and Deuteronomy) as their canon. Twenty-four books, classified in three groupings, make up the Hebrew canon: the Law (Torah: Genesis, Exodus, Leviticus, Numbers, Deuteronomy); the Prophets, comprising the Former Prophets (Joshua, Judges, Samuel, Kings) and the Latter Prophets (Isaiah, Jeremiah, Ezekiel, and the Twelve Prophets); the Writings (Psalms, Proverbs, Job, Song of Songs, Ruth, Lamentations, Ecclesiastes, Esther, Daniel, Ezra-Nehemiah, and Chronicles). Samuel, Kings, the Twelve, Ezra-Nehemiah, and Chronicles are each counted as one book.

Historically, Protestant churches have recognized the Hebrew canon as their Old Testament, although differently ordered, and with some books divided so that the total number of books is thirty-nine. These books, as arranged in the traditional English Bible, fall into three types of literature: seventeen historical books (Genesis to Esther), five poetical books (Job to Song of Solomon), and seventeen prophetical books. With the addition of another twenty-seven books (the four Gospels, Acts, twenty-one letters, and the book of Revelation), called the New Testament, the Christian scriptures are complete.

The Protestant canon took shape by rejecting a number of books and parts of books that had for centuries been part of the Old Testament in the Greek Septuagint and in the Latin Vulgate, and had gained wide acceptance within the Roman Catholic church. In response to the Protestant Reformation, at the Council of Trent (1546) the Catholic church accepted, as deuterocanonical, Tobit, Judith, the Greek additions to Esther, the Wisdom of Solomon, Sirach, Baruch, the Letter of Jeremiah, three Greek additions to Daniel (the Prayer of Azariah and the Song of the Three Jews, Susanna, and Bel and the Dragon), and 1 and 2 Maccabees. These books, together with those in the Jewish canon and the New Testament, constitute the total of seventy-three books accepted by the Roman Catholic church.

The Anglican church falls between the Catholic church and many Protestant denominations by accepting only the Jewish canon and the New Testament as authoritative, but also by accepting segments of the apocryphal writings in the lectionary and liturgy. At one time all copies of the Authorized or King James Version of 1611 included the Apocrypha between the Old and New Testaments.

The Bible of the Greek Orthodox church comprises all of the books accepted by the Roman Catholic church, plus 1

Priest holding an ancient bible in Ethiopia

Esdras, the Prayer of Manasseh, Psalm 151, and 3 Maccabees. The Slavonic canon adds 2 Esdras, but designates 1 and 2 Esdras as 2 and 3 Esdras. Other Eastern churches have 4 Maccabees as well.

The Ethiopic church has the largest Bible of all, and distinguishes different canons, the "narrower" and the "broader," according to the extent of the New Testament. The Ethiopic Old Testament comprises the books of the Hebrew Bible as well as all of the deuterocanonical books listed above, along with Jubilees, 1 Enoch, and Joseph ben Gorion's (Josippon's) medieval history of the Jews and other nations. The New Testament in what is referred to as the "broader" canon is made up of thirty-five books, joining to the usual twenty-seven books eight additional texts, namely four sections of church order from a compilation called Sinodos, two sections from the Ethiopic Book of the Covenant, Ethiopic Clement, and Ethiopic Didascalia. When the "narrower" New Testament canon is followed, it is made up of only the familiar twenty-seven books, but then the Old Testament books are divided differently so that they make up 54 books instead of 46. In both the narrower and broader canon, the total number of books comes to 81.

Format. The traditional division of chapters (previously ascribed to Hugh of St. Cher and dated about 1262) is now attributed to Stephen Langton, a lecturer at the University of Paris and subsequently Archbishop of Canterbury (d. 1228). The present method employed for verses was originated by the scholarly printer Robert Stephanus (Estienne), whose Greek New Testament with numbered verses was issued in Geneva in 1551. The first English Bible to employ Stephanus's system of numbering verses was the Geneva version (New Testament 1556; Old Testament 1560).

The English Revised Version of 1881–85 relinquished the separate verse division of older versions in favor of a format employing paragraphs; however, verse numbers were still provided in the margin for ease of reference. Before the employment of this modern system the many verses, or texts, of the Bible were the subject of much statistical and even superstitious research. Fortunes were divined or the "will of God" learned by random selection of biblical passages. Some individuals undertook the daunting task of tallying the verses, words, and even the letters of the words, as though some all-important information was encoded in the result. The example below is a typical compilation, made by Thomas Hartwell Home (1780–1862) over a three-year period. According to Home's computations, the Authorized or King James Version of the Bible is comprised of:

	Old Testament	New Testament	Total
Books	39	27	66
Chapters	929	260	1,189
Verses	33,214	7,959	41,173
Words	593,493	181,253	774,746
Letters	2,728,100	838,380	3,566,480

This type of analysis has also brought to light miscellaneous information such as the following: the word "and" occurs in the Bible 46,227 times; the word "Lord" 1,855 times; "reverend" only once; "girl" also only once; "everlasting fire" twice; also, no words are longer than six syllables. These students of the letter of the Bible (like the Masoretes in ancient times) inform us that the middle book is that of Proverbs; the middle chapter, Job 39; the middle verse, 2 Chronicles 20.17; that the longest verse is Esther 8.9, and the shortest John 11.35 ("Jesus wept").

BRUCE M. METZGER

BISHOP. In pre-Christian and extra-Christian usage the Greek word rendered "bishop," *episkopos*, and its cognates, refers primarily to caring for something or someone. This can involve a person's oversight of a task or a group of people, such as priests in a temple, or God's own oversight of a person or an event.

The word occurs rarely in the New Testament and only in later documents with the exception of Philippians 1.1; the other passages are Acts 1.20; 20.28; 1 Peter 2.25; 1 Timothy 3.1–2; Titus 1.7. Acts 1.20 is a citation from Psalm 109.8 used to legitimate the selection of a replacement for Judas among the disciples. Acts 20.28 is from a speech by Paul encouraging his audience to "keep watch . . . over all the flock, of which the Holy Spirit has made you overseers to shepherd the church of God." The three citations from the Pastoral Letters have to do with requirements for the position or role of *episkopos* within the church.

Much of the debate about the usage of the term in the New Testament and early Christianity has been concerned with the evolution of an office called "bishop." Is it an authoritative role within the church that existed from apostolic times? Or should it be understood as a general term giving some measure of honor and perhaps authority to any believer? Naturally, different Christian traditions have various stakes in how these questions are answered.

With the exception of Philippians 1.1, all of the texts cited above probably come from the very end of the first or the beginning of the second century CE. Acts 20.28 and the citations from the Pastoral Letters seem to have in mind a specific group of leaders who look out for the well-being of the larger church. Philippians 1.1 seems to have a similar sense; the overseers are mentioned together with deacons, but there is no further indication of how they might have functioned. The Pastorals associate certain responsibilities with the office. The *episkopos* is a teacher, a good host, possesses only one wife, is above reproach, and perhaps is good in a debate (Titus 1.7); there is no evidence that this overseer had responsibility outside the local church.

The letters of Clement of Rome (ca. 95 CE) and Ignatius of Antioch (ca. 115 CE) demonstrate the development of a hierarchical office that eventually became dominant. The office of bishop is thus an indicator of the evolution of Christianity from a popular Palestinian movement to a sophisticated institution with offices, authorities, and hierarchy.

J. ANDREW OVERMAN

BROTHERS AND SISTERS OF JESUS. Siblings of Jesus are referred to collectively twice in the Gospels. In the account of the "true kindred" (Matt. 12.46–50 par.), Jesus' mother and brothers come to speak to him while he is teaching. Jesus refuses to see them, however, saying that his true sister, brother, and mother are those who do the will of God.

When Jesus teaches at the synagogue in his hometown of Nazareth, the listeners react angrily to his wisdom and mighty works (Matt. 13.53–58; Mark 6.1–6). The crowd doubts that a local person could be endowed with such power, and they cite the presence of his parents, brothers, and sisters as proof. The brothers are listed by name (James, Joseph [Mark reads Joses], Simon, and Judas) but the sisters only as a group. In Luke 4.22, the crowd asks simply, "Is not this Joseph's son?"

References to brothers and sisters of Jesus conflict with some understandings of the virgin birth. For those who feel that Jesus' mother Mary remained a virgin for life, brothers and sisters must be read as cousins or as stepbrothers and stepsisters fathered by Joseph in another, unmentioned, marriage.

DANIEL N. SCHOWALTER

BURIAL CUSTOMS. A part of the story of Abraham is the record of his concern and care for the burying of Sarah (Gen. 23). He buys a cave for her tomb; this purchase is his first land acquisition in the land of Canaan. The Hittites offered one of their sepulchers, but Abraham preferred to buy and utilize his own cave. For those outside the Promised Land, burial in the ancestral territory continued to be important. For example, the body of Joseph was embalmed in Egypt and returned to Canaan (Gen. 50.26). In like manner, many Jews of the Dispersion of the Roman period preferred to be buried in the Holy Land. The burial customs and practices, as with Abraham, were carried out amid outside cultural influences but yet maintained their own distinctiveness.

Tomb construction saw considerable change and variety. Abraham, as noted above, used a cave. In later periods tombs were cut from the rock. Jesus mentions "whitewashed tombs" (Matt. 23.27), which implies buildings. One of the few monuments from the first century CE still intact in Jerusalem is the so-called Tomb of Absalom, a monument that exhibits both Greek and Nabatean influence. Extended families often had a single connected cluster of underground tombs with niches for the various individuals or families. Often these were reused. Individual rockcut tombs were also common. The bodies were generally not enclosed in coffins; after decomposition the remaining bones were then removed to a bone chamber in the floor or at the side of the burial ledge and the space reused. Rock tombs were sealed with a hinged door or a heavy wheel-shaped stone. Criminals were buried under a pile of stones.

With regard to the preparation of the body for burial, neither embalming (an Egyptian custom) nor cremation (called idolatry in *m. 'Abod. Zar.* 1.3) was allowed. The body was washed (Acts 9.37) and enclosed (John 19.40), and finally a napkin was placed over the face (John 20.7). The Greek custom of individual coffins was occasionally followed in New Testament times; the earlier period did not use coffins.

Secondary burial, in which the remains, after decomposition, were placed in a small stone or clay box called an ossuary, gradually increased over time. A coffin (sarcophagus) averaged 1.8 m (6 ft) in length, while the ossuary was often only .8 m (2.5 ft) long. Many tombs had numerous small niches (Hebr. *kôkîm*) into which the ossuaries were placed. Considerable new evidence on burial customs has been gleaned from the excavations of the extensive Jewish cemetery at Beth Shearim, where secondary burials dominated. Often the ossuaries were decorated with various geometrical patterns. Roman Jericho has yielded a significant collection of wooden coffins. It seems likely that the biblical phrase "to sleep with [or to be gathered to] one's ancestors" refers to secondary burial in the family tomb.

Burial in the Middle East has always taken place without delay; almost always the person is buried the same day. The warm climate and the lack of embalming has necessitated this practice. In the case of the burial of Jesus, the approaching Sabbath added to the desire to complete the burial formalities before sundown (cf. Deut. 21.23).

The Middle East has long known the tradition of demonstrative mourning. The walls of ancient Egyptian tombs often depict groups of professional women mourners as a part of the funeral procession. This profession was also known in Israel; Jeremiah explains the purpose of the presence of evocative funeral songs sung by the professionals: "that our eyes may run down with tears" (Jer. 9.18). Instruments used at funerals included the flute (Matt. 9.23); Rabbi Judah (140–165 CE) said, "Even the poorest in Israel should hire not less than two flutes and one wailing woman" (*m. Ketub.* 4.4).

The Bible records a number of poems composed for the deceased, the most famous being David's lament over Saul and Jonathan (2 Sam. 1.18–27). The prophets use the funeral lament satirically in speaking of the ruin of nations such as Babylon, Tyre, and Egypt (e.g., Isa. 14.4–21; Ezek. 27; 32), and the book of Lamentations uses the genre for Jerusalem after its destruction in 587/586 BCE.

In biblical tradition mourning continued for seven days (Gen. 50.10). The places of burial were generally apart from the dwellings of the people; in earlier periods some burials took place within the house. While the Egyptians made elaborate preparations for the dead and placed the surroundings of life in the tomb of the deceased, these customs were kept to a minimum in Palestine. Tombs were comparatively modest and ostentation was criticized (Isa. 22.15–16). Eighty percent of the tomb inscriptions in the Beth Shearim cemetery are in Greek, yet the inscriptions themselves display a minimum of Greek ideological influence. Resurrection as a concept remains dominant over the idea of the immortality of the soul.

KENNETH E. BAILEY

Tombs from the Roman period in the Kidron Valley, Jerusalem.

C

CAIAPHAS. Also named Joseph, Caiaphas was high priest at the time of Jesus' death. According to Josephus, he was appointed in 18 CE by Valerius Gratus, the Roman procurator before Pilate; his father-in-law, Annas, had preceded him, as had, for very short terms, several of Annas's sons (*Ant.* 18.2.35). He was removed from office in 37 CE and replaced by another of Annas's sons (*Ant.* 18.4.95). There is some confusion in the New Testament about whether Annas or Caiaphas was high priest at the end of Jesus' life and about their role in his death, but the Gospels are consistent in their depiction of hostility toward Jesus by the high priest.

In 1990, the family tomb of Caiaphas was found in Jerusalem. It contained twelve ossuaries, one of which had inscriptions with the full name of Caiaphas in Aramaic (*yhwsp br qyp'*; and *yhwsp brqp'*: Joseph, son of Caiaphas), and another with simply the family name (*qp'*).

MICHAEL D. COOGAN

CAIN AND ABEL. Genesis 4.1–16 relates the curious story of Cain and Abel. Cain (meaning perhaps "smith," possibly related to the Kenites), is the firstborn of Adam and Eve, and Abel (meaning "emptiness") is his younger brother or twin. As is generally the case among biblical siblings, they come into conflict. Cain, a farmer, offers a sacrifice of grain to Yahweh, while Abel, a shepherd, offers a sacrifice from the firstborn of his flocks. For no obvious reason, Yahweh rejects Cain's sacrifice; this appears to be a literary gap or blank. After some moral advice from Yahweh, Cain murders Abel in the field, which Yahweh discovers from Abel's blood "crying out" from the ground. Yahweh confronts Cain with Abel's absence, to which Cain feigns ignorance. As punishment, Yahweh condemns Cain to wander the earth, decreeing that the earth will no longer bear crops for him. In fear for his life, Cain pleads for mercy, which Yahweh grants by placing an unspecified sign on Cain so that no one will murder him. Cain finally departs to wander in a land called Nod ("wandering"), east of Eden.

Many themes appear in this story, including sibling rivalry, the attraction of sin, crime met with punishment, the futility of pretense before God, and the moral distinction between civilization and barbarism. Cain begins as a farmer, plying the fruitful earth, and because of his unchecked passion he commits a heinous crime, only to separate himself and be separated—morally, economically, and geographi-

An ossuary found in southern Jerusalem, which contained the bones of the high priest Caiaphas (see Matt. 26.57), whose name is written on the left side.

cally—from the proper realm of civilized life. Only a plea for God's mercy (perhaps implying a degree of repentance) saves his life, signaling the small worth of life outside of civilization, where one is "hidden" from God's face.

In later interpretation, the cause of Cain's evil nature is frequently explored, with a tendency to identify Cain as the son of either Satan (1 John 3.12), the wicked angel Sammael (Targum Pseudo-Jonathan on Gen. 4.1 and 5.3), or the serpent in Eden (4 Macc. 18.8). Other gaps in the story also receive much attention, such as the origin of Cain's wife (in Jubilees 4.9 she is his sister, Awan, meaning "Wickedness") and the fate of Cain and his offspring (identified as demons in the *Zohar* and medieval legend). An early gnostic sect, the Cainites, may have regarded Cain as a savior figure.

In the New Testament, Abel is the prototypical martyr, who died for his faith (Matt. 23.35 par.; Heb. 11.4; 12.24).

RONALD S. HENDEL

CAPERNAUM. A village on the northwest shore of the Sea of Galilee (Map 12: X2). The Greek name *Kapharnaoum* evidently represents a Semitic original, "village of Nahum." It is identified as Tell Hum, a mound that has now been extensively excavated.

Jesus is reported to have settled in Capernaum (Matt. 4.13) and made his home there at the beginning of his ministry (Mark 2.1). From here he carried on his early preaching and healed many, beginning with an exorcism in the synagogue (Mark 1.21–28). Here he healed the slave of the centurion who had built the synagogue (Luke 7.1–10; Matt. 8.5–13). The synagogue is also the scene of the discourse on the bread of life (John 6.22–59).

The first archaeological discovery was a magnificent synagogue, now dated to the fourth century CE. It is constructed of limestone, enclosed by columns and adorned with fine carvings, and the facade faces Jerusalem.

More recently a large area has been excavated, in which single-story basalt dwellings were grouped in squares, with streets in between. In this complex there is an octagonal church from about 450 CE. Beneath it is a house church (about 350 CE), which was remodeled from a dwelling that the Franciscan archaeologists identify as Peter's house (Mark 1.29). Near the great synagogue there is a smaller one, built of basalt, probably from the first century CE.

Capernaum was evidently a fishing village when its houses were built in the first century BCE and had a population of not more than one thousand.

SHERMAN ELBRIDGE JOHNSON

CHRISTIAN. According to Acts 11.26, Jesus' disciples were first called Christians in Antioch. Elsewhere in the New Testament the word "Christian" occurs in Acts 26.28 and 1 Peter 4.14–16.

The origin of the term "Christian" is uncertain. It comprises the word "Christ," the Greek word meaning "anointed one" with an ending meaning "followers of" or "partisans of." Jews who did not accept Jesus as the Messiah would hardly refer to Jesus' disciples as Christians—the Messiah's followers. According to Acts 24.5, such Jews referred to Jesus' followers as "the sect of the Nazarenes," apparently regarding Christians as a Jewish group.

Because followers of Jesus used "saints" (2 Cor. 1.1; Rom. 12.13; Acts 9.13, 32), "brothers" (1 Cor. 1.10; Rom. 1.13; Acts 1.16), "the Way" (Acts 9.2; 19.9), "disciples" (often in the Gospels; Acts 6.1–2; 11.26), and other designations

Cain murdering Abel (Gen. 4.8)

when referring to themselves, it is unlikely that the term "Christian" originated among Christians.

In Acts 26.28 Agrippa uses "Christian" sarcastically; in 1 Peter 4.14–16 it is a term of reproach used during persecution. Thus, the term seems to have been derogatory. The contemporary Roman historians Tacitus (*Annals* 15.44) and Suetonius (*Lives of the Caesars* 6.16) use the term that way. Tacitus refers to Christians as people hated for their evil deeds, and Suetonius calls them "a new and evil superstition."

If first applied to Jesus' followers in Antioch, Roman officials may have coined the word to distinguish the Christian group from Judaism. Perhaps "Christian" was used to designate the Christian movement as hostile toward Agrippa. No matter where the term originated, it was first a word of scorn or ridicule. But by the end of the first century CE Christians accepted the name as a comforting sign of God's glory (1 Pet. 4.1416; Ignatius, *Romans* 3.2).

EDWIN D. FREED

CHRISTMAS. The English word Christmas means Christ's Mass, the festival of Christ's birthday. 25 December was by the fourth century CE the date of the winter solstice, celebrated in antiquity as the birthday of Mithras and of Sol Invictus. In the Julian calendar the solstice fell on 6 January, when the birthday of Osiris was celebrated at Alexandria. By about 300 CE, 6 January was the date of Epiphany in the East, a feast always closely related to Christmas. The earliest mention of 25 December for Christmas is in the Philocalian Calendar of 354, part of which reflects Roman practice in 336. Celebration of Christ's birthday was not general until the fourth century; in fact, as late as the fifth century the Old Armenian Lectionary of Jerusalem still commemorated James and David on 25 December, noting "in other towns

C

Mary, Joseph, and Jesus from the Nativity Church in Bethlehem (Luke 2.7)

they keep the birth of Christ." When celebrated, the theme was the Incarnation, and the scriptures were not confined to the birth or infancy narratives. To Luke 2.1–14 and Matthew 1.18–25 were added not only John 1.1–18 but also, for example, Titus 2.11–14.

The year of Christ's birth is hard to determine. The enrollment by Quirinius in that year according to Luke 2.1–5 is dated by Josephus as equivalent to 6–7 CE (*Ant.* 18.2.26), but this enrollment was not of "all the world" (Luke 2.1), would not have taken place under Herod, during whose lifetime Quirinius was not governor of Syria, and would not have required the presence of Joseph, and still less of Mary, in Bethlehem. Although Luke 3.1-2 suggests no exact year, the passage seems to indicate between 27 and 29 CE as the times of John's baptizing and of Jesus' being about thirty years of age (Luke 3.23). Jesus' birth would then be about 4–1 BCE. The time of year is nowhere indicated.

The place of Jesus' birth also raises problems. If we had only the gospels of Mark and John we would assume that it was Nazareth (Mark 1.9; John 1.45-46; cf. Luke 2.4, 39). Luke 2.1–20 tells the story of the birth in Bethlehem and Matthew 2.1 follows a similar tradition, though introducing not a birth narrative but an infancy narrative, for the account of the wise men implies that Jesus might have been as much as two years old when they arrived (Matt. 2.16).

The exact place at Bethlehem is doubtful; the manger of Luke 2.7 may be rather a stall with almost no covering, or even a feeding trough in the open, the "inn" itself not being a building but a yard with partial shelter at its sides. The ox and ass of subsequent art are not in Luke's story but enter from Isaiah 1.3. Another early tradition, recorded in the second century apocryphal Protoevangelium of James (18–21) and Justin (*Trypho* 78.657), tells of a cave as the birthplace. It was apparently shown to Origen ca. 246, and by 333 Constantine had built a basilica over it, which was replaced under Justinian ca. 531. Still extant, the cave claims a stone as the manger. In early liturgies both the manger

and the shepherds' fields play a part, but at the inclusive feast of the Epiphany rather than at a celebration solely of Christ's birthday.

A. R. C. LEANEY

CHRONICLES, THE BOOKS OF.

Title. As with Samuel and Kings, the two books of Chronicles are in reality one: the counting of words and sections customary in the Hebrew text appears only at the end of 2 Chronicles. The division was first made in the Septuagint and thence in the Latin Vulgate; hence it was adopted in other translations and, by the sixteenth century, also in printed Hebrew Bibles. The Hebrew title is "book of the acts of the days," that is, annals, a phrase used frequently in this sense to describe royal acts or records (e.g., 1 Kings 14.29, and cf. Esther 6.1). The title is not entirely appropriate; there is much material of other kinds to be found in Chronicles. Even if it reasonably fits the larger part of the work, it too easily gives the impression that we are dealing with a work of history, which is only very partially the case. In the Greek, the title given is "the thing(s) left out" (*paralipomenon*); this is intelligible on the common assumption that Chronicles was intended to supplement the books of Samuel and Kings by providing information not given there, but it is an inaccurate description for what the work really is. Indeed, it may be recognized that this misunderstanding has often led to a use of Chronicles, for example in simplified histories of Israel and in church lectionaries, that does not do justice to a writing that needs to be read for its own sake and in the light of its own style of approach and not just to fill gaps in a differently conceived presentation.

Contents. Briefly, the contents are:

1 Chronicles	1.1–9.34: Genealogies from Adam onward, culminating in lists of those who returned from exile in Babylon
1 Chronicles	9.35–29.30: The kingship of David
2 Chronicles	1–9: The kingship of Solomon

2 Chronicles 10–36: The kingdom of Judah to its destruction by the Babylonians and the beginning of restoration under Cyrus the Persian.

The outline suggests a twofold approach to the story. In the first, the opening chapters (1 Chron. 1-8), consisting almost entirely of lists of names, offer a survey from the earliest figures of Israelite tradition, through a concentration on the tribes of Israel to the family of Saul, the first king; this ushers in chap. 9, where there is a leap forward to Judah's unfaithfulness that led to exile in Babylon and to the return, listing family groups, priests, and other religious officials. In the second approach, the story begins over again (at 9.35), with a repetition of the Saul genealogy (cf. 8.29-40), which here serves to introduce Saul's failure as a foil to the establishment and achievements of David in chapters 10–29. With its sequel in 2 Chronicles, this second approach offers a survey covering the whole period of the monarchy, itself to end with a short reference to Cyrus, and the promise of a return from exile. The question whether the books of Ezra and Nehemiah, which continue the story, are to be regarded as part of the same work or are independent of Chronicles will be considered subsequently.

Text. Like all other biblical books, the text of Chronicles presents numerous problems resulting from errors in transmission. But the more serious difficulties here arise from the considerable degree to which these books offer duplicate texts of material found elsewhere in the Bible. The main overlaps are with sections of Samuel and Kings; a substantial part of 1 Chronicles 10 to 2 Chronicles 36 contains such parallels. The relationship is not all at one level; there are passages where the Chronicles and Samuel or Kings texts are virtually the same but many more where numerous smaller and larger differences are to be seen. Some of these differences may derive from the simple substitution of more familiar words or forms than those found in what are clearly the older texts; some of the exact coincidences may be due to crossinfluence from one text to the other at a relatively late stage. Some differences are evidently the result of exegetical activity, as indeed at least some of the additional material, unparalleled in the older texts, is likely to be due to the interpretive inventiveness of the author of Chronicles. The study of the relationship is complicated by some evidence in the Qumran texts of Samuel which suggests that the text known to the writer of Chronicles may have been closer to those texts than to Samuel as it appears in the Hebrew Bible.

There are numerous other textual overlaps. Much of the genealogical material in 1 Chronicles 1–9 is paralleled in the Pentateuch or elsewhere. The psalm passage in 1 Chronicles 16.8–36 is paralleled in parts of Psalms 105, 96, and 106; and there are numerous other quotations or allusions to psalms and to other works, especially to various prophetic writings (e.g., 2 Chron. 20.20; cf. Isa. 7.9). These last are usually of greater interest as representing the exegesis of earlier material than for textual relationship.

Sources and Integrity. As has just been indicated, we may recognize the books of Samuel and Kings as the major source for Chronicles, allowing for the probability that the text used was not exactly the same as that familiar to us; other materials provided further sources on which the writer drew. In addition, however, we find a substantial number of passages where no parallel is known. Thus, in 2 Chronicles 28, in relating the reign of Ahaz, the Chronicler clearly knows the parallel in 2 Kings 16, but there is additional material not found there. In this particular case, we

may note the probability that some of the smaller differences—but no less important for that—are due to the Chronicler's own exposition of the already familiar material. But the whole of the war narrative in 28.5–15 is not so easy to explain. The same is true of archival material about fortifications (e.g., 2 Chron. 11.5-12) and of a good deal of what is devoted to modifications in the Jerusalem Temple, regarded favorably or unfavorably (e.g., 2 Chron. 28.24-25: Ahaz's antireforms; 2 Chron. 29.3–31.21: Hezekiah's reforms). These extra passages have been variously assessed. Some would regard them as genuine extracts from archival and other sources that existed alongside the books of Samuel and Kings. Others would see in such unparalleled material evidence of the Chronicler's imaginative inventiveness, but it is not easy to see why some of this material should be pure invention. It is more important that we attempt to link such embellishments of the narratives with what may be detected of the main purposes of the work and, at the same time, recognize that Chronicles does not simply reuse older material but offers exegeses of it. Thus, the portrayals of Ahaz and Hezekiah, already alluded to, may serve as examples of an interpretive process by which a bad king, according to 2 Kings, becomes the worst representative of the Judean monarchy, while a good king, again as 2 Kings describes him, has become a virtually ideal figure. For the latter, it is instructive to observe not only the enormous additional account of religious reform in 2 Chronicles 29-31 (contrast the extreme brevity of 2 Kings 18.4), but also the skilled reworking of the narrative material of 2 Kings 18–20 in 2 Chronicles 32.

It is in the light of this that the sources named in the books of Chronicles should be considered. At a number of points, in the summaries of the kings' reigns, allusion is made to the sources employed; thus 1 Chronicles 29.29-30 refers to "the records of the seer Samuel, and . . . the records of the prophet Nathan, and . . . the records of the seer Gad" (cf. the similar statement for Solomon in 2 Chron. 9.29, and for Hezekiah in 2 Chron. 32.32). In other instances, as in the books of Kings, reference is made simply to annals—"the Book of the Kings of Judah and Israel" and the like. It would appear that the Chronicler is here both following the pattern of the books of Kings in citing such annalistic works and also developing the understanding of the earlier writings and emphasizing the relationship between their stories of kings and the activity of prophets. The earlier works, from Joshua to 2 Kings, came in time to be known as the "Former Prophets" and were to stand alongside the "Latter Prophets," namely the prophetic books, Isaiah, Jeremiah, Ezekiel, and the Twelve. Such a description of the earlier writings suggests that, whatever precisely the Chronicler may have had at his disposal, he was accepting and developing a particular understanding of the writings familiar to him; whatever sources unknown to us were available, we must expect that they too were handled with the same kind of creative reinterpretation.

One further question needs a brief mention here: Does the work exist essentially as it came from its author, or has it been modified to a greater or lesser extent? Various theories of stages in its formation have been proposed, but none appears entirely convincing; there is insufficient evidence to support the idea of a "first" and a "second" Chronicler, or that of a first stage belonging to the early Persian period and second and third stages from a later date. The possibility that 1 Chronicles 1–9 is a later addition has also found some supporters; but the relationship between these chapters and what follows makes that view difficult. Perhaps, and this has been particularly argued for 1 Chronicles 24–27,

C

some expansions have been made; but unless it is possible to see clear evidence of a shift in standpoint, it is difficult to be sure. And even with such an apparent shift, we cannot be certain how far such a different emphasis was inherent in material being taken over from another source and incorporated by the author in spite of the fact that its outlook did not agree at every point with that of the main work.

The Place of Chronicles in the Canon. In English translations, Chronicles is placed, as in the Septuagint and the Vulgate, in the group of books that may be roughly described as "historical." Thus, it follows the books of Kings and is in turn followed by Ezra, Nehemiah, and Esther. (The canons of some churches include Tobit, Judith, and 1 and 2 Maccabees in this group as well). There is clear logic in this arrangement; all these writings, whatever their differences, are mainly narratives of one kind or another. The Hebrew Bible offers a different picture. As has been noted, the "historical" books from Joshua to Kings there appear as the Former Prophets. Chronicles, as also Ezra-Nehemiah (as one book) and Esther, appear in the third part of the Hebrew canon, entitled the Writings. Most commonly, in manuscripts and printed editions, Chronicles stands last, preceded by Ezra-Nehemiah; this is problematic, since clearly Ezra-Nehemiah provides a continuation of the Chronicles narrative. In some manuscripts, Chronicles stands first among the Writings, immediately before Psalms; in such a position it provides a context for the Psalter, traditionally associated with David, for much of 1 Chronicles is concerned with David and lays great stress on his organization of Temple worship and singing (for the latter, see especially 1 Chron. 16). When placed at the end of the Writings, it may be regarded as setting out by both warning and example how the true Temple and true worship must be maintained. It then follows Daniel, ostensibly concerned with the disasters of the sixth century BCE and the destruction of Temple

and worship then—though, in reality (see especially Dan. 9), it points to the defilement and hoped for reestablishment of the Temple in the second century BCE in the period of Antiochus IV Epiphanes; and Ezra-Nehemiah, which relates various stages in the restoration of Temple and people in the Persian period. By placing Chronicles at the end, the Hebrew Bible, which eventually reflects later concerns of the Jewish community, may be seen to look to a future restoration of Jerusalem and its shrine, beyond the still later disasters of Roman rule (especially the events of 70 and 135 CE).

A Literary Work and an Interpretation. The term "the Chronicler" is often used as a convenient shorthand to refer to the unknown author of the books of Chronicles. It has the advantage of simplicity, but it can too easily seem to imply that we know who the author was. In fact, nothing at all is known; the traditional view named Ezra, but there is no real evidence for this, and it must be regarded as part of the process by which the authority of biblical writings was associated with noteworthy biblical characters. Nor do we know when Chronicles was compiled. In part, a decision on this is connected with the relationship between Chronicles and Ezra-Nehemiah; if these together form a unity, then the final shaping must be later than the events there described, which would point to the late fifth or the fourth century BCE, or perhaps later still. It is clear that, with its dependence on Samuel and Kings, whose final form cannot be earlier than the sixth century BCE, we must look in all probability in the Persian period; there is no clear evidence of the change to Greek rule. A fourth century BCE date is reasonable, but remains a balanced guess.

There can be no certainty on whether the work is the product of a single author or was produced within a particular circle whose members shared views and ideals about the nature of their community. The very fact that so much earlier material has been reused makes the assessment of lit-

The Building of the Temple of Solomon (Luca Giordano)

erary unity very difficult. Indeed, we may wonder how far the idea of literary unity is really appropriate to such a writing. The supposition that an ancient writer would endeavor to produce a completely unified and consistent work is too much based on modern conceptions of how an editor should update older material. We should more probably expect to find general consistency, but expressed in a variety of ways.

This is particularly relevant to the debated question of whether the books of Ezra and Nehemiah are separate or belong to the same work. They are treated as separate in the Hebrew Bible, and, as noted above, they normally stand in the reverse order from that found in the Greek and derived translations. There is a small overlap between the two (2 Chron. 36.22–23 = Ezra 1.1–3a); in the alternative form in 1 Esdras, which covers from 2 Chronicles 35 to Ezra 10 plus Nehemiah 7.73b–8.13, the material runs continuously, but the evidence of 1 Esdras is problematic. It seems clear that, whatever the actual relationship, the reader is intended to see Ezra-Nehemiah as a sequel. Alternative views range from the assumption of unity, so that Chronicles-Ezra-Nehemiah are referred to as the Chronicler's work; to the maintenance of single authorship, but with the two parts written at different times, with either order of writing proposed; and to stress disunity, the marked differences between the two works in language, style, and ideology. Such differences of view suggest that certainty cannot be achieved. In part, the decision comes down to assessing whether and to what extent the differences within the books are too great for the books to be considered other than superficially related; to what extent unity in the literary sense demands complete unity of thought and style; and to what extent disunity is related to the use in all parts of the work of source material that has its own language and style and has often been taken over virtually unaltered. If we demand very strict unity of thought and style, then we will decide to separate them, but if we think in terms of a circle of thought, in which the main lines are shared but with differences of view on many matters of detail, then an overall unity may embrace variety of approach.

Whatever the decision in this delicate matter, it seems clear that the author of the books of Chronicles, as we know them, was setting out to give to his contemporaries an understanding of their current position as a small subject people under alien (Persian) rule, in the light of his interpretation of the past. This involved seeing that small community in the light of the whole story from creation to the restoration under Cyrus (so in 1 Chron. 1–9); a similar approach may be seen in the Pentateuch, which traces the story from creation to conquest. It also involved offering an understanding of the contemporary significance of the two major institutions of that history: kingship and Temple. The total loss of the former, with no realistic possibility of its recovery, is explained through a retelling of the story with the stress laid on David as creator, and on his worthy successors as continuers, of the religious life of the Jerusalem Temple; in this view, the real function of the monarchy was religious. The restoration of the Temple under Persian rule described in Ezra 1–6 is implicit in the material of 1 Chronicles 9 and set in motion in the final verses of 2 Chronicles. Whoever was responsible for Ezra-Nehemiah was providing the logical conclusion to the story. At the same time, the books of Chronicles provide an idealized picture of the true people, loyal to their God and to the law of Moses (Torah); the story does not shirk the recognition of failures by rulers and people, from the disastrous disloyalty of Saul (1 Chron. 10), to the secession of the north from the true inheritance

(2 Chron. 10), to the apostasy of other rulers, reaching a climax in Ahaz (2 Chron. 28), and so to the final disobedience that led to the exiling of the people to Babylon, leaving an empty land to recover by observing its forgotten sabbaths (2 Chron. 36.17–21). But the author does not merely paint a gloomy picture; numerous instances of repentance are included, the most remarkable being the total reinterpretation of the reign of Manasseh who, being the worst of the kings of Judah in 2 Kings, now becomes an exemplar—punished for evil by captivity in Babylon, he returns in repentance and becomes a reformer (2 Chron. 33.1–20), an interpretation that clearly understands Manasseh as a symbol of Judah in exile and return. Within the broad sweep of interpretation, which gives the work a clear unity of purpose, there is a rich mixture of story and comment, of homiletic development and imaginative depiction, almost like a series of sermons, all on central themes but developed in a variety of ways.

This is not a history of Judah; attempts to prove historical accuracy are as misguided as criticisms of it as fabrication. It is a work of literary skill, significant for its theological relevance to the needs of the postexilic community and to any period that demands the rethinking of long-held beliefs.

PETER R. ACKROYD

CHRONOLOGY. *This entry consists of two articles on dating systems used in the Bible and their correlation with modern historiography. The first article is on* Israelite Chronology *and the second,* Early Christian Chronology.

Israelite Chronology

Biblical chronology may be considered under two aspects: historical or scientific chronology, which deals with the real chronology of actual events, and theoretical or theological chronology, which considers the meanings and purposes of chronological schemes used as a literary vehicle of religious conceptions. Individual statements may often be considered from either point of view; both aspects will be taken into account here.

Dating Systems. The Hebrew Bible has no universal dating system like our BCE/CE system. There are several modes in which chronological information is given:

Simple addition from the datum point of creation: For example, Adam was 130 years old when his son Seth was born, Seth was 105 when his first son Enosh was born (Gen. 5.3,6). By such addition, we can reckon that the flood began in the year 1656 AM (= Anno Mundi, i.e., from creation); however, this figure is not made explicit, and readers must do their own addition. Such reckoning can produce a clear chronology, with only some uncertainties, from creation down to the start of Solomon's Temple.

Regnal years of kings, often synchronically correlated with another line of kings (e.g., years of a Judean king are stated along with years of a contemporary king of Israel). Such dates are relative, not absolute; they were doubtless adequate for people of the time, but they do not tell us the actual date unless we can bring some other source to bear.

Later books used the Seleucid era, commencing 312/311 BCE, for example, "in the one hundred thirty-seventh year of the kingdom of the Greeks" (1 Macc. 1.10); this was used long and widely in Jewish life.

Modern Jewish reckoning, by years from creation: the Jewish year 5754 is 1993–1994 CE, implying that the world was created in 3761 BCE. Although figures going back to creation were important, dates are not stated in this way in the

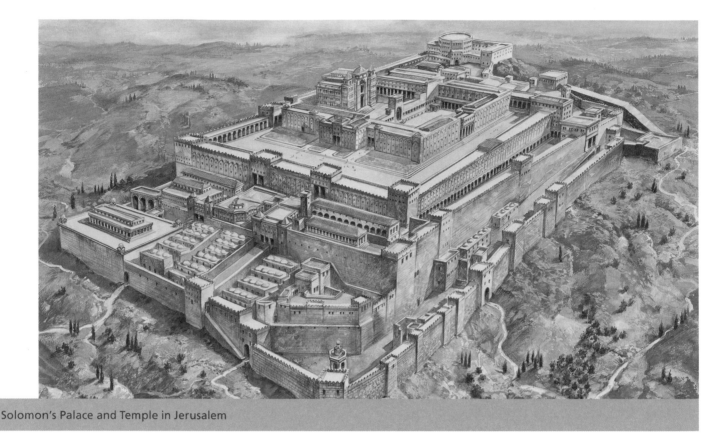

Solomon's Palace and Temple in Jerusalem

Bible; this mode of stating dates did not come into use until long after biblical times.

Basic Data. The main body of chronological material in the Hebrew Bible falls into three great segments:

From creation to Abraham's migration from Haran into Canaan. This is easily fixed by addition of the ages of the patriarchs, mainly in the genealogies of Genesis 5 and 11. The period is split by the central event of the flood. The figures differ in various texts, being mainly lower in the Samaritan and higher in the Septuagint (LXX); thus the flood, which is 1656 AM in the Hebrew Masoretic text, is 1307 AM in the Samaritan and 2242 AM in the LXX. One obscurity is the "two years after the flood" of Arpachshad's birth (Gen. 11.10), which is difficult to reconcile with the dates of his father Shem (Gen. 5-32).

From Abraham's migration to the start of Solomon's Temple. This segment falls into three smaller sections:

From Abraham's entry into Canaan to the entry of Jacob and his family into Egypt. This is easily calculated from the ages of the patriarchs and amounts to 215 years.

The period spent in Egypt is expressly given by Exodus 12.40 as 430 years. The Samaritan and the LXX, however, have the extra words "and in the land of Canaan" or the like; this means that the 430 years stretch back to Abraham's entry 215 years earlier, thus reducing the time in Egypt to 215 years. This reading, 430 years from Abraham to Moses, is followed by Paul (Gal. 3.17). According to the Hebrew text, subject to some minor uncertainties, the Exodus was probably in 2666 AM.

The time from the Exodus to the start of the Temple (not its completion) is clearly stated as 480 years (1 Kings 6.1). This comprehensive statement bridges over the times of Joshua, the Judges, Samuel, Saul, and David, for which there are many detailed chronological statements (e.g., the years of each of the Judges), but also many gaps (e.g., the dates of Joshua, Samuel, or Saul). The total of 480 bridges these uncertainties and provides a clear overarching connection

between creation and Temple. The Temple-building probably began in 3146 AM.

From Solomon onward we have figures for the years of each king. If we simply add up the figures for the Judean kings, from Solomon's fourth year, when the Temple construction began, to the destruction of Temple and kingdom, the figures in themselves are 430. Here, however, we can compare the figures with historical facts, and the period cannot have been more than about 372 years (Solomon's accession 962 BCE; start of Temple 958 BCE; destruction 587/586 BCE).The figures amounting to 430 have been accounted for through overlaps of reigns, co-regencies, textual errors, historical mistakes, and schematic periodization.

In addition, it is difficult to make the years of the Israelite kings fit exactly with those of the Judean.

After the destruction of kingdom and Temple, chronological information in the Hebrew Bible is fragmentary and sporadic. Some dates are given by the year of a Persian emperor (e.g., Zech. 1.1; Ezra 1.1; Neh. 2.1), but the Hebrew Bible itself does not tell us how long these kings reigned or in what order they came, nor did later writers preserve an accurate memory of this. Later Jewish chronography assigned only thirty-two or fifty-two years to the entire Persian empire, which had in fact lasted over two hundred years, and similarly the number of actual Persian monarchs was unknown, hence the "four" kings of Persia (Dan. 7.6; 11.2). This leads to another aspect.

Dependence on Extrabiblical Information. Chronology cannot be worked out from biblical data alone; it depends on some synchronism with points established from sources other than the Bible. Traditional biblical chronology dovetailed biblical data into Greek and Roman history. Classical sources give a fairly exact dating of events back to the sixth century BCE, and this can be synchronized with the latest events recorded in Kings, thus providing an entry from extrabiblical history into biblical chronology. In modern times, knowledge of ancient Egypt and Mesopotamia, as well as archaeological discovery, have provided a much richer network of evidence against which events reported in the Hebrew Bible can be set. Thus, an inscription of Shalmaneser III of Assyria mentions Ahab, king of Israel, in a battle (not mentioned in the Bible!) of 853 BCE, and Jehu in 841; Jehu's revolt against the dynasty of Omri (2 Kings 9–10) is now placed in 842 BCE. This correlation of biblical data with extrabiblical information carries us back to about 1000 BCE, and without it we would not know the true duration of the kingdom. Key dates to remember are:

962 BCE   accession of Solomon
842   revolt of Jehu and crisis in royal house of both kingdoms
722   destruction of Samaria and end of kingdom of Israel
587/586   destruction of Jerusalem and end of kingdom of Judah

When we go back beyond the time of David, extrabiblical information is often not sufficiently specific to provide chronological exactitude; it may suggest nothing more precise than historical circumstances or social conditions that might have fitted with an event mentioned in the Bible. Biblical dates in the earlier stages, taken alone, leave us to question whether they rest on accurate memory or on theoretical schematism. Later, in the Persian period, though the dates of kings are well known from Persian and Greek sources, the Hebrew Bible may leave it vague as to which king of a certain name was involved—for example, whether Artaxerxes I or II, an uncertainty that affects the content of Ezra and Nehemiah.

Theoretical Chronology. Taken as a whole, the chronology of the Hebrew Bible, though containing true historical data, may have been theological rather than historical in its interest, a literary or legendary device that bore a religious message. Thus, the Genesis figures are part of the genealogies, in which persons live to ages like 930 or 969 years; this is true of Mesopotamian legend as well, in which a king in the beginnings of the world might reign for thirty-six thousand years or more (and eight kings might last 241,000 years down to the flood), with the figures dropping rapidly after the flood. Chronology of this sort belongs to legend or myth.

Some essential dates have strikingly round figures: 215 years from Abraham to Egypt, 430 years in Egypt, 430 for the figures of the kings when added up; 40 on the march from Egypt to Canaan, 480 from the Exodus to the Temple. Are not such figures theoretical? If, as is possible, the Exodus took place in 2666 AM, is it perhaps significant that this is almost exactly two-thirds of 4000?

While some chronological material comes from ancient legend, there are signs that figures were being adjusted and modified at a late date, such as the variations between the Masoretic, Samaritan, and Greek texts in Genesis 5. The book of Jubilees, a rewriting of Genesis and Exodus 114 from the second century BCE with an intense chronological interest, measures time in "jubilees" of forty-nine years, and ends at the entry of Israel into Canaan, exactly fifty jubilees or 2450 years from creation; like the Samaritan Pentateuch, it dates the flood to 1307 AM.

Enoch, the seventh from Adam, lived 365 years—obviously a very significant number, and markedly different from others in the same genealogy—before he was taken away by God (Gen. 5.21–24). The book of Enoch has many contacts with Jubilees, and it is concerned with the calendar and the movement of the heavenly bodies; the number of days in a year was hotly debated in this period.

Eschatological expectation forms another likely aspect; it might be thought that the world would last a total round number of years. Major events like the Flood, the Exodus, and the construction of the Temple, were linked with that coming end by significant number sequences. Such sequences might also lead, not to the final end of the world, but to the establishment of a basic constitution (e.g., completion of Mosaic legislation and start of tabernacle worship) or to a decisive historical stage (the entry into Canaan in Jubilees). If, as has been suggested, a figure of 4000 was held in mind, the present biblical chronology might be predicated upon the rededication of the Temple (about 164 BCE) after its profanation by Antiochus, which would establish a connection with Daniel, as well as with the books of Enoch and Jubilees.

The antiquity of the Jewish people was an issue in Hellenistic times, when they were sometimes regarded as newcomers on the scene of world culture. Against this, Josephus insisted on the ancient origins of the Jews; their possession of books that went back without interruption to the beginnings of the world could be a powerful argument. This may have motivated the higher figures of the chronology in the LXX.

Conclusion. Chronological interest is a very important element in the Hebrew Bible, though it is not obtrusive as in Jubilees and not all biblical sources were equally interested in it. The chronology formed an important part of the total shape of the Bible. New Testament authors were well aware of its details: Paul quoted the 430 years exactly, though he did not need the precise figure for his argument; Acts 7.4 is precise, though contrary to the natural sense of the Hebrew, in saying that Abraham migrated from Haran "after his father died" (cf. Gen. 11.2632; 12.4). After New Testament times, biblical chronology continued as a normal and essential aspect of Christian culture, and was cultivated by such writers as Eusebius and Bede. Histories began with creation and continued up to what were then modern times. In the Reformation, Luther's *Supputatio annorum mundi* or chronological summary was regulative for German-speaking Protestantism. In the English-speaking world, James Ussher, Archbishop of Armagh (1581–1656), wrote his detailed chronology from creation (which he fixed in 4004 BCE) to just after the destruction of the Temple in 70 CE. In this he integrated biblical data with all known material of Greek and Roman chronology. Many English Bibles have enshrined his dates in their margins. Only in the nineteenth and twentieth centuries did biblical chronology lose its charm and come to be largely forgotten; even the more conservative and literalist reader of the Bible was no longer literal enough to take seriously the precision of biblical chronology. Now is the time for its literary and theological character to be appreciated once again.

JAMES BARR

Early Christian Chronology

No special era is used by the New Testament writers. While Jewish authors were familiar with the Syrian era, which began on 1 October 312 BCE (e.g., 1 Macc. 1.20, the year 143 = 169 BCE), no references of this kind are found in the New Testament. Here, as in the works of Josephus, dates are given simply with regard to the number of years during which a contemporary ruler had been governing when the event in question happened. Thus, John the Baptist is said to have begun preaching" in the fifteenth year of the reign of Emperor Tiberius" (Luke 3.1), which corresponds to 28 CE. Christian writers of subsequent centuries took over the Roman era in which the years were counted from the presumed foundation of Rome on 21 April 753 BCE *("ab urbe condita")*. In the sixth century CE this era was replaced by the Christian era which is based on calculations of the Greek monk Dionysius Exiguus in Rome. Commissioned around 532 CE to coordinate the festival calendar of the church, he dated the incarnation of Christ to 25 March of the Roman year 754, and this year became the year 1, starting from 1 January. Dionysius Exiguus made a slight error, since Matthew 2.1 dates the birth of Jesus to the days of King Herod, who died in 4 BCE.

Matthew explicitly connects the birth of Jesus with the government of King Herod (Matt. 2.1), and the reference to this ruler's successor Archelaus (2.22) proves that he meant Herod the Great. The years during which Herod was the king of the Jews are known from Josephus. According to his colorful reports, Herod was elected king of the Jews by the Roman senate in 40 BCE (Josephus, *Ant.* 14.14.385, confirmed by Strabo, Tacitus, and Appian), and he died at springtime thirty-six years later, which gives us the year 4 BCE (*Ant.* 17.8.191; *War* 1.33.665). Matthew thus reports that Jesus was born some time before the year 4 BCE. Attempts have also been made to base a more specific dating on the star discovered by the Magi (Matt. 2.2), but all identifications with a comet, a constellation, or a nova seem arbitrary, so that Matthew's reference to Herod remains the only fixed datum.

Luke likewise regarded Jesus as born under Herod when he dated the birth of John the Baptist to the days of this king (Luke 1.5) and indicated that Jesus was six months younger (1.26). In his infancy narrative, however, Luke connected the birth of Jesus with an enrollment for taxation ordered by Augustus and carried out under Quirinius (2.1–2). An enrollment arranged by Quirinius as governor of Syria is known only from 6 CE, when Judea was made the property of Augustus to be administered by a procurator in Caesarea whose task it was to collect taxes for the emperor. This taxation of 6 CE caused a revolt in Judea (*War* 7.8.253–56; *Ant.* 18.1.3–10, 23–25), but did not involve the population of Galilee, where Joseph and Mary lived and where Herod Antipas ruled as tetrarch. Luke had probably heard of an earlier registration within the whole kingdom of Herod the Great, but was attracted by the famous taxation under Quirinius.

Concerning the ministries of John the Baptist and Jesus, the only chronological information available is the above-mentioned reference to John's first preaching in 28 CE (Luke 3.1) and a notice that Jesus was reproached for speaking with authority though he was not yet a senior of fifty years (John 8.57).

The capital punishment of the Baptist resulted from his criticism of the marriage between Herod Antipas and Herodias, whom he accused of adultery because the latter had been the wife of the former's brother (Matt. 14.4 par.). A further consequence of this marriage was that Antipas was attacked in the year 36 by the army of the Nabatean king, whose daughter the tetrarch had divorced in order to marry Herodias (Josephus, *Ant.* 18.5.109-15). John's criticism of the tetrarch cannot have been uttered many years earlier, so that his death (ibid. 116-19) will have taken place around 32 CE.

Accordingly, the death of Jesus is preferably to be dated 33 CE, and in this year the political situation favored the trial against him. Shortly before, in 31 CE, Tiberius had deposed and executed Sejanus, who had been a cruel dictator in Rome and an especially great antagonist of the Jews; subsequently and most likely in 32 the emperor had ordered his representatives in the provinces to pay attention to Jewish interests (Philo, *Legation to Gains* 161). This explains the exceptional rapport between Pilate and the Pharisees that led to the crucifixion of Jesus.

As to a more exact dating of Jesus' last supper and his death, it has first to be observed that in Jewish tradition each

The Roman emperor Nero (54–68 CE) overseeing the torture of Christian subjects by burning at the stake in ancient Rome

day begins in the evening so that both events belonged to the same day. According to all four Gospels, the eucharist and the crucifixion took place just before Passover on the so-called day of preparation (Grk. *paraskeuē*), which that year was a Friday, so that it served to prepare Passover and the Sabbath at the same time (Matt. 27.62; Mark 15.42; Luke 23.54; John 19.31). Contrary to what is often stated, the synoptic and Johannine reports do not contradict each other in this point. In the Jewish calendar, the day of preparation for Passover, to which all four Gospels refer, had to be 14 Nisan. The beginning of this lunar month was established year by year according to the first visibility of the crescent moon in March, and though no exact timing was possible in those days, modern studies have shown that 14 Nisan fell on a Friday in two of the years in question: ca. 7 April in the year 30 and ca. 3 April in the year 33. The political factors mentioned above speak in favor of dating Jesus' last supper and crucifixion to an evening and the subsequent day around 3 April of the year 33.

The next New Testament events to be dated are the martyrdom of Stephen and the conversion of Paul (Acts 7.58; 9.4), and here the circumstances justify a dating to 36 CE. In this year, troubles with the Parthians led Vitellius, the governor of Syria, to secure Jewish goodwill; he deposed Pilate in Caesarea and appointed a dynamic high priest. He allowed the latter to rule independently, and thus created a Jewish interregnum until 37 CE, when a less powerful high priest was installed and subordinated to a new imperial procurator (Josephus, *Ant.* 18.4–5.88–125). Since, according to Luke, the high priest who sentenced Stephen to death is not reported to have sought consent from the Roman procurator as normally would have been required, and since he sent Paul as far as Damascus in order to arrest dissidents, he must have had unusual political authority. Thus he can be identified with the above-mentioned high priest of 36 CE, so that Stephen's martyrdom in Jerusalem and Paul's conversion at Damascus took place in that year.

Starting from the year 36, two later visits of Paul to Jerusalem can be dated with the aid of his letter to the Galatians, where he refers to a first visit "after three years" and to a second "after fourteen years" (Gal. 1.18; 2.1). As usual, the initial year is included in the numbers, so that the apostle refers to visits occurring two and thirteen years after his conversion; he thus came to Jerusalem in 38 and 49 CE. The latter date is that of the Apostolic Council, described from different perspectives by Luke and Paul (Acts 15.1–29; Gal. 2.1–10).

Before the Apostolic Council, Paul had undertaken his first missionary journey under the leadership of Barnabas (Acts 13.1–14.28), and for this a suitable date is 47–48 CE. Paul's second journey (Acts 15.36–18.22) can be supposed to have lasted from 50 to 54 for the following reasons: He probably came in 52 to Corinth and there met Aquila and Priscilla (Acts 18.2), who, together with other Jews, had been expelled from Rome by the emperor Claudius in 50 CE (Suetonius, *Claudius* 25.24). At any rate, it was in 52 that Paul was confronted with the proconsul Gallio in Corinth (Acts 18.12) because this governor of Greece is mentioned in an inscription at Delphi as holding office during that year. The eighteen months that Paul is said to have spent in Corinth (18.11) thus probably covered parts of the years 52 and 53, and so the whole second journey will have included the years 50-54.

The third journey of Paul (Acts 18.23–21.16) began shortly after his second journey, or around the year 55, and it probably ended in 58 CE. During this journey the apostle spent two years in the Roman province of Asia (19.10), then a considerable time in Troas and Macedonia (2 Cor. 2.12-13), and three months in Greece (Acts 20.3). The subsequent captivity in Caesarea lasted for two years, as long as Felix was procurator there (Acts 24.27), and when the new procurator Festus had sent Paul to the emperor, the apostle had to spend two more years in Roman custody (28.30). Since Felix was deposed in 60 CE (when Nero had overthrown his powerful brother Pallas in Rome), Paul's captivity can be dated to parts of the years 58–60. The continuation of his trial under Festus and his journey to Rome thus probably took place in the year 60, and so the date of his custody for two years in Rome will have been 61–62.

It is also possible to give approximate dates for the death of some early Christian leaders. The apostle James was killed around 42 CE during a persecution arranged by King Agrippa I (called Herod in Acts 12.2). James, the brother of Jesus, who had presided at the Apostolic Council held in Jerusalem in 49 CE, was stoned in the year 62 on the initiative of the high priest (Josephus, *Ant.* 20.9.197–203). According to later sources, Peter and Paul were killed in Rome. This happened some time after the city's destruction by fire in 64 CE, which caused Nero to persecute the Christians there (Tacitus, *Annals* 15.44.4), probably at the beginning of the year 65.

Shortly before the Jewish war of 66–70 CE broke out, the Christians of Palestine are said to have emigrated to Transjordan (Eusebius, *Church History* 3.5.3). After the destruction of Jerusalem in 70 CE, the separation of Judaism and Christianity became even more evident. Domitian's persecution of Christians (Rev. 1.9; etc.), which took place around 94–95 (1 Clement 1.1, 7.1; cf. Pliny, *Epistles* 10.96.6: twenty years before 114), is the last datable event referred to in the New Testament.

Since the New Testament books do not indicate when they were composed, their literary origin can be dated only approximately by such historical events as those mentioned above. Without this support, all scholarly theories on the age of New Testament writings are speculative, and one should not accept any general tendency or common opinion as established truth.

BO REICKE

CHURCH. In the Greek world, the term *ekklēsia* meant a group of citizens "called out" to assemble for political purposes. In the New Testament, *ekklēsia* signifies a group of believers in Jesus who are called together and is translated as "church." The original Greek sense survives, however, when the author of Acts describes an assembly at Ephesus in which citizens have a heated discussion about Paul and his preaching (Acts 19.32, 39, 41). The city clerk finally tells people to suspend their debate until the next regular *ekklēsia*.

In the Septuagint *ekklēsia* is used interchangeably with *synagogē* to render Hebrew terms that mean assembly. One such occurrence from Psalm 22.22 is cited by the author of Hebrews: "in the midst of the congregation (*ekklēsia*) I will praise you" (Heb. 2.12).

Paul regularly uses the term church (*ekklēsia*) in his letters to address individual communities of believers (Rom. 16.1; 1 Cor. 1.2; 2 Cor. 1.1; 1 Thess. 1.1; 2 Thess. 1.1), and he uses the plural form to speak in general about groups such as "the churches of God in Christ Jesus that are in Judea" (1 Thess 2.14) and "all the churches of the saints" (1 Cor. 14.33). Paul does not have a developed sense of the church as a universal institution but rather sees local assemblies of believers functioning independently in separate locations.

Churches and mosques in the old quarters of Jerusalem

In a few cases, however, especially in reference to his persecution of the church of God (Gal. 1.3, 1 Cor. 15.9, Phil. 3.6), Paul's use of the term seems more generalized.

The term church appears only two times in the Gospels, both in Matthew. One occurrence refers to a local community's role in disputes between believers (Matt. 18.17), while in the other, Jesus uses the term church in a much more expansive sense. Matthew's Jesus responds to Peter's confession by saying "on this rock I will build my church" (Matt. 16.18). Whether the "rock" refers to Peter or to his confession is strongly debated, but either way, the verse conveys a sense of the church as a universal institution.

This universal sense is developed further in the Deutero-Pauline letters. Ephesians and Colossians elaborate on a Pauline image by referring to the church as the body of Christ (Eph. 1.22; Col. 1.24) and to Christ as the head of that body (Eph. 5.23, Col. 1.18). In Ephesians 5.23, Christ's headship of the church is used as justification for a husband's authority over his wife.

Ignatius of Antioch (ca. 100 CE) is the earliest known author to use the phrase "catholic church" when referring to the universality of the body of Christ (*Smyrneans*, 8). Unanimity becomes a key concept in later discussions of the church, as orthodox leaders stress catholicity in the face of challenges from various heterodox groups. Some versions of the Nicene Creed conclude with the formula "one holy catholic and apostolic church."

DANIEL N. SCHOWALTER

CIRCUMCISION. Circumcision is the ritualistic removal of the male's foreskin, practiced by many African, South American, and Middle Eastern peoples. Often performed at puberty, it may have originated as a rite of passage from childhood to adulthood; some biblical texts have been interpreted in this way (Gen. 17.25; Exod 4.24‒26). In Jewish tradition, following biblical commandments (Gen. 17.12; 21.4; Lev. 12.3), males are normally circumcised at eight days of age. Proselyte males are circumcised before admission into the community.

Although some rabbis held that males who had been born Jews could maintain their status without circumcision, across the centuries others demanded excommunication for those not circumcised (e.g., Gen. 17.14). According to one passage, even Moses would have died had his son not been circumcised (Exod. 4.24‒26). Nevertheless, according to Joshua 5.2‒9, apparently those born in the wilderness were not circumcised until they entered Canaan. Then the Lord required that they be circumcised, presumably to enable them to celebrate Passover (Josh. 5.10; see Exod. 12.48). Later scribes modified this tradition by improbably having them be circumcised "a second time" (Josh. 5.2).

Antiochus Epiphanes had women and their sons who had been circumcised despite his proscription killed (1 Macc. 1.60). Some Palestinian Jews managed to undo their circumcisions, stood apart from the holy contract, yoked themselves to the gentiles, and sold themselves to do evil (1 Macc. 1.15). This does not necessarily mean that they performed some sort of surgical reconstruction, for these four items are all parallel ways of making the same statement, that liberal Jews became so completely Hellenized that orthodox Jews said they were no longer circumcised. This was probably insult rather than fact, just as male Jews who mingled with gentiles socially and in business were called "harlots," as if they had mingled sexually. There may, however, have been liberal Jews and Jewish Christians who stretched the remaining foreskin to make circumcision less obvious (1 Cor. 7.18). "Circumcision" was also used metaphorically. Someone who did not accept divine teaching was said to have an uncircumcised ear (Jer. 6.10), and a stubborn person had an uncircumcised heart (Lev. 26.41; Jer. 9.25‒26).

Circumcision was traced back to the covenant or contract God made with Abraham, and thus is widely practiced by Muslims as well as Jews. It was called the "sign of the covenant" (Gen. 17.11), the covenant in the flesh (Gen. 17.13), and the "covenant of circumcision" (Acts 7.8); the traditional European Jewish (i.e., Yiddish) term for circumcision, *bris,* is an alternate pronunciation of the word for "covenant" (Hebr. *běrît).* In earliest Christianity, there was considerable debate over the requirement of circumcision (Acts 15.121; Gal. 2.3–14); Paul, however, held that circumcision was part of the old contract that had been superseded and was therefore no longer required (Gal. 6.15), and his view ultimately became normative for Christians.

GEORGE WESLEY BUCHANAN

COLOSSIANS, THE LETTER OF PAUL TO THE.
Outline.
  I. Introductory greeting (1.1–2)
  II. Thanksgiving: Faith-love-hope and the gospel (1.3–8)
  III. Praying for knowledge and godly conduct (1.9–14)
  IV. Christ the Lord in creation and reconciliation (1.15–20)
  V. Reconciliation accomplished and applied (1.21–23)
  VI. Paul's mission and pastoral concern (1.24–2.5)
  VII. False teaching and its antidote (2.6–3.4)
     A. The all-sufficiency of Christ (2.6 15)
     B. Freedom from legalism (2.16–23)
     C. Seek the things above (3.1–4)
  VIII. The Christian life (3.5–4.6)
     A. Put away the sins of the past (3.5–11)
     B. Put on the graces of Christ (3.12–17)
     C. Behavior in a Christian household (3.18–4.1)
     D. Watch and pray (4.2–6)
  IX. Personal greetings and instructions (4.7–18)

Authenticity. The Pauline authorship of Colossians has often been challenged over the last hundred and fifty years. The grounds for this questioning concern the language and style of the letter; more recently it has been argued that there are major differences between Colossians and the theology of the main Pauline letters, particularly in relation to the person and cosmic work of Christ, the church as the body of Christ, and early Christian tradition.

But such arguments against the authenticity of Colossians are not conclusive. First of all, it must be admitted that many expressions used in Colossians show decided Pauline peculiarities of style. The similarities and points of contact extend to theological terminology, such as the expressions "in Christ" (1.2, 4, 28), "in the Lord" (3.18, 20; 4.7, 17), and "with Christ" (2.12, 20; 3.1, 3), including exposition about being united with Christ in baptism (2.11–12). Second, the thirty-four words that occur in Colossians but nowhere else in the New Testament ought to be considered in light of the fact that such hapax legomena also turn up in considerable numbers in other letters that are acknowledged to be Pauline (Galatians, for example, has thirty-one words that recur nowhere else in the New Testament). It is reasonable to assume that several unusual terms appear in Colossians because of the heresy that Paul is combating. Third, the theological developments are consistent with the apostle's earlier teaching.

Colossians, as well as its companion letter Philemon, is present in the Pauline corpus as far back as we can trace its existence, that is, at least as early as Marcion, about 140 CE.

Date. Colossians is one of three or four letters written by Paul at about the same time and sent to various churches in the Roman province of Asia. He was then in prison (probably in Rome), and so these letters are called the captivity

A panel depicting the circumcision of Jesus (Luke 2.21), from an altar. (Master St. Severin, 1490)

epistles. Colossians seems to have been written fairly early in this imprisonment, about 60–61 CE.

The Church at Colossae. The Christian community at Colossae came into existence during a period of vigorous missionary activity associated with Paul's Ephesian ministry (ca. 52–55 CE), recorded in Acts 19. Paul was assisted by several coworkers through whom a number of churches were planted in the province of Asia. Among these were the congregations of the Lycus Valley, Colossae, Laodicea, and Hierapolis (Map 14:E3), which were the fruit of Epaphras's endeavor (Col. 1.7, 8; 4.12, 13). A native of Colossae (4.12) who probably became a Christian during a visit to Ephesus, Epaphras was "a faithful minister of Christ;" as Paul's representative (1.7) he had taught the Colossians the gospel.

The many allusions to the former lives of the readers suggest that most were gentile converts. They had once been utterly out of harmony with God, enmeshed in idolatry and slavery to sin, but God had reconciled them to himself (1.21–22). As gentiles who had previously been without God and without hope, they had been united to Christ in his death, burial, and resurrection (2.11, 12, 20; 3.1, 3). As members of his body, they had his life within them and could look forward to the day when they would share in the fullness of his glory (3.4).

The picture is thus drawn of a Christian congregation obedient to the apostolic gospel, and for which the apostle can give heartfelt thanks to God (1.4–6). He knows of their "love in the Spirit" (1.8) and is delighted to learn of their orderly Christian lives and the stability of their faith in Christ (2.5).

Occasion of the Letter. Epaphras had paid Paul a visit in Rome and informed him of the state of the churches in the Lycus Valley. While much of the report was encouraging, one disquieting feature was the attractive but false teaching recently introduced into the congregation; if unchecked, it would subvert the gospel and bring the Colossians into

The Court of Justice in the Forum of Corinth. Paul may have preached from the monumental rostrum shown here. The ancient citadel of Corinth (Acrocorinth) is in the background.

spiritual bondage. Paul's letter, then, is written as a response to this urgent need.

The Colossians' "Heresy." Nowhere in the letter does Paul give a formal exposition of the Colossians' "heresy"; its chief features can be detected only by piecing together and interpreting his counterarguments. Some have questioned whether there was a "Colossian heresy" at all. But in light of 2.8–23 with its references to "fullness," specific ascetic injunctions ("Do not handle!" etc., v. 21), regulations about food and holy days, unusual phrases that seem to be catchwords of Paul's opponents, and the author's strong emphasis on what Christ has already achieved by his death and resurrection, it is appropriate to speak of a "heresy" that had just begun to make inroads into the congregation.

The teaching was set forth as "philosophy" (2.8), based on "tradition" (an expression that denotes its antiquity, dignity, and revelatory character), which was supposed to impart true knowledge (2.18, 23). Basically, the heresy seems to have been Jewish, because of the references to food regulations, the Sabbath, and other prescriptions of the Jewish calendar. Circumcision is mentioned (2.11) but did not appear as one of the legal requirements.

This Judaism was different from that against which the churches of Galatia had to be warned; rather, it was one in which asceticism and mysticism were featured, and where angels, principalities, and powers played a prominent role in creation and the giving of the Law. They were regarded as controlling the lines of communication between God and humankind, and so needed to be placated by strict observances. This teaching is to be read against the background of ascetic and mystical forms of Jewish piety (as evidenced, for example, at Qumran). It was for a spiritual elite who were being urged to press on in wisdom and knowledge so as to attain true "fullness." "Self-abasement" (2.18, 23) was a term used by the opponents to denote ascetic practices that were effective for receiving visions of heavenly mysteries and participating in mystical experiences. The "mature" were thus deemed able to gain spiritual entrance into heaven and join in the angelic worship of God as part of their present experience (2.18).

Paul's Reply. The apostle issues a strong warning to the Colossians to be on their guard lest the false teachers carry them off as spoil "by philosophy and empty deceit" (2.8),

from the truth into the slavery of error. Although they had set forth their teaching as "tradition," Paul rejects any suggestion of its divine origin. It was a human fabrication, and in reply he sets it over against the tradition of Christ—not merely the tradition that stems from the teaching of Christ, but that which finds its embodiment in Christ (2.6). Jesus Christ is the image of the invisible God (1.15), the one who incorporates the fullness of the divine essence (2.9). In a magnificent hymnic passage in praise of Christ as the Lord in creation and in reconciliation (1.15–20), it is asserted that Christ is the one through whom all things were created, including the principalities and powers that figured so prominently in the Colossian heresy. All things have been made in him as the sphere, through him as the agent, and for him as the ultimate goal of all creation (v. 16).

Those who have been incorporated into Christ have come to fullness of life in the one who is master over every principality and power (2.10). They need not seek perfection anywhere else but in him. It is in him, the one in whose death, burial, and resurrection they have been united (2.11, 12), that the totality of wisdom and knowledge is concentrated and made available to all his people—and not just in some elite group.

The apostle's criticisms are trenchant, even devastating (2.16–23). To place oneself under rules and regulations like those of v. 21 is to return to slavery to the forces overthrown by Christ (v. 20). Any teachers who lay claim to exalted heavenly visions as a prelude to fresh revelations are puffed up. Worst of all, the arrogance in these private religious experiences comes from not maintaining contact with Christ the head: they are severed from the source of life and unity (v. 19).

Ethical Teaching. Often in Paul's letters, doctrinal instruction is followed by ethical teaching (cf. Rom. 12.1; Gal. 5.1). The same feature is evident in Colossians where the conjunction "therefore" (3.5) links the practical injunctions with the theological basis for right behavior. A lengthy hortatory section (3.5–4.6) follows, with four distinctive catchwords of early Christian catechesis at the head of each paragraph: "put to death" (3.5–11; cf. also "put away," v. 8); "put on" (3.12–17); "be subject" (3.18–4.1); and "watch and pray" (4.2–6). In the third of these, "be subject," directions about the mutual duties of members of a Christian household are given.

PETER T. O'BRIEN

CORINTHIANS, THE LETTERS OF PAUL TO THE. Though edited as two separate letters, the canonical letters of 1 and 2 Corinthians most likely consist of several shorter letters or notes written by Paul to the church at Corinth in the early 50s CE. Because of their length, content, and influence they rank among the major Pauline letters. Except for certain subsections, Pauline authorship is undisputed.

The Corinthian Church. Not only do the letters contain reminiscences of his founding visit (1 Cor. 1.14–16; 2.1–5; 2 Cor. 11.9; 12.12), but the narrative account in Acts also provides independent confirmation of certain details about the church's beginning (Acts 18.1–17). Especially valuable for dating the letters is the mention in Acts of Paul's appearance before Gallio (Acts 18.12–17), whose proconsulship is reliably dated ca. 51–53 CE on the basis of an inscription discovered in 1905 at Delphi. Accordingly, Paul's founding visit, which lasted eighteen months (Acts 18.11), could have occurred as early as 50–51 CE during his ministry in the Aegean. After Paul's departure from Corinth, he remained in continual contact with the church, even though he was engaged in a mission in Ephesus, from which he wrote 1 Corinthians and at least part of 2 Corinthians (1 Cor. 16.8, 19; Acts 19.1–40; 2 Cor. 1.8; 7.6, 13). The letters reflect at least two different stages in Paul's relationship to the church after his founding visit.

In the first stage, Paul responds to the needs and questions of a fledgling church experiencing internal tensions (1 Cor. 1.10–13; 3–3; 11.1819) and trying to work out the implications of Paul's gospel in a heterogenous setting. The relationship between Paul and the church is still, for the most part, amicable, even though his departure and absence seem to have diminished the church's loyalty to him. In the second stage, Paul's relationship with the church is severely strained, primarily because of the arrival in the church of outside teachers whom Paul regards as opponents of his gospel. He now has to deal with issues relating to the source, nature, legitimacy, and extent of his apostolic authority. Generally, 1 Corinthians relates to the first period, whereas 2 Corinthians relates to the second.

1 Corinthians. A letter preceded the writing of 1 Corinthians (1 Cor. 5.9, 11). This letter may be preserved in 2 Corinthians 6.14–7.1, a self-contained literary unit that calls for Christians to keep their distance from non-Christians.

Situation addressed. 1 Corinthians addresses a church divided not so much by doctrinal differences as by personal loyalties to different religious teachers and by interpersonal tensions (1 Cor. 1.10–13; 3–3; 11.18–19). Some in the church were self-confident, indeed arrogant (4.19; 5.2), probably because they claimed special knowledge and spiritual wisdom (3.18; 8.1–2). Whether this outlook is "gnostic" in the nontechnical sense that it merely placed an unusually high premium on "knowledge" (*gnōsis*) and "wisdom" (*sophia*) or in the more technical sense that it stemmed from a system of thought resembling second-century gnosticism is a matter of ongoing debate. In any case, such a claim to spiritual superiority grounded in a higher wisdom seems to be a common denominator of several problems addressed in the letter: the fragmentation beginning to appear within the church (1.10–13), the sense of perfection some were claiming to have achieved (4.8), a blasé attitude toward sexual immorality (5.1–2), a refusal to be conciliatory in dealing with internal disputes (6.1–8), an insistence on individual freedom (6.12; 10.23–30), an expressed preference for celibacy over marriage (chap. 7), an inability, or refusal, to consider the needs of weaker Christians in deciding how to behave (chaps. 8–10), an urge to be unconventional (11.2–16), a lack of sensitivity to the needs of others within worship (11.17–34), and an insistence on the superiority of the more visible gifts, most notably speaking in tongues (chaps. 12–14). Whether there is one group within the church whose theological outlook and ethic are the underlying problem or whether there are actually several groups with different theological outlooks and ethics it is difficult to say. But it is clear that the church is faced with an almost bewildering variety of pressing questions on which it needs further instruction.

Structure and content. The letter exhibits three clear divisions: chaps. 1–4, 5–6, and 7–16.

The first section, introduced by Paul's characteristic greeting and opening prayer of thanksgiving (1 Cor. 1.1–9), is a formally constructed Pauline exhortation. It opens with an exhortation to unity (1.10–17) and closes with an exhortation to heed Paul's teaching, follow his example, and listen to his messenger Timothy (4.14–21). Within this exhortation, Paul articulates his theology of the cross as a message of divine power and wisdom (1.18–2.5), expounds the nature of the higher wisdom reserved for the mature (2.6–16), and delineates his own role and that of Apollos as God's ministers (3.1–4.13). Throughout this first section, Paul insists on the radical priority of God and thereby undercuts the arrogant self-sufficiency that he sees within the church (1.18–2.5; 3.9, 23).

In the second section (1 Cor. 5–6), Paul provides the church with what appears to be unsolicited instruction. Two questions are treated: how the congregation should deal with a case of blatant sexual immorality (5.1–13) and how the congregation should resolve disputes that have been taken before courts (6.1–11). Paul then provides further teachings on sexual morality (6.12–20).

In the third section (1 Cor. 7–16), Paul addresses a list of questions that the church had written to him (7.1). His first response concerns marriage (7.1–40). A second extended response is given to the question of eating meat offered to idols (chaps. 8–10). A third topic treated is congregational worship (11.2–34). Two issues are treated: the proper attire (veils) to be worn in worship (11.2–16), and the proper observance of the Lord's Supper (11.17–34). The Corinthians had also inquired about spiritual gifts (or persons), to which Paul devotes extended treatment (chaps. 12–14). The final major topic treated is the Resurrection (15.1–58), in which Christ's own resurrection is presented as the basis for the resurrection of Christians (15.12–58). A final question concerned the collection for the poor Christians in Jerusalem, about which Paul provides brief procedural instructions (16.1–4). This third major section is then concluded with miscellaneous exhortations and personal greetings (16.5–24).

2 Corinthians. Scattered references in 2 Corinthians suggest that after the writing of 1 Corinthians, the situations of both the church and Paul had changed dramatically. Their relationship became severely strained, and the resulting turbulence is mirrored within the letter itself, which is much more uneven than 1 Corinthians. Abrupt changes in style, tone, and content suggest several self-contained sections (6.14–7.1; chaps. 8–9; chaps. 10–13; perhaps 2.14–6.13), which some scholars regard as separate letters written by Paul to the church throughout this second period, as well as, in some cases, earlier. Consequently, numerous theories of composition have been suggested for this letter. The relationship between the historical situation and the literary structure of 2 Corinthians is a major question in interpreting the letter.

Situation addressed. Generally, the letter reflects a worsened situation that was directly related to the arrival of outside teachers within the church (2 Cor. 3.2; 10.2, 7–12; 11.4–6, 11–15; 12.11). So seriously was Paul alienated from the church that he made a "painful," and apparently unsuccessful, visit from Ephesus to the Corinthian church (2.1, 5–8; 13.2). This was followed by a "severe letter" sent by Paul to the church (2.4, 9; 7.9, 12).

One widely accepted reconstruction regards 2 Corinthians 10–13 as the "severe letter," written from Ephesus after the unsuccessful "painful" visit. Shortly thereafter, Paul was forced to leave Ephesus (1.8–11), and journeyed to Troas

The destruction of the Temple in Jerusalem by Titus in 70 CE

anxious about the letter's reception (2.12–13). Still unrelieved, he went to Macedonia, where he eventually learned from Titus that the letter had been well received (7.5–16). Buoyed by this good news, while still in Macedonia he wrote to the church a much more positive letter of reconciliation (1.1–6.13; 7.2–16; perhaps 6.14–7.1 and chaps. 8–9), in which one still hears echoes of the earlier controversy.

Regardless of the theory of composition one adopts, and the historical reconstruction into which it is fitted, the canonical letter of 2 Corinthians reflects different concerns from those mentioned in 1 Corinthians. Throughout the letter, Paul himself is the focus of controversy.

Criticism of Paul, which was subdued in the first letter (1 Cor. 4.3–5; 9.3), is much more open and pronounced. He is accused of being vacillating and acting inconsistently (2 Cor. 1.17; 10.1), of being intimidating (2 Cor. 10.9), crude in speech (2 Cor. 10.10; 11.6), and calculating and manipulative (12.16). "Acting according to the flesh" (2 Cor. 10.2) may serve as the general rubric for several criticisms, pointing to what his critics believed to be a boorish life-style unbecoming someone with apostolic status.

As criticisms of Paul's behavior are more explicit in 2 Corinthians, so are polemical references to his opponents, who are Christian missionaries (2 Cor. 11.4, 23, 33) of Jewish background (2 Cor. 11.22). Whether they originated in Palestine or the Dispersion is much debated and still unresolved, as is their relationship to the original apostolic circle, most notably Simon Peter. Because they had gained an entrance into the church, Paul viewed them as evil forces set on undermining his authority. The opponents appear not to have been judaizing teachers who insisted on circumcision as a prerequisite to salvation, as was the case in Galatia (Gal. 5.1–12). The issue may have been one of territorial infringement (2 Cor. 10.13–16), which threatened the success of

Paul's collection for the Jerusalem poor (2 Cor. 11.7–11; 12.14). In any case, what emerges from the letter is a debate about apostolic legitimacy: whether true apostleship is more properly authenticated by dazzling signs, rhetorical ability, and displays of power (2 Cor. 12.1–7, 12), or by divine power experienced through suffering, weakness, and deprivation (2 Cor. 11.23–33; 12.8–10; 13.3–4)

Structure and content of the letter. The canonical form of the letter can be divided into three sections: chaps. 1–7, 8–9, and 10–13. Each of these sections may be a composite of smaller letters or fragments of letters.

The first section (chaps. 1–7) is introduced by a Pauline greeting and opening prayer of blessing (2 Cor. 1.1–7). This is followed by recollections of mortal threats experienced in Ephesus (1.8–11) and a defense of his recent behavior toward the church and actions on their behalf, including the "painful visit" and writing the "severe letter" (2.13).

There follows an extended set of reflections on Paul's theology of ministry (2 Cor. 2.14–6.13). The tone is apologetic (2.17–3.3; 4.2–3), but what unfolds is a positive treatment of Paul's self-understanding. Basic features include his theology of the new covenant of Christ as superior to the old, Mosaic covenant (3.4–18), a ministry illuminated by the light of the new creation (4.1–6), Paul's suffering as manifesting the death and life of Jesus (4.7–15), outward change and inward transformation grounded in a future hope (4.16–5.10), ministry compelled by the love of Christ (5.11–15), existence in Christ and the ministry of reconciliation (5.16–21), and working with God in the new age as servants embodying the paradox of power experienced through suffering (6.1–10).

This first section concludes with Paul's final appeal for the Corinthians to receive him affectionately (2 Cor. 6.11–13; 7.2–4). His recollections of the encouraging report received from Titus and the effects of the "severe letter" (7.5–16) echo sentiments expressed earlier (1.8–2.13). Also included in this section is an arguably parenthetical set of instructions urging the separation of believers from unbelievers (2 Cor. 6.14–7.1).

The second section (chaps. 8–9) consists of instructions concerning the collection, a program of relief for poor Christians in Jerusalem.

The third section (chaps. 10–13) is marked by a conspicuous change in tone and content. The pervasive mood of the section is apologetic, as Paul defends his apostolic commission against the charges of detractors (e.g., 2 Cor. 10.1–12). Prominent within this section is the "fool's speech" (11.1–12.13), in which Paul insists that he has been motivated to act toward the Corinthians out of genuine love (11.1–6), as seen in his willingness to forfeit financial support for their sake (11.7–11). After characterizing the opponents as fraudulent apostles (11.12–15) and the church as undiscriminating hearers (11.16–21), Paul engages in "foolish boasting" by listing his vicissitudes (11.16–33). His supreme boast is of a heavenly vision (12.1–10), from which he learned the paradox of gaining strength through weakness. He concludes his defense by insisting on the adequacy of his apostolic witness within the church (12.11–13). Toward the conclusion of this section, Paul discusses his future plans with respect to the Corinthian church (12.14–13.10) and closes with miscellaneous appeals and a benediction (13.11–14).

Significance. Naturally these letters have figured prominently as sources for understanding Paul's life and thought. Because of the variety of topics treated, they touch on almost every aspect of Pauline theology, ranging from his theology of the cross to his theology of ministry, even though some major Pauline themes, such as justification by faith, play only a minor role. While he provides concrete instructions about such matters as sexual morality, settling disputes, marriage, eating sacrificial meats, liturgical protocol, and the collection, they are intended for congregational praxis. To be sure, Pauline theology emerges in these letters, but it does so in the service of the congregation. Even in those sections in which he treats more broadly his theology of ministry, he does so in order to clarify the nature of his apostolic commission vis-á-vis a local church.

Specifically, they serve as valuable sources for reconstructing Pauline Christianity and especially Christianity at Corinth. Sociological analysis of the New Testament and efforts at constructive social history of early Christianity have found the Corinthian letters to be especially valuable as sources.

The Corinthian letters have also figured prominently in discussions about gnostic influence in the New Testament. Such passages as 2 Corinthians 1–4 and 2 Corinthians 12 have figured centrally in such discussions. Another debate in which these letters have played a central role is the identification of Paul's opponents and their relationship to early Christian heresies; in particular, the polemical section of 2 Corinthians 10–13 has received extensive attention. Because of the amount of space devoted to the collection (1 Cor. 16.1–4; 2 Cor. 8–9), these letters are a primary source for understanding this project.

CARL R. HOLLADAY

COVENANT. One of the fundamental theological motifs of the Hebrew and Christian scriptures. Eventually the expressions "old covenant" and "new covenant," which once referred to two eras (Jer. 31.31–33) or dispensations (2 Cor.

3.4–11), came to designate the two parts of the Christian Bible, the Old Testament (Covenant) and the New.

The Hebrew term for covenant (*bĕrît*) seems to have the root meaning of "bond, fetter," indicating a binding relationship; the idea of "binding, putting together" is also suggested in the Greek term *synthēkē*. Another term used in the New Testament is *diathēkē* ("will, testament"), pointing more to the obligatory or legal aspect of a covenant. The meaning of covenant, however, is not determined primarily by etymology but by how these and related terms function in various literary contexts. In general, covenant signifies a relationship based on commitment, which includes both promises and obligations, and which has the quality of reliability and durability. The relationship is usually sealed by a rite—for example, an oath, sacred meal, blood sacrifice, invocation of blessings and curses—which makes it binding.

In the Hebrew Bible, various secular covenants are mentioned: covenants between leaders of two peoples (Abraham and Abimelech, Gen. 21.25–32), between two heads of state (Ahab and Ben-hadad, 1 Kings 20.34), between king and people (David and the elders of Israel, 1 Chron. 11.3), between a revolutionary priest and the army (Jehoiada, 2 Kings 11.4), between a conquering king and a vassal (Nebuchadrezzar and a Judean prince, Ezek. 17.13–19; cf. 1 Sam. 11.1). These treaties or pacts were usually thought to be supervised by the deity. This was the case for instance, in the covenant between Jacob and Laban, which was sealed with a sacred meal and which concluded with a prayer that God would see to it that both sides lived up to the terms of the agreement (Gen. 31.44–54). Likewise the covenant between Jonathan and David, based on the loyalty *(hesed)* of friendship, was "a covenant before Yahweh" (1 Sam. 23.18).

In the ancient world, covenants or treaties often governed the relations between peoples. There were parity treaties between two equal sovereign states, and there were overlord treaties between a powerful monarch and a vassal state. Illustrative of the latter is the suzerainty treaty form of the second and first millennia, which apparently influenced Israel's Mosaic covenant theology found in the book of Deuteronomy. These treaties included such elements as a summary of the benevolent deeds of the overlord, the stipulations binding on the vassal who receives favor and protection, and the sanctions of blessings and curses in case of obedience or disobedience.

Covenant expresses a novel element of the religion of ancient Israel: the people are bound in relationship to the one God, Yahweh, who makes an exclusive ("jealous") claim upon their loyalty in worship and social life. In a larger sense, the relationship between all creatures and their creator is expressed in the universal covenant with Noah (Gen. 9.1–17), which assures God's faithful pledge to humanity, to nonhuman creatures, and to the earth itself. In the Pentateuch, however, primary emphasis is given to God's covenant with the Israelite people, portrayed in the migration of Abraham and Sarah in response to the divine promise (Gen. 11.31–12.7) and the special relationship between God and their descendants (Gen. 15.1–21; 17.1–22). In the biblical narrative, the covenant with Israel's ancestors is the prelude to the crucial events of the Exodus and the Mosaic covenant at Sinai and is supplemented by the covenant between God and the Davidic monarch, who mediates God's cosmic rule, manifest in the anointed one (the reigning ruler) and in the Temple of Zion (Ps. 78.67–72; 2 Sam. 7).

The covenants between God and the people are all covenants of divine favor or grace (Hebr. ḥesed). They express God's gracious commitment and faithfulness and thus establish a continuing relationship. They differ from one another theologically at the point of whether the accent falls upon God's loyalty, which endows the relationship with constancy and durability, or upon the people's response, which is subject to human weakness and sin. The Abrahamic and Davidic covenants belong to the type of the "everlasting covenant" (běrít ʿōlām), for they rest upon divine grace alone and are not conditioned by human behavior. On the other hand, the Mosaic covenant, set forth classically in the book of Deuteronomy, has a strong conditional note, for its endurance depends on the people's obedience to the covenant commandments.

Furthermore, all of God's covenants with Israel include divine promises, as well as human obligations, though they differ as to which is emphasized. The Abrahamic covenant is primarily a promissory covenant. In it God imposes no conditions (circumcision is a sign, not a legal condition of the relationship) but rather gives promises: the land as an everlasting possession, numerous posterity, and a special relationship between God and the descendants of Abraham and Sarah (Gen. 17.7–8). Similarly, the Davidic covenant, perhaps on the analogy of royal grants of the ancient Near East, does not impose legal conditions, but offers a gracious promise of an unbroken succession of kings upon the throne of David (2 Sam. 7). Although unfaithful kings will be chastised if they behave badly in office, God will not abrogate the covenant promises of grace made to David (Ps. 89). The Mosaic covenant, however, like the suzerainty treaties of the ancient world, is a covenant of obligation, subject to the sanctions of blessings and curses (Deut. 30.15–20). If the people are unfaithful and disobey the covenant stipulations, they will be punished for breaking the covenant. Carried to the extreme, this covenant could even be annulled, so that no longer would Yahweh be their God and no longer would Israel be God's people (Hos. 1.9). The renewal of the covenant, in this view, would be based solely on God's forgiving grace (Exod. 34.6–9; Jer. 31.31–33; Ezek. 16.59–63).

The New Testament draws upon all of these covenant traditions. In some circles, however, there was a strong preference for the promissory covenants associated with Abraham and David (cf. "the covenants of promise," Eph. 2.12). Paul's interpretation of the new relationship between God and people, shown by the display of God's grace in Jesus Christ, sent him back beyond the Mosaic covenant of obligation to the Abrahamic promissory covenant (Gal. 3.6–18). And the promissory Davidic covenant, found especially in the prophecy of the book of Isaiah, provided a theological context for the announcement that Jesus is the Messiah (Christ), the Son of God.

BERNHARD W. ANDERSON

CRUCIFIXION. The act of nailing or binding a person to a cross or tree, whether for executing or for exposing the corpse. It was considered the crudest and most shameful method of capital punishment.

According to ancient historians such as Herodotus and Diodorus Siculus, various kinds of crucifixion (e.g., impalement) were used by the Assyrians, Scythians, Phoenicians, and Persians (see also Ezra 6.11). The practice of crucifixion was taken over by Alexander the Great and his successors, and especially by the Romans, who reserved it for slaves in cases of robbery and rebellion. Roman citizens could be punished in this way only for the crime of high treason. In the Roman provinces, crucifixion served as a means of punishing unruly people who were sentenced as "robbers." Josephus tells of mass crucifixions in Judea under several Roman prefects, in particular Titus during the siege of Jerusalem; the same also occurred in the Jewish quarter of Alexandria, according to Philo. Before the execution, the victim was scourged (Mark 15.15; War 5.11.449–51). He then had to carry the transverse beam (patibulum) to the place of execution (John 19.17), and was nailed through hands and feet to the cross (see Luke 24.39; John 20.25), from which a wooden peg protruded to support the body; some of these literary details are confirmed by archaeological finds of the bones of crucifixion victims.

Crucifixion, though not mentioned in the list of death penalties in Jewish law (m. Sanh. 7.1), might be suggested in Deuteronomy 21.22–23, which requires that a person put to death must be hung on a tree and buried on the same day. While this is interpreted by the Mishnah (m. Sanh. 6.4) as the exposure of the corpse of a man who was stoned because of blasphemy or idolatry, the order of the verbs is reversed in the Temple Scroll of Qumran: the delinquent must be hung up so that he dies (11QTemple 64.8), which amounts to crucifixion. The same source also specifies that it must be applied in a case of high treason, for example, if an Israelite curses his people or delivers it to a foreign nation. Though such a crime is not mentioned in the Hebrew Bible, it must be derived from the ambiguous term "God's curse" (Deut. 21.23). Delivering up or cursing Israel is also regarded as blasphemy, because the nation belongs to God.

The same interpretation of Deuteronomy 21.22–23 underlies 4QpNah, which mentions "hanging men up alive [on the tree]," presumably a reference to the atrocious deed of Alexander Janneus when he crucified eight hundred of his Pharisean enemies who, in his view, had committed high treason (Josephus, War 1.4.9297; Ant. 13.14.378–81). Other references to crucifixion include the hanging of eighty "witches" (probably Sadducees) by Rabbi Shimon ben Shetah (m. Sanh. 6.5; see War 1.3.79–80), the crucifixion of Rabbi Jose ben Joezer (Gen. Rab. 65 [141a]), and Matthew 23.34.

In rabbinic writings crucifixion is the death penalty for "robbers" (bandits [t. Sanh. 9.7, Qoh. Rab. 7:26 (109b)]) and for martyrs (Gen. Rab. 65 [141a]; Mek. 68b). Isaac, carrying the wood for his sacrifice, was compared to a man bearing the cross on his shoulders (Gen Rab. 56 [118b]). Similarly, a disciple of Jesus must take up his cross and follow him (Mark 8.34 par.; Matt. 10.38).

According to Matthew 20.19 and 26.2, Jesus said that once delivered to the gentiles he would suffer crucifixion. The predictions of suffering by Jesus are not necessarily prophecies after the fact. The inscription on the cross told that Jesus was crucified as "king of the Jews" (Mark 15.26). In his trial before the high priest (Mark 14.62) and before Pilate (15.2), Jesus had admitted to being the Messiah of Israel and Son of God. The members of the Sanhedrin declared that Jesus deserved death because he had uttered blasphemy (Mark 14.63–64); they must have understood Deuteronomy 21.22–23 in a way similar to the Temple Scroll (cf. John 19.7, 15). A false messiah could deliver the people of Israel and the Temple to the gentiles (see John 11.4850). According to the Babylonian

Jesus before Pilate (Mark 15.1–2)

Talmud (*b. Sank*. 43a), Jesus was executed because he had led Israel astray, a judgment based on Deuteronomy 13.1 –11.

By delivering Jesus to Pilate (Mark 15.1), the members of the Sanhedrin could expect the sentence "death by crucifixion," for the claim to be the Messiah could be understood as a rebellion against Rome. It is for this reason that Jesus was compared with the revolutionary Barabbas (Mark 15.7). After the people had asked for Barabbas (v. 11), Pilate had no other choice than to crucify Jesus, who was scourged (v. 15), mocked by the legionaries (vv. 16–19), and crucified together with two "robbers" (vv. 25–27).

Before the crucifixion Jesus had refused wine mingled with myrrh, which was intended to ease the pain (Mark 15.23). The mockery (vv. 2932), in which the guilt of Jesus is reiterated, may have been intended in the first place to make him understand his error and to lead him to a confession of sins (see *m. Sanh.* 6.2). While the crucifixion was carried out by Roman soldiers, the burial in the evening of this day was done by a Jew in accordance with Deuteronomy 21.23 (Mark 15.42–46; see John 19.31).

Deuteronomy 21.22–23 is also related to crucifixion by Paul in Galatians 3.13 (see Acts 5.30; 10.39). Because a person hanging on a tree is cursed by God (Deut. 21.23), the cross of Jesus became a stumbling block to Jews (1 Cor. 1.23).

OTTO BETZ

CYRUS. Cyrus (II) "the Great" founded the Persian (Achemenid) empire in 559 BCE and controlled the ancient Near East by the time of his death in 530. "Cyrus" may have been a dynastic rather than a personal name, for his grandfather Cyrus (I) was king of Anshan and a contemporary of Ashurbanipal, king of Assyria (669–627 BCE). Cyrus took over the territories of the Medes around 550 BCE and united them into a strong alliance, which clashed with Croesus of Lydia and captured Sardis, thus inaugurating a prolonged war with the Greek states. Cyrus's empire, which extended far to the east as well, was administered by local district governors (satraps).

In October 539, Cyrus defeated the Babylonians at Opis, and his troops took control of the capital into which the gods from surrounding cult centers had been withdrawn for safety. When Cyrus entered the city he was warmly welcomed as a man of peace, and he demonstrated his religious tolerance with decrees returning the exiled deities to their shrines. In an edict he allowed the exiled Judeans to return home (Ezra 1.1; 2 Chron. 36.23) and later supported the restoration of the Temple in Jerusalem. The references to Cyrus in Isaiah (44.28; 45.1, 13) are significant, both for the usual dating of Isaiah 40–55 ("Second Isaiah") to the mid-sixth century BCE and for their description of him as the divinely designated shepherd and as the Lord's anointed ("messiah"), the agent of the divine plan for Israel. Parts of the narrative of the book of Daniel are also set in the reign of Cyrus, but this has been interpreted as the use of Cyrus as a dynastic name, as is the case with Darius in the same context (Dan. 6.28).

Cyrus is depicted on sculptures in his palace at Susa. He was buried in Pasargadae in 530 BCE and succeeded by his son and co-regent, Cambyses II.

DONALD J. WISEMAN

DANIEL, THE BOOK OF. According to the book that bears his name, Daniel was a pious and wise Jewish youth who was deported to Babylon by King Nebuchadrezzar (spelled Nebuchadnezzar in the book), together with his three young friends, Shadrach, Meshach, and Abednego, the royal household, and other prominent citizens. Presumably, this was the first deportation ordered by Nebuchadrezzar in 597 BCE (2 Kings 24.10–16; the date implied in Dan. 1.1 is 606 BCE). In Ezekiel 14.14, 20, a Daniel (Hebr. *Dānī'ēl*) is mentioned alongside Noah and Job as one of the outstandingly righteous men of history; in Ezekiel 28.3, the wisdom of the king of Tyre is said to exceed even that of this Daniel. Many commentators believe that the Daniel of the Ezekiel text is to be identified with the Canaanite Dan'il (*dn'il*) of "The Tale of Aqhat" preserved among the fourteenth-century BCE texts found at Ras Shamra (Ugarit) in Syria. There, Dan'il is described as one who "judges the cause of the widow / tries the case of the orphan." It would therefore appear that Daniel was a legendary figure, represented in this book as a youth of outstanding wisdom and piety who matures into a seer capable of receiving visions of the future.

Content. The structure of the book of Daniel is straightforward:

I. Six tales from the Babylonian exile
  A. Daniel and his friends at the table of the king (chap. 1)
  B. Daniel interprets the king's dream of the colossal statue (chap. 2)
  C. Three young men in the fiery furnace (chap. 3)
  D. Nebuchadnezzar's madness (chap. 4)
  E. The handwriting on the wall (chap. 5)
  F. Daniel in the lions' den (chap. 6)
II. Apocalyptic visions and Daniel's prayer
  A. The vision of "the one like a son of man" (chap. 7)
  B. The vision of the ram and the he-goat (chap. 8)
  C. Daniel's prayer and the meaning of the seventy years of "the devastation of Jerusalem" (chap. 9)
  D. The final vision and the promise of resurrection (chaps. 10–12).

The internal dates throughout the book show that the narratives of Part I partially overlap the visions of Part II. The latter culminates in the final vision dated in "the third year of King Cyrus of Persia" (10.1), 535 BCE. In effect, the book records both the external and the internal history of Daniel, the former (chaps. 1–6) consisting of the stories of his virtuous deeds and wonders, and the latter (chaps. 7–12) his visionary experiences and revelations regarding the future of the world.

It should be noted that the Daniel tradition in ancient Israel was considerably larger than what is now preserved in our canonical text. We know this from the additions to the book of Daniel found in the Septuagint (the older Greek translation of the book of Daniel, ca. 100 BCE) and in Theodotion (a more literal Greek version of the first century CE, and the one usually included in ancient Greek manuscripts). These include the Prayer of Azariah and Song of the Three Young Men (inserted after 3.23 of the Hebrew text); the story of Susanna and the elders (chap. 13 in the Septuagint), and the story of Bel and the Dragon (chap. 14 in the Septuagint). In addition, a number of extracanonical Daniel materials have appeared among the Dead Sea Scrolls at Qumran, the most interesting of which is the "Prayer of Nabonidus." Although put in the mouth of a different Babylonian king, this text parallels the story of Nebuchadnezzar's madness and recovery found in Daniel 4.

Unity and Language. The artful arrangement of the diverse subject matter of the book might suggest a single redaction, if not a single author. But the problem is further complicated by the circumstance that the book of Daniel is written in two languages, Hebrew and Aramaic.

The Hebrew text of Daniel 2.4a begins: "The Chaldeans said to the king (in Aramaic)." From that point until the end of chap. 7, the Masoretic text of Daniel is written entirely in Aramaic, in the same dialect as that found in the other Aramaic texts of the Hebrew Bible (Ezra 4.8–6.18; 7.12–26, the single verse Jer. 10.11, and two words in Gen. 31.47). Why the text of Daniel switches so suddenly from Hebrew to Aramaic and back again, no one has ever been able to determine. One obvious solution would be that another writer, living at a different time and place and more deeply rooted in the literary culture of Official Aramaic, composed these chapters. Composite authorship is not the only possible solution, though. For centuries, Aramaic, a linguistic cousin to Hebrew and possibly even the language of the ancestral period (see Gen. 31.47; Deut. 26.5), was the lingua franca of the Babylonian and Persian empires, and it continued in use throughout the Hellenistic period in Palestine. Jews knew it well and used it freely—so freely, in fact, that by the Roman period it was displacing Hebrew as the language of Palestine. Perhaps a single writer of Daniel freely moved from Hebrew to Aramaic for no reason other than to tell the stories of the Babylonian diaspora in the language that was in fact being used there at the time.

Were the Aramaic portion of Daniel exactly coequal with the narrative portion, chaps. 1–6 the case for at least dual authorship would be almost irresistible—but it is not. Not only is the first tale (down to Dan. 2.4a) written in a late biblical Hebrew enriched by Persian loan words, but chap. 7, the first of the apocalyptic visions and in many ways the most central chapter in the whole book, is written in Aramaic. Literary genre and theological intention thus do not correlate with language.

One of the most frequently offered explanations of the bilingual character of Daniel is that the entire book (except for the prayer of 9.4–20) was originally written in Aramaic, and that 1.1–4a and chaps. 8–12 were later translated into Hebrew, perhaps in the interest of rendering the book more acceptable and authoritative to a community whose estimate of the sacredness of the Hebrew tongue waxed even as its vernacular use of that language waned. The case is supported by the fact that the Hebrew of the last five chapters in particular contains many Aramaisms and can often be clarified by translation "back" into Aramaic. While such a view of the bilingualism of the book would certainly imply an ongoing history of development of Daniel even after the text was essentially fixed, it would not necessarily demand that the book be regarded as composite in authorship. And even this modest theory faces the difficulty that the earliest fragments of the text of Daniel among the Dead Sea Scrolls of Qumran, written perhaps little more than a century after the composition of the book itself, already exhibit the same Hebrew/Aramaic/Hebrew transitions at the same points in the book.

The strongest arguments for multiple authorship are these. First, the literary style of chaps. 1–6 differs radically from that of chaps. 7–12. The former have all the flavor of heroic tales of the kind that would emanate from courtly or wisdom circles (compare Daniel 2 with the Joseph story and with Esther); the latter chapters belong to that late descendant of prophetic eschatology, apocalyptic literature. Second, the stories about Daniel in chapters 1–6 reflect a diaspora outlook. By their language and their knowledge of cultural details, they show considerable exposure to both Persian and Hellenistic influences. In their essentials, these stories are assumed to come from the third century BCE or even somewhat earlier. The apocalypses of Daniel 7–12, on the other hand, focus on Judah, Jerusalem, and the sanctuary. They can be dated rather more precisely (see below) to the first quarter of the second century BCE. If they were not composed by one writer who supplemented and revised the earlier work several times during a period of two or three years, then they were composed by persons working in close proximity in time and place. The writer(s) of Daniel 7–12 knew of the earlier cycle of Daniel stories, and for reasons of their own they used that collection as a basis from which to extend its ministry into their own realm of apocalyptic dreams and visions.

Date. The book of Daniel is one of the few books of the Bible that can be dated with precision. That dating makes it the latest of all the books of the Hebrew Bible, and yet it is still early enough to have been known by the sectarian community at Qumran, which flourished between the second century BCE and 68 CE.

The lengthy apocalypse of Daniel 10–12 provides the best evidence for date and authorship. This great review of the political maelstrom of ancient Near Eastern politics swirling around the tiny Judean community accurately portrays history from the rise of the Persian empire down to a time somewhat after the desecration of the Jerusalem Temple and the erection there of the "abomination that makes desolate" (Dan. 11.31) in the late autumn of 167 BCE by the Greco-Syrian king Antiochus IV Epiphanes. (The story of this first of all pogroms of the Jews is told in 1 Macc. 1.41–61) The portrayal is expressed as prophecy about the future course of events, given by a seer in Babylonian captivity; however, the prevailing scholarly opinion is that this is mostly prophecy after the fact. Only from 11.39 onward does the historical survey cease accurately to reproduce the events known to have taken place in the latter years of the reign of Antiochus IV. The most obvious explanation for this shift is that the point of the writer's own lifetime had been reached. Had the

Daniel in the den of lions (Dan. 6.16–23)

writer known, for example, about the success of the Jewish freedom fighters led by Judas Maccabeus in driving the garrison of the hated Antiochus from the temple precincts (an event that occurred on 25 Kislev, 164 BCE, according to 1 Macc. 4.34–31), the fact would surely have been mentioned. But evidently it had not yet happened!

The discussion of the date of the book of Daniel can be summed up as follows. With the possible exception of minor glosses, the book reached its present canonical form approximately in the middle of 164 BCE, though the translation of 1.1–2.4a and chaps. 8–12 from Aramaic into Hebrew may have taken place later. One of the best pieces of evidence available for the rapid acceptance of the book of Daniel as scripture is the inclusion of Daniel and his three friends in the list of the heroes of the Jewish faith in 1 Maccabees 2.59–60, thought to have been written in Hebrew about 100 BCE. In contrast, in Ben Sira's similar list (Sir. 44–49), written about 180 BCE, Daniel figures not at all.

D

Audience. To determine to whom the book was addressed in the first place, and in what circles the author or authors might have moved, two bits of internal evidence must be taken into account. First of all, the heroes of the stories of chaps. 1–6 must represent the kind of piety that would have been considered exemplary by the book's audience. These were observant Jews, heroes of the faith who refused to compromise with idolatry or, to put it another way, to participate in the syncretizing practices of the upper classes of their people during the Hellenistic reign of Antiochus IV Epiphanes (see 1 Macc. 1.41–43). In Daniel 7–12, the heroes are "the people who are loyal to their God" (11.32), "those who are wise. . . those who lead many to righteousness" (12.3). To these "holy ones of the Most High" (Dan. 7.18) is awarded the everlasting kingdom to be their dominion forever.

Given these clues internal to the book, modern commentators have frequently identified the authors of Daniel and the audience to which they spoke with the observant party of the "Hasideans" or *hasidim*, a title variously translated "the righteous ones," "the godly ones," or even "the saints." These people are known from 1 Maccabees 2.42 and 7.13–17, where they are presented as devout persons who reluctantly join in the war of liberation raised by the Maccabean rebels and who stay with that rebellion until they are convinced that the desecration of the Temple has been removed and that the authentic Zadokite priestly line has been restored. According to some scholars, their descendants among the observant wing of Judaism of the first century BCE branched into the covenanters at Qumran, on the one hand, and into the Pharisees, and perhaps even the Zealots, on the other. For several centuries, this party in Judaism stood against syncretism and accommodation and may even have organized themselves into secret conventicles to oppose the corruptions in worship and in politics indulged in by the priestly classes.

Significance. The theological value of the book of Daniel does not lie in its ability to predict the future. According to the text of Daniel 7.9–27, the great judgment of the kingdoms of the earth and the establishment of "one like a son of man [NRSV: human being]" (7.13)—who may be "the holy ones of the Most High" themselves (7.19)—should have occurred during the reign of Antiochus IV Epiphanes, the "little horn" with the "mouth speaking arrogantly" (7.8). Such an eschatological crisis did not, of course, happen in the reign of Antiochus. The canonizers themselves must have known this; perhaps they had already reinterpreted the four beasts who rise out of the sea in chap. 7 in such a way as to make Rome the fourth beast and the little horn some Roman emperor. By means of reinterpretation of the symbols of the apocalypse, it would have been possible to keep the timetable of events leading up to the last judgment open, and it was that openness that enabled the writer of Revelation 20 to transform Daniel 7 into a vision of the imminent worldwide crisis known as the day of judgment.

But all attempts to discern an actual timetable in the apocalyptic scenario of Daniel finally are doomed to failure. As Jews and Christians affirm, the Bible is a human word, and therefore cannot accurately predict events of the distant future in the manner of history written in advance. As Jews and Christians also affirm, however, the book of Daniel is at the same time a word from God to God's people. It teaches that the God of justice and righteousness is not mocked by the powers of oppression that hold sway in the world. God will emerge from history as the victor, and those who choose to serve the causes of justice and righteousness are on the victor's side. In their own lives they can give a foretaste of life in the kingdom of heaven, just as Daniel and his three friends do in the stories of chaps. 1–6. In prayer and proclamation, God's people can announce the good news that those who hope for equity and the vindication of the just need not wait forever. Although our age no longer shares the confidence of an earlier age that it is possible to give a timetable or to write a historylike narrative about God's coming victory, the deep faith remains fundamental to our western theological tradition that history is meaningful. It gains its meaning from the end of history, which is God's triumphant intervention on behalf of God's own goodness. And it gains its meaning in movements along the way in which the saints have opportunities to enact in their own lives of righteousness and obedience the reality of God's coming kingdom.

W. SIBLEY TOWNER

David's Victory over Goliath (1 Sam. 17.50–51) (Caravaggio, 1599)

DAVID. One of the best-known biblical characters, David is a curiously elusive figure. The Bible tells of his carving out an empire unmatched in ancient Israel's history. Elsewhere, however, in historical records from near that period (tenth century BCE), he is not so much as mentioned. He is known to generations of scripture readers as "the sweet psalmist of Israel" (2 Sam 23:1 KJV) and the man whom God had chosen (1 Sam. 16.12; 2 Sam, 10.5). Yet his story in the books of Samuel pivots on the episode of his adultery with Bathsheba and murder of her husband, Uriah.

The Books of Samuel and Kings. David's story emerges primarily in the books of Samuel, concluding in 1 Kings 1–2. Scholarly attempts to reconstruct the history of the composition of these books remain highly speculative. On the one hand, there is general agreement that the final form of the work belongs to the period of exile in the sixth century BCE. On the other hand, dates for individual component units of the work vary from near the time of the events depicted to the time of final compilation, a span of some five hundred years.

Few critics, however, would deny David a significant place in the history of the ancient Israelite state. Recent scholarship views him as a paramount chief with a genius for mediation, a man supremely able to command diverse tribal, economic, and cultic allegiances and to consolidate them into the centralized power needed for the formation of a nation-state.

According to Samuel and Kings, this youngest son of a Bethlehem farmer is sought out and anointed by the prophet Samuel on behalf of the Lord (1 Sam. 16). He gains access to the court of Saul, first king of Israel, initially by virtue of his musical prowess (1 Sam. 16.14–23) and then by defeating the Philistine champion Goliath (1 Sam. 17)—there is some inconsistency in the plot here. Jonathan, Saul's son, loves him. A period of deadly rivalry with Saul, however, ensues. During this time, he marries Saul's daughter, Michal, and establishes his own independent military power as an outlaw in the Judean wilderness and as an ally of the Philistines (1 Sam. 18–30).

After Saul's death (1 Sam. 31), David becomes king over Judah in the south (2 Sam. 1–2) and then over Israel in the north (2 Sam. 3–5), hence king over "all Israel." In 2 Samuel 5–10, he is depicted as coming to the peak of his power: he wins victories over external enemies, including the Philistines, establishes "Jerusalem as a capital and a cult center, and is assured by the prophet Nathan of an enduring dynasty (2 Sam. 7). His dealings with Bathsheba and Uriah (2 Sam. 11–12), however, elicit divine denunciation, conveyed by Nathan. Rape and murder now erupt within David's own house (2 Sam. 13–14), his son Absalom rebels, and civil war ensues (2 Sam. 15–20).

A coda of short stories, anecdotes, and poetry (2 Sam. 21–24), connected to what has preceded by theme and allusion rather than by plot, caps the books of Samuel. The main plot itself is brought to a close with the story of David's death and Solomon's succession at the beginning of the next book (1 Kings 1–2).

This story of David belongs to the larger story, told in Genesis through 2 Kings, of Israel's origins, nationhood, and eventual removal from the Promised Land. David's story belongs with the account of the emerging nation-state's attempt to adapt religious and political institutions, especially leadership, to changing circumstances. His story is also part of the story of Yahweh's attempt to maintain or re-create a relationship of loyalty between deity and people. The people's desire for a human king is taken as a rejection of divine sovereignty. Thus Saul, designated by God at the people's insistence, must be rejected in favor of David, the one whom God has chosen freely (1 Sam. 13.14).

In a sense, the reader's first glimpse of David comes even earlier in 1 Samuel (2.1–10). The childless Hannah gives thanks for the gift of a baby (Samuel) and speaks, prophetically, of the king, the "anointed one" to whom Yahweh will give power. As the child is a special gift to the woman, so the kingdom is a special gift to David. Both gifts are freely given by God.

Giving and grasping lie at the story's heart. At critical moments David seems to allow choice to rest with others, especially Yahweh. At those moments he moves with a favorable tide; he may provoke a reader to contemplate forbearance, to consider providence as reality (e.g., 1 Sam. 14 and 26; 2 Sam. 15–16). At other times he falters, unwilling to take the risk, or to accept injured esteem issuing from rejection (e.g., 1 Sam. 25; 2 Sam. 11–12). In these instances, a reader may be confronted with a more familiar reality, the reality of deceit, greed, and violence that makes many judge the David story in Samuel realistic and plausible.

God gives David the kingdom, the house of Israel and Judah (cf. 2 Sam. 12.8). David's life, however, has a private as well as public dimension. What happens, privately, in his own house (palace and family) impinges on the nation. While his mighty men are besieging Rabbah, the Ammonite capital, David seizes Bathsheba (2 Sam. 10–12). Thus, as the one house (the house of Israel) is secured, another (the house of David) begins to crumble. In the brutal story of Amnon, Tamar, and Absalom that follows, first Tamar, David's daughter (2 Sam. 13), then both family and nation will be rent (2 Sam. 14–20).

The kingship arose out of the people's search for security, but security readily generates corruption. David's son, the builder of Yahweh's house, falters in turn; the great Solomon falls prey to the expanding glory of his own house (see 1 Kings 11). Kingship—even Davidic kingship, Yahweh's gift—turns out to be no talisman (see 1 Sam. 8 and Deut. 17). In Yahweh alone, the story suggests, is true power and security to be found. The larger story (Genesis–2 Kings) ends with the house of Yahweh ruined, the people dispersed. A brief note about the house (dynasty) of David concludes the work (2 Kings 15.27–30): the exiled Davidic king sits powerless in the house of his Babylonian conqueror, like Mephibosheth, grandson of Saul, in the house of David (2 Sam. 9.13). The wheel has turned full circle. The promise of an enduring house for David seems, in 2 Samuel 7, to be unconditional. It turns out to have limits; Yahweh, after all, is unwilling to be taken for granted.

The New Testament designation of Jesus as "son of David" has predisposed many Christian readers to idealize the king. Yet David in Samuel and Kings is a complex character. Often, to be sure, the narrator elicits for David the admiration of readers—as the heroic slayer of Goliath (1 Sam. 17), for example, or the man who twice spares Saul, his persecutor (1 Sam. 24, 26), or the king who denounces Joab for killing Abner, the enemy general (2 Sam. 3), or who grants life to the cursing Shimei (2 Sam. 16, 19). Yet, equally, the narrator opens other possible perspectives even in these same narratives; David is a man with an eye for the main chance, adept at clothing his power-seeking and self-interest in the rhetoric of piety and morality, but exposed for all to see in the story of Bathsheba and Uriah.

The undercutting of the hero is ubiquitous. The account of his incarceration ("until the day of their death") of the ten concubines whom he abandoned to be raped on the roof of the house he fled hardly conjures a character of courage or responsibility (2 Sam. 15, 16, 20). The story of Solomon's accession in 1 Kings 1 pictures the king in gray tones as the dupe of a Solomonic faction's power play. His dying charge to Solomon (1 Kings 2.1–9) to kill Joab, his long-serving general, and Shimei, to whom he had granted pardon, evokes admiration only for its tidy ruthlessness. Or the coda to 2 Samuel (chaps. 21–24) may prompt a reader to ponder, for example, the difference between Rizpah's courage and David's compliance (2 Sam. 21), or the incongruity between David's treatment of Bathsheba and Uriah and the psalmist king's proclamation of his innocent righteousness ("I was blameless before [Yahweh] and I kept myself from guilt," 2 Sam. 22.24). Is this perhaps not righteousness but self-righteousness, not piety but hypocrisy? Even the tale of the slaying of Goliath, the foundation story of the heroic David, is placed in question by the coda. Without warning, tucked in amongst miscellaneous anecdotes, is the narrator's devastating remark that it was Elhanan who slew the mighty Gittite (2 Sam. 21.19).

In the subsequent narrative (1 and 2 Kings) David is viewed as a standard by which most other kings are judged unfavorably (e.g., 1 Kings 14.8; 15.3–5, 11), yet even these passages harbor a sardonic quality. David, the narrator informs us, "did what was right in the sight of Yahweh and did not turn aside from anything that he commanded him all the days of his life, except in the matter of Uriah the Hittite" (1 Kings 15.5). That little word "except" is powerfully subversive.

In Samuel and Kings the tensions in the depiction of David are never resolved. They are, perhaps, what give him life.

The Books of Chronicles. 1 and 2 Chronicles offers quite a different version of David's life. This work is later than Samuel-Kings, composed perhaps in the fifth century BCE, and draws upon a version of those books which it revises and supplements.

After a genealogical prologue, the main story line starts (1 Chron. 10–12) with the death of Saul and David's crowning as king of all Israel; gone are the divisions between north and south. Jerusalem is taken. A great muster of mighty men is transformed into a cultic congregation conducting David and the ark to the new capital with singing and celebration (1 Chron. 12–16). Battles (1 Chron. 14; 18–20) and plague (1 Chron. 21) are mentioned but bracketed by this greater purpose of establishing the place where Yahweh will be worshiped. From 1 Chronicles 22 to the end of the book and David's death, the focus is upon worship. David gathers the congregation once more and issues plans for the building of

Yahweh's house and the organization of those who will sustain it. Priests and Levites, musicians and gatekeepers, commanders of this, chief officers of that, all are ordered to such an end. It is in ordering and implementing the great praise due to God that David finds life in the Chronicler's narrative.

The Psalms. Elsewhere in the Bible, the theme of a promise to continue David's line (the Davidic covenant) surfaces, for example, in the prophecy of Isaiah 9.7 and in Isaiah 55.3–4, a message of hope addressed to the Judean community in exile. Otherwise, David's presence is most marked in the Psalms where many of the psalm titles use the term *lĕdāwīd*—of, to, or about David.

Modern scholars (and a few in ancient times) have generally considered these psalm ascriptions to be later additions to material that is itself mostly post-Davidic. Most interpreters over the centuries, however, have read the psalms in the light of these Davidic titles. In western iconography, for example, David is instantly recognizable as the man with crown and harp or psaltery, David the psalmist king; in popular culture he is often found with these attributes as the king of spades in playing cards. The image connects with the story of David's coming to Saul's court in l Samuel 16, but much more with 1 Chronicles, where the king's concern with the promulgation of music in the temple worship is such a dominant theme (see also Amos 6.5). Moreover, one psalm is shared by both the Psalter and 2 Samuel (Ps. 18 = 2 Sam. 22).

Davidic authorship of the psalms has a special attraction for those who would flesh out the inner life of David, especially the David of Samuel-Kings whose piety is so tenuously pictured. Thus Psalm 51, linked by its title to the crucial Bathsheba episode, may be read as a window into the soul

An ultra-orthodox Jew is symbolically beaten during the "Malkot" ceremony at the Western Wall in Jerusalem shortly before the start of Yom Kippur.

of the great king. His repentance, indicated in the narrative with but a few words (2 Sam. 12.13), is here paraded impressively. Problems of interpretation remain, however. The last verses of Psalm 51, for example, conjure a postexilic context (sixth century BCE or later) and strain any reading that takes the poem too literally as the outpourings of the tenth-century king.

The New Testament. The New Testament shows little interest in the personality of David, though the account of Jesus' plucking of the ears of grain on the Sabbath (Mark 2.23–28 par.) explicitly recalls David's taking the holy bread from the priest at Nob (1 Sam. 21) and is in character with the David of the books of Samuel. In the Gospels, Jesus is linked to the royal dynasty of Judah and to the Davidic covenant by both genealogy (Matt. 1.1–17; Luke 3.23–38) and address—he is called son of David, mostly in the context of healing/exorcism stories (e.g., Matt. 15.21–28; 20.29–34). Above all, in the New Testament, David is author—and prophet—of the psalms (see, e.g., Mark 12.36; Acts 1.16 20), which are interpreted where possible as messianic prophecies fulfilled by Jesus.

DAVID M. GUN

DAY OF ATONEMENT. Known in Hebrew as *yôm (ha)kippūr(îm)*, the Day of Atonement is the most solemn festival in the Jewish religious calendar. It is celebrated on the tenth day of the seventh month, Tishri (= September/October). The name is found in Leviticus 23.27–28; 25.9 and is explained in Leviticus 16.30: "for on that day the Lord will make atonement (*yĕkappēr*) for you to purify you from all your sins." Leviticus 16 describes the elaborate rites performed by the high priest in the Temple at Jerusalem. The priest drew lots between two goats, one of which was presented as a sin offering to God, and the other dispatched to Azazel in the wilderness. It was only on this day that the high priest entered the holy of holies, the most sacred part of the Temple enclosure in which the ark of the covenant was situated. He would enter bearing incense whose fragrance symbolized God's forgiveness of the sins of Israel.

In antiquity as well as today Yom Kippur was considered a festival of spiritual accounting. Leviticus 16.29, 31 ordains that "you shall afflict yourselves." This term was interpreted to signify a day of fasting when all food and drink were avoided. Tradition has added to these abstentions other deprivations, such as refraining from bathing, the use of cosmetics, and sexual intercourse. The people spend the day within the synagogue reciting and chanting a specially composed liturgy, the core of which includes confessional prayers, thanksgiving hymns, and petitions to God for favor in the coming year. According to Leviticus 25.9–10, Yom Kippur was the day of the jubilee year (i.e., the fiftieth year) when slaves were freed, debts canceled, and land returned to its original owners. This aspect of the ancient festival is preserved in the modern collection of pledge contributions for the assistance of those in need.

Jewish tradition regards Yom Kippur as a day of judgment. On this day God passes judgment on the past deeds of every individual and decrees who shall live and who shall die during the ensuing year. The judgment process actually begins ten days before Yom Kippur, on the first day of Tishri, or Rosh Hashanah, the Jewish New Year, and reaches its culmination on Yom Kippur.

Even after the early Christians ceased to observe the day of fasting, some of the symbolism of Yom Kippur was retained in certain formulations. Note, for example, such New Testa-

The Last Judgment

ment expressions as "the blood of Christ" or "the day of judgment," as well as the parallel made in Hebrews g.1–14.

BEN ZION WACHOLDER

DAY OF JUDGMENT. The "last day," the end of the present world, when God or his agent will preside over a final, universal judgment of the living and the resurrected dead. A definitive assessment of human actions will be made, and each person rewarded or punished accordingly.

Hebrew Bible. Neither the phrase "day of judgment" nor the full-blown apocalyptic eschatology supporting it is found in the Hebrew Bible. But the cluster of ideas and images surrounding the day of the Lord contribute significantly to its eventual development: the forensic character of "that day" when God will judge his enemies (Joel 3.2, 1, 14); its universal perspective, with judgment directed against both Israel's enemies, "the nations," and Israel herself, or at least the enemies of God in her midst (Isa. 2.6–19); and the opposing imagery of light and darkness (Amos 5.18–20), with far greater emphasis placed on the latter (Zeph. 1.14–16; the somber medieval hymn *Dies irae* draws its opening line from the Vulgate rendering of v. 15).

Early Judaism. The factors that lead eventually to the emergence of the idea of a final day of judgment in particular are as disputed as those that lead to apocalyptic eschatology in general. Some degree of foreign influence (Persian, Egyptian, and/or Hellenistic) is plausible, but difficult to prove. What is clear is that both the phrase "day of judgment" and its substance appear in a wide variety of Jewish texts of the Greco-Roman period, along with the first undisputed reference to the resurrection of the dead (Dan. 12.2). In Daniel

D

Byzantine mosaic of Saint Mark conducting a baptism with assistance from a deacon.

New Testament. The New Testament references to the day of judgment are rooted in contemporary Jewish apocalyptic thought. This is evident from such texts as 2 Peter and Jude, in both of which the fate of the rebel angel Azazel (1 Enoch 10.4–6) is extended to his fellow rebels. In Jude 6, these angels are enchained "in deepest darkness for the judgment of the great Day;" in 2 Peter 2.4, the rebels are to be kept in hellish pits "until the judgment" (expanded in 2.9 to "until the day of judgment"). And, as in 1 Enoch 22 and other texts, that same day of judgment will signal the "destruction of the godless."

In two noticeable respects, however, early Christian views of the last judgment tend to distance themselves from traditional Jewish apocalyptic. Judgment is now seen almost exclusively in individual rather than national terms (Matt. 10.15 is something of an exception), and the judge is increasingly identified as Jesus, returned to serve as God's agent (Rom. 2.16), rather than God himself. Both of these features are present in Matthew 25.31–46, where it is the Son of man who sits on the throne of judgment, and where the nations are judged not communally but individually, based on their treatment of the needy. The second development leads also to an expansion in terminology particularly noticeable in Pauline literature. Alongside "the day" (Rom. 2.16; 1 Cor. 3.13), "that day" (2 Tim. 1.12; 4.8; cf. 4.1), and "the day of wrath" (Rom. 2.5), we find "the day of Christ" (Phil. 1.10; 2.16), "the day of Jesus Christ" (Phil. 1.6), the "day of the Lord" (1 Thess. 5.2; 2 Thess. 2.2), "the day of the Lord Jesus" (1 Cor. 5.5; 2 Cor. 1.14), and "the day of our Lord Jesus Christ" (1 Cor. 1.8). The forensic role of Jesus on the day of judgment becomes central in later Christian tradition. In the Apostles' and Nicene Creeds, Jesus "will come again (in glory) to judge the living and the dead;" and artists from Giotto and Michelangelo to William Blake have placed him at the center of their depictions of the Last Judgment.

PAUL G. MOSCA

the link between resurrection (12.2) and judgment (7.9–27) is implicit. In becomes explicit in 1 Enoch, where the angel Raphael shows Enoch the places appointed for all human souls "until the day of their judgment" (22.4); this is "the great judgment" (22.5), "the great day of judgment and punishment and torment" (22.11) that will affect even the rebel angels (10.6; cf. 90.24–27). In these earlier strata of 1 Enoch, judgment will apparently come from God himself (91.7); in the later Similitudes, however, God's "chosen one" is repeatedly named as judge (45–55).

The apocryphal book of 2 Esdras (4 Ezra) contains the most coherent account of the day of judgment. Judgment day will be preceded by a temporary messianic kingdom (7.28–29), a week of "primeval silence" (7.30), and the resurrection of the dead (7.32). Only then will the Most High sit in judgment; both righteous and unrighteous deeds shall stand forth clear and unchangeable, and paradise and hell be disclosed (7.33–36). Without sun, moon, or stars, noon or night, this "day" will in fact last "as though for a week of years" (7.43). During it, God will judge all nations, the few righteous and the many ungodly (7.51). This "day of judgment" will be definitive because it marks "the end of this age and the beginning of the immortal age to come" (7.43 *[113]*).

Other early Jewish texts that speak of a day of judgment include the Septuagint of Isaiah 34.8 (rendering the Hebrew for "day of vengeance"); Judith 16.17 (against the nations); Jubilees 5.10–14 (the great day of judgment that awaits the generation of the giants and all creation) and 22.21 (against Canaan and all his descendants); Testament of Levi 3.2–3 (the second and third heavens prepared to punish unrighteous humans and spirits at the day of judgment); and Pseudo-Philo's *Biblical Antiquities* 3.10 (following a pattern similar to that of 2 Esdras 7-30-33. *43 [113]*).

DEACON. The Greek noun *diakonos* underlying the English word "deacon" has in general usage the meaning of "servant," especially in the sense of one who waits on tables (cf. Matt. 22.13; John 2.5, 9). Perhaps the word was originally applied to early Christian leaders who assisted at celebrations of the Lord's supper. It has often been suggested that the establishment of the diaconate is sketched in Acts 6.1–6, and this may be Luke's intention, although neither here nor elsewhere does he use the noun *diakonos*.

The understanding of Jesus as servant (e.g., Mark 10.45, using the verb *diakonein*) informs later Christian concepts of ministry, though the New Testament applies *diakonos* to Jesus in a positive sense only once (Rom. 15.8). The term occurs twenty-eight other times in the New Testament but only rarely in relation to a special church office.

In Philippians 1.1 Paul addresses a letter to all the Philippian saints "with the bishops and deacons." Generally the Pauline letters do not imply the existence of fixed church offices with distinctive functions, but in this passage "deacons" clearly refers to a particular group of church leaders. No function is specified, but perhaps Paul mentions them here (along with bishops) because they helped provide the material assistance that partly occasions his letter (4.10–18).

In Romans 16.1–3 Paul mentions a certain Phoebe as a *diakonos* of the church at Cenchreae (a port city of Corinth) and "benefactor" of many Christians, himself included. Nothing specific is said about her work, but there is no indication that she is a deacon in a lesser or different sense from that of the persons addressed in Philippians 1.1.

One passage in the Pastoral letters (1 Tim. 3.8–13) follows a list of qualifications for bishops with those for deacons. Deacons must be of good character, not avaricious, and good managers of their private households. Such requirements suggest that deacons are administrators with special responsibility for money. Nothing is said about teaching ability. A sentence about women (1 Tim. 3.11) may allude to women deacons or to the wives of male deacons.

Although the Pastoral letters seem to reflect an advanced stage in the development of church organization and differentiation of clerical roles, it is noteworthy that here and elsewhere *diakonos* can also be used as a general term for Christian "minister" (1 Tim. 4.6). Paul several times applies the term in this broad sense to himself and to other church leaders (1 Cor. 3.5; 2 Cor. 3.6; 6.4; 11.23; cf. Eph. 3.7; Col. 1.23, 25).

DAVID M. HAY

DEAD SEA SCROLLS. Since 1947, hundreds of Hebrew and Aramaic scrolls have been discovered near the Dead Sea, at first in unorganized searches by Bedouins and later in orderly archaeological excavations. The main location where these scrolls were found is Qumran (Map 12:X5), roughly 16 km (10 mi) south of Jericho; other sites still farther to the south include Murabba'ât, Seelim, and Masada (Map 12:X5). Some of these locations are more inland, so that the term "Judean Desert Scrolls" is more appropriate than "Dead Sea Scrolls." In eleven caves at Qumran, hundreds of scrolls were discovered, some in jars and almost complete, such as the large Isaiah scroll from Cave 1, but others mere fragments, often very difficult to read. Their antiquity, disputed at first by a few scholars, is now beyond doubt, and dates between 250 BCE and 70 CE have been secured by carbon-14 tests, archaeological evidence, and paleography. The scrolls are kept in the Rockefeller and Israel Museums in Jerusalem, and only the major ones are shown to the public.

The caves in which the scrolls were found are located near the ruins of a settlement near the Dead Sea. These ruins (Khirbet Qumran) have been excavated; they consist of a walled site comprising various community buildings, such as a bakery, a potter's workshop, a dining hall, and possibly a scriptorium.

No external evidence on the settlement is available, but probably there was a close link between its buildings and the scrolls found in nearby caves. Some of the artifacts found near the scrolls are identical with artifacts found in the community buildings. Furthermore, the sectarian writings found in the caves describe the lifestyle of a community that would suit the buildings.

The identity and nature of the community of the scrolls has often been discussed by scholars, and most now agree that they are the Essenes described in ancient sources. The Essenes were an ancient Jewish sect with a status similar to that of the Samaritans, Sadducees, and early Christians, all of whom departed from mainstream Judaism, embodied in the Pharisees. While most of the Essenes lived elsewhere in Palestine, the Qumran group decided to depart physically from society when they chose to dwell in the desert of Judea. The characteristics of the Essenes (the origin of the name is

unknown), described in detail by Philo and Josephus, agree in general with the evidence from the scrolls. These are of three types: sectarian compositions, apocryphal works, and biblical scrolls.

The sectarian compositions found in Qumran reflect a secretive community about whose life much is still unknown. The main information is found in the so-called *Manual of Discipline* (in Hebrew, "The Rule of the Community"), detailing the daily life, behavior, and hierarchy of the sect. The principal source for the history of the community is a letter supposedly written by its leader, the "Teacher of Righteousness," to the priests of Jerusalem, outlining points of difference between both groups (4QMMT).

Other details can be learned from the *Damascus Covenant*, which tells about the beginning of the sect's existence, and from *pĕšārîm*. The special laws of the community are outlined in the *Damascus Covenant* and in smaller legal collections. The sect's views are reflected especially in the *pĕšārîm*, exegetical writings focusing on the relevance of biblical books to the sect. The *Temple Scroll*, the largest preserved scroll, rewrites the laws of the Pentateuch in apparent agreement with some of the sect's views. The *War Scroll* depicts the future war of the "Sons of Light" (i.e., members of the sect) against the "Sons of Darkness." The sect's expectations and grievances are expressed in the *Thanksgiving Hymns*.

Among the scrolls found in Qumran and at Masada are several Hebrew and Aramaic apocryphal and pseudepigraphal works, previously known only in ancient translations or from medieval sources. Of these, the books of Jubilees, Enoch, Sirach, and the Testament of Levi are now known in their original Hebrew or Aramaic form.

A large group of scrolls found in Qumran and at other places in the Judean desert consists of biblical manuscripts,

A portion of a Dead Sea Scroll, discovered in 1947, in jars found in caves above Khirbet Qumran, Israel

dating from 250 BCE until 70 CE. Similar scrolls from the beginning of the second century CE have been found in other places in the Judean Desert. These finds inaugurated a new era in the study of the text of the Hebrew Bible, previously known almost exclusively from medieval sources.

In eleven Qumran caves, roughly 190 biblical scrolls have been found, some almost complete and others very fragmentary. Different scrolls are distinguished by their script. With the exception of Esther, all books of the Hebrew Bible are represented at Qumran, some by many scrolls (Deuteronomy, Isaiah, Psalms), others by a single copy. The great majority of the scrolls are written in the Aramaic script, while sixteen are written in the paleo-Hebrew (or Old Hebrew) script.

Most of the scrolls have the same spelling as the Masoretic Text (MT), but a significant number are written with a previously unknown form of spelling, which frequently uses letters to indicate vowels. Some scholars argue that the scrolls displaying this special spelling were written by the Qumran scribes, for all the sectarian scrolls are written in this spelling as well. The biblical scrolls from the Dead Sea area show what the biblical text looked like in the last three centuries BCE and the first century CE.

Of similar importance are the new data about the content of the biblical scrolls, since different texts are recognizable. Some texts reflect precisely the consonantal framework of the medieval MT. Others reflect the basic framework of the MT, although their spelling is different. Still others differ in many details from the MT, while agreeing with the Septuagint or Samaritan Pentateuch. Some texts do not agree with any previously known text at all, and should be considered independent textual traditions. Thus, the textual picture presented by the Qumran scrolls represents a textual variety that was probably typical for the period.

Although most of the scrolls have been analyzed, the nature of the collection of scrolls found in the Qumran caves is still not known. While some scholars continue to refer to the contents of these caves as the "library" of the sect, others consider it a haphazard collection of works deposited there for posterity in the difficult days of the destruction of Jerusalem in 67–70 CE.

Because the nature of the collection is not known, it is also not clear how one should evaluate the fact that biblical, apocryphal, and sectarian works were found in the same caves. Probably this does not show anything about the sect's views, but some scholars believe that the sect's concept of scripture was more encompassing than the collection that eventually became the Jewish canon.

EMANUEL TOV

DEBORAH. A name which means "bee" in Hebrew, Deborah is the name of two women mentioned in the Hebrew Bible. Two passages (Gen. 35.8; 24.59) call Rebekah's nurse Deborah. Much more prominent is the Deborah mentioned in Judges 4 and 5, whose fame in the biblical record emerges from her role as a military leader. With her general, Barak, she successfully led a coalition of Israelite tribal militias to victory over a superior Canaanite army commanded by Sisera. The battle was fought in the plain of Esdraelon (Map 13:X3), and the mortal blow to the Canaanite general was delivered by another female figure, Jael.

The account of this war, ending with an important victory for the Israelites in their struggle to control central and northern Palestine, is recounted in two versions, a prose narrative in Judges 4 and a poetic form in Judges 5. The literary and chronological relationship of these two versions is a matter of debate; but most scholars see in the archaic language of the poem evidence that it comes from a very early stage of biblical literature and may be the oldest extant Israelite poem, perhaps dating from the late twelfth century BCE, not long after the battle it recounts.

Deborah occupies a unique role in Israelite history. Not only is she a judge in the sense of a military leader, but also she is the only judge in the law-court sense of that title (Judg. 4.5) in the book of Judges. Of all the military leaders of the book, only Deborah is called a "prophet." She is also the only judge to "sing" of the victory, illustrating the creative role played by women as shapers of tradition (cf. Exod. 15.20–21). While some would see Deborah, a female, as an anomaly in all these roles, her contributions should be set alongside those of other women who are pivotal figures in the premonarchic period (Miriam, Jael, Jephthah's daughter, Samson's mother). All emerge as strong women with no negative valuation, perhaps because during the period of the judges, a time of social and political crisis, able people of any status could contribute to group efforts. In the rural, agrarian setting of the period of the judges, with the family as the dominant social institution, the important role of women in family life was more readily transferred to matters of public concern than during the monarchy, with its more formal and hierarchical power structures. Deborah as a strong woman reflects her own gifts as well as a relatively open phase of Israelite society.

CAROL L. MEYERS

Deborah addressing Barak (Judg. 4.6–9) in an etching by Marc Chagall (ca. 1935)

DEUTERONOMY, THE BOOK OF.

Content. The book of Deuteronomy received its title from the Greek translation of Deuteronomy 17.18, where the Hebrew word indicating "copy" has been understood as meaning "second law" (*deuteronomion*, hence "Deuteronomy"); in Hebrew it is called *děbārîm*, "words," from the opening verse. Despite the misunderstanding, this is a good description of a book whose main part is a second corpus of laws given to Israel through Moses, supplementing those given at Horeb (see 29.1). This second corpus was delivered to the Israelites in the plains of Moab on the eve of their entry into the land of Canaan. The central part of the book lies between 4.44 and 30.20, which must once have formed its beginning and ending. Deuteronomy 29.1 describes them as "the words of the covenant [between God and Israel]," and 4.45 describes them as made up of "decrees, statutes, and ordinances." Presenting "law" or Torah (Hebr. *tôrâ*) is the major concern of the book as it formulates the covenant between God and Israel, the basis for the nation's life in the land of Canaan. Because such laws are to be found primarily in chaps. 12–26, the material of 4.44–11.32 can be seen as a general introduction made up of Moses' exhortations in the form of long speeches directing Israel to obey the laws; 27.1–30.20 is an epilogue with admonitions, warnings, and curses against failing to do so. The whole of the book may be described as "preaching law;" often the laws themselves take the central place, but at other times a passionate preaching and admonitory manner are foremost.

The laws at the heart of the book are in many cases laws in our familiar juridical sense, specifying offenses and defining the appropriate punishments for them. At other times, however, they are essentially religious instructions and regulations for worship, as in the festival calendar of 16.1–17, or an even broader type of ethical admonition and instruction, as in the Ten Commandments of 5.6–21. The speeches broaden this sense of the demands for godly living still further by emphasizing the need for a right attitude toward God and society. Consequently, there is much urgent warning to remember God and his dealings with Israel, not to forget the divine gifts, and to love God with a deep love in the heart (esp. 6.5).

The book thus aims to provide both the framework for a national constitution of Israel and a basic summary of every citizen's rights and duties, as well as to exhort the proper feelings and attitudes toward God and fellow citizens; it strongly endeavors to bring all of life—its private, social, and more openly religious aspects—under an awareness of obligation and duty toward God.

Sources. The sources of the book can be determined only with a degree of probability, since in many cases there is limited evidence on which to base conclusions. Clearly, a significant part of the central law collection in chaps. 12–26 repeats, with additions and modifications, many of the laws given earlier in the Book of the Covenant (Exod. 20.22–23.19). Approximately half of the laws are covered, and in a way that shows the Deuteronomic version to be later, either fuller or adapted to a more complex economic and social order. These laws provide a handbook for administration in civil or criminal cases where wrongs have been perpetrated and society must act against the wrongdoers. Why all the cases present in the earlier laws are not dealt with remains unclear.

The book's brief historical framework presupposes an earlier Pentateuchal narrative tradition, which scholars have usually assigned to the sources J and E. Where a few traces of the P (Priestly) source are to be found, these are thought to have been added after the main book of Deuteronomy had been completed. The detailed festival calendar similarly presupposes earlier forms of this material (Exod. 23.14–17; 24.18–23), now elaborated extensively. We must assume that much of the contents of Deuteronomy rests on far older tradition, partly oral and partly written, which has not otherwise survived in biblical tradition.

The consistency of style and continuity of dominant themes suggests strongly that there was a community of scribes and legislators, often loosely described as the Deuteronomists or the Deuteronomic School, who composed the present work. This undoubtedly took place over a long period of time, perhaps as much as a century, for the book shows signs of having been elaborated, adapted, and extended until it attained its present form.

Most important from a literary perspective is the variety of patterns of addresses to the audience, which is variously referred to in the singular and the plural. In all cases, however, the reader is assumed to be an ordinary Israelite, rather than a priest, prophet, or administrator; the book is addressed to the laity, both men and women. Furthermore, it is evident that this lawbook of Deuteronomy provided the opening part of the historical narrative of Israel's fortunes as a nation, which is continued in the books of Joshua, Judges, 1 and 2 Samuel, 1 and 2 Kings. This corpus has come to be known as the Deuteronomic (or Deuteronomistic) History because it presupposes throughout the lawbook of Deuteronomy as the primary constitution of Israel, which is frequently referred to as the "law" and sometimes as "the covenant." Deuteronomy 1.1–4.43 can best be regarded as an introduction to the whole work consisting of both law and historical narrative. Only at a late stage was this lawbook detached from its subsequent history and combined with the other laws and traditions about Israel's origins, now found in Genesis, Exodus, Leviticus, and Numbers, in order to compose the Pentateuch. This must have taken place after the Babylonian exile, in order to bring together in one work all the primary instructional material about the origins, nature, and responsibilities of Israel.

Date of Composition. We read in 2 Kings 22.8–20 that a lawbook was found in the Jerusalem Temple while the Temple was undergoing repairs in the eighteenth year of the reign of King Josiah. The authors of this narrative and of the account of the subsequent kingdomwide reform of worship undertaken in accordance with this lawbook (2 Kings 23) intend it to be understood as the lawbook of Deuteronomy in some form. Since 1805, when the German scholar W. M. L. de Wette briefly noted the point, scholars have recognized that the date of this reform (622 BCE) has some bearing on the date of the composition of Deuteronomy. The main part of the book was most likely composed during the previous half-century, in the reigns of Manasseh (696–642 BCE) and Josiah (639–609 BCE). A probable time is the early years of the latter's reign, when the century-long Assyrian domination of Judah and Israel was coming to an end. Other elements of the book were composed in the later years of Josiah, and it was undoubtedly still being supplemented after his death in 609 BCE.

This period can be viewed confidently as the time when Deuteronomy was composed, and serves to explain many of its most distinctive features. Although the book evinces an air of crisis that has not passed, it does not presuppose the catastrophes that took place in the years of Babylonian rule, when the Temple was destroyed and the Davidic dynasty removed (587/586 BCE). It regards the land of Israel, the demand for national unity ("all Israel"), the gift of kingship, and the very "name" of God dwelling in the sanctuary as the supreme spiritual endowments of the nation. These precious institutions are threatened and may even have been neglected, but clearly they had not been lost when the major part of the book was composed. It is, when viewed comprehensively, a last appeal to Israel to regain its sense of a

Moses with the tablets of law (Deut. 9.9–17)

religious observance provide keynotes for all that the book of Deuteronomy understands by "law" (*tôrā*). To tolerate, let alone to encourage, the worship of other gods is capital offense (13.1–18; 17.2–7). Thus, an insistence on the purity of religious observance pervades all the Deuteronomic legislation and appears to have given rise to the desire to control the administration of worship. Even the king, the supreme head of the people, must subject himself and his conduct wholly to the terms laid down in the Deuteronomic law (17.18–20). This concern to regulate the administration and observance of all forms of religion is extended further to cover the activity of prophets, who fulfill a role like that of Moses (18.15). The danger of false prophets is noted (13.1–5; 18.20–22), but the true prophet's teaching conforms to that of Moses.

Alongside this stress on purity of worship, there is a surprising and far-reaching emphasis on its essential inwardness. The primary purpose of a festival even so great and deeply rooted as Passover, with the Feast of Unleavened Bread—which Deuteronomy now for the first time firmly conjoins with it (16.1–8)—is to serve as an occasion for remembering the great acts of God toward the people's ancestors: "so that all the days of your life you may remember the day of your departure from the land of Egypt" (16.3). Worship itself, then, is valued primarily for its spiritual and psychological potential as a remembrance of the goodness of God and a demonstration of gratitude toward him. Particularly appropriate is a special concern for the oppressed and downtrodden members of the community: "Remember that you were a slave in Egypt; and diligently observe these statutes" (16.12). This deep and religiously motivated attention to the poor is a prominent moral feature of Deuteronomy (15.7–11).

The combination of an inward psychologizing and spiritualizing of worship with a regard for the poor leads to a remarkable desacralising of tithes, the offering of which becomes a holy opportunity for rejoicing before God and for sharing gifts with the poor and disadvantaged (14.22–29). The entire people is conceived as a single entity, whose members are regarded as being "brothers," from the king at the head (17.20) to the slave at the bottom of the social ladder (15.12–18). Likewise, the foreigner is to be accorded a certain status providing the possibility of full entry into the people (23.7–8).

The target of the religious hostility expressed in the Deuteronomic legislation is the worship of Baal and Asherah, more often described as the male and female deities who represent the older forms of religion practiced by the previous inhabitants of the land (7.4–5, 16, 25; 11.28; etc.). In view of the period when the Deuteronomic legislation was probably composed, it is surprising that the book never explicitly condemns the symbols and evidence of Assyrian imperial control over Judah. To what extent there had been such visible signs of Assyrian rule is not known, but the aims of the Deuteronomic reform were established when this rule was in serious decline and had largely disappeared. Deuteronomy regards the great variety of religious traditions that had survived in the land of Israel as the cause of the divine anger that led God to punish the Israelites by bringing "a nation from far away" (28.49).

In sharp contrast with this emphasis upon the inwardness of true religion and a just and caring social order is the vehement condemnation of any deviation from absolute loyalty to God. Veneration of other gods is to be ruthlessly opposed and its practitioners exterminated (7.2, 16; 13.8–10; etc.).

God-given destiny, which Mesopotamian imperialism and internal apostasy were weakening perilously.

Distinctive Feature. A distinctive feature of the book is its stress on the three great unities. First, Israel is one people, which Moses can address as such (Deut. 5.1, 6.4, etc.), and which is viewed as remaining one through all its subsequent generations. Second, it must worship one God alone, the God who reveals himself to Moses on Mount Horeb; this finds expression in the great formulation (the Shema) "Hear, O Israel: The Lord our God is one Lord" (6.4). This should not be understood as originally implying that there is only one God, though it later came to be interpreted in this fashion. Rather, it declares that the Lord (Yahweh) is a deity who is not to be worshipped alongside, or in conjunction with, any other deity. Furthermore, though there were many sanctuaries where the Lord God was worshipped, this was not to be taken as implying that he existed in different forms or manifestations, as was the case with Baal. The third great unity is the sole place of worship where an altar is to be set up and sacrifices offered (12.5–14). This is described as "the place that the Lord your God will choose out of all your tribes as his habitation to put his name there" (12.5). This location is not further defined, but Jerusalem was obviously intended and is later identified by the historians of the Deuteronomic school (1 Kings 8.16–21; etc.).

These three great unities of people, God, and sanctuary form the visible and outward expression of the one purpose of God first revealed to the ancestors of Israel (6.3) and confirmed and realized through the covenant made through Moses on Horeb (5.1–5). The concern for centralization of worship and a kingdomwide consistency of

The most enduring expression of concern for complete loyalty of religious practice and a just social order is to be found in the Ten Commandments (5.6–21). Since this series of injunctions, with only minor modifications, is also found in Exodus 20.2–17, scholars have been divided in their views as to whether the collection is of Deuteronomic origin or derives from a much earlier time. Clearly, the subject matter of the commandments reflects ancient and fundamental concerns in any society, but this recognition does not itself suffice to determine the actual date when this short didactic compendium of ten basic religious and moral duties was brought together. Many think that such a brief teaching form was of early date, but underwent revision and modification over a long period of time. In any case, they wholly accord with the aim of Deuteronomy to bring as much of life as possible under a sense of obligation toward God.

Authorship and Readership. The book of Deuteronomy, formulated as an address by Moses to all Israel, presupposes a literate reading public who could benefit from a book of instruction. It also recognizes, however, the need for orally teaching the law (esp. 6.7, 31.10–13) and regards the preservation of the lawbook and its placement beside the ark in the Temple (31:24–26) as serving primarily as a "witness." Since the Levitical priests are made the custodians of this lawbook (31.9), it is certain that they were expected to fulfill some teaching role in promulgating its contents. Clearly, Levites would form the bridge between the custodians of the law and the laity of Israel. This suggests that some elements of the Levitical priesthood were closely linked to, and supportive of, the lawbook's authors.

The presumption of literacy by the lawbook's originators, combined with the pronounced rhetorical style of persons skilled in public speech-making, also points to scribes. There are, in addition, numerous indications of expertise in legal affairs, which leads us to conclude that the Deuteronomic authors included among their number several major state officials. It is the only law collection in the Bible to include a statute defining the office of the king (17.14–20). All of this suggests strongly that the authors of Deuteronomy formed a body of religiously motivated reformers, drawn from a circle close to the centers of state administration but apparently not directly associated with the king and royal household. They are, in any case, too critical of many of the basic assumptions regarding priestly service and its ritual obligations to have been priests themselves.

It is important to recognize the warm interest in prophecy and the belief that certain prophets continued to fulfill a role in Israel comparable to that of Moses. Such interest, which becomes more marked in the history that elaborates the lawbook, suggests that some prophetic element may also have contributed to the Deuteronomic movement for reform in Israel. Yet the understanding of prophecy is highly distinctive, and too removed from its most fundamental forms, for the authors of the book to have been prophets themselves. Prophecy is viewed essentially as a means of promoting the knowledge and claims of the Deuteronomic law.

As to the first readers of the book, we must assume that these were the lay men and women of Judah who so eagerly watched the decline of Assyrian control during the years of Josiah's reign. With the king's untimely death, the setbacks caused by Egyptian attempts to fill the power vacuum in Judah, and then the firm assertion of Babylonian rule over Judah from 604 BCE, the first expectation of the reformers presumably gave way to a more considered hope. There is much to indicate that this took effect by a sharp shift of emphasis from the soughtafter outward political changes to striving for a basic change of heart and a renewal of faith among Judah's citizens. All of this finds expression in the numerous expansions, modifications, and exhortations that were added over a long period to the original lawbook.

The Significance of the Book. The significance of the book in the growth of biblical tradition is considerable. More than any other book, it establishes the general tone and character of the Pentateuch, and it is likely that the Deuteronomic classification of "law" (*tôrâ*) gave this title to the Pentateuch more generally. In many prominent features, it was Deuteronomy's claims to represent an embodiment of Israel's religious tradition superior to that of prophet, priest, or king that established the notion of a canon of sacred legislative tradition.

In literary influence, it is demonstrable that the historical work consisting of Joshua, Judges, 1 and 2 Samuel, and 1 and 2 Kings (the Deuteronomic History) was a direct development of the lawbook of Deuteronomy and emanates from the same general circle of authors. Furthermore, the edited book of the prophecies of Jeremiah, which now constitutes one of the major texts dealing with the final downfall of the state of Judah at Babylonian hands (604–587/586 BCE), has also been shaped by the Deuteronomic circle of reformers. Jeremiah's prophecies are presented as the final proof of the Deuteronomic interpretation of the reasons for the collapse of Israel as a nation; they serve also as the vehicle of hope and guidance for the nation's renewal and eventual restoration.

Deuteronomy's religious ideas, which more directly than any prior element in Israel's religious traditions express a coherent and comprehensive theology, are a milestone in Israel's intellectual development. It is surprising that when

Jewish Passover

the restoration of a fully organized religious life took place in Judah and Jerusalem after the initial returns from Babylonian exile, the Deuteronomic legislation was much altered and left aside. A staunchly priestly tradition, more conducive to the thinking and aims of a traditional pattern of ritual, merged with it, heavily modifying the relatively rational and spiritualized features of Deuteronomic religion. Among the Jews of the dispersion, however, who formed an increasing element of the surviving Jewish people after 587/586 BCE, the currency and clarity of a simple lawbook able to embody so many aspects of the Jewish tradition was of inestimable importance. With Deuteronomy, the first major step had been taken to promote the existence of Judaism as a religion of a book. Formal worship in a temple came to be simply an adjunct to a more comprehensive code of religious attitudes and duties prescribed in an instructional text.

RONALD E. CLEMENTS

DINAH. Jacob and Leah's daughter, Leah's seventh child, born after her six sons (Gen. 30.21; 46.15); her name, like that of her half-brother Dan, is derived from a root meaning "to judge." In Genesis 34, Dinah is raped by Shechem, who then falls in love and wants to marry her. Enraged at their sister's treatment, Dinah's brothers agree to intermarriage, but only if the men of Shechem (the city) will be circumcised. While they recuperate, Simeon and Levi (full brothers to Dinah) kill them, and Jacob's other sons plunder the city, taking women and children as well as wealth and livestock and risking retaliation from neighboring groups.

The narrative in Genesis 34 gives a remarkable glimpse into Israelite history and customs, including the complicated relationships between the "sons of Israel" and the inhabitants of the land of Canaan and the association of circumcision with marriage (cf. Exod. 4.25–26).

JO ANN HACKETT

DISCIPLE. The term *disciple* (Grk. *mathētēs*) occurs many times in the New Testament, but only in the Gospels and Acts. It is used both of the twelve who according to the Gospels originally followed Jesus, and also of a wide range of Jesus' followers. The Gospels speak not only of disciples of Jesus but also of Moses (John 9.28), "John the Baptist (Mark 2.18; Luke 11.1; John 1.35), and the Pharisees (Matt. 22.16). But above all the term refers to followers of Jesus, who are literally "learners," students of Jesus of Nazareth.

The somewhat amorphous group called disciples constitutes a vital feature of all the Gospel narratives, but the authors used the term to communicate different aspects of being a follower of Jesus. In Mark, the disciples are agents of instruction for the author, but as negative examples. They teach the audience or readers, but mostly through the things they do wrong or fail to understand. The constant questions and concerns of the disciples, particularly in the central section of Mark's gospel, provide an opportunity for the author to explain the purpose of Jesus' mission and the hidden meanings of his teaching. Discipleship in Mark involves fear, doubt, and suffering, as 8.31, 9.31, and 10.33 make explicit; nowhere is this more poignantly captured than in the character of Simon Peter. The disciples in Mark, whomever this broad term may include, never fully understand and never quite overcome their fear and apprehensions. There is actually the hint in Mark that the disciples' fear is in some sense the beginning of wisdom.

The gospel of Matthew on the other hand offers a rather different portrayal of the band of disciples, a term he uses with much greater frequency than the other Gospels (forty-five times without parallel in Mark or Luke). A disciple in Matthew is one who understands, teaches, and does (5.19) what Jesus taught and did. Discipleship in Matthew is not a distinctive office or role but rather describes the life of an ordinary follower of Jesus in the Matthean community. Disciples have authority to teach (5.19; 13.52; 23.8–10; 28.20), and so naturally, unlike the Marcan disciples, they understand the teachings of Jesus, himself portrayed as the authoritative teacher, as the Sermon on the Mount illustrates. Matthew alone among the Gospel writers ascribes the authority to forgive sins to the disciples (6.15; 9.8; 16.19; 18.18). As in Mark, the figure of Peter embodies all aspects of discipleship, but in contrast to the Marcan Peter, in Matthew he understands, can teach, and is granted unusual authority (16.16–19; cf. 18.18).

The meaning and content of the term "disciple" varies in the four Gospels. Each writer uses this broad term, which tends simply to designate a follower of Jesus, in ways that support their understanding of the community of the followers of Jesus and impress on their audience the contours and complexities of the life of a contemporary disciple.

J. ANDREW OVERMAN

EASTER. From Eostre, a Saxon goddess celebrated at the spring equinox. In Christianity, Easter is the annual festival commemorating the resurrection of Christ, observed on a day related to the Passover full moon but calculated differently in eastern and western churches.

In the Bible, the Passover (Hebr. *pesaḥ*, Grk. and late Lat. *pascha*, hence the adjective "paschal") is part of the divine order, Israel's annual commemoration of deliverance (Exod. 12; Deut. 16; Heb. 11.28). For New Testament writers, Christ is the Christian Passover victim (1 Cor. 5.7), and the Gospel presentation has often a Passover background; see Luke 2.41 and the synoptic passion narrative (Matt. 26.2 par.), according to which the Last Supper appears to be a Passover. In John, there are three Passovers: John 2.13, which is associated with the cleansing of the Temple; John 6, where the feeding of the five thousand has paschal and eucharistic echoes (the synoptic accounts may also have a paschal origin); John 11–13; 18.28, 39; and 19.23–37, where Jesus dies on the cross according to this Gospel's chronology at the time when the Passover lambs were being slaughtered in preparation (19.31) for the feast. Christ is thus the eternal paschal lamb; see John 19.36 (cf. Exod. 12.46) and John 1.29, 36.

Easter is therefore the Christian Passover, celebrated for some time on the night of fourteenth of the Jewish month Nisan (Passover night) on whatever day of the week that date fell. This custom continued long in Asia Minor (as in Celtic Britain), with those maintaining it being called Quartodecimans ("fourteeners"), but in Rome, Easter was observed on a Sunday from a date that is difficult to determine but earlier than 154 CE, when Polycarp of Smyrna, a Quartodeciman, on a visit discussed the different observances with Anicetus, head of the Roman church.

The transfer of Easter to the first day of the week was no doubt because Sunday had become the Christian weekly day for worship. That this was owing to the Lord's resurrection on Sunday is not provable but suggested strongly by the New Testament evidence and the absence of any convincing alternative theory. The first day of the week marks the discovery of the empty tomb (Matt. 28.1 par.), while on the same evening the meal recalls the Last Supper (Luke 24.30). See also John 20.1, 19 and 26, the last being the Sunday a week later, and Acts 20.7, which again suggests the custom of a Sunday evening Eucharist. Paul calls the Eucharist the Lord's supper (1 Cor. 11.20); the word for "Lord's" recurs in the New Testament only in Revelation 1.10 in "the

The Entombment

The Resurrection, right hand predella panel from the Altarpiece of St. Zeno of Verona, 1456-60 (Andrea Mantegna, 1456–60)

Lord's day." It was probably "the Lord's" because it was the day for the Lord's supper or Eucharist, at which the Lord had been physically present before his crucifixion, and especially on the day of his resurrection and subsequent days (to which Acts 1.4 and 10.41 probably refer), and invisibly ever since, anticipating his final coming.

A. R. C. LEANEY

ECCLESIASTES, THE BOOK OF. The title of the book in Hebrew is *qōhelet* (also transliterated *qōheleth* and *koheleth*), a particular form of the verb "to assemble," which led to the Septuagint translation *Ekklēsiastēs*, one who addresses an assembly, frequently rendered "The Preacher." The content of this short treatise, however, is less ecclesial than sapiential, displaying a skepticism and dry wit that would be incongruous in a formal religious gathering. Even the ethical theory of moderation smacks of the academic, and the editorial epilogue, by another hand (12.8–10), shows the author in the guise of a scribe-teacher, adding the definite article: *haqqôhelet,* or "The Assembler," suggesting that it may well be a student's nickname for a well-known character.

Written probably in the third century BCE, it belongs among the wisdom books, being one of the Megillot. Its unity is much disputed, ranging from twofold or fourfold authorship to a loose collection of short sections or chapters attributed to different hands. However, the recurrence of idiosyncratic phrases and sophistication of language may point to a single author. In spite of what appears to be a lack of sequence and an overlapping of ideas, there is real unity in the thought pattern. It presents a running dialectic: the "vanity of things" set over against the goodness of life. Being to some extent gnomic wisdom, an extended proverb, it restructures accepted truths

about life, death, pleasure, and toil, and reevaluates them realistically, holding experience up to the light and refracting it. The seeming contradictions are a deliberate teaching tool, and the heterodox atmosphere comes from this dialectical style rather than from the ideas.

Philosophical more than religious, the work consists of a sequence of reactions to the question presented in 1.2–3: "What does one gain by all one's toil?" Beginning and ending with this theme, the book falls into two parts: a philosophical treatise on life and the absurd (chaps. 1–6), and an ethical discussion on how one should live one's life as a result (chaps. 7–12). Quite often a traditional maxim of the schools serves as a launching pad for a personal observation. The thesis of 1.2–3 is the starting point: "vanity," or universal contingency, qualifies cosmos, human environment, and all human effort. The idea refers more to the way Qoheleth experiences life than to a clear metaphysic. There follows a demonstration of this thesis by a study of cosmic circularity (1.4–11). All things are in perpetual flux, ending where they began—an order presumably fixed by God but to mortals quite arbitrary. One finds oneself swept up in a flood of time and destiny that cannot be controlled. Even the human desire for knowledge is contingent. The subsequent proof of this thesis (1.12–2.26) begins in typical sapiential style, from experience. Adopting the mantle of Solomon and thus vested with perfect wisdom (1.1, 12, 16), the author looks for meaning where traditionally it is to be found: in pleasure, in riches, in work. All end in death. Even wisdom itself avails nothing. Absurdity remains, and not simply in personal experience but rooted in human nature: "God has given to human beings" the innate urge to reason why, but even this is "vanity." Paradoxically, the inevitability of death focuses the mind on the "now," and so human life, with its limitations and pleasures, takes center stage. Indeed, 2.16–26 suggests that the only norm is the individual. Although time rolls around fruitlessly, again and again (3.1–9), and people can find no permanent foothold, yet they still study and inquire and dream, for God "has made everything beautiful in its time, and has put eternity into their minds, yet they cannot find out what God has done from beginning to end" (3.11). From chap. 3 on the thesis is viewed from every side, philosophical and existential (3.1–12 is answered in 3.13–15; 3.16–21 in 3.22; 4.1–5.17 in 5.18–20). The mystery of existence is seen in the pattern of the cosmos and in time, both of which impose themselves on humanity, though to some extent one can control the latter and limit its mystery by judging the propitious moment. There is further the enigma of right and wrong: good is not invariably rewarded (3.16–20; 7.15); the same end comes to all (3.1920), and all that results from human effort is bitterness (6.2–3). Contingency is as near a rule of life as one can find.

The practical conclusion is drawn in the second half of the book (7.1–11.6) in what is effectively a moral treatise, proverbial in style. If effort and toil, if even piety and justice avail so little, the only profitable attitude to adopt is to live in the world as one finds it, to be moderate in all things (even piety), and to enjoy the good pleasure that life gives, for even this is a gift, and fulfillment may not come with success (7.1525; 8.14–17). In these chapters many familiar themes reappear, such as human destiny, God's providence, wisdom, and folly; but now they are given a moral twist, and Ecclesiastes becomes a wisdom dialectic in the service of a humanistic ethic. The fact of death and the problematic nature of moral retribution lead to the belief that life remains the only good—as long as one recognizes its precarious nature and lives within the sane limits of prudence.

The presence of God acts as a moderating influence on the harder skepticism of the contemporary scene, while a strong belief in free will and human responsibility modifies its determinism. The author does of course present an enjoyment ethic, but he is quite careful to impose restrictions on the enjoyment of life's good things, which must never exceed human limits. Abuse is never acceptable. Pleasure is a practical ideal, not an absolute. This appears to be the best solution to the vanity of things.

The final word, suitably, is found in an allegory of youth and age (11.7–12.8). Life is short, and youth in particular should enjoy it, for soon will come old age when energy fades and passions die. The editorial epilogue (12.9–14), perhaps by two hands, is an orthodox footnote, sympathetic but cautious.

Ecclesiastes represents an individual's experiential view of the world and human existence and a resultant ethic based on reason applied to that experience. Without rejecting his tradition, the author's rational, universalistic tendencies made blind allegiance to that tradition impossible. God remains the God of Judaism, but the author sees him rather as Elohim, the universal creator and sovereign who remains beyond human understanding. It is this that makes the ethic so important; in an unpredictable world one maintains human values of integrity and decency. One maintains one's humanity, and perhaps this is the only certain value.

How this book found a place in the Hebrew canon remains a puzzle. Perhaps it is a tribute to the fact that a religious scholar, heir to a tradition, could face a world of cultural ferment and make a personal contribution by offering an intellectually valid answer to the problem of existence.

DERMOT COX, O.F.M.

EDEN, THE GARDEN OF. A garden of trees and lush vegetation planted by God and occupied by Adam and Eve (Gen. 2–3). The meaning of the word "Eden" in Hebrew is uncertain. Some scholars connect it with a Sumerian word meaning "wilderness" or "plain," while others have proposed a derivation from the Hebrew word for "delight" or "pleasure." Thus, Eden came to be identified as an ideal garden of delight, or paradise.

The location of the garden of Eden that the author of Genesis had in mind is difficult to determine. Genesis 2.8 places the garden "in the east," which in general indicates Mesopotamia. Genesis 2.10–14 appears to draw from a Near Eastern tradition of an idyllic garden from which rivers flowed. Two of the four rivers named in Genesis are known, the Tigris and the Euphrates. The other two are not known (although Gihon, meaning "gusher," is also the name of Jerusalem's primary spring), making any precise geographical location hypothetical.

In Genesis 2–3, the garden of Eden has at its center the tree of life and the tree of the knowledge of good and evil. The garden is not simply a luxurious paradise but a place created by God in which human beings live and eat and work (Gen. 2.15). Eden functioned as a paradigm of the unbroken relationships between God and humans, and between humans and nature, which no longer obtained after the first couple's disobedience.

The image of the garden of Eden reappears in somewhat altered form in the later prophets. The expulsion from Eden functions as a metaphor for the coming judgment against the nations (Tyre: Ezek. 28.11–19; Egypt: Ezek. 31.8, 9, 16, 18), and for the coming judgment of the day of the Lord (Joel 2.3). The garden of Eden is also an image of promise; in parallel with "the garden of the Lord," Eden appears in Isaiah 51.3 as a metaphor for the renewal of the land of Israel after the Babylonian exile (see also Ezekiel 36.35; Revelation 22.2–3).

DENNIS T. OLSON

EDOM. A kingdom that neighbored Judah on its southeastern border during the Iron Age. It encompassed the area southward from the Wadi Hesa in Jordan to the Gulf of Aqaba, and, during part of this period, included the area called Seir, southwest of the Dead Sea and south of Kadesh-barnea (see Map 1:Y7).

Very little is known about Edom. Virtually no Edomite inscriptions have been found, apart from some seals and a

Adam and Eve in the Garden of Eden (Gen. 3.1–7), from the Holy Trinity Cathedral, the largest Orthodox church in the world, in Addis Ababa, Ethiopia

few ostraca. The primary literary source for the history of Edom is the Bible, but only the barest outline can be constructed from that source. Some information comes from Assyrian records, and archaeological excavations and surveys have enabled a general picture of the development of the region to be sketched.

The early development of Edom remains largely unknown. The stories in Genesis that describe family relationships between Israel's ancestors and those of all the surrounding kingdoms are generally understood to be artificial. For Edom this is particularly clear, since the connection between Isaac's brother Esau and Edom is tenuous and awkward in the narratives of Genesis 25:19–34 and is almost certainly a later imposition on the stories.

Archaeological surveys indicate that the land of Edom was occupied fairly sparsely during the Late Bronze Age (ca. 1550–1200 BCE), with only a few small fortified towns and some tiny villages. The geographic name Edom appears for the first time in an Egyptian document of the thirteenth century BCE.

Numbers 20.14–21 suggests that Edom was already a monarchy at the time of the Exodus in the thirteenth century. Recent studies, however, have cast considerable doubt about the historicity of this and related stories. Even the so-called Edomite king list in Genesis 36.31–39 has been shown to be garbled and unreliable.

Saul is said to have fought Edom successfully (1 Sam. 14:47), but it was David who conquered it and incorporated it into his empire, setting up garrisons throughout the land (2 Sam. 8.14). Although a certain Hadad tried to rebel against Solomon, he does not appear to have been successful (1 Kings 11.14–22). Edom remained under Israelite control, ruled by an Israelite governor until the reign of Jehoram of Judah in the mid-ninth century (2 Kings 8.20). At that time the Edomites successfully rebelled and set up their own king.

During the reigns of Amaziah of Judah (797–769) and Uzziah (769–734) Edom again came under Judean domination. Uzziah recaptured and rebuilt Elath on the Gulf of Aqaba early in his reign. But in the reign of Ahaz Edom decisively threw off Judean control and remained independent of Judah from that time on.

In Judah's place, however, came Assyrian domination, but as was the case also for Ammon and Moab, the Assyrian presence appears to have been economically and politically beneficial to Edom. Excavations at Buseira (probably the Edomite capital Bozrah), Tawilan, and Tell el-Kheleifeh (Elath), show that the late eighth through the mid-sixth centuries BCE saw the peak of Edomite prosperity and expansion. It is from these centuries that monumental architecture is known, and there are indications that Edom expanded its influence into the southern hinterlands of Judah.

Edom seems to have survived the violence of the Babylonian campaigns under Nebuchadrezzar, and, although Buseira, Tawilan, and other sites suffered destruction later in the sixth century, the region recovered and continued to play a role in international trade during the Persian period. With the rise of the Nabateans, a significant proportion of the Edomites seem to have moved westward, so that, by the Hellenistic period, Idumea (the Greek form of Edom) was the name of the region directly to the south of Judah (Map 10:W-X5–6; see 1 Macc. 4.29). The most famous Idumean was Herod the Great.

Attested Edomite names suggest that the Edomites worshiped the well-known West Semitic gods, Hadad/Baal and El. But it appears that the primary deity of Edom was a god named Qaus/Qos. Little is known of this god, and even his basic characteristics (is he a war god or a storm god?) are debated. Some scholars have speculated that in the late second/early first millennium BCE, Yahweh may have been an important deity in Edomite religion, since a few biblical passages link Yahweh closely with Edom and Seir (Judg 5–4; Deut. 33.2; Hab. 3.3).

Although Deuteronomy 23.8 expresses a tolerant attitude toward the Edomites, most biblical passages dealing with the kingdom display a severe hostility toward it, reflecting the almost constant conflict between Judah and Edom. Considerable bitterness is evident in the biblical texts concerning Edom's attitudes and actions after the destruction of Jerusalem in 587/586 BCE (see, e.g., Jer. 49.7–22; Obad.; Isa. 34). Edom, in fact, became a symbol of Israel's enemies in postexilic literature.

WAYNE T. PITARD

EGYPT (Map 6:E–F5). The name is derived from the Greek *Aiguptos*, itself a rendering of the Egyptian *Ḥwt-Ptaḥ*, "Temple of Ptah." The Egyptian name for the country was *Keme*, "the Black Land;" in Hebrew it appears as *Miṣrayim*.

Apart from the delta region, formed by silt deposited for millennia by the Nile, the rest of Egypt consists of a narrow river valley, bounded on its eastern and western sides by vast arid and inhospitable deserts. The delta is similarly bounded on the east by the Sinai desert and on the west by the Libyan des-

Clouds beginning to hover over the hills of Edom in Transjordan.

ert. In the south, the turbulent waters of the First Cataract at Aswan form a natural boundary, as does the Mediterranean Sea in the north. In ancient times, these natural geographical borders effectively isolated Egypt from the rest of the Near East, thereby favoring the uninterrupted development of the civilization distinctive to the Egyptians, generally undisturbed by foreign invasions. Blessed with a stable climate and extremely fertile lands, regularly watered by the river Nile, the Egyptians developed a rich agricultural economy, producing wheat, barley, vegetables of many kinds, various fruits, and grapes (see Num. 11.5). Very early on, Egypt became the granary of the ancient Near East, especially in times of famine (see Gen. 41.57). Although rich in fine types of stone suitable for building and carving—among them, limestone, alabaster, sandstone, and granite—Egypt was poor in metal ores workable at the time. The one exception was gold from the eastern desert, Nubia, and the northern Sudan. Egypt also was and still is poor in trees suitable for woodworking. External trade in this commodity dates back to early times.

The exact origin of the Egyptians is uncertain. They themselves claimed that their ancestors migrated northward from a region bordering on the Red Sea. Their language, essentially Hamitic, nevertheless reveals certain affinities with the Semitic family of languages. The latest form of Egyptian is Coptic, developed during the early period of Christianity in Egypt. It is still used in the liturgy of the Coptic church, though since the Arab conquest in the seventh century CE the ordinary language of the people has been Arabic.

Egypt's geography, largely a river valley some six hundred miles in length, led to the development of many local dialects of the native language. During the early pharaonic era, in order to overcome the difficulties caused by this diversity of speech, a special form of writing was developed. Based on many hieroglyphic figures, it was a kind of Mandarin written language, strictly consonantal but capable of coping with the vocalic differences of the various dialects. The work of interpreting and more particularly writing the hieroglyphs was performed by a large body of trained scribes, who might be described as forming an early civil service that maintained the successful administration of Egypt.

Both from original sources and from a history written in Greek ca. 300 BCE by an Egyptian priest, Manetho, it appears that the unification of the two ancient kingdoms of the north and the south was effected by Menes, the founder of the first historical dynasty and the builder of the city of Memphis. In his history, Manetho lists the rulers of Egypt under thirty dynasties, but many of the kings he names have left no tangible records of their reigns. A simpler scheme of the long history is provided by these divisions: the Archaic Period, ca. 3100–2700 BCE; the Old Kingdom, ca. 2700–2500 BCE; the Middle Kingdom, ca. 2134–1786 BCE; the New Kingdom, ca. 1575–1087 BCE; the Late Period, until the beginning of the Greek or Ptolemaic Period, ca. 1087–332 BCE.

The Old Kingdom was a period of remarkable building and artistic excellence. In particular, the rulers of Dynasty IV erected the immense pyramids at Giza, reckoned by classical antiquity as one of the seven wonders of the world. The drain on the kingdom's economy in building the pyramids, intended as the secure burial places of the rulers, eventually so weakened the succeeding dynasties that at the end of Dynasty VI a period of anarchy and decline occurred.

Able monarchs, originating from Thebes, during Dynasty XI established effective control over the whole of Egypt and founded the Middle Kingdom. The most powerful rulers were those of Dynasty XII, who conquered and held Nubia.

During the Middle Kingdom there was a revival of artistic excellence, especially in portraiture.

As had been the case with the Old Kingdom, toward the end of the Middle Kingdom a period of weakness in the central government allowed the entry into the delta region of a group of foreigners, known as the Hyksos or "Chieftains of Foreign Lands," probably of pastoral origin. They were powerful enough to hold northern Egypt for a considerable time; some ancient and modern scholars regard this period as the setting of the Joseph narratives in Genesis. During the same period, people from Nubia (the northern Sudan) overran most of the region south of Aswan.

Despite these reverses, the rulers of Thebes eventually succeeded in defeating the forces in Nubia and expelling the Hyksos from the delta. With the founding of the powerful Dynasty XVIII, a period of military advance into Palestine and Syria began. Under warlike kings such as Tuthmose I and his later successor Tuthmose III, greatest of all the pharaohs, Egyptian armies advanced as far as the headwaters of the Euphrates. Conquest brought vast quantities of booty into Egypt to swell the treasury of the state god, Amun-Re. This period also witnessed the entry of many foreign artisans into the country, and with them new ideas. Toward the end of the dynasty, internal religious strife and external administrative weakness followed the accession of Amenhotep IV, better known as Akhnaton (also spelled Akhenaton and Ikhnaton). He attempted to change the long-established religion, bitterly opposing the priesthood and eventually removing his capital city from Thebes to Tell el-Amarna. Opinions about Akhnaton have varied from seeing him as the first monotheist to a pleasure-loving materialist. It is not easy to form a just assessment, for after his death his capital city was abandoned, the ancient religion restored, and every possible record of him destroyed. Some correspondence with Asiatic rulers in such cities as Byblos, Jerusalem, and Shechem has survived and is known as the Amarna letters; it is an important source for our understanding of Syria-Palestine in this period. Among his successors was the youthful Tutankhamun, who reigned briefly, and whose tomb, filled with splendid treasures, was found in the Valley of the Kings by Howard Carter in 1922.

A significant restoration of Egypt's former glory was achieved during Dynasty XIX under the Kings Seti I and his son Ramesses II, both of whom advanced once more into Palestine and Syria; the Exodus of the Hebrews from Egypt is dated to this period by many scholars. Ramesses warred inconclusively with the Hittites in northern Syria, but his greatest achievements during a long reign were his building projects, especially at Thebes, and his massive rock-cut temples at Abu Simbel in Nubia. His successor, Merneptah, had to deal with foreign invasion in the north. On a triumphal stele from his reign occurs the first mention of the name of Israel, as a defeated people. In Dynasty XX, a far more serious invasion of northern Egypt by land and sea occurred. This was crushed by Ramesses III, not generally recognized as militarily the greatest of the kings bearing that name. Among the various people who attempted the invasion by sea were the group known in the Bible as the Philistines.

A succession of kings bearing the name Ramesses followed, but each proved weaker than his predecessor, and Egypt declined in power. The geographical barriers that in times past ensured so many centuries of isolation no longer sufficed to prevent foreign invasion. Thus, Dynasty XXII was founded by a Libyan general, Sheshonq I. Called Shishak in the Bible, he invaded Palestine during the reign of Rehoboam, ca. 920 BCE, removing some of the vessels of the Temple (1 Kings

Osiris pillars line a temple dedicated to Ramses II in the ancient Egyptian city of Thebes.

at the apex, and, in descending layers, the royal family and the local princes, the priests, the scribes, the artisans, and at the base the workers of the land.

To modern minds, the religion of ancient Egypt appears to be a strange, chaotic mixture of pantheism and animal worship, frequently full of contradictory beliefs. Long isolation from the rest of the ancient Near East had tended to breed in the Egyptians a strongly conservative outlook with a deep reverence for the past, so that what might seem to be contradictory was accepted as complementary. Over the centuries, purely local deities merged into larger groupings so that the god of one locality might be regarded as the husband of the goddess of another locality. In some instances, the deity of a third locality, merged into a larger grouping, might be regarded as the child of a divine marriage, thus creating a triad. In many instances, the only clues to the former existence of local gods are their names alone. It should be noted that the many gods of Egypt were essentially deities of the Nile Valley, and that of their vast number only one, the goddess Isis, was successfully translated abroad.

The many temples, supported by great estates, were established to serve the various gods, who in their turn served humankind by preserving the physical fabric of the world. The temples were in fact state institutions and not places of individual devotion and prayer. The temples played a very practical role by training able boys, regardless of their social standing, to become scribes in the service of the state. There was a widespread belief in a resurrection and a future realm of rewards and punishments, presided over by the god Osiris, who had been slain by his evil brother Set, but who was afterward restored to life. From various writings it appears that at all times there existed a sense of personal religious morality as distinct from the state religion.

J. MARTIN PLUMLEY

11.40; 14.25–26). A record of some of the places he claimed to have captured appears on one of the walls of the temple at Karnak. Dynasty XXV originated from Nubia. In the time of Taharqa (the Tirhakah of 2 Kings 19.9), the fourth ruler of the Dynasty, Egypt faced invasions by the Assyrians. During the last of the Assyrian invasions in the time of Taharqa's successor, in 663 BCE, the great city of Thebes, No-Amon, was captured and sacked (Nah. 3.8).

For a period after the withdrawal of the Assyrians, Egypt revived under a number of able rulers only to fall eventually to the Persians under Cambyses. In 332 BCE, Alexander the Great was welcomed by the Egyptians as their deliverer from the rule of the hated Persians. Following Alexander's death and the division of his empire among his generals, Ptolemy gained Egypt in 322 BCE, becoming the first ruler of the Ptolemaic or Greek Dynasty. The last of the Dynasty was Cleopatra, who like her lover Antony committed suicide after their defeat at the Battle of Actium (31 CE). Egypt then became part of the Roman empire.

Under the Pharaohs, the government of Egypt was essentially theocratic, the king as a child of the gods being semi-divine, and as such high priest of the land. His general title, pharaoh, meaning "the Great House," can be compared with "the Palace" or "the Sublime Porte." It is not until the time of the Pharaoh Sheshonq that the throne name of the ruler of Egypt is recorded in the Bible. Two other names of rulers recorded are So (2 Kings 17.4) and Neco (2 Kings 23.29; Jer. 46.2). The order of precedence in Egyptian society can be illustrated by the figure of a pyramid: the pharaoh

ELDER. The designation and role of the elder (Hebr. *zāqēn*; Grk. *presbyteros*) dates to premonarchic times in Israel. In the legislation concerning the Passover in Exodus 12.21 Moses addresses "all the elders of Israel." Similarly, in Numbers 11.16 Moses is commanded to gather together "seventy of the elders of Israel whom you know to be the elders of the people and officers over them" and bring them to the tent of meeting. As this passage and others suggest, the elder, as head of the extended family, had authority over it and also represented it in larger assemblies. These elders functioned primarily on the local level as judges, leaders in battle, and intermediaries between the people and their leaders or God. These functions continued during the monarchy, as the story of Naboth's vineyard (1 Kings 21.8–14) and other passages (e.g., Jer. 26.17; Prov. 31.23) make clear, and in the Second Temple period as well (see Ezra 6.7–8; 10.14), both in Judea (1 Macc. 12.35) and in the Diaspora (Sus. 5).

In the New Testament, the "elders of the people" figure throughout the Gospels (e.g., Mark 15.1 par.) and Acts (5.21; 22.5) as leaders of the Judean community who frequently counsel with other leadership groups and have some role in judging capital crimes. Perhaps related to such a group is the phrase "the tradition of the elders" (Mark 7.3, 5 par.) against which Jesus argues and which is associated with the Pharisees in both the Gospels and Josephus.

When Christianity began to institutionalize in a formal sense, it understandably drew on Jewish tradition to accomplish this task; thus the title and office of elder make their way into New Testament history and texts. Though not found in the authentic Pauline letters, there are elders mentioned in Acts in the churches at Antioch (14.21), Jerusalem (15.6; 21.18), and Ephesus (20.17). The author of 2 and 3 John identifies himself as a *presbyteros,* as does the writer of 1 Peter (5.1). The office of elder occurs frequently in the Pastoral Letters. 1 Timothy 5.1 uses the term in the context of one who is deserving of respect, but not necessarily as a technical term; in 5.17, however, an office is clearly meant, and an elder is defined as one who both teaches and preaches. Functions such as laying on of hands (1 Tim 4.14), anointing the sick (James 5.14), and general governance (Tit. 1.5; 1 Pet. 5.2–3) are also mentioned. There are also repeated references to the office of elder in the apostolic fathers, but as time went on hierarchical episcopacy became the normative form of church administration; the English word "priest," however, is ultimately derived from the Greek word *presbyteros.*

The title, and to some extent the functions, of elder were revived by the sixteenth-century reformer John Calvin, and the Greek word was adopted for the name of the Presbyterian church.

J. ANDREW OVERMAN

ELIJAH. Elijah ("Yah[weh] is my God") was a prophet in the northern kingdom of the divided monarchy during the reigns of Ahab, Ahaziah, and Jehoram (873–843 BCE). The circumstances of his birth and early life are not recorded, nor, somewhat unusually, is the name of his father. He was a native of Tishbe in Gilead, an unknown Transjordanian site.

The stories about Elijah, which once circulated separately, have been incorporated into the Deuteronomic history as part of its extensive account of the reign of Ahab of Israel (1 Kings 16.29–22.40) and of its briefer account of the reign of his short-lived son Ahaziah (1 Kings 22.51–2 Kings 1.18). Elijah's translation to heaven and his sucession by Elisha in 2 Kings 2.1–18 are outside the regnal frame and are part of the Elisha cycle; they take place sometime in Jehoram's reign.

The Elijah cycle records the battle in the north for the survival of authentic Yahwism. Both Ahab and his successor Ahaziah looked not only to Yahweh but also to Baal and to his consort Asherah for the winter rains and summer dew that fertilized the land (1 Kings 17–19), and for healing (2 Kings 1). Elijah had to contend not only with the many prophets of Baal and Asherah but with other prophets of Yahweh; 1 Kings 20 and 22 (though not mentioning Elijah) show disagreements among prophets speaking in Yahweh's name. To Elijah, Yahwism involved more than proper worship; the king was accountable to Yahweh's word delivered through prophets such as Elijah and was bound by Mosaic laws protecting the poor (chap. 21). The royal house, influenced by the Phoenician Queen Jezebel, looked to non-Israelite models of kingship, in which the patron gods supported the dynasty.

The section 1 Kings 17–19 is artfully arranged from short stories into a coherent demonstration of Yahweh's control of fertility and protection of his prophet. Elijah announces a drought in 17.1, then in 17.2–24 is protected from its effects and from the king. In 18.1–40 Elijah challenged Ahab and his prophets to a contest to determine which deity could end the drought. Yahweh's consumption of the bull offered to him proves that he alone is God; the rain of vv. 40–46 is therefore from Yahweh and not from Baal.

The prophetic word ending the drought, like the word that began it (17.1), puts Elijah in danger from the king. Chap. 19 tells how Yahweh protected Elijah at Horeb, the source of authentic Yahwism. Like Moses, he encounters God. The theophany, however, is not in the traditional storm but in "a still small voice" (19.12; NRSV: "a sound of sheer silence"), commissioning him to anoint new kings in Syria and Israel (Hazael in place of Ben-Hadad and Jehu in place of Ahab), and a prophetic successor, Elisha. The sole divinity of Yahweh, proved in the drought-ending storm at Carmel, is asserted in a different way at Horeb; the God of Israel has authority to reject and appoint kings and to provide for a continuing prophetic word.

Chap. 21 is another confrontation of king and prophet, this time about the judicial murder of Naboth, who, in accord with the Israelite conception of land tenure, had refused to sell his family plot to Ahab. Elijah's curse upon Ahab takes effect only in the next generation, occasioning Elijah's last recorded confrontation, with Ahaziah in 2 Kings 1. The king in his illness had sent to Baal of Ekron for healing, and so he must die.

Outside the books of Kings, the Chronicler reports a letter from Elijah condemning Jeroboam (2 Chron. 21.12–15). Malachi (4.5 [Heb. 3.23], commenting on 3.1) identifies the messenger of the last days with Elijah; taken up to heaven (2 Kings 2.11), the prophet shall return to prepare the nation for the day of the Lord in judgment. Elijah's role as precursor continues in Jewish tradition, with the development of messianic expectations; at the Passover table a place is set for Elijah in case he returns to inaugurate the messianic age. This belief is also present in the New Testament; Mark (6.15; 8.28; 9.11–13; pars.)

The Dream of Elijah (1 Kings 19.5)

The prophet Elisha heals the Syrian Naaman (2 Kings 5). (Cornelis Engebrechtsz, 1520).

upon seeks out Elisha, who is plowing, and casts his mantle, the symbol of his prophetic office, upon him; Elisha becomes his servant and eventually his successor, when Elijah's mantle definitively is given into his hands (2 Kings 2.1–18). The first two tasks given to Elijah—the anointing of Hazael in 2 Kings 8.7–15 and of Jehu in 2 Kings 9—were in fact performed by Elisha.

There are two types of Elisha stories. One type is the lengthy narratives in which the prophet, sometimes with his servant Gehazi, is involved with the great figures of the day. He advises the kings of Israel, Judah, and Edom in their war with Moab (2 Kings 3.4–27); he assists the king of Israel in the matter of Naaman the Syrian (2 Kings 5); he plays a role in wars between Syria and Israel (6.8–7.20); and he foments the rebellion of Jehu (2 Kings 9). The other type is brief stories in which Elisha alleviates the distress of individuals: he makes a spring's water nontoxic (2 Kings 2.19–22); he punishes irreverent boys (vv. 23–25); he feeds the Shunammite widow and raises her son from the dead (2 Kings 4.8–37; 8.1–6); he detoxifies a cooking pot and multiplies loaves of bread (2 Kings 4.38–44); and he makes an ax head float (2 Kings 6.1–7). Both types of stories, especially the latter, emphasize the miraculous. Their emphasis upon the extraordinary resembles that of the Elijah stories and the plague narratives in Exodus; biblical signs and wonders, generally, are more soberly portrayed.

Elisha is mentioned only once in the New Testament, in Luke 4.27, which cites the cure of Naaman the Syrian as an instance of God's caring for non–Israelites. The miracles of Elisha, like those of Elijah, have, however, influenced the narratives of Jesus' miracles, especially in Luke, such as the raising of the widow's son (2 Kings 4–32–37; cf. Luke 7:11–17) and the multiplication of loaves (2 Kings 4.42–44; cf. Mark 6:30–44; 8:1–10; par.).

RICHARD J. CLIFFORD

and John (1.21, 25) speak of Elijah as the precursor of the last days. The Elijah of the book of Kings appears in Luke 4.25–27; Rom. 11.2; James 5.17; and is dramatically presented in Felix Mendelssohn's oratorio *Elijah*.

RICHARD J. CLIFFORD

ELISHA. Elisha ("God has granted salvation"), son of Shaphat, a native of Abel-Meholah in the northern kingdom of Israel (Map 3:X4), was a prophet during the reigns of Jehoram, Jehu, Jehoahaz, and Joash (849–785 BCE). The stories about him in 2 Kings 2–9 and 13.14–21 directly continue those about his prophetic predecessor Elijah in 1 Kings 17–2 Kings 1. The Deuteronomic history (Deuteronomy to 2 Kings), a vast work narrating the story of Israel from Moses to Josiah and into the sixth century BCE, incorporated these stories with little editing. Most scholars assume there was once a cycle of stories about Elisha, perhaps more extensive than those preserved in 2 Kings, which was then joined to the slightly older Elijah cycle before being incorporated into the Deuteronomic history. Elisha is portrayed as a disciple of Elijah (1 Kings 19.16–21; 2 Kings 2.1–18; 3.11). Elisha, however, is quite different from the solitary Elijah with his unswerving hostility toward the house of Omri. He leads prophetic guilds, "the sons of the prophets" (NRSV: "company of prophets"; 2 Kings 2.15–18; 4.38–44; 6.1–7; 9:1), and is sometimes, though by no means always, in friendly contact with the Israelite kings.

Elisha is first mentioned in 1 Kings 19. Elijah, renewed by his visit to the source of Yahwism at Mount Horeb, is commissioned to three momentous tasks: to anoint Hazael to be king of Syria in place of Ben-Hadad, to anoint Jehu to be king in Israel in place of Jehoram, and to anoint Elisha "as prophet in your place . . . and whoever who escapes from the sword of Jehu, Elisha shall kill" (vv. 16–17). Elijah there-

EPHESIANS, THE LETTER OF PAUL TO THE.
Structure and Contents.
I. God's great work is completed through Jesus Christ and his Spirit (chaps. 1–2). (a) 1.3–14: God's love has been poured out as an abundant blessing; through grace and forgiveness Jews and gentiles now praise God's glory (1.6, 12, 14). (b) 1.15–23: Thanksgiving and intercession for the congregation issue in praise of God's power, which has raised Jesus Christ from death and made him the head over all things, especially over the church, (c) 2.1–10: Christ's resurrection reveals the omnipotence of God's love; all were dead in their sins, but they are freed by grace to do works

pleasing to God. (d) 2.11–22: Peace between the divided, hostile parts of humanity, and peace of all with God, was established by the crucifixion of Jesus and his announcement of peace. The church, as yet the unfinished house of God, is evidence of God's presence among all peoples.

II. The publication and continuation of God's work (3.1–4.16). (a) 3.1–13: To Paul and other apostles before him, it was revealed that Jews and gentiles are common heirs of God's fulfilled promises. The suffering of the apostle in prison, for the sake of this message, is reason for joy, not despair, (b) 3.14–21: In his prayer Paul asks the Father for Christ's presence in every heart, and for increased appreciation of the love bestowed through Christ, (c) 4.1–16: A call to unity prepares the way for an outline of the constitution of the universal church. The one and only God (Deut. 6.4) has now revealed himself as Spirit, Lord (Jesus), and Father. The exalted Lord provides the church with diverse gifts to maintain its unity. The diversity of the members of his body supports its harmony.

III. The testimony of daily life (4.17–6.22). (a) 4.17–32: The only way to affirm God's full revelation in Christ is to make a radical break with non-Christian behavior and to put on Christ. (b) 5.1–20: By experience Christians will learn to discern and do God's will, being inspired by God's Holy Spirit rather than by alcoholic spirits! (c) 5.21–6.9: The so-called *Haustafeln* (home rules) deal with the three essentials of the human condition: sexuality (husband-wife relationship), historicity (generation problems), and economics (owner/slave; rich/poor; strong/weak). While Greek philosophers and other teachers used to direct their moral advice to the stronger groups only (fathers, kings, slaveholders), in Ephesians the weaker are addressed more extensively than are their stronger counterparts. They are declared worthy and capable of a voluntary co–responsibility for the common good (cf. Rom. 13.1–7; 1 Cor. 7.21–23). (d) 6.10–20: Threatened by the attacks of superhuman forces, Christians can trust God to provide them with an armor first used by himself, then given to the Messiah. Their active life and the tribulations they suffer reveal their solidarity with Paul's mission and suffering.

Date and Authorship. According to 1.1; 3.1–13; 4.1; and 6.19–22, the letter was written while the author was in prison. A very few postscripts to ancient Greek manuscripts state that Ephesians was written in Rome; if this is true, the date of the letter would be about 61–63 CE However, the Caesarean imprisonment of the apostle (between 58 and 60?; see Acts 23–26) and an Ephesian captivity (in the mid 50s) have also been suggested.

In 1792, the English divine Edward Evanson first questioned Pauline authorship. During the nineteenth century, German scholars gathered arguments in favor of pseudonymous origin, and today most researchers treat the letter as non–Pauline, dating it between 70 and 100 CE, mainly in the 90s. Some think that the author was Onesimus, the runaway slave mentioned in Paul's letter to Philemon, who is then further identified with the bishop of Ephesus bearing the name Onesimus (mentioned in Ignatius's letter to the Ephesians 1.3; 2.1; 6.2). The arguments against Pauline origin include the following, which are balanced with counterarguments.

Style. Ephesians has to a large extent a liturgical and/or hymnic style; it has a tendency to be heavy, baroque, if not bombastic (e.g., 1.18–19, 21; 3.5; 4.15–16, 30). Extremely long sentences frequently contain vocabulary not found in unquestioned Pauline letters; well–known words occur with a new meaning; favorite Pauline terms and phrases are missing. On the other hand, whenever in his undisputed letters (such as in Romans 8.38, 39; 11.33–36) Paul breaks out in prayer, his diction is similarly pleonastic and/or liturgical. Since Ephesians contains numerous citations of or allusions to pre-Pauline confessional and hymnic elements (see 2.4–8, 10, 14–18; 3.5, 20–21; 4.4a, 5–6, 9, 21C–24, 25b–27), it is not astonishing that its style and vocabulary differ from Pauline prose usage.

Historical reasons are spearheaded by the observation that a mutual acquaintance between Paul and the readers is denied in 1.15; 323; 4.21. But Acts 18.17–20.1, 17 clearly speaks of short and lengthy periods of Pauline activity in Ephesus. The alternatives seem inescapable: either this is a genuine Pauline letter that was addressed not to Ephesus but to an unknown city that Paul never visited, or Ephesus is the correct address, as it were, but Paul is not the author. Still, even this dilemma can be resolved if one assumes that Paul wrote to only a part of the congregation in Ephesus, namely to former gentiles (2.2, 11, 19; 4.17–19; 5.8) who had joined the church after the apostle's departure. Just as Paul warns against triumphalism over the Jews in Romans 11.17–24, so Ephesians is a call to remember that the church owes its existence to inclusion of gentiles into God's people, Israel.

Other arguments against authenticity are based upon historical developments. The absence of a sharp dispute with judaizers seems to presuppose that the struggle about justification by faith, not the Law, belongs to the past. The dynamic Pauline preaching of justification appears to be replaced by the proclamation of apostolic and church authority, transmitted in a fixed tradition. Dualistic, deterministic, and mythical gnostic elements are said to have invaded formerly pure doctrines of sin, Christ, salvation, and the church. Although it is acknowledged that the letter contains elements of antignostic reaction, it is yet considered a victim of the enemy it tried to battle: since no one wants to burden Paul with such weakness and defeat, the letter is not considered Pauline. On the other hand, since about 1960 the Nag Hammadi documents have shown that the composition and the spread of the "gnostic myth" is to be dated no earlier than the second century CE. In consequence, Ephesians could neither have fought it nor have fallen prey to it.

Personal elements in Ephesians, together with original elaborations on doctrines less developed elsewhere, discourage the notion that Ephesians is no more than a composite of quotations from genuine Pauline letters. Paul was not bound always to speak of justification, nor to lash out against misuse of the Law. In other letters he also speaks of reconciliation and peace. A development of his teaching about the church's relation to Israel cannot be excluded on historical grounds: it is certainly a long way from sharp reference to God's wrath upon the Jews in 1 Thessalonians 2.14–16, to the statement that the legalistic part of Israel was driven out (Gal. 4.30), to the proclamation of God's faithfulness to his promises, which even finally may lead to the regrafting of cut-off branches (Rom. 9–11), and finally to the irenic stance taken in Ephesians 1–3, where the gentiles are described as adopted into God's eternally beloved people, Israel. At the same time, it cannot be proven that Paul was unable to learn, to develop, even to correct himself. Paul changed his teachings about the presence of salvation, the nature of the church (universal rather than local), marriage, and other issues. A plagiarist would hardly have dared to be so independent of earlier Pauline letters.

Literary dependence of Ephesians upon the Pauline letters, especially Colossians, revealed by many almost identically phrased sentences, seems to exclude the pen of a man

E

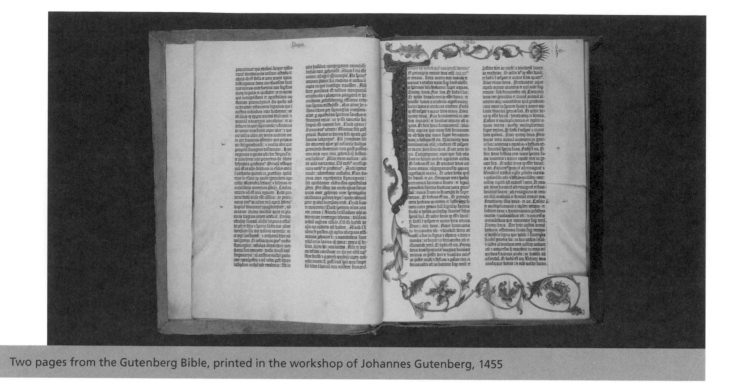

Two pages from the Gutenberg Bible, printed in the workshop of Johannes Gutenberg, 1455

who in his undisputed letters is a wellspring of ever-new ideas and formulations. Thus, 6.21–22 appears to be copied to a large extent from Colossians 4.7–9. In Colossians 1 and Ephesians 1 and 3, Christ, the head of the church and the world, is described in similar terminology, though in Colossians Christ's cosmic rulership is emphasized more than in Ephesians. The latter concentrates attention upon the universal church's function, and it contains several explicit biblical quotations, together with interpretive sentences or hints (see 1.18–22; 2.13–17; 4.8–10; 5.31–33; 6.14–17), while Colossians never explicitly cites the Bible. Scholars tend to favor dependence of Ephesians upon Colossians, making Colossians more likely to be authentic. A secretary or a later disciple of Paul may have written the letter. Pseudonymous authorship was often a sign of respect toward the one whose name was put at the head of a document; to speak of falsification and plagiarism misses the point.

Still, not even the undisputed letters (except Galatians) were written without secretarial help. The similarity between Ephesians and Colossians might have a simple reason: at about the same time of his life, Paul may have used the same general outline to address the Colossians in polemical terms and to send a peaceful message to the Ephesian church, a kind of encyclical to all the churches in Asia Minor.

Theology. The distinct theology of Ephesians appears to tip the scale in favor of pseudonymity. Protestant scholars point out that in this letter ecclesiology overshadows Christology; that gnosticizing knowledge and cosmological speculation encroach upon the genuine, existential faith; that institution and tradition replace trust in grace and eschatological hope; that biblical ethics have yielded to petit–bourgeois moralism. In short, though under protest by Orthodox and many Roman Catholic scholars, Ephesians is considered, together with the Pastoral Epistles and Acts, to expound what is called "early Catholicism." Others have dubbed it a "Marseillaise of church triumphalism."

Indeed, if the theology of Paul has been fully grasped and described by the Augustinian, Lutheran, and existentialist understanding of justification, then salvation has to do primarily with the encounter between God and the individual.

Because in Ephesians salvation is a social event with cosmic dimensions, the letter is thought to contradict the core of Paul's message and to be spurious. On the other hand, even in undisputed letters Paul not only speaks of justification but also of the reconciliation and solidarity of Jews and gentiles under God's grace. He also speaks of peace, of mission, of the final liberation of the whole cosmos, though these topics often receive only minor attention. The special theological features of Ephesians may reveal how much there is still to learn of Paul's complete message.

In conclusion, Ephesians should be considered an authentic Pauline letter. Its irenic and embracing character distinguishes it among the more bellicose letters of Paul. It deserves to be called his testament.

Highlights and Influence. At least four traits distinguish Ephesians from most other Pauline writings. First, this letter speaks of only one mystery. This *mystērion* is unlike the numerous apocalyptic-historical and theological–interpretative mysteries that will be disclosed only at the end of time. Whenever the term "mystery" occurs in this letter (1.9; 3.3–4, 9; 9.19; cf. "wisdom" in 3.10), it designates a secret that has recently been disclosed, first to a few chosen people and now to be communicated to all. Its substance is the eternal will of God to save the gentiles as well as the Jews, to whom alone he had first given the hope of an inheritance and of the Messiah to come. Especially in 1.10 and 2.11–12, God's means to carry out his will are described: since the time of fulfillment has come, the Messiah, long ago promised to Israel, has come and has died on the cross to make peace between formerly hostile groups. The Holy Spirit continuously confirms ("seals" 1.13–14; 4.30), based upon Christ's completed work, that all sinners are forgiven and now enjoy equal rights as children in one family and as citizens of God's kingdom (2.1–19). In this letter, the "new person" is not an individual, but two former enemies (of one another and of God) now joined together in peace by the removal of what had formed a legal wall of separation (2.14–16). Even more clearly than in Romans 3.21–31 and 9–11, Ephesians reveals that the intervention of the God-sent mediator terminates segregation, hostility, and strife. Nowhere is it denied that salvation pertains also to persons and their souls. According to Ephesians, however, the liberation of individuals takes place within the framework of God's kingdom, in the victory of his love and righteousness over all injustice and misery.

Second, together with Matthew 16.17–19 and John 17.17–22, Ephesians is, within the New Testament, the magna carta of the one, holy, apostolic, and catholic church (4.4–6). The church is the palpable evidence of the work of unification accomplished by Jesus Christ (2.20–22). It is a beacon for all the world (5.8) and is the still-incomplete structure of God's house, waiting for the insertion of the capstone, that is, Christ who will come again (2.20; 4.13, 15–16).

Since the Jews have been and remain the first members of God's people, there is no unity of the church available without them. When the church is depicted as Christ's bride (5.25–27, 31–32), and when the relationship between Christ and his church is explained in terms of the union of a man and a woman (Gen. 2.24 is quoted), then love is shown to be the bond of unity. On the other hand, it is also made clear that an identification of Christ and the church is not in question. Further, Ephesians does not support the claim that certain sacraments are to be administered exclusively by ordained clergy, nor that the difference between clergy and laity constitutes the church. In this letter, God's love for Jews and gentiles, not the church, is the "mystery of God," "mystery of Christ," and "mystery of the gospel." Since the reconciliation of Jews and gentiles with one another and with God is the paradigm of the unification of all human groups (as the *Haustafel* in 5.21–33, compared with the text about the broken wall in 2.11–22, shows), in this letter the doctrine of the church is identified with social and personal ethics.

Third, in Ephesians, the situation of the church in the world is described in an apparently antiquated way. Above, around, and perhaps even within the church and its male and female, older and younger, free and dependent members, and in the same position over against all human beings, there are good and evil principalities and powers, and a devilish realm high up in the air (1.21; 2.2, 7; 3.10; 6.11–12). Rather than imposing a mythological or demonic worldview upon the readers, the author of Ephesians probably means by these terms biological and psychological, social and political, cultural and religious forces that are unseen and yet encountered in human existence (cf. Rom. 8.38–39; also Colossians and Revelation). Ephesians intends to assure the tempted, suffering, and desperate among humankind that God has made his own cause not only the suffering that must be endured, but also the resistance, combat, and victory over the superhuman ruling powers.

Finally, traditional interpretations of the passage about husbands and wives (5–21–33) have required women to be submissive toward men. Feminists disdain this part of Ephesians and call for removal of allusions to it in marriage liturgies. The biblical text, however, speaks first of mutual subordination (5.21), never of submission, and only of married persons. It controls and qualifies the husband's headship by making it clear that only an unselfish and self–giving love characterizes such a "head." Speaking to wives, the text is far from requiring a forced subordination: Ephesians encourages wives to place themselves at the disposition of the common good. In the same way, which has nothing to do with loss of honor and selfhood, Christ subordinates himself to the Father (1 Cor. 15.28; cf. Phil. 2.6–8), and the church to Christ when it acknowledges the love he has bestowed upon it (Eph. 5.24). Since already in 1 Corinthians 7 and Galatians 3.28 Paul has spoken of the interrelationship of equally free partners under the unifying lordship of Christ, his marriage counseling in

Ephesians must not serve to substantiate male superiority; rather, it promotes the partnership of those married.

MARKUS K. BARTH

ESAU. The older son of Isaac and Rebekah, and the twin brother of Jacob (Gen. 25.24–26). His ruddy and hairy appearance, as well as his preference for hunting and the outdoor life, distinguished him from his brother. Despite the apparent connection between his name and his hairiness in Genesis 25.25, the etymology of Esau remains uncertain. Esau also is considered the ancestor of the Edomites (Gen. 36.9).

Genesis 25.29–34 relates how Esau foolishly sold his birthright to Jacob for the price of a meal whose name in Hebrew (*'ādōm*) resembles Edom, another name for Esau (Gen. 36.1). Jacob, acting on the advice of Rebekah, then tricked Isaac into making him the principal heir by disguising himself as his older brother and obtaining his father's blessing (Gen. 27). Esau eventually shunned revenge, was reconciled with Jacob, and settled in Seir (Gen. 33).

Most scholars view the stories of Jacob and Esau not only as folktales about fraternal relationships and reversals of fortune but also as Israelite depictions of the ambivalent and sometimes treacherous relationship between Edomites (sons of Esau) and Israelites (sons of Jacob) over territorial claims and other ethnopolitical issues (2 Sam. 8.12–14; 2 Kings 8.20–22; Obad.). Ethnopolitical relationships are ostensibly reflected in notices about Esau's marriages to women of various ethnic origins (Gen. 26.34; 28.9) and about his progeny (Gen. 36).

Within Christianity Esau became a central example in debates concerning the right of Christians to the blessings promised by God to the descendants of Isaac (Rom. 9.6–14) and in debates about predestination.

HECTOR IGNACIO AVALOS

ESTHER, THE BOOK OF.

The Hebrew Book. Deriving its title from the name of its heroine, the book of Esther presents the story of an unsuccessful attempt to kill the Jews living in the Persian empire during the reign of a certain Ahasuerus, probably meant to be Xerxes (486–465 BCE). The threat was averted by the courage and shrewdness of Esther and her cousin Mordecai, with the aid of a series of fortuitous circumstances. Since it purports to explain the origin of the festival of Purim, the book has been read aloud in the synagogue at that feast since antiquity.

Neither the date nor the location of the book's composition can be determined with any precision. While it is clearly one of the latest books in the Hebrew Bible, the absence of clear historical allusions or perspectives renders the questions uncertain; nor is there sufficient linguistic evidence to resolve them. It may be as late as the second century BCE, just before the Maccabean period, or as early as the late fifth century, from the Persian period. Doubtless, it contains traditions and information that go back to the Persian period. In part because of its lack of interest in Palestinian religious institutions and its concern with the problems of Jews in foreign lands, it is likely that the book was composed in the eastern Diaspora.

As a well-constructed story that creates interest by developing and resolving tension, the book of Esther's plot structure includes the following elements:

I. Exposition, or setting the scene (1.1–2.23)
   A. Life in the Persian palace: the king banishes
      Queen Vashti (1.1–22)

B. Esther becomes queen, and her cousin Morde-
cai exposes a plot against the king (2.1–23)
II. The crises and their resolution: the lives of Morde-
cai and of all the Jews are in jeopardy but they are
saved (3.1–8.14)
A. Haman plots to kill Mordecai and all the Jews
(3.1–4.17)
B. Esther and Mordecai take actions that avert the
threat (5.1–8.14)
III. The resolution and the results (8.15–10.3)
A. The Jews celebrate the edict (8.15–17)
B. The Jews' victory over their enemies (9.1–15)
C. Date of the celebration (9.16–19)
D Mordecai's records and letter scheduling the
feast of Purim (9.20–28)
E. Esther's letter concerning the feast (9.29–32)
F. Epilogue in praise of Mordecai (10.1–3)

Although the details of its setting are entirely plausible and the story may even have some basis in actual events, in terms of literary genre the book is not history. Nor is it legend, though the sequence of events is as unlikely as those in legends, and folkloristic traditions probably underlie the story. Missing are the conventional legendary features of the miraculous, as are characters who reveal the power of God in human affairs and thereby serve as models for future generations. Rather, because of the extended and well–developed plot and its point of view, the book is best understood as a novella, a type that arose not as oral tradition but as a written composition. The closest biblical parallels are the story of Joseph (Gen. 37–50) and the books of Ruth, Jonah, and Tobit.

The author sacrifices characterization and, to a lesser extent, description of setting in order to emphasize the plot. Three main characters (Esther, Mordecai, and Haman) and two lesser ones (King Ahasuerus and Queen Vashti) are set forth in the account; all lack depth and complexity. The author deals only in passing with the actors' motivations and feelings, drawing them in such sharp profile that they are almost caricatures. Haman is evil incarnate, while Esther and Mordecai are synonymous with beauty, wisdom, and the good. The storyteller gives us no opportunity to sym-pathize with Haman, nor to criticize or question Mordecai and Esther. The king is shown to be something of a buf-foon, always acting on the spur of the moment, at the mercy of his emotions and whims.

Most of the action transpires in the palace, and is orga-nized in series of scenes, with relatively clear markers indi-cating changes of time and location. The author takes pains to provide the reader with every reason to believe in the cir-cumstances, giving particularly detailed descriptions of the palace and the king's frequent banquets.

By means of a relatively straightforward plot, the book of Esther tells the story of how the Jews were saved from persecution and death. It is a simple story of the triumph of good over evil, but the narrator takes some care to pace the tale, keeping the outcome in doubt as long as pos-sible. Ironic twists appear—first, when Haman hears the king ask, "What shall be done for the man whom the king wishes to honor?" and, assuming the monarch has him in mind, he answers only to discover that the king intends to honor Mordecai (6.6–11). The final irony for Haman is that he is hanged on the gallows he had built for Mor-decai (7.9–10). Moreover, the story is not without humor, and possibly satire as well, particularly in the portrayal of Ahasuerus.

As the outline above indicates, the first two chapters set the scene and mood for the events of the story itself. In chap. 1, though the main characters have not yet appeared, we learn how the king behaves capriciously, how much plot-ting and conflict there is in the court, and that when the king banishes Vashti he will need a new queen. Two events equally important for the outcome of the story are reported in chap. 2: after an empirewide search, the Jewish girl Esther becomes the queen; and her cousin Mordecai discovers a plot against Ahasuerus and reports it.

Two distinct but related threads run through the body of the story: the threat against Mordecai and the threat against the Jewish people as a whole. The first is set in motion when Mordecai refuses to bow down before Haman (3.1–3), thus disobeying one of the king's laws. The story does not state directly why Mordecai puts his life in danger, but it implies that he does so because he is a Jew. When Haman learns this (3.4–6), he vows to kill all the Jews. Then Haman schemes to accomplish his goal, bribing the king to proclaim the destruction of the Jews (3.7–15) on a date set by the casting of a lot (Hebr. *pûr;* hence the festival is called Purim [the plural form]). The first thread of the plot is brought to a cli-max when Ahasuerus, finding Haman in what he takes to be a compromising position with Esther, decrees Haman's death (7.1–10). It was not just Esther's appeal but a chance encounter that brought the enemy's downfall.

Still, the terrifying danger hangs over the Jews, for the king's edict has gone out and cannot be recalled. As the book stresses more than once, royal proclamations cannot be changed (1.19; 3.12–15; 8.8). Ahasuerus can and does, however, promulgate another edict, this one authorizing the Jews to defend themselves. When this document is circulat-ed (8.11–14), the main plot has reached its resolution. What follows, including the extermination of the Jews' enemies, is the denouement of the conclusion's results.

On the surface, the book's theme is a simple one, that good triumphs over evil. The more specific form of this theme is one of the favorites of oppressed and persecuted people everywhere, that their persecutors are defeated by their own hostile plans. Moreover, the good triumph over the evil so long as they are shrewd, courageous, and fortu-nate. More significant, the story encourages those who see themselves threatened by hostile oppressors, and teaches those who wield authority over the weak how contemptible they are in the eyes of the powerless.

Although the story proceeds as the conflict between a Jewish minority and others bent on genocide, the book's attitudes toward foreigners and toward power are by no means unambiguous. Neither the Persians in general nor the Persian authorities are evil, but only the "enemies of the Jews" (9.1), epitomized by Haman. On the one hand, the capricious king and the immutable Persian laws are ridi-culed, but on the other, Esther and Mordecai work through the channels of power to save their people. As in the book of Ruth, intermarriage between Jews and gentiles is not only condoned but even approved.

One of the major issues in the book concerns the relation between law and justice. Mordecai disobeys the law, and on that basis he and all his people are jeopardized; Esther like-wise violates the law by entering the king's presence (4.11; 5.1). But the storyteller leaves no doubt in the minds of the readers that these laws are unjust, and not simply by the standards of the Mosaic Law—which is never mentioned— but by common sense. Haman is held in contempt for his self-serving legalism; the king's laws are shown to be petty and capricious. Thus, the book criticizes a narrow legalism with neither heart and soul, nor justice.

Behind the story stand certain views of how human history moves. The book is optimistic about the future, for history moves in a beneficent direction. Moreover, the development of events is viewed as the interaction of human wills with chance or destiny (and the latter is not a hidden reference to the will of God, who is never mentioned in the book). On the one hand, the Jews, through the hero and heroine, take care of themselves; on the other hand, they are fortunate, as is seen most clearly in Haman's downfall, when his foolish attempt to plead with the queen is misinterpreted by the king (7.7–8). These two forces, destiny and human initiative, are explicitly linked in Mordecai's words to Esther, "Who knows? Perhaps you have come to royal dignity for just such a time as this?" (4.14). In the right time and place, human individuals can hold the destiny of their people in their hands.

Additions to the Book. Jerome, in preparing his Latin Vulgate, recognized some 107 verses as additions to the book of Esther. Since the passages in question appeared in his Greek text but not in the Hebrew, he removed them from the body of the book and placed them at its end. A further step was taken during the Protestant Reformation, when the Apocrypha was created by placing in a separate part of the Bible those books found in the Greek Old Testament but not in the Hebrew. It was then that the Additions to the Book of Esther became a separate book.

The traditional Greek text (Codex Vaticanus) of Esther contains six additions not found in the Masoretic Hebrew text. One appears at the beginning, another at the end, and the others are interspersed through the book at appropriate points in the narrative. Their versification is somewhat confusing because when Jerome moved the additions to the end, he left the last one in place as the book's conclusion, thus disrupting the chronology of the closing passages.

The six additions, with their traditional English chapters and verses, are:

A (11.2–12.6): The beginning of the Greek version, before Hebrew 1.1. The first unit (11.2–12) reports Mordecai's dream of what will transpire in the Esther story, and the second (12.1–6) is a variation on the account of Mordecai's discovery of the plot against the king (Esther 2.19–23).

B (13.1–7): Following Hebrew 3.13, this addition contains the text of the king's decree ordering that the Jews be killed.

C (13.8–14.9): Following Hebrew 4.17, the first part (13.8–18) is Mordecai's prayer, and the second (14.1–19) is Esther's prayer.

D (15.1–16): Replacing Hebrew 5.1–2, this is an expanded report of Esther's appeal to the king.

E (16.1–24): Following Hebrew 8.12, this gives the contents of the king's second decree, allowing the Jews to defend themselves.

F (10.4–11.1): Following Hebrew 10.3, this addition tells how Mordecai recalls his dream, which has now come true, and interprets the meaning of the figures in it; 11.1 is a colophon validating the copy of the book, called here "The Letter of Purim," brought to Egypt in the time of Ptolemy and Cleopatra.

Four of the additions, A, C, D, and F, generally are considered to rest upon a Hebrew original, but B and E, the proclamations of the king, were composed in Greek. Therefore, if one considers only the textual differences between the traditional Hebrew (Masoretic Text) and the Septuagint B (Vaticanus), there were three clear stages of composition: the short Hebrew text, the Hebrew with four additions, and the Greek with two further expansions. The process of the text's growth and composition would have been even more complicated than that, for another Septuagint text (A [Codex Alexandrinus]) appears to rest on a different Hebrew tradition.

Esther and Ahasuerus (Esth. 7.1–7)

It follows, then, that the Additions to the Book of Esther were composed at different times and by different persons. The original book would have been written perhaps as early as the late fifth century BCE but no later than the early second century BCE. The fullest form of the book, represented in the two Greek editions, probably was written not long before when it claims to have been brought to Egypt in the "fourth year of the reign of Ptolemy and Cleopatra" (11.1), probably 114 BCE. In any case, the additions show that the book of Esther did not stabilize until relatively late.

The additions make the book of Esther a dramatically different work, and indicate that some of those who transmitted it were uneasy with the original. What had been a tale of the triumph of good over evil through the skills and courage of the hero and heroine, assisted by fortuitous circumstances, becomes a religious story stressing piety and the will of God. Whereas the book of Esther does not mention God, the additions constantly refer to the deity, to prayer, and to the sacred traditions and practices of Judaism.

The important human qualities are not shrewdness or power or royal position, but piety and humility. If Esther is eloquent before the king, it is because God has answered her prayer (14.1–9). The exercise of genuine religion leads to the salvation of the people. The authors of the additions must have been offended by all the story's pomp and circumstance, for they present Esther belittling her royal position and apologizing for her royal garb.

In the additions, one finds a significantly different understanding of history. In the first place, the story is now set between Mordecai's almost apocalyptic dream and its interpretation. This framework tells the reader that God not only knows the future but reveals it to the elect. Second, it is not chance or heroic actions that saves the Jews from extermination, but divine intervention. To be sure, that intervention was not by means of a dramatic miracle, but through influencing the human heart. Ahasuerus issued his second proclamation because "God changed the spirit of the king to gentleness" (15.8).

GENE M. TUCKER

EVE. The name given to the first woman by the first man (Gen. 3.20). The Bible interprets this name to mean "the mother of all living," both because Eve is, through her sons, the female ancestor of the entire human race and because the name sounds similar to the Hebrew word for "living being." The wordplay is probably etymologically incorrect, and later rabbinic tradition proposed a connection with the Aramaic word for "serpent." The actual linguistic derivation of the name remains uncertain.

According to the account in Genesis 2–3, the woman is created to be a companion corresponding to (not originally subordinate to) the man. Because the two of them eat the forbidden fruit, the man is destined to toil as a farmer in fields of thorns and thistles, and the woman is destined to suffer pain in childbearing. It is in the aftermath of these divine pronouncements that the man names the woman as he had earlier named the animals, thus indicating dominion over her.

Both Jewish tradition and the New Testament offer a very negative view of Eve, presenting her as representative of the alleged weaknesses of women. Paul feared that the Corinthian Christians would be led astray from Christ as Eve was deceived by the serpent (2 Cor. 11.3). In 1 Timothy 2.13–15, Eve's deception by the serpent and also her creation subsequent to the man are cited as reasons that women must keep silent in church (cf. 1 Cor. 14.34–35) and hold no authority over men.

Early Christian theologians contrasted Eve's sinfulness with the perfection of the "new Eve," Mary, the mother of Jesus.

This traditional emphasis on the gullibility of Eve and her tendency toward sin is one possible interpretation of the Genesis narrative; it is not, however, inherent in the text of the narrative itself. Genesis 3 gives no indication why the serpent addressed the woman and even indicates that the man and the woman were together when the serpent spoke. It has been suggested that the serpent might have addressed the woman as provider of food or as theological thinker, not as the more gullible of the couple, and that the woman's addition to the divine prohibition about the fruit ("we may not touch it") represents not a lie, but a desirable exaggeration meant to make sure that the basic command would not be broken. The man and the woman together discover their nakedness, together make fig leaf garments, and together hide from the deity. Both are destined to a life of pain (neither is cursed) because of their actions, and together they are expelled from the garden. Thus, once the reader sets aside the portrait of Eve based on later traditions, the great skill of the Genesis narrator in presenting a character open to diverse interpretation becomes apparent.

KATHARINE DOOB SAKENFELD

EXODUS, THE. The Exodus, the escape of the Hebrews from slavery in Egypt under the leadership of Moses, is the central event of the Hebrew Bible. More space is devoted to the generation of Moses than to any other period in Israel's history, and the event itself became a model for subsequent experiences of liberation in biblical, Jewish, Christian, and Muslim traditions. The Exodus is ancient Israel's national epic, retold throughout its history, with each new narration reflecting the context in which it was rendered. The Exodus entails not only the actual events in Egypt but all those encompassed within the period from Moses to Joshua, from the actual escape from Egypt to the conquest of the land of Canaan, including the wilderness wanderings. This epic is not preserved in the Pentateuch as such; within its boundaries the promise of land made to Abraham remains unfulfilled. But the structure of Pentateuchal narrative presumes it, and indeed the conclusion of the story is found in the book of Joshua, the beginning of the Deuteronomic History that has apparently displaced an earlier ending to Israel's original epic. The full story is also found in summary form in other passages (Exod. 15; Deut. 26.5–9; Josh. 24; Pss. 78; 80; 105; 114; cf. Ezek 20.6), some of which are quite old.

Historical Context. The Bible itself is virtually devoid of concrete detail that would enable the Exodus to be dated securely. It names none of the Pharaohs with whom Joseph, the "sons of Israel," and Moses and Aaron are reported to have dealt. Egyptian records are also silent about the events described in the later chapters of the book of Genesis and the first half of the book of Exodus; they make no mention of Joseph, Moses, the Hebrews, the plagues, or a catastrophic defeat of Pharaoh and his army. The first mention of Israel in a source other than the Bible is in an inscription written to commemorate the victory of the Egyptian Pharaoh Merneptah at the end of the thirteenth century BCE; there Israel is associated with places in Canaan rather than in Egypt. Because of this lack of direct correlation between biblical and nonbiblical sources, scholars have to resort to indirect evidence in assigning a date to the Exodus. Two principal views have been proposed. The first associates the flight of the Hebrews with the expulsion of the Hyksos kings from Egypt at the end of the Middle Bronze Age (ca. 1550 BCE).

First proposed by Josephus (*Against Apion* 1.103), this date approximates the figure of 480 years from the Exodus to the dedication of the Temple by Solomon (1 Kings 6.1; cf. Judg. 11.26) and, with some variations, is held by a minority of modern scholars. Biblical chronology itself is, however, not consistent, and most scholars date the event to the mid–thirteenth century BCE, during the reign of Ramesses II, because of a convergence of probabilities, including the identification of the store cities of Pithom and Rameses (Exod. 1.11) with recently excavated sites in the Egyptian delta and the larger context of the history of Egypt and of the Levant.

The Narratives. The account of the Exodus in the Pentateuch is multilayered, being composed of various traditions, some very ancient, such as the "Song of the Sea" in Exodus 15, and the bulk a prose narrative combining the Pentateuchal sources J, E, and P, to be dated from the tenth to perhaps as late as the sixth century BCE. The existence of these traditions enables us to observe a virtually continuous process of revision; thus, for example, the place names vary, apparently reflecting those current when a particular tradition was set down.

Embellishment, heightening, and exaggeration can also be observed. The simplest account of the event at the Sea of Reeds is found in Exodus 14.24–25. This passage may be understood in its simplest terms as a summary of how a group of Hebrew slaves escaping on foot was pursued by Egyptian guards, who were forced to give up the chase when their chariots became mired in the swampy region east of the Nile delta (see Map 2). This account is ultimately transformed into a miraculous intervention of Yahweh at the sea, when through the agency of Moses he makes a path through the sea, with walls of water on both sides (Exod. 14.21–23). Still later, in the Septuagint, the Hebrew phrase meaning "sea of reeds" is translated as "Red Sea," further enhancing the miracle. Likewise, the number of those escaping, according to Exodus 1.15 a small group whose obstetrical needs could be handled by only two midwives, becomes six hundred thousand men, as well as women and children (Exod. 12.37), an impossible population of several million.

Another tendency is to mythologize. The escape of the Hebrews at the sea is recast as a historical enactment of an ancient cosmogonic myth of a battle between the storm god and the sea, found also in biblical texts having to do with creation (Job 26.12–13; Jer. 31.35; Pss. 74.1217; 89.9–12; 93; 104). This mythology is explicitly applied to the Exodus in Psalm 114, where the adversaries of the deity are the personified Sea and Jordan River, who flee at God's approach at the head of Israel (cf. Judg. 5.4–5; Ps. 68.7–8; Hab. 3.3–15); Sea and Jordan are clearly related to Prince Sea and Judge River, the parallel titles of the adversary of the Canaanite storm god Baal in Ugaritic mythology (note the echoes of this motif in the New Testament, in such passages as Mark 4.35–41 par.; Rev. 21.1). The adversaries of the God of Israel, however, are not cosmic but historical—the Egyptian Pharaoh and his army, and sea and river are not primeval forces but geographical realities.

The same historicizing tendency is apparent in the treatment of the Passover, originally two separate springtime feasts from different socioeconomic contexts now given historical etiology associated with the Exodus. The "festival of unleavened bread" was originally an agrarian pilgrimage feast in which the first spring harvest of barley was offered to a deity without being contaminated with older leaven. In the Exodus narrative, the unleavened bread is explained by

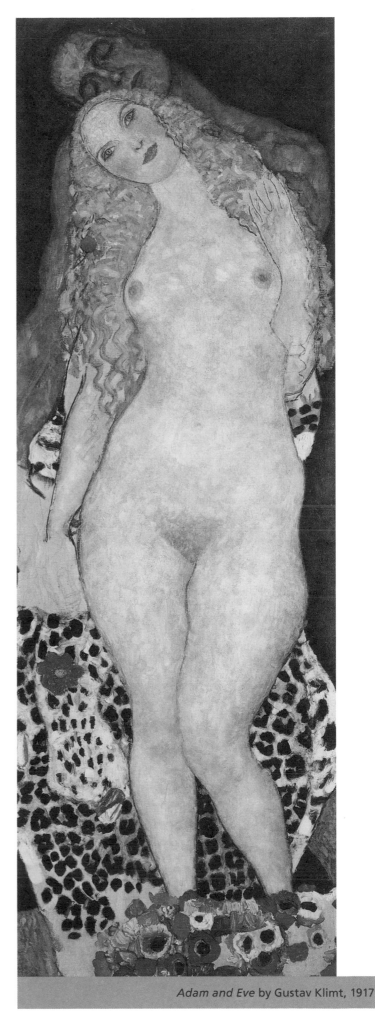

Adam and Eve by Gustav Klimt, 1917

the need for haste as the Hebrews left Egypt (Exod. 12.34, 39; Deut. 16.3; cf. Isa. 52.12). Similarly, the slaughter of the firstborn lamb, originally an offering by pastoralists to the deity thought responsible for their flocks' increase, is linked to the protective mark of the lamb's blood on the doorposts of the Hebrews, which spared them from the last plague.

In a similar way, other laws and institutions that developed later in Israel's history were legitimated by placing their origins in the formative period of the Exodus; the formative period thus became normative. This is one way of understanding the large amount of legal and ritual material found in the books of Exodus, Leviticus, Numbers, and Deuteronomy: set in a narrative context, these laws and religious practices are thereby linked with the central event of the Exodus and with Moses, the mediator of the divinely ordained instructions.

In view of these multiple tendencies, it is impossible to determine with any certainty what may actually have occurred to Hebrews in Egypt, probably during the thirteenth century. Literary analysis of the narratives suggests that what may in fact have been several movements out of Egypt by Semitic peoples have been collapsed into one. But whatever happened, this event was also formative in the sense that ancient Israel saw its origins here. A group of runaway slaves acquired an identity that, against all odds, they have maintained to today. It is understandable, then, that the event would be magnified in song and story, in part to praise the God thought responsible for it. It is also understandable why the Exodus became a dominant theme of later writers, who saw in the events of their times a kind of reenactment of the original Exodus.

Allusions to the Exodus. *Hebrew Bible.* Much of biblical narrative can be seen as shaped by or alluding to the Exodus both by anticipation and in retrospect. Thus, the division of the waters and the appearance of dry land at creation (Gen. 1.6–10) foreshadows the division of the Reed Sea (Exod. 14.21; both passages are P); the allusion to the P account of creation in Exodus 14 is an interpretation of the Exodus itself as a new creation. Likewise, the brief story of Abram (Abraham) and Sarai (Sarah) in Egypt (Gen. 12.10–20) is a proleptic summary of the longer narrative of Israel in Egypt that will be told later in the Pentateuch: the two ancestors go down to Egypt as aliens because of a famine (Gen 12.10; cf. 47.4); subsequently Yahweh afflicts Pharaoh and his house with great plagues (12.17; Exod. 11.1) so that the Egyptian ruler lets them go (12.19; Exod. 12.32).

The linking of Exodus and conquest in biblical poetry (Exod. 15; Ps. 114) is elaborately developed in Joshua 3–4. The Deuteronomic narrative of the crossing of the Jordan River parallels that at the Reed Sea, as the conclusion to the narrative explicitly states (Josh. 4.23).

Biblical literature as a whole is permeated by allusions to the Exodus. The prophet Elijah is described as returning in the darkest moment of his life to the mountain of God, called Horeb in Deuteronomic style, where the theophany experienced by Moses is repeated, but with a difference: Yahweh is not in the wind, the earthquake, or the fire, all manifestations of his presence in Exodus (19.18; 24.17; cf. Deut. 4.12; etc.), but in the "still small voice" (1 Kings 19.12). The prophet Hosea sees hope for Israel's restoration in a return to the wilderness (Hos. 2.14–15), the scene of Israel's honeymoon with its God (see Jer. 2.2). Scholars have also seen echoes of the Exodus in such texts as Jonah and Psalm 23.

The most sustained set of references to the Exodus in the prophets is found in the collection of oracles attributed to Second Isaiah. Writing in the context of the Babylonian captivity in the sixth century BCE, this anonymous prophet foresaw a return of Israel to its land, describing it as a new Exodus (43.2, 19–21; 52.4–5). Yahweh, who had shown his power in the defeat of the primeval sea and at the Sea of Reeds, would act again to bring his people in joy through a wilderness to Zion (51.9–11; 40.3; 41.17–20; 44.3).

Dead Sea Scrolls. The Essene community at Qumran in its sectarian writings continued the interpretive tradition of applying the experience of the Exodus to itself. These self-styled "covenanters" saw themselves as the new Israel, living in camps in the wilderness at the very edge of the promised land, preparing for the ultimate triumph of God after a war of forty years, reliving both Israel's original formative experience and that of the Babylonian exile, in fulfillment of the "new covenant" of Jeremiah 31.31.

New Testament. The appropriation of the Exodus as the model for prior and subsequent events in Israel's history was continued in the New Testament. The life of Jesus is frequently understood in the Gospels as a reenactment of Israel's experience. Luke 9.31 describes Jesus' passion, death, and resurrection as an "exodus" (NRSV: "departure"), the subject of his conversation with Moses and Elijah, both associated with the original Exodus of Israel (see above). Among the quotations from the Old Testament in the gospel of Matthew which the evangelist explicitly describes Jesus as fulfilling, one identifies Jesus as the new Israel, come out of Egypt just as the old Israel had (Matt. 2.15; cf. Hos. 11.1; Exod. 4.22). There are many other allusions to events and figures of Israel's Exodus throughout Matthew's gospel. Jesus is represented as another Moses, rescued at an early age from persecutors (2.21; cf. Exod. 4.19). He gives his teaching in five major discourses like the five books of Moses (the Torah), of which the first is a proclamation of the new law for the new Israel, the Sermon on the Mount, just as Moses had proclaimed the original law at Mount Sinai. Like Israel in the wilderness, Jesus' followers are fed miraculously in a deserted place (Matt. 14.13; 15.33; par.; cf. Exod. 16.4; John 6.31–32). The gospel of John carries this typology further by identifying Jesus with the Passover lamb (1.29; 19.36, quoting Exod. 12.46), an equation made earlier by Paul (1 Cor. 5.7) and later considerably amplified in the book of Revelation (5.6; etc.). Paul also identifies Christ with the rock from which water miraculously flowed in the wilderness (1 Cor. 10.4; cf. Exod. 17.1–7; Num. 20.2–13).

Postbiblical traditions. It is not surprising that a similar correspondence was made between the experience of ancient Israel and the life of the Christian. Baptism is understood as a personal exodus from slavery to sin to a new life of holiness made possible by passage through water; in the Roman liturgy the second reading of the ritual for blessing the baptismal water during the Easter vigil is Exodus 14.24–15.3. Thus, Christians, like Moses (Exod. 34–29–35), behold the "glory of the Lord" unveiled (2 Cor. 3.16–18). Likewise, at death, a traditional prayer asks that God save the soul of the dying person as he once saved Moses from Pharaoh. The Christian Eucharist is directly descended from the Passover service, because the Last Supper of Jesus was itself a Passover meal; the bread (often unleavened) and the wine of the Passover assume a specifically Christian symbolism, but the older Exodus themes are still present (1 Cor. 10.16–18; 11.23–25).

In Islam, the Qur'ān and subsequent traditions echo the biblical account of the Exodus in their description of the Hejira, the flight of Muhammad from Mecca to Medina.

The self–identification with the ancient community of Hebrews has continued into modern times. Various groups experiencing oppression have identified themselves with the Hebrew slaves in Egypt. Throughout the centuries of persecution and attempts at extermination, Jews have seen in the original Exodus a reason for hope: the God who had saved their ancestors would also save them. In the Diaspora, since the Roman destruction of Jerusalem in 70 CE, the longing for a return to the land of Israel has been expressed by the words "Next year in Jerusalem!" at the end of the Passover meal. Exodus symbolism was also adopted by the Zionist movement, especially in the aftermath of World War II and the Holocaust, and continues to be used by Jews seeking to emigrate from oppressive situations.

In the ideology of the Puritans immigrating to the "New World," the Exodus also served as a model and a divine guarantee: once again a divinely chosen group had escaped from oppression across a body of water to a new Canaan, a "providence plantation"; note the many biblical place names used in New England and throughout the United States. This conviction has continued to shape the American self–image, notably in the notion of "manifest destiny": the view that the Americans of the United States are a chosen people is commonplace in American political discourse. Ironically, in the early nineteenth century, after the founding of Liberia, American blacks used the same imagery in their spirituals; the "river" to be crossed was the Atlantic Ocean, but in the opposite direction from the Pilgrims, and Africa became the goal of their journey, the "greener pastures on the other side."

In the latter part of the twentieth century, the Exodus has been paradigmatic for liberation theology, a radical Christian movement of Latin American origin whose goals are political and social reform. Liberation theology has been criticized for its appropriation of the Exodus as sanction for views and actions espoused for other, quite legitimate, reasons. The appeal to biblical authority is highly selective and raises complicated questions: how, for example, can a God who rescues the Hebrews from Egyptian bondage be reconciled with one who immediately thereafter gives explicit commands in which the institution of slavery is not just presumed but condoned? Still, there is no denying the power of the Exodus story as a model for hope and even action to counter oppression.

MICHAEL D. COOGAN

EXODUS, THE BOOK OF. *Wĕʾelleh šĕmôt* begins the book of Exodus "And these are the names." This phrase serves as the Hebrew name for Exodus, and as a convenient linking of its narrative with the preceding narratives in the canon. Indeed, the beginning of the list of the descendants of Israel in Genesis 46.8 employs precisely the same words as does Exodus 1.1, and much as the narrative of Genesis 12–50 is concerned with the promise of Yahweh to Abraham, Isaac, and Jacob of progeny and land, the narrative of the book of Exodus is concerned with various dimensions of the fulfillment of that promise.

Contents. Most of the book of Exodus is prose, as straightforward narrative, as lists of laws in apodictic (universal) or casuistic (specific case) form, or as instructions related in one way or another to worship. One important section is poetry (15.1b–18, 21), and there is one three-line poetic stanza at 32.18.

The subject matter of the book of Exodus is far more disparate in content than in form. There are narratives about Moses alongside narratives of Israel's oppression and narratives of the intransigence of the Pharaoh of Egypt alongside narratives

of rescue and provision by Yahweh. There are instructions appropriate to an agricultural setting alongside instructions appropriate to an urban life. There are dramatic accounts of the coming and appearance of Yahweh alongside the most elaborate descriptions of the objects designed to suggest and memorialize Yahweh's nearness. There are stories intended to prove that Yahweh is present alongside stories of Israel's fear of both his presence and his absence. And there are reports of the authentication of Yahweh's representative alongside the instructions for the ordination and the specifications of the vestments designed to symbolize that authority.

All these quite different sequences are set into a loose geographical and chronological framework. For roughly the first third of the book of Exodus, the setting is Egypt (1.1–13.16). For the next five chapters, the setting is the wilderness en route to Sinai (13.17–18.27). And for just over the second half of the book, as also for Leviticus and nearly the first third of Numbers (through Num. 10.11), the setting is the plain before Mount Sinai (19.1–40.38). The chronological sequence of the book extends from the rise of a new dynasty in Egypt some time after Joseph's death to the birth of Moses in the context of a bitter oppression of Israel, through Moses' growth to maturity, his flight to Midian, his call there and his return to Egypt to lead Israel, through the sequence of the mighty acts demonstrating Yahweh's presence with his people, through the event of the Exodus and Israel's deliverance at the sea to the subsequent journey in the wilderness to Sinai. There, after an appropriate preparation, Israel experienced the advent of Yahweh, received the revelation of the "ten words" (Exod. 34.28) and the gift of covenant relationship. The remainder of the sequence of Exodus, involving special instructions for the apparatus and personnel of worship, the rebellion involving the golden calf, Yahweh's punishment and mercy, the renewal of the covenant relationship, and the execution of the special instructions all occurs within what is represented as a brief period of time.

Unfortunately, there is no way to locate this admittedly loose chronological sequence with any precision, either in an Egyptian setting or in a wilderness setting. A wide variety of dates has been suggested, from the first half of the fifteenth century BCE to the early part of the thirteenth century BCE.

Literary Structure. From the beginning of critical inquiry into the Bible, the disparity of the various sections of the book of Exodus has been noted, and during the latter third of the nineteenth century and the first third of the twentieth, this disparity was generally attributed to the differences in vocabulary, style, and interest of the Pentateuchal or, more recently, Tetrateuchal sources. The Yahwistic (J) and Elohistic (E) sources were regarded as present, usually in a kind of foundational amalgam onto which the Priestly (P) material had been grafted or attached as extended addenda here and there. In commentaries published in the sixty years following 1875, the assignment of verses and verse fragments to these "documentary" sources was made with both assurance and precision. This procedure sometimes led, however, to an absurd fragmentation of the text of Exodus, so much so that the source hypothesis came to be put forward with more caution, and eventually to be emphasized or deemphasized according to the format of a given commentary series and the interests of individual authors.

Attention to the motifs underlying these sources has led to a larger view of the book of Exodus, both as a part of a continuing narrative and also as a whole within itself. Exodus continues a narrative begun by Genesis and provides the foundation for another continued by Numbers and Deuter-

An artistic interpretation of the Exodus from Egypt (Exod. 15) by Richard Mcbee.

onomy. Indeed, Exodus is a foundation for the entire Bible, for it sets forth a kind of first presentation of the themes of coming and presence, relationship and responsibility, which are so much a part of the biblical message.

The literary structure of the book of Exodus is certainly composite, whether by that one means the joining of traditions, the weaving of sources, or the exposition of themes. There is, however, an important sense in which Exodus is in itself a whole, one that needs to be taken seriously. Whatever may lie behind the book, in a literary history that can only be speculated, the canonical text of Exodus presents a whole that cannot be denied, whether or not it can be understood. On a first reading, that whole may appear somewhat more disjointed than it really is, in part because of the prejudice of years of thinking of the book of Exodus in pieces. A closer reading reveals a literary structure that is not only deliberate but also quite effective in organization.

Composition and Compilation. The composition of the book of Exodus took place over a long period of time. That much is established by the patchwork nature of the book's literary structure. Yet just how long that period of time may have been, or just when it may have begun, can only be speculated. No assignment of any part of the book of Exodus to a definite author can be made; many minds are evident in the forty chapters that comprise the book.

Tradition has ascribed Exodus, along with the other four of the first five books of the Bible, to Moses, both because of his significant role as Yahweh's representative and also on the basis of such references as Deuteronomy 1.1; 2 Kings 14.6; Ezra 6.18; 2 Chronicles 25.4; and Mark 12.26. This tradition and such references were probably never intended to suggest a Mosaic authorship, but rather to establish a Mosaic authority, a kind of guarantee of an ancient and accurate record. From the earliest history of the Bible, the book of Exodus has been recognized as a collage of sometimes conflicting and often very different traditions. Also from an early period, both Jewish (Philo, Josephus, the Talmud) and Christian literature

have connected Moses with the Pentateuch, and for appropriate reasons. The historicity of Moses is the most reasonable assumption to be made about him. There is no viable argument why Moses should be regarded as a fiction of pious necessity. His removal from the scene of Israel's beginnings as a theocratic community would leave a vacuum that simply could not be explained away. Moses may be connected with the earliest substratum of the book of Exodus, specifically with the accounts of call and theophany and perhaps also with the Ten Commandments. What cannot be said, of course, is that there are, anywhere in Exodus or in the Bible, words that can be said certainly to be Moses' own.

What may be proposed in theoretical reconstruction of the composition of the book of Exodus is a substratum of narrative, cultic instruction, covenant formulary, hymnody, authorization sequences, etiological legends, and wilderness routes, gathered across the years from the time of the Exodus itself until at least the postexilic period of Israel's history. Through that period of approximately seven centuries, the book of Exodus was being composed and, in a sense, recomposed, as the gathering strata that comprise the canonical book were created, then joined, often in new arrangement. It is through these centuries that the process of composition became a process of compilation, and the canonical book is the product of this latter process.

The compilation of Exodus was by no means the haphazard arbitrary shuffle frequently implied by literary-critical essayists and commentators. Too much attention is given to the book of Exodus that might have been, and not enough to the book that is. The discontinuity and disparity in content, style, vocabulary, and organization are the result of an inevitable variation in source material, along with the growth of the book to its present form across a lengthy period of time. By no means are they the sign of careless or ignorant editorial work. Indeed, given this inevitable variation, the book of Exodus displays a remarkable unity of purpose and wholeness of organization.

The material often regarded as intrusive and even disruptive of the sequence of Exodus, such as the "Book of the Covenant" (20.22–23.33), and the two Priestly sections dealing with the media of Israel's worship (25.1–31.18 and 35.1–40.38), may be seen as deliberately placed pieces of a whole concept. The "Book of the Covenant" functions not as a displaced collection of loosely assembled laws, but as a practical and specific application of the principles of relationship set forth in the Ten Commandments. And the section on the symbols and acts and ministers of worship in Yahweh's presence are logically located, even in a narrative sequence that they disrupt. The revelation of the instructions for the creation of the media of such worship is placed immediately after the long composite narrative describing the promise of Yahweh's presence, the demonstration of Yahweh's presence, and the advent of Yahweh's presence, brought to a climax by the establishment of the covenant between Yahweh and Israel. The report of the fulfillment of those instructions is appropriately placed after the narratives describing the breaking of the covenant relationship, the consequent judgment upon Israel, the return of Yahweh's presence, and the renewal of the covenant commitment. The places of worship and their furnishings are not to be constructed until the relationship between Yahweh and Israel has been reestablished, and only when all the work of building has been determined to be in exact accord with Yahweh's direction does his presence settle upon the tabernacle (Exod. 39.42–43; 40.34).

An even more dramatic example of the literary and thematic unity of Exodus as a compilation is provided by Exodus 18, a chapter often considered dislocated in the narrative sequence of the book because it describes events that occur in the camp at the foot of Sinai/Horeb before Israel is said to have reached there and because it is concerned with the administration of Yahweh's requirements before they have actually been given. These inconsistencies of narrative sequence cannot, of course, have gone unnoticed by the compilers of the book of Exodus, so some other reason must be sought for the location of Exodus 18 where it now stands in the received text instead of after chap. 24 or even after chap. 34—a reason that sets aside the advantages of logical or chronological sequence. That reason is to be found in a thematic consideration: the reunion of Moses with his Midianite family, specifically Jethro, particularly in company with his people Israel freed from bondage in Egypt, amounts to an important reuniting of the two parts of a family divided by the expulsion of Cain (Gen. 4.10–16), by Abraham's sending forth of Keturah's sons (Gen. 25.1–6) and his disinheriting of Hagar and Ishmael (Gen. 21.8–21), and by the conflict between Jacob and Esau (Gen. 25.19–34; 27.1–45; 28.6–9; 32.36; 33.1–20). The redactors who compiled the book of Exodus were eager to have a reunited family of Israel before the great theophany and covenant–making at Sinai, and so they set what is now Exodus 18 where they did, ignoring other considerations.

Theology. What makes the book of Exodus as it stands a carefully organized whole is neither literary form nor authorship, neither historical sequence nor uniformity of content. Exodus is bound together by a theological intention: the presentation by narrative, by didactic device, by song, by dialogue, by legal specification, by liturgical arrangement, by a round of festival and solemn ceremony, by high drama, by symbol, by a witty and very direct picture of human nature, and by a soaring depiction of the majesty and the mystery of God, of theological memes that are foundational to the Bible and to Judaism and Christianity, as well as to Islam.

The most important of these theological themes is the repeated assertion that Yahweh is present in the ongoing daily life of Israel, his people of promise and covenant. This theme functions as a kind of center from and to which other themes are connected, as spokes to a hub. Yahweh, who made promises to Abraham, Isaac, and Jacob, is present and hence those promises are being kept; with the development of that assertion, the book of Exodus is begun. Yahweh, to be present with his people, must come to them, must bring them to himself; thus, there are in Exodus the narratives of his advent, in chaps. 3 and 4, 19 and 20, 24, 33 and 34, and 40. Yahweh must be known to be present, by his people and by those who would oppose them alike: therefore a proof-of-the-presence sequence, dramatically moved forward by Pharaoh's recalcitrance, increasing in seriousness and brought to a climax in the deliverance at the sea, is provided.

If Yahweh is present, his people will be cared for; so there are accounts of guidance through a great and terrible wilderness, and stories of the provision of water and foodstuff in the form of the manna and the quails. Because Yahweh is present, the enemies of his people must be bested; as a result, the Egyptian learned men are in due course frustrated, the Egyptians are humbled and despoiled, Pharaoh himself is defeated, and Amalek is vanquished at Rephidim. Since Yahweh is present, his people should know that presence in a unique manner; hence, he prepares them and comes to them at Sinai/Horeb, having given them already through Moses his unique and descriptive name, a name suggesting his very nature as the "one who really is." The presence of Yahweh realized can only mean a response of some kind; thus, Yahweh gives his guidance for life in his presence, in the Ten Commandments, and opens himself to his people in covenant with them. The direction of life in Yahweh's presence involves a concrete application of the broad principles of life in relationship with him;

The Youth of Moses, a fresco in the Sistine Chapel (Exod. 2.11–3.12) (Sandro Botticelli, 1481)

therefore the Ten Commandments are applied by a rambling collection of specific case provisions.

The living memory of Yahweh's proof of his presence to Israel is essential for the generations to come; thus, provision is made for the seasonal reenactment of event, in the ritual testimony of the requirement of the firstborn, the feast of unleavened bread, the feast of the Passover, and perhaps even a covenant–renewal festival (see Exod. 19.4–6 and 24.3–8). A constant reminder of Yahweh present among his people is also important; hence, the lengthy and detailed chapters on the media of worship, media that symbolize the circles of nearness to Yahweh's presence in the tabernacle of Israel's devotional life, moving from the primary symbol of Yahweh's presence, the Ark in the holiest space, to the altar of wholly consumed offerings in the circle of the outer court, the area of preparation for entry into Yahweh's presence in worship. The instructions for the creation of the media of worship (Exod. 25–31) are ended with the specification of the Sabbath as a sign in perpetuity of relationship with Yahweh present. The narrative of the fulfillment of those instructions (Exod. 35–40) is begun with this emphasis on the Sabbath and ended with an account of the settling of Yahweh's presence onto the place of worship erected in their midst. Thus, the theology of Yahweh present is asserted in the book of Exodus as a presence incarnate in both the worship and the life of Israel.

Appropriately, the extended sequence of symbol is interrupted, between instruction and fulfillment of instruction, by a narrative of disobedience and forgiveness that affords a context for still other motifs of the theology of coming and nearness. Israel's sin of the golden calf is a fundamental violation of the covenant relationship, involving disobedience to at least the first two of the Ten Commandments. As a result, Israel falls under the threat of the cancellation of the gift of Yahweh's presence, in effect a negation of the remainder of the book of Exodus. In a narrative filled with tension, Israel is judged and forgiven, and Moses witnesses a unique revelation, by Yahweh, of his own nature and atti-

tude (Exod. 34.6–7), a revelation that extends the earlier revelation of his unique name, at the time of Moses' call. It is a sequence that provides a setting for two additional symbols of Yahweh's nearness, the tent of promised presence (Exod. 33.7–11) and the shining face of Moses (Exod. 34.29–35).

In the book of Exodus, one is brought to the thematic beginning of the Bible. For in Exodus, the biblical story and its major themes are presented, in narrative, in symbol, in expectation, or in promise. The book that begins "And these are the names" ends with a declaration that the cloud of Yahweh's presence, filling the tabernacle, provided for all Israel a vision of Yahweh's nearness to them by day and by night. And there, given all that lies between that beginning and that ending, one is in the middle of a story that is unfolding still.

JOHN I DURHAM

EZEKIEL, THE BOOK OF.

Author. The book of Ezekiel tells relatively little that is explicit concerning the figure for whom it is named, and apart from brief references in Sirach (49.8–9) and 4 Maccabees (18.17) he is not mentioned by name elsewhere in the Bible. Ezekiel, whose name means "God strengthens," was of priestly lineage, son of Buzi (1.3). Along with other Judeans, he suffered deportation to Babylon following the surrender of Jehoiachin in 598/597 BCE (1.1; cf. 2 Kings 24.12–16). Ezekiel received his prophetic calling in Babylon in 593 (1.1); his age at the time is not recorded. It is disputed whether some or even all of Ezekiel's ministry actually took place in Jerusalem rather than in Babylonia, as various of his words could suggest. According to the book's dates, he continued to receive divine communications until at least 571 (29.17). Nothing is mentioned in the Bible concerning the circumstances of his death; much later tradition states that he was murdered by one of the leaders of the exiles whose idolatry he had denounced, and that he was buried near Babylon.

Unlike his near contemporary Jeremiah, Ezekiel appears as an outwardly stoical, highly self-controlled and some-

Moses and Aaron before the Pharaoh (Exod. 12.31)

what passive personality, who, for example, follows without demur Yahweh's directive not to mourn the death of his beloved wife (24.15–18). On occasion, however, he does venture a protest or appeal in the face of what is communicated to him (4.14; 9.8; 11.13). It is likewise clear that Ezekiel's call to herald Judah's doom caused him profound distress (3.14–15). The response to Ezekiel's message seems to have been much less overtly hostile than was true in the case of Jeremiah. In fact, there are several references to his being respectfully consulted by the leaders of the exiles (8.1; 14.1; 20.1). Finally, the content of Ezekiel's book reveals him as a man of wide learning.

Arrangement/Divisions. The individual units of Ezekiel's material have been arranged in their present sequence on the basis of considerations of chronology and content. First of all, more so than with any other prophetic book, there seems to have been a concern with giving the dated texts of Ezekiel—there are some fifteen of these—in their correct chronological order; only twice does a deviation occur (29.1; 29.17). The materials, however, are grouped by content into three large-scale segments. Words of doom against Judah/Jerusalem are concentrated at the beginning of the book (chaps. 1–24); oracles against various foreign nations follow (chaps. 25–32); and texts concerning the eventual restoration of Yahweh's people predominate in the concluding segment (chaps. 33–48). The intention behind this sequencing (which can be seen also in the book of Zephaniah, Isaiah 1–35, and the Septuagint text of Jeremiah) is for the book to culminate on an upbeat note. This principle of arrangement, however, is not followed with complete consistency; chaps. 1–24 contain promises of salvation (e.g., 17.22–24), while an oracle against Edom (chap. 35) stands with the concluding segment (chaps. 33–48).

Within each of these three major divisions, one may readily identify various distinct blocks of material. Within chaps. 1–24, the vision sequences of 1.1–3.27 and 8.11–11.25 stand out. In chaps. 25–32, brief oracles against Judah's near neighbors (chap. 25) are followed by extensive discourses of doom concerning Tyre (chaps. 26–28) and Egypt (chaps. 29–32). The final segment, chaps. 33–48, comprises a series of generalized promises of Jewish revival (chaps. 34–37) and a detailed blueprint for the reconstruction of the cult (chaps. 40–48), with chap. 33 serving as transition from what precedes and the Gog oracles (chaps. 38–39) as a kind of interlude.

Literary Features. As a piece of writing, the book of Ezekiel presents a variety of noteworthy peculiarities, four of which are singled out here. First, certain fixed expressions, which are either unique to Ezekiel or especially favored by him in the Bible as a whole, recur repeatedly, thereby unifying the book terminologically. Examples include "son of man" (NRSV: "mortal") as a title/address for the prophet (roughly one hundred occurrences: 2.1; etc.); "rebellious house" (twelve times: 2.5; etc.); "to execute judgments on" (nine times: 5.10; etc.); "set your face toward/against" (nine times: 6.2; etc.); "and they/you shall know that I am the Lord" (about fifty times: 6.7; etc.); "to bear disgrace" (eleven times: 16.52; etc.). Second, in articulating its message, the book makes use of a rich variety of literary forms: vision accounts (e.g., 37.1–14), sign narratives (e.g., 12.1–11), allegories (e.g., 17.1–24), laments (e.g., 27.1–36), judgment speeches (e.g., 13.1–23), salvation oracles (e.g., 36.37–38), disputations (e.g., 33.10–20), legal prescriptions (e.g., 44.15–31). Frequently, too, Ezekiel's literary forms are complex entities, incorporating into themselves a number of subgenres; see, for example, chap. 17, an allegory that contains both a judgment

Michelangelo's *The Prophet Ezekiel* from the Sistine Chapel

speech (17.15–21) and a salvation oracle (17.22–24). Third, Ezekiel's style evidences a consistent tendency toward prolixity and a graphic excess in the handling of traditional imagery; see, for example, his treatment of the conjugal metaphor for Israel's relation to Yahweh in chaps. 16, 20, and 23. Last, in its heavy use of metaphorical language and avoidance of proper names for contemporary figures (curiously, "Ezekiel" occurs only twice: 1.1; 24.24), the book makes a somewhat disembodied impression. Accordingly, it is not surprising that both the locality of the prophet's ministry and the date of the book's composition—it has been dated variously from the age of Manasseh in the mid–seventh century BCE to the Hellenistic period—have long been controverted.

Theology. Ezekiel's God is above all a "holy" being (36.23), that is, one who utterly transcends human comprehension, manipulation, and calculation. This quality of Yahweh finds manifold expression throughout the book. Ezekiel refrains from any direct claims to have seen the deity (see 1.26–28; cf. Isa. 6.1). Yahweh remains free to rebuff human inquiries (14.3; 20.3); he can void the schemes of practitioners of magic (13.20–23). The movements and fates of the great world powers, such as Babylon (29.20) and Gog (38.23), are just as much under his control as is the destiny of Israel itself. Yahweh has the capacity to manifest himself outside the land of Israel (1.1); he is able to withdraw his presence from the Temple (11.23), and later to return there as he wills (43.1–4). He acts, unconstrained by any human claim, for his own purposes (36.22).

At the same time, however, the holy Yahweh is also a God who has freely but passionately and irrevocably committed himself to the people of Israel. Like Hosea and Jeremiah, Ezekiel develops this dimension of Yahweh's being and activity by using conjugal imagery (chaps. 16; 20; 23). Yahweh carefully and tenderly nourished the cast–off child

Israel as his future bride (16.3–14). At present, he is punishing her for her persistent infidelities, but ultimately he will not abandon his spouse to her misery and sinfulness. Rather, he will restore her prosperity and give her the inner capacity to live in faithfulness to him (see, e.g., 36.26–30). In all of this, the transcendent God is intimately and continuously involved in human history, to the end that, finally, both Israel and the nations will know him as the sole, truly efficacious deity (39.22–23, 28).

Anthropology. Ezekiel's anthropology is characterized by an underlying unresolved tension. On the one hand, he is the Hebrew Bible's great advocate of individual responsibility (18.1–32). Ezekiel is likewise commissioned precisely in order to summon his hearers to conscious decision about their behavior options (3.16–21; 33.7–16). On the other hand, however, Ezekiel's words disclose an overwhelming pessimism concerning the people's capacity ever to choose rightly. For him, unlike Hosea (3.15) and Jeremiah (2.2–3), there never was a honeymoon period in Israel's relation to Yahweh. Already during her time in Egypt (16.26; 20.8), as well as ever since, Israel has consistently chosen other gods in preference to Yahweh. Judah learned nothing from Yahweh's punishment of the northern kingdom, only redoubling her own idolatry in the face of that experience (23.11). Although Ezekiel's hearers may not actively persecute him, neither do they give much attention to his warnings (12.26; 20.49; 33.20–33). Such circumstances suggest that the exhortations Ezekiel is sent to deliver are futile (2.7); what is needed, rather, is a direct intervention by Yahweh that will produce a transformed, obedient heart in his people (11.18–19; 36.26–27). Ultimately, like so many theologians after him, Ezekiel is left affirming both realities, human freedom and divine grace, without being fully able to account for their interplay.

Biblical Affinities. The book of Ezekiel manifests significant links with a wide range of other biblical traditions. Ezekiel is familiar with the creation myths incorporated into the primeval history of Genesis (29.16; 31.8–9; 36.35). From the historical traditions of Israel, he cites the figures of Abraham (33.24), Jacob (37.25), and David (34.23; 37.24). In common with Deuteronomic tradition, he emphasizes the centrality of the Law, its observance, and especially its nonobservance, in the unfolding of the Yahweh-Israel relationship. His affinities with the Priestly (P) material of the Pentateuch, above all the "Holiness Code" (Lev. 17–26), both in content and phraseology, are especially marked; compare, for example, Ezekiel 44.22 with Leviticus 21.7, 13–15, and Ezekiel 44.25–27 with Leviticus 21.1–3. Similarly, Ezekiel displays many similarities with the teachings of the contemporary prophetic figures Jeremiah and Second Isaiah, including marital imagery, hopes for an inner transformation of the people, renewal of their covenant with Yahweh, and recognition by the nations of Yahweh's sole deity. The elaborateness of the accounts of his vision and the cosmic terms in which he describes God's interventions against the enemies of his people (32.7–8; 38.19–22) anticipate later apocalyptic writing.

The book of Ezekiel is cited directly in the New Testament only rarely; see, for example, 2 Corinthians 6.16 = Ezekiel 37.27. On the other hand, its imagery often provides a point of departure for presentations of various New Testament authors, such as the allusions to Ezekiel 34 in Jesus' contrasting of himself as good shepherd with the Jewish leadership (John 10), and the use in Revelation 22.1–2 of Ezekiel 47.1–12, which describes elements of the vision of water from the temple. Thus, the book of Ezekiel, which itself brings together so many earlier streams of tradition,

came to serve as a source of still more comprehensive literary and theological developments in early Christian writing.

CHRISTOPHER T. BEGG

EZRA, THE BOOK OF. At an early stage, the books of Ezra and Nehemiah were regarded as a unity. From the time of Origen (third century CE), they were divided as we have them today.

Historical Background. Ezra 1–6 describes the return of the Jews to Jerusalem under Sheshbazzar (539 BCE) and the initial attempts to rebuild the Temple; their efforts, however, were frustrated by their enemies. Later, Zerubbabel, influenced by the prophets Haggai and Zechariah, resumed the building of the Temple with the permission of the Persian king, Darius. The Temple was completed in 515 BCE.

Ezra 7–10 describes a much later situation and tells of the return of Ezra and a certain group of Jews to Judah in the time of the Persian king Artaxerxes (presumably Artaxerxes I, 465–424 BCE). According to Ezra 7.7, this happened in the seventh year of Artaxerxes (458 BCE). However, in view of disturbed conditions early in his reign, scholars have found this reference to royal permission for the return exceedingly difficult to accept. Another problem arises with the memoir of Nehemiah, in which Ezra and his important religious activities are totally ignored. It is certainly difficult to explain why Ezra and Nehemiah, if they were contemporaries, would avoid mention of each other almost completely in their memoirs. Scholars have proposed various solutions to this problem. Some have pointed out that with only a slight emendation in Ezra 7.7, where "thirty" may have fallen out as a result of haplography, one can read the "thirty-seventh" year of Artaxerxes I. Thus, Ezra would have accompanied Nehemiah on his second visit to Jerusalem about 428 BCE; this solves some of the problems created by the traditional date of 458 BCE. Other scholars, assuming that the activities of Ezra and Nehemiah must be totally separated, have held that "in the seventh year of Artaxerxes" refers to Artaxerxes II (404–359/358 BCE), which brings us to 398 BCE. However, the traditional view, that Ezra arrived in 458 BCE, is still held by a number of modern scholars. In such a case, it is likely that Ezra's initial visit to Jerusalem was only a few months long. It is possible that he later returned to Jerusalem, but particulars about this are vague. Thus, it appears that the book of Ezra describes the history of certain Jews from 539 to 516 BCE and for a short period in 458 BCE.

This description, however, presents several problems: either the author assumed too much knowledge of certain events on the part of readers, or he himself was uncertain how events developed. One problem involves the role played by Sheshbazzar during the initial return, and his relationship to Zerubbabel. At a certain stage, Sheshbazzar completely vanishes from the sources; what happened to him? No satisfactory reply can be given, and some scholars identify him with Zerubbabel. But the root of this problem lies in the nature of the author's concerns. He is interested not in giving a full account of the life and acts of individuals but in the role that God played in Jewish history, namely, in allowing the people to return to Judah where they rebuilt the Temple. Another problem involves Zerubbabel: like Sheshbazzar, he simply vanishes from the sources. Yet, that he and the high priest Jeshua were active in the second attempt to rebuild the Temple is testified also by the books of Haggai and Zechariah (in both of which Jeshua is called Joshua); Zerubbabel was instrumental in obtaining permission from Darius to continue building, but in the description of the inauguration of the Temple, no mention is made of Zerubbabel. Since the sources imply that at a certain stage Zerubbabel may have been tempted to regard himself as a messiah-king, some assume that he was forcefully removed by the Persians. Yet another problem involves the return of the exiles. Did a large number return with Sheshbazzar, or did various groups return on different occasions? Is the list in Ezra 2 (cf. Neh. 7) representative of one such group of those returning, or is it a list of several groups over a long period? Although there are indications that the list is made up from several groups, one cannot be certain.

It is clear from chaps. 7–10 that Ezra was dispatched by the Persian king Artaxerxes to Jerusalem to establish the Israelite law (Torah) among the Jews. A number of exiles returned with Ezra, a kind of ideal group consisting of, among others, priests and Levites. To his dismay, Ezra discovered that there had been intermarriage with the neighboring nations, and he ordered all foreign wives to be repudiated, so as to keep the religion of Jews pure of contamination by the worship of different gods.

From a historical perspective, the book of Ezra starts with the hegemony of a new imperial force in the ancient Near East, namely the domination of the Persians under Cyrus. The Persians' tolerance in religious matters is well known. The book of Ezra begins with Cyrus's decree allowing the Jews to restore their sanctuary in order to serve their God according to their prescribed laws. After Cyrus, there is a lapse of time until the description of the chaotic circumstances that took place just before Darius I assumed full control. It was at this stage that Zerubbabel and his compatriots started in earnest to rebuild the Temple. When Darius had gained firm control in 520–519 BCE, he granted the Jews the right, according to Cyrus's decree, to continue their building activities. This culminates in the dedication of the Temple in 515 BCE.

In 458 BCE, Artaxerxes I gave permission to Ezra and certain Jews to return to Judah; this was not without political motives, for in 460 BCE a revolt had broken out in Egypt under Inarus against the Persians. Pericles, the Athenian leader who had first decided to attack Cyprus, changed his plans and assisted the Egyptians against the Persians. In 460 and 459 BCE the rebels, with the aid of the Athenians, succeeded against the Persians. The latter kept only a small strip of land under their control, but they bribed the Spartans to start a war against the Athenians. In 458, the Persian general and satrap, Megabyzus, was fighting a successful war against the Egyptians, who were subdued in 456 BCE. It was thus expedient for Artaxerxes to send Ezra out in all goodwill to the Jews so that Judah, so close to the border of Egypt, could be pacified.

Author, Composition, and Sources. The authorship of the book is difficult to determine. No doubt various persons worked on it during its long history of transmission before it reached its present form. Most scholars accept that the Chronicler is responsible for the final form of the book of Ezra, for the history of Israel is not concluded at the end of 2 Chronicles (36.22–23), but continues into Ezra 1. The Chronicler is thus, from this viewpoint, responsible for editing Ezra and the commentary on the sources that he incorporated into the book.

Other scholars have held that Ezra was written and edited by an author quite different from the Chronicler, one who held a different ideology. It is true that the book of Ezra expresses some religious ideas not shared by the Chronicler. One's assessment, however, depends on how thoroughly the Chronicler edited his materials. It is probable that he did not radically change the view represented in his sources, and that this explains the differences. Although we cannot be certain, it seems likely that in the fourth century BCE the book of Ezra was edited by a later Chronicler.

In any case, it is obvious that the author of the book of Ezra used various sources and put them in chronological order. In Ezra 1–6, various documents are quoted or summarized in the final author's own words. Some of these documents are of Persian origin. Until recently, most scholars rejected the authenticity of these Persian documents, because, it was thought, no Persian king would be interested in finer details of the Jews' religious activities. However, extrabiblical texts have been discovered that show the special interest of Persian authorities in their subjects' religious activities; the edict of Cambyses on the sanctuary of Neith in Egypt and the Passover papyrus from Elephantine in Egypt are two examples. Like the Elephantine papyri, some of the official documents in Ezra are written in Imperial Aramaic with a number of Persian loanwords. Imperial Aramaic was at that stage the chancellery language of the Persian empire. The greatest majority of Persian loanwords occur in these documents and must be regarded as a further proof of the documents' authenticity. The use of Aramaic in Ezra is not restricted to these documents, however; Ezra 4.8–6.18 and 7.12–26 are in Aramaic, providing further evidence of the book's complicated literary history.

An important source in Ezra 7–10 is the Ezra memoir, written in the first person with some parts in the third person. It is probable that we have here an actual memoir used by the Chronicler. In the sections using the first person, the Chronicler has quoted from the memoir, and in those parts using the third person he has rendered it in his own words. Scholars have pointed out that the language and style of the first-person and third-person sections are similar, and that both are in the common language of the postexilic period.

We may conclude that the book of Ezra was compiled in its present form by the later Chronicler in the fourth century BCE. All indications are that the sources used for this compilation were carefully selected and edited.

Theology. In the book of Ezra, typical religious conceptions of the postexilic period predominate. The Chronicler has not changed conceptions of Ezra to agree with his own, and this is why certain differences between the conceptions of the Chronicler and Ezra can be discerned. In the first place, the role of Yahweh as the God of history is emphasized. This is a common characteristic of Jewish thought in postexilic times. Yahweh is God not only of the Jews, but also of the whole world. He can move the heart of a mighty Persian king in favor of his own people (Ezra 9.8–9). Also, the book of Ezra clearly displays a sense of guilt for sins committed in the past by Israel. In Ezra 9.6, the Israelites' sins and guilt are represented as mounting higher than their heads and even as reaching up to heaven. This view is not present in the work of the Chronicler, but it is discernible in the work of the Deuteronomic school. Finally, heavy emphasis is laid on the observance of the law of God. The recording of legal stipulations started before the exile, but it was a continuous process that lasted into the time of Ezra and even later. The law was used by Ezra as a new platform to discipline the Jewish people and give them something tangible to cling to in times of distress.

F. CHARLES FENSHAM

FAITH. In the Hebrew Bible, forms of the noun *'ĕmûnâ* or the verb *'mn* are usually translated as "faith" or "having faith/believing." Such faith can be expressed toward God (Jon. 3.5), toward a human being (Exod. 4.1–9), or toward both: "So the people feared the Lord and believed in the Lord and in his servant Moses" (Exod. 14.31). The terms are also used to express adherence to an idea or a set of principles, "I believe in your commandments" (Ps. 119.66).

There are other ways of expressing this kind of regard for or confidence in someone or something. In fact, forms of the verb *btḥ* are much more frequent in the Hebrew Bible but are usually translated "to trust" rather than "to have faith/believe." This difference can be explained on the basis of semantic development, but there are some instances where the meanings are very close. "He [Hezekiah] trusted in the Lord, the God of Israel" (2 Kings 18.5).

One of the best-known instances of faith in the Bible concerns Abram (Abraham), who asks how God would make of

Abraham, Sarah, and an Angel (Gen 18.9–15)

him a great nation when he was old and his wife was sterile. The Lord asserts that Abraham will indeed have offspring that will be as numerous as the stars in the sky. In response to this promise and against all tangible evidence, Abram has faith in God and is considered to be a righteous person (Gen. 15.6; NJV: "he put his trust in the Lord").

Abram's willingness to trust God in this and other situations makes him a primary example of the biblical concept of faith. His willingness to believe and to obey God is the fulfillment of the covenant that God had made with him. Throughout the Hebrew Bible, Abraham's descendants struggle with the issue of how to continue as a faithful people. The Psalms rejoice in the faithfulness of God (Pss. 31.5; 111.7) but lament the lack of faith shown by the people (Ps. 78.8). Isaiah warns the people, "If you do not stand firm in faith you shall not stand at all" (Isa. 7.8), and Habakkuk states that "the righteous live by their faith" (2.4).

The Greek translation of the Hebrew Bible, the Septuagint, usually translates the *'mn* family of words with a form of the Greek word *pisteuein*, "to trust" or "to believe/have faith." This same family of words is used frequently in the New Testament. The author of the letter to the Hebrews defines faith as "the assurance of things hoped for, the conviction of things not seen" (11.1) and then goes on to list the great deeds that the people of Israel had accomplished "by faith" (11.4–40).

Paul also makes use of images of faith from the Bible, especially the faith of Abraham. In the process of justifying the mission to the gentiles, Paul argues that Abraham was said to be righteous by having faith in God before he was circumcised and therefore is the father of the gentiles who believe, as well as of the Jews (Rom. 4; Gal. 3).

The actual content of faith—what is believed—is described in different ways in Paul's letters. In Romans, righteousness will be credited to those who have faith in God who raised Jesus (Rom. 4.24) and those who believe in their hearts that God raised Jesus from the dead will be saved (Rom. 10.9). Elsewhere Paul refers to believing "in Christ Jesus" (Gal. 2.16), but it can be argued that this is an abbreviation for "faith in God who raised Jesus."

Several times Paul refers to faith with a grammatical construction that can be interpreted either as "faith in Christ" or "faith of Christ" (Gal. 2.16, 20; 3.22; Rom. 3.22, 26; Phil. 3.9). Scholarly debate centers on whether Jesus is referred to in the first sense as the object of faith or in the second as an example of faith. The NRSV translation includes footnotes that offer the latter reading as an alternative. It has also been suggested that Paul is being intentionally ambiguous with the construction, leaving both possibilities open. In this case it is interesting to note that later documents tend to specify "faith in Christ," eliminating the possibility for ambiguity (e.g., 1 Tim. 3.13; Acts 20.21).

The Fall of Man and Expulsion from the Garden of Eden, from the Sistine Chapel (Gen. 3)

In the synoptic Gospels faith is the operative factor in many of Jesus' miracles. Jesus is impressed by the faith of the centurion and so heals his son (Matt. 8.5–13 par.). Jesus marvels at the faith of those who brought the paralytic man (Matt. 9.1–8 par.) and tells the woman with a hemorrhage that her faith has made her well (Matt. 9.20–22 par.). When Jesus tells the father of a demon-possessed boy that "all things are possible to the one who believes/has faith," the man responds "I believe; help my unbelief" (Mark 9.23–24).

John's gospel emphasizes having faith (always in the verbal form) throughout and states its purpose as leading people to believe that Jesus is the Messiah, the Son of God (John 20.31).

"The faith" as a descriptive term for Christianity is found most clearly in Acts and the Deutero-Pauline material (e.g., Acts 6.7; 1 Tim. 4.1).

DANIEL N. SCHOWALTER

FALL, THE. The Fall refers to the disobedience and the expulsion of Adam and Eve from the garden of Eden. According to the J account of creation (Gen. 2–3), humanity—represented by Adam and Eve—initially enjoyed a life of ease and intimacy with God, but their desire to become "like gods" (Gen 3.5) led them to disobey God's prohibition against eating from the tree of knowledge. They were punished with expulsion from paradise and condemned to a life of suffering that was passed on to their descendants.

The biblical myth of the Fall is similar to other legends that contrast humanity's present state of suffering with an earlier time of perfection, a lost paradise or golden age. The biblical narrative is unique, however, in implying that humanity's degradation was indirectly caused by its own free choice.

The fall of divine beings played a central role in the writings of the gnostics (second and third centuries CE), many of whom believed that creation and even human existence were caused by a precosmic error. According to the gnostics, the physical cosmos was a concrete nightmare from which the divine sparks of humanity sought to escape.

In the New Testament Paul explained that Adam, the man of flesh, brought sin and death to the world while Christ, the second Adam and the man of spirit, brought life (1 Cor., 15.21–22). Paul's view that Adam's fall introduced sin and death (Rom. 5.12) led Augustine (fifth century CE) to develop the doctrine of original sin: that Adam's fall perverted all humanity and that its effects were passed by hereditary transmission from generation to generation. The belief that Adam, as a corporate personality, was responsible for the sins of humanity was never adopted by Judaism and was resisted by Christian thinkers such as Pelagius and Julian of Eclanum (fifth century CE), but Augustine's interpretation of the Fall became the accepted doctrine of Catholic Christianity. Like all myths of a lost paradise or golden age, the story of the Fall, whether of gods or humans, is an index of humanity's yearning for a better world and an attempt to account for the problems of evil and human suffering.

GREGORY SHAW

FEASTS AND FESTIVALS. Sacred feasts and festivals punctuated the calendar of ancient Israel. New moons were a function of a lunar system in which the month functioned as the basic unit for measuring time. The Pesah festival (Passover) in the spring, on which unleavened bread was eaten, was historical in character, a commemoration of the Exodus from Egypt. By contrast, the spring and autumn harvest festivals were seasonal celebrations linked to the agricultural economy of ancient Israel. All three annual festivals were occasions for pilgrimage (Hebr. *ḥag*).

How feasts and new moons were celebrated depended in great measure on where sacrifices could be offered. Israelites seeking to celebrate these occasions fully were required to do so at a proper cult site, in other words, to undertake a pilgrimage to an altar (*bāmâ*) or temple. The Bible records a protracted movement toward cult centralization and the elimination of all local and regional cult sites. The doctrine that all sacri-

F

The symbolic meal of Passover

fice should be restricted to a central temple was to have serious practical implications for the scheduling of pilgrimage festivals and all occasions when sacrifices were offered.

In 622 BCE King Josiah of Judah issued a series of edicts, recorded in 2 Kings 22–23, for-bidding all sacrificial worship outside the Temple of Jerusalem. Deuteronomy 12 restricts the offering of sacrifice to a single cult place (*māqôm*) to be selected by the God of Israel. It has recently been argued that the policy of cult centralization originated in the northern Israelite kingdom of the mid- to late-eighth century BCE before its fall to the Assyrians in 722 BCE. The Judean king Hezekiah had attempted to implement this policy (2 Kings 18.3–4,22), but since he was succeeded by Manasseh, the heterodox king who ruled throughout most of the seventh century BCE, no progress was made in eliminating the *bāmôt* before the time of Josiah. A young king who had returned to the Lord sincerely (2 Kings 23.25), Josiah acted effectively to eliminate places of worship throughout the land.

It is logical, therefore, to conclude that most of the significant changes in the celebration of Israelite festivals went into effect only after Josiah's edicts were promulgated and that most of them were heralded in Deuteronomy. Some scholars dispute this reconstruction, however, and date the priestly codes (P), which reflect basic changes in worship, to an earlier period.

The New Moon. The new moon (1 Sam. 20.5, 18; 2 Kings 4.23; Isa. 1.13; Hos. 2.11) is sometimes referred to as "the head of the month" (Num. 28.11; etc.). By all indications, the celebration of the new moon was an important occasion in biblical times. This importance may have diminished in time, since the growing importance of the Sabbath eventually reduced reliance on the lunar calendar, introducing the week as a unit of time.

The account in 1 Samuel 20, set in the early monarchy, suggests that the new moon was the occasion of a sacred feast (*zebaḥ*) celebrated by the family. Fixing the precise time of the moon's "birth" was necessary for scheduling the festivals, whose dates are formulated as numbered days of the month. According to priestly law (Num. 28.11–15), the new moon was to be celebrated in the public cult by a triad of sacrifices—the burnt offering, the grain offering, and the libation, preceded by the purificatory sin offering. The

new moon of the seventh month, in the early autumn (Tishrei), enjoyed special status because it heralded the autumn ingathering festival, the main pilgrimage festival of the year (Lev. 23.23–25; Num. 29.1–16; Ps. 81.3). On that new moon, the ram's horn was sounded to announce the autumn pilgrimage. In later Judaism, the new moon of the seventh month became Ro'sh ha-Shanah, the Jewish New Year.

The Festival of Unleavened Bread and the Passover. The first pilgrimage festival in the spring commemorated the Exodus from Egypt. In the Book of the Covenant, the earliest of the law codes in the Torah, this festival is called "the pilgrimage festival of unleavened bread" (*ḥag hammaṣṣôt*; Exod. 23.15). It is preceded on the eve of the festival by the "paschal sacrifice" ([*ze-baḥ*] *pesaḥ*; Exod. 12.21–13.10).

This festival began on the new moon of the month of ripening grain ears (*'ābîb*) and lasted seven days, during which only unleavened bread was to be eaten. The pilgrimage occurred on the seventh day. On the eve of the first day the paschal sacrifice, consisting of a lamb, was offered by the family near its home. According to Exodus 12.8–9, it was roasted whole over an open fire, a practice still followed by the Samaritans. Blood from the sacrifice was poured on the threshold and then spattered on the lintel and doorposts with a twig of hyssop. The application of the blood expressed the theme of protection. The sense of the Hebrew verb *pāsaḥ*, from which Pesah derives, has been misunderstood to mean "skip, pass over" (whence the name "Passover"), whereas it more properly means "to straddle, stand over," hence "protect" (Isa. 31.5). The God of Israel was pictured as standing over the homes of the Israelites in Egypt to protect them from the plague of the firstborn.

Egyptian bondage was symbolized by the bitter herbs, eaten together with the unleavened bread and the paschal sacrifice. This festival is a *mô'ēd*, "appointed time," a term that indicates its observance on the same date annually (Exod. 13.10; 23.15), and the same is true of the other annual festivals.

In Deuteronomy 16.3 a rationale is given for the unleavened bread. It symbolized affliction, and its preparation was reminiscent of the hasty departure of the fleeing Israelites. Most significant in the provisions of Deuteronomy 16.1–8 is the requirement that the paschal sacrifice be offered at the single cult place selected by God and that it be prepared in the usual manner by boiling major portions of the meat in pots (1 Sam. 2.11–17), with the rest of the victim burned on the altar.

The shift of venue from the home to the central sanctuary parallels the provisions of Josiah's edict (2 Kings 23.21–23) proclaiming the celebration of the paschal sacrifice in the Temple of Jerusalem, something that, we are told, had never occurred before (but see 2 Chron. 30). The paschal sacrifice now did double duty as the festival offering of the first day. This is indicated by the composite term, "the sacred feast of the pilgrimage festival of the Pesah" (Exod. 34.25).

According to Deuteronomy 16, the pilgrimage began with the paschal sacrifice. Israelites would rise the next morning and return home, continuing to eat unleavened bread for the remaining six days of the festival, and observing the seventh day in their settlements as a solemn assembly, on which labor was prohibited. The result of the Deuteronomic legislation was a brief pilgrimage that allowed farmers to return home at the busiest time of the year.

The priestly prescriptions for this festival reveal even further changes in its celebration. The date is the fifteenth of the first month (Nisan), preceded by the paschal sacrifice on the fourteenth, in the late afternoon (Exod. 12.18; Lev. 23.5–6; Num. 28.16–17). From the formulation of these priestly laws it is clear that the paschal sacrifice, like those offered on each of the seven days of the festival, occurred in the Temple. On both the first and the seventh days there is to be a "sacred assembly," on which labor is forbidden. Numbers 28.19–24 specifies the offerings of the public cult. The difficulty implicit in ordaining a seven-day pilgrimage to a central sanctuary would be dealt with, as we will see, by deferring the second pilgrimage. Proclaiming both the first and the seventh days as sacred assemblies satisfied the earlier pilgrimage of the Book of the Covenant as well as the Deuteronomic pilgrimage of the first night.

The Spring Harvest Festival of the First Grain Yield. In the Book of the Covenant (Exod. 23.16) this festival is named "the pilgrimage festival of reaping" (*ḥag haqqāṣîr*), that is, of the first yield of the barley crop. No specific date is provided in Exodus, but we may assume that it would occur quite soon after the Pesah early in Iyyar.

In Deuteronomy 16.9–12 we observe the dramatic effects of the Deuteronomic requirement of celebration at a central sanctuary: the spring festival of reaping is deferred seven weeks; thus, the festival is named "the pilgrimage festival of weeks" (*ḥag šābū'ōt*). The Israelites were to count off a period of seven weeks and then present an offering of first fruits, now consisting of wheat, not barley (Exod. 34.26; Deut. 26.1–11; Lev. 2.14–16).

The most logical reason for the deferral was the anticipated difficulty of undertaking two extended pilgrimages to a central temple at the busiest season of the agricultural year. Priestly law, represented by Leviticus 23.9–22, retains the deferral instituted by Deuteronomy. An earlier desacralization of the new barley crop is, however, ordained for the day of the original festival of reaping, soon after the Pesah festival. In Leviticus 23 the spring festival of reaping is not designated a pilgrimage at all; the first fruits were merely to be delivered to the central temple from the Israelite settlements (v. 17). This celebration, on the fiftieth day of the period of counting, was rendered more elaborate by including the "sacred gifts of greeting" (*šĕlāmîm* [v. 19; NRSV: "sacrifice of well-being"]), along with loaves made of semolina wheat. The counting of seven weeks was to commence on a Sunday and end on a Sunday, seven weeks later, so that seven actual sabbatical weeks would have passed, not merely forty-nine days. The fiftieth day is designated "a sacred assembly," on which labor is prohibited. Numbers 28.26–31 prescribes a complete regimen of sacrifices to be offered in the Temple and it curiously no longer includes the "sacred gifts of greeting."

In summary, we observe major changes in the celebration, scheduling, and essential meaning of the spring festival.

The Autumn Pilgrimage Festival of Ingathering. In the Book of the Covenant (Exod. 23.16) the autumn festival is called "the pilgrimage festival of ingathering" (*ḥag hā'āsîp)*, namely, "when you gather in your products from the field." It was to occur "at the outset of the year," more precisely, soon after the start of the two-month period of ingathering, corresponding to Tishri-Marheshvan (September—October). Psalm 81.3 indicates that this festival began on the full moon, at the middle of the month, rather than on the new moon. The pilgrimage lasted one day.

Once again, Deuteronomy (16.13–15) introduces a dramatic change. There this festival is named "the pilgrimage festival of booths" (*ḥag hassukkôt)* and is scheduled to last seven days. It was to occur somewhat later than the ingather-

ing, at the time when the produce of the fields, vineyards, and groves was processed, in the vat and on the threshing floor.

This autumn pilgrimage was the major event of the year, bringing large numbers of Israelites to the Temple. For this reason it was an appropriate time for the dedication of Solomon's Temple (1 Kings 8.2).

Leviticus 23, in two successive statements (vv. 33–36; 39–42), elaborates on the festival of booths, which was a particularly joyous occasion. A rationale is provided for living in booths, namely, the conditions characteristic of the wilderness experience. Greenery was utilized to symbolize the fertility of the land, and an eighth day with a solemn assembly was added. Like Leviticus, Numbers 29.12–38 specifies sacrifices for all eight days, with the first and eighth days designated as days of rest.

A more realistic approach would seem to suggest that the theme of "booths" was introduced in Deuteronomy as a consequence of the restriction of pilgrimage to one central temple, which also accounts for the extension of the festival to last longer than initially intended. Dwelling in temporary booths became necessary for the numerous pilgrims arriving in the capital from all over the land and, in later times, from the Diaspora as well (Neh. 8.13–18; Zech. 14.16).

The Day of Atonement. The first reference to the Day of Atonement (*yôm hakkippūrîm*) is found in Leviticus 16, which sets forth the rites of expiation and purification to be performed by the high priest in the sanctuary. The principal function of this day was the purification of the sanctuary and priesthood, in advance of the autumn pilgrimage festival.

The rites of expiation were quite elaborate, and they included the dispatch of the scapegoat into the wilderness, bearing the sins of the people. On this day, the high priest

Trumpeter blowing the Shofar at the time of Rosh Hashanah and Yom Kippur

Part of the epic of Gilgamesh telling the Babylonian legend of the flood, written in Babylonian cuneiform

entered the Holy of Holies to seek expiation for sins. In Zechariah 7.5 this day is referred to as "the fast-day of the seventh month," and its importance seems to have increased during the exilic and postexilic periods, in the wake of the national disaster of 587/586 BCE. The postexilic prophet whose words are preserved in Isaiah 58 emphasizes that the God of Israel wants more than cultic purification and sets down ethical, human goals whose pursuit alone may render the atonement process acceptable to God.

Purim. The book of Esther relates the saga of deliverance that accounts for the annual Purim feast on the fourteenth day of Adar (and, in some areas, on the fifteenth day as well). Set in the reign of Ahasuerus (possibly Artaxerxes I), the Persian ruler of the fifth century BCE, the story emphasizes divine providence over Israel, in which Esther, the queen, and Mordecai, the court counselor, foil the conspiracy of Haman, the wicked enemy of the Jewish people residing in the far-flung provinces of the Achaemenid empire. Jewish custom is to read the Esther Scroll on this occasion and to exchange gifts in celebration of deliverance.

Hanukkah. There is an additional festival, unmentioned in the Hebrew Bible, which became part of later Judaism. The generic word *ḥanukkâ*, "dedication," occurs in such passages as Numbers 7.10–11; Psalm 30 (title); and Nehemiah 12.27; but the festival of that name is first mentioned in 1 Maccabees 4.59 in its complete form as "the Dedication of the Altar" and referred to simply as "the Dedication" in John 10.22. Hanukkah is an eight-day festival whose celebration begins on the twenty-fifth day of Chislev and which was patterned after the Tabernacles festival of the harvest season, as is indicated by statements in 2 Maccabees 1.9, 18; 2.1; 10.6–8.

Hanukkah celebrates the rededication of the Second Temple of Jerusalem in 164 BCE by the victorious Maccabees, members of the priestly Hasmoneans of Modein, after its defilement by the Seleucid ruler Antiochus IV Epiphanes, acting with the collaboration of hellenizing Jews. It is the practice to kindle lights on Hanukkah, adding one light

each day throughout the eight days of the festival, and to recite psalms of praise, the Hallel (Pss. 113–118).

Conclusion. After the Roman destruction of Jerusalem and of the Second Temple in 70 CE, when all sacrificial rites became inoperative, major changes in observance affect virtually all biblical feasts. Yet all biblical feasts continue to be celebrated to this day, both in Israel and wherever Jewish communities exist.

BARUCH A. LEVINE

FLOOD, THE. Today, as in the past, catastrophic floods are experienced universally, and stories are told about them. The stories share many features: land submerged, multitudes drowned, survivors in a boat. People living in basically similar ways in separate places will react similarly; hence, common features in flood stories are predictable and are not proof that all such ancient stories refer to one great flood.

On the other hand, the Babylonian and Hebrew stories share so much that a connection between them can hardly be denied. Surviving copies of the Babylonian story come from the seventeenth and seventh centuries BCE (the Epic of Atrahasis and the Epic of Gilgamesh, respectively); the age of the account in Genesis 69 in its present form is debated. Both narratives have a pious hero warned by his god to build a great ship and to load it with his family and selected animals in order to escape the coming deluge. Once all others have perished, the ship grounds on a mountain in Armenia, a sacrifice pleases the god, and a divine oath follows never to send another flood. The later Babylonian version describes the hero releasing birds to seek vegetation, but the clay tablets on which the earlier text is recorded have been damaged where that episode might have occurred.

Both the older Babylonian account (Atrahasis) and the Hebrew account belong to larger compositions passing from the creation of human beings to later history, the flood, and its aftermath. Other Babylonian records show a wider tradition preserving the names of kings from the beginning of the human race onward, interrupted by the flood. Genesis 5 and 11 present comparable lists in a comparable context. All these similarities indicate a close connection. Scholars often claim that the Hebrew flood story depends on the Babylonian, with modifications in the interest of Israel's monotheistic faith. Consideration of certain differences, however, makes it more likely that both depend upon a common original.

Whether such a flood occurred or not is impossible to prove. Archaeologists finding layers of silt in three Babylonian cities associated them with the flood, but each was confined to one place and they were not contemporary. What physical traces such a flood would leave is debatable; though Genesis may imply a global flood, it need not, for the Hebrew word translated as "earth" (6.17; etc.) also means "land, country" (e.g., 10.10), so the narrative could report a deluge limited to the writer's known world.

According to Genesis 8–10, God promised never again to send "a flood to destroy the earth." The covenant with Noah (9.12–17) sets human society on a basis of individual responsibility, and Genesis goes on to trace this concept in the special revelation that God gave to the line he chose.

ALAN MILLARD

GALATIANS, THE LETTER OF PAUL TO THE.

GALATIANS, THE LETTER OF PAUL TO THE. A letter addressed by Paul to "the churches of Galatia" is fourth in the usual arrangement of the Pauline letters in the New Testament. It is a sustained and passionate expostulation with a group of churches that Paul had planted, whose members were in danger of abandoning the gospel that they had received from him. They were inclined to pay heed to certain teachers who urged them to add to their faith in Christ some distinctive features of Judaism, particularly circumcision. These teachers also endeavored to diminish Paul's authority by insisting that he was indebted to the Jerusalem church leaders for his apostolic commission and had no right to deviate from Jerusalem practice.

Contents. The opening salutation (1.1–5) is followed immediately by an expression of indignant astonishment that the readers are so quickly departing from the gospel that brought them salvation (1.6–10).

An autobiographical account follows. Paul received his gospel not from others but when God revealed his Son to him. Before that, he had become an expert in the study and practice of Judaism; he showed his zeal by persecuting the followers of Jesus. But when he received his revelation, together with the commission to preach Christ among the gentiles, he began to fulfill his commission at once without consulting the Christian leaders in Jerusalem. Not until three years later did he go to Jerusalem for a fifteen-day visit to Cephas (Simon Peter), during which he also met James, the Lord's brother. After that visit he went to Syria and Cilicia, and continued preaching the gospel there (1.11–24).

Several years later he visited Jerusalem with Barnabas and had a conference with the three pillars of the mother church, James, Peter, and John. They recognized that Paul and Barnabas had been specially called to evangelize gentiles, whereas their own responsibility was rather to evangelize their fellow Jews; they agreed to an appropriate demarcation of the two spheres of missionary activity. But they conferred no authority on Paul; he was in no way commissioned by them (2.1–10).

Indeed, his independence from them was shown during a visit paid by Peter to Antioch, when Peter withdrew from sharing meals with gentile Christians because of representations made to him by messengers from James in Jerusalem. As Paul saw it, Peter's action compromised the gospel by implying that there was some difference in principle between Jewish and gentile believers. In fact, Paul maintained, there was none; both had been accepted by God through faith in Christ, not through the Jewish law (2.11–21).

Paul wonders whether the Galatians have been hypnotized: how otherwise could they imagine that the saving work was to be completed by their own endeavors when it had begun with their reception of the spirit of God through faith (3.1–5)?

Abraham in his day received the promise that through him and his offspring all the gentiles would be blessed. Since it was on account of his faith that Abraham received this promise, it is on the basis of faith that the gentiles are to experience

Raphael's depiction of the Apostles Paul and Barnabas rejecting the sacrifice at Lystra in Galatia (Acts 14.8–18)

its fulfillment. The Law brings no blessing; instead, it brings a curse on those who fail to keep it, but from that curse Christ has redeemed those who have faith (3.6–14). When the promise to Abraham mentions his offspring, Christ is meant. The promise is like a deed of covenant, whose terms cannot subsequently be modified by codicil (3.15–18). The Law was given in order to bring the latent sinful propensity of humanity into the open in the form of specific transgressions, during the interval before the coming of the expected offspring. The Law was like a guardian, keeping children under restraint until their coming of age. With the coming of Christ and the exercise of faith in him, the people of God attained their maturity and enjoyed their liberty as his fully grown sons and daughters (3.19–4.7).

But the Galatian Christians are turning their backs on their liberty and placing themselves in bondage to legal ordinances. Paul appeals to them to remember the affection they showed for him when he first visited them: he is not jealous because they are listening to other teachers but concerned because those teachers are robbing them of their liberty. They are trying to make them accept circumcision, but Paul warns them that, if they submit to this demand, they must keep the whole Jewish law. Those who have seduced them into this false course will have much to answer for (4.8–5.12).

Christian liberty means liberty to live according to the spirit of Christ, to fulfill the comprehensive commandment to love one another. The way of the spirit is the way of life; the "works of the flesh" lead to destruction (5.13–26). Mutual helpfulness is the hallmark of men and women of faith. Those who do good to others reap the harvest of eternal life (6.1–10).

Let others boast of their achievements; Paul will boast of nothing but the cross of Christ. The scars he has received in his apostolic service mark him as Christ's property (6.11–17). With this he takes his leave of them (6.18).

Authorship. None of the letters bearing Paul's name is so indubitably his as Galatians. Galatians is, indeed, the criterion by which the authenticity of other letters ascribed to him is gauged.

Recipients. The "churches of Galatia" addressed in this letter were situated in the Roman province of Galatia (Map 11: F3), but which part of the province is a matter of dispute. Until 25 BCE the area had been the kingdom of Galatia. The original Galatians were Celts from central Europe who invaded Asia Minor and established themselves there in the third century BCE. But the rulers of Galatia extended their authority over neighboring territories populated by other ethnic groups; these groups were included in the province of Galatia and were Galatians in the political but not in the ethnic sense. To some of these groups belonged the cities of Pisidian Antioch, Iconium, Lystra, and Derbe, which were evangelized by Paul and Barnabas around 47 CE (Acts 13.14–14.23). One view is that the churches of those cities were recipients of the letter. Another view is that the recipients were churches established later in the northern part of the Roman province, among the ethnic Galatians. It is true that Acts makes no mention of Paul's visiting north Galatia, but Acts does not give a complete account of his missionary activity. The precise identity of the recipients does not greatly affect the argument of the letter.

Date. The date of the letter has been fixed at various points between 48 and 55 CE. If it was sent to the churches of Pisidian Antioch, Iconium, Lystra, and Derbe, a date around 48 CE is possible, even probable; if it was sent to churches in ethnic Galatia, its date would be later. The affinity between

Galatians and Romans has been thought to point to a date not long before the writing of Romans (early in 57 CE). The affinity should not be exaggerated, however; Paul's assessment of the Law, for example, was considerably modified between Galatians and Romans. Again, wherever Galatians may be dated within the limits mentioned, one's appreciation of its argument is affected only slightly.

Opponents. The traditional view, accepted here, is that those against whom Paul polemicizes in Galatians were judaizing intruders, eager to make the churches in Galatia, which were mainly gentile in composition, conform to the Jewish way of life and probably also to bring them under the control of the church of Jerusalem.

Other features, however, have been discerned in the situation implied in the letter. If Paul warns his readers not to pervert their liberty into license (Gal. 5.13–21), it might indicate that a campaign on two fronts has been simplified by one line of interpretation, according to which the one target of Paul's attack is a form of christianized Jewish gnosticism. If it is objected that Paul gives no clear hint of this in the letter, the answer is that he did not fully understand the nature of the teaching being urged on his converts. But this is not plausible. Our sole source of knowledge about the opponents and their propaganda is found in Paul's argument; if these references cannot be trusted, there is no other source of information.

The letter can be read against the background of revived militant nationalism in Judea in the years after 44 CE. These militants (who came to be called Zealots) treated Jews who fraternized with gentiles as traitors. Jerusalem Christians were sensitive to the charge that some of their leaders, if not they themselves, practiced such fraternization. Hence, perhaps, the representations to Peter at Antioch, which made him break off his table fellowship with gentile Christians in that city (Gal. 2.11–14); hence too, perhaps, the judaizing mission to Galatia. For if gentile converts could be persuaded to accept circumcision and conform to Jewish customs in other ways, for example, by observing the sacred calendar (Gal. 4.10), the militants (it was hoped) would be pacified.

Immediate Sequel. What effect the letter had in the churches to which it was sent we do not know. Paul's insistence on gentile believers' equal status with Jewish believers, his refusal of any procedure that compromised his converts' liberty, isolated him in large measure from his peers in the Christian movement as a whole. He was disillusioned when "even Barnabas," hitherto his closest colleague, joined those who found it expedient to stay aloof from association with gentile Christians at Antioch (Gal. 2.13). He continued to feel affection and respect for Barnabas, but confidence was no longer possible. He made no further use of the church of Antioch as a base for his missionary work, and he and the leaders of the Jerusalem church never again felt totally at ease with each other.

As for the churches of Galatia, their response to the letter is unrecorded. Certainly, circumcision soon ceased to be an issue throughout the gentile mission field. This could have been due in part to Paul's argument, but it may have been due even more to a ruling by the church of Jerusalem that circumcision was not to be required from gentile converts (Acts 15.23–29). When Paul began to organize a relief fund for the church of Jerusalem, toward the end of his Aegean mission, he sent instructions to the churches of Galatia about their participation in this effort (1 Cor. 16.1), but it is not clear whether they made a contribution. Perhaps some of them did: one of Paul's companions on the journey to Jerusalem to hand over the contributions was Gaius, a man from Derbe (Acts 20.4).

F. F. BRUCE

GALILEE, SEA OF (Map 12:Y2–3). A large, heart-shaped expanse of water, 20 km (12.5 mi) long by 11 km (7 mi) wide at its maximum points. It forms a deep basin surrounded by mountains on both sides and a narrow, shoreline plain where several important cities and towns are located. This pattern is broken only at the northwestern corner, where this strip opens out into the plain of Gennesar, the fertility of which was extolled by Josephus (*War* 3.516–21). The lake surface itself is ca. 210 m (700 ft) below sea level, thus forming a large basin for the waters of the Jordan River. According to Josephus and Pliny its original name was the Lake of Gennesaret, although both authors are aware that it was also called the Lake of Tiberias (Josephus) or the Lake of Taricheae (Pliny), after two of the more important settlements on its shores in Roman times.

The gospels of Matthew (eleven times) and Mark (seven times) call it the Sea of Galilee, a designation also found in John 6 and 21. This may reflect the Hebrew (*yam*), which can mean either a freshwater lake or the sea properly understood. It has been suggested, however, that Mark's usage (followed by Matthew) has a more symbolic significance in terms of Jesus' control of the forces of evil that are associated with the deep (Job 38.8–11; Ps. 107.23–25, 28–29). Luke reserves the word "sea" for the Mediterranean and always speaks of the "lake of Gennesaret" (5.1, 2) or "the lake" (8.22–23, 33) when referring to the Sea of Galilee. The significance of this usage is that it suggests that Luke, although presumably not a native of Palestine, was able to project himself into that context and accurately reflect local usage in differentiating between sea and lake.

The lake provided a natural boundary between Jewish Galilee and the largely gentile territories of Gaulanitis and the Decapolis directly across. Despite differences of religious affiliation among the populations on either side of the lake, archaeological evidence suggests a real continuity in terms of lifestyles, trading, and other relations. The Gospels also testify to this frequent movement, even when it is not always possible to detect accurately the points of embarkation and arrival (see Mark 6.45, 63; 8.10; John 6.22–24). Josephus too mentions fleets of boats on the lake, thus suggesting a busy and thriving subregion within Galilee and linking it to the larger region.

In addition, the lake was a natural resource for Galilee because of the fish industry. Strabo, Josephus, and Pliny, as well as the Gospels, all mention the plentiful supply of fish in the lake. Both Bethsaida and Taricheae are generally believed to have derived their names from the fish industry; the latter is most probably the Greek name for Magdala and is derived from the Greek term for preservation. Salting of fish, which made their export possible on a much wider scale, was, we know, a technical skill that was developed during the Hellenistic age. It is likely, therefore, that there was a genuine expansion of this industry in Palestine also. Josephus mentions (*War* 3.8.520) one type of fish, the *coracin* belonging to the eel family, which was also found in the Nile, suggesting perhaps that the early Ptolemaic rulers had expanded the fish industry to Galilee as a commercial enterprise. In this regard it is worth noting that James and John, the sons of Zebedee, would appear to have abandoned a thriving business, when they left their father and his hired servants to follow the call of Jesus (Mark 1.16–20).

SEÁN FREYNE

GENESIS, THE BOOK OF. Genesis is the book of beginnings. Its account of primeval history (chaps. 1–11) extends from the creation of the world and humankind (chaps. 1–2) through its near destruction and preservation in the Flood (chaps. 6–9) to the spread of humankind over the earth (chaps. 10–11). The subsequent history of the ancestors extends from Abraham to the sons of Jacob.

Chapters 1–11: Primeval History. Chapters 1–11 of Genesis form an internally coherent unity. The creation (chaps. 1–2) and Flood (chaps. 6–9) belong together; the crime against a brother (chap. 4) belongs within the story of rebellion against God (chap. 3).

The building blocks of chapters 1–11 are narratives (chaps. 1; 2–3; 4; 6–9) and genealogies (chaps. 5; 10). The narratives recount the beginnings of the world and its people; they cover the creation of the earth and of human beings (chaps. 1–2), wrongdoing and punishment (chaps. 3; 4; 6–9; 11), the first signs of cultural development, and the scattering of tribes and tongues. It is through the genealogies that the events in Genesis 1–11 become a coherent story. The creator's blessing causes the expansion of humankind through the course of time (chap. 5: genealogy from Adam to Abraham) and the reach of space (chap. 10: the table of nations). Between the two genealogies stands the catastrophe of the Flood (chaps. 6–9), which is caused by the corruption of humankind and threatens to destroy its existence. The accounts of wrongdoing and punishment demonstrate the many possibilities for transgression; both the individual (chaps. 3; 4; 9) and the group (6.1–4, 5–9; 11) can overstep the boundaries set for human beings.

The narratives of creation. The creation of the world and the creation of humankind are independent traditions, each found in early religions throughout the world; the creation of humankind is the earlier of the two. Creation stories did not arise out of a curiosity about origins but from a sense

The Creation of Man (Gen. 2.7)

of the menace to human existence in an endangered world. The older narrative (chaps. 2–3) emphasizes the creation of the human race, intertwined with the story of its failure; the limits of sin and death are an integral part of human existence. Human beings themselves, formed from earthly elements, become living beings by receiving the breath of God. They are creatures in all aspects of their existence; these include territory (the garden), food (the fruit of the garden), labor (the tilling and keeping of garden), community (the creation of woman), language (the call and naming), and their relationship to God.

The later narrative (1.1–2.4) emphasizes the creation of the world. In early religions, creation occurs through action, through generation and birth, and through combat. In Genesis 1, everything that exists or becomes has its origins in God's commanding word. The distribution of creation over seven days forms a temporal unity that recalls the week and its culmination in the Sabbath, and it suggests that the history of creation and humanity also has an aim. The creation of plants and animals according to species show that a created order can include evolution rather than excluding it. The creation of the human "in God's image" means "corresponding to God," that is, as a creature to whom God can speak and who can respond to God. Human dignity is based on this likeness to God. Human rule over the rest of creation is understood in terms of the rule of a king who is responsible for the well-being of his subjects. The growth of humankind involves human effort and the advancement of culture. The refrain, "And God saw that it was good," signifies that creation was good in God's eyes, that it was in accord with God's purpose.

The narratives of wrongdoing and punishment: human limitations. The present human condition is explained as having emerged from the basic and polarized experiences of being at once secure in God and alienated from God. Created by God, the human creature can turn against God and thus incur guilt. This is recounted in the expulsion from the garden (chap. 3). The serpent, the source of temptation, is a creature of God; there is no explanation for the provenance of evil. But God seeks out even the guilty ("Where are you?" [3.9]), and they are able to defend themselves. The punishment is expulsion from the garden, from God's presence and from access to the tree of life (although mortality is already part of the human condition [3.19]). In chap. 4, crime against a brother augments the disobedience to God's command ("Where is your brother Abel?"). Separated from God, human beings become capable of murder and, in 9.20–28, of dishonoring their parents. To this is added the overstepping of boundaries by human communities, as in 6.1–4 (the sons of God), chaps. 6–9 (the destruction of humanity), and 11.1–9 (the tower of Babel).

Development of the text. The development of the book of Genesis was a long process extending over centuries. The first book of Moses, or Genesis, as we know it, is only the final stage of this process. Oral tradition—narratives, genealogies, itineraries—played a large part in the evolution of this book; it was a long way to the present unity that combines all of primeval and ancestral history. The question of the identity of the author (in the modern sense) of Genesis is irrelevant. It was not writers or poets who desired and first formulated these accounts; their origins lie in the human communities to whose life they belonged. Thus they express an understanding of God, of the world, and of humanity, which did not yet make distinctions between knowledge and belief, between science, philosophy, history, and religion. This explains in part the parallels to the themes of the creation story in many other cultures. These parallels were not necessarily due to literary derivation; rather, questions about origins were asked everywhere in early human history. Therefore, primeval events cannot be understood or described as the beginning of history; it is misguided to inquire about their "historicity." The appropriate question to ask of this material is not, "Did it really happen that way?" but, "Is it our world that is being portrayed? Is this description of human beings accurate?" The essential fact is that, in describing creation, people for the first time grasped the world, and humanity, as a whole.

Chapters 12–50: History of the Ancestors. The narratives of the ancestors extend from Abraham and Sarah to the sojourn of Jacob's family in Egypt. For the most part, they are family stories, dealing with the basic relationships within a familial community: the relationship of parents and children (chaps. 12–25: Abraham, Sarah, and Hagar; Ishmael and Isaac), of siblings (chaps. 25–36: Jacob and Esau), and of both (chaps. 37–50: Joseph, his father, and brothers). In these stories the family is the paradigm of community from which all others arise. Human existence is experienced through the succession of generations. One's own identity is preserved in the tales of the ancestors, and only by telling those tales is a link with them established.

Three epochs are reflected in the three generations of Genesis. The first (chaps. 12–25) is dominated chiefly by primal events; life and death are repeatedly at stake. In the second (chaps. 26–36), institutions such as property rights, judicial practice, and sacred rites in sacred locations begin to play a role. The third (chaps. 37–50) reflects the confrontation of kin and kingship in Joseph's rule over his brothers.

The ancestral narratives grew out of oral traditions. They consist of various types of stories, genealogies, itineraries, and divine oracles. In the oral stage of transmission, these elements simply occurred in various versions and underwent many changes in the course of their existence. This is also true of the divine oracles, which trace their origins back to the ancestral period but owe their further development to a later time. Our concept of history cannot be applied to these narratives; they are not historical writing. Rather, they grew out of an interest in telling of one's own ancestors in order to preserve their memory, and this only made sense if the accounts did include true reports of actual persons: in a preliterary age, past events are narrated in order to allow their hearers to share in them.

In its written form, the text in chaps. 12–36 developed from the union of two independent texts, J ("Yahwist", the earlier of the two) and P ("Priestly," the more recent). The older text in chaps. 12–25 and 25–36 knits together stories and accounts from the era of the ancestors into a coherent history; the author functioned simultaneously as transmitter, poet, and theologian. This work subsequently underwent a series of expansions. The more recent work grew out of a priestly theology. In addition to its narratives, this text is dominated by genealogies and itineraries that describe the course of Abraham's life (Isaac's is only alluded to) and that of Jacob and Esau. Divine promises and calls occupy a central position in both sections (chaps. 17 and 35), and the concept of covenant is of prime significance. Characteristic of P are the etiologies of precultic rites, such as circumcision (chap. 17), kin marriage (chaps. 27–28), and burial on one's own land (chap. 23), which establish the family as the basic cell of the nation. This more recent text has radically altered the history from a theological point of view. A redactor (R) created a coherent presentation of ancestral history out of these two texts.

The time of the ancestors cannot be determined with certainty (attempts to fix its beginnings have ranged from 2200 to 1200 BCE). At any rate, it is the era before the Exodus and the settlement of the tribes in Canaan. The individuals and the societal structures belong to the prepolitical life-style of pastoral nomads before they become settled, lacking economic or political safeguards, and passing by walled cities at a distance. They live with elemental threats to their survival: hunger and thirst, natural catastrophes, danger from those in power. For them, temporal continuity exists only in the succession of generations; the future is embodied in their offspring.

Chapters 12–25: the Abraham cycle. These chapters contain a variety of tales about Abraham, framed by genealogies (11.27–32; 25.1–18) and connected by itineraries. The narratives follow two trajectories: one begins with Sarah's sterility (11.30) and leads to the birth of Isaac (21.1–7) through 12.10–20; 15.2–4, 16, 21; and 17.15–17; in addition there are the later accounts in chaps. 22; 23; and 24. This trajectory concerns the continuation of a family's life from one generation to another among threats and tensions. The Abraham-Lot narratives (chaps. 13; 18; and 19) form a second trajectory, which deals with a family's territory. At the center are the destruction of Sodom and the rescue of Lot.

Beside the narratives, an independent line of tradition is found in the divine pronouncements. Their point of departure and core is the prophecy foretelling a son (15.2–3; 16.11; 18.10–14; 17.15–21), one of the earliest Abraham stories. The prophecies of blessing, multiplying, and landowning belong to a later tradition. At the center (chaps. 15–17), prophecies accumulate and form their own narratives.

Between the first ending (chap. 21) and the final one (chap. 25), three detailed stories belonging to a late phase of the Abraham tradition have been inserted (chaps. 22; 23; and 24). Abraham's questioning of God concerning the destruction of Sodom (chap. 18.16–33) also belongs to this late phase. The account of Abraham and the kings (chap. 14) is a very late addition.

Chapters 26–36: the Jacob-Esau cycle. The heart of chaps. 26–36 is the conflict between the brothers Jacob and Esau; at its center is Jacob's indenture to Laban (chaps. 29–31) and the birth of Jacob's sons (chaps. 29.31–30.24: the quarrel between Leah and Rachel). These too are tales of conflict. Genealogies form the introduction and conclusion, and the theme of flight and return (chaps. 29–33) provides a larger narrative framework. The conflicts concern territory, food supply, and social standing. Accounts of holy places and encounters with God have been inserted in this context (chaps. 28, 32, and 35). Chap. 26, a remnant of the oral tradition, and chap. 34, an episode from the time of the Judges, do not belong in this context. The conflicts in the Jacob-Esau cycle take place in a familial setting and must be resolved there, since they all endanger the survival of the group; consequently, the narratives tend toward a peaceful resolution of conflict, as in the reconciliation of Jacob and Esau (chap. 33).

The religion of the ancestors. The religion of the ancestral period differs from that of Israel in later times. It is entirely determined by a personal relationship to God, which corresponds to the life-style of the ancestors. They are dependent on God's blessing; he bestows fertility on humans and their livestock, grants success in enterprise, and lets flocks increase and children mature. God is with them on their path; he helps them to find watering places, directs their journeys, and guides their departures and settlings. They are as dependent on God's promises as on his guidance, for they have no other safeguards for the future. While in chaps.

12–25 God's promises carry a vital significance for the whole, in chaps. 26–36 it is his blessing that occupies this position; God's blessing is the outcome even of the brothers' quarrel as well as of several other episodes.

God not only blesses, he is also the one who saves. He answers the lament of the childless with the promise of a child (17.15–19), which constitutes deliverance. God hears the cry of a thirsty child and leads the mother to a spring (21.15–19). In this relationship with God there is no need for laws. The curse does not yet stand beside the blessing, and the covenant is not yet paired with the threat of judgment. This is a prepolitical form of religion; the God of the ancestors has nothing to do with waging war.

In all these narratives, the ancestors are dealing with only one God. There is no sense of polytheistic influence from the surrounding culture. It is the single God on whom they call and in whom they trust, although one cannot describe the religion of the ancestors as a studied monotheism. They do not yet have an institutional cult; they have no temple, no priesthood, and no cultic laws. Whatever passes between God and human beings happens directly. Only expansions such as 18.16–38 contain intellectual reflections. It is only in such later passages, and not in the ancestral period, that theological concepts, such as faith, righteousness, trial, and covenant, receive significance. The later text of P begins to use language of a theological cast; and only in the later layers of tradition does one find the idealization of the ancestors and the accentuation of their merits.

Chapters 37–50: the Joseph story. The narrative begins with a quarrel between Joseph and his brothers (chap. 37) and ends with their reconciliation and reunion (chaps. 45–46). In chaps. 46–50 as in 37, the Joseph story is connected with that of Jacob. These connections at the beginning and the end show that the Joseph narrative is meant to continue the ancestral history. The Joseph story in the narrow sense (chaps. 37–45 [except 38] along with sections of chaps. 46–50) is a unified work, complete in itself, from the hand of an unknown writer who was also a theologian. It is an extensive family history, which proceeds from an imminent rift in the family of Jacob to the healing of that rift. The story is structured around two settings: the house of Jacob and Pharaoh's court. It starts with the quarrel of Joseph and his brothers (chap. 37). Chaps. 37–41 tell of Joseph's rise in Egypt; chaps. 42–45 take up the journeys of Joseph's brothers to Egypt and end with their reconciliation. The kingdom is incorporated into the narrative by setting parts of the story at Pharaoh's court; the restoration of peace in Jacob's family becomes possible through Joseph's high position at the Egyptian court, and at the same time, famine is averted from the Egyptian people. Thus, the Joseph story corresponds to two periods in the history of the people of Israel, that of the kings and that of the ancestors, and creates a connection between them. The end of the story concerns Jacob's testament and death, and finally the death of Joseph. Chaps. 38 (Judah and Tamar) and 49 (sayings of the tribes) are not part of the Jacob story but were inserted later.

The Joseph story is a unified literary narrative, the work of one author in the early monarchic period. The author is not the same as that of the older J tradition (chaps. 12–36); the technique and style are different, for the Joseph story is not compiled from separate narratives and contains no genealogies or itineraries. This story is meant to be heard, not read; thus, the shape of the narrative is clearly defined, both as a whole and in the individual sections. Narrative techniques include key words (three pairs of dreams, Joseph's coat,

G

Joseph recognized by his brothers (Gen. 45.1–15)

famine) and doublets (two settings, two journeys, pairs of dreams). The lively description of people and interpersonal relations is characteristic, as in Joseph's rise and fall at court and the danger of abusing power.

The Joseph story is not a didactic wisdom narrative. Only chaps. 39–41 have a connection to wisdom literature, conditioned by their subject: the wisdom of a statesman at the royal court. Pharaoh describes Joseph as a wise statesman, but his is no artificially learned, scholastic wisdom, but instead a wisdom bestowed by God and matured by hard experience.

God is with Joseph in the low and high points of his life. The effect of his blessing is directed at an individual, but it also gains a universal scope when he averts famine from Egypt. He is the God of peace who heals the rift in the family of Jacob. The God who blesses is also the God who saves. He seeks after the guilty and makes possible forgiveness and reconciliation. The interpretation in 45.5–8 and 50.19–21 summarizes the action of God in this story: God has incorporated the evil doings of the brothers into his working of good. It is God's action that fashions the sequence of events into a whole; at the same time, the whole sequence of events is encompassed within it.

CLAUS WESTERMANN

GENTILE. From the Latin *gens* (literally, "nation"; Hebr. *góy;* Grk. *ethnos*), "gentile" refers to a non-Jew or, more broadly, anyone outside the covenant community of Israel. Postexilic times witness references to individual gentiles as opposed to nations; concurrently, the possibility of conversion to Judaism appears. Gentiles depicted in the Bible are as diverse as are Jews: From Rahab to Ruth, Haman to Holofernes, they come from various locations and play various roles—helpers, oppressors, witnesses, tempters.

Joshua 24.11 mentions the seven nations from whom the covenant community is to maintain separation (see Exod. 23.23–33; Deut. 7; Josh. 23). Yet a "mixed multitude" accom-

panies the community escaping Egypt (Exod. 12.38), and rules for the resident alien permit the circumcised sojourner to participate in Israel's religious life (Exod. 12.48–49). The so-called promise motif (Gen. 12.3; see Ps. 72.17; Jer. 4.2) insists that by Abraham "all the families of the earth will bless themselves/be blessed"; Isaiah 42.6 (see 60.3) calls Israel "a light to the nations"; and Jonah is commissioned to preach to Nineveh. Yet Ezra (9–10) and Nehemiah (10.30; 13.23–30) require divorce of gentile wives (see also Exod. 34.15–16), and the condemnation of gentile nations is a common prophetic motif. The Hebrew book of Esther does not decry intermarriage, and the book of Ruth celebrates the union of a Judean man to a Moabite woman, but the Greek additions to Esther and the book of Tobit value endogamy.

Connections between Jewish and gentile communities existed in politics, trade, and even religious practices. Some gentiles became proselytes (Jth. 14.10; Acts 6.5); others were attracted to Jewish practices and synagogues (the "God-fearers"). The pseudepigraphical book of Joseph and Asenath presents the Egyptian priest's daughter whom Joseph marries as the archetypal proselyte. Gentiles also participated in worship in the Herodian Temple (Josephus, *War* 2.17.412–16; 4.4.275; 5.13.563).

Jewish reactions to gentiles are also diverse. Most Jewish groups in the Hellenistic and early Roman periods believed that the righteous among the gentiles would achieve salvation, but they would do so as gentiles and by divine decree at the end of time. Such dual soteriology may also underlie Romans 9–11. *Genesis Rabbah* 34.8 lists the Noachide commandments incumbent on gentiles. *Tosepta Sanhedrin* 13.2 mentions gentiles who receive a place in the word to come (but see 1QM; 4 Ezra 3.32–36; *'Abod. Zar.* 24a). Jews were to deal honestly with gentiles (*'Abod. Zar.* 26a) and relieve their poor (*Git.* 61a) even as they were warned against associating with idolaters. Neither scriptural warrant nor unambiguous historical evidence exists for an organized Jewish program to convert gentiles. Distinctions were to be kept between Jew and gentile, but the manner in which separation was maintained varied economically, socially, geographically, ritually, and philosophically.

Early Christian views of gentiles are generally positive; this is not surprising, given that the church found gentile territory fertile soil for its messages and that most of its canonical documents are addressed to gentile or partially gentile communities. Matthew's genealogy includes gentiles, and the gospel concludes with the command to make disciples of all the nations (or gentiles, *panta ta ethnē*; 28.19); Luke has Simeon predict that Jesus will be "a light for revelation to the Gentiles" (2.32). Paul is the apostle to the gentiles both in Acts and in his own letters. How Jesus himself regarded gentiles is not clear. In Matthew 10.5b–6; 15.24, he forbids his disciples to engage in a gentile mission (see also Rom. 15.8), but Luke 4 depicts his early willingness to extend the good news to non-Jews. And both comments may be redactional inserts.

Anticipated by the conversion of Cornelius in Acts 10, behavior incumbent on gentile Christians is confirmed by the Apostolic Council in Jerusalem (Acts 15): gentiles were to follow what was likely a combination of Noachide commandments and the laws incumbent on the resident alien (see also Gal. 2). Scholars debate whether Paul himself insisted that all ritual law was abrogated in light of the Christ event, or whether ethic Jews could retain ritual practices. Within a century, this debate ended: Christianity became predominantly gentile, and Jewish practices were labeled heresies. Today, especially in the United States, "gentile" is often viewed as synonymous with "Christian." This is not, however, the case among members of the Church of Jesus Christ of Latter-day Saints (Mormons), who refer to those outside their community (including Jews) as "gentiles."

AMY-JILL LEVINE

GEOGRAPHY OF PALESTINE. *(For this article map references are not given; Map 1 and the index to the maps should be consulted.)* From the time of the Greek historian Herodotus (fifth century BCE), the term "Palestine" (derived from the word for Philistine) designated the western tip of the Fertile Crescent, namely, the area on both sides of the Jordan River, limited on the north by the Litani River and Mount Hermon, on the east by the Syrian desert, on the south by the Negeb desert, and on the west by the Mediterranean Sea. It falls into six broad geographical regions: the coastal plain, the Shephelah, the central mountain range, the Judean desert, the Jordan Valley, and the Transjordanian plateau. These can be visualized as north-south strips set side by side.

The Coastal Plain. This strip is divided into three unequal portions by the Ladder of Tyre (Rosh ha-Niqra/Ras en-Naqura) and Mount Carmel. Above Rosh ha-Niqra, the plain widens to the north reaching its greatest width at the Phoenician city of Tyre, which in biblical times was an island. Between Rosh ha-Niqra and Mount Carmel, the plain averages 8 km (5 mi) in width. In addition to an annual rainfall of 600 mm (24 in), it is thoroughly watered, particularly south of Ptolemais (Akko), where the alluvium deposited by the Naaman and Kishon rivers has pushed the coastline forward into the Bay of Haifa. The two tips of the bay form natural harbors at Akko and Tell Abu Hawam.

South of Mount Carmel, the smooth coastline is devoid of natural harbors, but in antiquity there were lighterage stations at Dor, Strato's Tower, and Jaffa. In this area, the plain is much broader and runs all the way to Gaza. It is characterized by three parallel kurkar ridges, the remnants of prehistoric coastlines. The sand outside the first ridge gave way to swamps within, caused by the failure of rivers and wadis to drain completely. In biblical times, the third ridge was covered with oak, and the rich soil of the land reaching to the foothills was ideal for agriculture. The plain is divided in two by the Yarkon River, which begins at Aphek (Rosh ha-'Ayin). The plain of Sharon north of the Yarkon receives almost twice as much rain (300 mm [12 in]) as the plain of Philistia to the south. The great commercial highway, the Way of the Sea, had to pass through the 3 km (2 mi) gap between Aphek and the hills. This became a major crossroads when Herod the Great built the first artificial harbor at Strato's Tower and named it Caesarea Maritima.

The Shephelah. As the biblical name ("lowlands") indicates, this is an area of low, rolling hills roughly 45 km (28 mi) long and 15 km (9 mi) broad, lying south of the Aijalon valley. The soft chalk and limestone hills are cut by wide valleys running both north-south and east-west. Even the driest part in the south receives about 250 mm (10 in) of rain, and in the biblical period it was intensely cultivated. Olives, sycamore figs, and vineyards are mentioned explicitly in the Bible. The key cities were Gezer in the north, which dominated both the plain and the easiest access to the mountains, and Lachish in the south, which controlled the main route through the center to Beth-shemesh and also the lateral route to Hebron.

The Central Mountain Range. This region is by far the biggest, and can be divided into three areas, Galilee, Carmel and Samaria, and Judea.

Galilee. This mountainous area is bordered on the north by the Litani River and on the south by the Jezreel Valley, which runs along the north side of the Carmel range and broadens out into the great plain of Esdraelon (365 km² [140 mi²] before sloping gently to join the Jordan Valley at Beth-shean. Because ancient settlements appear only on the edges, it must have been subject to flooding in biblical times. It was, nonetheless, a very important east-west route.

The classical division into Upper and Lower Galilee is based on the simple fact that the three highest peaks of the former are all over 1000 m (3300 ft), whereas the two highest of the latter barely attain 600 m (2000 ft). Even though both benefit by an average rainfall of 800–500 mm (30–20 in), the terrain is generally unsuited to agriculture, and in the biblical period was covered by oak forests. The isolation of the perfectly rounded Mount Tabor (588 m [1929 ft]) gave it a numinous quality. Beside it ran the Way of the Sea, angling out from Hazor to the coast through the Carmel range.

Carmel and Samaria. Running southeast from the coast, the Carmel range is cut by two strategic passes, the Nahal Yoqneam and the Nahal Iron, the latter with Megiddo at its northern end. South of the Dothan Valley, the ridge coalesces with the mountains of Gilboa to create a much wider range with no Shephelah on the west and a steep drop into the Jordan Valley on the east. The central core of the area is constituted by Mount Gerizim (881 m [2889 ft]) and Mount Ebal (941 m [3083 ft]). The pass between them, controlled by Shechem (Nablus), carried the major east-west route coming from the Jordan via the verdant Wadi el-Far'ah, in which Tirzah, (Tell el-Far'ah) is located, and out to the coast just south of Samaria. This was the heartland of the northern kingdom of Israel, and the contrast between the closed site of Tirzah and the wide prospect to the west from Samaria is symbolic of the shift in policy that took place under Omri in the ninth century BCE (1 Kings 16.23–24). In this period, the hills were heavily wooded, but the valleys, which are wider in the north, produced grain, olives, and grapes. North-south travel was difficult, except on the crest running south from Shechem. The first 20 km (12 mi) of the route lay in the fertile Michmethath Valley, but after the ascent of Lubban the road wound in narrow wadis past the sanctuaries of Shiloh and Bethel.

Judea. Geographically, the Jerusalem hills are a saddle between Ramallah and Bethlehem, which is some 200 m (650 ft) lower than the highest points of Samaria to the north and Hebron to the south. This facilitated east-west travel, and there have always been relatively easy routes to the coastal plain and the Jordan Valley. The forests that covered the hills when the Israelites first occupied the area gradually disappeared. The demands of a growing city were intensified by the insatiable appetite for firewood of a sacrificial cult that endured almost a thousand years. After the hills had been denuded, terraces began to be built on the slopes. The small fields thus developed supported mainly olive trees, but some grain crops as well. The average rainfall is 560 mm (22 in). Enveloped by higher hills with a poor water supply and a location off the natural routes, Jerusalem would have been doomed to insignificance had David not given it political weight by making it a religious center.

South of Bethlehem, the hills rise toward Hebron (1000 m [3300 ft]) and then descend to the great plain around Beer-sheba. The tree cover in the biblical period was oak with patches of pine, but Genesis 49.11 attests the intense cultivation of the vine in the valleys and on terraces. The only significant route ran north-south with only one good branch route to the coastal plain. The geographic homogeneity of the Hebron hills helps to explain why it was always the territory of a single tribe, Judah.

The Judean Desert. This region borders the Hebron hills on the east. The rainfall decreases sharply some 5 km (3 mi) east of the watershed, and in 20 km (12 mi) the land drops 1200 m (4000 ft) to the Dead Sea. The vegetation is sufficient to support only sheep and goats. In biblical times, this was the grazing land of the settlements on the eastern edge of the hill country (see 1 Sam. 25.2). There are few springs, but runoff can be collected in cisterns to water the flocks. The character of the terrain makes travel difficult. It descends to the east in a series of steps, the most important of which is the Valley of Achor at the northern end. These are cut by the deep gorges of the Wadi Murabba'ât and Wadi Ghiar, which drain into the Dead Sea; both had extensive prehistoric occupation. In the biblical period, the only significant route was that from Tekoa to En-gedi.

The Jordan Valley. From its principal source at Banyas (303 m [995 ft]) in the foothills of Mount Hermon, the Jordan River runs south in a great crack in the earth's surface where two tectonic plates meet. It continues down the Gulf of Aqaba/Eilat to become the Rift Valley in Africa. In biblical times, the area south of Dan was an impassable swamp with Lake Huleh at its center. The Sea of Galilee (21 by 12 km [13 by 7½ mi] at its longest and widest) is a freshwater lake 210 m (700 ft) below sea-level. It contains twenty-two species of fish, and fishing has always been essential to the local economy.

Shortly after the Jordan leaves the lake it is supplemented by the waters of the Yarmuk. In the 105 km (65 mi) to the Dead Sea the valley drops 194 m (540 ft) but the river meanders through 322 km (200 mi). The river bed with its tropical undergrowth that sheltered large wild animals is some 7 m (23 ft) below the valley, which widens to 23 km (14 mi) near Jericho, where the rainfall averages only 150 mm (6 in).

The Jordan ends in the Dead Sea (404 m [1285 ft] below sea level), which has no outlet. Water is lost only through

evaporation (in the 40 °C [105°F] heat of summer about 24 mm (1 in) each day), producing a high concentration of all the chlorides (26 percent as opposed to the 3.5 percent salinity of the oceans); in Hebrew it is called the "Sea of Salt" (Gen. 14.3; etc; NRSV: "Dead Sea"). It averages 16 km (10 mi) wide, and its length was reduced to 50 km (30 mi) in 1976 when the area south of the Lynch Straits dried out. This may have been the size of the sea in the historical period, but some fifty thousand years ago the water level was 225 m (731 ft) higher, and the valley as far as Galilee was a long inlet of the Red Sea. The gradually rising continuation of the valley to the Gulf of Aqaba/ Eilat is now called the Arabah, though in the Bible that term generally means other parts of the Rift Valley.

The Transjordanian Plateau. This region is a strip roughly 40 km (25 mi) wide starting at Mount Hermon and limited on the west by the escarpment of the Jordan Valley. On the east it gradually shades into the Syrian desert. The Golan, lying north of the Yarmuk river, was biblical Bashan and is a basalt plateau characterized by the small cones of extinct volcanoes. The fertile volcanic soil of the southern part gives way to wild pastureland in the north. The center of biblical Gilead is located between the rivers Yarmuk and Jabbok (Nahr ez-Zerqa), but the term is also employed to designate the area as far south as the Arnon River (Seil el-Mojib), which is also called Ammon. The terrain and vegetation cover is very similar to that of the hill country of Samaria. At an average of 1000 m (3300 ft) above sea level, the plateau of Moab lying between the Arnon and the Brook Zered (Wadi el-Hesa) is higher than the land to the north. In biblical times, it was proverbial for its fertility, and 2 Kings 3.4 highlights the productivity of its sheep farming. Edom extends south of Moab as far as the Gulf of Aqaba/Eilat. Its average height parallels that of Moab, but the central peaks rise to 1700 m (5600 ft). Winters are very cold and the snows can last until March. Due to the altitude, the tree cover of this area extends much further south than the corresponding forests west of the Jordan. The great commercial route, the King's Highway, ran the length of the plateau linking Damascus with the ports of Elath and Ezion-geber on the Gulf of Aqaba.

JEROME MURPHY-O'CONNOR

GOLDEN CALF. Three "golden calves" appear in the Bible. The first is fashioned by Aaron at Sinai to replace Moses and Yahweh (Exod. 32; Deut. 9.8–21; Ps. 106.19–20; Neh. 9.18; Acts 7.39–41), and the second and third are a pair commissioned by Jeroboam, leader of the northern secession, to replace the ark; they were worshiped respectively at Dan and Bethel (1 Kings 12.26–33).

Hebrew *'ēgel* is generally rendered "calf," but a more mature beast may be intended. On the one hand, an *'ēgel* can be a prancing (Ps. 29.6), untrained (Jer. 31.18) one-year-old (Lev. 9.3; Mic. 6.6). On the other hand, the feminine *'eglâ* can denote a three-year-old heifer (Gen. 15.9), trained (Hos. 10.11) for plowing (Judg. 14.18) or threshing (Jer. 50.11 [translation uncertain]). Hosea 10.5 calls Jeroboam's images "heifers," although the reading is uncertain; elsewhere, Hosea describes the animals as male (8.5–6; 13.2). Most likely, the golden "calves" are young bulls, as the Septuagint renders in 1 Kings 12.

It is uncertain from 1 Kings 12.28 whether Jeroboam's images are solid gold or gold-plated wood; 2 Kings 17.16 calls them "molten." Aaron's image is "molten" (Exod. 32.4, 8; Deut. 9.16; Ps. 106.19; Neh. 9.18), yet it is destroyed by grinding and burning (Exod. 32.20), as if partly wooden.

Hosea 13.2 refers to molten image(s), idols, and calves (it is unclear whether these are the same), and speaks of silver, not gold, while Hosea 8.4 mentions both silver and gold, probably the constituents of the calf in 8.5. Judges 17–18 describes a molten silver image worshiped in Dan, conceivably a forerunner of Jeroboam's calf. In 1990, a silver-coated molten bronze bull 10 cm (4 in) high dated to ca. 1550 BCE was discovered at Ashkelon.

Aaron's and Jeroboam's calves are symbols of Yahweh; Aaron declares a "festival to Yahweh" (Exod. 32.5) and, throughout its history, the northern kingdom of Israel worshiped Yahweh, even while venerating the calves (2 Kings 3:3, 10.29; etc.). But it is unclear whether the calves represent Yahweh himself or a supernatural bovine on which he stands; Jeroboam's calves may even constitute the armrests of God's throne. All three interpretations have parallels in ancient Near Eastern art and literature, and perhaps more than one was current in Israel. The non-biblical name 'Egel-yo appears in the Samaria ostraca (eighth century BCE) and could mean either "calf of Yahweh" or "Yahweh is a calf."

The calf stories in Exodus. 32 and 1 Kings 12 are closely related. Both extol "your gods, O Israel, who brought you up out of the land of Egypt," and both culminate in priestly ordination. The simplest explanation is that Exodus 32 is a polemic against Jeroboam's movement; this would explain the plural "your gods" in Exodus 32.4 (contrast the singluar in Neh. 9.18). Alternatively, Exodus 32 might be a polemic against an older cult revived by Jeroboam—conceivably that of Judges 17–18.

WILLIAM H. PROPP

GOLDEN RULE. Since the eighteenth century CE the familiar saying "Do unto others as you would have them do unto you" has been known as the "Golden Rule." Often cited as the sum of Jesus' ethics, the saying also occurs in ancient Greek, Roman, and Jewish writings. For example, Rabbi Hillel (first century BCE) answered a question about the Law's central teaching with the statement: "What is hateful to you, do not do to your fellow creature. That is the whole Law; the rest is commentary" (*b. Sabb.* 31a).

Some seek to distinguish between the more common negative form just cited and the positive form found in Jesus' teaching by attributing the former to common sense based on self-interest and the latter to Jesus' higher ethical concerns. This distinction, however, fails to hold because the positive form also occurs in extrabiblical writings (*Letter of Aristeas* 207; *T. Naph.* 1; and 2 Enoch 61.1) and the negative form appears in Christian literature, such as a variant reading in Acts 15.20, 29; and *Didache* 1.1.

By itself the rule could indeed reflect a common-sense principle of conduct based on self-interest rather than conduct based on concern for others. But a closer look at New Testament usage reveals that the Golden Rule occurs in contexts calling for love for others. Matthew and Luke have the saying as part of Jesus' teaching in the Sermon on the Mount. In Luke 6.31 it is integral to Jesus' teaching about love for one's enemies (6.27–35). In Matthew 7.12 it comes at the conclusion of a series of demands pertaining to one's relation with others (5.21–48) and with God (6.1–7.11). Probably, therefore, Matthew took the saying from its traditional context of love for one's enemies (5.44–47) and used it as a summary of the preceding list of Jesus' demands. By adding the phrase, "for this is the law and the prophets," Matthew places the rule in the broader context of the Sermon on the Mount as well as of his entire gospel. In 5.17 he introduces the series of Jesus' demands (5.21–7.12) by noting that Jesus had come to "fulfill the law and the prophets"; a "greater righteousness" (5.20) is now demanded in one's relationship with others (5.21–48) and with God (6.1–7.11). In 22.40 Matthew directly relates the rule to the love commandment by having Jesus declare that the "law and the prophets" depend on the love commandment.

In the context of Jesus' teaching, therefore, the Golden Rule, rather than being merely a common-sense, ethical rule of thumb, is a practical expression of the love commandment growing out of love for God and one's neighbor. The same

The Adoration of the Golden Calf, from the Sistine Chapel (Exod. 32.6)

G

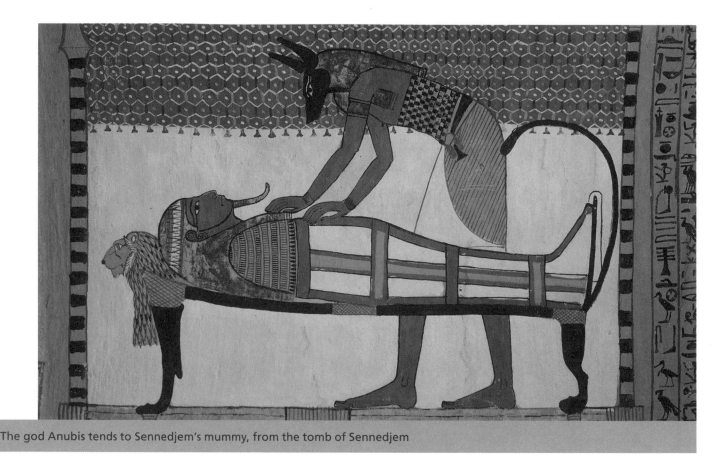

The god Anubis tends to Sennedjem's mummy, from the tomb of Sennedjem

connection between the Golden Rule and the love commandment is found in *Didache* 1.2, as well as in the variant reading in Acts 15.20, 29.

ROBERT A. GUELICH

GRAVEN IMAGE. Hebrew *pesel* is variously translated as "graven image," "idol," or "statue." Three-dimensional sacred images of metal, stone, wood, or clay were ubiquitously venerated in antiquity.

The Bible misrepresents idolatry by ascribing to worshipers the naive belief that the image is the deity. Egyptians, Canaanites, and Mesopotamians believed a god's spirit inhabited a statue after consecration, causing it to move, speak, or sweat. While the statue was the god in many respects, the god was not limited to its image. The idol's purpose was to allow the mortal a vision of the divine and to help god and worshiper focus their attention on each other. A few idols had moving parts—such as a movable jaw or dribbling breast—enabling priests to generate "miraculous" divine responses.

Since almost all ancient gods, including Yahweh (Gen. 1.26–27; 5.1; Ezek. 1.26–27), resembled humans, most idols were anthropomorphic. Some, however, portrayed animals, and Egyptian divine images often combined human and animal aspects. While humanoid idols depicted the god him- or herself, the wholly or partly animal representations metaphorically expressed aspects of its nature: a lion for ferocity, a frog for fecundity, a ram for virility, a hawk for mobility, and so forth.

The Bible forbids idolatry to Israelites (Exod. 20.4–5, 23; 34.17; Deut. 4.15–18; 5.8; 27.15). In Roman times, this proscription prevented compliance with the state cult of worshiping the emperor's statue (Rev. 13.14–15; 14.9, 11; 152; 16.2; 19.20; 20.4; cf. Dan. 3). Although archaeologists have uncovered virtually no representations of male gods from Israelite times, female figurines, probably representing goddesses, are common. Some equate these statuettes with biblical Asherah or teraphim.

Prayers might be spoken before the idol or food set before it, later to be removed for consumption by priests and/or worshipers. Among Jews and Christians of the Roman period, such food was strictly forbidden (Acts 15.29; 21.25; 1 Cor. 8; 10.18, 28; Rev. 2.14, 20).

The avoidance of divine images is called aniconism. While there is no inevitable link between monotheism and aniconism, it cannot be coincidence that the first monotheist, Pharaoh Akhnaton (1363–1347 BCE), abolished idolatry. Apparently both he and the biblical authors believed figurative representations limited the divine to a particular conception and place or encouraged identification of the one true God with other nonexistent deities. But while Akhnaton's god, the sun, was visible to all in the sky, Yahweh was hidden in his fiery cloud (Exod. 24.17; Deut. 4.15).

Although there were few if any images of Yahweh, Israelite shrines featured statues, carvings, and embroidery depicting celestial beasts associated with Yahweh: cherubim (winged sphinxes) (Exod. 25.18–22; 26.1, 31; 36.8, 35; 37.7–9; Num. 7.89; 1 Kings 6.23–35; 7–29' 36; 8.6–7; Ezek. 41.18, 20, 25; 1 Chron. 28.18; 2 Chron. 3.7–14; 5.7–8), bull calves (Exod. 32; 1 Kings 7.29; 12.28–30), and perhaps seraphim (winged snakes) (2 Kings 18.4). The Bible preserves vestiges of a debate over their significance: Are the cherubim God's throne or canopy? Are the calves pedestals or depictions of God? Is Nehushtan (2 Kings 18.4) a seraph sheltering Yahweh (Isa. 6) or a venomous serpent (Num. 21.4–9; cf. Isa. 14.29; 30.6)?

Jewish ritual art, like Muslim art, has generally avoided human images, but the third-century CE synagogue of Dura Europos features realistic illustrations of Bible scenes. Periodically, Christians have banned holy statues and pictures (iconoclasm), but they are still venerated in Roman Catholicism and Eastern Orthodoxy.

WILLIAM H. PROPP

HABAKKUK, THE BOOK OF. The book of Habakkuk is an integrated whole with the following outline:

1.1   Superscription
1.2–4   The prophet's initial complaint
1.5–11   God's answer to the prophet
1.12–17   The prophet's second complaint
2.1–4   God's answer
2.5–20   A series of "woe" oracles
3.1–16   A theophanic hymn, set within a biographical framework
3.17–19   The prophet's final song of faith

The central theme of the book has to do with God's purpose. It was composed between 609–598 BCE, when the Babylonian armies under Nebuchadrezzar marched into and captured the Palestinian landbridge. Habakkuk resides in the southern Israelite kingdom of Judah, and unlike the prophets who preceded him, Habakkuk addresses his words not to his compatriots but to God. His principal question is: When will God fulfill his purpose and bring in his reign of justice, righteousness, and peace on the earth? When is the kingdom of God going to come?

In the first oracle (1.2–4), Habakkuk raises his initial lament. He sees in Judean society around him nothing but violence and evil—the oppression of the weak, endless strife and litigations, moral wrongs of every kind. And despite Habakkuk's continual pleading with God to end the wrong, God seems to ignore him and to leave the righteous helpless to correct it.

But then God does answer his prophet (1.5–11). He tells Habakkuk that he is rousing the Babylonians to march through the Fertile Crescent and to subdue Judah, as punishment for her sin. The nation that has rejected God's order and rule will find itself subjected to the order and rule of Babylonia and her gods.

In the third section (1.12–17), the prophet acknowledges the justice of God's punishment of Judah. And because God's judgment is always finally an act on the way to salvation, Habakkuk knows that Judah will not die. But his problem remains, because the Babylonians, in their cruel conquests, are even more unrighteous than Judah has been. When will God bring that unrighteousness to an end?

To seek an answer, Habakkuk stations himself on his watchtower (2.1), a symbol of his complete openness to God. And God answers him, assuring him that the "vision"— that is, God's righteous rule, God's kingdom—will come, in faithfulness to the divine promise. Indeed, the fulfillment of God's purpose hastens to its goal. It may seem delayed to human beings, but it will surely come, in God's appointed time. In the meantime, the righteous are to live in faithfulness to God, trusting his promise, obeying his commands, and acting in a manner commensurate with the coming kingdom. Only those who live such trusting and obedient lives will have fullness of life. Those who rely on themselves and their own prowess, who are proud and self-sufficient, and who have no regard for the ways and will of God, will not prosper but will sow the seeds of their own destruction.

The "woe" oracles that follow in 2.5–20 illustrate the message of 2.4. V. 5 is corrupt, but probably should be read, "Moreover, wealth is treacherous; a mighty man is proud, and he does not abide"—a reference to the Babylonians. In the following verses, the prophet then shows the inevitable downfall of all who are unfaithful—of proud tyrants who oppress their captives, of corrupt and self-glorifying governments and military powers, and of idolaters.

The hymn of 3.3–15, with its introduction, confirms the message of 2.2–3. The prophet is granted a vision of God's final, future judgment of all, and of the establishment of God's rule over all the earth. The Lord is portrayed as a mighty warrior, marching up from the southern desert, to conquer all his foes and to give salvation to all who trust him. The portrayal presents the most extensive theophany (description of the divine appearance) to be found in the Hebrew Bible and depicts the overwhelming glory and might of God, before whose presence and promise of judgment Habakkuk both trembles and is reassured. Some scholars hold that this hymn

The Prophet Habakkuk

Abraham banishes Hagar and their son Ishmael into the wilderness (Gen. 21.8–14)

is an earlier, perhaps much earlier, liturgical composition, incorporated into the book in the postexilic period; if so, it has been skillfully integrated into its present context.

From such a vision of God's future triumph, Habakkuk has found his certainty. He therefore sings the magnificent song of faith (3.17–19) with which the book closes. The prophet's external circumstances have not changed. Violence and injustice still mar his community, strife still abounds, nations still rage and devour the weak, and the proud still strut through the earth. But Habakkuk has been given to see the final outcome of human history. God is at work, behind all events, fulfilling his purpose. His kingdom will come, in its appointed time, when every enemy will be vanquished, and God's order of righteousness and good will be established over all the earth. The prophet, and all the faithful like him, can therefore rejoice and exult.

Nothing more is known about the prophet, though he figures as a minor character in Bel and the Dragon 33–39. Paul quotes the book (2.4) in both Romans (1.17) and Galatians (3.11), in his discussions of justification by faith. Hebrews 10.37–38 identifies the coming "vision" of Habakkuk 2.2–3 with Christ, and uses it to strengthen a persecuted church. And believers throughout the years have affirmed the truth of Habakkuk's central thought: No matter what the circumstances, abundant and joyful life can be had from faithfulness to God.

ELIZABETH ACHTEMEIER

HAGAR. An Egyptian servant of Sarah, featured in the Genesis narratives about Sarah and Abraham. According to custom, Sarah, who was sterile, presented Hagar to Abraham so that Hagar might conceive and provide Abraham with an heir.

Two Hagar stories appear in the Bible. The first (Gen. 16.1–16) describes the expulsion of the pregnant Hagar from Sarah's household, her conversation in the wilderness with a messenger of God who urges her to return to the household, and the subsequent birth of her son Ishmael. In the second Hagar story (Gen. 21.8–21), set more than fourteen years later, when Sarah herself had at last borne a son (Isaac) and was celebrating the day of his being weaned, Hagar and Ishmael are cast out from Sarah's household into the wilderness. A divine messenger rescues them when their water supply runs out, and he proclaims that Ishmael will become a great nation.

The literary and chronological relationship of these two narratives is problematic, but certain themes common to both can be recognized. One is that Sarah is the dominant figure in the household with respect to management of domestic affairs, including determining the fate of household staff. In both narratives, Sarah makes a decision about Hagar's fate and Abraham acquiesces. Another theme is the tension between the main wife and a concubine or servant wife with respect to inheritance. Parallels with Babylonian laws suggest that Isaac, though born later, could still be considered firstborn. Sarah's desire to exclude Ishmael from any inheritance at all is partly to satisfy the narrative of Genesis 17, in which Sarah will be the mother of the covenantal heir; it may also reflect the difficult personal relations that arise when one son receives all.

A fourth theme involves the way in which disadvantaged individuals are portrayed as surviving and being blessed with the promise of great prominence. A final theme concerns the special role of Ishmael in biblical history. The Hagar stories establish the close relationship of the Ishmaelites ("the descendants of Hagar," according to Bar. 3:23) to the Israelites, relegating them to a separate territory but recognizing that God has protected and sustained their eponymous ancestor, the son of Hagar and Abraham. Finally, the narratives, while making Hagar a heroic figure, are also sensitive to her vulnerability as a woman, a foreigner, and a servant.

Paul interprets the Hagar stories with a tendentious allegory in Galatians 4:21–31.

CAROL L. MEYERS

HAGGAI, THE BOOK OF. The book tells us that Haggai prophesied in the second year of Darius the Persian (i.e., 520 BCE), his recorded ministry spanning a period of only three months, from the sixth to the ninth month of that year. The promises of Ezekiel and Second Isaiah, which must have spurred on many of the returning exiles, seemed not to have been fulfilled. A series of brief oracles in chap. 1 reveal the hardship of the situation of the pioneers, who were struggling to rebuild Judah after the Babylonian exile. They had known repeated droughts and failed harvests, with consequent famine, poverty, and inflation.

Haggai challenged the community about their priorities. He replies to their protests that they are too poor to rebuild the Temple (1.2) by saying that it is because they have not rebuilt it that they are so poor (1.4–6, 9–11). He thus draws on the old covenant traditions that had threatened the people, if they broke the Law, with drought, pestilence, famine, and the frustration of all their activity (Deut. 28.15–24). Similarly, the Zion tradition had linked God's presence in his Temple at Jerusalem with peace and prosperity for the land and community (e.g., Pss. 29; 72; cf. 2 Sam. 23.1–7). He therefore calls on them to rebuild the Temple (1.8).

A short narrative section (1.12–15) tells how the whole community under the leadership of Zerubbabel, the governor, and Joshua, the high priest (the Jeshua of Ezra and Nehemiah), was energized by Haggai's preaching to begin work, encouraged by a further assurance of Yahweh's presence by the prophet (1.13).

Evidently some grew discouraged in the work; they were not helped by the cynicism of those who had seen the grandeur of Solomon's Temple (2.3). The following verses show Haggai again encouraging them, not only by assuring them of Yahweh's presence in the task (2.4) but also with the promise that this Temple, once completed, would be the scene of Yahweh's reign as universal king (2.6–9). Earlier prophetic promises are taken up again, together with themes from the psalms that celebrate Yahweh's rule as king (the so-called enthronement psalms). So God appears, as on Mount Sinai (Exod. 19.16–18), accompanied by earthquake and cosmic upheavals (cf. Isa. 24.18–20; Jer. 10.10; Ps. 97.1–5); the nations come in pilgrimage to Zion (cf. Isa. 2.2–4, Mic. 4.1–4), bringing tribute to God as king (cf. Isa. 60.6). God will fill the Temple with his "glory" as he dwells there again (cf. Ezek. 43.1–5). That is why the new Temple will excel even the first and that is why it is worth building.

The oracle based on a priestly directive in 2.10–14 (cf. Zech. 7.1–3) shows that the postexilic prophets were seen as serving in a sanctuary setting and yet also were deeply concerned with ethical and moral purity.

In 2.15–19 the prophet describes the marked contrast in fortunes that he believed would be experienced after the Temple was rebuilt. The promises of 2.6–9 are renewed in 2.20–22, while 2.23 shows that Haggai saw Zerubbabel as continuing the line of the preexilic Davidic dynasty, which, it was believed, God had promised would last forever (2 Sam. 7.16). The picture of the Davidic king as God's "signet ring" echoes what was said of Jehoiachin earlier (Jer. 22.24). Haggai thus seems to have centered some kind of messianic hope on Zerubbabel.

We know nothing about Haggai himself. The book shows that he was seen as a prophet who assured the immediate postexilic community that earlier prophecies would be fulfilled and the hopes of the Zion/David theology of preexilic Jerusalem would be renewed. The Temple was completed in 515 BCE (Ezra 6.15), but we learn no more about or from Haggai after his three months of preaching spanning the dates given in the book (Ezra 5.1–2 adds nothing new). The addition of a gloss in 2.5 alluding to the presence of God in terms of the pillar of fire and cloud that accompanied the Israelites at the time of the Exodus (e.g., Exod. 13.21), and the description of the response of Haggai's hearers in terms reminiscent of that of the Exodus community to Moses (1.12–14; cf. Exod. 35.29; 36.2), suggests that his oracles were handed down among those who saw the return from exile as a second Exodus (as Second Isaiah had done) and Haggai as having exercised the ministry of a second Moses.

REX MASON

HALLELUJAH (Hebr. *halĕlû yāh*). The older English translation "Praise ye the Lord" makes it clear that the verb is in the plural; the command to praise is addressed to the members of the worshiping community. The ending "jah" (also written "yah") is a shortened form of Yahweh.

In the Hebrew Bible, the word occurs only in the Psalter, restricted to several groups of Psalms (104–106; 111–113; 115–117 and 146–150). It may stand at the beginning of a psalm, as in 111–112; or at the end, as in 104, 105, 115–117; or in both positions, as in 106, 113, 135, and 146–150. In Psalm 104, it concludes the praise of God in nature, and in 105–106, of the God of Israel. Psalms 146–150 are joyful, for use in public worship. It may be that these psalms were once an independent collection. The word also occurs in the Apocrypha (Tob. 13.17; 3 Macc. 7.13).

Like other Hebrew liturgical terms (e.g., amen), "Hallelujah" is used in the New Testament; in Revelation 19.1–8 it introduces several hymns of praise for God. Rabbinic writings use "Hallel" alone as the title for a song of praise. Christian liturgical usage employs the form "Alleluia," following the Greek and Latin transliterations of the Hebrew original.

GEORGE A. F. KNIGHT

HEBREWS. A name applied occasionally to the early Israelites, primarily to distinguish them from other cultures and peoples of the ancient Near East. An ethnic term, it antedated the common sociopolitical names Israel or Judah in the monarchic period, as well as the more ethnoreligious appellative Jew in later times. The word Hebrews, used thirty-three times in the Hebrew Bible, appears in only four texts (Jer. 34.9 [twice], 14; and Jon. 1.9) describing the period after the time of the Davidic kingdom. Contemporary sources outside the Hebrew Bible refer to the people not as Hebrews but as Israel.

The derivation of the word Hebrew (Hebr. *ʿibrî*) is uncertain. It may be related to the verb *ʿābar*, "to cross over or beyond." Thus, the Hebrews would be understood as "those who crossed over" or "the ones from beyond," meaning probably from the other side of the Euphrates River (Josh. 24.3) or perhaps the Jordan River (Gen. 50.10). Along this line, the Septuagint translates "Abram the Hebrew" in Genesis 14.13 as "Abram, the one who crossed over."

A second possible etymology is based on the genealogies (Gen. 10.21, 24–25; 11.14–17; 1 Chron. 1.18–19, 25; Luke 3.35) that identify Eber, the grandson of Shem, as one of the ancestors of Abraham and all his descendants, thus the "Eberites." No such explicit tie, however, is made in the Bible, and this connection would suggest that other peoples who are thought to derive from Abraham, including Edomites, Moabites, and Arabic tribes, should also be called Hebrews. The connections with Eber on the one hand and the motif of "crossing over" on the other, as well as a third possibility mentioned below, remain suggestive but inconclusive.

Virtually every reference to the Hebrews in the Hebrew Bible occurs in a context in which the purpose is to differentiate these people from those of neighboring countries, usually the Egyptians and the Philistines. Joseph, stemming from "the land of the Hebrews" (Gen. 40.15), is identified by this name (Gen. 39.14, 17; 41.12) in the story recounting his rise to prominence under the Pharaoh. A later Egyptian ruler charges the Hebrew midwives to kill all sons born to the Hebrews, but they refuse to do so, reporting deceitfully to the Pharaoh that "the Hebrew women are not like the Egyptian women; for they are vigorous and give birth before the midwife comes to them" (Exod. 1.19). Moses is recognized by the Pharaoh's daughter as a Hebrew child, and she calls for a Hebrew woman to nurse him (Exod. 2.6–7). Subsequently, Moses defends a Hebrew, "one of his people," from a beating at the hands of an Egyptian and then flees the land when he learns that other Hebrews have heard of it (Exod. 2.11–14). In confronting the Pharaoh to demand release of his people, Moses makes reference to "the Lord, the God of the Hebrews" (Exod. 3.18; 5.3; 7.16; 9.1). At all these points, the ethnic name serves to distinguish this people from the Egyptians, who are shown as using this designation as well. Genesis 43.32 reports that the Egyptians even considered it an "abomination" to eat with Hebrews, a custom for which there is no record in Egyptian sources.

H

In their dealings with the Philistines, the people are also often called Hebrews, especially by the Philistines themselves. At times it seems to be used as a term of contempt, parallel to the tradition in Genesis 43.32. In 1 Samuel 4.6, 9, the Philistines speak derisively of their opponents in battle and urge each other to fight courageously "in order not to become slaves to the Hebrews as they have been to you." In a later episode the Philistines, considering the Hebrews to be unworthy fighters who cower in caves (1 Sam. 14.11), are easily routed by the bravery of Jonathan and his armor bearer. This story also raises the question of whether the Hebrews and the Israelites are identical groups. When Saul issues the battle cry "Let the Hebrews hear," the text states that "all Israel heard" (1 Sam. 13.3–4)—which may not be the same as saying that all the Hebrews responded. It is in fact later reported that a number of Hebrews had previously attached themselves to the Philistines, and that after Jonathan's rout they disaffected and joined the Israelites (1 Sam. 14.21). This text may retain an ancient distinction that in later periods no longer applied: Hebrews as a larger socioeconomic group extending beyond Israel and Israelites as the particular ones who banded together in the Canaanite highlands to form a new nation. In that case, the Philistines may have simply considered the Israelites to be part of the larger class of Hebrews whom they were attempting to control, for example by restricting their access to metal-working (1 Sam. 13.19). A similar confusion occurs in 1 Samuel 29.3 when the Philistines prohibit David, who has been living with them, from joining them in battle against the Israelites—not because he is an Israelite but because he is considered a Hebrew.

There are only two other similar references to Hebrews in the Hebrew Bible. In Genesis 14.13, a context in which numerous peoples are mentioned, "Abram [Abraham] the Hebrew" appears parallel to "Mamre the Amorite." In a much later period, the prophet Jonah, when pressed by sailors of the boat on which he sought escape, calls himself a Hebrew and a believer in the Lord who created the sea and land (Jon. 1.9).

The ethnic and sociopolitical origin of the Hebrews remains a contested point. In many respects the ʿapiru (or Ḫabiru; in Sumerian SA.GAZ) seem to be a close counterpart, and it is often suggested that the word Hebrew is derived from ʿapiru (rather than from Eber or from the verb "to cross over," as indicated above). The ʿapiru were a diverse group of people with an inferior social status, living mostly on the fringes of settled civilizations from Mesopotamia to Egypt, and there is evidence of them in numerous sources throughout the second millennium BCE. They frequently were hired as mercenaries or sold themselves into servitude in order to survive. The Amarna letters (fourteenth century BCE) place them in the area of Syria-Palestine and describe them as basically outlaws and raiders, but such antagonism with resident populations may not have been common.

While there is no basis for equating the Hebrews with the ʿapiru, the proto-Israelites were probably a conglomeration of various Semitic groups, of which the ʿapiru was certainly one. Another was the shasu, pastoral nomads and plunderers also known to have been dwelling in Syria-Palestine as well as elsewhere in the region. The tradition of a "mixed multitude" (Exod. 12.38 [NRSV: "mixed crowd"]) or "rabble" (Num. 11.4) led by Moses through the wilderness is consistent with this picture of the early Israelites as an amalgamation of diverse peoples. Calling them "Hebrews" is an early means of distinguishing this new entity from other existing ethnic groups.

Hebrews are mentioned in one other notable context in the Hebrew Bible. Two laws dealing with slavery distinguish those who are Hebrews from others who are not (compare Lev. 25.39–55). Exodus 21.2–11 provides for the release of every male Hebrew slave after a seven-year period of service unless he should choose to remain for life with his master. Special rights are also reserved for a daughter who has to be sold into slavery. Deuteronomy 15.12–18 extends the law of manumission to include both male and female Hebrew slaves, stipulating that they are to be given ample provisions for starting their new life of freedom. Immediately before the fall of Jerusalem in 587/586 BCE, according to Jeremiah 34.8–22, King Zedekiah proclaimed the release of all male and female Hebrew (here also called Judean) slaves, but after this was accomplished the Israelite masters took them back, eliciting from Jeremiah an ominous pronouncement of doom. It may be that these Hebrew slaves, especially in the earlier laws, are reminiscent of the often-enslaved ʿapiru, but the Bible perceives them as compatriot Israelites deserving of treatment better than that normally afforded foreigners.

The name Hebrew, used rarely in the Hebrew Bible, thus occurs primarily to distinguish Israelites ethnically from non-Israelites. At times it is applied by foreigners (mainly Egyptians and Philistines); in other instances, by the Hebrews themselves when addressing foreigners. Except for the slave laws, Israelites normally identify themselves to each other—and often to others as well—as the people of Israel and Judah. Similar usage continues in later literature (e.g., Jth. 10.12; 12.11; 2 Macc. 15.37).

In the New Testament, the term designates Jews, hence Jewish Christians who maintained their ties with the Jewish heritage and the Aramaic or Hebrew language. Acts 6.1 contrasts them with Hellenists, perhaps Jewish Christians who accommodated more to the Hellenistic culture by speaking Greek and following certain Greek customs. Paul, born in Tarsus, proudly identifies himself as "a Hebrew born of Hebrews" (Phil. 3.5; also 2 Cor. 11.22; and Acts 22.2–3).

In modern usage, the term Hebrew is generally applied only to the language of ancient and modern Israel and of Jewish scriptures and tradition.

DOUGLAS A. KNIGHT

HERODIAN DYNASTY. Several members of the family of Herod governed Jewish Palestine during the period of Roman domination.

Sources. The primary source for the Herods is Josephus; for the later Herods, especially Herod Antipas, Agrippa I, and Agrippa II, the New Testament makes a small contribution to our knowledge. Josephus's two main works, *The Jewish War* and *The Jewish Antiquities*, overlap in their coverage of the Herods. Regarding Antipater and Herod the Great, Josephus depended primarily on Nicolaus of Damascus, who was Herod's court historiographer. For the period from Herod's death (4 BCE) to the First Jewish Revolt (66–70 CE), Josephus relied for the most part on oral tradition and hence has far fewer historical particulars. There has been debate about Josephus's historical credibility, but most would grant him to be reliable, taking note, however, of his biases. Archaeological discoveries in Jerusalem, at Qumran, and elsewhere have supported many details of his works.

Origin of the Herodian Dynasty. After the Maccabean Revolt (167–164 BCE), in 142 BCE the Jews became politically independent under the rule of the Hasmonean family. It was the Hasmonean Alexander Janneus (103–76 BCE) who appointed the Herodian Antipater, Herod the Great's grandfather, as governor of Idumea. After Alexander's death in the struggle for power among his family members, Hyrcanus II, his eldest son, after ruling only three months as king and high priest, was forced out by his younger brother, Aristobulus II (67 BCE). In 63 BCE Antipater II, son of Antipater and father of Herod the Great, was instrumental in having Hyrcanus II reinstated and in deposing his younger brother. With Rome's intervention in Palestine (63 BCE), both brothers appealed for Roman support, and Pompey sided with Hyrcanus II, reinstating him as high priest. Later Julius Caesar, who had defeated Pompey (48 BCE), reconfirmed Hyrcanus II as high priest and granted Antipater II Roman citizenship with tax exemption, making him procurator of Judea. Antipater II appointed his sons Phasael as governor of Jerusalem and Herod as governor of Galilee (47 BCE).

Herod the Great (47–4 BCE). *Governor of Galilee (47–37 BCE).* Although Herod was only twenty-five years old when he became governor of Galilee, he displayed efficient leadership. After the murder of Caesar in 44 BCE, Cassius, the Roman leader of Syria, appointed him as governor of Coele-Syria. After Antony defeated Cassius (42 BCE), he appointed both Herod and Phasael as tetrarchs of Judea.

In 40 BCE troubles arose for the two new tetrarchs. When the Parthians arrived in Syria, they joined with Antigonus (the son of Hyrcanus II's deposed brother Aristobulus II) to depose Hyrcanus II. The Parthians besieged Jerusalem and sued for peace. Herod was suspicious of the offer, but Hyrcanus II and Phasael went to meet the Parthian king, who put them in chains. On hearing of this treachery, Herod, his family, and his troops moved to Masada and then to Petra. Antigonus mutilated his uncle Hyrcanus II's ears to prevent his being reinstated as high priest and sent him to Parthia. Phasael died of either poisoning or suicide.

Herod departed for Rome, where Antony, Octavius, and the senate declared him king of Judea. On returning to Palestine, Herod was able to regain Galilee and eventually to lay siege to Jerusalem in the spring of 37 BCE. Meanwhile, before the fall of Jerusalem he married Mariamne, niece of Antigonus, to whom he had been betrothed for five years. He did this not only to spite Antigonus but also to strengthen his claim to the throne, since she was a Hasmonean. In the summer of 37, Herod defeated Antigonus and became de facto the king of the Jews.

King of the Jews (37–4 BCE). Herod's reign can be divided into three periods: consolidation (37–25 BCE), prosperity (25–14 BCE), and domestic troubles (14–4 BCE).

To consolidate his rule, Herod had to contend with four adversaries: the Pharisees, the aristocracy, the Hasmonean family, and Cleopatra of Egypt. The Pharisees, who disliked Herod because he was an Idumean, a half-Jew, and a friend of the Romans, had great influence over the majority of the people. Herod punished both the Pharisees and their followers who opposed him and rewarded those who were loyal to him. The Sadducean aristocracy, most of whom were members of the Sanhedrin, were pro-Antigonus. Herod executed forty-five of them and confiscated their property in order to pay the demands that Antony placed on him. The Hasmonean family was upset because Herod had replaced the mutilated high priest Hyrcanus II with Ananel of the Aaronic line. Herod's mother-in-law Alexandra successfully connived to have Ananel replaced with her seventeen-year old son Aristobulus (late 36 or early 35 BCE). Later Herod managed to have him drowned "accidentally," and soon after he put Alexandra in chains. His last adversary was Cleopatra, who wanted to eliminate Herod and Malchus of Arabia and confiscate their lands. When civil war broke out between Octavius and Antony (32 BCE), Herod was prevented from helping Antony because Cleopatra wanted Herod to make war against Malchus, hoping to weaken both and acquire their territories.

After the defeat of Antony at the battle of Actium (31 BCE) Herod proceeded to cultivate Octavius's friendship. Convinced of his loyalty, Octavius returned Jericho to him and also gave him Gadara, Hippos, Samaria, Gaza, Anthedon, Joppa, and Strato's Tower (later Caesarea).

The last years of consolidation saw much tension in Herod's domestic affairs. Owing to a bizarre series of events, Herod executed his wife Mariamne (29 BCE), his mother-in-law Alexandra (28 BCE) after she attempted to overthrow him, and his brother-in-law Costobarus (25 BCE). Hence, all male relatives of Hyrcanus II were now removed, leaving no rival for Herod's throne.

The period from 25 to 14 BCE was marked largely by success, although there were still occasions of stress. Herod constructed theaters, amphitheaters, and hippodromes and introduced quinquennial games in honor of Caesar, thus violating Jewish law. On the site of Strato's Tower a large urban port was built and named Caesarea. In 24 BCE he built a royal palace in Jerusalem. His crowning achievement in construction was his plan to rebuild the Jewish Temple; work on this began ca. 20 BCE and was completed in 63 CE. Herod's territory was also greatly expanded in this period with the addition of Trachonitis, Batanea, Auranitis, the area between Trachonitis and Galilee containing Ulatha and Paneas, the area north and northeast of the Sea of Galilee, and Perea (Map 12:Y5). To gain the good will of the people, in 20 BCE he lowered taxes by a third and in 14 BCE by a fourth.

As Herod grew older a considerable amount of intrigue engulfed his life, much of which arose from his ten wives, each of whom wanted her son(s) to become his successor. This is evident in his changing his will six times. His first wife was Doris, by whom he had Antipater; he repudiated them when he married his second wife, Mariamne (37 BCE), by whom he had five children, of whom only Alexander and Aristobulus were notable. In 24/23 BCE he married his third wife, Mariamne II, by whom he had Herod (Philip). His fourth wife was a Samaritan, Malthace (23/22 BCE), by whom he had Archelaus and Antipas. In 22 he took as his fifth wife Cleopatra of Jerusalem, who became the mother of Philip the tetrarch. Of the other five wives, none were significant and the names of only three are known.

The main rivalry was between Mariamne's two sons Alexander and Aristobulus and Doris's son Antipater. In 22 BCE Herod made his first will naming Alexander and Aristobulus as his successors. Because of the alleged plots of these two sons, Herod made a second will in 13 BCE, naming Antipater as sole heir. Later there was reconciliation between Herod and Alexander and Aristobulus, and in 12 BCE he made out his third will naming Antipater as the first successor and next after him Alexander and Aristobulus. Because Alexander and Aristobulus became hostile in their attitude toward Herod, he finally ordered them to be executed by strangulation in 7 BCE. Immediately after their execution Herod drew up his fourth will, naming Antipater as sole heir, and, in the event of his death, Herod (Philip) as his successor. With the discovery of Antipater's plan to kill Herod, he was tried and imprisoned. A fifth will was made in which Herod passed over the next two oldest sons, Archelaus and Philip, because Antipater had influenced him against them, and he selected Antipas as sole heir. Five days before Herod's death, he executed Antipater and made his sixth will, in which he designated Archelaus as

Salome, the niece and stepdaughter of Herod Antipas, with the head of John the Baptist (Mark 6.27–28)

ris, and moved his capital to a new city, Tiberias (named in honor of the emperor Tiberius).

Herod Antipas's greatest notoriety is the imprisonment and beheading of John the Baptist (Matt. 14.1–12 par.). This incident occurred after he had married Herodias, who was his niece and the wife of his brother Herod (Philip). John the Baptist boldly criticized the marriage, for according to the Mosaic law it was unlawful to marry a brother's wife (Lev. 18.16; 20.21), except for levirate marriage (Deut. 25.5). As a result, John was imprisoned, and eventually, at the instigation of Herodias with Salome's help, Herod beheaded John at Machaerus in 31 or 32 CE.

According to the Gospels, Antipas thought that Jesus was John the Baptist resurrected (Matt. 14.1–2; Mark 6.14–16; Luke 9.7–9) and desired to see him, but Jesus withdrew from his territories. Later, during Jesus' final journey to Jerusalem, the Pharisees warned him to leave Galilee because Herod wanted to kill him (Luke 13.31). According to Luke, during Jesus' trial Pilate sent Jesus to Herod when he heard that Jesus was from Galilee (Luke 23:6–12).

In 36 CE the Nabatean king Aretas IV defeated Antipas in retaliation for Antipas's deserting his daughter to marry Herodias. Although Antipas had hoped to get help from Rome, it was not forthcoming because of the change of emperors. On his accession, Caligula (37 CE) gave his friend Agrippa I, brother of Herodias as well as nephew of Antipas, the territories of Philip the tetrarch, who had died in 34 CE, and granted Lysanius the coveted title of king. His sister Herodias became intensely jealous and urged her husband to seek the title of king for his long, faithful service. When Antipas and Herodias went to Rome in 39 CE to request the title, Agrippa brought charges against Antipas, and consequently Caligula banished him to Gaul. Agrippa I obtained his territories.

Philip the Tetrarch (4 BCE–34 CE). Philip was the son of Herod the Great and Cleopatra of Jerusalem. In the settlement of Herod's will, he was appointed tetrarch over northern Transjordan, including Gaulinitis, Auranitis, Trachonitis, Bananea, Paneas, and Iturea (Map 13:Y2–3). He rebuilt two cities: Paneas, which he renamed Caesarea Philippi, the site of Peter's confession of Christ (Matt. 16.16), and Bethsaida, where Jesus healed a blind man (Mark 8.22–26). Philip married Herodias's daughter Salome, but they had no offspring. When he died in 34 CE, Tiberias annexed his territories to Syria and, when Caligula became emperor (37 CE), they were given to Agrippa I, Herodias's brother.

Agrippa I (37–44 CE). Agrippa I, the son of Aristobulus (son of Herod the Great and Mariamne) and Bernice (daughter of Herod's sister, Salome, and Costobarus) and the brother of Herodias, was born in 10 BCE. He lived extravagantly and with creditors pursuing him. Sometime ca. 27–30 CE Antipas provided him with a home and a position as inspector of markets in Antipas's new capital, Tiberias. Not long afterward he went to Rome and befriended Gaius Caligula. Owing to an unwise remark favoring Caligula as emperor, Tiberius put him in prison, where he remained until Tiberius's death six months later. In 37 CE when Caligula became emperor, he released Agrippa I and gave him a gold chain equal in weight to his prison chain. He also gave him the territories of Philip the tetrarch and of Lysanius, with the coveted title king. On Caligula's death in 41 CE, Claudius confirmed the rule of Agrippa I and added Judea and Samaria to his kingdom.

Of all the Herods, Agrippa I was the most liked by the Jews and, according to Acts 2, was a persecutor of early Christians. In 44 CE he died suddenly in Caesarea (Acts

king, his brother Antipas as tetrarch of Galilee and Perea, and their half-brother Philip as tetrarch of Gaulanitis, Trachonitis, Batanea, and Paneas. It is during this last period of Herod's life, complicated by illness and plots to obtain his throne, that the narrative of the Magi is set (Matt. 2.1–16).

In conclusion, although Herod was a successful king who was highly regarded by the Romans, his personal life was plagued by domestic troubles. After the death of Herod the Great in the spring of 4 BCE, Antipas and Archelaus contested his last two wills before the emperor in Rome. Antipas favored the fifth will because in it he was sole heir; Archelaus, of course, preferred the sixth. After some delay the emperor made Archelaus ruler over Idumea, Judea, and Samaria with the title of ethnarch, promising that he could become king if he showed good leadership. He appointed Antipas tetrarch over Galilee and Perea and Philip tetrarch over Gaulanitis, Auranitis, Trachonitis, Batanea, Paneas, and Iturea.

Archelaus (4 BCE–6 CE). Archelaus, the son of Herod and Malthace, was made ethnarch over Idumea, Judea, and Samaria in 4 BCE. Before he left for Rome to contest his father's will he was given control of the realm and proceeded to kill about three thousand people; after this there was a prolonged revolt at the feast of Pentecost. On his return he treated both Jews and Samaritans with brutality and tyranny; this is the background of Matthew 2.20–23. Archelaus continued the building policy of his father, but his rule became intolerable. Finally, in 6 CE, the emperor deposed him and exiled him to Gaul. His domain became an imperial province governed by prefects appointed by the emperor.

Antipas (4 BCE–39 CE). Antipas, the son of Herod and Malthace and a full brother of Archelaus, was appointed tetrarch over Galilee and Perea in 4 BCE. After Archelaus had been deposed, Antipas was given the dynastic title *Herod*, which had great political significance at home and in Rome. He rebuilt what had been destroyed in the widespread revolt after his father's death, including the largest city, Seppho-

12.22–23; Josephus *Ant.* 19.8.343–52). Because Agrippa's son was only seventeen years old, his territories were reduced to a Roman province. His daughter Drusilla eventually married the Roman procurator Felix (Acts 24.24).

Agrippa II (50–100 CE). Agrippa II, son of Agrippa I and Cypros, daughter of Phasael (Herod the Great's nephew), was born in 27 CE. Because of his young age he was not allowed to rule immediately, but in 50 CE Claudius appointed him king of Chalcis. In 53 Claudius gave him Abilene, Trachonitis, and Area in exchange for Chalcis. Shortly after the accession of Nero in 54 CE, he acquired the Galilean cities of Tiberias and Tarichea, with their surrounding areas, and the Perean cities of Julias (or Betharamphtha) and Abila, with their surrounding land.

The private life of Agrippa II was not exemplary, for he had an incestuous relationship with his sister Bernice. In his public life he was in charge of the vestments of the high priest and could appoint him. The Romans would seek his counsel on religious issues, and this may be why Festus asked him to hear Paul at Caesarea (Acts 25.13–26.32).

Agrippa II failed to quell the Jewish revolt against Rome in 66 CE and sided with the Romans throughout the war of 66–70. He died childless ca. 100 CE; with his death, the Herodian dynasty ended.

Conclusion. Herodian rule brought stability to the region. With its domination of the eastern parts of the Mediterranean Sea, it was important for Rome to have a peaceful Palestine, because it acted as a buffer state between Rome and the Parthians and was crucial for the trade routes north and south of Palestine. To be a ruler of the Jews was difficult primarily because of their religion. Although the Herods were enamored of Hellenism and adopted some of its elements, they were aware of Jewish religious sensitivities. After the deposition of Archelaus, direct Roman rule of Judea by prefects like Pilate brought instability, much of it due to lack of understanding of Judaism.

Although each of the Herods (except possibly Archelaus) contributed to this stability, it was the pioneering rule of Herod the Great that laid its foundation. As a vassal king, he made it possible for Judea to be somewhat independent. Rome allowed this because he brought stability to the area and because he had proved his loyalty to Rome both militarily and financially.

HAROLD W. HOEHNER

HOLOCAUST. The English word *holocaust* is derived from Latin *holocaustum* and Greek *holocaustos/holokautos* (*holos*, "whole," and *kaustos/kautos*, "burnt"). Forms of the latter appear more than two hundred times in the Septuagint, generally to translate Hebrew ' *lâ* (literally, that which goes up), the burnt offering, one of the most common, multipurpose, and ancient forms of Israelite sacrifice (Lev. 1; Num. 15; etc.). The slaughtered sacrificial animals, birds, or unblemished male quadrupeds such as sheep, goats, or cattle were wholly burned on the altar, with the exception of the skin, which was given to the priest who performed the ritual (Lev. 7.8). The holocaust offering is mentioned three times in the New Testament (Mark 12.33; Heb. 10.6, 8). Although the sacrificial system ceased with the destruction of the Temple in 70 CE, rabbinic literature includes traditions about and discussions of the burnt offering, the earliest of which is in the Mishnah, especially tractates Zebahim and Tamid.

The meaning of "holocaust" has evolved from complete burnt consumption in sacrifice to include complete or massive destruction, especially of people. It was used in this context in the aftermaths of World War I and II. Since the 1950s, "The Holocaust" has come to refer to the Nazi murder of European Jewry (1941–45). By extension, "holocaust" is sometimes used to designate massive atrocities against or destruction of large numbers of people. The biblical religious-sacrificial origins and connotations of the term are troubling to some who prefer the word used most often in modern Hebrew to refer to the Nazi murder of European Jewry, *Sho'ah*, whose biblical meanings include devastation, desolation, and ruin.

BARBARA GELLER NATHANSON

The Sacrifice of Noah (Gen. 8.20)

HOLY SPIRIT. There is no distinct term for spirit in the languages of the Bible; the concept was expressed by a metaphorical use of words that mean, literally, wind and breath (Hebr. *rûaḥ;* Grk. *pneuma);* the English word "spirit" is simply an Anglicized form of the Latin word for breath (*spiritus*). Wind is an invisible, unpredictable, uncontrollable force, which bears down on everything in its path; and people found early that they are exposed to influences that affect them like the wind. Breath is a miniature wind, and from this the metaphorical use of the term acquired a more precise and positive direction, for breath is essential to life (Gen. 6.17).

The Spirit of God in the Hebrew Bible. The action of the spirit is seen in a broad range of experiences, some of which seem less than "spiritual" as we now understand the word. Thus the source of (physical) strength that enabled Samson to kill a lion is ascribed to the spirit of God (Judg. 14.6). And there are several places where it is not clear whether *rûaḥ* bears the literal sense of wind or the metaphorical sense of spirit (e.g., Gen. 1.2 [cf. 8.1]; Ezek. 1.12). The action of spirit is more often seen in inner experiences, but some of these too are ambiguous (e.g., the evil spirit from the Lord that seized Saul, 1 Sam. 16.14; the lying spirit that the Lord put in the mouth of certain prophets, 1 Kings 22.22). Among the most distinctive experiences ascribed to the action of the spirit are the raptures that drove people to ecstatic speech and behavior (e.g., Saul after his anointing, 1 Sam. 10.6–11; the seventy elders, Num. 11.25); this was the original meaning of "prophecy."

None of the prophets of Israel before the exile ascribe their vocation to the action of the spirit or, indeed, have much to say about the spirit at all. Some references of a critical or ironical nature seem to indicate that these prophets wished to dissociate their prophetic calling from the ecstatic raptures that earlier went under the name (Hos. 9.7; Mic. 2.11; cf. 1 Sam. 9.9). It is only in the later prophets that the spirit comes into prominence, notably in Ezekiel. Ezekiel mostly used the term *rûaḥ* without the qualification "of God," and in many cases the literal and metaphorical senses of the term are hard to disentangle. A high point in the prophecy of Ezekiel is his vision of the valley of dry bones, over which he was commanded to invoke the life-giving breath, or wind, or spirit of God (Ezek. 37.1–14; the three words all render *rûaḥ*). The hope so dramatically envisaged here becomes a major theme in the latest phase of biblical prophecy. Recognizing that the renewal of God's people could come only from God, the prophets came to look for a general outpouring of his spirit (Isa. 32.15). In no case is the fulfillment of this hope ascribed to the mediation of an expected messianic king; but in the portrayal of this figure in the prophecy of Isaiah, he is to be the permanent bearer of the spirit (Isa. 11.2; 61.1)—perhaps in contrast to the charismatic leaders of Israel, such as Saul, from whom the spirit departed. The distinctive mark of the messianic era will be the bestowal of God's spirit on all, high and low, old and young, male and female (Joel 2.28).

The designation "holy spirit" occurs only in Psalm 51.11 and Isaiah 63.10–11.

The Holy Spirit in the New Testament. The New Testament announces the fulfillment of the eschatological hope of the spirit proclaimed by the prophets. Two elements are emphasized: the coming of the one who is the permanent bearer of the spirit and the outpouring of the spirit on "all flesh"; and both are linked.

Jesus is identified as the promised one on whom the Spirit will remain (John 1.33). This identification took place at his baptism by the visible descent of the Holy Spirit on him in the form of a dove. The story need not imply that the association of the Spirit with Jesus began at his baptism and that he was at that moment adopted as Son of God; John especially saw in the baptism of Jesus the epiphany of the preexisting Son (John 1.29–34), the one in whom the prophetic hope was fulfilled. According to Luke (4.16–21), Jesus explicitly claimed this identity in his sermon at Nazareth; and it is indicated in the nativity stories, where the emphasis is on the conception by the Holy Spirit rather than on the virginity of Mary (Matt. 1.18; Luke 1.35). Further references to the Holy Spirit are not frequent in the Gospels, but they occur at significant points, especially in Luke (4.1, 14, 16–21; 11.20 [cf. Matt. 12.28]; 12.10). It is preeminently in the presence and operation of the Holy Spirit in him that Jesus is authenticated (Matt. 12.28; cf. 1 John 5.6–12); and thus to refuse the testimony of the Spirit is a sin that is infinitely graver than the sin of refusing the testimony of Jesus to himself (Matt. 12.31; John 5.31–36). The life of Jesus is presented as wholly directed by the Holy Spirit (John 3.34), and this note recurs in the apostolic preaching in Acts (e.g., 10.38).

Jesus is not only the permanent bearer of the Holy Spirit; he is also the one who will dispense the gift of the Holy Spirit to others. But this action of Jesus (which is expressed in the future tense in the first three Gospels) does not coincide with his manifestation as the bearer of the Spirit; it is projected into a future beyond the earthly mission of Jesus. There is a stated interval between the epiphany of Jesus and the general distribution of the Holy Spirit. Luke concludes his account of the ministry of Jesus with his command to the disciples to wait for the promise of the Father (Luke 22.49), and in the sequel he measures the period of waiting as fifty days after Easter (Acts 2.1). John expressed the same point in a different way, even though he records the promise made at the baptism of Jesus in the present tense (John 1.33), and he disagrees with the Lucan chronology in placing the gift of the Spirit to the disciples on the evening of Easter (John 20.22); early in his gospel John states that the gift of the Spirit could not be bestowed before Jesus was "glorified," that is, before he had completed his mission (John 7.39), and later, in one of the Paraclete sayings (see below), he stressed that the departure of Jesus must take place first, no matter how that grieves the disciples (John 16.7).

The five sayings about the Paraclete, perhaps a separate collection before their inclusion in the gospel according to John (14.15–17; 14.25–26; 15.26; 16.4–11; 16.12–15), contain the only formal teaching about the Holy Spirit in the New Testament. The term "Paraclete" (NRSV: "Advocate") belongs to the language of the law courts, and means a defending counsel, or attorney, as opposed to the accuser, who is called *diabolos* ("devil," Rev. 12.10). Paraclete is applied directly to Jesus himself in 1 John 2.1, and, indirectly, in John 14.16, where the word "another" implies a similarity between the Paraclete and Jesus himself; the Paraclete will be to the disciples what Jesus himself has been, and the coming of the Paraclete will be equivalent to a coming of Jesus himself (John 14.18, unless this is an allusion to the return of Jesus to the disciples after the Resurrection). But there are important differences, in addition to the sequential relation. The similarities and the differences may be listed summarily: the teaching of the Paraclete will be centered on Jesus and his teaching (John 14.26; 15.26; 16.14); the Paraclete will extend the range of Jesus' teaching to the world (John 16.8); the Paraclete will advance the disciples' understanding of "the truth," which is identical with Jesus (John 16.13; cf. 14.6); the presence of the Paraclete with the disciples will be permanent, in contrast to that of Jesus, which had to be withdrawn (John 14.16; 16.7); the presence of the Paraclete will be invisible and inward (John 14.17).

The relation between Christ and the Holy Spirit is also close in Paul. The mission of Christ and the mission of the Holy Spirit are virtually indistinguishable; the presence of the Holy Spirit is equivalent to the presence of Christ. The Christ who is designated Son of God in power according to the Holy Spirit (Rom. 1.4) is no longer to be known according to the flesh (2 Cor. 5.16).

The distinction between Christ and the Holy Spirit, where it appears in Paul, is nowhere expressed in terms of a sequence but rather as one between two sides or aspects of the same act of God; the mission of Christ presents its objective, or exterior, aspect, the mission of the Spirit its subjective, or interior, aspect (1 Cor. 2; Gal. 4.4–6). Paul's main concern is with the reality of Christ for faith; for the reality of Christ is accessible only to faith, and it is made accessible through the Holy Spirit (Rom. 8.1–15). Thus to be "in Christ" (Rom. 8.1) is the same as to be "in the Spirit" (Rom. 8.9).

The notion of the "seven gifts" of the Holy Spirit, which was developed in Christian liturgical tradition, is based on Isaiah 11.2 (where the Septuagint and the Vulgate add "piety" after "knowledge"), but this number does not cover the endowments granted to different members of the church for the good of the whole; lists of these gifts, called "charismata," are found at various places in the New Testament (e.g., Rom. 12.6–8; 1 Cor. 12).

GEORGE S. HENDRY

HOPE. An attitude toward the future, an assurance that God's promises will be kept, a confidence that what is bad will pass and that what is good will be preserved. Hope is a theme in many places in the Bible, even when specific words for hope are not used.

In the Hebrew Bible, a number of words are translated into English as hope. As in English, hope can be a verb or a noun—the act of hoping, the thing hoped for or the person or thing in whom one hopes. There is no single root word that carries the major responsibility for conveying this concept. Each word provides a slightly different nuance to the process of hoping, though we may not be able to identify each subtle distinction. The related words *qāwâ* (verb) and *tiqwâ* (noun) may be connected with meanings like "twist," "cord," or "rope," possibly referring to the tension of a time of hoping or the rope to which one clings when in need of hope. The root of the words *yāḥal* (verb) and *tôḥelet* (noun) may mean simply "to wait," being neutral about what will happen at the end of the waiting. Similarly, the verb *śābar* means "to watch," "wait," "expect" (e.g., Ps. 104.27); it becomes hope when one waits with a positive expectation about what will come.

Two words sometimes translated as hope show the relational quality of hope. The verb *ḥāsâ* can mean "to flee for protection," "to take refuge," "to put trust." The word *bāṭaḥ* is usually translated as "trust," but it can be understood as "hope," as the Septuagint often does.

In the New Testament, the noun *elpis* and the verb *elpizein* are virtually the only words translated as hope. They are used widely in the epistles, rarely in the Gospels, and not at all in the book of Revelation. This shows clearly that hope may be expressed by a text (such as in the words of Jesus or in Revelation) even when the specific word for hope is not present.

Hope has both an objective and subjective aspect. There are promises from God to which one clings as one faces the unknown and often forbidding future. But as suggested by a

A detail of a stained glass window

word like *bāṭaḥ*, hope is also an inner sense of confidence in God, a serenity despite terrible present circumstances. Whatever strengthens faith will also increase hope. Experiences that bring on a crisis of faith, like the exile or persecution of the early Christians, will also make hope more difficult.

God's promises form the basis for the content of biblical hope. From the objective side, hope is dependent on the confidence that God will provide: (1) The necessities of life—food, water, land. Without food and water, there is no hope even for life. Land plays an important part in biblical hope—it is promised, given, removed, and promised again. (2) Protection from danger—both as a community called by God and as individuals. God sends leaders—judges, kings—to protect the nation. When the nation falls, God promises a new and better king from the line of David, one who will outdo his illustrious ancestor (messianic promises in Isaiah, Jeremiah, Micah, and elsewhere). God will also protect individuals from all that can hurt them (Pss. 4.8; 27.1, 5). (3) Justice—the good will be rewarded and the wicked will be restrained and punished. (4) Community—the assurance that God will never abandon the people he has chosen, and that they will live in peace and love with other human beings.

Generally speaking, there is in the Bible a growing pessimism that God's promises will be kept within historical time; this is most clearly seen in apocalyptic writings. Confidence in God remains and hope as relationship survives, but language that had been used to articulate hope for this world is now projected into a world beyond human experience: the land becomes a heavenly home, food and water become heavenly food and the water of life; the Messiah becomes a divine being; heaven and hell are the final solution to the problem of justice; communities broken by death and tragedy and sin can be restored in heaven. In spite of the failures and disillusionments of this life, however, there is still hope. God will win the heavenly battle. There will be a resurrection, life after death, and a new age where God reigns.

DANIEL J. SIMUNDSON

HOSEA, THE BOOK OF. Hosea is the second of the eighth-century BCE prophets whose messages became a separate book.

The first three chapters tell the story of the prophet and his family. Hosea was instructed by God to marry a woman who is described as adulterous, either because she was already immoral or in anticipation of her unfaithfulness. The three children carry the same stigma (1.2; 2.4), and they are given bizarre names to symbolize their degraded status (chap. 1).

The similarity between Hosea's experience with his wife and Yahweh's experience with Israel is worked out in the book in all its dimensions—heartbreak, enraged rejection, efforts at reconciliation. All these are interwoven in an allegory in chap. 2. The stories are really the same, because the sin of Gomer against Hosea is identical with Israel's sin against Yahweh: unfaithfulness to the covenanted relationship by resorting to the cult of Baal, the god of the Canaanites (2.8, 13). This rival religion provided sexual activity as part of its ritual (4.10–19), at once literal and spiritual adultery.

In spite of the hopeless situation, which called for the most drastic discipline and even for the death penalty for both the mother (2.3) and the children (2.12b; 9.12–16), the Lord was quite unwilling to give up the covenant relationship (11.8). Strenuous efforts were made to renew the marriage, to begin all over again (2.14–23).

The story and the allegory are fairly clear in chaps. 1–3, where Hosea's concerns are uppermost. The rest of the book (chaps. 4–14) deals with Yahweh and Israel. It contains prophetic discourses composed in the language of cult poetry. This language is dense, compact, often opaque. Most translations are clearer than the original due to a considerable amount of guesswork and interpretation. This is unavoidable, because the text of Hosea is notoriously difficult, perhaps the most obscure and problematic in the entire Bible. Its difficulties have been attributed to the peculiar dialect of the northern kingdom, but this has never been demonstrated. Again, the text, because of its great age, is suspected of having suffered much damage in transmission, and numerous attempts have been made to repair these supposed corruptions by textual emendations. Doubtless the surviving text is blemished from such causes, but it is more likely that most of our perplexity arises from our failure to understand the author's use of intricate poetic patterns and sophisticated rhetorical devices.

Even when the words are familiar and the grammar seems to be correct, the discussion is often oblique and enigmatic. There are references to a priest (4.4), a prophet (4.5), a mother (4.5), a king (7.3). Priests are implicated in a murder (6.9) and in other crimes (4.1–2). But no one is named, and none of the events referred to in the book can be connected with historical facts known from other sources.

None of the oracles is dated, so we cannot attach them to the political developments of the period. The military activity described briefly in 5.8–12 has been identified as one of the Assyrian invasions, but it could be one of the many wars between the two kingdoms of Israel and Judah.

The clue provided by the title (1.1) is curiously lopsided. The four kings of Judah cover most of the eighth century BCE, but only one king of Israel is named. The prophecy predicts judgment on Bethel and Samaria with death or exile for the king (10.7), but it does not show any awareness of the fulfillment of these threats, notably in the fall of Samaria in 722 BCE. Many of the criticisms of the religious life of Israel could have been made at most times in its history; but the deterioration of the situation fits well with the third quarter of the eighth century, when the northern kingdom went into a rapid decline after the death of Jeroboam II (745 BCE), whom Hosea evidently regarded as the last real king of the north. The discourses reflect the chaos and lawlessness that marked the last two decades of the Samarian regime, the anarchy that set in after the death of Jeroboam II in which many of his successors lost their lives through assassination or revolution.

The international scene is dominated by Assyria and Egypt, who are frequently mentioned together throughout the book. Many of the references to these countries reveal diplomatic moves by both Israel and Judah to seek security ("healing," 5.13) through alliance with the great powers (7.11; 8.9). All too often, the little countries in the buffer zone between the two imperial nations tried to play one off against the other, with even more disastrous results. Such moves were roundly condemned by the prophets as apostasy from Yahweh, their true and only Lord. Their new protectors became their captors (9.3).

The northern kingdom is consistently called Ephraim, new terminology not found in Amos a generation earlier. It probably represents the contraction of the territory ruled from Samaria to a region corresponding to the traditional homeland of that tribe, due to loss of the eastern and northern provinces to the Assyrians and through civil war.

Hosea's messages mostly attack the northern kingdom (1.4), but Judah is frequently mentioned side by side with Ephraim and similarly condemned, especially in the all-important chaps. 4–8. Some scholars wish to delete the references to Judah as secondary additions, but such a revision would seriously injure the fabric of the whole book. The references to Jacob in the latter part of the book secure a complementary historical perspective that shows a concern for all Israel as the covenant people. It reaches deeply into the past, and Judah could hardly be excluded from Jacob's descendants. The reference to David in 3.5 likewise recalls the original unity of the people, and looks forward to its future restoration.

The prophecy anticipates wholesale destruction of the state and the deportation of the population. Assyria will be the prime agent of this development. Conquest by Assyria is identified as punishment by God.

Beyond that the prophet anticipates a return from exile (11.11) and reconstitution of the old regime (3.5). With the benefit of hindsight, we connect such statements with the later history of the people, the dispersal first of Israel, then of Judah, and the revival of national life after the exile. And because the promises of a return seem to fit these later developments, some scholars suspect them of being added after the fact. Unless we recover a manuscript of Hosea of pre-exilic date, we shall never be able to settle such a point with certainty. But the forecasts are general, even vague, and do not betray actual knowledge of what would eventually take place. It cannot even be shown that the book has been edited with a Judean perspective of later times. It betrays no awareness of the differing fate of Judah or of the later importance of Babylon. It does not feature Jerusalem, let alone the Zion mystique that begins to emerge already in Hosea's younger contemporaries, Micah and Isaiah.

Hosea's vision of the future sometimes breaks out into an almost apocalyptic scenario, with echoes of the serenity and bliss of the original paradise (2.16–23; 14.4–8). Some scholars believe that such ideas did not develop in Israel until after the exile, but they are deeply woven into the fabric of the book, and any attempt to remove them would spoil the total structure.

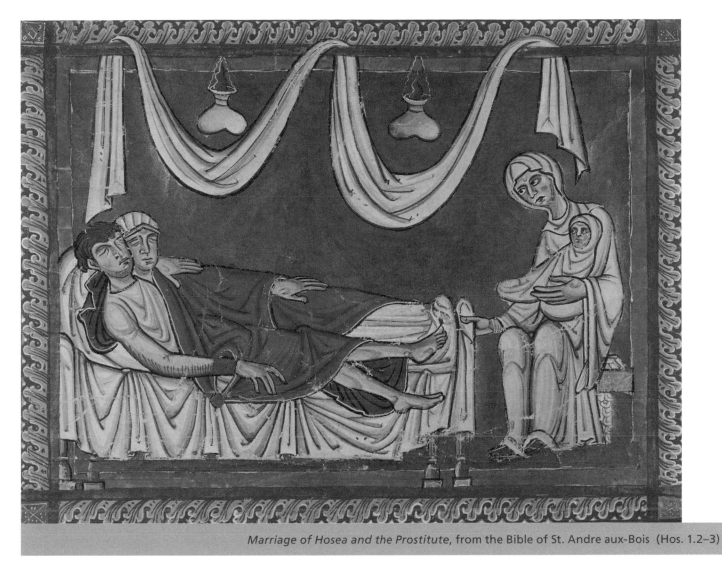

Marriage of Hosea and the Prostitute, from the Bible of St. Andre aux-Bois (Hos. 1.2–3)

Hosea is a book of conflicting passions. Extremes of rage alternate with the most moving expressions of tenderness and compassion. Its themes are the goodness and the severity of God. In passages of unexceeded savagery, Yahweh describes his execution and mutilation of his sinful partner (5.14; 6.5; 9.15; 13.7–8). In other places, the unquenchable affection of God for his people is expressed as grief over their loss, and as the yearning of a father for a beloved child (11.1), or of a husband for an estranged wife (chap. 3). The prophecy reveals the heart of God torn by powerful emotions: justice demands retribution; but grace cries out for forgiveness. How can both of these divine impulses be satisfied?

Hosea presents a radical solution to this problem. We do not know the outcome of his private tragedy and his heroic measures to recover his wife. He buys Gomer back (3.2), but we are not told how she responded. In God's parallel dealings with Israel, the book everywhere threatens and announces death as the inevitable punishment for sin (2.3, 12; 4.5, 9; 5.12; 7.2; 8.10; 9.9; 10.10; 11.6; 13.7–8, 16). But that will not be the end; once God's anger has been vented, the way of return is open. They may repent (14.1–2); then there will be healing and renewed love (14.4–8). Nothing less than resurrection from the dead can achieve this, and this is what is promised (13.14).

The story and the prophecy operate on several different levels at once, and it is impossible to separate the strands. The oracles have multiple meanings, personal and individual, national and historical. The figures of estrangement/reconciliation, sickness/recovery, death/resurrection are both lit-

eral and symbolic, realistic and fantastic. Beginning with one man's private tragedy and agony, the presentation expands to an analysis of Israel's past history and future destiny, reaching from the ancestors (chap. 12) to the eschaton (2.21–23). As one whose love was nurtured by the love of God, and whose experience then threw more light of understanding back into the love of God, Hosea reveals the Lord as both stern and sensitive, just and compassionate. He desires kindness (Hebr. *ḥesed*) rather than sacrifice (6.6), because kindness is an attribute in God even deeper than his justice.

FRANCIS I. ANDERSEN

HUMAN PERSON. The idea of the human person, so important in modern times thanks especially to the study of psychology, was not a focus of ancient Israelite thought. Because of the corporate identity of the people of Israel, the individual person did not receive much attention in the literature of Israel. However, as Israel moved into a later period, and particularly after its encounter with Hellenism, the nature of the individual and his or her fate became much more prominent both in Second Temple Judaism and early Christianity.

The Hebrew word for the human being is *nepeš*, which among its wide range of meanings connotes both flesh and soul as inseparable components of a person. A *nepeš*, or person, is first of all a living being, animated by breath. The life of a person is seen as residing in the blood as well as in the breath (Deut. 12.23, 24); therefore, it is unlawful to shed or to eat blood. Thus, an essential component of the person is the flesh (Hebr. *bāśār*), which is separate from

God and carries a connotation of weakness. All animals are composed of flesh, and the human animal is no different in this regard.

However, a person is also composed of "soul," so that less concrete attributes also belong to the person. Appetites such as hunger and thirst, emotions like desire, loathing, sorrow, joy, and love, and thought or mental activity all belong to the *nepeš*. This is how the human differs from animals, who are only flesh; the human, who has been animated by the breath of God (Gen. 2.7), shares in the attributes of God.

At death, the person's flesh dies, and the soul dwells in Sheol, a shadowy place for the dead. There is no notion in what may be called orthodox Israelite religion of a separate existence for the soul after death. Death is accepted as a natural part of the life cycle, but it is not welcomed, for the person who dies loses his or her being. In a prayer of thanksgiving, the psalmist says to the Lord, "What profit is there in my death, if I go down to the Pit? Will the dust praise you? Will it tell of your faithfulness?" (Ps. 30.9). Death is thus perceived to be the end of all sentient life. In later times, a doctrine of the resurrection of the dead developed, so that the best hope of the person after death lay in resurrection, when the soul and body would be reunited and live again (Dan. 12.2).

With the introduction of Hellenism into the ancient Near East, Israelite thought began to espouse the notion of a separation of soul and body. In Greek thought, body (*sōma*) is separate from soul (*psychē*), and the soul contains the true essence of a person. At death, the soul flees the prison of the body to seek a higher life, so that death is truly the liberation of the soul. As Jewish thought began to be influenced by Greek, these concepts emerge in its literature. Philo, an Alexandrian Jewish philosopher of the first century CE, assumes throughout his works a complete separation of soul and body, with flesh the chief cause of ignorance and soul the vehicle for a higher life. Josephus, the first-century CE Jewish historian, states that the Pharisees believe that souls have the power to survive death (*Ant.* 18.1.14), and that the Essenes believe that the soul is immortal (*Ant.* 18.1.18). It is probable, however, that the immortality both of these groups anticipate includes a bodily resurrection.

In the New Testament, the still prominent idea of bodily resurrection (see especially the resurrection narratives in the Gospels and also 1 Cor. 15) implies that the soul and body are inseparable, but the notion of a human being composed of a separate soul and body slowly gains ascendancy. There are several Greek words used to explain different aspects of the human person. The Greek word *sarx*, the equivalent of Hebrew *bāśār*, denotes the flesh of both animals and humans. It often appears with the word "blood," as in "flesh and blood," to signify the physical being of the human (as opposed to a supernatural being such as an angel, which is not composed of flesh and blood). As early as Paul, the word "flesh" begins to receive negative connotations, as the vehicle for sin in the human being (Rom. 7.5).

The body (Grk. *sōma*) is the physical being of the person animated by the soul. As such, it is both physical and spiritual, and sometimes is used as the equivalent of *nepeš*. Paul uses the term *sōma* in his metaphor of the church as the body of Christ, animated by Christ's spirit (1 Cor. 12.13).

The word *psychē*, or soul, occurs over a hundred times in the New Testament, illustrating its importance in early Christian thought. The soul is the seat and center of the inner life of the human, and the location of the feelings and emotions, especially love (1 Thess. 2.8). The soul is that part of the human person that survives after the death of the body, and receives the rewards and punishments of the afterlife (cf. Luke 16.19–31). Thus the soul is the vehicle of salvation. It cannot be injured by human instrumentality, but God can hand it over for destruction. Therefore the soul is the most important possession a person has (Mark 8.36–37). Thus the New Testament has moved beyond the Hebrew Bible concept of an inseparable *nepeš*, to the idea of a separate soul and body. The soul survives after death but may be reunited with the body in a physical resurrection (John 11.25).

The last word associated with the makeup of the human being in the New Testament is *pneuma*, or spirit. The spirit is the breath, that which gives life to the body; in fact, it is often used with "flesh" or "body" to denote the whole person (1 Cor. 5.3–5). The spirit is the seat of insight, often giving persons glimpses of things not visible to the naked eye (e.g., John 13.21). The spirit is also the location of feeling (particularly of love and grief) and will, so that at times the spirit and the flesh are in conflict: "the spirit indeed is willing, but the flesh is weak" (Matt. 26.41). The usage of the word "spirit" often overlaps with that of "soul," and the two together divide the inner life between them. However, the use of the term "spirit" in connection with Jesus emphasizes the most important aspect of "spirit": it is the divine attribute of the human being. God, who is spiritual, breathed his own spirit into the human at creation, and now the human spirit and the divine spirit are related. Often, it is the spirit of God that animates the life of the Christian, as at Pentecost (Acts 2.2–4). And it is the Holy Spirit which calls to the human spirit: "it is that very Spirit bearing witness with our spirit that we are children of God" (Rom. 8.16). Thus, early Christian writers pictured the human person as composed of flesh, soul, and spirit, with the flesh, as the vehicle of sin, as something to be tamed, and the soul and spirit, as the vehicles for salvation and participation in the divine, as those parts of the human to be emphasized and nurtured.

SIDNIE ANN WHITE

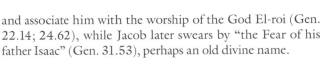

ISAAC. Son of Abraham and father of Esau and Jacob. The principal stories about Isaac are found in Genesis 21–28. Isaac is a more shadowy figure than the other patriarchs, and little if anything can be said of him as a historical figure. He is said to have been born when his parents were both advanced in years as a fulfillment of God's promise to Abraham to grant him posterity against all human expectation (see Rom. 4.16–22). In Genesis 22 God himself seems to challenge his own promise by demanding that Isaac be offered as a human sacrifice but rewards Abraham's unquestioning obedience by providing a ram as a substitute at the last possible moment. This story (the Aqedah) has been important in Judaism as a reminder of the precariousness of Israel's election and yet the sure promises of God, as well as in Christianity as a "type" of the sacrifice of Christ.

Of Isaac's maturity we learn little. Genesis 24 tells how he acquired a wife (Rebekah), but the principal characters in this tale are Isaac's servant and Rebekah's family. In Genesis 26 Isaac and Rebekah are involved in an incident with "Abimelech king of the Philistines" (an anachronistic reference), who takes Rebekah into his harem—essentially the same incident twice reported of Abraham and Sarah (Gen. 12 and 20). Isaac next appears as an old man, deceived by Jacob into giving him the blessing of the firstborn that should by right have been Esau's (Gen. 27). The stories about Isaac locate him at Beer-sheba in the far south of Judah (Gen. 26.23–33)

and associate him with the worship of the God El-roi (Gen. 22.14; 24.62), while Jacob later swears by "the Fear of his father Isaac" (Gen. 31.53), perhaps an old divine name.

JOHN BARTON

ISAIAH, THE BOOK OF. Isaiah is the first of the Major Prophets in both Jewish and Christian tradition. The book consists of sixty-six chapters that can be divided into five sections of roughly the same length (1–12; 13–27; 28–39; 40–55; 56–66). All except one begin with an attack on arrogance and an appeal for justice and culminate in a hymn or prophecy of salvation, and all except one are addressed to the people of Jerusalem. The one exception is chapters 40–55, which begins "Comfort, O comfort my people," and is addressed to an exiled community in Babylon during the sixth century BCE. The book is held together by common themes and phrases (e.g., "the Holy One of Israel," Jerusalem/Zion, justice and righteousness), by quotations from, or allusions to, earlier passages in later ones (e.g., 1.6 in 53.5; 6.1–13 40.1–8; 6.1 in 52.13 and 57.15; 11.6–9 in 65.25), and by other kinds of continuity, such as the life and times of the prophet (1.1; 6–9; 14.28; 20; 36–39; 40.1–8) and the downfall of Babylon (13–14; 46–47).

Contents. Chaps. 1–12 consist of prolonged and bitter attacks on the arrogance and hypocrisy of Jerusalem's leaders ("rulers of Sodom," 1.10; cf. Ezek. 16.49), interspersed

Eliezer asking for Rebekah to marry Issac (Gen. 24.34–51)

Sculpture by Claus Sluter of prophet Isaiah

with prophecies of a better age to come when swords will be beaten into plowshares (2.4; cf. Mic. 4.3) and "the wolf shall live with the lamb" (11.6). As the title suggests (1.1; 2.1), the prophet's visions place special emphasis on the role of Jerusalem and a royal savior from the line of David (9.2–7; 11.1–9). In such a context, it was inevitable that 7.14 would be interpreted as referring to the birth of either a royal savior, Hezekiah, or a future messiah.

These chapters also contain a memorable account, like those of other prophets (1 Kings 22.19–23; Jer. 23.18), of Isaiah's glimpse into the heavenly court where he was confronted by the awesome holiness of God and commissioned to convey God's judgment to his unhearing and unseeing people (chap. 6). This judgment theme continues into the narrative of his confrontation with King Ahaz during the Syro-Ephraimite crisis (chaps. 7–8; cf. 2 Kings 16). Like other eighth-century prophets, Isaiah prophesies that the Assyrians are the real danger and that they will sweep like a mighty river over the northern kingdoms and into Judah (8.5–8). He calls for faith (7.9; cf. 30.15) and sees beyond present gloom and anguish to future victory (9.1–5). Assyria is a tool in God's hand (10.5–7). Both the terror of a confrontation between human power and God's power, and the hope of the eventual victory of God's people, are expressed in the richly emotive term Immanuel, "God is with us" (7.14; 8.8; 8.10). The section ends with a short hymn of thanksgiving (chap. 12).

Chaps. 13–27 further proclaim God's sovereignty over history. Isaiah's oracles concerning the nations (cf. Jer. 46–51; Ezek. 24–32; Amos 1–2) begin with Babylon (13–14) and end with the entire earth (24–27). In addition to the customary taunts and mock laments (e.g., "How you are fallen from heaven, O Day Star, son of Dawn!" 14.12; cf. Amos 5.1–2), this series contains some unusual material: expressions of sympathy for the survivors of Moab (16.3–5), an unexpected blessing for Egypt and Assyria (19.24–5), and another glimpse into the trauma of a prophet's visionary experience (21.1–10).

The oracle concerning Tyre (chap. 23), an international seaport in contact with every part of the world, leads logically into the last part of this section in which the subject is the entire earth (24–27). These four chapters are often known as the "Isaiah apocalypse": although they do not have the literary characteristics of the book of Revelation and other true apocalypses, they do contain apocalyptic language and imagery. The whole earth is depicted as desolate, twisted, despoiled, and polluted; sun and moon are eclipsed (24.23); and the passage pictures an eschatological banquet (25.6), the resurrection of the dead (26.19; cf. 25.8), and God's ultimate victory over the host of heaven (24.21), Leviathan, the "fleeing . . . twisting serpent," and the "dragon that is in the sea" (27.1). The passage belongs firmly to Isaianic tradition, however, as is indicated by such recurring motifs as the city (26.1; cf. 1.21–26), the mountain of the Lord (25.6; cf. 2.2; 11.9), and the vineyard (27.2; cf. 5.1–7).

In chaps. 28–39, the prophet first directs the full force of his rhetoric against Israel and Judah again (28–31), just as Amos does after his oracles concerning the foreign nations (Amos 2.4–16). The whole preceding section (13–27) functions merely as a foil for this final condemnation of his own people. He takes up where he left off in 1–12: "Ah, the proud garland of the drunkards of Ephraim" (28.1; cf. 5.11–12). "The mighty flood" of an Assyrian invasion reappears from chap. 8, and the call for faith and courage in a city under siege is repeated (30.15; cf. 7.4, 9). This time the crisis is that of 701 BCE, when Sennacherib invaded Judah and Hezekiah was tempted to join forces with Egypt (31.1–3). Chaps. 36–37 tell the story of a miraculous victory over the Assyrians in that year, highlighting Isaiah's role. There were two other crises in the same year, Hezekiah's illness, when the prophet performs a solar miracle reminiscent of Joshua's at Gibeon (chap. 38; cf. Josh. 10.12, 14), and the visit of Babylonian ambassadors to Jerusalem, during which he foretells the Babylonian exile (chap. 39). Like chap. 39, the central chapters of this section, especially 34 and 35, point forward to the next section.

Chaps. 40–55 are often known as the "Babylonian chapters." They constitute the most distinctive and homogeneous part of the book, both stylistically and theologically, and are for that reason commonly referred to as "Second Isaiah" or "Deutero-Isaiah." Repetition is frequent (e.g., 40.1; 51.9; 52.1). The exiled community in Babylon is described and addressed collectively as "Zion" (feminine singular; e.g., 40.9; 51.17; 52.1–2) and "my servant" (e.g., 41.8; 44.1). The rise of Cyrus, king of the Medes and Persians, is described (45.1–3), as are the fall of Babylon (chap. 47) and the return of the exiles to Jerusalem in a new Exodus (48.20–21; 51.9–11; 52.11–12). The sheer scale of God's power in history and in creation is another recurring theme in these chapters (e.g., 40.12–20; 42.5–9; 45–9–13), as are explicit monotheism (e.g., 45.5, 6, 14, 21, 22), the ridicule of idolatry (e.g., 40.18–20; 44.9–20; 46.1–2), and feminine images for God (42.14; 46.3; 49.15; 66.9). Finally, the concept of healing and victory through the vicarious suffering of "the servant of the Lord" (52.13–53.12) marks out this section as unique in biblical prophecy.

The final section of the book (chaps. 56–66) is mainly concerned with the return of the exiles to Jerusalem and the building of a new society there. "Justice" and "righteousness" are again key motifs here as they were at the beginning (56.1; 59; 61.8; cf. 1.17). Foreigners and eunuchs will be admitted into the Temple (56.1). The poor and the oppressed will be set free (58.6–7; 61.1–2), and Temple sacrifice is finally rejected in favor of humility and repentance (66.1). The feminine imagery, introduced in chaps. 40–55, is further elaborated (62.1–5; 66.7–14). God is addressed as father (63.16; 64.8), and a striking variation on the God-as-warrior theme is the famous "grapes of wrath" passage (63.1–6) in which he is portrayed as a somewhat reluctant victor, limping home from war, bloodstained and stooping (v. 1; NRSV: "marching"). The last verse of the book, one of the few biblical texts on which a doctrine of hellfire can be based (66.24), is so gruesome that in Jewish custom the preceding verses about "the new heavens and the new earth" are repeated after it, to end the reading on a more hopeful and at the same time more characteristically Isaianic note.

Author. All that is known of Isaiah son of Amoz, the prophet to whom the book is attributed, is found in the book itself. He is not referred to elsewhere in the Bible apart from parallel passages in Kings and Chronicles (2 Kings 19–20; 2 Chron. 29–32). The book contains a few biographical details, which present the picture of a prophet in the traditional pattern: a glimpse into the heavenly court (chap. 6); the giving of symbolic names to his children (7.3; 8.1–4; cf. Hos. 2.1–9); dramatic appearances at the courts of kings (chaps. 7; 37–39; cf. 2 Sam. 12.1–15; 1 Kings 21.17–29; Jer. 22); prophesying through symbolic actions (20; cf. 1 Kings 22.11–12; Jer. 19; Ezek 12.1–7); the performing of miracles (38.7–8; cf. 1 Kings 18.20–46; 2 Kings 4.32–37); and the condemnation of injustice and oppression (1–5; cf. 2 Sam. 12.1–6; 1 Kings 21; Amos 5). According to an extrabiblical legend, he was martyred ("sawn in two"; cf. Heb. 11.37) in the reign of Manasseh.

The title informs us that he lived during the reigns of four kings of Judah (Uzziah, Jotham, Ahaz, and Hezekiah), that is to say, during the second half of the eighth century BCE. This was a period during which Judah's fortunes changed from affluence under Uzziah (see 2 Chron. 26) to defeat and humiliation at the hands of the Assyrians in 701 BCE (2 Kings 18). Many passages clearly reflect those traumatic years—the approaching Assyrian army (5.26–30; 10.28–32), the devastation of the land of Judah (1.7–8), the folly of Judah's leaders (chaps. 30–31)—and were probably composed at that time. Perhaps the hopes accompanying the coronation of Hezekiah in 715 BCE are expressed in the dynastic hymn 9–1–7.

A few sections of narrative, however, clearly reflect later ideas and attitudes. The story of Jerusalem's miraculous deliverance from the Assyrian army under Sennacherib in 701 (chaps. 36–37), for example, though based on the fact that Jerusalem was not destroyed on that occasion, probably owes much to an upsurge of national confidence during the reign of Josiah (626–609) when the Assyrian empire collapsed. The annals of Sennacherib, and 2 Kings 18.14–16 (omitted from the Isaianic version), suggest that the reality was very different.

Some passages, mainly in chaps. 40–66, contain no references at all to the Assyrians, but frequently allude to events and conditions in the Babylonian period (605–538 BCE):

Jerusalem and the Temple in ruins (44.28; 49.17); Babylonian idols (46.1–2); a Jewish colony at Syene (Elephantine) in Egypt (49.12); Cyrus (45.1). The bulk of the book was thus probably composed more than a century after the lifetime of Isaiah. The popular division into three sections, First Isaiah (chaps. 1–39) dated to the eighth century BCE, Second (Deutero-) Isaiah (chaps. 40–55) to the sixth, and Third Isaiah (chaps. 56–66) to the fifth, is a crude oversimplification. The literary and theological unity of the whole book is unmistakable; and some parts of First Isaiah, notably the two Babylonian chapters (13–14) and the Isaiah apocalypse (24–27), manifestly belong to the sixth century or later. Chaps. 24–27 should probably be dated to the fourth century BCE, contemporary with Joel. Each passage must be handled on its own, though both as a product of its age and in the context of the Isaianic corpus as a whole.

Key Concepts. Some development is evident from the earliest chapters to the latest. Different images and illustrations are used in different parts of the book, reflecting changes in historical context. But there are enough common themes running throughout the book for us to be able to discuss Isaianic tradition as a rich and distinctive entity within biblical theology. Concepts such as holiness, justice, righteousness, salvation, faith, and peace are brilliantly related to the two fundamental Isaianic themes, the idea of God as "the Holy One of Israel" and the centrality of the city of Jerusalem, which are epitomized in some of the most familiar biblical images and visions. Holiness, perhaps the most distinctive of these concepts, is expressed not only in the recurring epithet "Holy One of Israel" but also in the prophet's vision of God "in the year that King Uzziah died" (6.1–3). Holiness refers first to the transcendent majesty of the king of the universe, creator of all things (6.3; 40.12–23) and Lord of history (10.5–7; 45.1–7). But in Isaiah it has an ethical dimension too: the Holy One condemns moral uncleanness (6.5–7) and the holy city will be

The destruction of the army of Sennacherib, King of Assyria (704–681 BCE) (Isa. 37.36)

117

characterized by justice and peace (11.6–9; 56.1–8). Ritual purity and cultic practices are not enough in themselves; indeed, they are savagely condemned if they take the place of social justice (1.11–17; 58) or humility (66.1–4). The Temple plays only a minor role in the visions of a new Jerusalem (1.21–26; 2.2–4; 4-2-6; 26.1–6; 49.16–21; 65.17–25), and in those passages where it is mentioned, the emphasis is on opening its doors to foreigners (56.3–8) and to the nations of the world (2.2–4; 66.18–21).

Many of the most elaborate visions of a new age focus on an individual savior figure, champion of justice and righteousness. In some he is explicitly identified as a king from the royal lineage of David (9.2–7; 11.1–5), and this is no doubt implied in others (32.1–2; 42.1–4; cf. 55.3). In the context of the Babylonian exile, Cyrus is hailed as the Lord's anointed (45.1–7; cf. 41.2–3), and in one passage the savior figure is represented as a prophet, anointed to "bring good news to the oppressed" (61.1–4; cf. Luke 4.18–19). This prophetic model seems to underlie two others, in which he is described as "the servant of the Lord" (49.1–6; 50.4–9), though in both these cases the story of the "servant" may be understood to refer to the experience of Israel rather than any individual (cf. 49.3).

Finally, there is the celebrated "suffering servant" passage, which seems to tell the story of an individual who heals and redeems by vicarious suffering (52.13–53.12). At one time considered the last of four autonomous "servant songs" (42.1–4; 49.1–6; 50.4–9; 52.13–53.12), it is rather to be understood as an independent hymn of thanksgiving expressing the people's confidence in the power of God to intervene on their behalf, to heal their wounds, and to forgive their sins. There is no answer to the question of who the servant is or how he achieves this. The emphasis, here as elsewhere in the Isaianic tradition (1.21–26; 9.2–7; 35; 41.14–16; 49.14–26; 52.1–2), is on a transformation from humiliation to exaltation, defeat to victory. If it reflects the release of Jehoiachin from prison in Babylon in 660 BCE (2 Kings 25.27–30; Jer. 52.31–34), or the unexpected military successes of Cyrus that eventually led to the fall of Babylon in 538 BCE; it also draws on traditional religious ideas, such as the scapegoat ritual on the Day of Atonement (53.4, 6, 12; cf. Lev. 16.20–22) and the figure of Moses, the "servant of the Lord" (Deut. 34.5; Josh. 1.1, 2, 13; etc.), who offered to die for his people (53.7–9, 12; cf. Exod. 32.32). The Exodus and wilderness motifs are prominent throughout these chapters (e.g., 43.15–21; 48.20–21; 51.9–11; 52.11–12; 55.12–13).

Influence. The book of Isaiah has played a central role in Christian liturgy and theology. It is sometimes called the "Fifth Gospel" because, in the words of Jerome, Isaiah recounts the life of the Messiah in such a way as to make one think he is "telling the story of what has already happened rather than what is still to come." Isaiah is more often quoted in the New Testament than is any other book of the Hebrew Bible apart from Psalms and has provided the church with much of its most familiar language and imagery, including the ox and the ass (1.3), the *Sanctus* (6.3), the Immanuel prophecy (7.14), the key of David (22.22), the suffering Messiah (53), the winepress (63.3), and the New Jerusalem (65.18). The popularity of the Jesse tree motif (11.1) in Christian art, and of Handel's *Messiah* (largely based on excerpts from chaps. 7; 9; 34; 40; 52; 53; 60) have further extended the influence of Isaiah on western culture. Since the Second Vatican Council (1962–1965), which quotes 2.4 and 32.17 in an important statement on peace and social justice (*Gaudium et spes*, para. 70), Isaiah has provided liberation theologians and feminists with many of their key scriptural texts.

Isaiah is prominent in synagogue lectionaries, and has made a profound and distinctive impression on Jewish literary and religious tradition, in particular its Zion-centered visions of justice and peace (e.g., 2.2–4; 11.6–9).

JOHN F. A. SAWYER

Jacob wrestling with the Angel (Gen. 32.24)

ISHMAEL. Son of Abraham and Hagar. A generally positive attitude toward Ishmael and thus toward his descendants is found in the Genesis traditions. He is the recipient of a special divine blessing (Gen 17.20) and is present at the burial of Abraham (25.9). Like Jacob, Ishmael is the father of twelve sons, the ancestors of twelve tribes (Gen 25.16). Another indication of the generally favorable view of this patriarch is the fact that several other later Israelites have the same name. There are, however, hints of ethnic tension in the narratives as well. Like Cain, Ishmael is depicted as an outcast and prone to violence (Gen. 16.12), and as a wanderer (note the opening words of Melville's *Moby-Dick*). The Ishmaelites are elsewhere described as leading a typically nomadic life (Gen. 37.25; Ps. 83.6; 1 Chron. 27.30). The story of Ishmael and Hagar's separation from Abraham's household contains the kind of scurrilous sexual innuendo found elsewhere in J's etiological narratives concerning Israel's neighbors.

In Muslim tradition, the Arabs trace their ancestry back to Abraham through Ishmael. Because Ishmael was circumcised (Gen. 17.25), so are most Muslims. And, analogous to Paul's reversal of the figures of Isaac and Ishmael (Gal. 4.24–26), Muslim tradition makes Ishmael rather than Isaac the son Abraham was commanded to sacrifice.

MICHAEL D. COOGAN

ISRAEL. The name Israel ("he contended with God") is conferred on Jacob by a divine messenger after their struggle at the Wadi Jabbok (Gen. 32.28; 35.10; Hos. 12.3). The twelve sons of Jacob and their tribal descendants are therefore called "the sons of Israel" (the Israelites). The earliest nonbiblical reference to Israel occurs on the inscription of Merneptah, king of Egypt (ca. 1200 BCE).

Israel remains the normal designation for the entire nation until the division of the kingdom in 924 BCE (1 Kings 12.1–20). Biblical authors term the ten northern tribes (i.e., the northern kingdom) Israel and the two southern tribes (i.e., the southern kingdom) Judah. Hence, after the northern kingdom falls (722 BCE) and only Judah remains, its residents are called Judahites or Judeans.

In the postexilic period the residents of Judah or Yehud are regularly called Jews, but Israel is also used.

Samaria, the capital of the northern kingdom of Israel, falling to the Assyrians (2 Kings 17.5–6)

In postexilic writings (e.g., Chronicles) the term Israel can therefore denote Jacob, the united kingdom, the northern kingdom, Judah, or simply the descendants of Israel. In some cases, the meaning of Israel is, however, deliberately more restrictive (e.g., the returning exiles in Ezra 2.2, 70).

In rabbinic literature Israel refers to the Jewish people, and the land of Israel describes the country of the Israelite people. In the New Testament Israel can refer to the Jewish people (2 Cor. 3.12; Rom. 11.26) or to the church (Gal. 6.16).

GARY N. KNOPPERS

ISRAEL, HISTORY OF.

The Biblical Story of Israel. Genesis 32.28 reports God's words to Jacob: "You shall no longer be called Jacob, but Israel, for you have striven with God and with humans, and have prevailed." As the biblical narrative continues, one reads that Jacob/Israel immigrated with his family to Egypt where, during a long sojourn, his twelve sons fathered twelve tribes. Eventually, these twelve "Israelite" tribes were led out of Egypt by Moses, wandered for forty years in the wilderness, and finally reached the plains of Moab east of the Jordan River. At that point in the biblical narrative, Joshua succeeded Moses and led the tribes across the Jordan into Canaan, where they took possession of the land and divided it among themselves. The book of Judges finds the tribes settled in Canaan following Joshua's death, without stable leadership and often oppressed by surrounding peoples. "In those days there was no king in Israel; all the people did what was right in their own eyes" (Judg. 17.6).

In the time of the prophet Samuel, when the Philistines were oppressing Israel, the people cried out to Samuel to give them a king. Against his better judgment, Samuel accommodated their desire by anointing Saul to be the first king of Israel. Thus Saul, followed by David and then

Solomon, ruled over a kingdom that consisted primarily of the twelve Israelite tribes with their respective territories. When Solomon died, this Israelite monarchy split into two rival kingdoms—a northern kingdom, composed of ten tribes, which kept the name Israel, and a southern kingdom, composed of the two remaining tribes, Judah and Benjamin, which took the name Judah. These two kingdoms existed side-by-side for two centuries, sometimes at war with each other, sometimes at peace, until the northern kingdom was conquered by Assyria and its territory annexed by that great empire (722 BCE). Judah also fell under Assyrian domination, but it maintained its political identity for almost a century and a half, until it fell to the Babylonians (587/586 BCE).

Hopes of national recovery remained alive during the long years of Assyrian and Babylonian domination, however, and continued in the Jewish community (the remnant of the kingdom of Judah) that struggled for survival under Persian rule. These hopes are expressed in the prophetical books of the Hebrew Bible. Moreover, the hope was not just for recovery of Judah but for a united Israel as it had existed in the "golden age" of David and Solomon.

Thus, the biblical writers use the name Israel in different ways. It can refer to the patriarch Jacob (Gen. 35.21–22; 43.6–11); to the twelve tribes (constantly referred to as "the children of Israel" in the books Exodus through Judges); to the early united monarchy ruled over by Saul, David, and Solomon (1 Sam. 13.1; 14.47–48; 2 Sam. 8.15; 1 Kings 4.1; etc.); to the northern kingdom after the split of the united monarchy (1 Kings 14.19; 15–25; 2 Kings 17.21–23); or to the restored nation hoped for in the future (Amos 9.13–15; Zeph. 3.14–20).

Historical Uncertainties and Extrabiblical Sources. The biblical story of Israel, when examined in detail, presents numerous internal inconsistencies—for example, the several enumerations of the Israelite tribes do not always identify the same twelve (compare Gen. 49; Num. 1.20–43; 26.5–50; Deut. 33), nor do they take into account other important tribal groups such as the Calebites and Kenizzites. Moreover, the story presupposes concepts that were generally accepted in ancient times but not today, such as the idea that each of the world's nations descended from a single individual (see Gen. 10).

An Egyptian inscription from the reign of Pharaoh Merneptah (ca. 1200 BCE) provides the earliest known non-biblical reference to Israel, and the only such reference earlier than the ninth century BCE. The Merneptah inscription is a royal monumental text inscribed on a stele discovered at the site of ancient Thebes. Unfortunately, we learn no more from it regarding Israel than that a people known by that name was on the scene in Palestine by the end of the thirteenth century. Later texts from the ninth century are also royal inscriptions, one commissioned by King Mesha of Moab (see 2 Kings 3 and Moabite Stone), and several others from the reign of an Assyrian king, Shalmaneser III (858–824 BCE). Israel and Judah were separate kingdoms by the ninth century, and it is Israel that figures in these texts. Mesha reports that King Omri of Israel had "humbled" Moab and claims recovery of Moabite independence among the accomplishments of his own reign. Shalmaneser reports a series of military campaigns into Syria-Palestine and mentions in that context two Israelite kings, Ahab and Jehu. Occasional references to Israelite and Judean kings appear in later Assyrian and Babylonian documents, usually in the context of military campaign reports. These references in extrabiblical documents are especially useful for establishing a chronological framework for the Israelite and Judean kings and for correlating biblical history with international affairs.

Archaeological excavations at Palestinian sites provide information about the material culture of biblical times and also allow for some correlations. For example, the time of the "judges" in Israel would seem to correspond roughly to the opening centuries of the Iron Age (ca. 1200—1000 BCE), which was a period of transition and change in Palestine. Many of the old cities that had flourished during the Bronze Age, especially in the lowlands, were destroyed. Most of them were rebuilt but on a much smaller scale. At the same time, there was a marked increase in the number of small village settlements in areas such as the central hill country, which seem to have been only sparsely populated during the Bronze Age. Note that most of the stories of the book of Judges have their setting among the villages in the north-central (Ephraimite) hill country.

The writer of 2 Kings 9.10–14 credits Solomon with building (or fortifying) several cities including Hazor, Megiddo, and Gezer. Excavations at all three of these places have unearthed remains of buildings and fortifications that date from approximately 1000 BCE; their relatively impressive scale is suggestive of royal architecture, and for this reason archaeologists generally associate them with Solomon. A somewhat more impressive royal building program from approximately the ninth century seems to be indicated by the ruins at Hazor, Megiddo, and Samaria. This second building program generally is associated with the Omride rulers of Israel, particularly Omri and Ahab. Remains from later phases of the cities and villages of Israel and Judah show a marked decline in material wealth, many of them ending finally with destruction in approxi-

mately the seventh and early sixth centuries BCE. No doubt these later phases correspond to the years of foreign domination by the Syrians, Assyrians, and Babylonians.

Contemporary Views Regarding the History of Israel. Given the uncertainties that arise from the biblical story, the paucity of references to Israel or Israelites in extrabiblical documents, and the very generalized nature of evidence from artifacts, it is not surprising that present-day scholars hold widely divergent views concerning Israel's history. At one extreme are those who hold that the biblical story is an essentially accurate portrayal of Israel's past; at the other are those who see the Bible as a virtually useless source for historical information and regard it as futile even to speculate on the details of Israelite history. Most biblical scholars and ancient historians hold a moderate position between these two extremes. There seems to be a growing consensus, for example, on the following points.

Nothing can be said with certainty about the origin of the various tribes and clans that composed early Israel and Judah. For the most part, these tribal groupings probably emerged gradually from the diffuse population of Late Bronze and early Iron Age Palestine rather than having entered the land from elsewhere. The name Israel probably referred in premonarchic times primarily to the tribe of Ephraim, settled in the north-central hill country, but would have been understood to include certain surrounding tribes (such as Benjamin, Manasseh, and Gilead) that Ephraim dominated. This Ephraim/Israel tribal group would have been the Israel to which the Merneptah inscription refers; most of the stories in the book of Judges have to do with this tribal group; and it was the core of Saul's kingdom, which he appropriately called Israel.

One should not think of Saul's Israel as a highly organized kingdom with precisely defined boundaries. Moreover, loyalty to him probably varied from region to region, with Saul's strongest base of support being the Ephraim-Benjamin-Gilead-Manasseh zone. There is nothing to suggest that the Galilean tribes were part of his kingdom. His campaign against the Amalekites (1 Sam. 15) implies thoroughfare through Judahite territory. Saul also received some Judean support in his attempts to arrest David (1 Sam. 23.12–13; 26.1–5). This, however, does not necessarily mean that he exercised any sort of permanent control over Judah. In Judah, as in other peripheral areas, Saul's authority probably lasted only as long as he was present with his troops or the local people needed his protection against some other threat.

The battle of Gilboa, in which Saul and Jonathan were killed, left the kingdom on the verge of collapse (1 Sam. 31.1–7). A surviving son (Ishbaal [Ishbosheth]) claimed the throne but transferred his residency to Mahanaim in Transjordan and soon was assassinated (2 Sam 2.8–10; 4.1–3). Thereupon the elders of Israel went to David, who in the meantime had established a kingdom in the south-central "Judean" hill country, and recognized him as their ruler also (2 Sam. 2.1–4; 5.1–3). Later David would make Jerusalem his capital and expand his realm to include much of Palestine (2 Sam. 5.6–10; 8).

Thus, the Davidic-Solomonic monarchy was not exactly continuous with Saul's Israel. Moreover, the Israelites appear to have maintained their separate identity under David and Solomon—for example, there was some rivalry between the Israelites and the Judahites (2 Sam. 19.41–43), as well as ongoing opposition to Davidic rule. The Israelites played a central role in both Absalom's and Sheba's rebellions against David (2 Sam. 15–20); Solomon subjected them to forced labor in connection with his royal building projects (1 Kings 11.28); and when Solomon died they rebelled again, this time successfully (1 Kings 12.1–20). Thus was established the northern Israelite kingdom, which the biblical writers depict as a rebel and apostate state, but which the rebels themselves no doubt regarded as a restoration of pre-Davidic Israel. At the core of the rebel (or restored) kingdom was the old Ephraim/Israel tribal area, but it included additional territories (e.g., Jezreel and Galilee) and cities (e.g., Shechem) that had been annexed by David. The small tribal area of Benjamin became a disputed frontier between the rival kingdoms of Israel and Judah.

The northern kingdom of Israel lasted approximately two centuries (ca. 924–722 BCE), which may be divided into four phases.

Unstable beginnings (ca. 924–885). Separation left both Israel and Judah weak, while mutual warfare drained their strength even further. Moreover, Israel suffered dynastic instability that resulted finally in civil war. (See especially 1 Kings 15.25–16.22.)

The Omride dynasty (ca. 885–843). Omri, who emerged victorious from the civil war, founded a dynasty that continued through four kings. Under Omri and his son Ahab, Israel enjoyed a period of international prestige and internal prosperity that may have surpassed that of Solomon's day. Israel clearly overshadowed and probably dominated Judah during this period. Omri built a new capital for the kingdom, which he named Samaria. The Omride period was remembered, however, as a time of economic and social injustice, and of conflict between Baalism and Yahwism. Elijah and Jezebel were colorful characters of the Omride era. (See especially 1 Kings 15.21–2 Kings 10.27.)

The Jehu dynasty (ca. 843–745). Simultaneous and related palace coups brought a new ruler to the thrones of both Israel and Judah in approximately 843 BCE. Jehu, who seized power in Israel under the banner of Yahwism, founded a dynasty that lasted approximately a century.

Damascus, however, was already on the rise when Jehu seized the throne, and it totally dominated Israel during the reigns of Jehu and his son, Jehoahaz. Damascus, faced with problems from the direction of Assyria, eventually lost its hold on Israel, and Israel in turn enjoyed a brief period of recovery and prosperity. The moment of prosperity is to be associated especially with the reign of Jeroboam II. The Elisha stories reflect the difficult times experienced by the people of Israel during the early years of the Jehu dynasty, the years of Syrian domination. The book of Amos reflects the situation during the later years, when Israel is enjoying a recovery of prosperity, and implies that the problems of economic and social injustice remained. Zechariah, son of Jeroboam II, was assassinated soon after coming to the throne in approximately 745 BCE, and Tiglath-pileser III ascended the Assyrian throne the following year. Israel's end was near. (See especially 2 Kings 9–10; 12.17–13.25; 14.23–29; 15.8–12.)

Assyrian conquest and annexation (745–722). Already during the Omride era, Assyrian kings had threatened the little kingdoms of Syria-Palestine in general and Israel in particular. Now Assyria turned its attention to the west and, under Tiglath-pileser III (744–727), secured a firm grip on the whole region. Israel, which offered some resistance at first in coordination with Damascus, was reduced to vassal status and Hoshea confirmed as king. After Tiglath-pileser's death, however, Hoshea attempted to throw off the Assyrian yoke. This was a disastrous move: Assyria conquered Samaria, annexed the kingdom's territory, exiled thousands of its leading citizens, and replaced them with foreigners from other conquered lands. (See especially 2 Kings 15.13–31; 17)

The remnants of the kingdom of Israel usually are referred to in later literature as Samaritans, after the name of the kingdom's chief city founded by Omri (e.g., Luke 9.52; 10.29–41; John 4.1–42). A small group of Samaritans still survives in the vicinity of Nablus.

J. MAXWELL MILLER

A senior priest of the modern Samaritan community holds a Torah scroll at their most sacred site at Mount Gerizim.

J

JACOB. Son of Isaac and Rebekah and younger brother of Esau. The Bible presents Jacob in a double light. On the one hand, he is the revered ancestor of the people of Israel, and indeed the name "Israel" is said to have been given him by God after he had wrestled with God himself at Penuel (Gen. 32.28; but see also Gen. 35.10); on the other, he is a trickster, who deceives his brother into parting with his birthright (Gen. 25.29–34) and his father into giving him the blessing of the firstborn that should have belonged to Esau (Gen. 27). Hosea 12.2–6 and Isaiah 43.27 may well indicate that Jacob's acts were later regarded as sinful, although the accounts in Genesis seem to record them without censure. Jacob is presented as a pastoralist, whereas Esau is a hunter (Gen. 25.27), and the stories about them may reflect rivalries between these two groups in later times, as with the story of Cain and Abel (Gen. 4.1–16); equally, they are contrasted as the ancestors respectively of Israelites and Edomites (Gen. 32.3).

Jacob, like his father Isaac, seeks a wife in Mesopotamia (Gen. 28.1–5). On the way Jacob encamps at Bethel and there in a dream sees divine messengers ascending and descending on a staircase between earth and heaven and erects a pillar to commemorate the incident—perhaps a story to explain why Israelites worshiped at what had been a Canaanite sanctuary. Jacob the trickster is himself tricked by his uncle Laban into working fourteen years to obtain the wife he desires, Rachel; Jacob contracts to work for seven years but at the end of that time is given Leah, her elder sister, instead (Gen. 29.15–30). Jacob has his revenge on Laban by swindling him out of large flocks and herds (Gen. 30.25–31.21) and flees from Laban's house to return to the land of Canaan but is finally reconciled with his uncle (Gen. 31.36–54). After the mysterious incident at Penuel there follows a reconciliation also with Esau (Gen. 33.1–16).

The remaining stories of Jacob focus on the deeds of his children, the ancestors of the twelve tribes of Israel. Jacob' appears as an old man in the story of Joseph (Gen. 37; 39–50), where the theme of trickery recurs in the deceit by which he is robbed of his favorite son by Joseph's jealous brothers (Gen. 42.36). Eventually Jacob goes down to Egypt with his sons and dies there (Gen. 49.33), but his embalmed body (Gen. 50.2–3) is taken for burial to the land of Canaan by Joseph and his brothers (Gen 50.7–13). The blessing of Jacob (Gen. 49.2–27) is widely held to contain some of the oldest poetry in the Bible.

JOHN BARTON

JAMES. Four persons in the New Testament have the name "James" (Greek *Iakōbos*), which is one of two Greek forms of the Hebrew name Jacob (the other being the simple transliteration *Iakōb*). Since Jacob was a revered ancestor

Jacob blessing the sons of Joseph (Gen. 48.8–22) (Rembrandt van Rijn, 1656)

of Israel, James was a common name among Jews in the Roman period.

James, Son of Zebedee, was a Galilean fisherman in the area of Capernaum on the Sea of Galilee, a partner (along with his brother John) of Simon Peter (Luke 5.10). He was working in the family business headed by his father when called by Jesus to be his disciple (Mark 1.19–20). James and John along with Peter formed the inner core of three among the twelve apostles; they witnessed the raising of Jairus's daughter, were present at the transfiguration, and observed (and partially slept through) Jesus' agony in Gethsemane.

Apparently James and John either expressed themselves explosively or expected God to bring sudden judgment on the enemies of Jesus, for they were nicknamed "Boanerges" ("sons of thunder," Mark 3.17; cf. Luke 9.51–56). Their request to sit at Jesus' right and left hand in his kingdom earned them the anger of the other apostles and a mild rebuke from Jesus (Mark 10.35–45; Matt. 20.20–28; Luke 22.24–27).

Outside the synoptic Gospels James, son of Zebedee, appears only in Acts. He was present in the upper room with the group waiting for Pentecost (Acts 1.13). The only other reference to him in the New Testament is the cryptic note that Herod (Agrippa I) had him killed (Acts 12.2). He was thus the second recorded martyr of the church (after Stephen) and the first of the apostolic band to die (except for Judas Iscariot, who had been replaced as an apostle).

James, Son of Alphaeus, was a Galilean Jew and one of the twelve (Matt. 10.3; Mark 3.18; Luke 6.15; Acts 1.13); many believe he is the same person as James the younger (Mark 15.40). The Greek term translated "the younger" can also be translated "the little," which probably gives the correct meaning (i.e., he was shorter than James, son of Zebedee). If this identification is correct, this otherwise unknown apostle had a mother named Mary who was present at the crucifixion and was a witness of the resurrection and a brother Joseph (or Joses) who was probably a well-known early Christian (Matt. 27.56; Mark 16.1; Luke 24.10).

James, Father (KJV "brother") of the Apostle Judas (not Iscariot), is mentioned only by Luke (Luke 6.16; Acts 1.13). Nothing further is known about him.

James, Brother of Jesus, is named in Matthew 13.55 and Mark 6.3 along with three other brothers of Jesus. The Gospels indicate that neither James nor his brothers were followers of Jesus before the crucifixion (Mark 3.21, 1–35; Luke 8.19–20; Matt. 12–46–50; John 7.1–9). After the Resurrection, however, these same brothers are mentioned among the group of believers at prayer before Pentecost (Acts 1.14). Paul explains the reason for this change of heart (at least in James) in the statement that the risen Jesus had appeared personally to James (1 Cor. 15.7). James apparently rose quickly in the ranks of the church. In Acts 15.13 it is James, not Peter, who is named as the preeminent leader who summed up the deliberations of the council at Jerusalem (49 or 50 CE). Thus, he is viewed as the person who presided over the compromise that allowed Jewish and gentile Christians to remain unified without either forcing gentiles to become Jews or violating Jewish cultural sensibilities (see also Acts 21.18–26).

In his letter to the Galatians (2.9), Paul mentions James along with Peter and John, son of Zebedee, as "acknowledged pillars" of the church at Jerusalem. James's authority appears clearly in Galatians 2.12, for emissaries from Jerusalem are said to come "from James" and apparently therefore had authority as his official representatives. Scholars are divided over whether the effort of the emissaries to split Jewish from gentile congregations was James's position (in which case Paul and Acts give differing pictures of James) or whether he had sent them for some other purpose.

James's leadership was well enough known so that the letter of James is attributed to him with a simple "James, a servant of God and of the Lord Jesus Christ" (James 1.1), and the author of the letter of Jude identifies himself as "Jude, a servant of Jesus Christ and brother of James" (Jude 1). While the attribution of both these letters is debated, there is reason to believe that at least the material in the letter of James, if not the writing itself, stems from the brother of Jesus, and this material reveals an authoritative leader in a Palestinian context.

In 61 CE James suffered martyrdom at the instigation of the high priest Ananus after the sudden death in office of the procurator Festus (Josephus, *Ant.* 20.9.200). In the following centuries legends about James developed. For example, Hegesippus reports that James was known as "James the Just" because of his exemplary piety (Eusebius, *Hist. eccl.* 2.23), and Jerome connects him with the lost apocryphal *Gospel according to the Hebrews* (*De viris illustrious 2*). But other than the fact of his martyrdom and its approximate date, there is little evidence that any of these legends are accurate, and most are certainly apocryphal.

PETER H. DAVIDS

JAMES, THE LETTER OF.

Outline. The letter of James is a literary composition (i.e., a letter designed to be published rather than dispatched like a true letter) and follows the conventions of the literary letter in its structure:

I. Greeting (1.1)
II. Opening statement (1.2–27)
   A. Testing, wisdom, and wealth (1.2–11)
     1. Testing and faith (1.2–4)
     2. Wisdom and faith (1.5 8)
     3. Wealth and faith (1.9–11)
   B. Testing, speech, and action (1.12–27)
     1. Testing and sin (1.12–15)
     2. God's gift and sinful speech (1.16–21)
     3. Action and sin (1.22–27) (1.26–27 are transition verses)
III. Wealth and faith (2.1–26)
   A. Wealth and prejudice (2.1–13)
     1. Thesis (2.1)
     2. Illustration of the problem (2.2–4)
     3. Theological argument (2.5–7)
     4. Biblical passage 1 (2.8–9)
     5. Biblical passage 2 (2.10–11)
     6. Summary (2.12–13)
   B. Giving and faith (2.14–26)
     1. Thesis (2.14)
     2. Illustration of the problem (2.15–17)
     3. Theological argument (2.18–19)
     4. Biblical passage 1 (2.20–24)
     5. Biblical passage 2 (2.25)
     6. Summary (2.26)
IV. Wisdom and speech (3.1–4.12)
   A. Danger of sinful speech (3.1–12)
   B. God's gift of wisdom (3.13–18)
   C. Repentance from sinful speech and action (4.1–10)
   D. Example of sinful speech (4.11–12)

  V. Testing and wealth (4.13–5.6)
      A. Testing through wealth (4.13–17)
      B. Testing by the wealthy (5.1–6)
 VI. Closing: Patience and prayer (5.7–20)
      A. Conclusion: patience (5.7–11)
      B. Oaths (5.12)
      C. Prayer and health (5.13–18)
      D. Purpose of the letter (5.19–20)

Authorship and Date. The letter claims in 1.1 to come from James, the brother of Jesus, but this claim has been disputed frequently because of the theology of the letter (not that of an observant Jew) and the excellent quality of the Greek. Thus, the suggestion is frequently made that it is a pseudonymous letter from the late first century CE attributed to James because he had been a great leader of the church.

While this position is widely held, it is not the only possible one. First, the theology of the letter is not as difficult as it appears, especially if one accepts the portrait of James given in Acts over that of later legends. These legends portray James as being observant of the Law of Moses, but they contain so many improbable details that they cannot be trusted. On the other hand, Acts portrays him as a Jewish leader who was also a diplomat, concerned that both Jew and gentile live together in the church. There is no evidence that his teaching in Jerusalem (where the observance of the law was not an issue) had a particularly legalistic tone.

Second, while the Greek is good, among the best in the New Testament, it does from time to time employ obvious Semitisms. Furthermore, while there is a unity to the letter, the vocabulary is inconsistent (e.g., 1.12–15 and 4.1–10 use different words for the same concept). The best explanation of these data is that the letter is a collection of sermons and sayings from James (and possibly from Jesus as well, from whom 5.12 unquestionably comes) edited into letter form. This view also explains the simple attribution (as opposed to more flowery titles used for James by the end of the first

century) and the fact that the letter was first circulated in the eastern church and so is missing in some of the early canon lists in North Africa and the West (although it was known in Rome by the end of the first century, being used by the author of the *Shepherd of Hernias*). Finally, it accounts for the absence in the letter of a knowledge of Paul's writings on the one hand and the presence of depictions of Palestinian culture on the other.

If the material comes from James and reflects his setting, then the most likely place of editing is Jerusalem or at least Judea. Some of the material probably dates from before Paul's activity became well known in Jerusalem (49 CE or earlier), for it shows no awareness of Pauline formulations or at best knows only distorted oral reports of his teaching. But the final editing was probably triggered by the martyrdom of James and the desire to preserve and spread his teaching, that is, after 61 CE but probably before the fall of Jerusalem in 70 CE.

Unity. The letter of James has often been regarded as a collection of miscellaneous sayings without any internal unity other than an interest in some recurring themes. To a degree this is true, for the letter does contain sayings (1.26–27; 2.13; 3.18) and homilies (2.1–12; 2.14–26) that were originally not unified. But the discovery of the literary letter form with the doubled opening (i.e., A B C, A′ B′ C′) and the realization that the three main sections of the letter take up in reverse the topics mentioned in the opening (C B A) together show that these homilies and sayings have been edited into a unified whole. Even the ending fits this form. Thus, while the editor has been conservative and preserved the integrity of the various units (and even some Semitic expressions like "doers of the word" [1.23]), James is unlike Proverbs or similar wisdom literature, a mere collection of sayings; it has a unified structure.

Theology. James is writing in the context of a church under pressure, not facing impending martyrdom but discrimination and economic persecution. He is concerned about two tendencies, adopting the mores of the oppressors (e.g., valuing money over community) and attacking other members of the community (e.g., gossip, criticism). Thus his chief concern is the unity of the community and turning the community back from practices that threaten to disrupt it (5.19–20). Within this overriding concern there are several major themes.

The first is testing. Only true commitment to God will resist the overtures of the devil (4.7) made through the impulses of internal cravings. But it is this patient endurance, even when suffering, that God will reward when he comes to judge the world (5.7–8, 10). In this context James introduces the "double-minded" person (1.8; 4.8) and doubter. This is not the person who trusts in God but still struggles with doubt; it is the person who does the correct religious acts (because God might answer prayer) yet whose real trust (as seen in daily actions) is in human solutions. God does not tolerate such dual trust, for it is spiritual adultery (4.4).

The second major theme is wisdom. God offers people the gift of wisdom to help them stand firm in the test. One mark of this wisdom is the gentle attitude that it produces in speech and action (3.13–18). Conversely, conflict in the community is a mark of the love of the world rather than of God.

The third theme is wealth. In the culture in which James lives, the wealthy are by and large the oppressors of the Christians, many of whom are poor. Christians, however, must not accept the world's values or view their material poverty with concern; if they are truly committed to God,

'And the Prayer of Faith Shall Save the Sick' (James 5:15) (John Frederick Lewis, 1872)

they will show it in generous charity (2.14–26) and in seeking God's will in all their business plans (4.13–17).

Throughout the letter are found the themes of prayer and maintaining the proper perspective. When one is experiencing deprivation, it is easy to focus on the suffering, but James calls for joy (1.2) because the Christian has gained the perspective of God and realizes that the suffering is temporary, the return of Christ as judge imminent, and the rewards of God eternal. With this perspective the Christian should pray in confidence. This prayer is the key to endurance (chap. 1), to the supply of real needs (chap. 4), and to physical and spiritual healing (chap. 5). When he speaks of healing (5.14–18), James assumes this to be the normal practice of the church; unlike Paul (1 Cor. 12.9, 30), he does not look to the gifted healer for help, but to the elders.

James and Paul. Because of the famous section in 2.14–26, James has often been seen as opposing Paul's stress on justification by faith without the deeds of the Law. This appears true until one realizes that James uses his critical terms in ways that differ from Paul; in fact, James is using terminology in its older, original sense. Works for Paul are works of the Law, that is, ritual acts such as circumcision; works for James are deeds of charity such as, according to Jewish tradition, those that Abraham performed. Faith for Paul is a commitment to God, which produces good works; for James faith (i.e., in 2.14–26, for he uses the term in two or three different ways elsewhere in the letter) is mere intellectual belief (2.19), lacking commitment. Finally, "justified" for Paul means the pronouncing of a sinner righteous; "justified" for James means the declaration that a person did in fact act justly. Paul, of course, would have agreed with James that "faith" that does not produce appropriate deeds is a false faith (see Gal. 5.6, 16–21).

Given such differences in usage of common terminology, how are these two authors related? Two possibilities may be mentioned: either James is reacting to a misunderstood and badly distorted Paulinism, perhaps not even knowing who had originated it; or James is speaking to the fault of making intellectual religious commitments without the corresponding amendment of life. In neither case is James opposing Paul; he is simply arguing in his own context what Paul taught in his.

Peter H. Davids

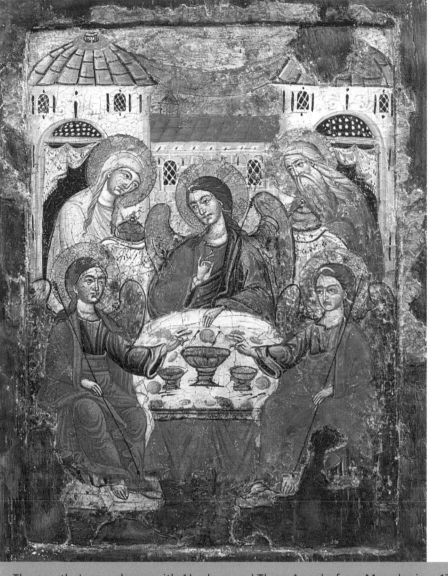
The apostle James, shown with Abraham and Three Angels, from Macedonia, c.1700

JEHOVAH. An artificially constructed name for Israel's God first attested in sixteenth-century CE Christian texts. The new construction was the result of changing attitudes toward the use of God's name. The Hebrew name "Yahweh" was not normally pronounced after about the third century BCE out of respect for its holiness. In its place, readers of the Hebrew used ʾadōnāy, "Lord." When vowels were added to the consonantal text of the Hebrew Bible (ca. 1000 CE), the consonants of Yahweh were preserved but the vowels of ʾadōnāy were used as a reminder to readers. Renaissance Christian tradition erroneously combined the consonants of Yahweh and the vowels of ʾadōnāy to produce "Jehovah," which is used occasionally in the King James Version and regularly in some revisions of it. More recent English translations tend to use "Lord" rather than "Jehovah."

Steven Friesen

JEREMIAH, THE BOOK OF.

The Background. The editorial introduction to the book of Jeremiah, 1.1–3, informs us that the book contains "the words of Jeremiah," that is, what Jeremiah said and did—the Hebrew term translated "words" can cover both—from the beginning of his prophetic ministry in the thirteenth year of the reign of Josiah, 627 BCE, until the fall of Jerusalem to the Babylonians in 587/586 BCE. This is not strictly an accurate account of the contents of the present book since chaps. 40–44 describe the activity of the prophet both in Judah and in Egypt after the fall of Jerusalem. Nevertheless the last forty years of the independent Judean state are the stage on which Jeremiah played out his major prophetic role. Since the book is full of historical references to events in this period, it is important for our understanding of the book to sketch briefly

Prophet Jeremiah

the political factors that shaped these years. They witnessed the gradual break up of the once all-powerful Assyrian empire and the resurgence within Judah of a religious nationalism that culminated in the reformation under King Josiah in 621 BCE (2 Kings 22–23). Although this religious nationalism must have received a jolt with the death of Josiah at the battle of Megiddo in 609 BCE, it still had a trump card: Jerusalem, the city of God, with its Temple where God dwelt, guaranteeing by his presence that this city could never be conquered or destroyed (see Pss. 46 and 48). Such self-confident religious nationalism clashed with the new imperial power of the day, the Neo-Babylonian empire. Under a succession of monarchs, Judah tried to play anti-Babylonian power politics with other small states, aided and abetted by Egypt, in an unsuccessful attempt to postpone the inevitable. In 597 BCE Jerusalem surrendered to the Babylonians, and the cream of Judean society went into exile. The last king of Judah, Zedekiah, came to the throne as a Babylonian nominee. But the anti-Babylonian lobby in Jerusalem prevailed until, ten years later in 587/586 BCE, the city was captured and destroyed. The curtain had fallen for the last time on the independent kingdom of Judah. The book of Jeremiah depicts a man who consistently protested against political and religious policies that sealed the fate of his country, a prophet who in the eyes of the establish-

ment of his day was both traitor and heretic. If the fall of Jerusalem had not vindicated his stance, we might now have been reading not the book of Jeremiah but the book of Hananiah (see chap. 28) or of some of the other prophets with whom Jeremiah clashed.

The Problem of the Book. But what do we mean by the book of Jeremiah? The prophets from Amos onward are sometimes called "the writing prophets" because in the Bible we find books to which their names are attached. If this conveys the impression that in such prophetic books we are dealing with a series of books each written by one person, then this is highly misleading, nowhere more so than in the case of the book of Jeremiah. In it we find duplicate accounts of the same events: twice we hear of Jeremiah's sermon in the Temple, once in chap. 7, once in chap. 26; and there are two versions of Jeremiah's arrest, imprisonment, and secret interview with King Zedekiah (37.11–21; 38.1–13). The same or very similar passages will appear in different contexts in the book: thus 6.13–15 reappears in 8.10b–12, and 23.19–20 in 30.23–24. A passage in 49.19–20, which occurs in the context of judgment against Edom, is repeated with minor variations in the context of judgment against Babylon in 50.44–46. Moreover, there is material within the book that is closely paralleled in other prophetic books; chap. 48 dealing with Moab has many similarities with Isaiah 15–16, while the section on Edom in 49.7–22 reads like a series of variations on Obadiah. At times we come across blocks of material dealing with a common theme or linked together by catchwords or phrases. Thus 3.1–4.4 deals with the infidelity and adultery of God's people; 21.1–23.6 gives us the prophet's verdict on various kings of Judah; 23.9–40 is headed "concerning the prophets"; 30, 31, and 33 (the "book of consolation") gather together words of hope for the future, and inserted in their midst (in chap. 32) is an incident from the life of Jeremiah that illustrates this theme. Within this book of consolation, brief independent sections are placed together and introduced by the same phrase. Thus three passages, each introduced by "The days are surely coming," are placed together in 31.27–40. The largest clearly defined collection of material in the book is chaps. 46–51, which contains "oracles against the nations." Such blocks of material, however, only serve to underline the general lack of order that runs through the book as a whole. There is no clear chronological ordering of material; chap. 21, for example, deals with events during the final siege of Jerusalem, chap. 26 with an event that happened more than twenty years earlier. The book keeps jumping about disconcertingly from topic to topic and seems to be needlessly repetitive. At times we are reading poetry, at other times prose. The book makes more sense as a collection or collections of varied material rather than as a work with a coherent theme or plot or any systematic historical framework.

There is a good reason for this. The preexilic prophets are not primarily writers but preachers, messengers of God who transmit their message by word of mouth. The message often takes the form of a brief poetic oracle that begins "Thus says the Lord" and often ends in the book of Jeremiah with another phrase that the NRSV renders "says the Lord," 2.1–3 being an excellent example; see also 2.5–8; 4.27–28; 5.14–15; 6.6–9, 9–12. The present book of Jeremiah contains collections of many such prophetic sayings, almost certainly preserved originally in oral form, supplemented by the addition of biographical and other editorial material. Behind it lies, as we shall see, a long and complex history of transmission, the details of which remain obscure.

The Text. We have spoken so far of the book of Jeremiah, but what book do we mean? The book of Jeremiah has come down to us in two forms, represented by the standard Hebrew Masoretic text (MT) and the Greek text (Septuagint [LXX]), and these two text forms differ significantly from each other. The LXX is approximately one-eighth shorter, lacking, it has been calculated, some 2,700 words of the MT. Furthermore, some of the material is differently placed in the two text forms. The "oracles against the nations" come in the MT at chaps. 46–51; in the LXX they are placed immediately after the words "everything written in this book" in 25.13a, and the individual oracles occur in a different order. Some further light on the problem of the two texts has been shed by the Dead Sea Scrolls. Among fragments of the book of Jeremiah from Caves Two and Four, there are some that support the MT where it differs from the LXX. From Cave Four, however, has come a Hebrew text that follows the LXX textual tradition against the MT in Jeremiah 10 in omitting vv. 6–8 and 10. Thus in Palestine prior to the common era there is evidence for the existence of two Hebrew textual traditions of the book of Jeremiah, a longer one corresponding to what became the standard Hebrew text and a shorter one corresponding to the Greek text. Which one takes us nearer to the earliest form of the text of the book is a matter of scholarly debate. On the whole, the balance of opinion favors the shorter LXX with the MT being regarded as a secondary, expanded text. It contains, for example, many descriptive titles of God not found in the LXX, and while "the prophet" appears as a designation of Jeremiah only four times in the LXX, it occurs twenty-six times in the MT. This is not, however, to say that in every case the shorter text is the superior text or that it represents the "original text" of Jeremiah, whatever that may mean. Each case must be treated on its merits. Since English Bibles follow the standard Hebrew text we shall continue to refer to the contents of the book as in this tradition.

Content and Sources. It is generally agreed that the material in the book of Jeremiah falls into three categories, each stemming from different sources or circles.

Poetic material, to be found in the main interspersed with prose passages in chaps. 1–25. These poetic sections consist largely of oracles in which the prophet functions as God's messenger, speaking in the name of God. They cover a variety of themes, including the nation's infidelity to the Lord and the call to repentance (3.1–5; 4.13–18; 6.15–17), with attacks on the religious and political establishment of the day (2.8–9; 6.13–15; 22.13–19). These poetic passages are on the whole undated and are given no clearly defined context, but it is widely held that in such passages we are in touch with the teaching of the prophet Jeremiah, and that much of the material in chaps. 1–25 represents the earliest stage of the book of Jeremiah. Such passages may well have been part of the scroll that King Jehoiakim, according to chap. 36, insolently consigned to the flames in the winter of 604 BCE, whereupon Jeremiah redictated the scroll to the scribe Baruch and for good measure added similar words. Certainly there is little in such poetic oracles that could not have come from the early years of the prophet's ministry between the time of his call (627 BCE according to 1.2) and 604 BCE.

In addition to these oracles in which the prophet speaks the word of God to his people, there are other poetic passages in 1–25 that are in the form of intensely personal poems that have been called Jeremiah's confessions or his spiritual diary (see 11.18–12.6; 15.10–21; 17.5–10, 14–18; 18.18–23; 20.7–18). Here we listen not to the word of God on the lips of the prophet but to a man baring his own soul and exposing some of the tensions involved in being a prophet. These passages are without parallel in prophetic literature. Attempts have been made to read them as cultic poems, modeled on the psalms of lament, that have no real roots in the life of Jeremiah. There seems, however, little reason to doubt that they reflect Jeremiah's experience. As such they are of the highest significance and interest. They show us that behind the apparently untroubled certainty of "Thus says the Lord" there may lie a host of unresolved questions and deep inner turmoil. This is a very human prophet committed to a vocation that tears him apart, agonizing over the apparent failure of his ministry, on the verge of giving up, consumed by a savage bitterness against those who opposed or ignored what he had to say, accusing God of betraying him.

There are two other blocks of material in the book outside chaps. 1–25 that similarly contain poetic prophetic oracles, often interspersed with and expanded by prose sections.

a) Chaps. 30, 31 and 33, the so-called book of consolation, consisting of oracles whose basic theme is that of hope beyond national disaster. This material is probably of very varied origin. The influence of an earlier prophet, Hosea, is very marked in some sections (e.g., 31.1–6), while the language and thought of other passages have close links with a later prophet, the author of Isaiah 40–55 (e.g., 31.10–14). That some of the material in this section goes back to Jeremiah, however, we need not doubt.

b) Chaps. 46–51, the oracles against the nations. The tradition of oracles against other nations, particularly those that threaten the existence of Israel, is one that can be traced back to Amos 1.3–2.3. Such oracles occur also in other prophetic books: Isaiah 13–23, Ezekiel 25–32, Nahum, and Obadiah. Inasmuch as Jeremiah was called, according to 1.5, to be "a prophet to the nations," it is hardly surprising that a substantial collection of such oracles appears in the book. Such oracles affirm that the God of Israel is lord over all nations and pronounce judgment on them not only for their treatment of Israel, but for the arrogant self-confidence that assumes that might is right and for actions that sacrifice justice and human rights to imperial ambitions. It is evident from the different setting in which these oracles are placed in the Hebrew and Greek texts, and the different ordering of the oracles within this material, that they once circulated as an independent collection. How much of it can be traced back to Jeremiah himself is a highly contentious issue.

Biographical narratives that claim to recount key incidents in the life of the prophet. There are two notable features of these narratives. First, there are more such narratives in the book of Jeremiah than in any other prophetic book, and thus, if authentic, they provide us with more information about Jeremiah than is available for any other prophet. Such narratives are to be found in chaps. 26–29, 32, 34–44. Second, these narratives are usually provided with precise dating, the earliest dated to 609 BCE (26:1). If therefore we assume, following 1.2, that Jeremiah's prophetic ministry began in 627 BCE, we have no such narrative for almost the first twenty years of his ministry. This, allied to the lack of any clear evidence in the book for Jeremiah's attitude to the key religious event of this period, the reformation under King Josiah in 621 BCE, has led a variety of scholars to believe that his ministry did not begin until 612 BCE or 609 BCE, with 627 BCE being the possible date of his birth. This is not, however, a necessary inference. The biographical narratives are often linked with the scribe Baruch, who appears in Jeremiah's company in chaps. 32, 36, 43, and 45. We could argue from the lack of biographical material prior to 609 BCE that Baruch first came into contact with Jeremiah in 609; perhaps he was drawn to Jeremiah as the result of the Temple sermon that chap. 26 dates to that year. We have spoken of biographical narratives, but we must not assume from this that it is possible to write a satisfactory biography of Jeremiah, even from 609 BCE onward. The narratives do not appear in chronological sequence, nor do they do any more than highlight what are taken to be certain key incidents that reveal the prophet often locked in conflict with the religious and political establishment of the day. It is no more possible to write a satisfactory biography of Jeremiah on the basis of these narratives than it is to write a life of Jesus on the basis of the gospel narratives. If we push this analogy further we would have to say that it is the events leading up to and surrounding the destruction of Jerusalem in 587 BCE that occupy in the book of Jeremiah the central place that the passion narratives occupy in the Gospels. It is perhaps not surprising that the book of Jeremiah ends in chap. 52 with an account of the fall of Jerusalem, derived in the main from 2 Kings 24–25.

Prose passages occur throughout the book, sometimes in the form of sermons or speeches attributed to Jeremiah, which are usually called Deuteronomic (or Deuteronomistic), since they reflect the style, language, and thought of the book of Deuteronomy and the Deuteronomic editors who shaped the history of Israel that we find in the books of Judges to 2 Kings. Typical examples of this material are the Temple sermon in chap. 7 and the covenant passage in 11.1–17. It is these Deuteronomic passages that have provoked the greatest controversy in the study of the book of Jeremiah. Some would trace them to Jeremiah himself; others argue that they reflect the characteristic rhetorical prose style of Jeremiah's day and present a tradition of Jeremiah's teaching as handed down in circles familiar with this style and sympathetic to the theology of the book of Deuteronomy. A variation of this view is to regard such passages as conventional scribal compositions and attribute them to Baruch. All such views trace the material in its present form back to the time of Jeremiah. Others, however, believe that such passages are later, either emanating from Deuteronomic preachers during the period of the exile in Babylon in the sixth century BCE or reflecting theological issues of a still later date during the Persian period. It is doubtful whether in their present form such passages can be attributed to Jeremiah, but it is unduly skeptical to deny that they may well have their roots in a tradition that builds on what Jeremiah said and did. Nor should we think that we necessarily solve problems by speaking about the Deuteronomists. They are at best shadowy figures. We do not know with certainty either who they were or when they functioned.

How or when such varied material came together to form the book of Jeremiah, either in its shorter or its longer form, we do not know, but it must have taken many decades, or even centuries, after Jeremiah's life. The very nature of the book—its varied components, the clear evidence of editing within it, the amalgamation of different traditions—raises the question as to what extent the book provides us with reliable historical data concerning the life, words, and deeds of the prophet. Some deny that the book provides us with any access to the historical Jeremiah. Behind the editing, however, and in and through the varied material, there does

seem to emerge a prophetic figure of striking individuality, God's spokesman to Judah at a major crisis point in the life of the nation, and it is hard to see why such a figure should be nothing other than the invention of later ages.

Key Religious Issues. In addition to much that the book of Jeremiah shares with other prophetic books, there are two issues to which specific attention may be briefly drawn. First is the problem of prophecy. The book speaks not only of one prophet, Jeremiah, but of many prophets. Chap. 28 describes the clash between Jeremiah and the prophet Hananiah, a representative of the Jerusalem religious establishment. Both preface their words by "Thus says the Lord," both use the same prophetic techniques to communicate the message, both are no doubt equally sincere, and both speak a diametrically opposite message. Hananiah declares that the Lord will protect his people and break the power of Babylon, and there was much in Israel's past faith to support his view (e.g., Isa. 31.1–5; Ps. 48); Jeremiah insists that such a message of peace, that all is well with the people basking in God's favor, must be false (6.13–15). But how would anyone witnessing such a clash know who had the true prophetic word? The tests for identifying false prophecy in Deuteronomy 13.1–5 and 18.16–20 would have been little help. In Jeremiah 23.9–40 it is claimed that prophets who proclaim a word that presents no challenge to the conscience of the nation stand in no relationship to God and have no access to his word. They do no more than spout lies they themselves have invented. But how could Jeremiah know this? Did he never wonder whether he himself was mistaken when he heard the confident "Thus says the Lord" of such prophets? This may be the implication of 20.7. The book of Jeremiah highlights the difficulties that people in Judah faced in deciding what was the authentic word of God for them in their day. They had to take choices and live with the consequences.

The second issue is the message of hope. Throughout the book of Jeremiah we find oracles of judgment that insist that Jerusalem must be destroyed, its fate sealed not by the Babylonians but by God. But there are also words of hope, not hope that sidesteps disaster, but hope of a new future beyond disaster. Many of the pictures of hope beyond the richly deserved judgment are modest and homely: people returning to the towns they were once forced to leave, the renewal of life in the countryside, the resumed worship of God in Jerusalem (31.23–25; 33.10–13). But there is another strand. Again and again the prophet draws attention to the stubborn evil heart or will that grips the people (e.g., 3.17). It means that the call to repent falls on deaf ears; it turns the most serious attempt to reform the nation's life into a dead letter. If things are ever to be lastingly different, it can only come through a new initiative of God that will transform human nature. This is the theme of the new covenant passage in 31.31–34, a vision that, drawing on Israel's relationship with God in the past symbolized by the covenant at Mount Sinai, sees a new relationship in the future, based as was the past on God's grace, but a relationship in which the people will be able to give the obedience for which God looks. Thus the book of Jeremiah, which draws richly on Israel's past religious traditions, reaches out to the future. In terms of the new covenant theme, the New Testament claims that that future became the present in Jesus (1 Cor. 11.25; Heb. 8.6–13).

ROBERT DAVIDSON

JERUSALEM. *This entry consists of two articles, the first on the History of Jerusalem and the second on the city's Symbolism.*

History

Name and Description. The earliest attestation of Jerusalem's name is in the Egyptian Execration Texts of the nineteenth and eighteenth centuries BCE in a form that must be a transcription of the Semitic *Urusalim*, which appears in the Amarna letters of the fourteenth century BCE. It is a combination of two elements meaning "the foundation of [the god] Shalem." The second element, rendered Salem, is used alone in Genesis 14.18 and Psalm 76.2. The pronunciation of the Hebrew name is reflected in the Greek *Ierousalem*, which predominates in the Septuagint. In 1 Esdras, Tobit, and 1–4 Maccabees, however, the Septuagint has the strongly Hellenized *Hierosolyma*. Both forms appear in the New Testament.

The biblical city spreads across two hills (average altitude 750 m [2500 ft]) in the central mountain range. It is limited on the west and south by the Hinnom valley, and on the east by the Kidron valley, which separates it from the Mount of Olives. Josephus alone records that the central valley was called the Tyropoeon ("Cheesemakers"). The western hill is slightly higher than the eastern hill, and both slope to the south. There are two springs, Gihon ("gusher"; see Gen 2.13) and Ein Rogel ("the fuller's spring"), in the Kidron valley. The climate is temperate, and all the rain (annual average 560 mm [22 in]) falls during the four-month winter (December to March). It occasionally snows.

Before the Exile. The original city was on the southern extension of the eastern hill known as Ophel, excavated principally by Kathleen Kenyon and Yigal Shiloh. Scattered pottery attests occupation from the third millennium BCE and the site was defended by a heavy wall from about 1800 BCE. Houses built on artificial terraces climbed the slope to the acropolis. After the Israelite conquest the territory of Jerusalem was absorbed by the tribe of Benjamin, but the city of the Jebusites, with its mixed population of Amorites and Hittites (Ezek. 16.3), was left alone. It thus served David's need for a capital independent of the twelve tribes. He took it ca. 1000 BCE (2 Sam. 5.6–10) and made it an effective center by bringing into it the ark of the covenant, to which all the tribes gave allegiance. In order to house the ark appropriately David bought a threshing floor to the north of the City of David from one Araunah (2 Sam. 24.18–25), which is both a title ("lord") in Hittite and a personal name in Ugaritic. Here Solomon built the First Temple ca. 960 BCE, which he linked to the city by a palace (1 Kings 6—7), effectively doubling the size of the original Jebusite city. The Jebusite water-shaft was retained for use in military emergencies, but Solomon dug a tunnel from Gihon along the edge of the hill. Sluice gates at intervals facilitated irrigation of the King's Garden in the Kidron valley. The population of Davidic and Solomonic Jerusalem was a few thousand at most.

The excavations of Nahman Avigad in the Jewish Quarter have unearthed evidence, notably a massive wall 7 m (23 ft) wide, that the city had expanded to cover the western hill in the late eighth century BCE. When Sennacherib menaced Jerusalem, King Hezekiah built the wall (Isa. 22.10) to protect refugees from the northern kingdom of Israel, who had settled outside the crowded city. He thus created two new quarters, the *mišneh* ("second"; 2 Kings 22.14) on the western hill, and the *maktēš* ("mortar"; Zeph. 1.11) in the Tyropoeon valley. The City of David was given a new wall just inside the Jebusite wall that had served for a thousand years. In order to guarantee the water supply, Hezekiah dug a 533 m (1750 ft) tunnel from Gihon through the Ophel ridge to the pool of Siloam in the Tyropoeon valley (2 Chron. 32). An inscription found inside the exit details the construction technique. A new wall was built to protect the vulnerable north side of the city in the seventh century BCE. Both it and houses in the City of David bear traces of the savage attack that brought Jerusalem under Babylonian control in 587/586 BCE.

After the Exile. The Israelites who returned from the exile in 538 BCE rebuilt the Temple under the direction of Zerubbabel (Ezra 5–6), but were authorized to reconstruct the walls only when the Persians appointed the first Jewish governor, Nehemiah, about 445 BCE. A complete description of these walls is given in Nehemiah 3, but the passage abounds in textual problems, and it has proved impossible to translate the data into a precise line on the ground. The

Jerusalem in her Grandeur, an engraving based on the painting by Henry Courtney Selous

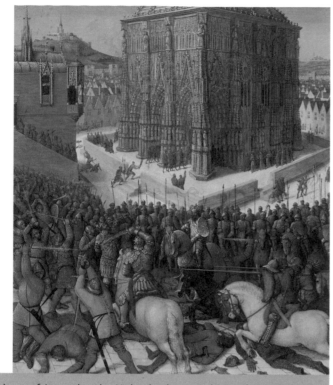

The siege of Jerusalem by Nebuchadnezzar, king of Babylon, in 587 BCE (Jean Fouquet, mid-15th century)

complete absence of Hellenistic remains on the western hill, however, indicates that they encompassed an area barely equal to that of the city of David and Solomon.

Jerusalem suffered three sieges in the wars between the Ptolemies of Egypt and the Seleucids of Syria (201, 199, and 198 BCE). Sirach 50.1–4 praises the high priest Simon (220–195 BCE) for his rebuilding program, but the differences between the Hebrew and Greek versions create a certain obscurity as to what he actually achieved. After Jerusalem passed into the hands of the Seleucids in 198 BCE, the Hellenizing faction among the Jews built a gymnasium in the city (1 Macc. 1.14). In 167 BCE Antiochus IV Epiphanes forbade all Jewish religious practices. In order to forestall any resistance he threw down the walls of Jerusalem, and built a great fortress, the Akra, to hold a Syrian garrison (1 Macc. 1.29–35). Nine different sites have been proposed for the Akra, but it seems likely that it was south of the Temple. It is not to be confused with the Baris sited northwest of the Temple.

The refortification of the city was begun by Jonathan Maccabeus (1 Macc. 10.10–11) and completed by his brother Simon (1 Macc. 13.10), i.e., between 160 and 134 BCE. Josephus's description of this line (*War* 5.4.142–45), which he calls the First Wall, has been given precision by excavations. It ran due west from the Temple along the southern edge of a tributary of the Tyropoeon valley, followed the rim of the Hinnom valley, and mounted the eastern edge of the Ophel ridge to join the Temple. Descriptions of the Hasmonean city appear in the *Letter of Aristeas* (83–106) and in Josephus (*Ant.* 12–14), but both must be used with great caution. The date of the information in the former is uncertain, and the latter is at times guilty of anachronism.

The Herodian City. The Romans, who asserted their authority over Palestine in 63 BCE, appointed Herod the Great king of Judea in 40 BCE. A three-year campaign to establish his sovereignty culminated with the capture of Jerusalem in the summer of 37 BCE. The fact that he had to break two walls in order to reach the Lower City (*Ant.*

14.16.476–77) suggests that what Josephus calls the Second Wall (*War* 5.146), which ran from the Gennath Gate in the First Wall to the northwest corner of the Temple, was already in existence at this time. No certain elements of this wall have been discovered, but the section running north from the First Wall cannot be farther west than the present Suq Khan ez-Zeit. Excavations beneath the Holy Sepulcher and in the Muristan reveal that this area was not within the city of the late first century BCE or early first century CE. There is unambiguous evidence that it was an abandoned quarry. A Jewish catacomb was cut in the west wall. The six kokhim graves still visible in the Holy Sepulcher are typical of the first centuries BCE and CE. A projecting corner in the south wall, which sloped to the southeast, was called Golgotha ("[the place of] the skull"). The relationship of these two elements corresponds perfectly with the description of Jesus' crucifixion and burial in John 19.17–42.

While he presumably repaired, and in some cases certainly strengthened, the walls of the city, Herod did not alter the lines he had inherited. The prime contemporary written source for data on the area they enclosed is Josephus's *Jewish War*. The principal passages are 5.4.136–83 and 6.4.220–442, but other topographical references are scattered throughout the work. He consistently refers to the western hill as the Upper City, and alludes to the old City of David on Ophel as the Lower City. Cemeteries bordered the city on the north and east; the tombs of the families of Herod the Great (*War* 5.108) and of the high priest Caiaphas have been located west of the city.

Herod's Buildings. Herod's first concern was for his own security. On the site of the Hasmonean Baris at the northwest corner of the Temple he built the Antonia fortress (*War* 5.5.238–45). Since it was named for Mark Antony, it must have been completed prior to the latter's defeat in 31 BCE. Paul was imprisoned there (Acts 21.27–22.30). The Roman garrison based there after 6 CE may have influenced the growth of the healing shrine outside the walls to the east, which figures in John 5.1–9. For the entertainment of his supporters Herod built a theater and an amphitheater (*Ant.* 15.8.268). The latter has not been located, but the former was in a little valley south of the Hinnom. The hippodrome (*War* 2.3.44) must have been in the Kidron valley. The quadrennial contests for which these were built gave great offense to pious Jews. In order to further elevate his splendid palace (*War* 5.4.161–82), excavations show that Herod erected a podium at the highest point of the Upper City. It was protected by three great towers, Hippicus, Mariamne, and Phasaelis. The latter surpassed the Pharos of Alexandria, one of the seven wonders of the ancient world. Its great base (today part of the Citadel) is the only element of the palace to have survived.

After the Romans assumed direct control of Palestine in 6 CE, Herod's palace became the residence of the procurators when they came to Jerusalem (*War* 2.14.301–308); Philo calls it "the house of the procurators" (*Leg. ad Gaium* 306). It is here then that we must locate the praetorium in which Pontius Pilate judged Jesus (John 18.28). This is confirmed by the geographic term used in John 19.13, because Gabbatha ("high point") can only apply to this part of the Herodian city. At this stage the descendants of Herod used the Hasmonean palace on the western edge of the Tyropoeon valley (*Ant.* 20.8.189–90; cf. Luke 23.7–12).

Starting in 20 BCE it took Herod nine and a half years to complete rebuilding the Temple on a much grander scale than its predecessor on the same site (*War* 5.5.184–247; *Ant.* 15.11.380–425). Nothing remains except the huge retaining walls supporting the platform, the western side of which became a site for Jewish prayer (the "Wailing Wall") after the destruction of the Temple. Such building activity inspired others, and the quality of life of the wealthy in first century CE Jerusalem is nowhere more evident than in the magnificent mansions excavated in the Jewish Quarter.

The sources make no mention of any concern on the part of Herod for the water supply of the city, but Josephus's mention of the Serpent's Pool (*War* 5.3.108; today Birkat es-Sultan), which served a large catchment area west of the city, probably implies the existence of the serpentine 67 km (42 mi) low-level aqueduct that brought water from Arrub via Solomon's Pools to the Temple. Herod certainly constructed the great reservoir, Birkat Israel, against the north wall of the Temple, and it is likely that he refurbished the Pool of Siloam (John 9.7). Other known reservoirs are Struthion (*War* 5.11.467), adjacent to the Antonia, and Amygdalon (*War* 5.11.468), just north of the palace; the latter was fed by aqueducts from Mamilla and from the north. When the water stored in house cisterns is added, it has been calculated that the population ceiling must have been about seventy thousand.

After Herod the Great. Pilate is credited with having constructed a new aqueduct soon after 26 CE (*War* 2.9.175), but it cannot be identified with the 15 km (9 mi) high-level aqueduct from Bir el-Daraj that supplied the Upper City, and which inscriptions date to 195 CE. The prosperity of Jerusalem increased the demand on space, and the climate of peace meant that there was no risk in building outside the Second Wall. Herod Agrippa I (41–44 CE) tried to wall in this New City or suburb of Bezetha, but the attempt was blocked by the Emperor Claudius (Ant. 19.7.326–327). This wall, completed by the rebels during the First Revolt (66–70 CE), is the famous Third Wall of Josephus (*War* 5.4.147–55), which has given rise to intense debate, because the data given by Josephus are both vague and incoherent. Only two elements have been identified archaeologically, the north gate beneath the present Damascus Gate, and the east gate, which is the Ecce Homo arch near the Antonia. When eighteen thousand men were made redundant on the completion of work on the Temple in 62–64 CE, Herod Agrippa II employed them to pave the city with white stone (*Ant.* 20.9.219–22).

The Roman siege began at Passover 70 CE, while internecine warfare raged in the city. All Jerusalem was in the hand of the legions by late August. By order of Titus it was levelled to the ground, the only exceptions being the great towers, Phasaelis, Hippicus, and Mariamne, which were left as a memorial to Jerusalem's former strength and glory (*War* 7.1.1–2).

JEROME MURPHY-O'CONNOR

Symbolism

Although the sixteenth century was a period of great scientific advances among European mapmakers, one of the best known maps of that period is more imaginative than accurate: a woodcut in the form of a cloverleaf, with Jerusalem depicted as the center of the world from which emanate the continents of Europe, Asia, and Africa. The idea of the centrality of Jerusalem has been a mainstay in Christianity, in various ways, since its inception. It has also been integral to Judaism since the time of King David in the tenth century BCE and, together with the sacred cities of Mecca and Medina, to Islam since its beginnings in the seventh century CE. In the modern era of nation-states, Jerusalem is both the capital of Israel and, for Palestinians, the capital of the state of Palestine. Thus, Jerusalem has long been a focus of powerful and intertwined passions of religion and politics. Although its name probably originally meant "foundation of [the god] Shalem," it has often been interpreted to mean "city of peace" (Hebr. *'ir šālōm*). But peace has remained an elusive goal for most of Jerusalem's entire history.

In his meditation on this most holy and painful city (*Jerusalem: City of Mirrors*, [Boston, 1989]), the "capital of memory," the Israeli writer Amos Elon observed that it is as if the very name Jerusalem (Hebr. *yĕrûšālaim*) is a reflection of the city's contradictory, even dualistic nature (*aim* is the Hebrew suffix indicating a dual or pair), manifesting itself even in its location on the boundary between Israel's cultivated grasslands and arid desert regions. There has always been a tension between the present and the future, the earthly and the heavenly, the real and the ideal Jerusalem, a city of diverse peoples struggling to accomplish their daily activities and the city of religious visionaries.

The name Jerusalem occurs 660 times in the Hebrew Bible; Zion, often used as synonymous with Jerusalem, especially in biblical poetry, occurs another 154 times. The former appears most frequently in the historical narratives of 2 Samuel, Kings, Chronicles, Ezra and Nehemiah, and in the prophetic books of Isaiah, Jeremiah, Ezekiel, and Zechariah. Except for Salem in Genesis 14.18, it is absent from the Pentateuch, achieving importance in ancient Israel's self-understanding only after David brought the ark of the covenant, symbol of God's presence, to the newly conquered city: The ark would find its permanent home in the Jerusalem Temple, the house of God, completed by David's son Solomon, and strategically situated very near to the house of God's loyal servant, the king. The belief in the inviolability of Jerusalem, the chosen dwelling place of God, was challenged by such prophets as Micah and Jeremiah, who

Booty, including a menorah, from the Temple in Jerusalem, taken by the Romans in 70 CE, as shown on the Arch of Titus in Rome

The Western Wall and Temple Mount

warned that the city would be destroyed as a result of its transgressions (Mic. 3.12, quoted in Jer. 26.18). But after the Babylonian destruction of Jerusalem and its Temple in 587/586 BCE, the exilic prophets envisioned a new Jerusalem, which was simultaneously a rebuilding and restoration of the old and also an idealized city, both grander and more enduring than its predecessor, offering its inhabitants a relationship with God and concomitant peace and prosperity. For Jeremiah, the rebuilt Jerusalem was well grounded in the old, even in its physical contours (30.18; 31.38–40). Ezekiel, who understood Jerusalem as "in the center of the nations, with countries all around her" (5.5), celebrates a new city and a new Temple, areas of radiating holiness, fruitfulness, and well-being (chaps. 40–48), where God's glory will again reside: "And the name of the city from that time on shall be, The Lord is There" (48.35). Second Isaiah is consoling in its assertion that Jerusalem "has served her term, that her penalty is paid" (Isa. 40.2). The gates of the new city will always be open (60.11), and the Lord will be its everlasting light (60.19–20). "No more shall there be in it an infant that lives but a few days, or an old person who does not live out a lifetime" (65.20).

The hopes and expectations of the exilic prophets were realized in part with the rebuilding of the city and Temple during the latter half of the sixth century BCE, the first generation of Persian rule. Both, however, would be destroyed by the Roman army in 70 CE. The Temple was never rebuilt. In the generation before its destruction, the Alexandrian Jewish philosopher and statesman Philo wrote that the Jews "hold the Holy City where stands the sacred Temple of the most high God to be their mother city" (*Flaccum* 46). The destruction of the Temple and "mother city" was both a great blow and a great challenge to Jews, inside and outside of Israel. Some Jewish apocalyptic texts from this period envisioned that at the end

time, the heavenly Jerusalem, fashioned by God, would descend to earth; others envisioned a heavenly Jerusalem that awaited the righteous above. In either case, the renewal of Jerusalem was integral to the vision of the end time, a role already suggested in the eschatological visions of the exilic and postexilic prophets.

The formative texts of rabbinic Judaism, which date from roughly the third to the seventh centuries CE, share with the earlier apocalyptic texts both the centrality of the renewal of Jerusalem in the messianic age and a lack of uniformity in the description of that future, ideal city; in some texts, an earthly Jerusalem, and in others a heavenly city; in some an earthly city that ascends to heaven, and in others a heavenly city that descends to earth. What is striking, however, are the linkages and interdependencies between the earthly and the heavenly Jerusalem. In the anti-Roman messianic Palestinian Jewish revolt of Bar Kochba (132–135 CE), the rebels struck coins with the image of the Temple facade and the inscription "of the freedom of Jerusalem," indicating their hopes for the rebuilding of Jerusalem and its Temple. Similarly, the Jewish rebels of the First Revolt (66–70 CE), with their constellation of religious, nationalist, and messianic apocalyptic motivations, issued coins with the inscription, "Jerusalem the holy." As noted above, however, the consequence of the first revolt was not the reinvigoration of Jerusalem, but rather its destruction.

Early rabbinic literature did not focus only on the Jerusalem of the messianic age. The Mishnah, Talmuds, and midrashic collections celebrated the memory of the historic Jerusalem as well. Some texts describe Jerusalem as the center or "navel" of the world; others depict in glowing language the grandeur and uniqueness of the city. Jerusalem's uniqueness was reflected also in the halakhic requirements associated with the city, most of which were not practiced, given the destruction of the Temple and city, and the banning of Jews from Jerusalem by the Roman emperor Hadrian, in the aftermath of the war of Bar Kochba.

As if in response to the words of the psalmist of a long-gone era, "If I forget you, O Jerusalem, let my right hand wither" (Ps. 137.5), the memory of Jerusalem and its Temple and the hope for their restoration were reflected in evolving Jewish liturgy, to be evoked on occasions of joy and mourning and perhaps, most importantly, to be recited as part of the Grace after Meals and the daily Amidah prayer, which together with the Shema, constitute, in a sense, the foundation of Jewish liturgy. The ninth of the month of Av developed as a day of fasting and mourning for the destruction of the First and Second Temples, becoming associated also with other calamitous events in Jewish history (see, e.g., *m. Taʿan.* 4.6).

It is not clear to what degree and for how long Hadrian's decree banning Jews from Jerusalem was enforced. Jews were permitted to reside in Jerusalem, however, during its many centuries of Muslim rule, beginning with its conquest by Caliph Umar in 638, interrupted only by the brief and, in many ways, violent rule of the twelfth-century Crusader Kingdom of Jerusalem. During the years of Ottoman rule (1517–1917), notwithstanding the rebuilding of Jerusalem's walls (1537–1541) by Suleiman I, Jerusalem remained a small and impoverished city. Only in the mid-to-late nineteenth century did the Jews, Latin Christians, Armenian Christians, and Muslims leave their traditional quarters in the walled city to establish new ongoing neighborhoods, the Jews settling generally to the west of the Old City.

The expansion of Jerusalem outside of the walled city developed at roughly the same time as European Zionism. Many factors contributed to the evolution of the latter, including the anti-Jewish policies of the Russian czarist governments, the overall political, social, and economic conditions of Eastern European Jewry, the evolution of anti-Semitic movements and agitation in Western Europe, and the presence and vitality of other European nationalist movements. Notwithstanding the generally nontraditional religious orientation of most of the early Zionist leaders, one cannot underestimate the significance for them of Jewish historical connections with the land of Israel and the city of Jerusalem, suggested even in the term "Zionism." Nonetheless, many of the early Zionist leaders expressed a kind of ambivalence about Jerusalem, reacting seemingly both to the physical squalor of the city and, from their perspectives, to Jerusalem's tired and outdated Jewish religious practices and passions. The ultra-Orthodox Jewish communities of Jerusalem were a counterpoint to the Zionists' visions of a transformed Jewish society. As late as 1947, the Zionist leadership was willing to accept the United Nations resolution to partition Palestine into a Jewish state and an Arab state, and to make Jerusalem a separate political entity under international administration. Following the war of 1948 and the bloody battle for Jerusalem, however, neither the internationalization of Jerusalem nor the Arab state in Palestine was established. Instead, the land fell under Israeli or Jordanian rule with western Jerusalem under Israeli control and eastern Jerusalem, including the Old City and its holy places, under Jordanian control. Jerusalem was declared the official capital of Israel in December 1949. As a result of the 1967 Six Day War, Israel began to govern formerly Jordanian-held East Jerusalem, which was later officially annexed and incorporated by the Israeli government into the state of Israel. Within the Old City stood the Western or Wailing Wall, a retaining wall from the Second Temple as renovated by Herod in the first century BCE. It continues to function as a complex religious-national symbol, a focus of prayer, and an object of pilgrimage for Jews inside and outside of Israel. Today, even most of the significant number of Israeli Jews who support territorial compromise with the Palestinians in exchange for peace, including the establishment of a Palestinian state in the West Bank and Gaza, are reluctant to give up any portion of Jerusalem, or to see the city come under international rule or be divided again. Analogously, the significant number of Palestinians who also support a "two state solution" insist that eastern Jerusalem serve as the capital of Palestine. Thus the "city of peace" remains a stumbling block in Arab-Israeli and Palestinian-Israeli negotiations.

Although the Christian population of Jerusalem, two to three percent of the total, has been in decline for the last fifty years, the number of Christian visitors and pilgrims to Jerusalem remains very large. The roots of this fascination with Jerusalem date both to the origins of Christianity as a first-century Palestinian Jewish apocalyptic movement and to the depictions of the ministry, death, and resurrection of Jesus in the four New Testament Gospels. The Gospels mention Jerusalem sixty-seven times. Matthew refers to it as the "holy city" (4.5; 27.53). Although the texts vary, each of the Gospels depicts Jesus as moving seemingly inevitably to Jerusalem, the site of the pivotal events of the life of Jesus and of Christianity's self-understanding, that is Jesus' death and resurrection; and, for first-century Palestinian Jewry, their national and religious center.

As was the case with other kinds of Judaism of this period, early Christianity knew of both an earthly and a heavenly Jerusalem (e.g., Gal. 4.25–26; Heb. 12.22–24). The book of Revelation, drawing heavily on Ezekiel's vision of the new Jerusalem and very reminiscent of contemporary Jewish apocalyptic texts, describes "the holy city, the new Jerusalem, coming down out of heaven from God" (21.2). Unlike Ezekiel's city, however, this Jerusalem has no Temple, "for its temple is the Lord God the Almighty and the Lamb (21.22)." As Robert Wilken has noted, speculation concerning God's future kingdom on earth with Jerusalem as its center dominated Christian eschatology of the first and second centuries, as, for example, in the writings of Justin Martyr and Irenaeus. Later church fathers, however, such as Origen, who spent more than twenty years in third-century Caesarea, disputed the teachings of Justin Martyr and Irenaeus, as well as Jewish beliefs in the future restoration of some kind of Jerusalem on earth, and spoke only of the heavenly Jerusalem, which remained above and entirely separate from the earthly city.

The fourth century was a period of tremendous change for Christianity. It entered the century as the religion of a persecuted minority, and exited as the official state religion of the Roman empire. Emperor Constantine made Christianity a legal religion in 313, and became its patron and protector. Palestine and in particular Jerusalem became a Christian showplace of sorts. From the time of Constantine, massive church building projects were undertaken to create a visible and glorious manifestation of the legitimacy and permanence of Christian rule—an outward sign of the truth and victory of Christianity. Money poured in from both the government and private persons, bringing with it increased material prosperity and cosmopolitanism for all of fourth- and fifth-century Palestine. Hadrian's Jerusalem, Roman Aelia Capitolina, named after the emperor and the gods of the Capitoline in Rome, would be transformed into a Christian Jerusalem. Constantine himself sponsored the building of three major Palestinian churches, all connected with the life of Jesus, and two of which were in Jerusalem:

Church of the Holy Sepulcher, Chapel of Calvary, showing the crucifixion of Jesus

the Church of the Holy Sepulcher; a church on the Mount of Olives; and the Church of the Nativity in nearby Bethlehem. Already, in the writings of Eusebius, the early fourth-century Caesarean church historian, one can see intimations of the Palestinian church's understanding of itself as guardian of a very earthly Christian Palestine with its center at Jerusalem—a land in which Christians lived and visited, and in which one could see and touch the very places in which the saving events of biblical history had taken place.

Christian pilgrimage to Palestine and especially Jerusalem became widespread in the fourth century. Early pilgrims included Helena, the mother of Constantine. Fourth-century Christian pilgrims, as part of their quest for perfection, would undertake the dangers of travel to Palestine to visit the holy places, and therein both confirm and strengthen their faith. As pilgrimage flourished, some church leaders questioned its value, drawing attention to the contrast between "Jerusalem the Holy" and the city that awaited the pilgrim. For example, Gregory of Nyssa in his "Letter on Pilgrimage" pointed to the "shameful practices" of the people of Jerusalem as evidence that God's grace was no more abundant in Jerusalem than elsewhere.

Echoes of early Christian speculations on the role and nature of Jerusalem in the end time, as well as an interest in the earthly city itself, can be found both in the constellation of factors that shaped the Crusades of medieval Europe, and in the voyages of Columbus who, influenced by late fifteenth-century apocalyptic thought, sought to acquire the gold to finance the final crusade, which would capture Jerusalem and place it again in Christian hands—all part of God's plan for the end time.

Columbus failed in his plans, but Christian interest in and pilgrimage to Jerusalem has endured. For many pilgrims, the

Church of the Holy Sepulcher, consecrated in 335, was the highlight of their trip. Today it remains the major Christian holy place in Jerusalem, although most of what can be seen dates from the period of the Crusades, the Church having been destroyed and rebuilt several times since the time of Constantine. Several Christian denominations have rights to various sections of the Church. In their stories of conflict and cooperation, they are illustrative of the diversity within Christianity and the long, complex, and vital history of the Christian community in Jerusalem.

Although an overview of the symbolism and significance of Jerusalem for Islam is beyond the scope of this article, one must note both the importance of Jerusalem for Islam, and the importance of the city's Muslim communities since their inception in the seventh century CE for the history of Jerusalem, in Arabic "al-Quds," "the Holy." Today, Jerusalem's major Muslim holy place, the magnificent Dome of the Rock, a rotunda on an octagonal base, built by the Umayyad Caliph Abd al-Malik and completed in 691/692, dominates the Haram al-Sharif, or Noble Sanctuary, also the site of the Temple Mount of the Jews. The Dome, reminiscent on a grander scale of the nearby Church of the Holy Sepulcher, was constructed in the architectural style of the Byzantine martyrium to serve as a shrine for the holy rock beneath it—a rock which by the time of the Muslim conquest of Jerusalem in 638 was already associated with the Temple and with Abraham, the common traditional ancestor of Judaism, Christianity, and Islam. The Dome affirmed the triumph of Islam in the midst of the Christian showplace, Jerusalem, "The Holy City," and in a place, atop the Temple Mount, which the Byzantine Christians had kept in ruins to concretize Christian beliefs that the destruction of the Jerusalem Temple was both a fulfillment of prophecy and a proof of the victory and truth claims of the "New Israel."

The sanctity for Islam of the Rock, the Haram, and Jerusalem, in general, was strengthened by the identification by early Muslim authorities of Jerusalem as the destiny of the Prophet Muhammad's night journey (Sūrah 17:1), and the Rock as the place from which he ascended to heaven (Sūrah 53:4–10). As in Judaism and Christianity, Jerusalem assumed an important role in Muslim beliefs concerning the end time and the day of judgment. So too, Muslim sources reflect the tensions between the holy city, setting of the last judgment, and Jerusalem in its daily activities. Thus Muqaddasi, a tenth-century geographer and historian, and a native of Jerusalem, would celebrate Jerusalem as "the most illustrious of cities" where the advantages of the present and the next world meet, and also describe the city as a place oppressive to the poor, lacking in learned men, "a golden basin filled with scorpions."

Jerusalem is today a city of approximately 750,000 people, a city which both celebrates and is haunted by its history, a city in which the tensions between the ideal and the real Jerusalem are lived and witnessed daily, and in which the rages and passions of religion and politics bring to mind the words of the psalmist, "Pray for the peace of Jerusalem" (Ps. 122.6).

BARBARA GELLER NATHANSON

JESUS CHRIST.

Life and Teaching. *Introduction: critical method.* By accepting the modern critical method of studying the New Testament, we need not attempt to write a life of Jesus in the modern sense of a psychological study. We can hope only to reconstruct the barest outline of his career and to give some account of his message and teaching.

We shall assume that Mark is the earliest of the four Gospels and that, apart from the passion narrative (14.1–16.8), the individual units of material are arranged in an order determined more by subject matter than by historical or chronological concerns. Moreover, these units of material (stories about Jesus, pronouncement stories, miracle stories, parables, and aphorisms) were adapted to the needs of the post-Easter community and circulated in oral tradition for some forty years before Mark was written down. The authors of the two later synoptic Gospels—Matthew and Luke—used Mark as their primary source, plus a common source consisting mostly of sayings, unknown to Mark. This source is hypothetical and only recoverable by reconstructing the non-Marcan material common to Matthew and Luke. It is generally known as Q, from the German word *Quelle*, "source." In addition, Matthew and Luke have their own special traditions. Like Mark, the three sources—Q, Special Matthew, and Special Luke—contain material previously passed on orally for some fifty years. The evangelists, in their use of sources and oral traditions, shaped them according to their theological interests; this editorial work is known as redaction. Thus, the synoptic Gospels contain material that developed in three stages: authentic words and memories of Jesus himself (stage I), materials shaped and transmitted in oral tradition (stage II), and the evangelists' redaction (stage III). The gospel of John, however, is very different. It contains some stage I and stage II materials independent of the synoptics that can be used sometimes to confirm or supplement the synoptic evidence in reconstructing the career and teaching of Jesus. But the Fourth Gospel contains much more material belonging to stage III. In reconstructing our account of Jesus, we shall attempt to recover stage I materials from all four Gospels. We shall be assisted by certain tests of authenticity. We may be reasonably certain that materials go back to stage I if they meet some or all of the following criteria: (1) have multiple attestation (i.e., are attested in more than one source or in more than one type of material); (2) are distinctive to Jesus (i.e., they are without parallel in Judaism or in the post-Easter community; this test should be used with caution and generally applied to confirm rather than exclude; principle of dissimilarity); (3) cohere with other accepted Jesus traditions (test of coherence); and/or (4) exhibit indications of originating in Aramaic (in the case of sayings), since this was Jesus' normal language (though he probably knew some Greek), or in a Palestinian milieu or social setting.

The birth and upbringing of Jesus. The birth stories in Matthew and Luke are relatively late, and belong to stages II and III. But they contain certain items that go back to earlier tradition. Some of these are clearly theological: Davidic descent, conception through the Holy Spirit while his mother remained a virgin, homage at birth. Factual data in these common items include: the date of Jesus' birth in the last years of the reign of Herod the Great (died 4 BCE); the names of Jesus' parents, Mary and Joseph; the fact that the child was conceived between betrothal and wedding; the birth at Bethlehem (though this may be a theological assertion, associated with the Davidic descent). In any case, Jesus was brought up in Nazareth. His father is said in Matthew 13.55 to have been a carpenter, and Jesus is said to have been one himself in Mark 6.3. Since sons habitually followed their father's trade, this is not improbable. Presumably, Jesus received the education of the devout poor in Israel, with thorough instruction in the Hebrew scriptures.

Leonardo Da Vinci's The Virgin and Child with Anne and John the Baptist

135

The beginning of Jesus' public ministry: his message.
Jesus' public career began when he left home for the Jordan River to be baptized by John the Baptist. Jesus looked back to the Baptist as the source of his mission and authority (Mark 11.27–33). For a time, he appears to have conducted a ministry of baptizing parallel to that of the Baptist (see John 3.22; 4.1), presumably continuing the Baptist's message by demanding repentance from Israel in view of the impending advent of God's kingdom. After the Baptist's arrest (Mark 1.14), Jesus embarked upon a new kind of ministry. The message of the kingdom acquired a new urgency, perhaps as a result of the temptation (Mark 1.12–13), which included a vision of God's victory over Satan (Luke 10.18). Abandoning the practice of baptism, Jesus went to the synagogues for a time and then spoke in the open air, reaching out to the people instead of waiting for them to come to him; but still like the Baptist, he continued preaching the coming kingdom. Jesus never defined what he meant by the kingdom, but it means God's coming in saving power and strength, defeating the powers of evil and inaugurating salvation for Israel. It is basically future ("your kingdom come" in the Lord's Prayer) but also presently operative in Jesus' words and works (Matt. 12.28 || Luke 11.20 Q). In the parables of the kingdom, Jesus seeks to engage his hearers, persuading them to see the present operation of the kingdom in his own words and works, and to secure from them the response of faith and confidence in its future consummation—parables of the sower, the seed growing secretly, the mustard seed (Mark 4.3–32); also the leaven (Matt. 13.33 || Luke 13.20–21 Q).

Jesus preaching to the crowds

An inescapable conclusion is that Jesus was influenced by the prophecies of Isaiah 40–66, where the coming of the reign of God is a central theme (Isa. 52.7). Indeed, much of Jesus' teaching is shot through with allusions to Isaiah 40–66. Jesus is represented as quoting Isaiah 61.1–2 and 58.6 in the inaugural sermon in the synagogue at Nazareth (Luke 4.18–19), but the content of the sermon was probably shaped in stage II or III. There are, however, clear echoes of these passages in the Beatitudes (Matt. 5.3–6 || Luke 6.20–23 Q) and in the answer to John (Matt. 11.5–6 || Luke 7.22–23). Jesus thus appeared first and foremost as eschatological prophet, one who announced the definitive coming of God's kingly rule, the salvation of the end time.

Jesus' teaching: ethics. Jesus was also recognized as a rabbi and teacher. Like the rabbis, he taught in synagogues, collected a band of disciples, and discussed Torah with them as well as with inquirers and critics. The forms of his teachings were similar to those employed by Pharisaic teachers: parables and aphorisms, that is, sayings, often of a wisdom type, enunciating general truths about human life and manners (e.g., the teaching on anxiety in Matt. 6.25–34). Like the Pharisees, Jesus took the authority of the Hebrew Bible for granted. It enunciates the demands of God: prohibition of divorce (Mark 10.6–8; Matt 5.32; Luke 16.18); the second tablet of the Ten Commandments (Mark 10.19); the Shema and the summary of the law (Mark 12.29–31).

Yet there are differences between Jesus' teaching and those of the Pharisees. He emphasizes more strongly than they that God demands not just outward conformity to the law but the whole person, and not just love of neighbor but love of enemy (see the antitheses of the Sermon on the Mount, Matt. 5.21–48). The rich young man must not only keep the commandments but sell all he has and follow Jesus (Mark 10.21).

For Jesus, God's demand is summed up in the double commandment of love. This raises the question of the relationship between Jesus' preaching of the kingdom and his enunciation of God's demand, between his prophetic preaching and his wisdom teaching. Jesus never relates the two; in fact, he relates his wisdom teaching to creation rather than to the coming of God's kingly rule. Thus, the command to love one's enemy is based on the fact that God causes the rain to fall and the sun to shine upon the just and the unjust alike (Matt. 5.45; cf. Luke 6.35). Similarly, the absolute prohibition of divorce shows that the reversion to the situation at creation is now possible because of the shift in the ages: the age of Moses is coming to an end, and God's kingly rule is coming. Therefore, Jesus' prophetic preaching presupposes his wisdom teaching. The coming of that rule makes possible the realization of God's original intent in creation. The same unspoken presupposition operates in the double commandment of love: only the coming of God's kingly rule makes it possible for people to love God in radical obedience and to love one's neighbor, including one's enemy. For God's coming in his kingly rule is an act of mercy and forgiveness (an important aspect of Jesus' message; see, e.g., Mark 2.5; Luke 7.47; Matt. 18.23–35; also Jesus' preaching of repentance is connected with his offer of forgiveness: Mark 1.15; 6.12; Matt. 11.20); and forgiveness as a human response to God's forgiveness is the supreme expression of love. Jesus' prophetic message is the indicative and his enunciation of the will of God is the imperative that the indicative implies.

Jesus' teaching about God. Jesus brought no new teaching about God. God is the creator, though this is understood in an immediate way. God did not merely create the world in

J

the beginning, rather, it comes from him as his creation in every moment (Matt. 6.26, 30, 32, and the fourth petition of the Lord's Prayer). For Jesus, God is also the God who acts in history, the climax of which is the coming of the kingdom (see e.g., Matt. 13.16–17 || Luke 10.23–24 Q, and the tradition behind Matt. 23.34–35 || Luke 11.49–50). Also, Jesus frequently adduced biblical characters whose situation in their day was analogous to the situation of his contemporaries in the face of the coming kingdom (e.g., Lot and his wife, the Queen of Sheba, Jonah).

Although the address of God as Father is not unknown in the Hebrew Bible and Judaism, and even the familiar abba is not completely without precedent, that usage was characteristic of Jesus. He did not enunciate the fatherhood of God as an abstract doctrine or a general truth but himself experienced God as his own Father (i.e., in his call to his unique mission mediated through his baptism and temptations), and he offered to those who responded to his prophetic message a similar experience and the privilege of addressing God as abba (note the opening address of the Lord's Prayer in its original Lucan form, Luke 11.2).

Jesus' conduct. Jesus appeared as a charismatic healer as well as a preacher and teacher. This was a further implementation of the prophetic mission set forth in Isaiah 35 and 61 (Matt. 11.5–6 || Luke 7.22–23). Jesus performed exorcisms, which he claimed were the action in him of the Spirit (Matthew) or finger (Luke) of God. To deny this spirit at work in his exorcisms was blasphemy, a sin for which there would be no forgiveness (Mark 3.29). Thus, both healings and exorcisms are related to his message. The actual miracle stories may not be direct reports, but they reflect a general memory that Jesus did do such things. More problematic are the so-called nature miracles. There are three raising stories—Jairus's daughter (Mark 5.21–24, 35–43), the widow's son at Nain (Luke 7.11–17), and Lazarus (John 11.1–44)—but all these belong to stage II. The answer to John (Matt. 1.1.5–6 || Luke 7.22–23), however, may enable us to take back the fact of resuscitations to stage I, in which case the three stories of the raising may rest upon a general memory that Jesus did perform such deeds. Another special instance of a nature miracle is the feeding of the multitude. This miracle has multiple attestation (Mark 6.30–44, Mark 8.1–10, and John 6.1–15 represent three independent traditions). The shaping of the stories originated early in stage II, where they were modeled partly on the eucharistic tradition and partly on the Elisha story (2 Kings 4.42–44, whence the miraculous multiplication of the loaves derives). But such a meal itself may well be historical: Jesus met with his followers in a remote place and ate with them. This meal may have been one of a series of events constituting a crisis at the climax of the Galilean ministry.

Jesus also celebrated meals with the outcast, and for this too there is multiple attestation. In the parables of the lost (Luke 15), Jesus interprets this action as a celebration in advance of the joy of the great banquet of the kingdom of God.

Like John the Baptist, Jesus addressed his message of repentance in view of the coming kingdom to Israel as a whole. But he called some to follow him, accompany him, and share in the work of proclaiming the message. From these he selected twelve to symbolize the restoration of Israel (Mark 3.14; 6.7; Matt. 19.28; cf. Luke 22.28–30). It would seem that much of Jesus' radical demand was intended for these followers, who constituted a band of wandering charismatic preachers and therefore had to dispense, as he did, with the normal secu-

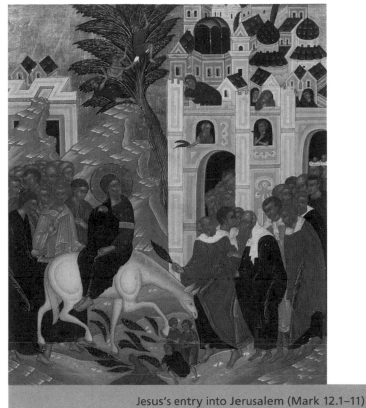

Jesus's entry into Jerusalem (Mark 12.1–11)

rities of human life (Mark 6.8–9), including family ties (see Mark 3–34–35; 8.34–37; 10.28–30).

The central crisis. It is clear that at one point Jesus broke off his Galilean ministry and transferred his activities to Jerusalem. There are indications of a series of events starting with the feeding of the multitude (Mark 6.30–52; 8.1–9.13; John 6.1–71), followed by a withdrawal from the crowds, a crossing of the lake, and a period of solitary communication with his disciples (represented by the confession of Peter and the Transfiguration), after which Jesus set out for Jerusalem. We may suppose that during this period of solitude Jesus resolved that it was now God's plan for him to go to Jerusalem and carry his message to Israel at the very center of its life. Two circumstances may have contributed to this decision. First, Jesus' ministry evoked a dangerous messianic enthusiasm among the crowds (John 6.15, clarifying Mark 6.45). Second, the execution of John the Baptist (Mark 6.14–29; cf. 9.13) made Jesus fear that Herod Antipas might arrest him before he could challenge the authorities in Jerusalem (Luke 13.31–34).

The chronology of the Galilean ministry. Since Mark mentions only one Passover during Jesus' public career, it is often supposed that his entire ministry lasted but a few months, less than one year. True, John mentions two Passovers before the final one (2.13; 6.4), but these references belong to stage III. There are, however, indications of two springs during the Galilean ministry. In Mark 2.23, Jesus' disciples plucked ears of grain, while in the first feeding the crowds sit on the "green grass" (6.39). If we can trust these items and if they do not refer to the same spring, it would permit us to conclude that the Galilean ministry lasted over a year, for the grainfields episode requires that Jesus should have had time to collect a band of followers, and the feeding presumes a longer ministry. According to Luke 3.1, the Baptist's ministry began in the fifteenth year of Tiberius's reign (27 CE). Jesus' baptism could have occurred in that year, his Judean ministry would have covered the intervening period, and the Galilean ministry would have begun in late 27 or early 28 and ended after the spring of 29. But this is highly speculative.

The journey to Jerusalem. John's gospel has obscured the decisiveness of Jesus' final journey to Jerusalem by bringing him to the holy city on two earlier occasions (John 2.12; 5.1), but these episodes probably belonged to the final Jerusalem period. John may be right, though, in making the Jerusalem ministry last for several months rather than for a single week, as it does in Mark. Indeed, Luke offers some support for a longer Jerusalem ministry (Luke 13.34). This would mean that the journey would have occurred some months earlier than the final Passover, perhaps bringing Jesus to Jerusalem in time for the feast of tabernacles (John 7.2). This would be in the fall of 29 CE.

The purpose of the trip is stated in Mark's three passion predictions (8.31; 9.31; 10.33–34). It is generally agreed that these predictions in their present form are prophecies after the event and therefore reflect a knowledge of the passion story (stage II). But they may well contain an authentic nucleus (stage I), such as "the Son of man will be delivered into the hands of men" (Mark 9.31), where we have an Aramaic play on words (Son of man/men). Jesus hardly went up to Jerusalem in order to die; that, it has been suggested, would be tantamount to suicide. But he may well have realized that death would be the inevitable outcome of his mission.

The ministry in Jerusalem. Jesus continued to preach and teach in Jerusalem as he had done in Galilee. He also engaged in conflicts with his adversaries. These conflicts, Mark indicates, were of a different kind from the earlier ones in Galilee. Jesus is now a marked man and his enemies engage him on specific issues, seeking to entrap him into self-incrimination. John likewise presents Jesus as engaged in theological conflict with the religious authorities in Jerusalem.

Jesus' challenge reached its climax in his entry to Jerusalem and the "cleansing" of the Temple (so the Synoptics; John shifts the "cleansing" for theological reasons to the beginning of the ministry). It is not at all clear what the precise issues were that led the Sanhedrin to plot Jesus' execution (for the plot see Mark 14.1–2; 10–11; John 11.45–54). The Synoptics attribute the plot against Jesus to the Sanhedrin's reaction to the cleansing of the Temple (Mark 11.18 par.), while John, less convincingly, attributes it to the raising of Lazarus. Yet John's report of the Sanhedrin meeting (John 11.47–53) seems to be based on reliable tradition: the Sanhedrin decided to get rid of Jesus out of fear that any disturbance of the peace would lead to Roman intervention and destroy the delicate balance between Jewish and Roman power.

On the eve of Passover (following the more plausible chronology of John), Jesus celebrated a farewell meal with his disciples. In the course of it, he interpreted his impending death as the climax of his life of self-giving service (Luke 22.24–27; cf. John 13.1–11; Mark 10.42–45a may originally have belonged to this context). The exact words Jesus spoke over the bread and cup are impossible to recover, since the various accounts of the institution (1 Cor. 11.23–25; Mark 14.22–24 || Matt. 26.26–28; Luke 22.19–20) have been colored by liturgical developments in the post-Easter community. But they all agree that Jesus associated the bread with his body (i.e., his person) and the wine with his blood (i.e., the giving of his life in death) and with the inauguration of a (new) covenant. He also assured his disciples that beyond his death lay the coming of the kingdom of God (Mark 14.25; Luke 22.15–18).

After the supper, Jesus and the disciples went out to the garden of Gethsemane (Mark 14.32; John 18.1) where he was arrested by Temple police, and also, if John 18.3 is correct, by Roman soldiers. This would indicate that the priestly party and the Roman prefect Pilate were in close collusion over the matter. A preliminary investigation was held before the Jewish authorities (Mark 14.53–64; see also John 18.12–14, 19–24, which may be more accurate). This was not a formal trial, but more like a grand jury proceeding. By this investigation they established to their satisfaction that there was sufficient ground to warrant an accusation of high treason before Pilate's court (Mark 15.1–15). There Jesus was condemned to death as a messianic pretender. He was then taken out to Golgotha and crucified with two criminals who were guilty of sedition (Mark 15.20b–32; John 19.16b–19). Jesus died later that same day and was buried, according to the gospel tradition, by sympathizers (Mark 15.42–47 par.; John 19.38–42). This marks the end of his earthly career.

Jesus' self-understanding. While Jesus' career evoked messianic hopes among his followers and fears among his enemies, stage I material shows him reluctant to assert any

The Last Supper (Mark 14.22–25) (Leonardo da Vinci, 1498)

overt messianic claim. The self-designation he uses is son of man. This is so widely attested in the gospel tradition and occurs (with one or two negligible exceptions) only on the lips of Jesus himself, that it satisfies the major tests of authenticity. It occurs in all primary strata of the gospel tradition (Mark, Q, Special Matthew, Special Luke, and the pre-Gospel tradition in John). It is not attested as a messianic title in earlier Judaism and occurs only once outside the gospels (apart from citations of Psalm 8.5–7), in Acts 7.56. So there should be no reasonable doubt that it was a characteristic self-designation of the historical Jesus. It is not a title but means "human one," and it is best understood as a self-effacing self-reference. It is used in contexts where Jesus spoke of his mission, fate, and final vindication.

Jesus certainly thought of himself as a prophet (Mark 6.4; Luke 13.33), but there was a final quality about his message and work that entitles us to conclude that he thought of himself as God's final, definitive emissary to Israel. He was more interested in what God was doing through him than in what he was in himself. He did not obtrude his own ego, yet his own ego was included as part of his message: "Whoever welcomes you welcomes me, and whoever welcomes me welcomes the one who sent me" (Matt. 10.40 || Luke 10.16 Q); "Follow me" (Mark 1.17; etc.); "Those who are ashamed of me . . ." (Mark 8.38); "Blessed is anyone who takes no offense at me (Matt. 11.6 || Luke 7.23 Q); "If it is by the Spirit [Luke: "finger"] of God that I cast out demons. . ." (Matt. 12.28|| Luke 11.20 Q). Jesus dared to speak and act for God. This is clear in the antitheses of the Sermon on the Mount (Matt. 5.21–48: "It was said to those of ancient times . . . but I say to you"), in his pronouncement of the forgiveness of sins (which only God could do, Mark 2.5–12; Luke 7.36–50), his acceptance of the outcast and healing of lepers who were shunned under the law. Coupled with such features is the tremendous authority with which Jesus spoke and acted, an authority for which he offers no credentials save that it is intimately bound up with the authority of the Baptist (Mark 11.27–33) and rests upon God's final vindication (Mark 8.38 and Luke 12.8 Q). Jesus does not claim overtly to be Son of God in any unique sense. Passages in which he appears to do so belong to stage II or III of the tradition. But he does call God "abba" in an unusual way, which points to God's call to which he has responded in full obedience, and therefore we may speak of his unique sense of sonship. But we must bear in mind that in this Palestinian milieu sonship denoted not a metaphysical quality but rather a historical call and obedience. Jesus did challenge his disciples to say who they thought he was, which elicited from Peter the response that he was the Christ or Messiah (Mark 8.27–30; cf. John 6.66–69). According to Mark, he neither accepted nor rejected Peter's assertion. What did Peter mean, and in what sense did Jesus take it? It is commonly thought that it was meant in a political-nationalist sense and that Jesus rejected this. It seems more likely, however, that Peter meant it in the sense of the anointed prophet of Isaiah 61.1. Such a response to Jesus would have been wholly appropriate as far as it went. What Peter and the other disciples did not realize, of course, was that this mission extended beyond the terms of Isaiah 61 and that it also involved rejection, suffering, and death. It is possible, though much disputed, that Jesus modeled this further insight upon the figure of the suffering servant in Isaiah 53. We could be sure of this if Mark 10.45b belongs to stage I.

A very early tradition (Rom. 1.3) asserted that the earthly Jesus was of a family descended from the royal line of David. We cannot be sure that this played any role in his self-understanding. For the post-Easter community this title was important as qualifying him for the messianic role he assumed after his exaltation.

The use of "Rabbi" and "my Lord" in addressing Jesus during his earthly ministry did not denote majesty: these were titles of respect accorded a charismatic person. However, as the conviction grew among his followers that he was the final emissary of God, these terms would acquire a heightened meaning.

In sum, we find in the Synoptics only limited evidence for an explicit Christology in Jesus' self-understanding, and such evidence as there is is critically suspect. He was more concerned with what God was doing in him than who he was, especially in any metaphysical sense. But what God was doing through him in his earthly ministry provided the raw materials for the christological evaluation of Jesus after the Easter event.

Person and Work. *Introduction: critical presuppositions.* In reconstructing the New Testament interpretation of the person (Christology) and work (soteriology) of Jesus, we are concerned with the Christian community's response to the Christ event in its totality. This event embraces both his earthly career, culminating in his crucifixion, and also the Easter event, that is, the community's subsequent experiences, the empty tomb, and the appearances, together with their ongoing sense of his presence and the hope of his coming again.

The earliest Christian writings we have are those letters of Paul that are beyond question authentic, namely, 1 Thessalonians, Galatians, 1 and 2 Corinthians, Romans, Philemon, and Philippians. These letters contain formulae that give us evidence of the theology of the pre-Pauline communities (e.g., 1 Thess. 1.9–10; 1 Cor. 15.3–5; Rom. 1.3–45 3.25–26; 4.25; 10.9). Some of these formulae go back to the earliest Palestinian community, others to the Hellenistic communities (Greek-speaking communities before Paul). In addition, we have the kerygmatic speeches, proclamations of the Christ event, in Acts; though composed by the author of Luke-Acts, they probably enshrine samples of early Christian preaching (e.g., Acts 2.22–24, 32–33 36; 3.13–15, 21). Putting the evidence afforded by these materials together, we can form a general idea of the Christologies and soteriologies of the early communities. The letters of Paul provide ample evidence for the apostle's understanding of these matters. We have no other writings that can be said with any certainty to derive from the apostolic age, but there are a number of New Testament writings that, though ascribed to apostolic authors, were probably written in the subapostolic age (i.e., the period from ca. 70 to 110 CE). This would include the "deutero-Pauline" letters, that is, those letters which though ascribed to Paul were with varying degrees of probability written by later writers. Their purpose was to perpetuate Paul's teaching after his death. They consist of 2 Thessalonians, Colossians, Ephesians, and the Pastorals (1 and 2 Timothy and Titus). Other writings for this period are Hebrews, together with the catholic letters (James, 1 and 2 Peter, 1, 2, and 3 John, Jude, Revelation), and stage III of the four Gospels.

The person of Christ. The Easter event established in the first disciples the conviction that, despite Jesus' crucifixion, God had vindicated him and his message. The Christ event was indeed God's saving act. The earliest Christians expressed this conviction by ascribing to Jesus titles of majesty, such as Messiah (Grk. *christos*, Eng. "Christ," which was originally a title and is not a proper name), Lord (*kyri-*

os), and Son of God. Some of the early christological patterns suggest that Jesus was "appointed" Christ, Lord, or Son of God (Acts 2.36; Rom. 1.4; Phil. 2.9–11) at his exaltation. These patterns are often called "adoptionist," but this is misleading. The meaning is not that Jesus became something he was not before, for example, a divine person; rather, he was appointed to a new office and function, that of being the one in whom God would finally judge and save the world (Acts 3.21; 1 Thess. 1.10), and through whom he was already offering salvation after Easter in the church's proclamation (Acts 2.38). Moreover, this type of Christology does not mean that the earthly life of Jesus had no christological or salvific significance. It was not nonmessianic, for God was present and acting in the earthly Jesus (Acts 2.22). But its messianic significance was initially expressed by a different set of terms, such as the end-time prophet promised in Deuteronomy 18.15 (Acts 3.22–23; 7.37). It is notable that the emphasis of these Christologies is on the end of Jesus' career; in short, they are paschal Christologies.

Over time, the titles that were first applied to the post-Easter phase of Jesus' saving activity were pushed back into his earthly life. This was notably the case with the title Son of God. As the story of Jesus' baptism developed in stage II, this title was featured in a heavenly voice ("You are my Son," Mark 1.11), perhaps replacing an earlier use of "servant" in this context. Later in the birth stories, the title Son of God is pushed back to the moment of Jesus' conception or birth (Luke 1.35; cf. Matt. 2.15). This does not mean that some sort of metaphysical divinity is being ascribed to Jesus. In a Jewish context, it meant that like the kings of Israel Jesus was chosen for a unique role in history. Jesus' conception through the Holy Spirit is not meant to imply any metaphysical quality; it means, rather, that Jesus was a historical person elected from the womb for his unique role through the direct intervention of God (cf. Isa. 49.5; Jer 1.4).

A similar type of Christology is expressed in the so-called sending formulae. These follow a regular pattern: a verb of sending with God as the subject and the son as the object, followed by a purpose clause stating the saving intention behind the sending. The earliest occurrence of such a formula is: "God sent his Son . . . to redeem those . . ." (Gal. 4.4–5). From such formulae it will be clear that the title "son" denotes a historical person with a saving mission. Notice that, unlike the paschal type, this type of Christology focuses upon the beginning rather than the end of Jesus' career.

In Hellenistic Christianity, a new pattern began to develop in which Christ existed in heaven before his birth. Here is a Christology of preexistence and incarnation. It is generally agreed that this pattern developed from the identification of Jesus with the wisdom of God. In Judaism, especially in the Greek-speaking world, the notion of the wisdom of God had undergone a remarkable development. Originally it had been no more than the personification of a divine attribute (see, e.g., Prov. 8.22–31), like God's righteousness or salvation (Isa. 51.6; Ps. 85.10–11). In the later wisdom literature, however, and in the writings of Philo, the concept of the wisdom or Word (logos) of God developed in the direction of hypostatization—it became the distinct personal entity within the being of God, something like a person in the sense in which that term was later used in the Christian dogma of the Trinity (see, e.g., Wisd. of Sol. 18.14–15). Wisdom or "Word" was that aspect of the being of God which was God turned toward the world in creative, revelatory, and saving activity (see, e.g., Wisd. of Sol. 7.22–27).

The ground for this identification of Jesus with the hypostatized wisdom of God was the fact that Jesus himself had appeared as a sage or wise man and had used the speech forms of wisdom literature. He thus came to be regarded not merely as a spokesperson of wisdom but as wisdom's final envoy who acted as the mouthpiece of wisdom (cf. Matt. 11.28–30 with Sir. 24.19 and 51.23–26). From there, it was but a short step to identify him in person with wisdom itself. This happened first in certain christological hymns (Phil. 2.6–11; 1 Cor. 8.6; Col. 1.15–18a; Heb. 1.3–4; John 1.1–18). In these hymns, the same grammatical subject, usually the relative pronoun "who," governs all the verbs that speak of wisdom's activity before the incarnation, of the activity of the incarnate one in history, and of the exalted one after Easter. Thus, we now have a three-step Christology: (1) wisdom's activity in creation, revelation, providence, and salvation history before Christ; (2) the career of the historical Jesus; (3) the exalted life of Jesus after Easter. Like the sending formulae, this Christology focuses upon the origin rather than the fate of Jesus.

Outside the Fourth Gospel and the Letters of John, this preexistence-incarnation Christology is for the most part confined to hymns. It does not widely affect the Christological thinking of Paul, the deutero-Pauline writings, or Hebrews outside the hymns. There are, however, a few exceptional passages where we do see the influence of this type of Christology. When Paul says that the rock that followed the Israelites in the wilderness was Christ (1 Cor. 10.4), this implies the identification of Christ with a preexistent wisdom who was active in Israel's salvation history, especially in the exodus. Again, when Paul says that God sent his Son in the "likeness of sinful flesh" (Rom. 8.3), the sending formula has apparently been widened to include the idea not just of historical sending but of preexistence and incarnation.

Hebrews also shows the influence of this incarnation Christology when the author applies Ps. 8.5–7 to Jesus' career in 2.6–9, and goes on to say "since, therefore, the children share flesh and blood, he himself [Christ] likewise shared the same things" (Heb. 2.14). There are signs in Hebrews that the three-step Christology is beginning to be integrated into the author's thinking.

It is in the gospel of John, however, that the preexistence-incarnation Christology was fully integrated into the thought of the evangelist. True, the Fourth Gospel does contain earlier materials reflecting the more primitive sending formula (e.g., John 12.44, a pre-Johannine saying with synoptic parallels). There are also passages in John where, like Matthew 11.28–30, Jesus is presented as the spokesperson of wisdom (e.g., John 6.35, 37). This may also have been the original sense of the great "I am" sayings, including John 8.58, which originally was intended not to be a personal utterance of Jesus but of God's wisdom speaking through Jesus. Other parts of the evangelist's stage III materials, however, present Christ as one who was personally preexistent. He came down from heaven (3.31). God sent him into the world (3.17). He came into the world (3.19). At the Last Supper, Jesus prays that he may resume the glory that he had before the world was made (John 17.5; cf. 13.3). Thus, in the later phases of stage III, John moves beyond the idea of Christ as wisdom's spokesperson to the idea that he is the personal incarnation of the eternal wisdom of God. This doubtless affected the understanding of the earlier sending formulae and the sayings' in which Jesus is the spokesperson of wisdom. He is now perceived to be the incarnation of wisdom in person. But never does John call Jesus the wisdom of God; rather, the titles that describe him as such are "son" and, in the prologue, Word (Grk. *logos*). The consequence is that the title Son of God, or son, which had earlier been used functionally to denote historic mission, now acquired a metaphysical sense. We may now properly speak of the divinity, or better, the deity, of Christ. In three instances the Johannine writings actually call Jesus "God" (John 1.18; 20.28; 1 John 5.20). Other instances of this in the New Testament are doubtful on textual or interpretative grounds (Rom. 9.5; Tit. 2.13). When we call Jesus God, it must be carefully nuanced: Jesus is not all that God is. He is the incarnation of that aspect of the divine being which is God going forth from himself in creative, revelatory, and saving activity. In terms of later dogma, he is the incarnation of the Second, not of the First, person of the Trinity.

We may ask what motives propelled Christian writers to such a high Christology within such a relatively short period. The God whose presence had been discerned in the Christ event was the same God they had known all along, the God who created the world, the God who was known in general human experience, and, above all, the God who was known in Israel's salvation history. The Christ event was an experience of recognition. Also creation and salvation were closely related. Salvation was not salvation out of the world but salvation of the world.

The work of Christ. By the work of Christ is meant the saving significance of the Christ event (soteriology). The earliest Christian preaching as recorded in Acts (chaps. 2; 3; 10) does not highlight the death of Christ, but speaks of the Christ event in its totality as God's act of salvation. These speeches do feature the death of Christ, but always in the so-called contrast scheme: the death of Christ was Israel's rejection of God's offer, and the Resurrection was God's act of vindicating his offer (Acts 2.23–24; 313–15; 10.39–40). Mark's passion predictions, which in their present form belong to stage II, have the same contrast scheme. Yet these passages also state that Israel's rejection of the Messiah was in accordance with God's purpose (Acts 2.23 and the "must" of the passion predictions). It was also explicitly predicted in scripture (Acts 3.18). Thus, the way was prepared for conceiving the death of Christ not only as Israel's active refusal but also as God's act of salvation.

It was the celebration of the Lord's Supper which appears to have provided the context for reflection on the saving significance of Christ's death. The earliest traditions that do so consist of liturgical materials. First, we have the expansion of the cup word in the Supper tradition itself (Mark 14.24; cf. Mark 10.45b). Here we get for the first time the so-called *hyper*-formula, which asserts that the death of Christ was for (Grk. *hyper*) us. Next, the *hyper*-formula appears in creedal or catechetical traditions (1 Cor. 15.4).

Over the course of time, more precise imagery was introduced to interpret the meaning of Christ's death. One pre-Pauline hymn compares the death of Christ and its effects with the ritual of the Day of Atonement. We are "justified . . . through the redemption that is in Christ Jesus, whom God put forward as a sacrifice of atonement by his blood. . . . He did this to show his righteousness, because in his divine forbearance he had passed over sins previously committed" (Rom. 3.24–25). "Justify" is a metaphor from the law courts referring to the judge's pronouncement of the verdict "not guilty." This is another way of saying that Christ's death conveyed the forgiveness of sins, an idea that occurs later in the hymn when it speaks of God's "passing over sins."

Christ's death is then described as an act of "redemption" (Grk. *apolytrōsis*). Although this word is often thought to derive from the manumission of slaves, it has a more likely background in salvation history. God redeemed Israel by bringing it out of the land of Egypt and by restoring it after the exile, and Israel continued to hope for redemption at the end. The Song of Zechariah announces the fulfillment of this hope (Luke 1.68). Redemption thus came to denote deliverance from all the ills of history in the messianic age.

Next we have the word translated "sacrifice of atonement" (Grk. *hilastērion*). Its precise meaning is disputed. Some translate it "propitiation," which suggests appeasing or placating an angry deity—a notion hardly compatible with biblical thought and rarely occurring in that sense in the Hebrew Bible. It requires God as its object, whereas in this hymn God is the subject: "whom God put forward." Luther translated it as "mercy seat," an item of the Temple furniture which was sprinkled with blood on the Day of Atonement (Lev. 16.14–16). But applied to Jesus the metaphor would be confused: Jesus did not cleanse himself through his own blood as the priest did with the mercy seat on the Day of Atonement. Accordingly, the rendering "expiation" is the most probable. In Israelite sacrifices, especially those of the Day of Atonement, sins were expiated, that is, they were covered over or cleansed and thus removed (Lev. 4.1–6.7; 6.24–7.1). This seems to give the best meaning in Romans 3.24–25. There is, however, an element of truth in the idea of propitiation, for it calls attention to the fact that sin is not only a defilement but a breach of the human relationship with God. As a result of Christ's saving work, this broken relationship has been restored. The last soteriological term in this hymn is the word "blood." This comes from the cup word in the supper tradition and denotes not a substance but the death of Christ as a sacrificial and saving event. Another early formula is found in

Crucifixion with a Darkened Sun by Egon Schiele (Mark 15.22–41)

Romans 4.25: Christ "was handed over to death for our trespasses and was raised for our justification."

Paul took over these earlier traditions about the saving work of Christ and developed them significantly in two directions. He speaks both of the work of Christ in itself (the objective side) and of the work of Christ in believers (the subjective side). Here we will be concerned with the former, the objective side.

The central term in Paul's soteriology is justification. Together with its cognates, including "righteousness" as applied to God, it occurs some forty-eight times in the undisputed letters. It is the major focus of Paul's arguments in Galatians 3–4 and in Romans 3.21–5.11. It is almost synonymous with reconciliation (Rom. 5.11). This gives it a more personal twist, for reconciliation is a metaphor derived not from the law court but from relationships between persons and between social groups. Thus, justification comes to mean not merely to pronounce not guilty but also to bring into a right relationship with God. Paul tries to explain how this happened. On the cross Christ took upon himself the curse of the Law (Gal. 3.10–14) and endured its consequences. God made his son to be "sin" for us (2 Cor. 5.21). Christ put himself in the place of sinners, and as the sinless one he exhausted God's wrath against sin, thus making it possible for humanity to enter into a right relationship with God. The metaphor reconciliation also gives a social and cosmic dimension to justification (2 Cor. 5.19). These dimensions received further emphasis in the deutero-Pauline letters (Col. 1.20–22; Eph. 2.16).

Paul occasionally speaks of Christ's death as a sacrifice but only in traditional formulae (in addition to Rom. 3.25–26, see 1 Cor. 5.8). He once uses the term "blood" as shorthand for Christ's death as a saving event, in the phrase "justified by his blood" (Rom. 5.9). Otherwise, in the genuine Pauline letters "blood" occurs only in connection with the Lord's Supper.

Christ's death is also regarded by Paul as a victory over the powers of evil, another item that comes from earlier tradition (Phil. 2.10). In speaking about victory, however, Paul is careful to emphasize that the powers, though decisively defeated, await final subjugation at the end (1 Cor 15.25–27). The apostle includes among the powers of evil not only cosmic forces but existential realities like law, sin, and death. This victory-soteriology becomes more important in the deutero-Pauline letters (Col. 2.15; Eph. 1.21), which abandon Paul's reservation about its present incompleteness. All that remains is for everything to be united (NRSV: "gathered up") in Christ at the end (Eph. 1.10).

In itself, the term "salvation," with its cognates "save" and "savior," is a rather colorless word in the Pauline writings. As with the other words we have studied, its background is found in the Hebrew Bible, where it is applied to the Exodus and to the restoration from exile (Exod. 15.2; Isa. 43.11; 52.10). Like similar words, it also became part of Israel's hope for the end. Paul uses this word group in an all-embracing way. Believers have been saved, though only in hope (Rom. 8.24–25); they are being saved (1 Cor. 1.18); and they will be saved at the end (Rom. 5.10). Once again, the deutero-Pauline letters abandon this reserve and insist that believers have already been saved (Eph. 2.5,8).

The only New Testament work to develop the doctrine of Christ's saving work is the letter to the Hebrews. This letter makes an elaborate comparison between the levitical high priests and their sacrifices, on the one hand, and Christ and his sacrifice, on the other. The author took up certain items from earlier Christian tradition. One was the comparison of Good Friday with the Day of Atonement, which we have already seen in Romans 3.24–25 (note the expression "sacrifice of atonement," Heb. 2.17). Another was the supper tradition with its language about blood and covenant (Heb. 8.6–13). Yet a third theme, that of Christ as high priest after the order of Melchizedek, was suggested by Psalm 110, which led the author on to verse 4 (Heb. 5.6; etc.).

In developing his argument, the author of Hebrews had first to prove that Jesus was qualified to be a high priest despite his lack of levitical descent (Heb. 5.1–10). Then, in the central part of his work (7.1–10.18), he compares Jesus and his sacrifice point by point with the levitical high priests and their sacrifices, demonstrating at every point the superiority of Jesus and his self-offering. As the comparison with the Day of Atonement shows, Christ's sacrifice is not confined to his death but includes also his ascension into heaven. For the action of the priest in taking the blood of the victim into the Holy of Holies was an essential part of the ritual, in which the slaying of the victim was only a preliminary. Thus, Christ's sacrifice was completed only when he entered into the presence of God and sat down at his right hand (Heb. 10.12). Henceforth, Christ lives to make intercession for us (Heb. 7.25).

How does the author of Hebrews understand Christ's sacrifice to be effective in taking away sin? He follows the biblical belief that sin is a ritual defilement that can be cleansed only with the blood of a victim (Heb. 9.22). Yet he points beyond a merely cultic interpretation of this imagery when he observes that Christ's death was the offering of a perfect obedience of his human will (Heb. 10.5–10). On the strength of his perfect obedience, believers too can draw near to God's presence and offer the sacrifice of praise that leads to the obedience of a holy life (Heb. 10.19–25; 13.15).

The author of 1 Peter takes over the earlier tradition that compared Christ's sacrifice to that of the Passover lamb (1 Pet. 1.19). In a remarkable hymnlike passage (1 Pet. 2.21–25), the author describes Christ's passion in terms of the suffering servant of Isaiah 53. Christ's sufferings are to serve as the example for Christian slaves to follow (v. 21). This treatment of the death of Christ as an example is characteristic of the moralism of the subapostolic age.

We turn now to the treatment of the death of Christ in stage III of the four Gospels. Each evangelist presents the death of Christ from his own perspective. For Mark, the death of Jesus was the occasion for the unveiling of the messianic secret. Only at the crucifixion could he be publicly acknowledged as the Son of God (Mark 15.39). Mark was probably countering the view that overemphasized the miracles, as revelations of Christ's deity. The miracles are important to Mark but only as prefigurations of the supreme act of salvation on the cross.

For Matthew, the cross was Israel's rejection of the Messiah. Because of it, God's judgment came upon the nation at the fall of Jerusalem in 70 CE (Matt. 27.25). A new nation, the Christian church, would arise in Israel's place (Matt. 21.43). Meanwhile, Matthew emphasizes the saving significance of the cross by adding to the cup word at the supper the phrase "for the forgiveness of sins" (Matt. 26.28).

For Luke, the death of Jesus at Jerusalem and his consequent assumption into heaven (Luke 9.51) constituted a major turning point in salvation history, inaugurating the new period of the church and its universal mission. This period would be covered by the book of Acts. Luke is wrestling with the problem created by the delay in Christ's second coming. The time of the church will be marked by persecution and martyrdom, and Christ's passion is presented as an example for Christian martyrs to follow, such as Stephen in Acts 6–7.

John seems to shift his interest away from the cross to the revelation that Jesus brings in his earthly life (John 1.18). The death of Jesus seems to be no more than the occasion when he returned to the Father from whom he came (John 13.3; 16.5). But this is to underestimate the importance of Christ's death in the Fourth Gospel. The words and works of Christ are all overshadowed by the hour of the passion (John 2.4, etc.). The signs or miracles point to what Christ would finally accomplish on the cross. It is there that he brings in the new order symbolized by the changing of the water into wine (2.1–11). It is there that he makes his flesh available for the life of the world (6.51–58), that he cures the blindness of human life (9.1–41), and that he confers eternal life (11.1–44). It is also in the cross that all the claims made in the great "I am" sayings are substantiated. It is because of the cross that he is the true bread that comes down from heaven (6.33), that he is the light of the world (8.12), the door of the sheep (10.7), the good shepherd (10.14), the resurrection and the life (11.25), the way, the truth, and the life (14.6), and the true vine (15.1). Moreover, it is through the cross that the Spirit-Paraclete is released which leads the Johannine community into all truth (7.39). Thus it was the death of Christ and his glorification that made it possible for the Fourth Gospel to ascribe the "I am" sayings to Jesus.

Despite the apparent preoccupation of the author of Revelation with the events leading up to the end and with the new heaven and the new earth that lie beyond, the cross for him plays a crucial role in salvation history. The central christological image in Revelation is the Lamb that was slain. In the cross, the Lamb has conquered and taken his seat beside the Father on the throne of heaven (3.21). Because of that victory, the Lamb alone is qualified to open the scroll and its seven seals (5.5). In other words, his victorious death determines the future course of history. It becomes clear that the cross is the central and controlling event of the whole book. Meanwhile, Christ has "ransomed" believers "from every tribe and language and people and nation, and . . . made them to be a kingdom and priests serving our God" (Rev. 5.9–10).

REGINALD H. FULLER

JEW. The English word "Jew" is derived from Hebrew *yĕhûdî* (fern, *yĕhûdît*, "Judith"; see Gen. 26.34; also the book of Judith), meaning "Judean," by way of Greek *ioudaios* and Latin *judaeus*. The term is first used for citizens of the southern kingdom of Judah in 2 Kings 16.6; previously, male inhabitants of the kingdom, or of the tribe of Judah from which the kingdom took its name, were referred to as *'îš yĕhûdâ*, literally "man [men] of Judah" (e.g., 1 Sam. 11.8). As a consequence of the exile of many members of the upper classes of Judah by the Babylonians in 597 and 587/586 BCE, many Jews were forcibly settled in Mesopotamia (2 Kings 24–25; Jer. 52). Others, including the prophet Jeremiah, fled to Egypt (Jer. 43). This was the beginning of the Jewish dispersion, or Diaspora, across the globe, which continues to this day. After the exile the term Jew came to be used for all descended from or identified with this ethnic or religious group, whatever their race or nationality. Thus, in Esther 2.5, Mordecai is identified both as a Jew and as a member of the tribe of Benjamin. The term "Jew" thus began to parallel the much more ancient designation "Israelite."

The Jews who returned from exile after 538 BCE (Ezra 2; Neh. 7.6–73) settled in the Persian province of Yehud, which eventually became the Roman province of Judea and preserved its name until it was suppressed by the Romans in reaction to the Jewish revolts of 66–73 and 132–135 CE.

In the New Testament "Jew" can designate both Jesus (Mark 15.2) and many of his followers (Acts 21.39), as well as some of his adversaries (1 Thess. 2.14–16). However, the rivalry between Christianity and Judaism, coupled with the often uncomplimentary portrait of Jews in the New Testament and the similarity in sound to the name of Judas, often made the word *Jew* pejorative in the Christian world.

The question of how to define a Jew, put more simply as "who is a Jew," has engendered much discussion through the ages. Are the Jews to be understood as a social, religious, national, or ethnic community? Basically, the answer of the Jewish tradition, the *halakhah*, has been that one born of a Jewish mother or one converted to Judaism is a Jew. But this definition has been challenged in recent years. The murder of many of Jewish descent who, however, were not halakhically Jewish during the Holocaust has raised questions regarding inclusion and exclusion in the Jewish community. The high court of Israel, in the Brother Daniel Rufeisen case, ruled that an apostate from Judaism cannot apply for automatic citizenship as a Jew under the Law of Return. And in recent years the American Jewish Reform movement has attempted to redefine the term "Jew" to include, in addition to converts, anyone of Jewish descent, whether that descent be matrilineal (the halakhic position) or patrilineal (excluded by *halakhah*), who practices Judaism and identifies himself or herself as a Jew. A strict definition is therefore impossible to reach.

CARL S. EHRLICH

JEZEBEL. Princess of Tyre who married Ahab, king of Israel (mid-ninth century BCE). Jezebel was the daughter of Ethbaal, king of Tyre ("Sidonians" in 1 Kings 16.31 is a biblical term for Phoenicians in general); according to genealogies given in Josephus and other classical sources, this would make her the great-aunt of Dido, the founder of Carthage. Jezebel was an ardent worshiper of Baal and Asherah who supported their worship from the throne in Israel (1 Kings 16.31–33; 18.4, 19; 19.1–2); her name is best understood as meaning "Where is the Prince?", the cry of Baal's divine and human subjects when he is in the underworld. Jezebel exercised royal prerogatives to acquire Naboth's vineyard for her husband (1 Kings 21) by plotting to have Naboth executed. This incident prompted Elijah to predict that dogs would eat Jezebel's corpse in Jezreel (1 Kings 21.23; see 2 Kings 9.30–37). Jehu, the commander of King Joram's army in Israel, was anointed king in Ramoth-gilead in order to destroy Ahab's house because of what Jezebel had done to the prophets and the faithful of Yahweh (2 Kings 9.1–10). When Jehu met King Joram, son of Ahab and Jezebel, to kill him, he remarked that there could be no peace in Israel while the "whoredoms [apostasy] and sorceries" of Jezebel continued. After killing Joram of Israel and King Ahaziah of Judah (Ahab and Jezebel's grandson), he went to Jezreel to kill Jezebel. Adorned like a queen, she appeared to him in a window, regally defiant in the face of his violence. She was thrown out of the window by her own attendants, who sided with Jehu, and was trampled to death.

Jezebel's sons and daughter also ruled. Ahaziah was king of Israel for two years after Ahab died and Joram succeeded him (1 Kings 22.51–53, 2 Kings 1.17–18; 31–3; 10.12–14). Jezebel and Ahab's daughter Athaliah married Jehoram of

Jezebel

Judah, and was the mother of Ahaziah, king of Judah (2 Kings 8.25–27). When her son was killed by Jehu (9.14–28), Athaliah set out to kill all his heirs, and she herself ruled for six years (11.1–20).

Jezebel later becomes an insulting epithet for a woman, and is used in Revelation 2.20 to describe a prophet in Thyatira of whose teaching and practice the author disapproves.

Jo Ann Hackett

JOB, THE BOOK OF. The book of Job is the most consistently theological work in the Hebrew Bible, being nothing but an extended discussion of one theological issue, the question of suffering. Its chief literary feature is that it does not expound or defend a dogma from one point of view, but portrays a debate in which conflicting points of view are put forward, none of them being unambiguously presented as preferable. This makes it perhaps the most intellectually demanding book of the Hebrew Bible, requiring of its readers a mental flexibility and even a willingness, in the end, to be left with no unequivocal message.

It is not only a work of intellectual vigor, though; it is also a literary masterpiece that belongs with the classics of world literature, with the *Iliad*, the *Divine Comedy*, and *Paradise Lost*. In design it has both the form of an unsophisticated prose narrative, which nonetheless contains intriguing surprises, and that of a series of subtle speeches in poetry of great delicacy and power. The interplay between prose and poetry, between naïveté and rhetorical finesse, mirrors the interplay among the six participants in the book—Job, the four friends, God—and the narrator.

Structure. The book can be most easily analyzed as narrative framework surrounding poetic core:

1.1–2.13	Framework	prose: narrative
3.1–42.6	Core	poetry: argument
42.7–17	Framework	prose: narrative

Another way of reading the shape of the book follows the indications given by the book itself about the speakers. The whole book may be seen as speech, the narrator speaking in prologue and epilogue, and the characters in the dialogue—the three cycles of conversation between Job and the first three friends, the speeches of Elihu the interloper, and the exchanges between God and Job:

  I. Prologue (1.1–2.13)
    Narrator
 II. Dialogue (3.1–42.6)
    A. Job and the three friends, First Cycle
       Job (3.1–26)
       Eliphaz (4.1–5.27)
       Job (6.1–7.21)
       Bildad (8.1–22)
       Job (9.1–10.22)
       Zophar (11.1–20)
    B. Job and the three friends, Second Cycle
       Job (12.1–14.22)
       Eliphaz (15.1–35)
       Job (16.1–17.16)
       Bildad (18.1–21)
       Job (19.1–29)
       Zophar (20.1–29)
    C. Job and the three friends, Third Cycle
       Job (21.1–34)
       Eliphaz (22.1–30)
       Job (23.1–24.25)
       Bildad (25.1–6)
       Job (26.1–14)
       Job (27.1–28.20)
       Job (29.1–31.40)
    D. Elihu
       Elihu (32.1–33:33)
       Elihu (34.1–37)
       Elihu (35.1–16)
       Elihu (36.1–37.24)
    E. Yahweh and Job
       Yahweh (38.1–40.2)
       Job (40.3–5)
       Yahweh (40.6–41.32)
       Job (42.1–6)
III Epilogue (42.7–17)
    Narrator

This analysis shows, first, that the narrator's words enclose those of all the characters, which has the effect of predisposing the reader to understand how all the speakers in the dialogue are to be understood, and at the end leaving the narrator's perspective uppermost in the reader's mind. Second, it is Job who for the most part initiates conversation; he speaks, and the friends reply to him. But when Yahweh speaks, it is he and not Job who takes the initiative; though Job has summoned Yahweh to speak, Yahweh's speeches are less a reply than a new approach. Third, all the speaking moves toward silence; Job, who has done most of the talking, in the end lays his hand on his mouth (40.4–5); the friends run out of words and do not even finish the third cycle of speeches. Does the book perhaps imply that the real resolution to the problem of suffering comes not at all through talking but only when Yahweh too stops speaking and actually restores Job's fortunes (42.10)?

Argument. Although it is generally agreed that the chief issue of the book is the problem of suffering, we need to be clear on just what that problem is.

Sometimes it is thought that the question is why is there suffering, what are its origins and cause, or why has this suffering happened to a specific person? To these serious questions the book of Job gives no satisfactory answer. It does indeed say that suffering is sometimes punishment for sins, sometimes a warning against committing sin in the future, and sometimes, as in Job's case, for no earthly reason at all, but for some inscrutable divine reason. In the end, though, readers cannot learn from the book any one clear view about what the reason for any particular suffering, or for human suffering in general, may be.

A second problem about suffering is whether there is such a thing as innocent suffering. Against cut-and-dried theologies of retribution, the book of Job, without of course denying the possibility that sometimes suffering is richly deserved by the sufferer, denies that such is always the case. Job is an innocent sufferer, whose innocence is not only asserted by himself (6.30; 9.15) but is attested to by the narrator (1.1) and above all by God (1.8; 2.3; 42.7–8).

There is a third, and more important, problem about suffering that the book does address, however indirectly. It is more existential: In what way am I supposed to suffer, or what am I to do when I am suffering? Two different but complementary answers are given. First, in the opening two chapters, Job's reaction to the disasters that come upon him is a calm acceptance of the will of God; he can bless God not only for what he has given but also for what he has taken away (1.21; 2.10). The patient Job is thus a model for sufferers. But second, Job does not remain in that attitude of acceptance. Once we move into his poetic speeches, from chap. 3 onward, we encounter a mind in turmoil, a sense of bitterness and anger, of isolation from God and even persecution by God. Job makes no attempt to suppress his hostility toward God for what has happened to him; he insists that he will "speak in the anguish of [his] spirit" and "complain in the bitterness of [his] soul" (7.11). What makes this protesting Job a model for other sufferers is that he directs himself constantly toward God, whom he regards as responsible, both immediately and ultimately, for his suffering. It is only (we may suppose) because Job insists on response from God that God enters into dialogue with Job. Even though Job's intellectual questions about the injustice of his suffering are never adequately answered, he himself is in the end satisfied, as a sufferer, by his encounter with God.

Origins. The composition of the book of Job can be dated to some point between the seventh and the second centuries BCE, but hardly more precisely than that. Quite probably there was a much older tale of an innocent sufferer, and the general theme is found also in Jeremiah and in the poems of the Suffering Servant of the Lord in Second Isaiah, both of these prophetic texts stemming from the sixth century. Perhaps the inexplicable suffering of Job was intended to symbolize the suffering of the Jews in Babylonian exile in that century.

The earliest reference to Job outside the book is found in Ezekiel 14.14, 20, where Job is mentioned along with Noah and Daniel as an ancient hero. But this sixth-century reference may well be not to the book of Job but to the more ancient folktale, so no inference about the date of the book can be drawn.

There can be little doubt that the author of the book was an Israelite. Job's homeland is depicted as north Arabia or possibly Edom, and in most of the book Job himself does not know God by the Israelite name Yahweh. Nor does the book refer to any of the distinctive historical traditions of ancient Israel. But these facts only mean that the author has succeeded well in disguising his own age and background in his creation of the character of his hero, who is intended to have universal significance.

In the history of scholarship on the book, several critical questions have commonly attracted attention. One is whether the prose framework of the book (the prologue and epilogue) once existed as an independent story before the poem (3.1–42.6) was composed. The tendency now is to assume that although there was a prose story of Job older than the present book, the prologue and epilogue that we have now were written for their place in the book, since the prose framework by itself does not tell a completely coherent story. The other major question is whether the present allocation of speeches in the third cycle (chaps. 21–31) is the one intended by the author—for it seems strange that there is no third speech of Zophar, that the third speech of Bildad is so short that Job is credited with three speeches in a row, and that some of what Job says seems more suitable in the mouth of one of the friends. Most scholars therefore suspect that there has been some error in the manuscripts of Job, and that, for example, 26.5–14 was originally part of Bildad's speech and 27.13–28.28 was originally Zophar's third speech. A third question often raised is whether the speeches of the fourth friend Elihu

Satan Asking God to Tempt Job (Job 1.9–12) (Bartolo di Fredi, 1356–67)

(chaps. 32–37) were originally part of the book, since Elihu (unlike the other friends) is not referred to in either the prologue or the epilogue. But it is not possible to settle this question, and in any case these speeches need to be treated as a significant part of the present book whether or not they were contained in the original book.

Job among the Wisdom Literature. The book of Proverbs affirms that wisdom—which means the knowledge of how to live rightly—leads to life, while folly leads to death (e.g., Prov 1.32; 3.1–2, 13–18; 8.36). Everywhere the principle of retribution is asserted or taken for granted: that righteousness is rewarded and sin is punished (e.g., Prov. 11.5–6). And the world of humans is divided into two groups: the blessed righteous, or wise, and the unhappy wicked, or foolish.

Ecclesiastes, while not disparaging the quest for wisdom, asks, What happens to one's wisdom at death? Since death cancels out all values, not excepting wisdom, life cannot be meaningful if it is made to consist of gaining something that will inevitably be lost.

As for Job, from the viewpoint of the book of Proverbs, he is an impossibility. If he is truly righteous, he finds life, and wealth, and health. If he is in pain, he is one of the wicked and the foolish. In the end, of course, the book of Job does not completely undermine the principle of retribution, for Job ends up pious *and* prosperous; but once the principle is successfully challenged, as it is in the book of Job, even in a single case, its moral force is desperately weakened. For once the case of Job becomes known, if a person who has a reputation for right living is found to be suffering (the fate Proverbs predicts for wrongdoers), no one can point a finger of criticism; the book of Job has established that the proper criterion for determining whether people are pious or not is the moral quality of their life and not the accidental circumstances of their material existence.

DAVID J. A. CLINES

JOEL, THE BOOK OF. In both the Hebrew and the Greek canons of the Bible, the book of Joel appears in proximity to that of the eighth-century BCE prophet Amos, a circumstance that is easily explained by the close correspondence between Joel 3.16–18 and Amos 1.2; 9.13. There can hardly be any doubt that this correspondence is the result of the dependence of the text of Joel on that of Amos; from internal evidence it seems clear that the book of Joel is the work of a late postexilic prophet who was indebted for his images and metaphors to the much older prophetic traditions to which he laid claim and in which he presumed to participate.

The Author and His Times. We know nothing about the person of Joel (whose name means "Yahweh is God") other than that he is identified as the son of an equally unknown Pethuel. All the knowledge that we can derive about him and his times comes from the examination of his prophecy. He is, on the one hand, much concerned with the proprieties of the Temple worship (1.9, 13–14; 2.14–16; etc.), a trait that connects him very closely with the anonymous prophet Malachi, who was possibly one of the very last to appear in the Judahite prophetic tradition. This trait, however, was by no means characteristic of preexilic prophecy of either Israel or Judah. Joel presupposes, therefore, the existence of a Temple—presumably the Second Temple of Zerubbabel, which came to be in the aftermath of the initial return from exile, following the liberating decree of Cyrus the Persian after his defeat of the Babylonian empire in 539 BCE (Ezra 1.1–4). Furthermore,

contrary to the picture drawn in the preexilic Deuteronomic history of Israel and Judah, so much concerned with kings and politics, and even contrary to that of the Chronicler's depiction of the period of Ezra and Nehemiah (ca. 458–443 BCE), when Judah and Jerusalem, still under the domination of the Persian empire, were regaining a relative political autonomy with a secular (although concomitantly religious) leadership of native governors (like Nehemiah), Joel's text seems to presuppose a polity not unlike that presupposed by Sirach (Sir. 50.1–24) or the book of Judith, where it is taken for granted that the political leadership of the Jews has, by default, devolved upon the high priesthood. Since there is no hint of a disruption in Joel of this peaceful coexistence between religion and alien domination, we are probably not far off the mark when we assign this work to the latter stage of the Persian period of Palestine, which was disrupted only by the conquests of Alexander the Great beginning in 333 BCE. These considerations would date Joel about 400 BCE.

Outline. The book of Joel consists of two sharply distinguished parts. There is, first of all, the graphic and highly descriptive depiction of a locust plague and a drought (the Hebrew vocabulary for "locusts" is virtually exhausted in 1.4) that descends on Judah and Jerusalem, demanding of everyone, class by class, profession by profession, repentance and prayer as the price of the Lord's continual toleration of a recalcitrant people (1.2–2.27). In the second part (2.28–3.21 [3.1–4.21 in the Hebrew Bible]), the Day of the Lord is announced in apocalyptic language. There is a series of salvation prophecies: Judah and Jerusalem will be restored, Israel will triumph over her enemies, and the gentiles will be requited for their misdeeds.

Interpretation. Is Joel a prophet of judgment (against Israel) or of salvation (of Israel in the face of its gentile enemies)? It is really difficult to say. Was the locust plague of the first verses an attempt to describe a real happening, as in Amos 7.1–3, or is it merely a literary device borrowed from the text of a prophetic predecessor? Is this plague a cloak for physical invasion of Israel or simply a symbol of national disintegration? Is the lifting of the plague potential or real? How much and to what extent is the repeated "Day of the Lord" intended to apply to Israel's future destiny and its relation to the gentile world? And by no means let us forget the outpouring of the spirit foretold by this prophet (2.28–323) and the fulfillment that was discerned by New Testament writers seeking religious continuity (Acts 2.16–19). Whether Joel is to be considered a "cult" or "nationalist" prophet, a prophet of "judgment" or of "salvation," are questions that truly indicate that we have not yet fully comprehended the phenomenon of Israelite prophecy.

BRUCE VAWTER, C.M

JOHN THE BAPTIST. If John was born of priestly parentage (Luke 1.5), he must have abandoned the priesthood and taken up an ascetic mode of life in the Judean wilderness, where he subsisted on locusts and wild honey (Mark 1.6). Those who came out to him encountered a man dressed in camel-hair homespun with a leather belt around his waist, the explicit garb of a prophet (2 Kings 1.8; Zech. 13.4). With prophetic zeal he preached a new message and offered a new rite. The message was that lineal descent from Abraham would not guarantee salvation. Abraham's merits would not suffice, but only an act of repentance that included the renunciation of all presumptions based on election or ethnicity would ensure salvation (Matt. 3.9). The God that had called Israel out of Egypt and led it across the Jordan River was now creating a new people by passing them through the waters of baptism in that same river. The twelve stones that had been set up to mark Israel's crossing of the parted Jordan (Josh. 4) would themselves be raised up into twelve new tribes if the people of Israel would not repent. John was not founding a·new religion but attacking the use of all religiousness as a defense against the demand of God for authenticity and justice.

This message of radical repentance was enacted in a rite of immersion in which the sin of presumption and the whole of one's old life were washed away. Those who rose out of the waters were as newborn infants (John 3.3–8), or as those who had passed from death to life, having been buried and raised from the dead (Rom. 6.1–11). These later Christian interpretations seem to have carried forward at least Jesus' own understanding of what John was about, for he spoke of his own baptism not as an event in the past but as a metaphor for his own approaching death (Mark 10.38–39; Luke 12.50).

John himself may have shared the idea, common in that period, that the last judgment would be enacted by a river of fire through which everyone would have to walk. In anticipation of that imminent judgment, John was inviting one and all to submit to God's judgment now, and by undergoing baptism to cleanse themselves of sin, in advance of that terrible day. Those who had surrendered themselves to this washing would be preserved through the coming tribulation. They would be wheat gathered into God's granary, while the rest would be chaff burned in unquenchable fire (Matt. 3.12 par.).

John's message fell on Israel like fire on stubble. The Gospels report that "all" went out to hear him (Mark 1.5; Matt. 3.5, Mark 11.32 par.; Luke 7.29; Acts 13.24), and Josephus comments that he was highly regarded by the whole Jewish people (*Ant.* 18.5.116–119). The crowds that attended him included tax collectors and prostitutes (Matt. 21.32; Luke 3.12; 7.29). This simple act of immersion, unlike circumcision, made salvation accessible even to women. It was John, not Jesus, who opened a way to God for those who before had felt themselves excluded. And by his dress and diet, even by the metaphors he chose (a tree cutter, a thresher), John identified himself, and the one whom he awaited, with the lowly.

Judaism had never encountered anything quite like this, yet virtually everything recorded of John had parallels in Isaiah. These parallels include the following: an eschatological outpouring of the Holy Spirit (Isa. 32.15; Mark 1.8 par.) associated with the wilderness (Isa. 35.1–10; 40.3; 41.18–19; 43.19–20; Mark 1.3, 8, 10 par.); a spirit-endowed one to come who will act as judge (Isa. 11.2–5; 42.1–4; 61.1; Mark 1.7–8 par.); Israelites as children of Abraham (Isa. 29.22; 41.8; 51.2; 63.16; Matt. 3.9 par.); unfaithful Israel portrayed as a brood of vipers (Isa. 59.5; 1.4; Matt. 3.7 par.) or as trees that God will hew down with an axe (Isa. 6.13; 10.15–19, 33–34; 14.8; Matt. 3.10 par.); wind/breath/spirit (Hebr. *rúah*), and fire compared to a river in which one is immersed (Isa. 30.27–28, 33; 43.2; Matt. 3.12 par.); Israel as the threshed and winnowed one (Isa. 21.10; Matt. 3.12 par.); Israel washed clean (Isa. 1.16; 4.4; 52.11; Mark 1.4 par.); and works of righteousness mandated subsequent to washing (Isa. 1.16–17; Matt. 3.8 par.; Luke 3.10–14).

Despite such extensive parallels, John burst on the scene as a virtual mutant, for his rite of baptism, though outwardly similar to Temple lustrations, was wholly without precedent in its meaning. Nowhere in any Jewish source is rebirth made a metaphor for redemption. One is born a Jew. Proselytes might be "reborn" as Jews, but proselyte baptism was not practiced in the first century CE, applied only to non-Jews, lacked an eschatological setting, and did not require running water. John's rite was so unique that he was named by it ("the Baptizer"), and Jesus clearly regards it as given to John by revelation from God (Mark 11.27–33). It circumvented the Temple and its rites; perhaps John's rejection of the priesthood is related to widespread revulsion against the corruption of the Temple and its priesthood in the first century CE.

John's presence in the wilderness has suggested to some that he might have at one time belonged to the community at Qumran, possibly even being raised by them as an orphan (Luke 1.80; his parents were elderly at his birth [Luke 1.7]). Both John and the settlers at Qumran glowed with eschatological fervor, expecting an imminent judgment and preparing for it in the wilderness. Both called on all Israel to repent, denying that mere Jewishness could save. Both used washings, broke with the Temple cultus, taught prayer and fasting, and focused on Isaiah as their guide to the future. But these qualities seem to have been shared by other sectarians who had located in the wilderness. The Jerusalem Talmud indicates that twenty-four such distinct sects had come into existence by 70 CE (*Sanh.* 29c). And much of what John and Qumran held in common derives from Isaiah.

In key respects, moreover, John was quite different from the community at Qumran. They wore white linen; he dressed like the poor, in homespun. His disciples did not settle a community but wandered about with him. John required no three-year period of probation but accepted whoever came, and they returned home rather than remaining with him in the wilderness. He was prophetic, public, missionary, inclusive; Qumran was exclusive, secretive, and withdrawn. His opening of salvation to prostitutes, tax collectors, and sinners must have scandalized that sacerdotal sect. Qumran's ethic applied only to its own community; John's was addressed to the entire nation, even the king (Mark 6.18). He called not

St. John the Baptist, from the Triptych of the Braque Family

for the communal sharing of goods but for sharing with the wretched who had nothing (Luke 3.11). Instead of demanding that his hearers abandon lives of moral ambiguity and move to the desert, John offered an ideal attainable in society by people unable to abandon everything (Luke 3.12–14). John's baptism, unlike Qumran's washings, was not daily, but once for all, and was not intended to achieve levitical purity, but to secure the forgiveness of sins in anticipation of the coming day of wrath. Even their common use of Isaiah 40.3 was different. Qumran interpreted it to mean that the preparation for the Lord's way was to be done in the wilderness by moving there and studying scripture. John seems to have understood the wilderness only as the place where the voice cries out. And Qumran expected a prophet, a messiah of Aaron, and a messiah of Israel; John expected only a coming judge different from all three.

The evangelists each employ the traditions about John in the service of the proclamation of Jesus. Each handles him differently, but all see him as the one who stands at the beginning of the gospel story, demanding of the hearer a beginner's mind and the jettisoning of all previous securities, so that a new word can be heard.

WALTER WINK

JOHN, THE GOSPEL ACCORDING TO.

Structure and Content. The story of Jesus in John's gospel is presented as a drama, consisting of a prologue, two main acts, and an epilogue. By considering the gospel in this light, its distinctive character may be understood and its teaching illuminated.

The prologue (chap. 1 as a whole) introduces the main theological themes developed in the body of the gospel, such as "life," "light," and "glory." It also includes the leading characters who are to be involved in the main action. John the Baptist is there, and so are the disciples who will form the nucleus of the early Christian community: Andrew and Peter, Philip and Nathanael. But the stage is dominated by the central character of Jesus himself, whose identity begins already to be disclosed, for in this single chapter he is described as Word, Son, Christ (Messiah), Son of God, King of Israel, and Son of man. The climax of the prologue is reached in 1.51 ("you will see heaven opened, and the angels of God ascending and descending upon the Son of man"). Jesus, as the incarnate and exalted Son of man and Son of God, joins earth and heaven decisively together and makes it possible, even in this world, for every believer to share the life of eternity.

Act I (chaps. 2–12) describes the revelation of the Word of God to the world. For those with eyes to see, Jesus during his ministry reveals through his words and actions the glory of God the Father. To demonstrate this truth, John makes his own selection from the miracles, or "signs," that Jesus performed and narrates six of them dramatically. To these six signs are attached explanatory discourses, all of which deal with the leading theme of "life" through Christ, and several memorable "I am" sayings, which act as a text for each sermon. These may be set out as shown in the table on page 150.

Act 2 of John's drama (chaps. 13–20) deals with the glorification of God's Word for the world. At its heart is the story of the passion and resurrection of Jesus, prepared for by the farewell address to the disciples (John 14–17), a discourse that deals with the life of the believer.

The drama ends with an epilogue, chap. 21, which may have been written later but is now firmly related to the body of the gospel. This final section narrates the seventh sign, the catch of 153 fish, and the recalling of Peter. Together these incidents point to the unlimited scope of the Christian good news, an idea retained throughout John's gospel, and provide an agenda for the church of the future. The mission of the disciples to the world can now begin on the basis of the revelation and glorification of the messianic Word of God.

Throughout his dramatic portrayal of the ministry, death, and exaltation of Jesus, John is anxious that readers should "see" the identity of the central character as Christ and Son of God (20.29–31) and "hear" his words. Verbs of seeing

Ancient mosaic from the Church of the Multiplication of the Loaves and the Fishes, Tabgha, Israel : (5th century CE) (John 6.1–14)

and hearing are important in John and are close in meaning to the activity of believing. As in a courtroom, witnesses are called throughout the drama to bear testimony to the life-giving Christ; and the sources of this evidence are divine (the Father, 5.37; the Spirit, 15.26; the scriptures, 5.39) as well as human (John the Baptist, 1.29–36; the Samaritan woman, 4.29, 39–42; the blind man, 9.35–38; Martha, 11.27; and, supremely, Thomas, 20.28).

John thus moves beyond the witness of the other gospel writers in exploring the nature of Jesus in relation to God and humanity, and the grounds for Christian belief and for the spiritual life that is its consequence. Jesus, in John's portrait, is both one with the Father (10.30) and one with his church on earth (16.28).

Origin. Since roughly the middle of the twentieth century support has been growing for the view that the basic tradition underlying John's gospel may be historically more reliable than previously acknowledged. After the rise of biblical criticism in the middle of the nineteenth century, scholarly opinion tended to regard this gospel as a theological rewriting of the others. The author knew Mark, Matthew, and Luke, it was thought, but went his own way when he wished to interpret their meaning. But that conclusion and the assumption that John knew and used the other Gospels in their finished form have now been seriously questioned. It is now thought possible that John drew more or less independently on common Christian sources about the life and teaching of Jesus.

This view may be supported in three ways. First, a straight literary comparison among the four Gospels reveals that, when material in John also appears in the other Gospels (such as the feeding of the five thousand [John 6; Mark 6 par.] and the anointing at Bethany [John 12; Mark 14 par.]), John preserves interesting points of circumstantial detail that appear to be historical rather than theological. Second, the evidence from the Dead Sea Scrolls has shown that before the common era a literary setting existed in which Jewish and Greek religious ideas were combined in a manner that was once thought to be unique to John and of a late, second century CE, date. The scrolls now make it clear that John may well have derived from Qumran itself his language of "truth," "knowledge," "wisdom," and "faith," as well as his theological conviction that life is a struggle between truth and perversity, the sons of light and the sons of darkness, good and evil, in which God will ultimately prevail. Third, archaeological discoveries in and around Jerusalem have indicated that, when John uses place-names hitherto unknown (such as Bethesda [John 5.2] and Gabbatha [19.13]), he was not being inventive but referring to sites now identifiable. In this case the stories associated with such sites need not be theological creations either and may well rest on an underlying historical tradition.

Composition. We have already noted that John's gospel is a literary unit, which may be analyzed in terms of its dramatic structure. But, despite the unity of the gospel as we now have it, there are some features that suggest it was composed in edited stages.

For example, there are differences of style and language in various parts of the gospel, especially chaps. 1 and 21. Second, some of the discourses contain material that seems to be largely repeated (as in 6.35–50 and 50–58; chaps. 14 and 16). Third, there are notorious breaks in sequence at a number of points in the gospel. Thus the first two signs performed by Jesus are numbered "first" and "second" (2.11;

454), yet in 2.23 we hear of other signs that he did, and the sequence is thus unaccountably interrupted. The geographical locations, also, do not appear to be consistently exact. So in 3.22 we read that Jesus went into Judea, whereas according to 2.23 he was already there; and in 6.1 it is implied that Jesus is in Galilee, although at the end of chap. 5 he is in Jerusalem. Similarly, there is a clear break between the setting of chaps. 20 (Jerusalem) and 21 (Galilee/Tiberias). Furthermore, the continuation of the farewell discourse in John 15–16 (17) is awkward after the command of Jesus at 14.31 ("Rise, let us be on our way").

It is possible to account for some but not all of these variations, repetitions, and breaks in continuity; the problem is thus to explain their presence in what now appears to be a carefully constructed literary whole. Some scholars have suggested that there is no problem, inasmuch as the author himself chose to write in this way. Others believe that displacements in John's material have occurred at the manuscript stage, for example, that chaps. 5 and 6 became reversed, resulting in the odd geographical sequence in John 4–7.

None of the proposed restorations, however, takes the problem seriously or resolves it adequately. A third (and more plausible) explanation suggests that behind the composition of the gospel lie a number of different sources, recording the signs, the teaching, and the passion of Jesus, that have been combined and edited at various stages in the writing of this document, until its final publication as a unified work. What follows is a suggested description of those stages.

First, John the apostle, who was traditionally identified as the "beloved disciple," transmitted orally to his followers an account of the deeds (especially the miracles, or "signs") and sayings of Jesus and of his death and resurrection. As we have already seen, these reminiscences preserved historical information about the ministry of Jesus in both Judea and Galilee.

Second, the beloved disciple and his circle of followers moved to Ephesus (a city associated, by strong tradition, with John), where the nucleus of the Johannine church was established. While there, John's disciples committed to writing the traditions preserved in their community for the purposes of worship and instruction. In this first draft of the final gospel what may now be recognized as distinctively Johannine thought emerged, as the ideas handed on by the apostle were dramatically treated and theologically developed by the fourth evangelist and his colleagues.

Third, after the death of John his church at Ephesus published a final edited version of the gospel. This included a summary introduction (1.1–18), based on a community hymn and now tied securely to the remainder of the chapter, some editing of the discourses, possibly the addition of the prayer of consecration in chap. 17, and an epilogue (chap. 21). The whole gospel thus assembled then carried an authenticating postscript (21.24–25).

If some such process were involved in the making of John's gospel, it explains many of the features in its composition already discussed. Thus, it accounts for the likelihood that more than one author was responsible for the writing of the gospel, at more than one stage; and also for the fact that at first the Fourth Gospel was not ascribed to John the son of Zebedee. If the witness of the beloved disciple lies behind this gospel (as the text suggests; see 19.35; 21–24) but others from his community actually wrote it, the work may be regarded as apostolic in character, even though it did not in

Resurrection of Lazarus (John 11.38–44)

J

the end come (as some would argue) from the hand of John the apostle himself.

Date. We have seen that there is good reason to regard the sources that were used in the final composition of John's gospel as early and historically reliable. But even if the Johannine tradition may be dated to the early first century CE, this still leaves open the question of the date of the gospel's publication in its final form.

An upper limit may set at 150 CE or a little earlier. Two manuscripts, written on papyrus and discovered in Egypt, are relevant to dating the gospel. One, known as the Rylands Papyrus, contains a few verses of John 18 and may be dated to 135–150 CE. A second papyrus (Egerton 2) includes part of an unknown gospel that probably used John as well as Mark, Matthew, and Luke; this manuscript dates from ca. 150 CE. The existence of these witnesses suggests that John's gospel must have been written at the very latest by the beginning of the second century CE, and probably earlier.

There are no other conclusive external grounds for an earlier date and no firm evidence that any writers before ca. 150 CE knew the gospel. We must therefore look to the contents of the gospel itself to see whether they can help us—although, here again, it is difficult to establish definite conclusions.

One important clue is provided by the reference in 9.22 and 16.2 (cf. 12.42) to the possibility of Jews who confessed Christ being "put out of the synagogue." This may be an allusion to the Test Benediction that was introduced by

Rabbi Gamaliel II (ca. 85–90 CE) as a means of excluding Nazarenes and other "heretics" from Jewish worship. If so, a date in this period (ca. 85 CE) may be assigned to the gospel. Such a date is also suggested by the fact that John's theology presumably took some time to develop. It is deeper and more sophisticated than that of the other evangelists, whose texts probably emerged earlier than 85 CE.

Purpose. Various motives have been suggested for the composition of John's gospel. For example, it has been argued that John's intention was to supplement or interpret the other gospels, to restate the Christian good news in Greek terms, to issue a polemical attack on the sect of John the Baptist, to adjust the sacramental teaching prevalent in the early church, to correct understanding about the return of Jesus, and to counter gnostically inclined theology.

John himself gives us (20.30–31) a reason for writing his gospel. He wants his readers to see and to hear who Jesus is: that he is the Christ and the Son of God. But this does not give us a complete picture. Who were these readers? It is unlikely that they were Jews, since by 85 CE the mission to Israel was over. It is possible that John was addressing Jewish Christians in the Dispersion, torn between loyalty to Judaism and their new-found faith in Jesus and increasingly pressurized by the recently introduced Test Benediction. This would account for the stress in this gospel on the fulfillment of Judaism. But, once again, such an interpretation of John does not take full account of his message about Jesus; nor does it relate the Fourth Gospel directly to a living church situation, in line with current thinking about John.

Let us suppose that John was addressing the needs of his own community and see whether this will provide a reason for the dramatically shaped version of the Jesus story that he preserves in his gospel. It could be that this community of Christians, gathered initially around the beloved disciple, included believers from different backgrounds, both Jewish and gentile. Some held a balanced view of Jesus: that he was both one with God and fully human. But some from a Jewish background, who still felt a loyalty to their heritage, regarded Jesus as human rather than divine. This would have been all the more likely if, after 70 CE, they were under pressure from their compatriots in the Dispersion and were tempted to return to Judaism by denying the messiahship of Jesus, as "the Jews" do throughout this gospel. On the other hand, those in the circle from a Greek background, including possibly some Hellenistic Jewish Christians, could have thought of Jesus as divine rather than human. This would be understandable if the "divine man" tradition of their original religious environment exercised influence on the Johannine church.

These two groups, it may be presumed, had begun to perceive the real identity of Jesus, but neither had seen that his nature, both human and divine, made it possible for him

SIGN	DISCOURSE	"I AM" SAYING
1. Changing water into wine (2)	new life (3)	the true vine (15.1)
2. Healing the official's son (4)	water of life (4)	the way, the truth and the life (14.6)
3. Making the sick man well (5) official's son (4)	Son, life-giver (5)	the door of the sheep (10.7)
4. Feeding the five thousand (6)	bread and Spirit of life (6–7)	the bread of life (6.35)
5. Restoring the blind man's sight (9)	light of life (8)	the light of the world (8.12)
6. Raising Lazarus from the dead (11)	shepherd, life-giver (10)	the resurrection and the life (11.25)

to be the savior of the world. Friction may have resulted; in this case John's emphasis on mutual love (15.12) and unity within the church (17.11, 21–23) would have been entirely in place.

We can find this story anticipated in the book of Revelation and concluded in the Johannine letters. Evidently the appeal of the fourth evangelist did little to ease the tensions that had beset his community. But his balanced estimate of the person of Jesus was exactly suited to the needs of his own adherents, and it has provided Christians ever since with important guidelines for assessing and maintaining a crucial part of their faith.

Teaching. John's theology is a theology of life. He bears testimony not only to Jesus, but also to the possibility of life through him (1.4). The repeated symbol of light makes the same point. The life that he mediates to every believer, on the basis of his revelation to the world and his glorification for the world, is the divine life that ultimately belongs to the Father himself (5.26).

Moreover, John's gospel speaks of life through Jesus in all its fullness. The seven signs make clear that Jesus is concerned about the physical dimension of human existence as well as its spiritual possibilities. And since the Word became flesh (1.14), as the signs again illustrate, all matter (not only water, bread, and wine) can point to and convey the abundant life of the life-giver (10.10). Such is John's particular "sacramentalism."

This eternal life is available to the faithful now. John's theology of salvation includes a future tense; so, for example, Jesus promises his disciples that he will eventually "come again" for them (14.3). But his emphasis is on the blessings of eternity that can be shared by the Christian in the present, when the judgment as well as the life of God are disclosed (3.16–18).

This understanding of salvation is determined by John's concept of sin. For writers of the other Gospels sin is essentially personal and communal wrongdoing: it is disobedience to God's law. Its consequence, as throughout the Hebrew Bible, is a breakdown of the covenant between creator and creature. Such a covenant relationship can be restored only by the sacrifice on the cross, echoed in the subsequent self-offering of obedience in the lives of the disciples (Mark 10.45; Matthew 7.21; Luke 9.23).

For the fourth evangelist sin is not, as in the other Gospels and in Paul, primarily ethical. It stems from a cosmic state of alienation from God, from a spiritual blindness, or darkness, or deadness (John 3.19; 12.35). This situation can be remedied only by restored sight (9.39) and a conscious return to the light through identification with, and incorporation into, the life of the Son who unites the dimensions of heaven and earth (12.46; 15.4). So in John's gospel the passion and crucifixion of Jesus are not seen as a sacrificial explanation for the forgiveness of sin but as glorification: the exultant transformation scene in a spiritual drama of revelation. In Johannine terminology, references to Jesus as the "Lamb of God" (1.29, 36; see Rev. 13.8) are correspondingly cosmic in character. In John's view, the cross is a timeless manifestation, mediated through a historical event: "I, when I am lifted up from the earth, will draw all people to myself" (John 12.32).

Those who are thus "drawn" to the glorified Christ are indwelt by the Spirit-Paraclete (14.16–17) and receive new life from the vine; and this not only sustains believers individually but also unites them with every other "branch" in the Christian community (15.1–5). At this point, ethical sinfulness can be eradicated by effecting the "new commandment" of love (13.34–35). The time of eternal life in Christ has yet to come; but through him, and decisively, it has arrived already.

STEPHEN S. SMALLEY

JOHN, THE LETTERS OF.

Situation. The three letters in the New Testament that bear the name of John form a composite unit. Although each possesses individual features, all have common characteristics of style, language, and thought and appear to belong to the same situation.

1 John, in contrast to 2 and 3 John, does not at first look like a personal letter. But it was evidently addressed to a particular church situation, in which problems of belief and behavior were being encountered. Indeed, a crisis had arisen, precipitated by some members of the Johannine circle who were spreading false teaching and encouraging secession from the community. As a result, dissident groups had already been established (1 John 2.19). In the face of division, John (as we may for convenience call the writer[s] of these three epistles) composed a "letter" that was designed to correct the inadequate and erroneous views of his readers and to recall them to the fundamental elements in the apostolic gospel.

The nature of the false teaching propounded by John's opponents is indicated in various places in 1 John. The heterodox members of the church claimed to have a special relationship with God (1.6; 2.4) and to be without sin (1.8, 10). They did not believe that Jesus was the Christ or Son of God (2.22; 5.1, 5), and denied his being incarnate (4.2–3; 5.6; 2 John 7). The emphasis in 1 John on right behavior (renouncing sin, rejecting worldliness, and being obedient, especially to the love command) suggests that the opponents were leading others astray regarding ethical as well as theological issues.

If we try to relate these ideas to known systems of opinion in the first century CE, a number of possibilities present themselves. The most widely accepted view is that John was confronted by some early form of gnostic thinking. Such an outlook stemmed from a sharp, characteristically Greek, division between the spiritual, regarded as good, and the material, deemed to be evil. In such a system no place for a real incarnation of the Son of God could be found; the consequence was docetism, a system that acknowledged Jesus as Son of God but claimed that this was merely a seeming or phantom advent. Views of this nature were entertained in the first century CE by Cerinthus, and in the second century by those whom Ignatius of Antioch attacked, and by Basilides.

An alternative approach is to identify John's opponents, as in the Fourth Gospel, with Jewish denials that Jesus was Messiah and Son of God. Thus, the false teachers countered by the writer claimed to know the Father but denied the Christhood of Jesus (2.4, 22–23). Those who object to this interpretation do so on the grounds that non-Christian Jews cannot have belonged to John's church (2.19) or have claimed to be guided by the Spirit (3.24; 4.1) and to be sinless (1.8, 10). But there is no problem involved if the Jewish opposition came from Jewish Christians. If so, we may combine these two solutions and say that some of John's opponents were Jewish and some were Hellenistic. In that case the situation addressed in 1 John closely approximates that in John's gospel.

Central to the theology of the fourth evangelist is his balanced understanding of the person of Christ: that he is both one with humankind and one with God (see John 16.28).

Some Johannine Christians had remained orthodox in their belief. But others, from a Jewish background, needed to be reminded of the divinity of Christ; while a third group, of gentile origin, required assurance about his real humanity.

If this is an accurate description of the volatile setting out of which John's gospel came, it will throw light on the situation behind 1 John and account for the nature of the false teaching that this writer was trying to resist. For by the time that the Johannine letters were written (say, ten years after the gospel), friction between the two heterodox groups had developed, and a polarization had begun to emerge. Those with a low view of Jesus had moved further toward a Jewish position and denied that Jesus was the Christ (2.22). Those who espoused a high Christology had become more clearly gnostic and docetic by inclination and refused to acknowledge that the Christ was Jesus (4.2). On both sides, problems of behavior accompanied those of doctrine (2.7–8, the Law is wrongly regarded as indispensable; 3.10–11, right conduct is falsely deemed unimportant). As a result, secession from the community began to take place (2.18–19).

So the writer of 1 John recalls his followers to the fundamental truths of the Christian faith. Often appealing to the teaching of John's gospel, elements of which may have been distorted by his opponents in support of their theological position, he summarizes the claims of the heterodox, provides a balanced theology of Christ's person (divine, [2.13–14], and human, [3.16]), and refutes ethical error, not least by stressing the command to love (3.11; see John 13.34).

The plea for love and unity, however, evident in both the Fourth Gospel and 1 John, seems not to have been widely heeded. The divisions in the community, already apparent when 1 John was written, deepened; and from 2 John we learn that "many deceivers" had gone back into the world (v. 7). Perhaps these were predominantly docetic in outlook (see 2 John 9), although, again, there is nothing in the Johannine letters to suggest that docetism is the only tendency in view.

By the time 3 John appeared, the unity of the Johannine circle seems to have been threatened from an organizational, as well as doctrinal, point of view. Diotrephes was "putting himself first" and excluding orthodox members from the church (3 John 9–10), and the writer's concern that the influence of such leaders should not increase suggests that he feared the final dissolution of the Johannine community. What actually happened we can only guess. Some of the group presumably went further into gnosticism; the Jewish secessionists may have returned to Judaism, while the orthodox adherents no doubt became absorbed into the life of the great church. At that time John's gospel, with the discussion of its doctrine provided by 1 John (supplemented by 2 and 3 John), came into its own, and the teaching of John's circle was finally secured for the cause of orthodoxy.

Character. 2 and 3 John are the shortest letters in the New Testament. They each consist of one chapter only, are roughly equal in length, and correspond to the conventionally brief length of a private letter that, at the time, would have been written on a single papyrus sheet about 20 by 25 cm (8 by 10 in) in size. Both are personal missives, written by one who describes himself as the elder. But 2 John (addressed to a community) conforms closely to the pattern of other New Testament letters; whereas 3 John (addressed to Gaius, an individual) reflects a secular form of first-century letter writing. Moreover, 2 John is closer than 3 John to 1 John in subject matter and style. None of these variations, however, compels us to infer that 2 and 3 John are

ultimately unrelated (there are evident points of contact between them) or that 2 John was written as a first draft of 1 John. The history of the Johannine community sketched above may be traced entirely naturally from the Gospel to the letters in their present sequence, despite some attempts to assign to them a different order of composition.

The literary character of 1 John, on the other hand, is more difficult to determine. It is not epistolary in character, as are 2 and 3 John; and its style is general, even if personal. Possibly it is best described as a paper or brochure. It was written in light of John's gospel, as a comment on the fourth evangelist's teaching, for purposes of teaching and debate within a troubled and slowly disintegrating community.

Structure. The ways of analyzing the structure of 1 John are numerous. One possibility is to subdivide the two main sections of the letter, which carry exhortations to live in the light as children of God, into four subsections, which set out the basic conditions for truly Christian living. These are stated in the first half of the letter and repeated in cyclical fashion (with one expansion, exemplifying the demand for obedience in terms of the command to love) during the second half. Together with 2 and 3 John this is their outline:

1 JOHN
    I. Preface (1.1–4): The word of life
   II. Live in the light (1.5–2.29):
      A. God is light (1.5–7)
      B. First condition for living in the light: renounce sin (1.8–2.2)
      C. Second condition: be obedient (2.3–11)
      D. Third condition: reject worldliness (2.12–17)
      E. Fourth condition: keep the faith (2.18–29)
  III. Live as children of God (3.1–5.13):
      A. God is Father (3.1–3)
      B. First condition for living as God's children: renounce sin (3.4–9)
      C. Second condition: be obedient (3.10–24)
      D. Third condition: reject worldliness (4.1–6)
      E. Fourth condition: be loving (4.7–5.4)
      F. Fifth condition: keep the faith (5.5–13)
  IV. Conclusion (5.14–21): Christian confidence

2 JOHN
    Living in truth and love

3 JOHN
    A plea for help.

Composition of 1 John. The difficulties involved in determining the literary character of 1 John and analyzing the structure of its material have resulted in a number of attempts to explain the present form of the letter. Two main proposals have been put forward by scholars.

According to one view, the original order has been rearranged. There is, however, no evidence for such transposition, which in the end introduces further dislocations in the text. According to others, various sources have been used and edited; theories under this heading vary considerably. Rudolf Bultmann, for example, has argued that two different styles of writing can be identified in 1 John and that one belongs to a source that may also be detected behind John's gospel while the other derives from the author himself. Wolfgang Nauck, who is critical of Bultmann's position, has proposed that 1 John stems from an earlier composition by the writer, which in due course he rewrote as a baptismal homily. But attempts of this kind to separate an underlying tradition from its edition are unsupported by firm evidence.

It is clear, therefore, that the history of this document cannot easily be explained in terms of rearrangement or written sources. The alternative view, that 1 John is a literary unity, is just as plausible; this suggestion is strongly supported by the theological coherence and balance of the letter and by its coherent structure.

Authorship. The identity of the author of the Johannine letters is a matter of considerable debate and raises the issue of the relationship between these documents and both the gospel and Revelation of John. The following scheme, which attempts to take account of all the relevant data, is only one solution to the problem.

The inspiration behind the tradition and distinctive theology of the Fourth Gospel came from John the apostle, the beloved disciple, himself. In 70 CE he wrote Revelation in order to encourage the members of his community to remain steadfast in the faith. Some of his followers later undertook the final publication of the gospel. A leading Johannine Christian (who may possibly have been involved in the composition of John's gospel) in due course wrote 1 John. An elder, close to the author of 1 John (or possibly the same person), was then responsible for 2 and 3 John.

All the Johannine documents in the New Testament are associated in some way, even if at times the links between them seem tenuous. That association is probably best accounted for by tracing their origin to a specific community, gathered in some way around John the apostle. Whatever answers are given to the question of authorship, therefore, the origin of the letters (as of the other parts of the Johannine literature) can well be assigned ultimately to an authoritative, apostolic tradition.

Date and Place of Origin. There are conflicting opinions among scholars about when and where the Johannine letters appeared. Assuming that 1, 2, and 3 John followed the gospel of John, the letters of John may be dated to the last decade of the first century CE. This allows time for a sharpening of the heterodox opinions within John's circle and for the first moves on the part of the secessionists.

Although some scholars have suggested Syria as the place of publication, the view that 1, 2, and 3 John were addressed to Johannine communities in Asia Minor, with their center in Ephesus, is more probable. This is the traditional setting for the birth of John's gospel; it could easily have produced the controversy with Judaism and Hellenism that may be detected in both the Johannine gospel and the letters; and its religious syncretism would readily have nurtured the tendencies in the situation behind the letters.

Postscript. The Johannine letters are often described as catholic documents. This does not mean that they were written for all in the early church but that they delivered to all believers in John's community a timeless message about the nature of Jesus in relation to God and humanity, about the importance of right behavior as well as right belief, and about the need for unity, however flexible, among all the churches. The tensions in John's community were probably not resolved by the appeal for love and unity built into his letters; but the truths that they preserve have proved indispensable for the life of the universal church ever since.

STEPHEN S. SMALLEY

JONAH, THE BOOK OF. The antihero of the book of Jonah is mentioned in 2 Kings 14.25 as a prophet of salvation during the expansionistic era of Jeroboam II. The choice of this

Initial 'E' depicting Jonah Thrown into the Sea (Jonah 1.15), from the Souvigny Bible, late 12th century

prophet as the target of didactic satire is doubly appropriate, first because he proclaimed nationalistic oracles on behalf of Israel and second because his name means "dove [of faithfulness or truthfulness]." The author wrote a short parable characterized by fantastic events to poke fun indirectly at a little man whose inner thoughts remain virtually hidden. Although certain similarities exist between this story and the prophetic legends of Elijah and Elisha, a greater kinship is with 1 Kings 13. Neither Jonah nor this unnamed man of God is intended for emulation; hence the term "legend" is not entirely appropriate.

The book of Jonah resembles later midrash, for it interprets biblical texts explicitly (Exod. 34.6) and implicitly (Num. 23.19; Ezek. 18.23). In each instance the issue is the nature of Jonah's God: Is divine mercy a more powerful attribute than justice? Can the deity actually repent? Does God's preference to grant life rather than death extend beyond Israel's borders?

Jonah's resistance to the divine call exceeds the usual reluctance, exemplified by Moses, Amos, and Jeremiah. Jonah actually flees from God, and after the deity has shown him the futility of his ways, he carries out the task with a vengeance. Then he resents the sparing of repentant Ninevites and argues that justice ought to prevail, although he has experienced undeserved compassion. This picture of Israelite prophecy is not flattering, for Jonah is unrepentant to the end. Furthermore, his manipulation of the facts in answering the sailors renders the prophet suspect and extols their superior ethics. When he does resort to prayer, Jonah exalts the ego and uses the occasion to accuse God. He is also spiteful, hoping that the sailors' repentance will be short-lived, and he eagerly awaits the destruction of Nineveh.

When was this unflattering depiction of prophecy written? Like many biblical books, this one yields few clues about its time of origin. The supposed Aramaisms may reflect a northern or Phoenician linguistic influence, so they do not necessarily indicate a postexilic date for the book. The expression "king of Nineveh" is no different from king of Samaria (1 Kings 21.1; 2 Kings 1.3); the same usage occurs in Neo-

Assyrian inscriptions. Moreover, the use of the past tense with references to Nineveh is not without stylistic precedent in Hebrew narrative (Gen. 29.17; Exod. 9.11; Num. 14.24). The literary relationship between the book of Jonah and other texts (Exod. 14; 32; Deut. 21; 1 Kings 19; Jer. 26 and 36; Ps. 139) does little to clarify the date of the book. Even the apparent citation of Joel cannot be proved, for both references may derive from a common source.

Another approach to dating the book is by searching for its probable setting. The negative attitude toward prophecy resembles Zechariah 13.1–6, but that text cannot be dated with any certainty. Furthermore, unflattering views of prophecy may have existed at various times and places. The antiparticularism is often thought to be a response to the narrow policy of Ezra and Nehemiah. Thus, Ruth and Jonah function to combat the view that would exclude foreigners from divine solicitude. Others suggest that the primary purpose of the book is to encourage repentance on Israel's part, and that was an important aspect of the message proclaimed by Jeremiah and Ezekiel. The search for an appropriate social and religious context for the book implies that its essential message is clear; this, however, does not seem to be the case. The favorable depiction of foreigners at Jonah's expense is striking, but is this openness to non-Israelites the central theme of the book?

The strange behavior on Jonah's part is given a rationale from sacred tradition. Jonah quotes (4.2) Exodus 34.6, the cultic confession that the Lord is both compassionate and just, as the reason for his flight from the divine presence. This conscious reflection on the nature of God offers a decisive clue to the purpose of the book. The conflict between Jonah and God concerns theodicy. Is it fair for the wicked inhabitants of Nineveh to escape the deity's wrath by repenting of their sins? Linguistic features link Nineveh and the cities Sodom and Gomorrah, a comparison in which the Israelites could concur because of the suffering inflicted on them by Assyrian hordes. Nevertheless, the object lesson involving a fast-growing plant that perished just as quickly offers a justification for God's repentance. The closing question addressed to the sulking prophet throws into relief divine compassion for all creatures in Nineveh.

The author may have had more than one purpose. The great prophets had predicted the destruction of foreign nations, but these oracles had failed to come true. Were the prophets false? No, this book suggests, for the Assyrians gained time by repenting. Again, from the perspective of several prophets, Israelites were entirely unrepentant. How could the nation escape God's wrath? By turning from their evil ways and evoking the Lord's pity. Is it too late for that? No, for God is so eager to save them that repentance even by the wicked Ninevites would result in forgiveness. Although the portrait of Israelite prophecy is troubling, the radical self-criticism goes a long way toward redeeming the profession.

Several literary features of the book have captured the imagination of modern critics. These include the repetition by God and the polytheistic sailors of key words such as "get up," "go," and "cry out/proclaim"; the presence of vivid terms like "throw," "go down," and "evil" (the last even in self-description by the people of Nineveh); and varied names for the deity, which do not appear to be used capriciously. Moreover, the book has numerous allusions to earlier biblical expressions, particularly in the psalm (chap. 2) that Jonah utters from the belly of the fish. Perhaps the grotesque and fantastic achieve their pinnacle in the attribution of thoughts to the endangered ship (1.4). The weighty message does not exclude humor: on hearing Jonah's facile confession that deliverance belongs to the Lord, the fish throws up. This entire psalm is a devastating mockery of Israelite piety as it is exemplified by the dubious prophet whose sole concern was his reputation for accuracy of prediction or a restriction of divine compassion to Israel.

JAMES L. CRENSHAW

Baptism of pilgrims in the Jordan River

JORDAN RIVER (Map 1:Y2–5). The major river in ancient Palestine, linking the two major inland lakes of Kinneret (the Sea of Galilee) and the Dead Sea (also known as the Salt Sea). The principal source of the Jordan is the precipitation on Mount Hermon and the three springs near Tel Dan, Banias, and Hasbaya. In antiquity some of the headwaters of the Jordan River flowed through the Huleh Valley, a lake until modern times, which is some 300 m (985 ft) higher than the Sea of Galilee; this rapid drop in elevation, which continues farther south, probably explains the river's name (from Hebr. *yārad*, "to go down"). These sources combine near the northern edge of the Huleh Valley, and from that point the river is called the Jordan.

The river flows out of Kinneret at its southern tip, possibly an artificial outflow; 10 km (6 mi) south the Jordan is joined by its main tributary, the Yarmuk. Another tributary from the east is the Jabbok, in the Wadi Zarqa, 56 km (35 mi) farther south. The Jordan valley receives virtually no direct rainfall south of the Yarmuk. The total annual flow of the river into the Dead Sea, another 194 m (600 ft) lower than the Sea of Galilee, is 1.2 billion m^3 (3 billion gal) of water. Despite this volume, the Jordan River has rarely served as a source of irrigation. The river bluffs of the flood plain of the Rift Valley (Arabic *Ghor*), which line both sides of the Jordan, are 500–1,000 m (1,500–3,000 ft) wide and constantly crumbling and rise at least 20–50 m (60–150 ft) above the river bottom. These factors constitute a serious impediment to irrigation, since the technology of pumping is fairly recent. The flood plain (Arabic *Zor*) is called "pride of the Jordan" (NRSV: "thicket"; Jer. 12.5; 49.19; 50.44; Zech. 11.3).

Because of the intense heat of the Rift Valley and the availability of moisture from the Jordan along its river banks, much of the vegetation there has the characteristic of a tropical jungle, which is typical of regions as far south as the Sudan. One plant that grows freely there is the papyrus. In addition there is much tamarisk and *spina Christi* on the river banks. In antiquity it was a haven for many wild animals, including lions. The river is fairly narrow and easy to cross, though the current is often swift.

Much of the importance of the Jordan River in the Bible derives from the fact that it assumes so central a place in the geographical nomenclature. It forms a natural boundary, so that Moab is "beyond the Jordan" and hence the Israelites must cross the Jordan in order to enter the Promised Land (Josh. 3). Although Israel often controlled territory east of the Jordan, the Jordan forms a natural eastern border, and Ezekiel's idealized nation is entirely to its west (see Ezek. 47.18). Jesus is reported to be baptized at "Bethany across the Jordan" (John 1.28). It is thus both as a primary water source, especially in the northern Ghor, and as a central feature of the Palestinian landscape that the Jordan River derives its importance.

ERIC M. MEYERS

JOSEPH (HUSBAND OF MARY). According to the opening chapters of the gospels of Matthew and Luke, Mary, the mother of Jesus, was engaged before his birth to Joseph, son of Jacob (Matt. 1.16) or of Heli (Luke 3.23). Matthew's infancy story is written largely from Joseph's point of view, even narrating his receiving messages from angels in his dreams. These dreams portray his struggle to determine how to deal justly with his fiancée's unexpected pregnancy (Matt. 1.18–25) and how to respond to threats against the infant Jesus (2.13–23).

Joseph's father, Jacob, weeps to see his son's coat, after his envious brothers sold him into slavery in Egypt (Gen. 37.29–36)

Matthew and Luke agree in their genealogies of Jesus that Joseph was a descendent of King David (Matt. 1.1–16; Luke 3.23–38). These genealogies imply that Joseph was in some way Jesus' father. Joseph is gone from the scene when the Gospels describe Jesus' adult life, though he was apparently remembered by those around Jesus as his father (Luke 4.22; John 1.45; 6.42) and as a carpenter (Matt. J3:55) The gospel of Mark makes no mention of Jesus' father, and calls him instead "Mary's son" (Mark 6.3). The second-century CE infancy gospel *Protevangelium of James* provides additional information of a legendary character. Later Christian tradition comes to view Joseph as an elderly widower, so that the "brothers and sisters of Jesus" in such passages as Mark 6.3 could be understood as Joseph's children from a previous marriage, not his children with Mary; later, he came to be seen as a saintly ascetic with no interest in sex, and Jesus' siblings as "cousins."

PHILIP SELLEW

JOSEPH (SON OF JACOB). Joseph, whose name means "May God give increase," was the son of Jacob and Rachel (Gen. 30.22–24), and the eponymous ancestor of the house of Joseph, one of the twelve tribes of Israel. Genesis 37–50 portrays Joseph as a patriarch through whom the promises to Abraham, Isaac, and Jacob are transmitted to later Israel. The God of the ancestors is not, however, called the God of Joseph, and Joseph the patriarch is seldom mentioned in the Bible outside Genesis.

The Joseph story begins in Genesis 37.1, "Jacob settled in the land where his father had lived as an alien, the land of Canaan," and comes to its preliminary end in 47.27, where the opening formula is transformed, "Thus Israel settled in the land of Egypt, in the region of Goshen." Its unity comes not from a single theme, but from sophisticated art, narrat-

J

ing the interaction of the human characters; God's direct action is hardly mentioned.

The story begins with the young, self-centered Joseph announcing to his father and brothers his double dreams of their obeisance to him. The doubling of his dreams here and later (41.1–8) proves their divine origin. Joseph later goes out to visit his brothers who are caring for their father's flock, apparently a rare event since he does not even know where they are camped (37.12–17). As he comes upon his brothers, they decide to kill him, but at the intercession of Reuben and Judah, he is spared; he ultimately falls into the hands of traders who sell him to the Egyptian Potiphar, captain of the guard. His brothers, however, tell Jacob that his son is dead, and offer as evidence his blood-stained garment, a preferential gift from his father (37.3, traditionally, although probably erroneously, translated as "a coat of many colors"). As if to indicate the passing of time and to build suspense about Joseph's fate, chap. 38 tells the story of Judah, the ancestor of the southern kingdom, a counterbalance to Joseph, the ancestor of the northern kingdom. Chap. 39 opens with Joseph as overseer of Potiphar's house. Even in prison, to which he is unjustly condemned, God protects him. His ability to interpret dreams brings him to Pharaoh's notice (40.1–41.14). He interprets Pharaoh's dream correctly as seven years of plenty and seven years of famine, and he is put in charge of preparing for the seven years of famine (chap. 41). That famine causes Jacob to send all his sons but Benjamin (the other son of his beloved Rachel) to Egypt to buy grain. In the first visit of his brothers (chap. 42), Joseph tests them by treating them roughly, holding Simeon as hostage, putting their money back in their grain sacks, and demanding that they return with Benjamin on their next visit. Joseph, the cool courtier, wants to learn his brothers' attitude toward him, his full brother Benjamin, and their father. The second visit of the now uneasy brothers is even more eventful (chaps. 43–45): Joseph surprises them by seating them at a banquet according to the order of their birth, Benjamin is arrested on a ruse, and, finally, Judah as spokesman for the group expresses the pain the family disunity has caused (44.18–44). Joseph, by now emotionally drawn into the family's crisis, reveals himself to his brothers, acknowledging that God, despite the selfish behavior of the family members, "sent me before you to preserve life" (45.5). The last chapters narrate Jacob's blessing of his grandsons Ephraim and Manasseh (chap. 48), his testament (chap. 49), his death, and Joseph's final days (chap. 50).

At one level, chaps. 37–50 explain how the sons of Jacob got to Egypt through the agency of Joseph. On a deeper level, the chapters tell movingly how God kept a disintegrating family united by the repentance and restraint of its members. The lesson is an important one for Israel because its unity is often threatened by the claims of one tribe against another.

The tribe of Joseph is divided into the tribes of Ephraim and Manasseh (Gen. 48; Num. 26.28–37; Josh. 14.4). "House of Joseph" may designate the northern kingdom as distinguished from the southern kingdom of Judah (2 Sam. 19.20; Ps. 78.67–68), or it may designate all Israel (Pss. 77.15;80.1–2).

In the New Testament, Hebrews 11.22 lists Joseph as a hero of faith; Stephen in his speech summarizes his career in Acts 7.13–17. Some have seen in Mark's episode of the youth who left his cloak behind (Mark 14.51–52) an echo of Gen-

esis 39.11–12. Among noteworthy modern retellings of the Joseph story is Thomas Mann's *Joseph and His Brothers.*

RICHARD J. CLIFFORD

JOSHUA, THE BOOK OF. Deriving its title from the name of its protagonist, Joshua is the sixth book of the Bible. It is a narrative that reports how Joshua, following the death of Moses (Deut. 34), led the people of Israel in occupying the Promised Land, apportioned it to the twelve tribes, and led them in the renewal of their covenant with Yahweh.

Structure and Literary Characteristics. The contents of the book may be outlined as follows:

I. Stories of Israel's occupation of the land (chaps. 1–12)
   A. Prologue, with an account of Yahweh's designation of Joshua as Moses' successor (chap. 1)
   B. The spies in Jericho (chap. 2)
   C. The crossing of the Jordan and the camp at Gilgal (chaps. 3–5)
   D. The fall of Jericho (chap. 6)
   E. Achan's sin and the conquest of Ai (7.1–8.29)
   F. A covenant on Mount Ebal (8.30–35)
   G. Treaty with the Gibeonites (chap. 9)
   H. Conflict with Amorite kings and the southern campaign (chap. 10)
   I. The northern campaign (11.1–15)
   J. Summary of the occupation (11.16–12.24)
II. Account of the division of the land (chaps. 13–21)
   A. Prologue, with an account of the unconquered lands and summary of trans-Jordanian territory (chap. 13)
   B. Allotments of Judah, Ephraim, and (Western) Manasseh (chaps. 14–17)
   C. Allotments of Benjamin, Simeon, Zebulun, Issachar, Asher, Naphtali, and Dan (chaps. 18–19)
   D. Cities of refuge and Levitical cities (chaps. 20–21)
III. Concluding events (chaps. 22–24)
   A. Dismissal of Transjordanian tribes (chap. 22)
   B. Joshua's last words (chap. 23)
   C. The covenant at Shechem (24.1–28)
   D. The graves of Joshua, Joseph, and Eleazar (24.29–33)

Although the book of Joshua is a narrative work, it does not have a carefully developed plot like the books of Ruth, Jonah, and Esther. As the outline indicates, the book is a composition made up of a great many individual and diverse elements. In terms both of contents and genre, each of the three parts of the book consists of quite different types of traditions. Most elements of the first part (Josh. 1–12) are stories of the events in the occupation of the land. With few exceptions, the elements of the second part (Josh. 13–21) are geographical descriptions or lists. Speeches and reports of ceremonies predominate in the final section (Josh. 22–24).

There is, however, narrative movement, if not an explicit and developed plot. At the beginning, the people stand on the edge of the land, poised to take it, and in the end they are in the land, making a covenant with their God. How they got there, and the details of their settlement are the questions answered by the book. What unifies the work is the movement of the people of Israel toward a particular goal, their settlement of the land. Although on close exami-

Detail showing Jericho, from a 6th-century CE mosaic (the Madeba Map)

nation one finds that this goal was not fully reached, it is nevertheless the major theme of the narrative. The book is also unified in the particular leader whose name symbolizes the era. Joshua was not only the person who led Israel in the realization of the promise of the land but also the last leader considered fully acceptable to Yahweh.

History of Composition. Consideration of the literary history of the book of Joshua must begin with an examination of its relationship to its context. The fundamental question is whether the book of Joshua should be seen more as a part of what precedes or what follows. Answers to this question have in large measure shaped interpretations of the book's literary history.

On the one hand, the book of Joshua continues the story begun in Genesis and brings to full circle the traditions of the Pentateuch, recording the fulfillment of the promises to the ancestors reported in Genesis 12–50. Thus, in the late nineteenth and early twentieth centuries, the source-critical analysis of the Pentateuch was extended into the book of Joshua, and scholars found there the same sources (J, E, D, and P) recognized in the earlier books. Later form-critical and traditio-historical study by Gerhard von Rad argued that Israel's most ancient story included the events now reported in Genesis through Joshua, that is, the Hexateuch. Whether or not there was an ancient little historical credo, as von Rad argued, certainly in a great many places Israel's past was summarized in terms of a series of saving events, including the promise to the ancestors, the Egyptian sojourn and Exodus, the wan-

dering in the wilderness, and the settlement of the land. In that circle, the subject matter contained in the book of Joshua would have been the concluding part.

In terms of the organization of the canon, however, there is a distinct break between the first five books (the Torah or Pentateuch) and the section that begins with Joshua (the Former Prophets in Jewish tradition). That organization is doubtless the last stage in a long history of development, and stems in large measure from the legal contents of the Torah and its association with the authority of Moses.

On the other hand, certainly in its present literary formulation, the book of Joshua is part of the history that begins with Deuteronomy. Whether there are traces of the other Pentateuchal documents or not, its clearest literary affinities are with the book of Deuteronomy. It was Martin Noth who recognized that the book of Joshua is the second major section of a Deuteronomic history, the account of Israel's past that includes the books of Deuteronomy through 2 Kings as they are organized in the Hebrew canon, that is, without the book of Ruth.

The diverse evidence points to the following conclusions. At an early stage in their oral transmission, Israel's traditions about the occupation of the land would have been the concluding element in the story that began with the promise of the land to the ancestors. At the latest stage, when the Hebrew books were being recognized as canonical, the book of Joshua was part of the second group of scriptures, the Prophets. But at the dominant level of their literary formulation, Joshua belongs with the Deuteronomic historical work that begins with the book of Deuteronomy.

There is abundant evidence in the book of Joshua for the Deuteronomic historians' editorial hand. These scribes—for there must have been more than one—did not create the story but rather drew upon older written and oral materials, organized and interpreted them, and at various points tied the story together with their editorial additions. These latter, recognizable by their similarities to the style and theology of the book of Deuteronomy, tend to occur at key transitions in the history, as well as to consist of speeches by the main characters in the story. Joshua 1 and 23 are such editorial contributions.

The final edition of the history must have been written not long after the last events it reports, in an anecdote concerning King Jehoiachin in Babylon. Thus it dates from ca. 560 BCE, during the Babylonian captivity, and could have been written in either Babylon or Judah. It is highly likely that there were earlier editions of the history. Evidence for two stages is seen in the two conclusions to the book of Joshua (chaps. 23 and 24), both of which bear the clear imprint of the style and theology of Deuteronomy.

In general, the final Deuteronomic editor(s) were at once historians and theologians. In a time of national disaster it was important to preserve the story of the people, especially since the institutions that transmitted the national memory were in disarray. As theologians, they interpreted their present—the Babylonian exile—as the results of a sinful past. Because of Israel's unfaithfulness to the covenant with Yahweh, the prophetic announcements of judgment had now come to pass.

Older Traditions. When the Deuteronomic editors began to compose the book of Joshua they had at their disposal a great many oral and written materials, some doubtless quite ancient, and some already organized into collections. Most of the individual traditions in chaps. 1–12 are etiological tales, at least in their structure and intention, that is, they tend to conclude with explanations of an existing place, practice, or name in terms of some event during the time of Joshua. Thus, twelve stones at Gilgal are to be explained to future generations as those taken from the Jordan during the crossing (4.19–24), and the name Gilgal is said to come from the first circumcision in the Promised Land (5.2–9; cf. also 6.22–25; 7.24–26).

Most of the individual stories in Joshua 1–12 relate to events in a single region, that of the tribe of Benjamin and the area near Gilgal (see Map 3:5X), an old sanctuary. What at first glance is an account of the conquest of the entire land turns out to concern the occupation of a small region. The exceptions are the reports of a southern campaign (10.28–43) and a northern one (11.1–23). It seems very likely, then, that the traditions of the tribe of Benjamin and of the sanctuary at Gilgal formed an old collection that became the core of other stories.

Most of the lists that form the basis for the account of the division of the land in chaps. 13–21 existed before the final edition of the book. These include a list of towns and a boundary list. The town lists (15.20–62; 18.21–28) present the names of cities belonging to various tribes. Although twelve groups are given, they do not correspond to the twelve tribes; rather, they list only cities in the southern part of the country. Thus, the town lists probably give the administrative districts of Judah during the monarchy, either from the time of Josiah (639–609 BCE) or earlier. The boundary lists (15.1–19; 17; 18.11–20; 19.10–16) trace out the frontiers between

the tribes as on a map. Although the actual tribal holdings might have changed frequently, it appears that the boundary lists give a premonarchic version of the land claimed by each tribe. This list is the basis for most contemporary maps of the tribal boundaries in the time of the judges.

Chaps. 13–21 also contain lists of the cities of refuge and of the Levitical cities (chap. 21) and some individual stories of specific groups such as the Calebites. Some of these, which appear also in Judges 1, concern territories not captured under Joshua; they probably reflect quite ancient tradition. In the final section of the book, chap. 24 calls for special comment. Although the account of the covenant at Shechem has been edited by the Deuteronomic historians, it probably rests upon early Israelite practice, as does the related passage in 8:30–35.

The History of the Settlement. As a source for the history of ancient Israel, the book of Joshua is useful but limited. In particular, as evidence for the period it reports, there are several reasons why its account cannot be read uncritically. First, while the Deuteronomic editorial framework gives the impression of an invasion of all of Canaan by all of Israel under the leadership of Joshua, a careful reading of the individual sections reveals a different picture. All of the stories account for only part of the land, mainly in the central hill country, and there is even a summary of unconquered territory (13.1–6). Second, the historian of this period needs to take into account a great many other passages that deal directly or indirectly with the period and its events, especially Judges 1. Others are Genesis 34, which appears to concern the settlement of the tribes of Levi and Simeon in the area of Shechem, and Numbers 13–14, which seems to assume the conquest of the southern plateau by the tribe of Judah. Third, the historian needs to take note of whatever external evidence can be brought to bear, including the results of archaeological research. There is, for example, evidence of the destruction of several Palestinian cities ca. 1200 BCE, and the appearance of a new and materially inferior culture at about that time, but the details of Israel's emergence in her homeland remain uncertain. One of the most useful historical sources in the book is the list of tribal boundaries, reflecting the situation in the period of the judges.

One general point is quite clear. It is far more accurate, both theologically and historically, to speak of what happened in the era of Joshua as the settlement rather than the conquest of the land. Theologically, virtually all levels of the tradition insist that Israel received the land as a gift from Yahweh, in fulfillment of the promise to the ancestors. The battles were understood as episodes in a holy war in which the conflict was won by Israel's God. Historically, Israel's movement into Canaan was not a sudden series of military campaigns but a gradual settlement over a long period of time, probably more than a century. Certainly, this settlement would have seen military conflict with the native population, but more often by individual tribes than by the entire people of Israel.

Theological Themes. The dominant theological perspective of the book of Joshua is that of its final editors, who wrote during the Babylonian exile to interpret that disaster for those who had experienced it. These thinkers viewed the history of Israel as a series of eras, each characterized by particular leaders. Moses was, of course, the leader without peer, the only one with whom Yahweh spoke face to face (Deut. 34.10; etc.). The period of Joshua was the last era of harmony, when an obedient people experienced the fulfillment of the promise of the land. In various ways, the life of Joshua is shown to parallel that of Moses; as Moses led the people through the sea, Joshua led them across the Jordan River, and both men led the people in the establishment and renewal of the covenant with their God. The next era, that of the Judges, was a time of testing, and the monarchy—with the primary exception of the reigns of David and Josiah—was a history of apostasy leading up to the exile.

In this scheme, the book of Joshua stresses the importance of the land as a divine gift, addressed finally to a people that has lost that inheritance. Thus, the lists of cities and tribal holdings in chaps. 13–21 are at least as significant as the stories of battles won in chaps. 1–12. The land belongs, ultimately, to the Lord, and the people hold it in trust as an inheritance. One message of the book is that the proper social structure for maintaining that trust is that of the family and the tribe. Land, therefore, is not a commodity to be traded.

Both directly and indirectly, the book addresses the problem of syncretism. To what extent can the people of Israel adopt the religious and cultural patterns of the Canaanites? The Deuteronomic tradition argued vigorously that any compromise with foreign religions and cultures was a betrayal of the covenant and would lead ultimately to ruin. By commanding the total destruction of the native population, the writers express the dogma of a radical means to avoid the problem. This dogma had its roots in the ancient holy war tradition, in which all captives and all booty were subjected to the ban. But the writers of the book of Joshua knew that the native population had by no means been exterminated; for the most part, they continued to live alongside the Israelites. Thus, the book of Judges reports that the Canaanites and their religious practices were left in order to test the faith of Israel (Judg. 3.1, 4).

Another theme that runs through the book is the relationship between obedience and blessing. Although Israel receives the land as an unmerited gift, in fulfillment of the promise to the ancestors, she will remain in the land and enjoy its fruits so long as the people are faithful to the covenant. The meaning of faithfulness is expressed in the law (even understood as the "book of the law," 1.8) and the covenant stipulations (8.30–35; 21.13–20; 23.6–13; 24.14–28). Above all, this relationship between obedience and blessing is a corporate rather than an individualistic one. As the story of Achan indicates (chap. 7), the people as a whole may suffer for the sins of some of its members.

GENE M. TUCKER

JUDAH, THE KINGDOM OF.

The Tribe of Judah. The tribe of Judah, which occupied the hill country between the vicinity of Jerusalem and Hebron (Map 3:x5), plays a minor role in the biblical narratives that pertain to premonarchic times. In the book of Judges, for example, there are only occasional mentions of Judah, and this tribe seems to have been very much on the fringe of Saul's kingdom. Judah comes into prominence, however, with David's rise to power, David himself being a Judean from the village of Bethlehem. Before conquering Jerusalem and transferring his residency there, David ruled over a kingdom centered at Hebron and consisting primarily of the tribe of Judah. Later, the tribal territory of Judah was to be the core of the southern kingdom, which remained loyal to the Davidic dynasty following Solomon's death.

Thus the name "Judah," like the name "Israel," is used in different ways in the Bible. It can refer to the eponymous ancestor of the tribe of Judah (Gen. 29.35; 35.23; 37.26), to the tribe itself (Num. 2.3; 7.12; 10.14; Josh. 18–55 19.1; Judg. 1.4), and to the kingdom of Judah, which covered more extensive territory and included peoples of other tribal origins (1 Kings 14.21, 29; 15.1, 7; Isa. 1.1; Jer. 1.2). These distinctions are not always clear in the biblical story. For example, the tribal boundaries and cities recorded for the tribe of Judah in the book of Joshua actually represent the ideal territorial extent of the kingdom of Judah. Likewise, the biblical genealogies tend to subsume under Judah various other southern tribal groups, such as the Calebites, which became constituents of the kingdom of Judah.

David's Judean Kingdom. David gained popularity as a Philistine fighter under Saul's command. Later he broke with Saul and led a rebel army that operated along the frontier of Judean territory. First we hear of David and his men camped at Adullam (1 Sam. 22.1–4). When Saul learned of their presence there, David and his followers moved to the barren slopes of the hill country southeast of Hebron (1 Sam. 23–26). Apparently, they received little support from the local population in either area; on the contrary, the villagers reported their whereabouts to Saul on more than one occasion.

Eventually, David found it necessary to move to Philistine territory, where he placed himself and his army under the command of Achish, the Philistine King of Gath (1 Sam. 27). Thus it happened that David was allied with the Philistines when they defeated Saul's army at the battle of Gilboa, the battle at which Saul and Jonathan lost their lives (1 Sam. 28–31). Saul's Israelite kingdom was left on the verge of collapse and without leadership. The crown fell to Ishbaal (Ishbosheth) who, realizing that the whole central hill country was now vulnerable to Philistine encroachment, moved his residency (and accordingly the administrative center of the kingdom) to Mahanaim east of the Jordan (2 Sam. 2.8–11). Thereupon David, presumably with Philistine approval,

David (right) and Solomon (left), (Lorenzo da Spirito, 15th century CE)

159

APPROXIMATE CHRONOLOGY OF THE KINGS OF ISRAEL AND JUDAH

Saul, David, and Solomon lived ca. 1000 BCE. The following dates may be regarded as accurate within ten years for the earlier kings and within two years for the later ones.

JUDAH	ISRAEL	JUDAH	ISRAEL
Rehoboam (924–907)	Jeroboam I (924–903)	Jotham (?–742)	
Abijam (Abijah) (907–906)			Shallum (754)
Asa (905–874)			Menahem (745–736)
	Nadab (903–902)	Jehoahaz I (Ahaz) (742–727)	Pakahiah (736–735)
	Baasha (902–886)		Pekah (735–732)
	Elah (886–885)		Hoshea (732–723)
Jehoshaphat (874–850)	Omri (885–873)	Hezekiah (727–698)	*Fall of Samaria* (722)
	Ahab (873–851)		
Jehoram (850–843)	Ahaziah (851–849)	Manasseh (697–642)	
Ahaziah (843)	Jehoram (849–843)	Amon (642–640)	
Athaliah (843–837)	Jehu (843–816)	Josiah (639–609)	
Joash (Jehoash) (837–?)		Jehoahaz II (609)	
Amazian (?–?)	Jehoahaz (816–800)	Jehoiachin (608–598)	
	Joash (800–785)	Jehoiachim (598–597)	
Uzziah (Azariah)	Jeroboam II (785–745)	Zedekiah (597–587/586)	
	Zechariah (745)	*Destruction of Jerusalem* (587/586)	

occupied the city of Hebron and its surrounding villages (2 Sam. 2.1–3). His kingship over the region was formalized when "the people of Judah came [to Hebron] and there they anointed David king over the house of Judah" (2 Sam. 2.4).

Thus, for the next seven years, according to 2 Samuel 5.4–5 and 1 Kings 2.11, David ruled over a kingdom centered in the hill country south of Jerusalem, composed largely of the tribe of Judah, with Hebron as its capital. David's realm of influence expanded rapidly during these years of rule from Hebron, so that by the time he conquered Jerusalem and moved his residency there (2 Sam. 5.6–10), the tribe of Judah was only one constituent part of the kingdom. This was to remain true throughout the reign of Solomon. Among other constituent elements of the Davidic-Solomonic kingdom, for example, were the Israelites.

The Post-Solomonic Kingdom of Judah. Following Solomon's death, the Israelites rebelled and established an independent kingdom of "Israel" (1 Kings 12.1–17). No doubt, many of them understood this as a restoration of the old Saulide kingdom. The people of Jerusalem and of the southern hill country, however, remained loyal to the Davidic dynasty, specifically to Solomon's son, Rehoboam, who was next in line for the throne. While Rehoboam continued to rule from Jerusalem, his realm of authority consisted essentially of the area that David had ruled from Hebron, that is, the old tribal territory of Judah and immediately adjacent regions—the southern hill country, the "wilderness" region between the hill country and the

Dead Sea, some of the Negeb, and some of the Shephelah (*see* Map 5:w–x5–6). Not surprisingly, this post-Solomonic kingdom came to be called Judah, even though its territory and population extended well beyond those of the tribe of Judah.

This post-Solomonic kingdom of Judah remained in existence for almost three and a half centuries, from Solomon's death in approximately 925 BCE to the destruction of Jerusalem in 587/586 BCE. During the first two hundred years of this period, the kingdoms of Israel and Judah existed side by side, sometimes at peace, sometimes at war; and for much of this time, during the Omride period for example, Judah was overshadowed by, and possibly subject to, Israel.

The article in this volume on "Israel, History of" summarizes key political developments during the two centuries that the two kingdoms existed alongside each other. The following summary covers some of the same material, but focuses on Judah and extends to the destruction of Jerusalem in 587/586.

Unstable beginnings (ca. 924–855). Rehoboam was left with a small and weak kingdom. Hostilities with Israel, whose frontier was only about 17 km (10 mi) from Jerusalem, would have drained his resources even more. As if that were not enough, the Egyptian pharaoh Shishak raided Palestine during the fifth year of Rehoboam's reign. Rather than challenge Shishak, Rehoboam paid a heavy ransom from the Temple treasury (1 Kings 14.25–28).

Apparently, Shishak's raid was a temporary episode with no lasting effect. The hostilities with Israel continued for four decades, however, through the reign of Rehoboam's grandson, Asa (ca. 905–874). 1 Kings 15.16–24 reports that Asa negotiated an agreement with Ben-hadad, the Aramean king of Damascus, which called for an Aramean attack on Israel's northern border. With Israel's king (Baasha, ca. 902–886) thus distracted, Asa secured his own northern frontier with fortifications at Mizpah and Geba (1 Kings 15.16–22).

In the shadow of the Omrides (ca. 885–843). Under the Omride rulers during the second quarter of the ninth century, Israel emerged as a powerful kingdom. Jehoshaphat of Judah (ca. 874–850) was roughly contemporary with the two most outstanding of the Omride kings, Omri and Ahab; and the biblical records suggest that he was an unwavering supporter of their military undertakings; probably he had little choice. Moreover, the two royal families were joined by the marriage of Jehoshaphat's son Jehoram (ruled ca. 850–843) to Omri's daughter (or granddaughter; compare 2 Kings 8.18 with 8.26). When the Omride dynasty fell, therefore, in approximately 843 BCE, there were significant political repercussions in Judah as well.

The circumstances are described in horrible detail in 2 Kings 8.28–10.27. On an occasion when Israel's troops were defending northern Transjordan against Aramean encroachment, Jehu, commander of the troops, assassinated the king of Israel (also named Jehoram, a son of Ahab), seized the government, and massacred the whole Omride family. Ahaziah, who by that time had succeeded Jehoram son of Jehoshaphat to the throne in Judah, also was assassinated, while visiting his Omride relatives in Israel.

A century of instability and decline (ca. 843–745). Jehu's coup initiated a period of hard times in both Israel and Judah (2 Kings 10.32–33; 12.17–18; 13.3). In fact, all of Syria-Palestine seems to have been dominated for the next four decades by the Aramean kings of Damascus. Judah was troubled as well with dynastic instability. After Ahaziah, who had been assassinated in connection with the Omride massacre, the next three Judean rulers (Athaliah, Joash, and Amaziah) were each executed or assassinated.

Athaliah, the Omride queen mother, seized the throne for herself at Ahaziah's death and ordered the execution of all others in Judah who could possibly have any claim to it. Her own downfall and execution, after seven years of rule, resulted from a palace coup orchestrated by a priest named Jehoiada (2 Kings 11). Joash, whom Jehoiada placed on the throne in her stead, was a seven-year-old child, supposedly a son of Ahaziah who had escaped the bloodletting at the time of his father's death. Not surprisingly, Joash was much influenced during the early years of his reign (ca. 837–?) by Jehoiada and the Jerusalem priests. Later, however, as Joash reached adulthood and especially after Jehoiada died, he began to exert more independence over the priests. Eventually he too was assassinated, apparently by persons in the royal court (2 Kings 12.1–16, 19–21).

By the time that Amaziah, the son of Joash, ascended the throne (sometime near the end of the ninth century BCE), the Aramean domination of Syria-Palestine had begun to relax. Once again, conflict erupted between Israel and Judah, with Israel overwhelmingly victorious. Not only was Amaziah unable to defend his frontier against Jehoahaz of Israel, but Jehoahaz captured Jerusalem, destroyed a large section of the city wall, and took royal Judean hostages to Samaria (2 Kings. 14.8–14). Soon thereafter, Amaziah was assassinated by his own countrymen, and Judah probably remained essentially a vassal to Israel through the reigns of Uzziah and Jotham.

Dates for the Judean kings of this period are impossible to establish with any degree of precision. Uzziah and Jotham would have lived during the latter part of the eighth and first part of the seventh centuries BCE respectively (2 Kings 15.1–7, 32–38). The prophets Amos and Hosea also belong to this period, as does the early career of Isaiah.

Assyrian domination (ca. 745–627). Judah, along with all the other little city-states and kingdoms of Syria-Palestine, succumbed to Assyrian domination during the latter half of the eighth century BCE. Unlike Israel, however, whose national existence came to an end at that time and whose territory was annexed by the Assyrian empire, Judah survived for another quarter of a century after the Assyrian empire itself collapsed. This does not mean, however, that Judah continued to enjoy any significant degree of independence. On the contrary, Tiglath-pileser's Palestinian campaigns in 734–732 left Judah a subject nation, and this situation remained essentially unchanged until the fall of Jerusalem in 587/586. When Hezekiah and certain other allied kings dared to challenge Assyrian domination during the reign of Sennacherib (705–681), the attempt failed miserably, and numerous Judean cities and villages were destroyed. Jerusalem itself narrowly escaped destruction, which was regarded as a miracle (2 Kings 18.9–19.37). The prophets Isaiah and Micah were active during these years of Assyrian domination.

Egyptian domination (627–605). Although the specific circumstances are not well known, it seems that the Assyrians and Egyptians established an alliance during the latter years of the Assyrian empire. As the Assyrians began to relax their grip on Syria-Palestine, the Egyptians tightened theirs. Specifically, Judah seems to have been subject to Egypt from approximately the end of the reign of Ashurbanipal (668–627 BCE) until the battle of Carchemish in 605. This was the political context of Josiah's cultic reform, his execution by Pharaoh Neco, and Jeremiah's early career (2 Kings 22.1–23.30; Jer. 2.18–19).

Babylonian domination and the end of the kingdom of Judah (605–587/586). The Babylonians, by defeating the Assyrians and their Egyptian allies at the battle of Carchemish in 605 BCE, became masters of Syria-Palestine as well as of Mesopotamia. Unfortunately, the Judeans persisted in challenging the new master, which resulted in the end of their kingdom. Jehoiakim (605–598) died while Jerusalem was under Babylonian siege. Jehoiakim's son Jehoichin was on the throne when the city fell in 597 and was exiled to Babylon with many other prominent Judeans (2 Kings 24.1–17). The Babylonians placed Zedekiah on the throne; when he too proved disloyal, they conquered Jerusalem again, sacked the city, sent many more Judeans into exile, and placed one Gedaliah in charge of the region (2 Kings 24.18–25.26).

The exact status of Gedaliah, who resided at Mizpah, is unclear—whether he was regarded as a vassal king or as a military governor over annexed territory. Apparently he was not, however, of the Davidic family; soon he was assassinated by a nationalistic group who presumably wished to restore the Davidic line. Very little is known about the situation in Palestine in the aftermath of Gedaliah's assassination, but certainly by this time Judah had ceased to exist as a kingdom.

The Hasmonean Kingdom of Judah. Mention should be made finally of the revolt of the Maccabees against the Seleucid rulers during the second century BCE. Not only was

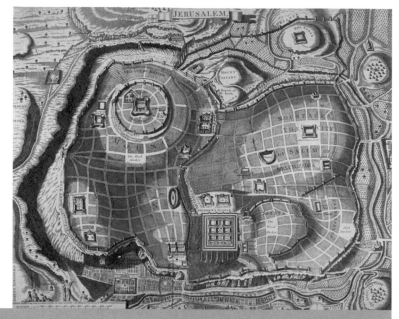

Scale in sacred and modern measures of a map of Jerusalem, engraved for Maynard's new translation of the works of Josephus.

the revolt successful in throwing off the Seleucid yoke, but it resulted in a Judean kingdom with Jerusalem as its capital, lasting for a century—from the Maccabean recovery of Jerusalem in 164 BCE to Pompey's eastern campaigns in 64–63 BCE. Ruled by the Hasmonean dynasty, the family of Judas Maccabeus, this kingdom included virtually all of Palestine when it reached its greatest territorial expansion under John Hyrcanus I (134–104 BCE) and Alexander Jannaeus (103–76 BCE).

J. MAXWELL MILLER

JUDAISMS OF THE FIRST CENTURY CE. The title of this article indicates a change in scholarly consensus from earlier in this century. Why Judaisms and not Judaism? It has become clear that in the first century CE Judaism was not monolithic but highly variegated throughout the Greco-Roman world, and diverse and complex even within the borders of Roman Palestine. No longer valid is George Foot Moore's characterization of "normative Judaism," by which he meant that Pharisaic-Rabbinic Judaism was the dominant and legitimate expression, against which all other Judaisms were judged to be aberrations or variants. Instead, the picture that has emerged is of multiple Judaisms, distinct Jewish religious systems, yet with connecting threads, indicators that they share a common legacy. Another characterization to be rejected is "late Judaism." This turn-of-the-century terminology was used to brand Judaism in the Greco-Roman period as a legalistic degeneration of earlier prophetic religion, moving toward the end of Judaism with its lack of acceptance of Jesus as the Messiah. Scholars today recognize that the Judaisms of the first century are early and not late, that they are much more at the beginning than at the end. Yet another contrast that has been laid aside is that of Palestinian versus Hellenistic Judaism; this is an artificial opposition which reduces an enormously complex picture into a simplistic one. Hellenization and its attendant issues were not confined to the Diaspora. Still, while the overlap between the Judaisms inside and outside of Palestine is significant, one should not deny the distinctive features of Diaspora Judaism, many of which were an outgrowth of two issues: the great distance between the Jerusalem Temple

and most Diaspora Jews, and the fact that Diaspora Judaism was a minority religion in a heavily hellenized and polytheistic setting. In short, it is difficult to compose a coherent picture of the Judaisms of this time because of the very diversity, complexity, and dynamic character which lead us to speak of Judaisms rather than Judaism, and also because of the nature of the sources.

Sources. The primary literary sources for the Judaisms of the first century provide only a limited picture. Those preserved are those which were important to the victors of history. From the Jewish perspective this is rabbinic literature (which dates from the third century CE on, though it may preserve earlier traditions), the foundational literature of what is known as Orthodox Judaism. It gradually came to regard itself as the heir to Pharisaic Judaism, and therefore either ignored or was hostile to other varieties of Judaism in the first century. From a Christian perspective, there is mid-first to second century evidence in the New Testament and other early Christian writings. These view first century Judaisms through the lenses of various Christian communities struggling to establish identities independent of the Judaism out of which they are emerging or with which they are competing, often polemically. Additional sources include two first-century Jewish figures, the historian Flavius Josephus and the philosopher Philo of Alexandria, the Dead Sea Scrolls, the Jewish literature written between the Bible and the Mishnah and preserved in the apocrypha and in the pseudepigrapha, and archeological and inscriptional evidence. Each source has its own problems of interpretation, and there are major gaps, such as data concerning women. Nevertheless, there is a wealth and variety of sources for the Judaisms of the first century which reflect diverse socioeconomic perspectives. Ironically, it is the very diversity of these perspectives which often limits historical reconstructions, because of their disagreements with one another and the gaping holes that they leave in their wake.

Pharisees. Of the named Judaisms of the first century, the best known are the Pharisees, attested in Josephus, the New Testament, and rabbinic literature. The evidence reveals nothing of the internal organization of this group—their criteria for membership, leadership structure, or educational system. Only two known individuals claim that they were themselves Pharisees: Josephus and Paul. There are reasons to question Josephus's claim that at the age of nineteen he became a Pharisee, and certainly many of his writings do not seem to be those of a Pharisee or someone who is more than neutral toward the Pharisees. Still, his later writings show a change of attitude and could support a later Pharisaic affiliation. Paul wrote from the perspective of one who had left Pharisaic Judaism. Josephus's and Paul's claims to be Pharisees open up the possibility that Pharisaic Judaism was found not only in Roman Palestine, but in the Diaspora, possibly as a way of responding to the wider world of Greco-Roman culture with a consciously Jewish way of life.

Josephus mentions the Pharisees fewer than twenty times, and the portrait that emerges is of a relatively small group (six thousand at the time of Herod the Great, *Ant.* 17.2.42) that for most of the first century played a minor role in Jewish society. They are portrayed as one of three philosophical schools of thought, alongside the Sadducees and Essenes, but seem to have been primarily a political interest group.

J

Lacking their own political power, the Pharisees sought influence with the ruling class to achieve their goals for Jewish society, attempts that succeeded especially during the latter part of Hasmonean rule, and at other times up through the beginning of the revolt against Rome in 66 CE. Josephus' selective description of Pharisaic beliefs—they believe in fate, free will, and God, that the soul is imperishable and that the souls of the wicked will be punished—reflects the interests of his Greco-Roman audience. A hint of the Pharisees' overall goals is that they had a reputation for interpreting traditional laws not recorded in the books of Moses; unfortunately Josephus does not elaborate.

Other clues concerning the Pharisees' goals for a renewed Judaism and their own internal rules come from the Gospels and rabbinic Judaism. The depiction of the Pharisees in the Gospels as the opponents of Jesus focuses the contention between Jesus and the Pharisees around issues of fasting and tithing, purity, and Sabbath observance, issues that overlap with the agenda of early rabbinic law. Further, the early rabbinic evidence for the Pharisees presents them as applying their own tradition of priestly piety to everyday life and business. According to Anthony Saldarini, "the Pharisees drew on an old tradition of using priestly laws concerning purity, food, and marriage in order to separate, protect, and identify Judaism" ("Pharisees," *Anchor Bible Dictionary*). Without denying that the rabbis are the ideological descendants of the Pharisees, the precise relationship between the Pharisees and the early rabbis who came after them is problematic, and there are considerable differences between the rabbis and the Pharisees. Apparently Pharisaic Judaism's rise to prominence is gradual, beginning after the war with Rome.

Sadducees. Evidence for the Sadducees is more meager and much more difficult to interpret than that for the Pharisees. None of the sources (Josephus, the New Testament, rabbinic literature) were written from a Sadducean point of view; the Sadducees rarely appear alone in them; and they are generally hostile in their treatment of the Sadducees. The sources agree, however, that the Sadducees were a recognized and well-established group of first-century Jews. Josephus further notes that while they had limited influence, they were respected within Jewish society. Their origins and history are obscure, though we hear of them as a political party during the Hasmonean rule of John Hyrcanus (134–104 BCE) and continue to hear of them throughout the first century CE until sometime after the war with Rome. Josephus portrays the Sadducees as drawn from the ruling class and therefore not popular with the masses. Several sources suggest some sort of connection between the Sadducees and the priestly establishment, and Acts 5 associates them with the high priest and makes them the dominant group on the Sanhedrin (though Acts 23 envisions the Sanhedrin as more evenly divided). Caution is needed here: the Sadducees cannot be equated with the priesthood and the ruling class. Not all Sadducees were priests and at best only a very small number of the ruling class were Sadducees. In rabbinic literature the Sadducees are identified with the even less well known Boethusians. It is unclear whether these were two distinct groups or whether the rabbis have conflated two sets of opponents. The little we can glean of Sadducean beliefs comports well with the conservative nature of a group drawn from the ruling class and with some connection to the priesthood: they rejected resurrection, the afterlife and judgment—a position connecting them with older Israelite religion and pitting them against newer beliefs. Josephus portrays them as denying fate and the traditions of the Pharisees and accepting no observance "apart from the laws." This hardly makes them scriptural literalists, and most likely they had their own traditions of interpretation opposed to those of the Pharisees. Certainly early rabbinic sources claim that the Sadducees differ from the Pharisees concerning ritual purity and Sabbath observance. Other beliefs concerning rituals such as those related to the Temple and the Sadducean/Boethusian method of reckoning Pentecost coincide with priestly practices.

Essenes. Largely due to the discovery of the Dead Sea Scrolls at Qumran, the best known group from ancient sources is the Essenes. The identification of the Qumran community with Essenes is not found in the Scrolls; rather, the impressive agreement of the evidence in the scrolls with that of the other key sources for Essenes (the Roman geographer Pliny the Elder, Philo, and Josephus) makes highly probable the identification of the Qumran community as Essenes. Still, discrepancies remain and the portrait that emerges is far from complete. Both Philo and Josephus number the Essenes at more than four thousand and say that the Essene communities were found throughout Palestine. Pliny locates a major settlement of the Essenes on the northwest corner of the Dead Sea, between Jericho and En-gedi, which all but names the site at Qumran. That site could accommodate about two hundred members at any one time; the majority of Essenes must have lived elsewhere. Both the Scrolls and Josephus seem to provide for two orders of Essenes: celibate men and those who married and had families. It is presumed that Qumran was a celibate community of Essenes and may have served as a center for Essenes from other locations—though the evidence does not rule out other interpretations. The history of the group is only imprecisely known. The Essenes may have originated in the early second century BCE. Even though the Qumran site was destroyed in the war against Rome, because the majority of Essenes lived at other settlements it is not impossible that the group persisted after 70 CE, though evidence to support their survival is hard to find.

Both the Qumran community and the other Essene groups were tightly organized. Those living outside of Qumran offered hospitality to other members, and in general the Essenes studiously avoided contact with outsiders. The penalties were severe for those who violated the rules and purity regulations of the community and for those who denigrated the community in any way. The Essenes were hierarchically organized according to seniority, standing within the community, and "perfection of spirit," with priests at the top. Admission to the group entailed a graduated process over two to three years, which was carefully regulated; there was also provision for expulsion. Full membership involved some form of communal property (even though there appears to have been some private ownership allowed), as well as communal meals and communal funds. The Essenes rigorously kept the Sabbath. The evidence concerning the attitude of the Essenes toward animal sacrifice and Temple worship is confusing. Possible interpretations include: there were times in the history of the group when they sent offerings to the Temple and times when they did not; or, the Qumran community dissented from the official Temple ritual, whereas the other Essene communities did not. Among their beliefs were theological determinism, present participation in "eternal life" as well as one which extended beyond the grave, and the notion of a final and universal conflagration.

Other Groups. Philo mentions the Therapeutae, a celibate community of men and women living outside of Alexandria. Their piety and communal practices resemble those of celibate Essenes, with whom there may be some connection. The evidence for scribes in the first century CE is at best sparse and confusing, and the portrait that emerges from the various sources is incoherent. Despite the presentation of the scribes in the New Testament, scribes do not seem to have formed an organization with its own membership. Rather, scribalism was a profession and a class of literate individuals who functioned as personal secretaries and public officials at all levels of Jewish society. Scribes who worked with the ruling class would most likely have been learned in all aspects of Judaism.

There are also first century Jewish groups whose activity seems to have been primarily political during the time leading up to and throughout the First Jewish Revolt. Josephus wrote of the Zealots mainly as a group in Jerusalem from 68–70 CE, who spent most of their energy struggling with other Jewish revolutionary groups until Jerusalem was surrounded, when they united against the Romans and mostly died fighting. Josephus also mentions the Fourth Philosophy, a group similar to the Pharisees except for their belief that only God should be acknowledged as king and ruler. The Fourth Philosophy spawned the Sicarii, who specialized in assassinating Jews who collaborated with the Romans. They may have been motivated in part by eschatological and messianic expectations.

Just as there was no "normative Judaism" in the first century CE, so too the borders of first century Judaism were not impermeable. Several groups attest to the porous nature of first century Jewish identity. Most clearly on the "outside" from all but their own perspective are the Samaritans, yet there are many reasons to view them as among the Judaisms of the age. The Samaritans believed themselves to be the authentic representatives of Mosaic religion. They are characterized by the building of their temple on Mount Gerizim and worship there rather than in Jerusalem, and by limiting themselves to their own version of the Pentateuch, which emphasizes the divine sanctity of Gerizim as the center for Israel's cultic life. Ranging from "inside" to "just outside" from a first century perspective, and yet clearly on the outside from twentieth-century Jewish and Christian perspectives are Jewish Christians, a label that encompasses a complex situation and a great variety. Examples include a number of named Jewish Christian groups mentioned in early patristic sources who share their adherence to Jewish beliefs and practices alongside their messianic understanding of Jesus and often a virulent anti-Pauline strain; the community underlying the gospel of Matthew, who seem to have understood themselves as recently and bitterly separated from the local synagogue because of their messianic beliefs, despite the fact that they were better at practicing their Judaism; the gospel of John may be appealing to Jews who have a secret and incipient belief in Jesus (represented by Nicodemus, the parents of the man born blind, and Joseph of Arimathea), urging them to grow in their understanding and not to be afraid of expulsion from the synagogue or of leaving their Jewish roots behind.

The above Judaisms present only a partial picture of the diversity of the first century. Josephus and Philo are examples of individuals who do not give us a clear sense of what, if any, Jewish group they might represent (despite Josephus's claim to have been a Pharisee from the age of nineteen). Most of the first-century Jewish writings preserved in the apocrypha and pseud-epigrapha are not linked to the above-named groups, yet they add significantly to the diversity and complexity of the picture. The several apocalypses and the apocalyptic features of other writings add another substantial dimension. There seem to have been a number of small groups that placed an emphasis on baptism, whether for ritual purification, initiation, or both. We have only glimpses of other features of the Judaisms of the first century: possible Jewish-Gnostic tendencies, peasant social banditry groups, popular messianic movements, prophetic movements and groups which formed around a wide range of charismatic leaders.

Common Elements. What do these diverse Judaisms share? In part it is what Lester Grabbe has termed "personal Jewish identity:" belief in one God; the concept of being part of the chosen people—Israel; the rejection of images in worship; the centrality of Torah; and the practice of circumcision. But even these characteristics are complex. Torah is a good example. The third part of Jewish canon (the Writings) was not yet closed; in general, different Jews had different ideas about what to include, which text or translation to read, which parts of the Torah, Prophets, and Writings were more authoritative, and how they should be interpreted. Also connecting the various first-century Judaisms was the Jerusalem Temple. The Temple was central both within Roman Palestine and in the Diaspora, despite the obvious problem of distance. In Jewish writings the Temple varies from concrete reality to metaphor to idealization. Long after its destruction, the Mishnah discusses the Temple as if it were still standing. Even those who were critical of current Temple practices, such as the Qumran community, did not contemplate permanently abandoning it. There are exceptions, like the Samaritans, who rejected the Jerusalem Temple, or the community of Leontopolis in Egypt, who built another. Yet even for such dissidents, temple cult in some form was central.

SARAH J. TANZER

JUDAS ISCARIOT. Judas Iscariot is mentioned only in the Gospels and Acts. The name Iscariot probably means "man from Kerioth" (a village in southern Judea) because "from" is used with the name in John (12.4; etc.) and because similar names occur in Josephus.

Only in John is Judas called Simon's son (6.71; 13.2, 26), and Simon is also Iscariot (6.71; 13.26). So was the name Iscariot given to Judas or to his father or to both? Only John says that Judas was "a thief" and "kept the common purse" (12.6; 13.29). Unlike the synoptic Gospels, John does not mention the kiss to indicate the one whom the authorities sought.

Judas was remembered for his betrayal of Jesus, an incident on which the sources agree (Mark 3.19 par.; 14.10–11, 43–45 par.; Matt. 26.25; John 6.71; 12.4; Acts 1.16). The motives for Judas's behavior cannot be precisely determined. Mark and Luke report that Jewish authorities promised Judas money for his action, but Matthew says that they paid him thirty pieces of silver immediately, a particular derived from the Hebrew Bible (Matt. 26.14–16; 27.3–10; Zech. 11.12–13; Jer. 18.2–3; 32.6–15). Judas repented, returned the money, and hanged himself. The authorities used the money to buy the "Field of Blood," but Acts 1.18–19 reports that Judas himself bought the field with his blood money and that he died as the result of a fall when "all his bowels gushed out." According to Acts 1.16, 20, his end was predicted in Psalms 69.25 and 109.8.

According to John 13.18, Jesus chose Judas deliberately so that the scripture (Ps. 41.9) might be fulfilled by his betrayal. John agrees with the Synoptics that at the Last Supper Jesus predicted his betrayal by Judas; but John, unlike the

The Kiss of Judas (Mark 14.43–46)

J

Synoptics, does not leave the identity of the traitor in doubt (13.26), since "the devil had already put it into the heart of Judas . . . to betray him" (13.2, 27). Luke also attributes Judas's action to Satan's influence (Luke 22.3).

Accounts of Judas are varied, inconsistent, and influenced by theological opinions of the writers, the belief in the fulfillment of scripture, and the idea that God brings death to ungodly persons (2 Macc. 9.5–12). It is therefore difficult to assess the historicity of Judas and his action. Why, for example, does Mark not mention the name of Judas in the story of the traitor (14.17–21)? Yet all sources list him among Jesus' disciples and know him as Jesus' betrayer. Perhaps as tradition grew the name of Judas became more infamous and the details of his demise more appalling.

EDWIN D. FREED

JUDE, THE LETTER OF. The letter of Jude was written to an unknown church or group of churches to combat the danger posed by certain charismatic teachers who were preaching and practicing moral libertinism. The author seeks to expose these teachers as ungodly people whose condemnation has been prophesied, and he urges his readers to maintain the apostolic gospel by living according to its moral demands.

Despite its brevity, the letter is rich in content, owing to its masterly composition and its economy of expression, which at times achieves an almost poetic effect. An analysis of the structure of the letter is essential to an adequate understanding of it:

I. Address and greeting (vv. 1–2)
II. Occasion and theme of the letter (vv. 3–4)
   A. Appeal to contend for the faith (v. 3)
   B. Background to the appeal: the false teachers (v. 4)
III. Body of the Letter (vv. 5–23)

   B¹. Background to the appeal: a commentary on four prophecies of the doom of the ungodly (vv. 5–19)
      1. Three biblical types (vv. 5–10)
      2. Three more biblical types (vv. 11–13)
      3. The prophecy of Enoch (vv. 14–16)
      4. The prophecy of the apostles (vv. 17–18)
   A¹. Appeal to Contend for the Faith (vv. 20–23)
      1. Exhortations (vv. 20–21)
      2. Advice on dealing with offenders (vv. 22–23)
IV. Concluding doxology (vv. 24–25)

It should be noted that the initial statement of the letter's theme (vv. 3–4) contains two parts that correspond, in reverse order, to the two parts of the body of the letter. The main purpose of the letter is the appeal "to contend for the faith," announced in v. 3 and spelled out in vv. 20–23. But v. 4 explains that this appeal is necessary because the readers are in danger of being misled by false teachers. The claim in v. 4 that these teachers are people whose ungodly behavior has already been condemned by God is then substantiated by the exegetical section (vv. 5–19), which argues that these are the people to whom the scriptural types and prophecies of judgment refer. This section establishes the danger in which the readers are placed by the influence of the false teachers and so performs an essential role as background to the appeal; it is not the main object of the letter, whose climax is reached only in the exhortations of vv. 20–23. Thus, the negative polemic against the false teachers is subordinate to the positive teaching of vv. 20–23. The letter concludes with a doxology (vv. 24–25), in effect a confident prayer that God will preserve the readers and achieve his purpose for them.

The form of the exegetical section (vv. 5–19) requires further explanation. It is not mere undisciplined denunciation, but carefully composed commentary that argues for the statement made in v. 4 that the condemnation of the false

Barak and Deborah (Judg. 4.6–9)

teachers has long been prophesied. Both the assumption that scripture is prophetic and the exegetical methods used to apply it to the present resemble the type of commentary (*pēšer*) found in the Dead Sea Scrolls.

Jude cites four main "texts" (vv. 5–7, 11, 14–15, 17–18) and comments on each (vv. 8–10, 12–13, 16, 19). The first two are summary references to biblical figures who are types of the ungodly of the last days. The third is a prophecy quoted from the book of Enoch (1.9), and the fourth gives a prediction of the apostles. The commentaries contain further allusions to scripture, the most prominent being the reference to an apocryphal account of the burial of Moses in v. 9. In each case, however, the transition from text to commentary is clearly marked by the word "these," indicating that the author's opponents are the people to whom the prooftext refers, and by change in tense to the present, indicating that the type or prophecy is now being fulfilled. Another feature of the exegetical method is the use of catchwords to link prooftexts with commentary and with each other; an example is "slander" in vv. 8, 9, 10.

Jude evidently had great respect for the book of Enoch, quoted in vv. 14–15 and echoed elsewhere (see vv. 6, 12–13). V. 9 refers to an apocryphal text no longer extant, perhaps the lost ending of the Testament of Moses. The use of such literature may locate the letter in a Palestinian Jewish context, in which these works were highly valued. Other indications that point in the direction of Palestinian Jewish Christianity as the milieu in which Jude wrote are his exegetical methods, his dependence on the Hebrew text of the Bible rather than its Greek translation (the Septuagint), his emphasis on the importance of ethical obligation rather than doctrinal orthodoxy, and his apocalyptic outlook, which expects the parousia in the near future. Some scholars therefore regard Jude as a relatively early work that affords a rare glimpse of early Jewish Christianity. But many other scholars date Jude relatively late (up to ca. 120 CE) and consider it an example of the post-Pauline development of early Christianity represented by

such works as the Pastoral letters and Luke-Acts. In favor of this latter view, two major claims are made—that Jude's view of "the faith" (vv. 3, 20) identifies Christianity with a fixed orthodoxy, and that v. 17 looks back to the age of the apostles as past—but both claims can be contested.

Two further issues related to the disagreement about the date and character of Jude are the identity of the opponents and the identity of the author. The false teachers whom Jude denounces have often been identified as gnostics, but there are no clear traces of gnostic teaching in what Jude says about them. What is clear is that the opponents were antinomians who understood the grace of God (v. 4) as a deliverance from moral constraints. They were evidently itinerant teachers (v. 4a) and were accepted at the churches' fellowship meals (v. 12a), where they laid claim to charismatic inspiration. They evidently regarded themselves and their followers as the truly spiritual people, distinguished from more conventional Christians by their Spirit-inspired freedom from all external authority (see v. 19). This kind of charismatic antinomianism may represent a distortion of Paul's teaching on freedom from the Law; it would have been possible at any time in the New Testament period.

Most scholars are agreed that the Jude (a shortened form of Judas, the author's actual name, which few English translations use because of the association with Judas Iscariot) to whom this letter is attributed is Judas the brother of Jesus (Mark 6.3). This identification is strongly implied by the phrase "brother of James" (v. 1), which distinguishes this Judas from others of the same name by mentioning his relation to James the brother of the Lord. A majority of modern scholars think the letter is pseudepigraphical, written by a later Christian who attributed his work to Jesus' brother, but a strong case for authenticity is made by others, who point to the features already mentioned that may place the letter in the context of Palestinian Jewish Christianity.

RICHARD J. BAUCKHAM

JUDGES, THE BOOK OF. The book of Judges follows Joshua and purports to cover the history of Israel from the time of the settlement until just before the establishment of the monarchy. The book's chronology is a problem since the sum of the periods mentioned in it comes to about four hundred years. The Exodus is usually dated to the thirteenth century BCE and the anointing of Saul to the middle of the eleventh century; consequently, the era of the judges as calculated by the book is far too long. The book presents the subjects of its narratives as referring to all Israel when originally these figures were associated with particular tribes. It is not possible to relate the stories of these savior-judges to each other chronologically. The book of Judges is a collection of stories about ancient tribal heroes; the chronological sequence of these stories is certainly artificial, and the fact that the total number of heroes is twelve also suggests editorial design.

The book begins with an introduction (1.1–36) that serves to connect it with the book of Joshua. This introduction, in contrast with the account in Joshua, portrays the settlement as only partially successful and still somewhat incomplete. A short discourse that follows (2.1–5) explains Israel's failure to complete the settlement successfully as the result of its disobedience. The purpose of this first introduction is to contrast the period of the judges with that of Joshua. Under Joshua's strong and effective leadership, the tribes enjoyed unity and success. No leader comparable to Joshua took his place, with the result that the unity of the tribes was broken: apostasy soon followed, then military defeat. Israel was

J

faithful to Yahweh during Joshua's lifetime; after his death it fell away. Because Israel turned to other gods, it placed itself in mortal danger. The stories of the judges show how a number of tribal heroes were able to ward off this danger—but only for a time.

A second introduction (2.6–3.6) presents the period of the judges as one during which Israel was guilty of a series of apostasies. Each apostasy was followed by divine punishment, a prayer for help, the rise of a "judge" who saved Israel from destruction, and a period of peace when Israel was ruled by its savior-judge. This pattern is not reflected in all the narratives themselves; rather, it represents the Deuteronomic interpretation of this period in Israel's life.

The stories about the judges themselves begin in 3.7 and conclude with 16.31. The portrait of Othniel (3.7–11) is rather ill-defined, though it follows the Deuteronomic pattern: Israel sinned by worshiping the gods of Canaan; God gave Israel into the hands of its enemies for a time; the people repented and God raised up a warrior to deliver them; then Israel had rest for forty years. The story about Ehud (3.12–30) is a coarse Benjaminite saga about one of that tribe's ancient heroes who outwitted and then killed Eglon, king of Moab. There is no narrative connected with Shamgar but only the statement that he "delivered Israel" (3.31).

The story of the prophet Deborah and the commander Barak is told in both prose (4.1–23) and poetry (5.1–31). The poem of chap. 5 is known as the Song of Deborah and is the most authentic literary source from the period of the judges, probably composed a short time after the victory it celebrates. The story of Deborah and Barak exposes the conflicts that took place when the Israelite tribes that originally settled in the largely unoccupied highlands attempted to make their way into the more fertile and therefore more populated valleys. The tribal forces led by Deborah and Barak defeated a Canaanite army and secured the Esdraelon

Valley for Israel. Archaeology has shown that Taanach was violently destroyed about 1125 BCE, when Megiddo was occupied (see 5.19).

The story of Gideon (6.1–8.35), also known as Jerubbaal, describes the fear with which Israelite farmers lived. There was the constant danger of having their harvest stolen by raiders. Gideon defeated the Midianites, whose raids threatened the Israelite population in central Canaan, but he refused the offer of kingship that the grateful tribes made. Gideon's son Abimelech, however, was quite different; he became king of Shechem. Abimelech was not really a judge but served as commander of the tribal militia. His story (9.1–57) describes the folly of the monarchy. When the people of Shechem withdrew their support from him, Abimelech did not hesitate to turn his army against them. The remains of ancient Shechem (Tell Balatah) give evidence of a violent destruction in the twelfth century BCE. Abimelech's story was recounted by those who considered the monarchy an infringement upon the rights of Yahweh.

Following Abimelech's story, there is a short note about Tola and Jair (10.1–4). They are credited with no military exploits. The lack of any information about their activities stands in marked contrast with the stories about the exploits of the savior-judges. The two mentioned here, along with three others cited in 12.8–15, had some type of judicial and administrative authority during the period before the monarchy and therefore were known as judges; because details of their activity are so scant, they are sometimes called "minor judges." Later their title was given to military heroes whose exploits are recounted in the major portion of the book; these are the "major judges."

The story of Jephthah (10.6–12.7) shows that social class posed no barriers to exercising leadership within the Israelite community at this period; Jephthah was a son of a prostitute. He led a mercenary army in the north and was called by

The sacrifice of the daughter of Jephthah (Judg. 11.29–40)

the elders of Gilead to deal with the Ammonites. Jephthah is remembered for the sacrifice of his daughter to fulfill a vow (11.34–40) and for his use of the password *shibboleth* during a civil war with the tribe of Ephraim (12.1–6).

Before the stories about Samson begin, there is another note about three judges who engaged in no military exploits but who, like Tola and Jair, were famous tribal leaders: Ibzan, Elon, and Abdon (12.8–15).

Samson hardly fits the figure of a judge. His stories (13.1–16.31) do not describe leadership he provided for the Israelite tribes against their enemies; rather, they recount a series of personal battles he fought with the Philistines. None of Samson's adventures have anything to do with the fate of Israel as a whole; he led no organized military campaigns. Samson is a tragic figure who was consumed in a Pyrrhic victory over his enemies. He is included among the judges because his final victory over the Philistines was remembered as a reaffirmation of God's presence with Israel.

The stories about the savior-judges portray them as heroes who led single tribes or groups of tribes in military campaigns in order to liberate Israel from periodic oppression by its enemies. Their rule was temporary. They led certain tribes in a specific military campaign and then, after the military threat was removed, they returned home. None of the judges succeeded in gaining the allegiance of all the tribes. They held power briefly and the area under their effective control was limited. In the present framework, however, these stories receive greater significance. They are not simply tribal sagas about famous heroes of the past; they have become testimonies to the power of Yahweh, who frees Israel when it repents and calls out for deliverance.

The predominant motif in these stories is Yahweh's deliverance of Israel through the judges. The judges are charismatic leaders upon whom has come the "spirit of Yahweh" (6.34; 11.29; 14.6,19; 15.14). This spirit enables them to accomplish what is apparently beyond their natural abilities. In Gideon's story, this receives special emphasis through the narrative about his call (6.11–23).

The remainder of the book of Judges (chaps. 17–21) is taken up with stories that illustrate the self-destructive forces at work within the Israelite tribes. These stories along with the introductions in 1.1–3.6 provide the work's basic theme. The introductory material raises the issue of strife among the tribes; the concluding chapters illustrate the extent to which this lack of unity threatened the very existence of the people of Israel.

Chaps. 17 and 18 deal with a certain Micah who set up his own shrine and introduced a Levite from Bethlehem to serve as his priest. This Levite was, in turn, recruited by the migrating Danites to serve as their priest. The tribe of Dan is depicted in a very unfavorable light. The Danites lack the courage to remain in their original place of settlement; they steal Micah's ephod, kidnap his priest, and massacre the peaceful village of Laish. The book ends with an internecine war between the tribes that almost succeeded in destroying the tribe of Benjamin (chaps. 19–21). The purpose of these last few chapters is to portray the period just before the emergence of the monarchy as a time of chaos. The book ends with this characterization of the era: "In those days

there was no king in Israel; all the people did what was right in their own eyes" (21.25). The picture of Israel in chaps. 17–21 makes the establishment of the monarchy inevitable if Israel was to survive.

Originally, stories about the most famous of tribal heroes circulated independently of one another. At some point during the period of the monarchy they were assembled in order to underscore the power and willingness of God to save Israel from those who would destroy it. This collection of stories did not involve extensive editing, which may explain some of the repetitions and apparent contradictions in the text. Under the influence of the book of Deuteronomy, the stories about the judges were incorporated in a much larger work that traced the story of Israel in the land from the entrance under Joshua to the exile under the Babylonians. The comprehensive purpose of this Deuteronomic history was to convince the people of Judah that their exile from the land was not due to some failure on God's part but, rather, that it was their own doing. Israel's peace in the land promised and given by God was constantly threatened by its disobedience and infidelity. The political and economic roots of Israel's problems with its neighbors were ignored in favor of a religious interpretation. Foreign invasions were divine punishment for Israel's infidelities with Canaanite gods. When Israel repented of its failure, foreign domination came to an end through the agency of a judge on whom had fallen the spirit of Yahweh.

For the Deuteronomists, the period of the judges was marked by apostasy after apostasy, which caused Israel to be given into the hands of oppressors. Though God saved Israel through the judges when the people cried for deliverance, Israel always repeated its infidelities. One result of this tendency to apostasy was God's determination not to drive out the nations, in order to test Israel's fidelity and to help instruct the people regarding the bitter consequences brought on by infidelity.

The book of Judges cannot be used to reconstruct the history of Canaan in the twelfth and eleventh centuries BCE except in the broadest possible terms. It describes this period as one of anarchy when the Israelites were competing with other peoples for the rich but limited resources of Canaan. It portrays the era of the judges as a time when Israel was in the process of achieving a sense of national unity and of laying its own claim to the land of Canaan. Both the book of Judges and archaeology have shown this time to be one of political, social, and economic disorder. The Deuteronomic history continues in the books of Samuel to show how Israel survived this difficult time.

Sometimes the perspective of the book of Judges is considered to be cyclical. The book does describe a cycle of apostasy, oppression, repentance, and deliverance followed by new apostasy, but this cycle is not endless: the anarchy of the era of the judges leads to the establishment of the monarchy. In addition, the text seems to be posing the question: How long can this cycle of apostasy, repentance, and deliverance go on? The conclusion of the Deuteronomic history states that there is a limit to the infidelities that Yahweh will countenance from Israel before expelling it from the land that had been promised and given to it.

LESLIE J. HOPPE, O.F.M

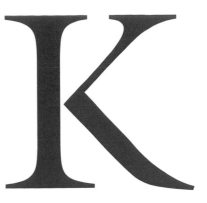

KINGDOM OF GOD. There is clear agreement among the synoptic Gospels that the kingdom of God was the principal theme within Jesus' message (Matt. 4.17, 23; Mark 1.15; Luke 4.42, 43), although each attests to this fact distinctively. In aggregate, they present some fifty sayings and parables of Jesus concerning the kingdom. In the gospel of John Jesus refers only once to the kingdom expressly, though the saying is repeated (3.3, 5). In that instance, however, the kingdom is presented as something that even the Pharisee Nicodemus is assumed to understand; the point at issue is not the nature of the kingdom but how it might be entered. It is, then, a matter of consensus within the canon that the kingdom constituted a primary focus of Jesus' theology.

The notion that God is king and as such rules, or wishes to rule, his people is evident in the scriptures of Israel. In the books of Judges and Samuel, the Lord's kingship is even held to exclude human monarchy as the appropriate government of the covenantal people (Judg. 8.23; 1 Sam. 8.7–9). It requires a distinctive fiat, by prophetic anointing, to establish Davidic kingship as the seal of the divine covenant (2 Sam. 7.5–17; cf. 1 Sam. 16.1–13). In no sense, then, does the Davidic royal house supplant God's ultimate rule. God could still be conceived of as reigning over all things (Ps. 145.13), and as about to reign on behalf of Israel (Isa. 52.7). In both Hebrew and Aramaic the verb "reigns" or "rules" is cognate with the nouns "king" and "kingdom" (all from the root *mlk*); furthermore, the noun "kingdom" refers more to the fact or force of rule than to the territory governed. The phrasing of the New Testament, although distinctive, is conceptually rooted in the Hebrew Bible.

The future orientation found in Isaiah 52.7 may be perplexing. Alongside the conviction of God's continuing, royal care, there was also the hope that God would finally—and unambiguously—be disclosed as king. Just that hope, in an ultimate and irrefutable exertion of the divine reign, is characteristic of early eschatology (e.g., Isa. 52.7). Within that perspective, the end of time is not dreaded but is rather the object of longing. The dissolution of the present age is a frightening prospect only for those who enjoy the rewards of this world; for Israel, the chosen people who had been denied the fruits of divine promise as a result of their sin and foreign domination, the end of this age—and the beginning of another—increasingly became an urgent hope. Only then, it was believed, would the promised peace of God reign supreme. Their hope seemed only to increase the more critical became the absence of a Davidic king, the presence of the Romans, and confusing controversies concerning the efficacy of worship in the Temple. Eschatologi-

God the Father (Victor Mikhailovich Vasnetsov, 1885)

cal urgency was a function of two collateral axioms within the faith of Israel: that God was just and that Israel is the elect people of God. Within their own understanding, the people of Israel could not agree that contemporary circumstances were consistent with either axiom. God, they felt, must be about to act in vindication of both his people and his own integrity.

"The kingdom of God" (or "the kingdom of the Lord") is precisely the phrase used in certain documents of early Judaism in order to express hope in God's ultimate disclosure as king. The Targums use the phrase chiefly to convey that eschatological hope (*Targum of Isaiah* 24.23; 31.4; 40.9; 52.7). The early (perhaps first-century CE) prayer known as the Kaddish also refers to the kingdom in that sense: "May He make his kingdom reign in your lifetime!" Later rabbinic texts conventionally use the phrase "kingdom of the heavens," as in Matthew. No difference in meaning is implied by replacing the word "God" or "Lord"; "heavens" appears to be a reverential periphrasis. In most rabbinic texts, however, the kingdom appears less as an eschatological than as a moral concept; the language refers to accepting God as one's king (by reciting the Shema) rather than to readying oneself for his rule.

The preaching of Jesus is far closer to eschatological expectation than to the moral emphasis of later rabbis. Although, in Jesus' thinking, the kingdom "has come near" (Mark 1.15), or has made itself available (Luke 16.16 par.; Matt. 12.28; par.), it was part of his programmatic prayer that the kingdom's coming should be sought (Matt. 6.10 par.). Care must be taken, however, to do justice to Jesus' distinctiveness as a rabbi or teacher as well as to his context within Judaism. By speaking of the kingdom, Jesus adopted the language of scripture (as used in synagogues) and of prayer and made that language his own. The kingdom in his preaching was not merely promised but announced as a divine activity that demanded repentance and that could be entered into by participating in its divine force. That stance is represented not only by the programmatic descriptions of his teaching but also by the parables. Those that involve images of growth or process (Mark 4.26–29; Matt. 13.24–30, 31–33 par.) particularly insist that the kingdom must not be limited to any single temporality, be it present or future. Such limitation would betray the dynamic unfolding such parables are designed to convey. For that reason, to describe the kingdom in Jesus' expectation as apocalyptic, in the sense of an anticipated calendar of divine unveilings in which God's rule can be dated, is misleading. The dearth of references to the kingdom in apocalyptic literature undermines that position, and much of the teaching attributed to Jesus militates against it (Luke 17.20, 21; cf. Matt. 24.36 par.; Acts 1.7, in addition to passages cited above).

A last element of Jesus' theology of the kingdom must be mentioned, which also tells against an apocalyptic construal of his message. Jesus' teaching was not simply futuristic in its eschatological orientation; he was also known as an ethical teacher (cf. Matt. 22.34–40; Mark 12.28–34; Luke 10.25–28). Many of his parables show how, within his vision of a single kingdom, Jesus could be both expectant of the future and demanding in the present. Parables of growth or process involve expectant readiness as the appropriate attitude toward the climax (Mark 4.29; Matt. 13.30; 13.32b, c par.; 13.33d par.); a king or lord who invites people to a banquet expects those invited to be prepared (Matt. 22.8, 9, 11, 12; Luke 14.24; cf. Matt. 8.11, 12 par.); even absent rulers anticipate their subjects' willing obedience during

their absence (Matt. 25.1–13; 14–30; Luke 12.35–38; 17.7–10; 19.11–27). The ethical themes implicit in such parables make sense once one appreciates that Jesus conveys by them a self-disclosing kingdom whose focus is irreducibly future and whose implications are pressingly present. Just as his claim to speak on behalf of that kingdom is perhaps the most obvious root of Christology, so his message gave to the movement that succeeded him a characteristic attitude of expectancy in respect of the future and, consequently, of responsibility within the present.

BRUCE D. CHILTON

KINGS, THE BOOKS OF. The perception of the Greek translation of the Hebrew Bible (the Septuagint) is that the first and second books of Samuel and of Kings should be regarded as four books of "Kingdoms," and a similar understanding of them appears in Jerome's view that they constitute four books of "Kings." They deal with the history of the monarchy from its inception and throughout its course. The narrative recounts the false starts beginning with Saul; the achievement of a united kingdom under David; the division of the kingdom under Rehoboam; and thereafter the record of two separate lines of kings until the northern kingdom disappears in 722 BCE. The history up to 587/586 BCE then focuses on Judean kings.

Summary of Contents. After a detailed treatment of Solomon's reign, an account of the circumstances in which the kingdom was divided and the early history of the two kingdoms, the emphasis falls on the northern kingdom (Israel); Jehoshaphat, king of Judah, enters the narrative only insofar as he is associated with Ahab (1 Kings 22) and Jehoram (2 Kings 3) in military enterprises. This latter section, which extends from 1 Kings 16.29 to 2 Kings 10.36, predominates in the books of Kings. The first part of it is taken up with the conflict between Elijah and Ahab, the second with Elisha's involvement in the overthrow of the house of Omri and his connection with Jehu. A narrative of the downfall of Athaliah, a Judean counterpart of Ahab (2 Kings 11) is followed by a series of short records of kings of Israel and Judah. After the final collapse of the northern kingdom has been described, there is a transition to kings of Judah: Hezekiah, who is praised for suppressing the high places (2 Kings 18); Manasseh, who is roundly condemned; and Josiah, in whom special interest is shown, for he is portrayed as an ideal king. The final kings of Judah and the circumstances of their reigns are then reviewed, and the history ends with the fall of Jerusalem to the Babylonians under Nebuchadrezzar.

The Compiler and his Criterion. Josiah is represented (2 Kings 22.1–23.30) as having suppressed all cultic centers of Yahwistic worship within his borders, on the grounds that they were infested with idolatry, and to have concentrated the worship of Yahweh in the Jerusalem Temple, as the only legitimate cultic site. This criterion is adopted by the compiler of 1 and 2 Kings. Consequently, when he deals with the reign of Josiah, the compiler has reached the heart of his own convictions; since the aims of the Josianic reformation correlate with some or all of the book of Deuteronomy's contents, he is revealed as a historian belonging to the Deuteronomic school.

Apart from applying his criterion, which he does by means of introductory and concluding formulae attached to accounts of individual reigns, the Deuteronomic compiler does not interfere much with his sources. He uses this material in order to achieve his effects, but only occasionally does he compose in the interests of his Deuteronomic interpretation of the history of the monarchy in Israel and Judah. For example, the narrative concerning the reform of Josiah may be the compiler's own composition, as also may be the account of the fall of Jerusalem in 587/586 BCE (2 Kings 25). A difference in style has been detected between the narrative of the finding of the book of the law and its effects (2 Kings 22.3–23.3, 9, 21–25), on the one hand, and the narrative of the cultic and political measures initiated by Josiah (23.4–8, 10, 15, 19–20), on the other; it has been supposed that the latter derives from a different source, namely the Book of the Annals of the Kings of Judah.

1 Kings 8 been widely regarded as a case of intervention by the Deuteronomic compiler, for in it Solomon, whose preparation for the building and furnishing of the Temple, with Tyrian cooperation, is described at length (1 Kings 5–7), appears to take on some of the features of Josiah. He is portrayed as presiding over a great religious festival in connection with the Jerusalem Temple's completion and legitimation by dint of the ark's installation—the ark before which he stood and sacrificed in Jerusalem after the theophany at Gibeon (1 Kings 3.15). As with the Deuteronomic view of this cult object, it is described as "the ark of the covenant" and is regarded as essentially a container for the stone tablets of the Law. Solomon is drawn as a man of great piety, full of noble religious sentiments and capable of giving utterance to a great prayer. Other compositions by the Deuteronomic compiler in this section of the books of Kings have been detected at 1 Kings 3.2–3, 14 and 11.1–13.

The Compiler's Sources. The sources on which the compiler of 1 and 2 Kings is said to have relied are given as the Book of the Acts of Solomon (1 Kings 11.41), the Book of the Annals of the Kings of Israel (e.g., at 1 Kings 14.19), and the Book of the Annals of the Kings of Judah (e.g., at 1 Kings 14.29). The Solomonic source has a different Hebrew title, and, judging from 1 Kings 11.41, it contains a variety of material and is not correctly described as either "annals" or "chronicles." The expression "Now the rest of the acts of Solomon, all that he did as well as his wisdom" (1 Kings 11.41) suggests that the source contained both annalistic and nonannalistic material (legends and sagas). Examples of the latter are the dream at Gibeon (1 Kings 3.4–15), the Solomonic judgment (3.16–28), and the visit of the Queen of Sheba (10.1–10,13). The "Book of the Acts of Solomon" was perhaps itself a composite that had been gathered together from other sources.

The other two sources are thought by some to have been essentially annalistic in character, records of particular reigns, registers of achievements, or calendars of events. If they had this form rather than that of a fully articulated historical narrative, there is a great deal in 1 and 2 Kings that could not be fitted into them. In any case, whatever precise literary form these chronicles or annals of the kings of Israel and Judah took, prophetic stories (in which the context is not in any sense royal and national, and which are especially associated with Elijah and Elisha) must be disengaged from them. Nor can we suppose that royal archives are a source for the account of the conflict between Elijah and Ahab or the episode of Naboth's vineyard and the murder of Naboth arranged by Jezebel, nor for the interventions of Elisha in the wars against Aram, where he appears as a national savior and his miraculous powers are heavily emphasized. The sources used by the Deuteronomic compiler were diverse and his criterion was not applied so stringently that he shaped all of them into a homogeneous whole. He is not so consumed with his narrow criterion of acceptability that he

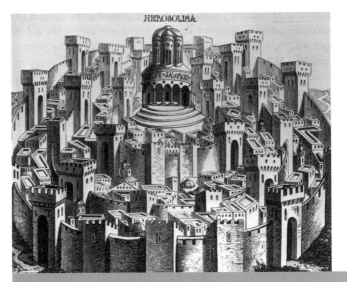

The walled city of Jerusalem, with the Temple of Solomon in the center, as depicted by a 15th-century German artist

does not allow his sources to speak with different voices and to indicate concern for other and broader issues.

The Framework Formulae. The compiler's narrowness, however, is particularly evident in the introductory and concluding formulae that bracket the accounts of individual reigns of kings of Israel and Judah. Apart from affording him an opportunity to assess each reign with an introductory formula, these formulae record the accession of individual kings, indicate death and burial, and provide a synchronic chronology relating the accession of the kings of Israel and Judah.

This chronological element has raised the question whether the formulae in their entirety are the creation of the Deuteronomic compiler or whether he is using a preexisting source comparable to the "Synchronic History" recovered from the library of Ashurbanipal, which correlates events of Babylonian and Assyrian history. The first complete example of these formulae occurs for Rehoboam (1 Kings 14.21–24, 29–31); note that the source is referred to in the conclusion. The concluding formula is missing for Joram and Ahaziah (2 Kings 9.22–28), and the introductory formula is missing for Jehu (2 Kings 10.34–36). Both are lacking for Athaliah (2 Kings 11), and the conclusion is omitted for kings violently deposed: Jehoahaz (2 Kings 23.31–34); Jehoiachin (2 Kings 23.8–17); Zedekiah (2 Kings 24.18–25.21).

Date of Composition. What is immediately striking about the criterion is its apparently anachronistic character. Insofar as the criterion derives from the Josianic reformation and its program, and therefore could not have been formulated before this event or series of events, it gives us some indication of the date of the Deuteronomic compilation of the books of Kings. One might attempt to date the work more precisely by appealing to individual passages, but the results thus achieved must be treated with reserve: we should not assume that the history is all of a piece, or that it was created in its entirety at one time by a single compiler.

More than this, for reasons that have been indicated, we should not expect reliable consistency from a compilation of this kind and so should not appeal to a single passage in order to reach conclusions about the date of the whole. Thus, because there is a passage (2 Kings 22.20) in which the disastrous death of Josiah at Megiddo in 609 BCE apparently lies in an unforeseen future should not lead us to conclude that the work must have been completed before that

K

The prophet Elijah

supposed to be legitimate Yahwistic sanctuaries at Bethel and Dan (1 Kings 12.30). The "man of God" who is represented as raising, his voice against the sanctuary at Bethel, while Jeroboam is sacrificing at its altar, is expressing a Deuteronomist view (1 Kings 13.1–3).

Ahab and his successors of the house of Omri are charged with a different kind of idolatry. Ahab, on whom attention is especially focused, permits Jezebel, his Tyrian wife, to establish a cult of the Tyrian Baal in his capital city of Samaria (compare the case of Solomon and his foreign wives). Hence, what is involved is the importation of the cult of a foreign god into Israel; although this is distinguishable from a contravention of the law of the single sanctuary, it is no doubt regarded as an aggravation of this offense (1 Kings 16.31–33). It is this contest between Yahweh and Baal which is dramatized in 1 Kings 18, where Elijah confronts Ahab and issues his challenge in the name of Yahweh. Elijah's miraculous victory over the prophets of Baal and Asherah is enhanced by the fact that the wood that has been set alight had been saturated with water; he then acts as a rainmaker, putting an end to the drought he enforced at his first appearance (1 Kings 17.1). Jehu, by whom foreign gods were expelled, and who is Yahwistic in his religion, politics, and cultural preferences, is condemned in terms of the law of the single sanctuary, as he was bound to be insofar as he maintained the cult of Yahweh within his own territory (2 Kings 10.31).

Elijah and Elisha Narratives. The narratives concerned with the conflict between Elijah and Ahab (1 Kings 18; 19; 21) cannot be satisfactorily interpreted on the assumption that they deal simply with an idolatry whose existence is established by the application of a narrow criterion of religious orthodoxy. We are confronted here with a criticism of a royal regime and style of life that are morally and culturally alien and unacceptable: they cannot be reconciled with the ethos of the Israelite community and its social institutions. The excavation of Samaria has revealed a grandeur of architecture not achieved by Ahab's predecessors, which certainly is another mark of Tyrian influence (cf. 1 Kings 5).

The story of Naboth's vineyard (1 Kings 21) focuses on a clash between Ahab's royal desires and Naboth's sense of the inalienability of his ancestral land. The way in which this is delineated is not totally unsympathetic to Ahab: he does not simply confiscate Naboth's land with a display of crude power; rather, he offers what he regards as a fair price and is distressed when Naboth refuses to bargain with him. Even so, the fact that he is represented as making an offer indicates the distance between him and an older set of Israelite social values, which separated family land from the marketplace and assumed an abiding connection between the continuation and well–being of the family and its land possessions. The villain of the piece is Jezebel, for whom a peasant's resistance to the will of the king is incomprehensible, and who removes the opposition by poisoning justice at its source and disguising murderous oppressiveness with a bogus legal process. We meet here a foreign queen who not only has established the worship of her gods in Israel but also, utterly lacking insight into Israelite social values, holds in contempt the right of her subjects to equality under the law.

The legal aspect of this is especially interesting, because there are other passages in the books of Samuel and Kings that emphasize the special responsibility of the king to ensure that justice is done to his subjects. Absalom fastens on to David's neglect of these matters as a prime source of public discontent (2 Sam. 15.1–6), and in connection with the praise of Solomon's wisdom his legal acumen is particu-

date. Nor does the fact that the work closes with reference to an event that took place in 566 BCE demonstrate that the entire compilation cannot be earlier than that. If, however, we suppose that the Deuteronomic history contained in 1 and 2 Kings was already under way during Josiah's reign, we have to conclude that there was a subsequent supplement that brought it down to the fall of Jerusalem in 587/586 BCE, and we should then also suppose that 2 Kings 25.27–30 is a final postscript about the fate of Jehoiachin in exile.

Interpreting the Criterion. The stringent application of the criterion is especially difficult to accept in relation to Israelite kings (as opposed to Judean kings). Too much should not be made of its anachronistic character, though, or, in stressing its apparent illogic, we might lose sight of the endeavor to understand the point of view it represents. The Deuteronomic historian regards the centralization of worship not as a new departure in the reign of Josiah but as the restoration of an ancient legitimacy. That is why the Jerusalem cult features so prominently in the account given of Solomon's reign. Before the Temple was built "he sacrificed and offered incense at the high places" (1 Kings 3.3), and it is only in his old age (so it is represented), under the influence of his foreign wives, that he becomes an idolater (1 Kings 11.1–13). Further, his political failures, which led to the division of the kingdom, are traced to his idolatry (1 Kings 11.14–25).

From this point of view, the division into two kingdoms, a political breach, had idolatry as an inevitable consequence. The political schism can then only have disastrous consequences for Yahwism: the kings of the northern part of Israel do not have Jerusalem within their territory and will set up what they regard as legitimate Yahwistic sanctuaries, which in the Deuteronomic view constitutes idolatrous worship. The narrow point, however, must be widened, otherwise the narrative would become unbearably tedious. It is made against the first of these kings who founded what he larly illustrated (1 Kings 3.16–28). The relation in respect of motif between 2 Samuel 12.1–7 and 1 Kings 20.35–43 should not be missed (the latter passage stands apart from the other contents of 1 Kings 20 and 22). In both these passages, a king is appealed to as supreme legal authority and he gives a verdict in which he unknowingly passes sentence on himself (cf. 2 Sam. 14).

In a more private context, Elijah is represented as a solitary prophet who works miracles for a widow of Zarephath, providing for her and her son when they are on the edge of starvation, and who subsequently restores the dead child to life (1 Kings 17.8–24). He is a marvelous provider and life-giver, but he is also a destroyer who calls up fire to consume soldiers sent by Ahaziah to take him, and he comes into the king's presence and tells him that he will die because he has asked guidance from Baal-zebub, god of Ekron (2 Kings 1.9–17). He runs with such great speed that he can keep up with horse and chariot (1 Kings 18.46), but he is also a prophet who loses heart and who encounters God not in what are usually portrayed as the majestic accompaniments of a theophany but as a "still small voice" (1 Kings 19.12: AV; NRSV: "sound of sheer silence").

Two chapters stand somewhat apart from the narratives that have just been described, even though prophets play a part in both of them (1 Kings 20.1–34; 22). The motif of provocative behavior by a king of Aram in order to provide a pretext for aggression against Israel (1 Kings 20) is repeated at 2 Kings 5, in connection with the cure of Naaman's leprosy by Elisha. In 1 Kings 20.1–34, Ahab is portrayed as conciliatory but firm, as capable of proverbial aptness (v. 11), as adopting the strategy advised by a prophet and as magnanimous in victory. Although his conflict with Micaiah, and so with a true prophetic word, is an important factor in 1 Kings 22, the account is not informed with marked animus against him, except at v. 38, where his death is linked to a prophecy uttered against him by Elijah (1 Kings 21.19). Ahab and Jehoshaphat, king of Judah, are allies in an attempt to wrest Ramoth–gilead from Aram, an attempt that ends disastrously. In the Septuagint, 1 Kings 21 follows chap. 19, and chap. 22, which is separated from chap. 20 in the Hebrew text and the English versions, is continuous with it.

Only when he is associated with Elisha is Elijah drawn into the context of prophetic communities (2 Kings 2): there is an audience of fifty prophets and Elijah is addressed by Elisha as "father," that is, perhaps, as leader of a prophetic community who is to be succeeded by Elisha. But it is Elisha's connections with prophetic communities, perhaps at Bethel, Jericho, and Gilgal (2 Kings 2.1–4), which are more firmly established (2 Kings 4.1–7, 38–41, 42–44; 6.1–7); and although the anointing of Hazael of Damascus and Jehu are attributed to both Elijah (1 Kings 19.15–18) and Elisha (2 Kings 8.7–9.13), it is Elisha's involvement in political intrigue which is more evident. He lends his prophetic authority to the coup d'état by which Jehu overthrows the house of Ahab, and to the bloodbath that disposes of Jehoram, Jezebel, all the members of the royal family, and all the practitioners of Jezebel's cult (2 Kings 9.14–10.14).

Nevertheless, Elisha is represented as having used his miraculous powers to assist a king of the house of Ahab (Jehoram) in his wars against Moab (2 Kings 3.4–27) and Aram (2 Kings 6.8–7.19), and on his deathbed he teaches Jehoash, of the line of Jehu, how to work magic against Aram (2 Kings 13.14–19). There are unpleasant features about the portrayal of Elisha: his powers can be malevolent (for example, when he calls up bears to destroy some boys

who had called him names; 2 Kings 2.23–25) or sensational (he brings an axe head that had sunk in the Jordan to the surface and makes it float; 2 Kings 6.1–7). This happens in the course of building extensions to a prophetic community, and other miracles have a similar context: a flask of oil is multiplied into a great supply (2 Kings 4.7); Elisha counteracts poison in a communal pot (2 Kings 4.38–41); he feeds a company of a hundred with twenty barley loaves and fresh ears of grain (2 Kings 4.42–44). It is in the setting of a family whose hospitality he has enjoyed that he puts an end to the sterility of the Shunammite woman and then restores her child to life after he dies in the harvest field (2 Kings 4.8–37; cf. 1 Kings 17.8–24).

Conclusion. The contents of 1 and 2 Kings are varied, and there are many topics that are not narrowly related to the law of the single sanctuary. This criterion influences the portrayal of Solomon, and it is influential in the view taken of Hezekiah and, above all, Josiah. The praise of Hezekiah is mixed with a criticism of his behavior during the visit to Jerusalem of Merodach-baladan, king of Babylon (2 Kings 20.12–19). Approval of other Judean kings is mingled with the criticism that they failed the acid test by not suppressing the high places: Asa (1 Kings 15.11–15); Jehoshaphat (1 Kings 22.43–44); Amaziah (2 Kings 14.3–4); Azariah (2 Kings 15.3–4) Jotham (2 Kings 15.34–35) The final kings of Judah, with whom the disaster of exile is linked, are condemned: Zedekiah did what was wrong in the eyes of the Lord as Jehoiakim had done. Jerusalem and Judah so angered the Lord that in the end he banished them from his sight (2 Kings 24.19–20).

WILLIAM McKANE

KINGSHIP AND MONARCHY. Ancient Near Eastern texts almost unanimously presuppose the institution of kingship as a social organizing principle. Kingship in Mesopotamia is "lowered from heaven" or is coeval with creation. The Assyrian King List, for example, can hypothesize a time when kings "lived in tents," but not a time before kingship. The image of the "first man" as the "image of God" and as lord over creation (Gen. 1.26–28) is not unrelated: YHWH is often portrayed in Israelite literature and iconography in solar terms; just as the sun, the "major" astral body, "rules" over the sky (Gen. 1.16–18), just as YHWH rules over creation, so the relationship between humanity and the world is modeled as one of royal domination from the very outset.

Near Eastern myths, too, principally portray the order of divine organization as monarchic. Egyptian, Greek, Hittite, Ugaritic, and Mesopotamian myths all recount tales of martial conflict whereby one of the gods emerges as their king. In most instances, the monarchic order is portrayed as an innovation, replacing an earlier paternal domination of children. Interestingly, in the cases of Mesopotamian and Greek myth, the new kingship is functionally elective: the pantheon appoint a king-elect from among their number, to lead them into battle; the appointee wins the battle; and, as a result, the appointee wins confirmation on the throne. The royal ideal is thus one of elective autocracy. In Babylonian myth, the winning of the throne is also the starting point for the creation of the cosmos, which is the foundation for the heavenly structure that serves as the high god's palace, the counterpart of his earthly temple.

Kings and other administrators in the ancient Near East regularly portray themselves, like the state gods, as champions of the weak and the oppressed. The king was the upholder of the social order—much like the divine king who

K

resisted the threats and encroachments of chaos. But fixing the social order, to judge from Mesopotamian law codes, involved attempting to fix prices and attempting to ensure the inviolability of property. It also involved occasional amnesties, and general release from debt. Ultimately, the king presented himself as the personification and defender of what was just, the supreme judicial authority.

Near Eastern kingship was overwhelmingly an urban phenomenon. Cities lent themselves to monarchic organization precisely because of the complexity of administration involved. Kings took responsibility for, and pride in, the fortification of towns: the Gilgamesh Epic ends with a return to the subject of the mighty walls of Uruk, which were the hero's immortality. Kings thus enjoyed the right not to tax, but to direct corvée and conscription for the public good—for defense, conquest, and the construction of irrigation and navigation systems.

Claiming the right to govern by divine election, kings also relate their temple-building activities. The completion of a temple is modeled by them as a mundane repetition of the heavenly creation myth. The building of a temple also is taken as a sign of the gods' imprimatur on the builder's royal dynasty. Likewise, the New Year ritual in Babylon, and, later, in Assyria, combines a rehearsal of the creation myth with a renewal of the high god's temple: the king leads the high god in procession to reoccupy the temple, and at the same time renews his own kingship, after a ritual battle against chaos. The king consistently presents himself as warrior, builder, creator, favorite, even adoptee of the gods.

Israelite conceptions of kingship reflect both continuity with, and departure from, earlier traditions. For one thing, earliest Israel was decidedly nonurban, consisting of small agricultural settlements principally in the central hill country, Transjordan, and the upper Galilee. It is impossible to identify any major urban center as Israelite before David's conquest of Jerusalem. Israelite monarchy, therefore, originated as a national monarchy, not as a city-state kingship. Correspondingly, Israel is the only ancient Near Eastern culture to have preserved written memories of a time before the evolution of kingship or to have constructed any account of a transition from what later tradition would construe as

a theocracy to monarchic organization. (There were, however, periods when Assyrian kings presented themselves as stewards of the gods, rather than as kings, and early Sumerian kings adopted the same recourse.)

In this connection, a number of Israelite texts express reservations about the institution of kingship—a sentiment elsewhere unparalleled. Offered a dynasty, for example, the premonarchic warrior Gideon makes the paradigmatic reply, "I will not rule over you, and my son will not rule over you; YHWH will rule over you" (Judg. 8.24). Although the text proceeds to condemn Gideon for appropriating priestly status and constructing an ephod (Judg. 8.24–27), similar sentiments recur in an account of the transition to monarchy (1 Sam. 8.4–20; 10.19; 12.12): the urge to enthrone a human king conflicts on this theory with the ideal of YHWH's kingship over Israel (and Hos. 13.10).

Scholars for the most part find two sources underlying the account of the origins of Israelite kingship in 1 Samuel 8–12, but differ about their precise delineation. Nevertheless, both sources seem to replicate the pattern for divine kingship: in one (1 Sam. 8; 10.17–27; 11; 12), Saul is elected king with YHWH's approval, defeats Ammon, and is confirmed as king; in the other (1 Sam. 9.1–10.16; 13–14), Saul is anointed king-designate, defeats the Philistines, and is said to have "captured the kingship" (1 Sam. 14.47). There is a homology with YHWH's kingship over Israel, said to have originated in his election in order to bring Israel out of Egypt and into Canaan, and confirmed at the completion of the Exodus (Exod. 3.16–17; 6.7–8; 19–23); the same pattern already occurs in the Song of the Sea (Exod. 15; twelfth—eleventh century BCE), where YHWH's perpetual kingship and acquisition of a shrine (Exod. 15.18) is predicated on his defeat of Egypt and the establishment of Israel in Canaan.

Numerous psalms follow the same pattern, praising YHWH as the creator or as the victor in some cosmic or mundane martial conflict, in the context of the celebration of his kingship. Likewise, the book of Judges describes the pattern of mundane leadership in terms of a leader's election by YHWH, defeat of a threat or oppressor, and assumption of administrative power (Judg. 2.11–19; 3.7–12.7). And the

books of Samuel-Kings let the same myth inform their historiography: kings whose succession is irregular win battles or overcome obstacles and threats, before their accession formulary (that is, their historiographic confirmation on the throne) appears. The "myth of the Divine Warrior" regularly informs Israelite views of mundane, as well as divine, leadership.

Other Near Eastern conceptions of kingship are equally pervasive among the Israelites. The first Israelite kings eschewed temple-building, no doubt out of deference to their constituents' distributed and varied cultic traditions. David did bring a central icon, the ark, to his capital. But Solomon was the first to build a temple, and in the capital, which articulated claims of an eternal Davidic dynasty—as well as claims that Solomon, and the later Davidides, are sons of YHWH,

The death of King David's son Absalom after his revolt (2 Sam. 18.9–15)

entrants into the court of the divine king. Notably, the Israelite kingdom established by Jeroboam by secession from the kingship of Solomon's successor prescinded from establishing its cultic centers in the political capital. Yet the leader of the secession, Jeroboam, was moved to erect cultic establishments at Bethel and Dan to establish himself, too, as a temple builder. His actions implied independence from Judah yet disavowed any unchangeable divine election of his dynasty. When Omri's son, Ahab, later erected a temple in Samaria, his capital, the same dynamic was in effect. The revolutionary, Jehu, destroyed the temple in the capital, ensuring a separation of capital and temple in the northern kingdom for the rest of its duration.

In the Israelite ideal, the king is one nominated (or anointed) by YHWH, by prophetic means, and adopted by the people—YHWH proposes and the people dispose. But the opportunity exists, in the aftermath of divine designation, for popular elements responsible for confirming the king to impose conditions on the king's sovereignty. The operation of this principle is evident in 1 Kings 12, where the Israelites propose to elect Rehoboam as their king, on the condition that he lower taxes. Rehoboam refuses; the people therefore reject him as king, and elect Jeroboam. Similarly, both David (2 Sam. 2.4–9; 5–1–3) and Absalom (2 Sam. 15.1–12) campaign for election; David actually campaigns for reelection after Absalom's revolt (2 Sam. 19.10–44). Although elements of the royal establishment laid claim to a perpetual divine dynastic grant (Ps. 89), even the laws of Deuteronomy 17.14–20 acknowledge that kingship, given divine nomination of the candidate, was elective. In practice, this often meant that the king was made by army democracy—as in the cases of Solomon, Baasha, Omri, Jehu, Uzziah, and others.

The laws of Deuteronomy 17–18 also attempt to limit the king's latitude in forming policy. They limit priesthood to "Levites," install Levitic priests as the supreme judiciary, and protect the institution of prophecy. They further attempt to restrict the king's ability to accumulate wealth. Scholars concur that the Deuteronomic law code is late in origin. Still, the attempt to limit the ability to tax, the urge to restrict the king's right to disenfranchise priesthoods, the urge to protect prophets (Deut. 18.18–22; 1 Kings 22.26–28; Jer. 26.16) all reflect traditional ideals and rural views of central governmental authority.

Notwithstanding popular resistance to royal encroachments on the economy in particular, Israelite kings enjoyed the power both to tax (1 Kings 4.7–19; 12; 2 Kings 15.20; 23.35) and to conscript for warfare (2 Sam. 20.4) and for public works (1 Kings 5.27–30; 11.28; cf. 9.22). Moreover, archaeological remains at important towns, such as Megiddo and Hazor, indicate that the kings projected their power into the countryside in the form of massive fortifications and impressive public buildings. To date, this phenomenon is less well represented in the Israelite heartland, the hill country. However, starting in the tenth century BCE, and accelerating in the eighth century, public buildings are constructed in proximity to the gate complexes of some urban centers, such as Tell Beit Mirsim, Lachish, and Tell el-Far'ah (biblical Tirzah).

In the same period, increasing royal intervention in local economies is documented by the standardization of weights, and probably, by indications of incipient industrialization, as at the site of Horvat Rosh Zayit, inland from Akko. And, at the end of the eighth century, Hezekiah of Judah was able to concentrate the rural population of his kingdom in a set of fortresses.

There had always been some tension between the royal establishment and the kinship structures—the rural lineages—which were the seat of succession and conflict resolution before the monarchy and continued to function as such after the introduction of kingship. Early on, the state acknowledged an interest in restricting the feud (2 Sam. 14.11), one of the nonstate forms of conflict resolution in the society. But as the revolt of Absalom ended with the complete triumph of the professional royal army over the irregulars of the countryside, central control could be asserted over not only the succession but other aspects of statecraft as well. As early as the time of Solomon, a system of royal administrators was set in place for the purpose of extracting taxation and corvée (1 Kings 4.7–19; 11.28), bypassing traditional tribal forms of organization. It is likely that Jeroboam and the later kings of the northern kingdom undid this innovation; the Samaria ostraca furnish evidence of at least dabblings in a system of such administrators only in the eighth century (one group of ostraca reflects administration through the lineages at that time). However, even the lineage heads through whom some kings administered taxation would have been royal appointees in some sense, and certainly familiars of the establishment (see 2 Sam. 19.32–41).

It was only in the seventh century, after Hezekiah's emergency urbanization, that the monarchy achieved complete domination over the lineages. The urban geography of that era in Judah (Israel having been deported) reflects the resettlement of Judah, after its depopulation by Assyria in 701 BCE, by state orchestration. Gone are the extended-family compounds that characterize Israelite settlements until the late eighth century. Gone are the large, rambling settlements of that earlier era. Instead, the state, and the kingship, were able to stamp the ideals of the royal cult, the Jerusalem Temple, onto the country as a whole, resulting in a policy, under Josiah, of centralization of worship and of power. This development, and the disappearance of the monarchy in the restoration community (538 BCE), paved the way for the detachment of the monarchic ideology from its origins in relations with the agrarian hinterlands of the capital. In the Second Temple period, the idea of YHWH's anointed—the messiah, notionally a son of YHWH—was transferred from the human king whose election was a matter of negotiation and limitation, to a future king, not wholly human, whose reign would usher in a regime of justice, of the defense of the oppressed, and of requital of the guilty. In the myth of a kingless postexilic Judah, the old, high ideals of Near Eastern kingship took renewed hold, without the brake of political realities to restrain the ambitions or the imaginings of their adherents.

BARUCH HALPERN

LAMENTATIONS OF JEREMIAH, THE.

LAMENTATIONS OF JEREMIAH, THE. The book of Lamentations, also commonly known as the Lamentations of Jeremiah, consists of five poems occasioned by the siege and fall of Jerusalem in 587/586 BCE. Beginning with very early times, perhaps not long after the events (see Jer. 41.5; Zech. 7.3–5; 8.19), these laments have been used in Jewish, and later in Christian worship, as an expression of grief at the destruction of the city and also for more generalized sorrow, as in Christian liturgies of Good Friday, as well as an appeal for divine mercy. The book has attracted special interest among biblical scholars because of its relatively strict poetic form, all the chapters being alphabetic acrostics or related in some way to the alphabet.

The title "Lamentations" of the English Bible comes from the Vulgate's *threni* or Greek *thrēnoi*, translating a Hebrew title *qînôt*, "laments." In Jewish tradition the book is most often called after its first word *'ēkâ*, "How!"

Contents and Plan. The contents and plan of the book are difficult to summarize, since the form of the poems is dictated more by the alphabetic acrostics than by a narrative or logical sequence. In the first two poems, there is an alternation between the viewpoint of an observer of the calamity and the personified city itself. The third chapter, formally the most elaborate, also reaches heights of poignancy. The anonymous speaker is "one who has seen affliction;" through this persona the causes of the fall of the city are explored, and then the poem moves to a tentative expression of patient hope. Chap. 4 is mostly taken up with recollection of the horrors of the final days before the collapse of the city, and chap. 5 is a kind of liturgical close to the book, ending in an appeal to God for help.

Authorship and Date. One ancient tradition ascribes the book of Lamentations to the prophet Jeremiah, and this has even affected the traditional depiction of Jeremiah in western art as the "weeping prophet." Another ancient tradition, however, is silent as to the authorship of the book, thus implying that the author was unknown, and this is also the commonly held modern critical opinion.

The Septuagint, the ancient Greek translation of the Hebrew Bible, groups Lamentations with the book of Jeremiah, and prefaces the book with these words: ". . . Jeremiah sat weeping and composed this lament over Jerusalem and said . . ." Other ancient versions, as well as rabbinic sources, make the same ascription to the prophet. Although there is no explicit warrant for this in the Bible, there is a kind of basis for it in the comment in 2 Chronicles 35.25 that Jeremiah produced a "lament" or "laments" for King Josiah.

In the Hebrew scriptures themselves, Lamentations is not placed with Jeremiah. It is always placed not among the Prophets but with the Writings, the third division of the Jewish canon. Within this division its position varies, though it is usually placed somewhere with the five short books known as the five "scrolls." This position is significant testimony to the original anonymity of Lamentations, for it is difficult to see why the book was separated from that of Jeremiah if from the beginning it was understood to have been composed by the prophet. In modern times, scholars have pointed out elements in Lamentations that seem so much at odds with the views and personality of the prophet Jeremiah that it becomes very difficult to think of him as their author. Lamentations 1.10 refers to the enemies' entry into the Temple as a thing forbidden by God, whereas Jeremiah (7.14) had predicted it. Jeremiah foresaw the failure of foreign alliances (2.18; 37.5–10), but the author of Lamentations 4.17 shared with his people a frustrated longing for help from "a nation that could not save." Still further evidence of this sort may be pointed out, leading to the common opinion that the book's author—or authors, since the work is not strongly unified—is best regarded as unknown.

It is clear that Lamentations was written after the fall of Jerusalem in 587/586 BCE, but otherwise the date is uncertain. Since it expresses no clear hope for relief from conditions of bondage and humiliation, it probably dates to a time well before 538, when Cyrus permitted the Jews to return from exile. The book may have been written in Judah (rather than Babylon or Egypt), since it displays no interest in any other locale.

Acrostic Form. Chaps. 1 and 2 are made up of three-line stanzas, with the first line of the first stanza beginning with the first letter of the alphabet (*'ālep*), the second with

The lamentations of Jeremiah

176

the second (*bēt*), and so on through the twenty-two letters of the Hebrew alphabet. Chap. 4 follows the same scheme, but with two-line stanzas. Chap. 3 is a tour de force, having three-line stanzas with each of the three lines beginning with the proper letter. Chap. 5 is not an acrostic, but has twenty-two lines, so the alphabet still to some extent determines the form.

The purpose of this alphabetic and acrostic form is unknown. It is unlikely to have been merely a mnemonic device, but no definite meaning or symbolism can confidently be attached to this formal feature, and it is safest to say that the author seems to have aimed at some aesthetic effect. In any case, the acrostics make it possible to be relatively sure where the lines of the poems begin and end, a situation unusual in Hebrew verse, which was ordinarily copied just like prose, without regard for lines of verse. With this foundation, scholars have found in most of Lamentations a special "lament meter," in which the second of two parallel lines is shorter than the first. Although the complete aptness of this designation may be questioned, Lamentations continues to occupy a prominent place in the study of ancient Hebrew metrics.

Lamentations and Sumerian Laments. The Sumerians, authors of the world's oldest written literature, cultivated a genre of composition known today as "lament over the ruined city and temple." Laments over the ancient southern Mesopotamian cities Ur, Sumer and Ur (together), Nippur, Eridu, and Uruk were composed in the early second millennium BCE and were copied in the scribal schools. These texts have survived in whole or in part, and most have been edited and translated. As a result, it is possible to trace parallels in conception and expression between this body of laments and the biblical book of Lamentations.

The subject matter in the two cases is very similar—a holy city is destroyed by the god of that city—and could be expected to produce similarities in diction quite apart from any literary contact, so that some scholars prefer to minimize the significance of parallels between the biblical book and Sumerian laments and their Akkadian descendants. Such a view likely underestimates the force of the evidence, and it is preferable to posit that Lamentations is a representative of an Israelite city-lament genre. This genre is reflected also in the prophetic books, and is related as a genre to the Mesopotamian works, though details of this process are only conjectural.

DELBERT R. HILLERS

LAW. *This entry consists of two articles, the first on* Israelite Law *in its ancient Near Eastern context, and the second on* New Testament Views *of what came to be known as "the Law."*

Israelite Law

Although laws and the concept of law played an overwhelmingly important role in the Hebrew Bible and in the life of ancient Israel, the Hebrew Bible has no term exactly equivalent to the English word "law." The Hebrew word most often translated as "law," *tôrâ* (Torah), actually means teaching or instruction. As such it expresses the morally and socially didactic nature of God's demands on the Israelite people. The misleading translation of *tôrâ* as law entered Western thought through the Greek translation (Septuagint) of the term as *nomos*, as in the name of the book of Deuteronomy ("the second law"). That the word *tôrâ* is a loose concept is indicated by its use for the first five books of the Hebrew scriptures, which contain the bulk of ancient

Dark stone obelisk bearing inscribed Laws of Hammurabi & illustration of the King before the sun god Shamash

Israel's purely legal material, as well as for the Hebrew Bible as a whole. The vibrant nature of the legal tradition is indicated by the later Jewish distinction between the written Torah, namely the Hebrew Bible, and the oral Torah, the legal and religious traditions which were eventually codified in the Mishnah (ca. 200 CE) and developed in the Gemara (ca. 500 CE; together they form the Talmud) and later commentaries. The human intermediary between the people and their God in both cases is viewed as Moses, through the revelation at Sinai (Exod. 19–Num. 10) and later in a valedictory address in Transjordan before his death (Deuteronomy).

Among other terms employed in the Hebrew Bible that belong to the legal sphere and refer to specific practices and enactments are *ḥoq* "statute," *mišpāṭ* "ordinance," *miṣwâ* "commandment," and *dābār* "word."

Law in the Ancient Near East. Although it was once felt that biblical Israel's legal and moral traditions were unique in the ancient world, archaeological activity over the course of the last century has brought to light a large number of texts, mainly written in cuneiform script on clay tablets, which help to place biblical law in its ancient Near Eastern context. These include texts that have erroneously been termed "law codes," in addition to international treaties, royal edicts, and documents from the daily legal sphere.

The Babylonian Laws of Hammurapi (eighteenth century BCE, copies of which have been found dating up to a millennium later) remain the most famous and comprehensive of the ancient legal collections, and include close to three hundred laws, in addition to a lengthy prologue and epilogue in which the divine mission of providing laws for the land is given to Hammurapi. Other important "codes" include: the Laws of Urnammu, a Sumerian collection dating to ca. 2100 BCE; the Laws of Lipit-Ishtar, also in Sumerian, ca. 1900 BCE, the Laws of the city of Eshnunna, written in Akkadian and to be dated in the nineteenth century; the Hittite Laws, which date in their original form to ca. 1600 BCE; and the Middle Assyrian Laws from the reign of Tiglath-pileser I, ca. 1200 BCE.

These so-called law codes are not comprehensive codices in the Roman sense. They are rather miscellaneous collections of laws, compiled in order to enhance the stature of the ruler as the originator of order in his land. Although they preserve important evidence of individual stipulations and of the legal structure of a given society, these legal compilations are best viewed as literary texts. In spite of the ancient fame of a text such as the Babylonian Laws of Hammurapi, it is significant that among the thousands of legal documents known from ancient Mesopotamia not one refers to that collection for a precedent, nor to any other.

Ancient Near Eastern treaties, while important as historical, political, and legal sources, have also played a role in understanding the nature of Israel's covenant with God as one of vassal with suzerain. Elements in treaties that have been found in the Hebrew Bible include the identification of the parties to the treaty, a historical prologue in which God's actions on behalf of Israel are listed, the treaty stipulations (i.e., the laws), and the blessings and curses to be expected, as a consequence of obedience or of noncompliance to the terms of the covenant. Among the most important treaties are those of the Hittite empire of the second millennium BCE, to which many scholars look for the origin of the genre as a whole, and the neo-Assyrian vassal treaties, especially those of Esarhaddon (early seventh century BCE).

By far the largest number of ancient documents come from the daily practice of law. Tens of thousands of documents have been found recording economic and social transactions of all kinds, many of which can be compared to biblical practices. The closest biblical parallel to the actual practice of documenting transactions may be found in the account of Jeremiah's purchase of a plot of land in his home town of Anathoth, a transaction recorded in duplicate as were countless cuneiform documents (Jer. 32.9–15). Although most of the documents found were written on cuneiform tablets in Mesopotamia, documents written on papyrus and other perishable materials have been found in Egypt, for example at the site of the Jewish military colony at Elephantine, and in caves in the Judean desert, near the Dead Sea.

Israel's Laws in Modern Research. In addition to the comparative study of Israel's legal traditions, which seeks to shed light upon Israel's laws in their ancient context through a comparison of similarities and differences with non-biblical legal materials, two major trends can be identified in modern research on ancient Israel's legal traditions. The first is form-critical and concerns itself with the classification of Israel's laws according to form and syntax. The second attempts to identify the basic principles of Israel's legal tradition that set it apart from its surrounding cultures.

Basic for the study of the forms of Israelite law is the work of Albrecht Alt. In his essay on "The Origins of Israelite Law" (1934), Alt identified two basic patterns of legal formulations in the Bible. The first he termed "casuistic" law, since it arose from the sphere of case law. These are the laws formulated in the "if. . . then. . ." pattern. Alt sought the origin of these laws in Canaanite and general ancient Near Eastern traditions, which the Israelites took over after their "conquest" of the land. The second he termed "apodictic" law. These are laws formulated as absolute pronouncements, such as the Ten Commandments. They are mostly formed in the imperative: "You shall (not). . ." Alt sought the origin of these formulations in Israel's ancient Yahwistic law, from Israel's preconquest traditions. While Alt's analysis of the origins of these two types of law has not withstood the test of time, since both casuistic and apodictic laws are to be found in most ancient Semitic legal collections in varying relative percentages, his basic formcritical distinction continues to serve as the starting point of contemporary discussion.

Once it could be shown that ancient Israel belonged to the cultural milieu of the world in which it lived, the question arose whether there was any aspect of Israelite law which could be identified as distinguishing it from its neighbors. Two considerations are basic to the discussion.

First is the issue of authority. Although in ancient Mesopotamia the king was guided by divine will in the establishment of (secular) justice, the source of law was the king himself. In the Bible, on the other hand, the source of law was conceived of as God. In distinction to other ancient Near Eastern practice, in Israel the king was not conceived of as the promulgator of law. Moses and others were simply intermediaries who transmitted God's rules to the people. Thus both secular and religious law were given divine origin. Obeying laws was hence both a legal and a religious requirement. Breaking a law was not simply a secular delict, but an infraction of the will of God, hence a sin.

The second is the valuation of human life, for which the case of the goring ox (Exod. 21.28–32) may serve as example. The case of an ox that injured or killed a human being appears in a number of ancient legal collections. There are differences between the various laws regarding the liability of the owner of the goring ox according to its prior behavior and to the status of the person gored. However, only in the biblical law, upon which similar medieval European legislation was based, is the ox itself subject to the death penalty for killing a human being, its flesh not to be eaten. Since the ox murdered a human being, it became taboo and hence not fit for human consumption, in spite of the fact that that inflicted a great financial loss on its owner. To give another example, in the code of Hammurapi the death penalty is adduced for theft. The killing of another human being did not necessarily warrant such severe punishment (depending on the relative societal status of the individuals involved). In the Bible, capital punishment is reserved for cultic offenses, which included murder (see Exod. 21.12–14; Num. 35.29–34). Theft of property, as long it was not cultic or under the ban (see the story of Achan in Josh. 7), was not punishable by death. Theft of another human being, however, was (Exod. 21.16). Thus it is postulated by Moshe Greenberg that, whereas the protection of property belonging to the upper echelons of society was of paramount concern in Babylonian law, in Israelite law the sanctity of the individual formed in the image of God was primary.

Major Collections of Biblical Laws. Among the many legal passages in the Bible are a number that have been identified as independent units by modern scholars. These include the Ten Commandments (Decalogue; Exod. 20.2–17; Deut. 5.6–21), the Book of the Covenant (Exod. 20.22 [or 21.1]–

23.19), the Holiness Code (Lev. 17–26), and the Deuteronomic laws (Deut. 12–26). The Ten Commandments can be understood as the heart of Israel's convenantal relationship with God, since they include an identification of the suzerain, God's acts on behalf of Israel, and Israel's obligations to God formulated in apodictic style. Most of the obligations incumbent upon Israel in the Decalogue deal not with cultic issues, but with the relations between people in an orderly society. The Book of the Covenant, containing casuistic laws with many parallels in other ancient Near Eastern traditions, is assumed by many to be the oldest collection of laws in the Bible. The Holiness Code forms the oldest core of Priestly (P) legislation and is so named on account of its concern with Israelite ritual purity and holiness. The Deuteronomic laws, although presented as a speech delivered by Moses in Transjordan before his death, are associated in modern scholarship with the cultic reforms of King Josiah of Judah (640–609 BCE; see 2 Kings 22.1–23.30; 2 Chron. 34–35). The major concern of this corpus of religious legislation is with the centralization and purification of the cult and its sacrificial system in the Temple in Jerusalem.

CARL S. EHRUCH

New Testament Views

The modern New Testament is a fourth-century anthology of mid- to late-first-century documents, composed in Greek and reflecting the social and religious stresses of a new religious movement seeking to define and eventually to distinguish itself from Greek-speaking synagogue communities. In such a charged and changing context, "the Law" (Grk. *nomos*) received widely divergent treatments, although its definition remains constant: the Law is God's revelation through Moses to Israel.

Paul. The earliest and most problematic source is Paul. Written to predominantly gentile communities, his letters often address questions of ethics and authority. On these occasions, Paul's statements concerning the Law can only be seen as unself-consciously positive. The Law is the key to decent community life and the standard for group behavior (Gal. 5.15; 1 Cor. 14.34). Gentiles "in Christ" should strive to fulfill it and keep its commandments (1 Cor. 7.19; Rom. 8.4, 13.8–10; Gal. 5.14, authorizing his instruction by appeal to Lev. 19.18; cf. his defense of his apostolic rights by quoting from "the law of Moses," Deut. 25.4, in 1 Cor. 9.8–9). One can and Paul did—obtain righteousness under the Law (Phil. 3.6). Faith in Christ, Paul says, upholds the Law (Rom. 3.31). In the largest sense, the redemption in Christ comes to gentiles in order to confirm God's promises to Israel's ancestors as preserved in Genesis, the first of the five books of Torah (Rom. 15.8–9; cf. 9.4–5).

Yet elsewhere Paul virtually equates the Law with sin, death, and the flesh—the worst aspects of the "old aeon" that, through Christ's death, resurrection, and imminent parousia, is about to be overcome (Rom. 6.14; 7.5–6). God gave the Law on account of transgression and in order to condemn: it is the "old dispensation," inglorious and incomplete, compared to the gospel of Christ (Gal. 3.16–21, 24–26; 4.10, 19–22; 5.21–31, a particularly tortured passage; 2 Cor. 3.12–15; Rom. 3.20; 4.15; 520; 10.4). How then can this same author possibly maintain that "the Law is holy, and the commandment is holy and just and good" (Rom. 7.12)?

Scholars have attempted to resolve this tension. Some, at one extreme, take Paul's negative statements as definitive of his (hence, *the*) gospel and his positive statements as the measure of an unthought-out sentimental attachment to his community of origin. Some at the other end maintain that Paul preached a two-covenant theology: Torah for Jews, Christ for gentiles. On this view, his only objection to the Law would be if Christian gentiles chose it, that is, opted as Christians for conversion to Judaism. But Paul's own statements—forceful, passionate, at times intemperate—defy a consistent interpretation. He himself seems aware of the tensions in his position. As Paul saw it, however, history would soon relieve him of the necessity to make sense of God's plan in electing Israel, giving the Torah, and then sending Christ. For Christ, Paul urged, was about to return, end history, and bring all under the dominion of God. This conviction, and not his statements on the Law, is the one consistent theme in all of Paul's letters, from first to last (1 Thess. 1.10; 4.13–17; Phil. 1.10; 2.16; 4.5; 1 Cor. 7.26, 29, 31; 15; Rom. 8; 9–11; 13.11–12; 16.20). It spared him having to work out a "theology" of the Law.

The Gospels. The evangelists, writing some 40–70 years after Jesus' death, turned a negative attitude toward the Law (or the Jewish understanding of it) into the touchstone of Christian identity. This tendency makes for considerable confusion when one tries to reconstruct the views of the historical Jesus. Jesus of Nazareth, living and working in a predominantly Jewish environment, very likely had his own views on the correct interpretation of Torah, and these views may well have differed from those of his contemporaries. Argument about the Law between Jews was and is a timeless Jewish occupation: controversy implies inclusion. Transposed to a gentile context, however, argument can seem like repudiation.

Thus Mark's Jesus turns an unexceptional observation (people are morally defiled by what they do or say, not by what they eat, 7.15–23) into a repudiation of the Law regarding kosher food ("Thus he declared all foods clean"; v. 19). John's Jesus condemns his Jewish audience as sons of the lower cosmos and children of the devil (chap. 8): the Law, characterized throughout as that "of Moses" is, implicitly, not "of God," from whom comes grace, peace, and the Son (1.16, 7.19–24). In his Sermon on the Mount, Matthew's Jesus presents his intensification of Torah ethics as if in contradistinction to Torah and Jewish tradition ("You have heard it said . . . but I say"; chap. 5). Luke, although retaining the theme of Jewish guilt for the death of Jesus both in his Gospel and in Acts, nonetheless wishes to present the new movement as continuous with a Jewish view of biblical revelation. Consequently he edits out or softens many of Mark's anti-Law statements. And all the Gospels, no matter how strong their individual polemic against Jews and Judaism, and hence the Law, still present a Jesus who worships at synagogue on the Sabbath, observes Temple sacrifice, pilgrimage holidays, and Passover rituals, and whose followers, honoring the Sabbath, come to his tomb only on the Sunday after his death.

Later Traditions. Both within the New Testament and without, later traditions are similarly ambivalent. Negative statements tend to occur in those passages where these new communities seek to establish their identity vis-à-vis Jews and Judaism; positive statements emerge where Christians wish to distance themselves from their Greco-Roman environment. Christian ethics are in the latter case a judaizing of gentile populations according to the principles of Torah: shunning idols, sorcery, astrology, hetero- and homosexual fornication; keeping litigation within the community; supporting the poor, especially widows; and so on—all themes found especially in Paul's Corinthian correspondence.

In the early decades of the second century, Christian dualists such as Marcion and Valentinus took the position that the God of the Jew the God of the Law, was a second, lower, cosmic deity; God the father of Jesus, they held, thus had nothing directly to do with material creation and, thus, with the events and legislation give in scripture. Other Christians, committed to the unity of creation and redemption, argued that the Law was of divine origin: only their particular group, however, knew how to interpret correctly (that is, for the most part, allegorically, see esp. Justin Martyr, *Dialogue with Trypho*). The church's ambivalence toward the Law eventually determined the structure of the Christian canon itself. Retaining the Septuagint even as it repudiated Judaism, the church incorporated the Law into it "Old" Testament, while maintaining that it was superseded or perfected by the "New."

PAULA FREDRIKSEI

LAW AND THE BIBLE. Municipal or national law is the set of rules that, within a state, orders it affairs and those of persons under its jurisdiction, and which, when necessary, is enforced by special organs of the state. There may be more than one municipal law in a state, as in the United Kingdom, which contains the Scottish English, and Northern Irish legal systems, or in the United States, where each state has its own legal system in addition to the federal system. Other states, such as India, have special rules for special communities (e.g., for Christians). International law is the law between states and between states and other international entities.

Municipal law can be divided into the law that regulates the affairs of the state itself and that which deals with the rights and duties, privileges and immunities of persons within it. This division is often described as one between public and private law, though these categories overlap

The Bible has influenced all those systems of law that can be traced, sometimes tortuously, to western European sources. By and large, the legal systems of other societies have been less subject to its influence, though sometimes that influence was historically present, as with the Russian system, in which a traditional Christianity molded society in former centuries and is still to be discerned in such rules as those regarding contract.

There are two main groups within the broad European legal tradition. Civilian legal systems form one group. These owe much to the legacy of Roman Civil Law, particularly as that Law was rediscovered and developed by scholars from the twelfth to the sixteenth century. The Civil Law lays emphasis on rationality and principle, and for that reason the civilian tradition has been adopted by many states that have consciously chosen their law. The other group, roughly encompassing the Anglo-American tradition, stems in large part from the English Common Law, and like it has tended to concentrate more on remedies. This group has spread more by conquest and imposition than by conscious adoption. There is also a third group, that of the "mixed" legal systems, which draws from both main traditions. Scots Law and that of Louisiana are examples of these.

The remote history of any legal system is obscure, for much of our understanding of particular influences at specific times is conditional upon the accidental survival of documentation, and deductions therefrom. It is, however, undeniable that the influence of the Bible on the legal systems that trace themselves to a western European root is extensive, though nowadays often diffuse. Biblical principles form a part of the foundations, which, like all good foundations, are well buried. Indeed, many in the twentieth century would deny biblical influence on many legal principles, which in former years were held to be sufficiently justified by the Bible. Much depends upon a willingness to accept parallels as indicative of influence and not a simple coincidence of result. Jews or Christians interpret the evidence differently from those who proceed from rationalist, agnostic, or atheist presuppositions.

When the modern legal systems of the European family were being formed, three main bodies of law influenced their development, namely the indigenous law of the community, Roman law, and canon law. The Bible's influence was mediated through each of these.

Indigenous law was that obtaining within a community, refined in accordance with the expectation of the community as to what was right in a given situation. Naturally, such expectations had much to do with religious belief and presuppositions. In each legal system, therefore, there came to be a body of "common law" manifested and developed through the decisions of judges and the reasoning that supported those decisions. Since the early judges in most countries were in holy orders (though they were not usually canonists), the opportunity for biblical influence was great. Specific recourse to the Bible as authority was unusual, but the principles it contained exercised their influence. Within the English tradition, the common law came to be highly significant, and it is only in comparatively recent times that the legislature has come to be considered of greater authority than the common law in the sense that what Parliament legislates takes precedence over the common law. By contrast, in the American tradition, the Constitution operates as the brake upon the lawmaking power of the Congress or of state legislatures.

Throughout Europe, indigenous law was directly influenced by Roman law, particularly as enunciated in the *Corpus Juris Civilis* (529–545 CE), the product of scholars working under instructions from the Emperor Justinian. Naturally, the empire having become Christian, there was a desire on the part of these scholars to make the civil law congruent with church teachings. Biblical influences therefore were strong. From the twelfth century onward, scholars (known collectively as the Glossators) worked on the *Corpus*, expanding its precepts through commentary, with considerable effect on their contemporary municipal law.

The indigenous law was also influenced to a greater or lesser degree by the canon law, a major contribution of the church to civilization. The Roman Catholic church had extended its authority even as the Roman empire waned and disintegrated, and it was considered by many to be the only body that could continue a tradition of universal law. The sources of church law, however, were many and various, and it was only as the church organized itself on a monarchic principle under the papacy that the need for systematization was dealt with. The eleventhcentury rediscovery of Roman Law in the form of the Justinianic legislation, and notably the *Digest* of 533 CE, provided a model that eventually resulted in the *Corpus Iuris Canonici*, though that was constantly augmented by interpretation and further legislation. Much of the canon law had to do with church organization, but large portions affected the daily life of the laity and influenced the development of national laws in various areas. The aim of the canonists was to make their system of law correspond as closely as possible to right Christian conduct, and to minimize the separation of law and morals. The Bible influenced their deliberations, though its principles were often mediated through the teachings of the Roman Catholic church.

One area of law affected by the canonists was the law of marriage, an area important in every society and subject to church procedures. Another was the law of wills, where the church rules were much more simple than those of the civil law. Naturally the canonists, keen to keep law and morals together, were concerned with matters of intention and of good and bad faith. In contract, therefore, good faith was made a major requirement, and bargains were enforced through the church courts without the insistence upon the formalities for their constitution that had grown up previously (Matt. 5.34–37). (It has to be said, however, that this development took greater hold in the civilian tradition than in the Anglo-American, which has retained certain elements of formal requirements such as the notion of "consideration," and which does not recognize a unilateral contract unless entered into under appropriate ceremonial.) Again, the canonists' stress on responsibility for the consequences of one's actions helped root the concepts of tort.

In the area of crime, intention also came to be insisted upon as a prerequisite for criminality of conduct (see Matt. 5.28), thereby bringing crime into closer association with notions of sin and allowing actions to be differently weighed in any consideration of "blame," and therefore also of punishment. (A modern extrapolation from such concepts is the Scottish defense to a criminal charge of "diminished responsibility," which stems from that root, and was only lately taken over into English law.) The emphasis on sin also produced a change in attitude to punishment. In more and more instances, prison as a place of repentance was accorded a higher priority than vengeance exacted through physical unpleasantness. In criminal procedure, the notion of God as judge, weighing the evidence, came to be accepted as a model, and human judges were 2 given a greater freedom in their conduct of trials than former formalities permitted.

Finally, like the theologians and philosophers, the canonists gave consideration to such social questions as the doctrine of the "just price" and the "just wage." Price fluctuations in response to market forces alone were considered contrary to notions of intrinsic value. Such matters and their attempted solutions are, of course, still with us, and still echo Exodus 20.9; 34.21; 1 Thessalonians 4.11; 2 Thessalonians 3.7, 10–12.

The Reformation produced an interest in principles taken directly from the Bible in contrast to those mediated through church tradition and canon law. In some instances, this interest produced formal legislation. To take examples from one "reformed" jurisdiction, in 1567 in the Scots law the "degrees of relationship" within which marriage could lawfully be contracted were set out in terms of Leviticus 20 and "the Law of God," and the "prohibited degrees of relationship" for the purpose of defining incest were set out specifically in terms of Leviticus 18—though inaccurately, since the Geneva version (1560) of the Bible was the source used. Again, marriage between divorced persons and their paramours was made unlawful (Matt. 5.32; 19.9; Mark 10.11–12), though this was soon administratively avoided, and adultery was made a crime (Exod. 20.14; Lev. 20:10). Divorce on the grounds of adultery (Matt. 1.18–19:5.32; 19.9) or desertion (1 Cor. 7.15) was introduced. In 1563, witchcraft was made a capital crime in terms of Exodus 22.18, and various Sunday observance statutes were passed (Exod. 20.10–11). In 1649, 1661, and 1695, blasphemy was made a capital offence, though the full penalty was exacted only once.

The other major element that the Reformation took from the Bible was the concept of the priesthood of all believers (Exod. 19.6; Isa. 61.6; 1 Pet. 2.9; Rev. 1.6; 5.10; 20.6), which eventually filters down to the modern institutions of democratic government.

The law books of the sixteenth to eighteenth centuries, in which the roots of much modern law are laid, contain a considerable mixture of sources for the principles that they assert. The Bible is often quoted, as is the Roman law. However, appeal is also frequently made to a "natural law," containing principles that are treated as axiomatic. At first, such "law" was said by writers to be given by God, but in 1625, in the *Prolegomena* to his *De Iure belli ac pacis* ("The Law of War and Peace"), Hugo Grotius pointed out that the legal principles so identified would have a degree of validity even if there were no God. Reason would deduce such principles from a consideration of the nature of human beings and from their needs in society. Others acted on that observation, and drove a wedge between "natural law" and any religious source. This was not, however, a sudden or a complete change of emphasis. Blackstone's *Commentaries on the Laws of England* (1765), for example, discusses law as stemming from God (Intro, s.2), but makes little appeal to biblical texts. Stair's *Institutions of the Law of Scotland* (2d ed., 1693), written from a Presbyterian background, also links law to God, making a number of biblical citations in so doing (e.g. Book I, tit. 1, 2–9), but again the bulk of the work treats such matters as a base to be acknowledged and not as an active source of law. In that train, Puritanism influenced English and American law in the seventeenth and eighteenth centuries, but since then the deduction of legal principle from biblical or theological sources has been largely abandoned by lawyers. The principles remain, but their source is usually not acknowledged or is otherwise explained on bases of social, economic, or political necessity. In Europe, anticlericalism gave that trend further impetus.

In the twentieth century, major advances in securing biblical principles have been made in international law, particularly through the United Nations' Universal Declaration of Human Rights, and other international Human Rights Covenants and Conventions following in its wake. In some measure, these have provided a statement of fundamental principles for human conduct that draw on biblical ideas among their unacknowledged sources. They provide a base from which municipal law can be criticized, and even, under certain human rights treaties, a remedy and change be obtained.

Within the municipal law of most states of the European tradition, the law generally now proceeds upon unexamined assumptions. The biblical roots acknowledged in the early texts are taken for granted, and go unmentioned in modern discussions of matters such as tort, contract, marriage, divorce, wills, and the like, where the canonists did their job well in former centuries. In some areas, however, there has been a revival of appeal to biblical notions, often with explicit citation of biblical texts. Thus medical ethics, euthanasia, abortion, and surrogacy are contro verted legal matters. Curiously, it is in the United States, where the Constitution requires a separation of church and state, that most modern legislation and court action has had a clear biblical base. The debate on such matters as school prayer, abortion, and the teaching of science in schools (creationism verses evolution) has had a considerable emphasis on biblical precept. In other states, the influence of the Bible and of Christianity is left as something inarticulate but nonetheless real. The principles are there, but only those who are willing to do so acknowledge their source. Legislators and judges act on them, but without reference to their origin. As noted, effective foundations are well buried.

FRANCIS LYALL

Cuneiform letter and envelope, early second millennium BCE

LETTER-WRITING IN ANTIQUITY.

Letter-writing arose in antiquity to serve official purposes. There were three broad types of official correspondence: royal or diplomatic letters, military orders and reports, and administrative correspondence used in managing internal affairs. Most letters embedded in the Hebrew Bible, along with several other nonbiblical Israelite and Jewish letters, are official in nature. Solomon's correspondence with King Hiram of Tyre, for example, is diplomatic (1 Kings 5.2–6, 8–9; see also 1 Kings 21.8–10; 2 Kings 10.1–6). The Lachish letters, written when Judah was under siege by Babylonia, are military communiqués. We may add to these the letter from the Jewish military settlement in Egypt at Elephantine, which was sent to the Persian governor of Judah, requesting his intervention against attacks on a Jewish temple.

Originally, messages were oral, carried by trusted couriers. With the passage of time, the principal message of the letter was delivered in written form, but the letter's sender continued to be identified orally by the messenger with the phrase, "Thus says . . ." (e.g., Ezra 1.1–2). A written message provided confirmation of the letter's authenticity, especially when signed with the sender's seal (1 Kings 21.8–10; Esther 8.10). The written message carried by Uriah from King David to the military commander Joab was clearly closed, because it commanded Uriah's own death (2 Sam. 11.14–15).

Though professional couriers were used by ancient states from the beginning of recorded history, the first organized postal system was not established until the sixth century BCE, when the Persian king Cyrus set up a network of highways and relay stations. This postal system served as a model for Alexander the Great and his successors, as well as for the Roman empire.

Even when the entirety of the letter was written, the messenger often continued to play a supplemental role. This was certainly the case with Paul, who usually employed trusted coworkers as couriers and who expected messengers to represent him to his correspondents (1 Cor. 4.17; 16.10–11; 2 Cor. 7.6–16; 8.16–18, 23–24; 12.18).

Various materials were used for written messages. Correspondence in Mesopotamia was written on clay tablets in cuneiform script by means of a reed with a wedge-shaped tip. It was common in a number of places to write with a brush or reed pen on potsherds (ostraca). Parchment and vellum (skins) were used for more important correspondence. Papyrus was the most widely used material during the Persian and Greco-Roman periods. When Hellenistic rulers proclaimed benefactions and edicts worthy of permanent record, they were inscribed on stone after delivery.

Gradually, the letter was adapted to serve personal and nonofficial purposes. We know from archaeological discoveries that, at least in Greco-Roman Egypt, all levels of society sent letters. Although many were written by scribes, literacy was not as rare as was formerly believed. Nonetheless, ancient postal systems existed to serve only state business, not private correspondence. Whereas wealthy families and business firms could use employees or servants to carry their mail, ordinary people depended on those traveling on business (e.g., by ship or caravan) or on friends and passing strangers.

Greek and Roman rhetoricians regarded the cultivated letter of friendship as the most authentic form of correspondence. The letter was conceived as a substitute for the sender's actual presence. Since the recipient, however, could not ask for immediate clarification on epistolary subjects, it was recognized that the letter had to be more articulate than face-to-face talk. Despite the more studied style of letter-writing relative to conversation, theorists warned that the discussion of technical subjects was not appropriate in a letter. Nonetheless, the democratization of knowledge in late antiquity, along with the dialogic character of popular philosophy at the time, made it almost inevitable that much philosophical and religious instruction would be communicated in epistolary form.

While none of the books of the Hebrew Bible takes the form of a letter, twenty-one of the twenty-seven New Testament books are letters (also known as "epistles"). This difference stems in part from the fact that New Testament letters were written by Greek-speaking Jewish Christians who were influenced by the Hellenistic practice of writing instruction in the form of letters. Moreover, letters were often used by Christian leaders, such as Paul, to maintain contact with widely separated congregations.

The New Testament letters and patristic letters of the first three centuries CE are much longer than most pieces of ancient Greek correspondence. This length corresponds directly to their purpose as letters of instruction. In this respect, Christian letters are more like philosophical letters of instruction than like ordinary letters. On the other hand, the hortatory rhetoric used in Christian letters differs significantly from that in literary letters. For example, the emphasis on the whole community's spiritual maturation brought about by Christ's return, rather than on building one's individual character, shows that Christian letters were written by a specific religious subgroup with an apocalyptic Jewish coloring. Their special character is evident in the way traditional Jewish materials are cited within the letter (doxologies, benedictions, hymns), as well as in the tone of familiarity and equality that frequently described Christian recipients and their senders as family members. Later, in the fourth and fifth centuries CE, letters from Christian leaders conformed much more to Greek literary models of letters.

JOHN L. WHITE

LEVI. Son of Jacob and Leah, and one of the twelve tribes of Israel. Leah associates Levi with the verb "to join" (Gen. 29.34). Aside from his involvement with Simeon in the attack against Shechem (Gen. 34.25–26), Levi is best known for the sacerdotal functions of his descendants. The Levites play a prominent role in assisting Moses quell the golden calf rebellion (Exod 32.25–29). Whatever Aaron's ancestry, his sons, and not Levi's, dominate the Jerusalem cult from the time of Solomon (1 Kings 2.26–27) until the overthrow of Onias III by the Seleucids in 174 BCE.

Biblical sources depict the Levites as porters, carrying the ark (1 Sam. 6.15; 1 Kings 8.4) and the tabernacle (Num. 1.47–54). Given no inheritance of their own (Num. 18.23–24; Deut. 12.12–19; 14.28–29), the Levites were to reside in forty-eight designated cities (Num 35.1–8; Josh. 21.1–8). Israelites were to support the Levites through tithes and offerings (Deut. 18.1–4).

Scholars disagree whether Levi was originally a secular tribe (Gen. 49.5–7) or whether the Levites were supposed to have secondary status. P prescribes a rigid division of duties for the descendants of Levi's sons, Gershon, Kohath, and Merari (Num. 4.1–33). Barred as priests, the Levites function under Aaronid supervision (Num. 3.10). Similarly, Ezekiel denounces the Levites and confirms their lesser status (44.4–14).

In contrast, Deuteronomy defines a priest as a levitical priest and accords Levites an equal share at the central shrine (18.6–8). In Deuteronomy, Levites are judges (17.8–9), guardians of the torah scroll (17.18), and they assist in covenant renewal (27.9). In a postexilic context, Malachi predicts Levite renaissance because of priestly corruption at the Jerusalem Temple (2.1–9; 33–4). Chronicles strikes a mediating position, depicting cooperation between the dominant Aaronids and the Levites and stressing levitical *roles* as Temple singers, gatekeepers, and teachers of torah (1 Chron. 6.31–48; 9.22–27; 2 Chron. 17.7–9).

Many commentators see competition between the Levites and the Aaronids as the most plausible explanation for the different duties and kinds of status ascribed to these groups by biblical writers.

GARY N. KNOPPERS

LEVIATHAN. A mythological sea monster who is one of the primeval adversaries of the storm god. In the Ugaritic texts, Baal defeats Lothan (*ltn,* a linguistic variant of Leviathan), described as a seven-headed serpent, apparently identified with Baal's adversary Prince Sea. In the Bible, Leviathan is also identified with the Sea (Job 3.8) and has many heads (Ps. 74.14), and his defeat by God is a prelude to creation (Ps. 74.15–17). According to apocalyptic literature, that battle will be rejoined in the end of time when the evil Leviathan will be finally defeated (Isa. 27.1; Rev. 12. 3; 17.1–14; 19.20; 21.1), and, according to later tradition, given along with Behemoth as food to the elect (2 Esd. 6.49–52), another recalling of creation (Ps. 74.14). In Job 41, Leviathan is described as fully under God's control, a divine pet (vv. 4–5;

cf. Ps. 104.26). Many commentators have equated the Leviathan of Job 41 with the crocodile, and some elements of the description seem to fit this identification. But others, like his breathing fire (vv. 19–21), do not; in light of the other biblical references as well as the Canaanite antecedents it is better to understand Leviathan as a mythological creature.

In Thomas Hobbes's work by this title (1651), Leviathan is the symbolic name for the absolute power of the political commonwealth, to whose sovereignty people must be subordinate but which is ultimately subject to divine control.

MICHAEL D. COOGAN

LEVITICUS, THE BOOK OF. Leviticus is the third book of the Pentateuch, named *wayyiqrāʾ* in Hebrew ("and he summoned") from its opening words. The English "Leviticus" is taken over from the Latin Vulgate's *Liber Leviticus* derived from the Greek Septuagint. The contents of Leviticus relate not to the tribe of Levi but more generally to matters of concern to the priesthood, especially the proper procedures for various sacrificial offerings, priestly ordination, determinations concerning ritual purity, and the celebration of holy days. The Pentateuch in its final form is intended to be a single composition, and its division into five books is a later development; however apt the division may be, it should not obscure the fact that Leviticus stands in continuity with what precedes it in the Priestly code (P) and with what follows; in some cases, it presupposes them. Thus, the ordination of Aaron and his sons, described in Leviticus 8–9, conforms to instructions given in Exodus 29, and the relation of Aaron's line to other elements of Levi is explicated, in part at least, by the conflict stories in Numbers 16 and the assignment of contributions and tithes in Numbers 18.

Since Leviticus pertains to P, its contents are thought to have attained a relatively fixed form only in postexilic times; the rituals described therein are basically those of the Second Temple. Since, however, priestly circles tended to be conservative (especially the Jerusalem priesthood), much of the ritual no doubt reflects that of monarchic times, and some of it possibly even earlier periods. The priestly hierarchy of Leviticus reflects that of postexilic times, as elsewhere in P, with Aaron and his sons alone functioning as priests. Aaron is not called high priest; he is, rather, "the anointed priest" who stands apart from other priests (Lev. 4.3, 5, 16), and his prerogatives pass to another by right of succession (Lev. 6.22; 16.32; cf. Num. 20.25–29). The legal prescriptions in Leviticus, as in other parts of the Pentateuch, are generally introduced by the formula, "The Lord spoke to Moses, saying, 'Speak to the people of Israel'" (1.1–2; 4.1; 7.22–23, 28–29; 12.1–2; 18.1–2; 19.1–2; etc.; cf. Exod. 20.22; 25.1; 31.12–13; Num. 5.1–2, 5–6, 11–12; 6.1–2; 15.1–2, 37–38), but for those that pertain strictly to priests, God commands Moses to speak to Aaron or to Aaron and his sons (6.8–9, 24–25; 16.1–2; 21.1, 16–17; 22.1–2; cf. Num. 6.22–23; 8.1–2); occasionally Aaron, his sons, and all Israel are included under the same rubric (17.1–2; 22.17–18).

In a sense, such formulas bind the contents of the book together. Whether or not one holds P to be a narrative source, the action is advanced very little in Leviticus; Israel, which had already encamped at Mount Sinai in Exodus 19, remained there through all that is recounted in Leviticus, departing thence only at Numbers 10. The only narrative portions are those that tell of the ordination of Aaron and his sons (chaps. 8–10, by the rite prescribed in Exod. 29) and of a blasphemer and his punishment (24.10–23), the latter narrative occasioning and including a number of laws (vv. 17–20). Although the

183

materials contained in Leviticus are rather disparate in nature, a degree of coherence is provided in the way that many of them are fitted in. Thus, the first sacrifices narrated in P after the erection of the tabernacle (Exod. 40) are those relating to the ordination of Aaron and his sons (Lev. 8.14–9.21), and these are logically preceded by extensive instructions on the offering of sacrifice (chaps. 1–7). Thus also, the detailed rules for the distinction between clean and unclean (i.e., that which defiles) in chaps. 11–15 logically precede the instructions for the great Day of Atonement (chap. 16), whose primary goal is the cleansing of the sanctuary, meeting tent, and altar from the defilements of the Israelites (16.16–19).

Despite the present title given the book, and despite the book's interest in priestly ritual, extensive portions were directed largely to the lay population, in particular 1.1–6.7, which describes how certain sacrifices are to be carried out; these are initiated by the offerer, who also did the slaughtering, although for the priests are reserved the offering of blood and burning of whatever parts are to be burned. In 6.8–7.10, on the other hand, many of the same matters are covered, but now from the vantage point of priestly concerns; in the outline below in this article, these sections are labeled "supplement," though in fact they must originally have formed a separate (albeit somewhat disorganized) collection, formulated, preserved, and transmitted in priestly circles. As might be expected, most sections within this block are addressed to Aaron and his sons. (This section, extended to 7.38, is sometimes labeled "manual for the priests," and the previous sections "manual for the laity.")

The Holiness Code (H), chaps. 17–26, probably stood as a separate collection before its insertion into P; it is so named because its provisions aim at maintaining the ritual purity required of God's people, and because of the formula, "You shall be holy, for I the Lord your God am holy" (19.2; cf. 20.7). The idea of holiness here, as in the rest of Leviticus and the Hebrew Bible generally, is that of being set apart. It is in Yahweh's nature to be apart and therefore holy, but people and even things can be set apart as Yahweh's possession and for his service, and in that sense they can be holy. Israel is to "set apart" the clean from the unclean, just as Yahweh has set Israel apart from the nations (20.25–26; cf. 22.32–33). Priests are set apart in a special way, but so is sacrificial meat, the sanctuary, veil, altar and utensils, the Sabbath, the jubilee year, tithes, and things vowed to the Lord—and so

all these can be called holy or consecrated (8.10–11; 19.24; 21.6, 8, 15, 23; 22.9; 23.3, 20; 25.10; 27.9, 28, 30). Nevertheless, the concept of holiness is broader than separateness, for the former relates to fitting worship of the all-holy God and to what is in accord with his nature. Some of the provisions, furthermore, especially many of those in chap. 19, express high ethical ideals, for example, concern for the poor, disadvantaged, handicapped, and aged (19.9–10, 13–14, 32), honesty in action, word, and judgment (19.11–12, 15–16, 35–36), and even the command to love one's neighbor (19.18), including the resident alien (19.33–34). The unevenness and repetition in H is attributable to the fact that it was made up of several smaller, somewhat overlapping collections before its insertion into P; later additions, intended to bring its provisions into line with those found in P, contributed further to the unevenness. The list of rewards (for obedience) and punishments (for disobedience) with which H concludes (chap. 26) forms an epilogue similar in form, content, and function to that contained in D (Deut. 28). Some scholars believe that H originally had a historical prologue that was detached when H was inserted into P. In its independent form, then, H may have resembled the treaty form, which is also found in the outline of D.

Chap. 27, on the redemption of votive offerings (i.e., things vowed to God), forms an appendix containing some early material that was probably added after the rest of Leviticus had reached its present form.

The book may be outlined as follows (primary references are given according to the Hebrew text; NRSV and some other translations differ from the Hebrew in parts of chaps. 5 and 6):

I. RITUAL FOR SACRIFICES
   Chap. 1: The burnt offering (*'ōlá*)
   Chap. 2: The cereal offering (*minḥá*)
   Chap. 3: The peace offering (*zebaḥ šĕlāmîm*)
   Chap. 4: The sin offering (*ḥaṭṭā't*) for priests (vv. 1–12) for the community (vv. 13–21) for the princes (vv. 22–26) for private persons (vv. 27–35)
   Chap. 5: The sin offering for special cases (vv. 1–13)
            The guilt offering *'āšām* (vv. 14–26; NRSV: 5.14–6.7)
   Chap. 6: Supplement on the burnt offering (vv. 1–6; NRSV: vv. 8–13)
            Supplement on the cereal offering (vv. 7–16; NRSV: vv. 14–23)
            Supplement on the sin offering (vv. 17–23; NRSV: vv. 24–30)
   Chap. 7: Supplement on the guilt offering (vv. 1–10)
            Supplement on the peace offering (vv. 11–21)
            Prohibitions concerning blood and fat (vv. 22–27)
            Portions for priests (vv. 28–36)
            Conclusion (vv. 37–38)
II. CEREMONY OF ORDINATION
   Chap. 8: Ordination of Aaron and his sons
   Chap. 9: Their installation
   Chap. 10: Revolt of Nadab and Abihu (vv. 1–7)
            Some rules of priestly conduct (vv. 8–11)
            Supplement on priestly portions (vv. 12–20)

Small piece of an ancient Torah scroll containing extracts in Hebrew from the biblical book of Leviticus, dating back to the last Jewish revolt against Roman rule in Judea around 135 CE

III. Laws Regarding Legal Purity
    Chap. 11: Clean and unclean animals
    Chap. 12: Purification after childbirth
    Chap. 13: Leprosy of persons (vv. 1–46)
            of garments (vv. 47–59)
    Chap. 14: Purification after leprosy (vv.
            1–32)
            Leprosy of houses (vv. 33–57)
    Chap. 15: Unclean discharges
    Chap. 16: Ritual for the Day of
            Atonement
            Sacrifices and incense (vv.
            1–19)
            The scapegoat (vv. 20–28)
            Observed as sabbath of rest
            and affliction (vv. 29–34)
IV. Holiness Code (H)
    Chap. 17: Sacredness of blood
    Chap. 18: Forbidden sexual relations
    Chap. 19: Various rules of conduct
    Chap. 20: Penalties for various sins
    Chap. 21: Holiness of priests
            Rules of conduct (vv. 1–15)
            Irregularities (vv. 16–24)
    Chap. 22: The holiness of offerings (vv.
            1–16)
            Unacceptable victims (vv. 17–33)
    Chap. 23: Calendar of feasts
            Introduction; Sabbath (vv. 1–4)
            Passover (vv. 5–14)
            Pentecost (vv. 15–22)
            New Year's Day (vv. 23–25)
            Day of Atonement (vv. 26–32)
            Feast of Booths (vv. 33–44)
    Chap. 24: Service of the sanctuary (vv. 1 9)
            Sanctuary light (vv. 1–4)
            Showbread (vv. 5–9)
            A case of blasphemy and its punishment
            (vv. 10–23)
    Chap. 25: Sabbatical year (vv. 1–7)
            Jubilee year (vv. 8–55)
            Introduction (vv. 8–22)
            Redemption of property (vv. 23–34)
            Redemption of persons (vv. 35–55)
    Chap. 26: Rewards and punishments
            False and true worship (vv. 1–2)
            Rewards of obedience (vv. 3–13)
            Punishment of disobedience (vv. 14–26)
V. Appendix
    Chap. 27: Votive offerings and their redemption
                         Joseph Jensen, O.S.B.

An engraving from 1650 depicting a congregation saying the "Lord's Prayer"

LORD'S PRAYER. Also known as the "Our Father" (Latin *Pater noster*) from its first words, the Lord's Prayer occurs in the New Testament in two slightly different forms. The longer form is included in Matthew's account of Jesus' Sermon on the Mount (6.9–13) and reads (in the NRSV):

Our Father in heaven,
    hallowed be your name.
Your kingdom come.
Your will be done,
    on earth as it is in heaven.
Give us this day our daily bread.

And forgive us our debts,
    as we also have forgiven our debtors.
And do not bring us to the time of trial,
    but rescue us from the evil one.

The doxology at the close ("For the kingdom and the power and the glory are yours forever. Amen") is absent in ancient and important Greek manuscripts, and is not mentioned in early commentaries on the Lord's Prayer by Tertullian, Cyprian, and Origen. It occurs in twofold form ("power and glory") in the Didache (8.2). In liturgical use, some kind of doxology (perhaps composed on the model of 1 Chron. 29.11–13) could have concluded such a prayer as this.

The shorter form of the Lord's Prayer is given in Luke 11.2–4, where Jesus responds to a disciple's request, "Lord, teach us to pray," with the following:

Father, hallowed be your name.
Your kingdom come.
Give us each day our daily bread.
And forgive us our sins,
    for we ourselves forgive everyone
    indebted to us.
And do not bring us to the time of trial.

Later manuscripts, on which the King James Version depends, include additions that assimilate the Lucan form of the Prayer to that in Matthew. Furthermore, two Greek manuscripts of the Gospels (no. 162, dated 1153 CE, and no. 700, of the eleventh century) replace the petition "Your kingdom come" with "Your holy Spirit come upon us and cleanse us." This adaptation may have been used when celebrating the rite of baptism or the laying on of hands.

It is likely that Luke's shorter version is closer to the original and that Matthew's is an elaboration. But, of course, Jesus may well have given the prayer in different forms on different occasions.

It would seem that the mode of address that Jesus habitually used in prayer to God was "Abba, dear Father" (the only exception is Mark 15.34, itself a quotation from Ps. 22.1). It seems that nowhere in the literature of the prayers of ancient Judaism does the invocation of God as "Abba" occur. Perhaps there is an intimacy of relationship implied here that others had hesitated to use. However, in teaching his followers to address God in this way, Jesus lets them share in his own communion with God. That they rejoiced to do so is apparent in the letters of Paul (see Gal. 4.6; Rom. 8.15). Ancient Christian liturgies reflect something of the sense of privilege in using this approach when they preface the Lord's Prayer with the words "We are bold to say 'Our Father.' "

But if the address "Our Father" suggests intimacy, not to say familiarity, the next words, "in heaven," speak of the "otherness," the holiness, the awesomeness of God. It is when these two aspects of approach to God are held together in creative tension that real prayer can be engaged in. Further, the plural "our" should be noted—not, at least in this instance, "my." This is the prayer that Jesus' followers as members of one family are bidden to say together (see Matt. 12.49–50 and par.); the Father presides over the family unit.

Following the invocation in the Matthean form of the prayer, the petitions fall into two parts: three "you" petitions are followed by "we" petitions. The former focus on God and his purposes in the world; the latter pertain to our provision, pardon, and protection. In other words, before any thought is given to human need ("our daily bread") or even to divine forgiveness of sins or to the problem of temptation, God's name, God's kingdom, God's will must first engage our attention. This is the order of precedence when human beings engage in communication with the God who is at once immanent and transcendent.

"Your will be done" is not a prayer of resignation, but one for the full accomplishment of the divine purpose (as in Matt. 26.42). The words "on earth as it is in heaven" may be taken with all three preceding petitions.

The Greek adjective (*epiousios*), usually translated "daily," is extremely rare; it may mean "[the bread we need] for tomorrow." In either case, the sense is that we are to pray for one day's rations, perhaps with the implied suggestion that asking for more would be to engage in needless concern for the future (cf. Matt. 6.25–34).

The petition for God's forgiveness is closely linked with our forgiveness of one another (the difference in tenses between the Matthean and Lucan versions should be noted); Matthew elaborates the teaching in the following verses (6.14–15). The Aramaic word for "debt" is used in rabbinic writings to mean "sin," and would be so understood by Jesus' hearers.

The petition often translated "lead us not into temptation" is best understood as a prayer to be kept in the hour of severe trial; it is an acknowledgment of spiritual frailty (cf. 1 Cor. 10.12) in the face of the evil one (or evil, for the Greek can mean either).

DONALD COGGAN

LORD'S SUPPER. In 1 Corinthians 11.20 Paul refers to a gathering of church members at Corinth to eat "the Lord's supper," complaining that the way in which they did so was not consistent with the true character of the meal. What was meant to be a proclamation of the Lord's death was being celebrated as an occasion for gluttony and even drunkenness. This is the only passage in the New Testament where the meal is described by this name. In what is no doubt a reference to the same meal, Paul states (1 Cor. 10.16) that the Christians came together to "break bread;" hence, we can assume that "the breaking of bread" (Acts 2.46) was another name for the same occasion. The same verse, with its reference to sharing (Grk. *koinōnia*) in the body and blood of Christ, is the source of the name "(Holy) Commu-

nion" for the meal, and the association with thanksgiving (Grk. *eucharistoun*) in 1 Corinthians 11.24 is the rationale for calling it the Eucharist.

The only full discussion of this meal in the New Testament is in 1 Corinthians 11.17–34, where Paul deals with irregularities that had arisen in the congregation at Corinth. They met, doubtless in the home of one of their members, to have a communal meal, and it is likely that the practice of meeting weekly on the first day of the week (Acts 20.7; cf. 1 Cor. 16.2) was developing. It was a full meal, but apparently each person brought his or her own food (11.21). Since the church consisted of richer and poorer members, differences in the amount and quality of the food and drink existed, so that the social differences in the church were emphasized rather than diminished by this communal occasion. At some point in the meal there was a more formal sharing in a loaf of bread and a cup of wine, which became the focus of significant symbolism.

Already in 1 Corinthians 10.16–17, Paul commented that those who shared in the loaf and the cup, for which thanks had been given to God, were participating in the body and blood of Christ. The reference must be to experiencing the benefits resulting from the death of Jesus, in which he gave himself and shed his blood for the sake of others. At the same time Paul emphasized that those who took part in this way constituted one body; their common participation in the gift of salvation, as symbolized by the one loaf, meant that they belonged together in a way that should overcome the social and other differences that had arisen in the church. Thus, the meal was a powerful sign of unity within the local congregation.

The tradition that Paul had passed on to the church at the time of his visit there is found here in its oldest written form. We also have it in slightly divergent forms in the three synoptic Gospels (Matt. 26.26–29; Mark 14.22–25; Luke 22.15–20, reversing the order of wine and bread). In all of these cases, we have a tradition of what Jesus said and did at his Last Supper with his twelve disciples shortly before his death. Analysis of the differences between the accounts shows that we have two basic forms of the tradition, one given by Mark (who is substantially followed by Matthew), and the other found in 1 Corinthians and Luke (though Luke has also been influenced by Mark). The major difference between the two traditions lies in the two sayings of Jesus:

MARK	1 CORINTHIANS
This is my body.	This is my body that is for you. Do this in remembrance of me.
This is my blood of the covenant which is poured out for many.	This cup is the new covenant in my blood (Luke: + which is poured out for you.) Do this, as often as you drink it, in remembrance of me.

There is no agreement among scholars as to which is the older form of the tradition, but the differences are not too significant.

What we have here, then, is an account of the essential elements in the Last Supper that formed the pattern for the church's meal. It has been argued that the story in the Gospels is not so much a part of the story of Jesus as a liturgical text that was preserved on its own and then inserted into the gospel narrative. Some scholars would go further and claim that the story is based on early Christian liturgies rather than on history, the accounts of what the church did having been read back into the lifetime of Jesus. Still others claim that the uncertainty in the tradition of Jesus' sayings and how they express early Christian theology suggest that they are the creation of the early church (or at least that the original form has been heavily modified in transmission), with the result that we can no longer be sure what Jesus said. For example, the presence of the command to "do this" in remembrance of Jesus, which is lacking from Mark's account, given once in Luke and twice in 1 Corinthians, could be due to the early church putting into words what it took to be the intention of Jesus. Even if this is the case, we would still be left with a tradition of Jesus' sharing a loaf and a cup with his disciples, and these actions would invite interpretation. In other words, to account for the origin of the church meal and the early Christians' appeal to Jesus we must surely postulate the historicity of some kind of meal he held.

The Gospels all suggest that the Last Supper of Jesus was associated in some way with the Jewish Passover, though the Synoptics and John disagree on the date of that festival. Like other Jewish formal meals, it began with the breaking and distribution of bread to the accompaniment of a prayer of thanksgiving, and it included the drinking of wine. If it was a Passover meal, the main items of food would have been treated as symbols whose significance needed to be explained. There would then be a precedent for Jesus' explaining the significance of the loaf and the cup. Whether or not a Passover lamb was served (as Luke 22.15 and the story of the preparations for the meal clearly imply), no record has survived of any interpretation of it. Instead, Jesus made three main comments. First, he spoke of this meal as the last that he would eat with his disciples until he ate with them in the kingdom of God (Luke 22.16). This may suggest his imminent death. Second, he made the loaf a symbol of his body, and his distribution of the broken pieces suggests his giving of himself for others. Third, he made the cup a symbol of his blood. Blood, however, signifies death. Jesus associated it with a new covenant, and the echoes of Exodus 24.8 suggest a sacrificial death inaugurating a new covenant. The words "for many" are an allusion to the self-giving of the Servant of the Lord "for many" in Isaiah 53.11–12, And the way in which Jesus performed this act before his death implies that he was giving his disciples a way of remembering him and enjoying some kind of association with him after his death and during the period before they would share together in the kingdom of God. Hence, the meal that his disciples were to celebrate could be regarded as in some sense an anticipation of the meal that the Messiah would celebrate with his disciples in the new age (cf. Matt. 8.11; Luke 14.15). Such a meal would not be merely a symbol or picture of the future meal but would be a real anticipation of it. This is clear from the language of 1 Corinthians 10.16. Here the believers who receive the loaf and the cup participate in the body and blood of Jesus. The language must not be pressed literally, since the body in fact includes the blood; rather, Paul is saying in two ways that believers have a share in Jesus who died for them. This interpretation is confirmed by his point that it is inconsistent for believers to take part also in meals at which food sacrificed to idols was consumed: such a meal was a means of being "partners with demons" (1 Cor. 10.20), that is, having some kind of spiritual relationship to them. It is also confirmed by Luke's implication that the "breaking of bread" in Acts (2.42; etc.) was a continuation of the meals described in the appearances of Jesus after the resurrection.

Last Supper of Jesus

We can now see how Paul meant the meal to be celebrated at Corinth. It certainly was an occasion for joyful celebration rather than a funeral meal, but some of the Corinthian Christians carried this element to excess. But it was supremely a way of proclaiming the death of Jesus as a sacrifice on their behalf and the inauguration of the new covenant. It was an occasion for bringing believers together in unity rather than in disharmony. It was a meal for the temporary period before the Lord would return in triumph, and during that period it was one of the ways in which the union between the Lord and his people was expressed.

In Acts we have further evidence that the believers met regularly to break bread (2.42, 46; 20.7, and possibly 27.35). Since there is no reference in Acts to the cup or to any relevant sayings of Jesus, it is sometimes argued that here we have evidence of a somewhat different meal from the Pauline Lord's Supper, a joyful celebration of fellowship with the risen Lord rather than a memorial of his death. There is, however, nothing incompatible between the two types of account, and the combination of solemn remembrance of the Lord's death and joyful communion with him is entirely appropriate.

John's account of the Last Supper lacks the eucharistic elements found in the other Gospels, because for John it was not a Passover meal; John recorded elsewhere teaching ascribed to Jesus about eating his flesh and drinking his blood (6.53).

There are other allusions to the Lord's Supper in the New Testament. For example, the way in which the stories of Jesus feeding the multitudes are told (Mark 6.30–44; 8.1–10 par.) suggests that the evangelists saw a parallel between Jesus' feeding the people with bread and his spiritual nourishment of the church. And the development of the understanding of the death of Jesus that we find in the New Testament most probably had its roots in the words of institution where the basic concepts of sacrifice and covenant are to be found.

I. HOWARD MARSHALL

LOVE (Hebr. *'ăhăbâ*; *ḥesed*). Human loves in all their rich variety fill the passages of biblical narrative: love at first sight (Gen. 29.18–20: Jacob and Rachel); sexual obsession (2

Sam. 13: Amnon and Tamar); family affection across generations (Gen. 22.2; 37.3; Ruth 4.15: between mother and daughter-in-law); long marital intimacy (1 Sam. 1: Elkanah and Hannah); servile devotion (Exod. 21.5); intense same-sex friendship (1 Sam. 18.1, 3; 20.17: David and Jonathan); enthusiastic loyalty toward a leader (1 Sam. 18.16, 28: Israel and Judah's love of David). But the religious significance of the Bible's view of love lies preeminently with its ways of speaking about God and most particularly about God's relationship with Israel. Israel's election, their redemption from Egypt (and, eventually, Babylon), the giving of the Torah, the promise of the land—all are ascribed in biblical narrative and later rabbinic commentary to the fundamental and mysterious fact of God's love for Israel and the people's reciprocal love of God.

Human love serves as the readiest analogy when speaking of this relationship. God loves Israel as a husband loves his wife (Hos. 3.1; Jer. 2.2; Isa. 54.5–8), a father his firstborn son (Hos. 11.1–3; Jer. 31.9), a mother the child of her womb (Isa. 49.15). God manifests his love in and through his saving acts, most especially in his bringing Israel up from Egypt (Exod. 15.13; Deut. 4.37; 33.3; Neh. 9.17; Ps. 106.7; Hos. 11.4). Narratively and theologically, this liberation culminates in the Sinai covenant, when God gives Israel his *tôrâ* (literally, "teaching"), instructing Israel on their social and religious obligations in light of their election. Chosen by God's love (Deut. 7.7–8; 10.15), Israel is to respond in kind: loving the God who redeemed them and revealed his will to them, teaching his ways to all future generations (Deut. 6.4–7).

The covenant binding God and Israel likewise binds together society. The individual is charged to "love your neighbor as yourself," kindred and foreigner both (Lev. 19.18, 34). The Bible specifies the concrete actions through which this love is to be expressed: support for the poor (Lev. 19.9–10); honesty in measurements and in social interactions (v. 11); prompt payment to laborers; just law courts, favoring neither rich nor poor; respect for the elderly (vv. 13, 15, 32). A system of tithes underlay the welfare both of the poor, the fatherless, and the widowed, and of priests and Levites who, unendowed with land, are "the Lord's portion" (Num. 18.20; Deut. 18.1–2). Right behavior, group affection, and communal social responsibility are thus the concrete measure of Israel's commitment to the covenant. And God, in turn, "keeps" or "guards" his steadfast love for Israel (Exod. 34.7; 1 Kings 3.6; Isa. 54.10; 55.3). Ultimately, Israel's confidence in redemption rests in her conviction that God's love is unwavering, his covenant eternal, his promises sure (Ps. 119.41; 130.7; Zeph. 3.17).

Much of this tradition, both social and theological, comes into the earliest strata of New Testament writings. Paul urges his gentiles in Galatia to be "servants of one another through love [Grk. *agapē*], for the whole law is fulfilled in one word, 'You shall love your neighbor as yourself'" (Gal. 5.13–14, quoting Lev. 19.18). In powerfully poetic language, he exhorts the Corinthians to be knit together as a community through love (1 Cor. 13–14; cf. Rom. 14.15). Mark's Jesus sums up the Torah with the first line of the Shema (love of God) and Leviticus 19.18 (love of neighbor; Mark 12.28–31). The Q material of the later synoptic Gospels extends this last: followers of Jesus are to love not just their neighbor but also and even their enemies (Matt. 5.43–48 par.). Perhaps, by the criterion of multiple attestation, this ethic of passive—indeed, even active (Matt. 5.39–41)—nonresistance may go back to the historical Jesus himself. Paul teaches similarly: persecutors should be blessed; vengeance eschewed; injustice tolerated (Rom. 12.9–13.14; cf. 1 Cor. 6.7; so too other first-century Jewish texts, such as *Joseph and Asenath* 29.3–4 [cf. Prov. 20.22]; Josephus, *Ag. Ap.* 2.30.212 [cf. Deut. 20.19–20; 21.10–14]).

Love became the theological lodestone of nascent Christianity. Christ's sacrifice on the cross was understood as the ultimate sign of God's love for humanity (John 3.16; cf. Rom. 8.39). The eucharist (a community meal celebrating this sacrifice) was referred to as the *agapē*, or "love-feast." Christians exhorted themselves to love one another (see esp. 1–3 John), calling each other brothers and sisters. Such designations and community enthusiasms, misheard at a hostile distance, fueled dislike of the new groups, who were often accused of expressing love carnally at their convocations (Tertullian, *Apology*; Minucius Felix, *Octavius*). Yet in their care for both their own poor and the poor of the late Roman city, Christians, like their Jewish contemporaries, distinguished themselves by acts of public philanthropy—a fact noted with some irritation by the non-Christian emperor Julian (the Apostate, ca. 360; *Epistle* 22). This philanthropy was the social expression of the scriptural injunction to love the neighbor.

The Christian concept of love, in both its social and its theological applications, underwent elaborate and idiosyncratic development in the work of Augustine. In the unprecedented ecclesiastical situation after Constantine (d. 337), with the church increasingly merging with late Roman imperial culture, Augustine argued that the state

The Trinity (Jacopo Robusti Tintoretto, 1564)

coercion of heretics (by which he meant most especially his schismatic rivals, the Donatists) at the behest of the church is an act of Christian love, since it is done for their ultimate spiritual welfare. Theologically, he explored the concept of the Trinity as a dynamic of divine (and, ultimately, of human) loves: the Trinity should be understood on the analogy of the relations between and process of human self-knowledge and self-love (*De Trinitate*). Finally, and most influentially, Augustine came to analyze all humanity (and thus, given his theological anthropocentrism, all reality) according to loves: those enabled by God's love to love God belong to the "heavenly city;" those whom God leaves to their own fallen state love carnal things and thus belong to the "earthly city."

The City of God, Augustine's great masterwork, may thus be seen as a lengthy survey of the history of love, from angels through pagan culture to Israel and finally to the ultimate revelation of God's love through Christ. Fifteen centuries of Western religious thinkers, such as Bernard, Francis, Dante, and Simone Weil, attest to the power of this essentially Augustinian notion of *caritas* and *amor Dei* as the Christian virtues par excellence.

PAULA FREDRIKSEN

LUKE, THE GOSPEL ACCORDING TO. The third gospel is "the first volume" (Acts 1.1) of a two-part work, Luke-Acts, composed by the same author and dedicated to Theophilus. In content, this gospel is related to the Marcan and Matthean gospels; collectively, these three Gospels form the group usually called synoptic, i.e., the tradition that developed independently of the gospel according to John.

Content. The content of the Lucan gospel may be summarized under eight headings. (1) A brief *prologue* (1.1–4), written in a stylized periodic sentence, states the author's purpose in writing. (2) Two chapters are devoted to an *infancy narrative* (1.5–2.52), recounting in studied parallelism the birth and childhood of John the Baptist and those of Jesus. (3) One and a half chapters (3.1–4.13) set forth the appearance of John in the desert, his preaching and baptist career, and his imprisonment by Herod Antipas as a *prelude to the events inaugurating Jesus' public career*, namely, the latter's baptism, sojourn in the desert, and temptation by the devil. (4) The story of *Jesus' Galilean ministry* (4.14–9.50) begins programmatically in a synagogue in his hometown, Nazareth, and moves on to Capernaum and other towns and villages, as Jesus preaches the kingdom of God, heals those who are afflicted, and associates himself with disciples whom he gradually trains. This Galilean activity serves also as the starting point for his "exodus," or transit to the Father through death, burial, and resurrection (9.31). (5) There follows the *travel account* (9.51–19.27), which has both a specifically Lucan form (9.51–18.14) and another form in 18.15–19.27 that parallels Mark 10.13–52. In this account, Jesus is depicted not only as moving without distraction toward Jerusalem, the city of destiny, but also as instructing crowds of people and especially the disciples, who would become the foreordained witnesses of his ministry, career, and destiny in Jerusalem (see Acts 10.41). (6) At the end of the travel account, Jesus is accorded a regal welcome as he enters Jerusalem itself, purges its Temple, and initiates there a period *of ministry and teaching in the Temple* (19.28–21.38), which serves as a prelude to the events of his last days. (7) The *passion narrative* (22.1–23.56a) forms the climax of his exodus, as the Jerusalem leaders conspire with Judas against him, and as he eats his last meal with the twelve and foretells Peter's denial of him. After praying on the Mount of Olives, Jesus is arrested,

The infant Jesus and the infant John the Baptist

brought before a morning session of the Sanhedrin, delivered to Pilate, sent to Herod, and finally handed over for crucifixion. This narrative ends with the notice of Jesus' death and burial. (8) The Lucan *resurrection narrative* (23.56b–24.53) tells of the women who discover the empty tomb and of Jesus' appearance as risen to followers on the road to Emmaus and in Jerusalem itself. The Lucan gospel ends with Jesus giving a final commission to the eleven and others and with his ascension (apparently on the night of the day of the discovery of the empty tomb).

Authorship. Unlike the Pauline letters, which bear the Apostle's name, the third gospel is anonymous, as are the other gospels. Ancient church tradition attributed the third gospel to the Luke who appears in Philemon 24 as Paul's "fellow worker" and is called "the beloved physician" in Colossians 4.14 (cf. 2 Tim. 4.11).

Most modern commentators on the Lucan gospel, however, are skeptical about the validity of this traditional attribution. They regard the tradition as based largely on inferences from the text of the New Testament made when people were first beginning to wonder who had written the Gospels. They further call in question Irenaeus's description of Luke as Paul's "inseparable" collaborator (*Adv. haer.* 3.14,1), which he inferred from the "we" sections of Acts (esp. 16.10; 20.6). The nature of these "we" sections has since been questioned. Are they fragments of a diary or notebook that the author of Acts kept as he journeyed with Paul? Or are they, rather, a literary form used by the author to enhance his narrative of sea journeys? A still larger part of the problem is the relationship of the author of Acts to Paul. In recent decades it has become evident that only with considerable difficulty can one reconcile much of the depiction of Paul in Acts with that which emerges from Paul's own letters. Hence, was the author of Luke-Acts really the "inseparable" collaborator of Paul? The difference between the Lucan Paul and the Pauline Paul is not minor; even though it is largely an issue of Acts and the Pauline letters, it bears on the authorship of the Lucan gospel. The result is that many modern commentators are uncertain about the authorship of Luke-Acts.

A minority of commentators, however, retain the traditional attribution as substantially correct. They recognize that in this tradition one must distinguish between what could have been inferred from the text of the New Testament (Luke as a physician; as Paul's fellow worker; as one who had not personally witnessed the ministry of Jesus; Luke as an author who wrote for gentile converts; who wrote after the Marcan and Matthean gospels; who began his gospel with John the Baptist and was also the author of Acts) and what could not have been so inferred (Luke as a Syrian of Antioch; who wrote in Achaia, Bithynia, or Rome; who died in Boeotia or Thebes, unmarried, childless, and at the age of eighty-four). Many of the latter details are legendary and of no value; but the substance of the tradition—that the author of the third gospel and Acts was Luke, an inhabitant of Antioch in Syria and a companion of Paul—is far from being untenable.

In this regard, one must read Irenaeus critically. The evidence he used, namely the "we" sections of Acts, may indeed show that the author of Luke-Acts was a companion of Paul, but not that he was "inseparably" so. If one accepts the "we" sections as excerpts from a diary or notebook of the author and reads them at face value, one finds that they reveal only that the author was a *sometime* companion of Paul. He would have traveled with Paul from Troas to Philippi (Acts 16.10–17), i.e., for a short time toward the middle of Paul's second missionary journey (49–52 CE). He would have stayed in Philippi and joined Paul again only as the latter departed from Philippi at the end of his third journey (when he returns to Jerusalem for the last time [58 CE; Acts 20.6]), and as Paul sailed for Rome to appear before Caesar (Acts 27.1–28.16). Reading the evidence thus, we see that the author was not with Paul during the main part of his evangelizing endeavors, when he faced the major crisis of his missionary activity in the eastern Mediterranean area (the judaizing problem, as he struggled against those who insisted that gentile converts must observe Jewish legal practices), or when he wrote his greatest letters. Moreover, there is no indication that the author of Luke-Acts ever read Paul's letters. Yet his brief association with Paul led him to idealize Paul and make him the hero of the second part of Acts. He has painted his own picture of Paul, which may not agree in all details with the Paul of the uncontested Pauline letters. Yet, since Luke is not prominent in the apostolic age, if the gospel and Acts were not originally written by him, there is no obvious reason why they should have been associated with him. In other words, the ancient tradition which holds that Luke is the author of the third gospel and Acts may in the long run prove to be substantially valid.

Sources. The prologue of the gospel reveals that Luke depends on other gospel narratives and on information gathered from "eyewitnesses" and "servants of the word" (who may or may not represent two distinct sources for him). From an internal analysis of the gospel, one recognizes that Luke used mainly three sources: the Marcan gospel (in a form more or less as we know it today), a postulated Greek written source, often called Q (some 230 verses common to his and the Matthean gospel but not found in Mark), and a unique source, often designated L, either written or oral (episodes exclusive to the third gospel).

From Mark, Luke has taken over six blocks of material largely in the same order, into which he has inserted matter

The entry of Jesus into Jerusalem (Luke 19.29–40)

(from Q and L); he has also omitted some Marcan material and transposed some Marcan episodes. The use of Marcan material can best be seen thus:

(1) Mark 1.1–15 = Luke 3.1–4.15
(2) Mark 1.21–3.19. = Luke 4.31–6.19
   Luke's Little Interpolation:
   6.20–8.3 (from "Q" and "L")
(3) Mark 4.1–6.44 = Luke 8.4–9.17
   Luke's Big Omission at 9:17
   (= Mark 6.45–8.26)
(4) Mark 8.27–9.40 = Luke 9.18–50
   Luke's Little Omission at 9.50
   (= Mark 9.41–10.12)
   Luke's Big Interpolation:
   9.15–18.14 (from "Q" and "L")
(5) Mark 10.13–13.32 = Luke 18.15–21.33
(6) Mark 14.1–16.8 = Luke 22.1–24.12
   The Lucan Ending: 24.13–53 (from "L")

Luke has not slavishly copied this earlier material; he frequently redacts or modifies the Marcan text, improving its Greek style and language. He has also transposed seven Marcan episodes: (1) the imprisonment of John the Baptist (Mark 6.17–18) is moved up to Luke 3.19–20 (to finish the Baptist story before Jesus appears); (2) Jesus' visit to Nazareth (Mark 6.1–6) is moved up to Luke 4.16–30 (to become the programmatic beginning of Jesus' ministry); (3) the call of the disciples (Mark 1.16–20) is postponed to Luke 5.1–11 (to develop a better psychological setting for the call of Simon the fisherman); (4) the choosing of the Twelve (Mark 3.13–19) and the report of the crowds following Jesus (Mark 3.7–12) are reversed in Luke 6.12–16, 17–19 (to improve the psychological setting for the Sermon on the Plain); (5) the episode about Jesus' relatives (Mark 3.31–35) is moved to Luke 8.19–21 (to follow the interpretation of the parable of the seed, thus making Jesus' own relatives examples of the seed sown on good soil); (6) the foretelling of Judas' betrayal of Jesus (Mark 14.18–21) becomes part of the discourse after the meal (Luke 22.21–23); (7) the order of the interrogation of Jesus, his mistreatment, and Peter's denials (Mark 14.55–643, 640–65, 66–72) is reversed in Luke 22.54c–62 (Peter's denials), 63–65 (mistreatment), 66–71 (interrogation).

It is often difficult to distinguish between L passages and those that Luke may have freely composed. It is also a matter of debate whether some of the L passages are related to the material in the gospel of John (e.g., the anointing of Jesus' *feet* by a woman; the single account of the multiplication of the loaves and fish; the mention of Lazarus, Martha, and Mary; one of the twelve named Judas; no night interrogation of Jesus before the high priest; three nonguilty statements of Pilate during Jesus' trial; postresurrection appearances of the risen Christ in the Jerusalem area). Although there is no real evidence that the Johannine evangelist knew the Lucan gospel, some contact in the oral traditions behind both the Johannine and the Lucan gospels is not impossible.

Attempts are sometimes made to associate L with specific persons from whom Luke would have derived information: Mary, the mother of Jesus (see Luke 2.19, 51); the disciples of John the Baptist (Acts 19.1–3); Joanna, "wife of Chuza, Herod's steward" (Luke 8.3); Cleopas (24.18). Luke could have obtained information from such sources, but such a list of candidates is based on speculation, more pious than critical, about possible informants.

Date and Place of Composition. If the Marcan gospel is rightly included among the sources used by Luke in composing his gospel, then the latter is to be dated after Mark. The Marcan gospel is commonly dated ca. 65–70 CE. How much later is the Lucan gospel? One cannot say for certain. Luke 1.1 refers to "many" others who had previously tried to write the Jesus story; even if Mark is included among the "many," more time must be allowed for the others to whom Luke alludes. Again, since the Lucan Jesus refers to Jerusalem as an "abandoned" house (13–35), this and other references to Jerusalem (21.20, "surrounded by camps"; 19.43–44, with earthworks erected against it) would suggest a date for Luke after the fall of Jerusalem in 70 CE. Some have sought to interpret these references as merely literary imitations of biblical descriptions of the fall of Jerusalem under Nebuchadrezzar, hence lacking in historical references to the Roman destruction. But this interpretation is not without its problems. In any case, it is widely held that the Lucan gospel was composed ca. 80–85 CE even though one cannot maintain this dating with certainty.

Nothing in the Lucan gospel hints at the place where it was composed. The author's knowledge of Palestine is at times defective, which would suggest that it was not composed there. Ancient tradition mentions Achaia, Boeotia, and Rome; modern conjectures include Caesarea, the Decapolis, or Asia Minor. No one really knows where it was written.

Intended Readers. Details in the Lucan gospel suggest that Luke was writing for a predominantly gentile Christian community. Among such details are the dedication of his two-volume work to a patron with what is clearly a Greek name (Theophilus), his concern to relate his narrative account of the Jesus story and its sequel to a Greco-Roman literary tradition, his elimination from his source materials of items with a pronounced Jewish preoccupation (e.g., the controversy about what is clean or unclean, Mark 7.1–23; the substitution of Greek titles like *kyrios,* "Lord," or *epistatēs,* "master" for *rabbi/rabbouni,* cf. Mark 9.5; 10.51 with Luke 9.33; 18.41; and the omission of other Semitic words). All such details suggest that Luke envisaged his readers as predominantly gentile Christians in a Greek speaking setting, but who were not wholly unacquainted with the Septuagint.

Lucan Teaching. Even a brief summary of Luke's interpretation of the Jesus story must cope with its sequel, for details in Acts sometimes bear on the message of the gospel itself. Though the Lucan picture of Jesus may not be as radical as the Pauline or the Marcan, or as sublime as the Johannine, it is nevertheless one of the major testimonies to Jesus in the New Testament.

The Lucan picture of Jesus is kerygmatic. The Christian "kerygma" has been defined by Rudolf Bultmann as the proclamation of Jesus Christ, crucified and risen, as God's eschatological act of salvation. Luke clearly depicts Jesus proclaiming himself in this way, not only as God's agent of promised salvation (4.16–21) but also as the preacher par excellence of God's kingdom: "that is what I was sent for" (4.43). Luke further depicts, no less than the other evangelists, Jesus' disciples sent out to announce the kingdom and to heal (9.1). Later, in Acts, Peter proclaims Jesus Christ not only as crucified and risen but also as "Lord and Messiah" (2.36). Indeed, Peter announces further, "Salvation is found in no one else, for there is no other name under heaven given to human beings by which we are to be saved" (Acts 4.12). Although Luke's gospel has become more of a "Life of Christ" than either Mark's or Matthew's, it has not lost its proclamatory character. It accosts Theophilus, and other readers like him, with God's eschatological salvation achieved in Jesus Christ. Luke's picture of Jesus, now rooted

L

in history in a way that none of the other evangelists root it, has played the kerygma in another key, but it still utters a time-transcending, ever-present, existential challenge to its readers to put personal faith in, and to make a deep commitment to, Jesus the risen Lord and "the Messiah of God" (9.20).

The Lucan picture of Jesus is also drawn in a distinctive historical perspective. Luke's concern is evident from the remark that he has Paul utter before King Agrippa, "None of these things has escaped his [the king's] notice, for this was not done in a corner" (Acts 26.26). Jesus' story and its sequel, intended by God's providence to challenge human beings to Christian faith, has been rooted in human history. This is the reason that Luke has not written a "gospel," as does Mark (1.1), a term he never uses in the first part of his work (but only in Acts 15.7; 20.24), preferring instead to designate his two-volume work as a "narrative account" (*diēgēsis*, Luke 1.1). In this account he roots the Jesus story in a threefold synchronization, connecting it with Roman history, Palestinian history, and church history. Its relation to Roman history is shown by the connection of Jesus' birth with a decree of Caesar Augustus ordering the registration of the whole (Roman) world during the governorship of Quirinius (Luke 2.1–2). The ministry of John the Baptist (and of Jesus, by implication) is connected with the fifteenth year of the reign of the emperor Tiberius (28–29 CE) and with the prefecture of Pontius Pilate in Judea (26–36 CE; Luke 3.1). Luke further connects events in the early Christian community with the famine in the days of Claudius (ca. 46 CE; Acts 11.18), with Claudius's expulsion of Jews from Rome (49 CE; Acts 18.2), and with the proconsulship of Gallio in Achaia (52 CE; Acts 18.12). Again, he connects the birth of Jesus with Palestinian history by linking it with the days of King Herod the Great (37–4 BCE; Luke 1.5); and John's and Jesus' ministry to the time of the high priesthood of Annas and Caiaphas, to the reigns of Herod Antipas, tetrarch of Galilee, of Philip, tetrarch of Ituraea and Trachonitis, and of Lysanias, tetrarch of Abilene (3.1)—even though only Galilee further figures in the Jesus story. Finally, he connects the Jesus story with Christian history in a way that no other evangelist does, by recounting its sequel in Acts. All of this historical perspective, which is exclusively Lucan, is in the long run related to his view of salvation history. Luke sees all of human history divided into three phases: the period of Israel (see Luke 16.16), the period of Jesus (from the coming of John the Baptist to the ascension), and the period of the church under stress (from the ascension to the parousia). This historical perspective is central to the unique Lucan presentation of the Christian kerygma.

The Lucan picture of Jesus is also drawn in a geographical perspective. Luke is preoccupied in his gospel to depict Jesus as moving resolutely from his Galilean ministry, once the travel account begins (9.51), toward Jerusalem, the city of destiny—where his "exodus" is to be achieved (13.32–33). Such a perspective gives Jerusalem a distinctive centrality; towards it, all in the gospel is aimed. Then in Acts it becomes the focal point from which "the word of the Lord" (8.25) goes forth as Jesus' disciples are commissioned as "witnesses" to carry it from Jerusalem to "all Judea and Samaria" and "to the end of the earth" (1.8). Since the last expression can mean "Rome" (see Ps. Sol. 8.15), and since Rome is where the story of Acts ends (see 28.16), Paul becomes the one who in effect carries the word "about the Lord Jesus Christ openly and unhin-

dered" (28.31) from Jerusalem to that "end." Both the historical and the geographical perspectives enhance the status of the church as the sequel to Jesus' ministry in the Roman world of its time.

The Lucan picture of Jesus' ministry and its sequel also has an apologetic perspective. This is Luke's secondary purpose in writing his "narrative account," for he wanted to show that Christianity had as much right to legitimate recognition in the Roman world as did Judaism. Hence, he was concerned from the outset of the gospel to depict Jesus, the founder of Christianity, as born into a pious Jewish family, circumcised, and faithfully observant of Jewish customs. Later on, it emerges in Luke's account that Christianity, a "sect" of Judaism (Acts 24.5, 14), is the logical outgrowth of Pharisaic Judaism. He depicts Paul as stoutly maintaining his Pharisaic connection, by siding with the Pharisees against the Sadducees with respect to "the resurrection of the dead" (Acts 23.6). He further portrays Paul, once he has been taken captive at the end of Acts, as being declared innocent on several occasions (23.9, 29; 25.12, 18–20, 25; 26.31–32). These declarations of innocence imply indirectly that Christianity likewise stands in the same relation to the Roman government.

The key figure in Lucan salvation history is Jesus himself, about whom the evangelist makes not only christological but also soteriological affirmations about who Jesus is and what he has done for humanity. Certain aspects of Jesus, who is otherwise portrayed as a human being, hint at his transcendent condition: his virginal conception through the power of the Holy Spirit; his ministry under the auspices of the holy Spirit; his special relation to his heavenly Father; his resurrection and exaltation to glory. Luke applies many traditional christological titles to Jesus: Messiah (or Christ), Lord, Savior, Son of God, Son of man, Servant, Prophet, King, Son of David, leader, Holy One, Righteous One, Teacher. Particularly noteworthy are the distinctive Lucan use of "Savior" (2.11; Acts 5.31; 13.23), "suffering Messiah" (24.26, 46; Acts 3.18; 17.3; 26.23), and the retrojection of the title "the Lord" (originally used of the *risen* Christ) even into the infancy narrative (2.11; cf. 1.43) and the ministry account, when the evangelist himself is speaking (7.13, 19; 10.1, 39, 41; 11.39; 12.42a; 13.15; etc.). When Luke speaks of the soteriological function of Jesus Christ and the effects of what he has done for humanity, he depicts them as "salvation" (1.69, 71, 77; 3.6; 19.9; Acts 4.12; 13.26, 47; 16.17; 28.28), "forgiveness of sins" (24.47; Acts 2.38; 5.31; 10.43; 13.38; 26.18), "peace" (2.14; 19.38, 42), and "life" (10.25–28; 24.5; Acts 11.18; 13.46–48), and once even as "justification" (Acts 13.39, where the context provides the interpretation of it as "forgiveness of sins"). In a way that surpasses that of the other evangelists, Luke portrays not only the ministry of Jesus itself but even the movement begun by him as especially Spirit-guided. In at least seventeen instances in the gospel and fifty-seven in Acts the influence of the Spirit is seen both on the activity of Jesus himself and on that of his followers.

Hence, though Luke may have introduced a historical perspective in the gospel tradition, he did not simply imitate Flavius Josephus, who composed the *Jewish Antiquities*, by writing merely annalistic *Christian Antiquities*. He has preserved the proclamatory aim of the gospel tradition, and that is why we refer to it as "the gospel according to Luke."

JOSEPH A. FITZMYER, S.J.

MAGI.

The term "magi" customarily refers to the anonymous wise men who followed a star until it led them to Bethlehem (Matt. 2.1–12). While in Luke's gospel shepherds come to worship the child, Matthew introduces mysterious figures from the east who offer gifts from their treasure boxes.

Many details about the Magi are supplied by later tradition. In western Christianity they are assumed to have been three in number since three gifts are mentioned; eastern tradition gives their number as twelve. They traveled by camel, as is normal practice in the desert regions even today. Their names (Balthasar, Melchior, and Caspar, in the west) are supplied later. The fact that they are wealthy and converse with King Herod leads to their identification as three kings.

In fact, the Greek word from which "magi" is derived does not refer to royalty but to practitioners of eastern magical arts. The connection between magic and astrology is reflected in the visitors' fascination with the star that had led them to Bethlehem. Elsewhere in the Bible the portrayal of magi is not so positive. Greek versions of the book of Daniel refer to magi who were ineffective advisers to King Nebuchadrezzar. In Acts, apostles interact with Simon, a magician in Samaria (8.9–24), and Bar-Jesus, who was a magician and false prophet on Cyprus (13.6–12).

DANIEL N. SCHOWALTER

MALACHI, THE BOOK OF.

Since Malachi in Hebrew means "my messenger," it is unclear whether this is the name of the prophet or a description of his office. Usually the book is dated after the time of Haggai and Zechariah but before the coming of Ezra and Nehemiah in the mid-fifth century BCE. A postexilic date is indicated by the reference to a "governor" (1.8) and the fact that the Temple is standing. The abuses Malachi attacks are thought to show the need for the reforms that Ezra and Nehemiah were soon to carry out.

Malachi's question-and-answer style usually begins with a statement from the prophet of some theological truth followed by a question from his hearers. His answer then expounds the original theme. This is a literary device but it may contain echoes of the teaching and preaching practices current in the Second Temple.

A theme prominent in the book is covenant. The stark expression in 1.1–5 of the teaching that God chose Jacob (i.e., Israel) while rejecting Edom, a nation that became a symbol of oppression during and after the exile, is elaborated in the manner of earlier prophets—divine choice is not a ground for complacency but for obedience. The priests (1.6–2.9), for all their status under the covenant (2.8; cf. Jer. 33.21; Num. 25.11–13; Neh. 13.29), have been less zealous in their duties toward God than to the governor. Malachi thinks it would be better for such Temple worship to stop altogether and even contrasts it unfavorably with the offerings of other nations (1.10–11). The whole nation has violated the covenant in their cruel treatment of each other, denying their family status as children of one God, especially in their practice of casual divorce (2.10–16; a warning against intermarriage with foreigners has been inserted into this section, vv. 11–12).

Later, Malachi charges them with neglect of payment of tithes for the upkeep of the Temple and its personnel (3.6–12). Obedience here will result in material prosperity (cf. the words of Haggai about the rebuilding of the Temple, Hag. 1.9–11; 2.15–19). It is important to see that, for Malachi, proper observance of cultic worship was an expression of a true relationship to God ("Return to me," 3.7). Two passages address the despair and disillusionment of his contemporaries as they see no signs of God's activity or of the fulfillment of the old prophetic promises (2.17–3.5; 3.13–4.3). Both bring the assurance that God is about to act in righteousness and that therefore his people should hold the faith. (The passage 3.1b–4, with its switch to the third per

The *Adoration of the Magi* (Rogier van der Weyden, c.1455)

son and introduction of another figure, "the messenger of the covenant," may be a later insertion.)

The book ends with a call to keep the Law of Moses (4.4) and a promise that God will send Elijah the prophet to prepare the people for the final "day of the Lord" (4.5–6) so that it may prove to be a day of salvation and not a repetition of the old judgment of the "curse" (Hebr., Josh. 6.17; Lev. 27.28). Perhaps Elijah was thought of in this role because he had not died but had been taken up to heaven (2 Kings 2). This idea was repeated in Sirach 48.10 and in Mark 9.11.

Malachi shows how the postexilic prophets were deeply concerned for the Temple and its worship and yet held such concern in creative tension with a call for right ethical living. They recognized the dangers the preexilic prophets had warned against, whereby external worship could easily become a substitute for genuine relationship with God, yet challenged their hearers with the call to hold both aspects of the religious life together. Their call was not for mercy rather than sacrifice (cf. Hos. 6.6) but for mercy and sacrifice. They also held together concern for obedience to the Law and a strong eschatological hope of God's future saving action.

The final verses (4.4–6) should be seen as a conclusion not just to the book of Malachi but to the whole prophetic corpus, which ends with "The Book of the Twelve" (i.e., the so-called minor prophets). At a time when the prophetic collections were on the way to being regarded as canonical in status and authority, the function of these verses is to place such collections alongside the Torah as equally authoritative expressions of God's word.

REX MASON

Gathering of the Manna (Exod. 16)

MANNA. Of uncertain origin, in Exodus 16.15 the word "manna" is given a popular etymology by Israelites who asked, when they saw it, "What is it?" (Hebr. *mān hû'*). This was the miraculous food supplied by the Lord to the Israelites during the forty years of their wandering in the wilderness from Egypt to Canaan. Manna is also called, poetically, "bread of the mighty ones [NRSV: angels]" (Ps. 78.25) and "food of angels" (Wisd. of Sol. 16.20).

Early in their Exodus from Egypt, the Israelites came to the wilderness of Sin. There the whole congregation accused Moses and Aaron of bringing them into the wilderness to kill them with hunger. In response the Lord promised to rain down bread for them from heaven (Exod. 16.4). Manna came six days a week. Only one day's portion was to be gathered except on the sixth day; a double portion gathered that day permitted Israel to keep the Sabbath rest. Each morning when the dew had vanished, "there on the surface of the wilderness was a fine flaky substance, as fine as frost on the ground" (Exod. 16.14). It was "like coriander seed, white, and the taste of it was like wafers made with honey" (Exod. 16.31). Its appearance was like "gum resin" (Num. 11.7). The people "ground it in mills or beat it in mortars, then boiled it in pots and made cakes of it; and the taste of it was like the taste of cakes baked with oil" (Num. 11.8). An urn containing a quantity of manna was kept in or in front of the ark of the covenant as a reminder of this divine provision (Exod. 16.32–34; Heb. 9.11).

From ancient to modern times, manna has been linked with natural phenomena in the Sinai region. The traditional identification has been with a granular type of sweet substance thought to be secreted in early summer by the tamarisk bush. More recent investigations suggest that this "manna" is produced by the excretion of two kinds of scale insects that feed on the sap of the tamarisk. Because the sap is poor in nitrogen, the insects must ingest large amounts of carbohydrate-rich sap in order to consume enough nitrogen. The excess carbohydrate is then excreted as honeydew rich in three basic sugars and pectin. The amount of the substance thus produced would, of course, fall far short of Israel's need for bread; in any case, to give a natural explanation for what the Bible describes as miraculous is perhaps to miss the point.

According to the gospel of John, when Jesus was challenged to validate his ministry with a sign comparable to that of manna, he identified himself as the "true bread from heaven," come down to give life to the world (John 6.32–35).

JAMES I. COOK

MARK, THE GOSPEL ACCORDING TO. Mark is the shortest of the four canonical Gospels and was almost certainly the first to be written. Although the use of narrative to record God's salvation of Israel is common in the Hebrew Bible and although there is an obvious correspondence between the story told by Mark and the very brief summaries of the gospel found elsewhere in the New Testament (e.g., Acts 2.22–24), there are no parallels to this precise literary form before early Christianity. In all probability, therefore, the author of this book was responsible for creating the literary genre we know as "gospel."

Contents. Attempts to analyze this gospel run the risk of imposing our interpretation on it. In explicating a text, it is natural to look for an overall pattern, but Mark's story was almost certainly intended to be read aloud, and the impact it made on its first hearers is more likely to be discerned by noting connections between one paragraph and the next rather than by analyzing it into sections, which may obscure such links. This gospel has been built up out of many short units, and one of the features of Mark's arrangement is the frequent sandwiching together of incidents (e.g., 11.11–25). Notable also is the way in which he builds up evidence by a series of stories (e.g., about outsiders, 1.40–2.17; uncleanness, 7.1–30) or by repetition (three passion predictions, 8.31; 9.31; 10.33; two blind men healed, 8.22–26; 10.46–52; two feeding miracles, 6.31–44; 8.1–10; cf. 8.14–21; three summaries of Jesus' activity, 1.32–4; 3.7–12; 6.56). All these devices would help to convey the significance of the story as it was read.

For convenience, the following brief summary is set out in a geographical scheme, but this was not necessarily of particular importance to Mark himself.

The first thirteen verses, which establish Jesus' identity, are set in the wilderness. In 1.14 Jesus moves into Galilee, where he proclaims the kingdom, calls disciples, teaches, exorcises evil spirits, and heals (1.15–4.34); his activity brings him into conflict with the religious authorities. A series of notable miracles follows, as Jesus moves back and forth across the lake, but they are met with unbelief (4.35–8.26). In 8.27–30 Jesus reaches Caesarea Philippi in the far north, where Peter declares him to be the Messiah. As he moves south, Jesus three times foretells his death and resurrection and explains the meaning of discipleship (8.31–10.52). He reaches Jerusalem and the Temple (chaps. 11–13), and the passion narrative unfolds (chaps. 1415). In the final paragraph (16.1–8), women find the tomb empty. Chapter 16.9–20 and the alternative ending given in the NRSV footnote represent attempts by later writers to "complete" the gospel.

Author and Date. The ascription of the gospel of Mark goes back at least to Papias, Bishop of Hierapolis, who in about 130 CE reported that he had been told that it was written by Mark "the interpreter of Peter;" this is presumably the Mark referred to in 1 Pet. 5.13 as "my son Mark." Traditionally, he has been identified with the John Mark mentioned in Acts 12.12, but the latter was associated with Paul and Barnabas, not Peter (Acts 12.25; 15.37, 39; Col. 4.10; 2 Tim. 4.11), and the name "Mark" was one of the most common in the ancient world.

This gospel is usually dated between 65 and 75 CE. The first of these dates is set by Irenaeus (late second century CE), who said that Mark wrote after Peter's death. If we accept Marcan priority, then we must allow time between the composition of Mark and that of Matthew and Luke, which suggests a date before about 75 CE. The only clue in the gospel itself is chap. 13, which predicts the destruction of the Temple; many commentators contrast the vague references to the fate of Jerusalem in Mark 13 with the clear reference to the siege of the city in Luke 21.20 and suggest that this indicates that Mark was written before 70 CE. But Mark 13 is concerned to separate the disasters that are going to overwhelm Judea from the supernatural chaos at the end, and it is arguable that it was written in the period following the former to explain why the end was "still to come" (13.7). The gospel of Mark was probably written, therefore, either immediately before or immediately after the destruction of Jerusalem in 70 CE.

Tradition at least as early as Irenaeus held that it was composed in Rome, but this may have been a deduction from the association with Peter. Support for a Roman origin is sometimes found in Mark's use of Latinisms (e.g., *quadrans,* a coin, 12.42), but these were probably familiar throughout the Roman empire. Explanations of Jewish words and customs, together with a poor knowledge of Palestinian geography, suggest that Mark was writing for gentiles living outside Palestine, but they do not point to any particular place. The emphasis on the inevitability of suffering for Jesus' followers could well be explained if this gospel were written for a community that was suffering for its faith: although the Roman church was persecuted in the time of Nero, it was by no means alone, since persecution of Christians was common at the time.

Sources. Mark's gospel contains very little material that is not included by Matthew, and the earliest explanation, given by Augustine, was that it was an abbreviation of Matthew's gospel. But Luke has to be taken into account also, since he, too, includes a great deal of this material. According to the most commonly held solution to the synoptic problem, Mark's gospel was used as a major source by Matthew and Luke. This solution is not without problems, and the suggestion that they used an earlier version of Mark (*Urmarkus*) is an attempt to explain some of the differences from Mark that Matthew and Luke have in common. An alternative theory (known as the Griesbach hypothesis) argues that Mark used both Matthew and Luke as sources, but careful study of the parallels suggests that the Marcan version was probably the earliest.

The belief that Mark's gospel was a record of Peter's reminiscences was challenged by the work of form critics who argued that it was based on short units of oral tradition that had been handed down to the Christian communities and had been shaped by their situations and beliefs. C. H. Dodd suggested that Mark had fitted these units into a chronological outline of the ministry of Jesus, but the supposed outline proved too vague to be of value. It is possible that some of the material used by Mark, such as the conflict stories in 2.1–3.6, had already been gathered together at the oral stage, and it is commonly believed that the passion narrative had already been written down as a continuous narrative. The rise of redaction criticism, however, with its emphasis on the evangelists as authors rather than as mere collectors, has led to the realization that Mark himself may have been responsible for almost all the arrangement of the material and that his only sources may have been the individual units of tradition.

Readers. Mark probably wrote his gospel for one specific Christian community, and the problems and situation of that community will have governed the way in which he has set out the story; but these can only be deduced from the book itself. The way in which the passion narrative dominates the story suggests that the nature of Jesus' death caused Mark's readers difficulty: Mark's answer to the scandal of the crucifixion is seen in the paradoxical revelation of Jesus as Messiah and Son of God through his death. The suggestion that Mark was concerned to attack a "false Christology" is an anachronistic notion; we should think rather of a community that had not yet come to terms with the idea of a crucified Messiah. Similarly, the teaching about discipleship may indicate that its members had not grasped what this entailed: warnings that it involved following in the steps of Jesus suggest that persecution was either an imminent danger or had already taken them by surprise, while those warnings in Mark 13 that the end is "still to come" and that suffering will continue, suggest that the community was puzzled by the delay in the promised arrival of the kingdom.

The portrait of the twelve as slow to comprehend the truth about Jesus has been interpreted as an attack on the church leaders in Mark's day, but it should probably be understood in relation to the "messianic secret".

M

The Healing of the Woman with an Issue of Blood (William Blake, 1818)

Interpretation. For many centuries Mark was the least used of the gospels, being overshadowed by the longer synoptics, but the theory of Marcan priority, linked with the Petrine tradition, led to the belief that this gospel was the most reliable historically and so brought Mark into the forefront of critical study toward the end of the nineteenth century. In 1901, Wilhelm Wrede challenged this assumption in his study of the secrecy motif in the Gospels and argued that Mark was a theological presentation, not a historical record. In the 1920s, the development of form criticism strengthened the realization that Mark could not be treated as an eyewitness account of Jesus' ministry; attention came to be focused on the beliefs of the community that had shaped the tradition collected by the evangelist. The subsequent growth of redaction criticism shifted scholarly interest to Mark himself and to his role in the final shaping and arranging of the material; the evangelist was now acknowledged to be a theologian rather than a historian or a collector-editor. This led in the 1970s to the recognition that Mark's gospel had to be considered in relation to the community in which Mark lived, since he was influenced by that community and sought to influence it; we may thus hope to learn about the situation and beliefs of the community through him.

In studying this book, therefore, we need to ask questions at several historical levels. We can ask, first, about the way in which Mark understood the gospel and about the circumstances of the community for whom he wrote. Moving backward, we may ask about the traditions he inherited, and about the beliefs of the earliest Christians. Only then should we move to the final stage and raise questions about what Jesus himself may have said and done.

The historical problems are so complex that some commentators have abandoned them altogether and looked for other ways of interpreting Mark. Literary analysts insist that the text itself has a meaning, and some, such as structuralists, have no concern for the original intention of the author; since, however, the meaning discovered differs from one interpretation to another, it would seem that it is imposed by the reader rather than found in the text. In fact, all interpretation involves a large subjective element, since all readers of Mark's gospel (or any other text) inevitably interpret it in terms of their own experiences, but when historical criticism is abandoned there is no control over the process.

Mark's Presentation of the Gospel. Mark begins by setting out the identity of Jesus: he is the Messiah (1.1); his coming fulfills scripture (1.2–3), since he is the mighty one announced by John the Baptist, the messenger of the Lord (1.4–8); he is proclaimed by God as his Son, and the Spirit of God is with him (1.9–11); in the power of the Spirit he confronts Satan in the wilderness (1.12–13).

These first thirteen verses provide vital information that enables us to understand the rest of the story. From this point on, however, the truth about Jesus is stated only rarely, and then obscurely, until the very last chapters. If we compare these opening verses with the prologue of a Greek drama, we will realize that in reading them we have been privileged to receive information that is hidden from the characters of the story, who are bewildered by the events that follow. Although Jesus' identity is known to unclean spirits (1.24) and confirmed again from heaven (9.7), it remains hidden from the religious authorities, the crowds, and even the disciples, who only half comprehend. This is partly because of human obtuseness (8.18), but Mark also depicts Jesus as silencing anyone who comes near the truth (1.25, 34; 3.12; 8.30).

The messianic secret can no longer be explained as historical reporting; nor is it, as Wrede suggested, the result of imposing a messianic interpretation on a nonmessianic tradition. Rather, from the standpoint of Christian faith the significance of Jesus' words and deeds seem clear, and the failure of his contemporaries to recognize him as Messiah needs explanation. Mark's solution is that the truth was concealed from them, partly by divine purpose, partly by their own obstinacy; but to those with eyes to see and ears to hear, all is now plain: Mark's story is thus concerned with messianic revelation as much as messianic secrecy.

Miracles play an important role in Mark's gospel, and he makes clear in editorial summaries that there were in fact many more healings and exorcisms than those he describes. The miracles are greeted by onlookers with amazement and incomprehension, though their significance is recognized by unclean spirits (1.24; 3.11; 5.7) and implied by Jesus in 3.22–30: through the power of the Holy Spirit he has defeated Satan and is saving men and women from his clutches. Jesus' authority to heal encompasses not only the exorcism of unclean spirits, but restoration of all kinds: cleansing a leper (1.40–45), forgiving sins (2.1–10), raising the dead and giving new life (5.21–43). His power extends over nature, so that he is able to control the sea (4.35–41; 6.45–52) and give the people bread (6.31–44; 8.1–10), both manifestations of divine power reminiscent of the Exodus; yet the scribes accuse him of working under Satan (3.22), his family think he is mad (3.21), he meets with disbelief in his hometown (6.1–6), the Pharisees demand a sign from him (8.11–13), and his own disciples are unable to grasp the significance of what they have seen (8.14–21). To Mark's readers, however, the miracles demonstrate Jesus' authority, since they know the answer to the disciples' bewildered question, "Who then is this?" (4.41).

It is only those with faith who can receive healing (5.34, 36; 6.5–6; 7.29; 9.14–24), and the stories themselves become paradigms for the meaning of faith. The man who has ears but cannot hear until Jesus touches them (7.31–37), the blind man who has eyes but cannot see, and who receives his sight gradually (8.22–26), the man who cries, "I believe; help my unbelief" (9.24), and the beggar who receives his sight and follows Jesus on the way to Jerusalem (10.46–52) all tell us something of what belief in Jesus means.

Mark emphasizes also Jesus' role as teacher and makes use of a considerable amount of teaching, though less is included than in Matthew and Luke. According to Mark 1.14–15, the gospel announced by Jesus concerned the kingdom of God. Yet by his arrangement of the material, Mark makes it plain that the gospel is about Jesus himself: the kingdom is given to those who become his disciples. By their response to Jesus, men and women are divided into those who belong to his community and those who remain "outside" (4.11; cf. 3.31–35). Much of the teaching is thus appropriate only to those who are disciples and even they find it difficult to understand. As with the miracles, however, the significance of the teaching is plain to those readers of Mark's gospel who have eyes and ears to understand.

The major block of teaching occurs in chap. 4, in which Jesus teaches the crowd in parables. Mark believes the teaching to be deliberately enigmatic: the disciples should have understood, yet they require an explanation (4.10–12). In 8.31–10.52, Jesus teaches the disciples about his own destiny as the Son of man, together with the understanding of discipleship that necessarily follows, but they are unable to comprehend. The final section of teaching (chap. 13), addressed to four disciples, warns them of future judgment on Jerusalem and of persecution for themselves.

Other sayings occur in conflict stories and are thus addressed to Jesus' opponents. Notable examples are the debates about purity (7.1–23) and divorce (10.1–12), where Jesus challenges the Pharisees' interpretation of Mosaic teaching, and the parable of the vineyard (12.1–12). All demonstrate Jesus' authority, and because his opponents reject it, they are naturally outraged by this teaching.

Jesus acts with authority, but makes no direct claims for himself; when referring to himself he uses the enigmatic phrase "the Son of man." It is others who, with varying degrees of understanding, declare his identity. The truth is partly grasped by the disciples at Caesarea Philippi: in contrast to outsiders, who regard Jesus as some great prophet figure (8.28; cf. 6.14–16), Peter acknowledges him to be the Messiah; but the need for Jesus to suffer and die cannot yet be understood at this stage (8.27–33), and for Mark, the identity of Jesus is revealed fully only through his death and resurrection (9.9). The great irony of his story is that when we come to the passion narrative, those responsible for Jesus' death unknowingly identify Jesus. The high priest announces the truth when he asks whether he is "the Messiah, the Son of the Blessed One" (14.61); Pilate executes him on the charge of being "King of the Jews" (15.2, 9, 12, 18, 26, 32); and when he dies, his executioner proclaims him "God's Son" (Mark 15.39). Since this title earlier came from heaven (1.11; 9.7), it may be assumed that Mark believed it to be the fullest expression of the truth about Jesus. In the mouth of the Roman centurion, the phrase is remarkable: Mark appears to be affirming that through the crucifixion Jesus is fully revealed and faith is born. For Mark, the death and resurrection of Jesus provide the key to the whole story. The cross is thus no accident, but part of the divine plan.

The declaration of faith (as Mark interprets it) by a gentile brings to a climax another of Mark's important themes. Jesus proclaims the kingdom to Israel, but he is rejected by his own people—by family (3.21–35), hometown (6.1–6),

religious leaders (14.1–2), one of his disciples (14.10–11), and finally by the crowd (15.6–15). He pronounces judgment on the nation's religious leaders (3.28–30; 7.6–13; 11.11–20; 12.1–12, 38–40), and foretells destruction for Jerusalem (13). His ministry appears to end in failure. Yet he dies as "a ransom for many" (10.45; cf. 14.24) and promises future vindication for his disciples (8.35; 13.27). Who, then, are the "many?" The word probably refers to all those who belong to the people of God, and for Mark that means those men and women who have responded to Jesus. There are occasional hints that gentiles will be included: in 7.24–30, a gentile woman receives help because of her faith; in 13.10 we are told that the gospel must be preached "to all nations" (cf. also 14.9); moreover, Mark is clearly writing for gentiles (7.3). The centurion's confession, together with the rending of the Temple curtain, confirms that the vineyard has been taken away from the original tenants and given to others (12.9).

The gospel of Mark ends abruptly, at 16.8, and early attempts to add an ending show that it was felt to be incomplete. It is possible that the book was never finished or that it was damaged at an early stage. Yet it may be our knowledge of the other Gospels that makes us expect this one to end with appearances of the risen Lord. Certainly, it ends in an appropriate way for Mark—with fear, human failure, and the call to discipleship: it is those who respond and who follow the risen Lord who will see him.

MORNA D. HOOKER

MARY MAGDALENE. Mary Magdalene is one of the inner circle of the followers of Jesus in the Gospel narratives. Her

St. Catherine of Alexandria, St. Mary Magdalene and St. Margaret of Antioch (Master of the Trebon Altarpiece, 1380)

M

name suggests that she came from Magdala, a large city on the western shore of the Sea of Galilee, also called Taricheae (Map 10: Y3). Magdala was known for its salt trade, for its administrative role as a toparchy, and as a large urban center that was part of the contiguous cities and large villages along the western shore of the lake from Tiberias to Bethsaida/Chorazin.

Mary Magdalene is mentioned sparingly but at crucial points in all four Gospels. During the events surrounding the crucifixion of Jesus, she is depicted as watching the proceedings and waiting near the tomb to attend to the body (Matt. 27.56, 61; 28.1; par.; John 19.25). She is also one of the first witnesses to the resurrection (Matt. 28.9; John 20.11–18). These passages probably gave rise to the romantic portrayals of Mary as the devoted follower whom Jesus had saved from her errant ways.

Contrary to subsequent Christian interpretation, reflected in popular belief and recent films, there is no evidence from the Gospels that Mary Magdalene was a prostitute or for the later identification of Mary Magdalene with the women who anoint Jesus' feet (Luke 7.36–50; Matt. 26.613 par.) or with Mary of Bethany (Luke 10.38; John 11.1–2). In Luke 8.2 it is said that Mary Magdalene was healed of seven evil spirits by Jesus. But this is in the context of a list of women who were followers of Jesus, who had also been healed, and who supplied the material support for his mission. Since Mary Magdalene, Chuza (the wife of a steward of Herod) and Susanna are the only women mentioned, it is likely that these three were the benefactors of the Jesus movement according to Luke.

J. ANDREW OVERMAN

MARY, MOTHER OF JESUS. According to ancient Christian sources, Mary was the child of Jewish parents Joachim and Anne and was born in Jerusalem or Sepphoris in Galilee. If, as the sources suggest, Mary's first child Jesus was born around 4 BCE and she was espoused around the age of

fourteen, as was common, then Mary was probably born in 18 or 20 BCE.

During her childhood she lived in Nazareth, where she became engaged to the carpenter Joseph, who was descended from King David. The gospel of Luke relates that an angel of God appeared to Mary and told her that she would become pregnant with God's son by the Holy Spirit, even though she was not yet married. Mary and Joseph traveled to Bethlehem where Jesus was born in a stable or, according to later traditions, cave. According to Jewish custom, Jesus was circumcised and then presented at the Temple in Jerusalem. He was raised by Mary and Joseph and perhaps other relatives in Nazareth and probably learned the carpentry trade. One relative specifically mentioned by Luke is Mary's cousin Elizabeth, who in her old age gave birth to John the Baptist shortly before Jesus' birth. Some of the sources indicate that other children were born to Mary and Joseph after Jesus (e.g., Acts 1.14).

The gospel of Luke, the principal biblical source for Mary in the narratives of Jesus' infancy and childhood, also tells how, when Jesus was twelve years old, Mary and Joseph took him to the Jerusalem Temple—again, in fulfillment of Jewish law—for initiation into the faith. On the return journey, they lost him in the crowd and subsequently found him in the Temple impressing the religious leaders with his wisdom (Luke 2.41–52).

Joseph, probably considerably older than Mary, disappears from the sources at this time, and Mary's role becomes smaller as Jesus' becomes larger. She is mentioned in the context of the marriage feast at Cana (John 2.1–12), at Jesus' crucifixion (but only by John 19.25–27), and in Acts 1.14, the story of Pentecost. The accounts of Mary's later years, death, and assumption into heaven are found only in traditions outside the Bible, some as late as the fourth century CE. It is not known where she spent her final years, but it is generally believed that she lived with John the son of Zebedee in Jerusalem and died there. The date of her death is almost impossible to determine.

In addition to the gospel accounts, Mary is mentioned in the writings of some of the church fathers, including Justin Martyr, Ignatius, Tertullian, and Athanasius; in apocryphal works such as the Protevangelium of James (second century); and in the deliberations of the Council of Ephesus (431 CE), where she was proclaimed Theotokos, "God-bearer." A gnostic gospel of Mary and a Latin work from the Middle Ages called *The Gospel of the Birth of Mary* also exist.

It is through these and other sources that the powerful cult of Mary was born and grew, especially in the Roman Catholic, Anglo-Catholic, and Orthodox churches. Various feast days commemorate her importance for devotees: the Immaculate Conception (8 December), her purification in the Temple (2 February), the annunciation of the angel (25 March), her visit to Elizabeth when both were pregnant (2 July), and her assumption into heaven (15 August). Throughout the centuries, Mary has been revered not only as the Mother of God but also as a pure, ever-virgin woman, the perfect mother, the intercessor between human beings and God, and one who knows the deepest of human suffering, having borne witness to the agonizing and humiliating death of her firstborn son. She has been the object of pilgrimages and visions even to the present day, and the "Magnificat," attributed to her by Luke at the time of her visit to Elizabeth (Luke 1.46–55), has been part of Christian liturgy and music for centuries. Mary has

Michelangelo's *Pieta* in St. Peter's Basilica in Rome

been widely honored and even worshiped as representing inner strength and the exaltation of the oppressed over the oppressor.

Non-Christian sources are instructive in tracing parallels to the cult of Mary. Virgin Birth stories (e.g., Hera, Rhea Silvia, Brigid) were circulated in other cultures, as were tales of mothers mourning lost and deceased children (e.g., Demeter and Persephone; Isis and Horus). Iconographically, just as Mary was often portrayed holding or nursing the infant Jesus, so too was the Egyptian goddess Isis depicted suckling her infant son, Horus. Even as Mary was called Queen of Heaven and sometimes depicted surrounded by the zodiac and other symbols, so too were the deities Isis, Magna Mater, and Artemis.

Such parallels show that Mary's cult had roots in the cults of the female deities of the Greco-Roman pantheon, cults ultimately eradicated by Christianity. While Mary in some ways represents qualities impossible for human beings, especially women, to emulate—ever-virgin yet motherly; always gentle and obedient to God's will—her attributes nevertheless represent for many devotees important female properties not provided by the traditional all-male Trinity. For many, the adoration of a female figure is a vital psychological supplement to their faith.

VALERIE ABRAHAMSEN

MATTHEW, THE GOSPEL ACCORDING TO.
Matthew's gospel proclaims the message that in Jesus, Son of God, God has drawn near with his eschatological rule to dwell to the end of time with his people, the church (1.23; 16.16; 28.20). The purpose of this message is to summon the reader or hearer to perceive that God is uniquely present in Jesus and to become Jesus' disciple. As Jesus' disciple, one becomes God's child, lives in the sphere of his end-time kingdom, and engages in mission so that all people may find him in Jesus and also become Jesus' disciples.

Structure. Matthew is a gospel story in three parts. The main divisions derive from the formula that appears in 4.17 and 16.21: "From that time Jesus began to proclaim [to show his disciples] . . ." Embedded in this story are also five great speeches of Jesus. The following outline marks off the three parts of the story and indicates the distribution of the speeches:

I. The presentation of Jesus (1.1–4.16)
II. The ministry of Jesus to Israel (4.17–11.1)
    A. The Sermon on the Mount (5.1–7.29)
    B. The missionary discourse (9.35–10.42) and Israel's repudiation of Jesus (11.2–16.20)
    C. The discourse in parables (13.1–52)
III. The journey of Jesus to Jerusalem and his suffering, death, and resurrection (16.21–28.20)
    A. The ecclesiological discourse (17.24–18.35)
    B. The eschatological discourse (24.1–25.46)

As is apparent, the story that is told is of the life and ministry of Jesus. It begins with his miraculous conception and birth and closes with his death and resurrection.

Jesus drives the money changers from the temple, saying they have made the Lord's house a den of robbers (Matt. 21.12–13).

The temporal setting in which this story of Jesus takes place is the history of salvation. This begins with Abraham, the father of Israel, and extends to the consummation of the age and the return of Jesus for judgment (1.17; 25.31–46). It divides itself into two distinct epochs. The first epoch is the time of Israel, which is the time of prophecy (e.g., 2.5–6). The second epoch is the time of Jesus (earthly-exalted), which is the time of fulfillment (e.g., 1.22–23). For its part, the time of Jesus (earthly-exalted) encompasses the ministries to Israel of John (3.1–2), of Jesus (4.17), and of the pre-Easter disciples (10.7), as well as the ministry to the nations of the post-Easter disciples (24.14; 28.19–20). Central to this time, however, is the ministry of Jesus himself, for the ministry of John prepares for it and the ministries of the pre-Easter and post-Easter disciples are an extension of it.

In combination, the twin features of structure and view of salvation history advance a weighty theological claim on behalf of Jesus. As was noted, the structure of Matthew's story focuses on the life and ministry of Jesus. The view this story projects of the history of salvation describes Jesus both as the one in whom the time of Israel attains its fulfillment (1.17) and the one who is at the center of the gospel of the kingdom that is to be proclaimed to the nations (24.14; 26.12–13). Accordingly, the theological claim these two features advance is that for the salvation of all people, Jews and gentiles, the life and ministry of Jesus is of decisive significance.

Author, Date, Place. It is commonly held that Matthew was written about 85 or 90 CE by an unknown Christian who was at home in a church located in Antioch of Syria. A date toward the end of the first century seems probable because the destruction of Jerusalem, which occurred in 70 CE, appears to be an event that was rapidly receding into the past (22.7). Although the apostle Matthew may have been active in founding the church in which the gospel story attributed to him arose (9.9; 10.3), it is unlikely that he was the story's author. On the contrary, the author exhibits a theological outlook, command of Greek, and rabbinic training that suggest he was a Jewish Christian of the second rather than the first generation (cf. 13.52). Also, Antioch of Syria commends itself as the place where he may have been at home, because the social conditions reflected in his story correspond with those that seem to have prevailed there: the city was Greek-speaking, urban, and prosperous, and it had a large population of both Jews and gentiles.

Readers. Scholarly opinion holds that the church for which Matthew was written was made up of Christians of both Jewish and gentile origin. Socioculturally, this church was almost certainly living in an atmosphere of religious and social tension. Its mandate was to make disciples of all nations, and this was apparently provoking hostile reactions from both Jews and gentiles. Seemingly, Christians were being hauled into court by gentile authorities, judicially harassed, hated "by all," and even put to death (10.18, 22; 13.21; 24.9). Similar persecutions were likewise taking place at the hands of the Jews: Christians were being made to submit to such ill-treatment as verbal abuse (5.11), arraignment for disturbing the peace (10.17), perjured testimony in court (5.11), flogging in the local synagogues (10.17; 23.34), pursuit from city to city (10.23; 23.34), and even death (10.28; 23.34–35).

As a body, the church of Matthew appears to have achieved organizational autonomy and to have been materially well off. Religiously, these Christians were no longer living under the jurisdiction of contemporary Pharisaic Judaism (15.13; 16.18). Quite the opposite, they already had in place the means for making their own decisions concerning matters of church doctrine and church discipline (16.19; 18.15–20). Identifiable groups within the church were prophets, or itinerant missionaries, and teachers (10.17–18, 41; 23.34). Socioeconomically, the way in which both monetary matters and ethical and religious questions associated with the topic of riches are treated in Matthew indicates that the church in which it arose was relatively prosperous.

But Matthew's church was also rife with dissension. Under the pressure of persecution, some Christians apostatized (13.21; 24.10), while others betrayed fellow Christians to enemies (24.10); still others fell victim to the "cares of the world and the lure of wealth" (13.22). Hatred broke out among Christians (24.10), false prophets arose who led others astray (7.15; 24.11), and disobedience to the law of God was so rampant that the "love of many was growing cold" (24.12). It was to meet the religious and moral needs of this multiracial, prosperous, yet divided and persecuted church that the author of Matthew told afresh the gospel story.

Sources. Some scholars hold that Matthew was the first gospel story written, that Luke was the second, and that Mark is a synopsis of both Matthew and Luke. Most scholars, however, espouse the two-source hypothesis in resolving the synoptic problem. According to this view, Mark was the first of the gospel stories, and both Matthew and Luke are based on Mark, a sayings source called "Q," and

traditions peculiar to each ("M" and "L," respectively). Although the latter hypothesis is to be preferred, one ought not to be misled by source analysis into thinking that, in its final form, Matthew presents itself simply as a sum of layers of tradition. Instead, it constitutes a coherent story possessing a recognizable beginning, middle, and end.

Story of Jesus. In the first part of the gospel story (1.1–4.16), Jesus is presented to the reader. Initially, the narrator describes him as the Messiah, son of David, and son of Abraham (1.1). Jesus is the Messiah, the Anointed One, Israel's long-awaited King (1.17; 2.2, 4; 11.2–3). He is the son of David because Joseph adopts him into the line of David (1.16, 18–25), and he fulfills the eschatological expectations associated with David (9.27–31; 12.22–23; 15.21–28; 20.29–21.17). He is the son of Abraham, as well, because in him the entire history of Israel attains to its culmination, and the gentiles, too, find blessing (1.17; 8.11).

Upon Jesus' birth, the Magi arrive in Jerusalem and ask where they might find the King of the Jews (2.1–2). To Herod, and later to Pilate as well, this title denotes that Jesus is a pretender to the throne or an insurrectionist. Thus, Herod plots to have Jesus found and killed (2.13), and Pilate hands him over to be crucified (27.26, 37). In Matthean perspective, Jesus is in truth the King of the Jews, but not because he aspires to the throne of Israel or foments rebellion against Rome, but because he saves his people by submitting to suffering and death (27.27–31, 37, 42).

John the Baptist is Elijah returned, the forerunner of Jesus (3.1–12; 11.10, 14). He prepares Israel for the coming of Jesus by calling for repentance in view of the nearness of God's endtime kingdom and the final judgment (3.2, 10–12).

The baptismal scene constitutes the climax of the first part of Matthew's story (3.13–17). After John has baptized Jesus, God empowers Jesus with his Spirit and declares him to be his unique Son whom he had chosen for messianic ministry (3.16–17). This declaration by God reveals that the Matthean Jesus is preeminently the Son of God. The significance of this title is that it points to the unique filial relationship that Jesus has to God: conceived and empowered by God's Spirit (1.18, 20; 3.16), Jesus is "God with us" (1.23), the one through whom God reveals himself to humankind (11.25–27) and who is God's supreme agent of salvation (1.21; 21.37; 26.28; 27.54).

Guided by the Spirit, Jesus submits to testing by the devil (4.1–11). Three times the devil endeavors to get Jesus to break faith with God. Jesus, however, rebuts the tempter and shows himself to be the Son who knows and does his Father's will. Returning to Galilee, Jesus is poised to begin his public activity (4.12–16).

The second part of Matthew's story (4.17–16.20) tells of Jesus' ministry to Israel (4.17–11.1) and of Israel's repudiation of him (11.2–16.20). Through his ministry of teaching, preaching, and healing (4.23; 9.35; 11.1), Jesus summons Israel to repentance (4.17; 11.20–21). Israel, however, repudiates Jesus (chaps. 11–12), yet wonders and speculates about his identity (11.3; 12.23; 13.55; 14.2; 16.14). In sharp contrast to Israel's false view that Jesus is a prophet of whatever identity (16.14), the disciples correctly confess him to be the Messiah, the Son of God (14.33; 16.16).

The third part of Matthew's story (16.21–28.20) describes Jesus' journey to Jerusalem and his suffering,

M

death, and resurrection. The passion predictions sound this theme (16.21; 17.22–23; 20.17–19; cf. 26.2), and the motif of the journey binds together disparate materials (16.21–21.11). In Jerusalem, Jesus makes the Temple the site of his activity, where he teaches, debates, and speaks in parables (21.12–23.39). Addressing the parable of the wicked husbandmen to the Jewish leaders, Jesus raises the claim that he is the Son of God whom the leaders will kill (21.37–39). In wanting to arrest Jesus for telling the parable (21.45–46), the leaders show that they reject Jesus' claim.

At his trial, it is the claim that Jesus made in his parable, to be the Son of God, that the high priest uses to secure Jesus' condemnation (26.63–66). When Jesus replies to the high priest's question in the affirmative (26.64), he is sentenced to death for blaspheming God. The irony is that God has indeed affirmed Jesus to be his Son (3.17; 17.5).

Upon Jesus' death, the Roman soldiers also affirm Jesus to be the Son of God (27.54). What the reader knows and the soldiers do not is that the death of Jesus Son of God constitutes the climax of his earthly ministry and the act whereby he atones for the sins of humankind (1.21; 26.28). Atop the mountain in Galilee, Jesus appears to the disciples as the resurrected Son of God who remains the crucified Son of God (28.5, 16–20). Seeing Jesus as such, the disciples at last perceive not only who he is (16.16) but also what he has accomplished (26.28). In consequence of this, they receive the commission to go and make of all nations Jesus' disciples (28.18–20). Matthew's story ends, therefore, with both the disciples and the reader sharing the same perception of Jesus and receiving his commission.

Story of the Opponents. Entwined with the story line of Jesus in Matthew is the story of his opponents. These are the Jewish leaders, who form a united front against him and comprise such groups as the Pharisees, Sadducees, chief priests, elders, and scribes. Not until Jesus' arrest do the Jewish crowds turn on him (26.55).

The story of the Jewish leaders develops in close correlation with that of Jesus. In the first part of Matthew (1.1–4.16), the leaders are presented to the reader and cast in an unfavorable light. Thus, they make their debut as the supporters of King Herod who place their knowledge of scripture in his service (2.1–6). Like Herod and all Jerusalem, they are frightened at hearing the news that the Messiah, the King of the Jews, has been born. Subsequently, as John the Baptist readies Israel for the coming of Jesus (3.1–12), the Jewish leaders too go out to him. Instead of receiving them, however, John denounces them as a "brood of vipers" (3.7) and in so doing characterizes them as "evil" (cf. 12.34). How such evil is to be construed comes to light in the temptation and other pericopes. In the temptation (4.1–11), the devil, the fountainhead of all evil, three times puts Jesus to the test in order to get him to break faith with God (4.1–11). Later in Matthew's story, the Jewish leaders likewise repeatedly put Jesus to the test in order to best him in debate (16.1; 19.3; 22.18, 35). Accordingly, the Jewish leaders are evil in Matthean perspective because they have affinity with Satan.

In the second part of Matthew's story (4.17–11.1; 11.2–16.20), conflict erupts between Jesus and the Jewish leaders (chap. 9), but it does not immediately become mortal (chap. 12). At the point it does become mortal, three features characterize it: it is sparked by a question having to do with the Mosaic Law itself (12.1–8, 9–14); it is acutely confrontational in nature, in the sense that Jesus is himself directly attacked for an act he himself is about to perform (12.9–14); and it engenders such rancor in the Jewish leaders that they go off and conspire about how to destroy Jesus (12.15). Once the conflict takes this turn toward irreconcilable hostility, death looms as Jesus' certain fate.

As Jesus journeys toward Jerusalem in the third part of Matthew's story (16.21–28.20), only once does he clash with the Jewish leaders, and the purpose this serves is the instruction of the disciples (19.3–12). Not until after Jesus has reached Jerusalem, therefore, does his last great confrontation with the Jewish leaders prior to his passion take place (21.12–22.46). As Jesus teaches in the Temple, the various groups of Jewish leaders approach him, one after the other, in order to challenge him or, at the last, to be challenged by him (21.15, 23; 22.15–16, 23, 34–35, 41). The note on which all of these controversies end is that Jesus reduces all of the leaders to silence (22.46). The result is that they withdraw from the Temple to plot the immediate arrest and death of Jesus (26.3–5).

From their own standpoint, the Jewish leaders believe that by bringing Jesus to the cross, they are doing the will of God and purging Israel of a fraud (26.65–66; 27.63). Nevertheless, God shows, by raising Jesus from the dead and exalting him to all authority in heaven and on earth, that he puts Jesus in the right in his conflict with the Jewish leaders (28.6, 18). The upshot is that the death of Jesus becomes in Matthew not the occasion of Jesus' destruction but the means whereby God accomplishes the salvation of all humankind, Jew and gentile alike (26.28).

Story of the Disciples. The third story line in Matthew is that of the disciples. Because Jesus gathers no followers until he begins his public ministry to Israel, it is not until the second part of Matthew's story that the disciples make their appearance (4.17–16.20).

The focus in the first half of the second part of Matthew (4.17–11.1) is on the call and the task of the disciples. As Jesus bids Peter and Andrew and James and John to come after him (4.18–22), he directs attention to the nature and the purpose of discipleship. The purpose of discipleship is as absolute as engaging in worldwide missionary activity (4.19). Its nature reveals itself in the fact that when Jesus summons the four fishermen, they forsake nets, boat, and father (profession, goods, and family) to give him their total allegiance. Through their being "with him" (12.30), he grants them to live in the sphere of God's end-time rule and makes of them a family (12.48–50), or brotherhood (23.8; 28.10), of the "sons of God" (5.9, 45) and of his disciples (10.24–25).

In the Sermon on the Mount, the Matthean Jesus describes the piety the disciples are to practice. As those who live in the sphere of God's end-time rule, their piety is to be that of the greater righteousness (5.20). To do the greater righteousness, they must be "perfect," that is to say, they must be single-hearted in their devotion to God (5.48). What such single-hearted devotion entails is loving God with heart, soul, and mind, and one's neighbor as oneself (5.44–48; 7.12, 21; cf. 22.34–40).

Further interaction between Jesus and the disciples or a would-be follower provides additional insight into the significance of the call to discipleship. In turning away the scribe who would arrogate to himself the authority to become a disciple (8.19–20), Jesus shows that one cannot, apart from his enabling call, either enter upon or sustain the life of discipleship. In commanding the disciple who would go bury his father to follow him instead

M

into the boat (8.21–22, 23), Jesus discloses that the life of discipleship brooks no suspension. In chiding the disciples for displaying cowardice in the face of a storm while at the same time calming the winds and sea, Jesus reveals that although he does not condone their succumbing to the weakness of "little faith," he nonetheless stands ever-ready to assist them as they carry out whatever mission he entrusts to them (8.23–27). And in calling the tax collector Matthew to be his disciple (9.9), Jesus teaches all the disciples that he has come to gather not only the good and upright but also the despised.

As Jesus called his first disciples, the task he set before them was that of mission (4.19). With the circle of the twelve now closed (10.2–4), Jesus summons them for instruction in the first mission they are to undertake, to Israel (10.5–42). This mission is an extension of Jesus' own mission: like him, they too are to go "to the lost sheep of the house of Israel" (10.6; 15.24); and like him, they too are to proclaim the nearness of the kingdom and to heal the sick and exorcise demons (10.1, 7–8).

In the latter half of the second part of Matthew's story (11.2–16.20), the disciples stand out as the recipients of divine revelation. In contrast to Israel, which repudiates Jesus and shows itself to be uncomprehending, the disciples receive from God the gift of understanding (11.25–26; 13.11, 51). This encompasses insight into the mysteries of the kingdom of heaven (13.11) and knowledge of Jesus' identity: far from being a prophet as the Jewish public imagines, Jesus is, the disciples affirm, the Messiah, the Son of God (14.33; 16.13–16).

In the third part of Matthew (16.21–28.20), the story of the disciples describes how Jesus finally overcomes their unwillingness to accept the truth that the essence of discipleship is servanthood. Although the disciples know that Jesus is the Son of God, they do not know that the fate of the Son of God is suffering and death. In the first word Jesus speaks to the disciples in the third part, he predicts his passion (16.21). Peter takes offense at this (16.22), but Jesus rebukes Peter and solemnly warns all the disciples that only those can belong to him who are prepared to take up their cross and follow him (16.23–24). The proper response to suffering sonship is suffering discipleship or servanthood (20.25–28). Because the disciples resist this notion, they are unable to persevere with Jesus in his passion and fall away: Judas betrays him (26.49); all desert him (26.56); and Peter denies him (26.69–75).

But though the disciples fall away, the risen Jesus again gathers all of them except Judas (27.3–10) through the word he sends to them that they should meet him in Galilee (28.7, 10, 16). In gathering his scattered disciples, Jesus reconciles them to himself. Moreover, as the disciples, standing on the mountain, see the risen Jesus bearing on his person the marks of crucifixion, they are at last able to comprehend that Jesus' sonship has indeed been suffering sonship. In comprehending this, they likewise comprehend that suffering sonship is a call to suffering discipleship or servanthood. So enlightened, they recast their lives in accord with Jesus' earlier words: "If any want to become my followers, let them deny themselves and take up their cross and follow me" (16.24).

JACK DEAN KINGSBURY

Stained glass Menorah

MENORAH. The seven-branched candelabrum of the wilderness tabernacle and Jerusalem Temples, it was typical of Iron Age elevated metal structures combining the functions of lampstand and lamp. The tabernacle menorah, anachronistically described in the postexilic Priestly code (P) (Exod. 25.31–40 and 37.17–24), was said to have been hammered, together with all of its lamps and utensils, from one whole talent (ca. 44 kg [96 lb]) of pure gold by the craftsman Bezalel. Based on a tripod, three branches curved from both sides of a vertical shaft; these, with the central stem, were decorated with cups carved in the shape of open almond blossoms, the uppermost holding the lamps. These botanical motifs may reflect tree of life symbolism, common in the ancient Near East.

According to 1 Kings 7.39 (and 2 Chron. 4.7), ten pure gold lampstands, which are not described in detail, together with gold accoutrements, adorned Solomon's Temple, five on the south side of the main hall, and five on the north. The Second Temple, following the priestly directions for the wilderness tabernacle, had one golden menorah. According to Josephus (*Ant.* 3.8.199), three of its lamps burned all day; the rest were lit in the evening. The Talmud relates that the westernmost lamp, closest to the Holy of Holies, was never extinguished (*b. Yoma* 33a). The menorah was removed in 169 BCE by Antiochus Epiphanes IV (1 Macc. 4.49–50) during his desecration of the Temple. Judas Maccabee supplied a new menorah, together with other vessels, during the Temple's cleansing (1 Macc. 4.49–50; 2 Macc. 10.3). Josephus recounts that when Herod's Temple was destroyed in 70 CE, the menorah was carried by the Romans in Titus's triumphal march (*War* 7.5.148–9). The Temple menorah seems to be depicted on the Arch of Titus in Rome, although there is some controversy over this rendition's accuracy, particularly regarding the double octagonal pedestal, since according to all Jewish sources and considerable archeological evidence, the menorah stood on three legs. After 70 CE, the menorah became an enduring Jewish religious and national symbol, frequently appearing in synagogue, domestic, and funerary art; it appears today on the emblem of the State of Israel.

JUDITH R. BASKIN

MESSIAH. The term denotes an expected or longed-for savior, especially in Jewish tradition, where some applied it to the revolutionary Simon Bar Kokhba (d. 135 CE), the mystic Shabbetai Zevi (1626–1676), and other "false messiahs," and in Christianity, where it is exclusively applied to Jesus Christ.

The word is derived from the common biblical Hebrew word *māšíah,* meaning "anointed." In Greek it is transcribed as *messias* and translated as *christos.* In the Hebrew Bible, the term is most often used of kings, whose investiture was marked especially by anointing with oil (Judg. 9.8–15; 2 Sam. 5.3; 1 Kings 1.39; Ps. 89.20; Sir. 46.13), and who were given the title "the Lord's anointed" (e.g., 1 Sam. 2.10; 12.3; 2 Sam 23.1; Pss. 2.2; 20.6; 132.17; Lam. 4.20). It is even used of Cyrus, king of the Medes and Persians (Isa. 45.1). There is a possibility that some prophets may have been anointed (see 1 Kings 19.16; cf. Isa. 61.1), and according to some texts the investiture of priests includes anointing too (Exod. 29.7; Lev. 4.3, 5, 16; Sir. 45.15), though this probably reflects political developments after the fall of the monarchy; the title is not normally given to priests or prophets. In a passage from Zechariah dated 520 BCE, where king and priest are described as "the

Christ at the Column (Antonello da Messina,1475)

two anointed ones," the term *māšíah* is avoided (Zech 4.14; cf. 6.9–14). By Maccabean times, however, it is used of the high priest (Dan. 9.26).

In its primary biblical usage, then, "anointed" is, virtually a synonym for "king," in particular David and his descendants, and it should be understood in the context of the royal ideology documented in the books of Samuel, Kings, and Psalms, even when it is applied secondarily to priests and others. The king was appointed by divine command (1 Sam 10.1; 16.1–13; Ps. 45.7), and he was adopted as son of God (2 Sam 7.14; Ps. 2.7; cf. 89.26). His own person was sacrosanct (1 Sam 24.6), the future of his dynasty was divinely protected (2 Sam 7.12–16; 22.51; Ps. 89.4, 36–37), and he was the unique instrument of God's justice on earth (2 Sam. 23.3; 1 Kings 3.28; Pss. 45.4; 72.1–4; cf. 2 Sam. 14.4; 2 Kings 3.28). As with the ideals and the realities of Zion, the Temple, the priesthood, and other institutions, the gap between the ideals of Davidic kingship and historical reality widened (e.g., 1 Kings 11.6; 2 Kings 16.1–4; 21.118; cf. Deut. 17.14–17), and eventually royal language and imagery came to be applied primarily to a hoped-for future king, whose reign would be characterized by everlasting justice, security, and peace (Isa. 11.1–5; 32.1; Jer. 33.14–26; Ezek. 37.24–28). Such a figure is popularly known as "the messiah," and biblical texts that describe him are known as "messianic," though the term "messiah" itself does not occur with this sense in the Hebrew Bible.

At the heart of biblical messianism is the idea that God intervenes in history by sending a savior to deliver his people from suffering and injustice. Influenced by the Exodus tradition (e.g., Exod. 2.19; 3.7–12), the stories of Joshua and Judges (cf. Judg. 2.16, 18), and established religious institutions, this messianic hope crystallized into several models. The first is that of a king like David who would conquer the powers of evil by force of arms (Gen 49.10; Num. 24.17; Pss. 2.9; 18.31–42) and establish a reign of justice and peace (Isa. 9.2–7; 11.1–5). In some passages his wisdom is referred to (Isa. 9.6; 11.2; cf. 1 Kings 3.9; Prov. 8.15–16; 24.5–6), in others his gentleness and humility (Isa. 42.2–3; Zech. 9.9–10). Emphasis is on the divine initiative (2 Sam. 7.8–16; Jer. 33.14–16; Hag. 2.21–23) and on the result of the action, so that some visions of a "messianic" age make little or no mention of the messiah himself (e.g., Isa. 2.2–4; 11.6–9; 32.1, 16–20; 65.17–25; Amos 9.11–15).

Belief in a priestly messiah, son of Aaron, who would arise alongside the Davidic messiah to save Israel, appears in the Dead Sea Scrolls (e.g., 1QS 9.1). The mysterious figure of Melchizedek (Gen 14.18) provides a title for one who is at the same time both king and priest (Ps. 110.4; Heb. 7). A third model is that of a prophet, anointed to "bring good news to the oppressed" (Isa. 61.1; 11Q Melch. 18; Luke 4.18). The belief that a prophet like Moses would arise (Deut. 18.18; Acts 3.22), known as Taheb ("he who brings back"), is central to Samaritan messianism (cf. John 4.25).

Finally, the tradition that the divinely appointed savior should suffer (Luke 24.26; Acts 3.18) has its roots in numerous psalms attributed to David (e.g., 22; 55; 88), as well as in the traditional picture of Moses and the prophets as rejected and persecuted by their people (Exod. 16.2; 17.2–4; Jer. 11.18–19; 20.7–10; Matt. 23.37). The notion that his suffering or selfsacrifice is in itself saving (cf. Exod 32.32; Isa. 53.5, 10, 12) is given a unique emphasis in Christian messianism (e.g., Rom. 5.6–8; Gal. 3.13; cf. Acts 8.32; 1 Pet. 2.24–25).

JOHN F. A. SAWYER

METHUSELAH. One of the long-lived ancestors before the Flood. In the Sethite genealogy in Genesis 5.21–27 (see also 1 Chron. 1.3; Luke 3.37), which lists one male for each of the ten generations from Adam to Noah, Methuselah is listed eighth, the son of Enoch and the grandfather of Noah. Methuselah is the longest lived (969 years), but all ten live to remarkably high ages, as do the pre-Flood ancestors of Mesopotamian tradition. The name Methusaleh is very like Methushael, listed as Lamech's father and Enoch's great grandson in the similar genealogy in Genesis 4 (seven male ancestors from Cain to Noah).

JO ANN HACKETT

MICAH, THE BOOK OF.

The Author. Micah, a shortened form of Micaiah (which occurs in Jer. 26.18), means "Who is like Yah(weh)?" He was a person of whom we know practically nothing other than his place of origin, which was Moresheth (Mic. 1.1) or Moresheth-gath (1.18), a tiny village in the Judean foothills (Map 8:W5). (Mic. 1.8–16, doubtless Micah's own words, confirms the information in the title of the book supplied late by an editor at 1.1, since here he seems to be speaking of the small part of the world that he knew best.) From other internal evidence it is likely too that the other data of the opening title are valid, namely, that he spoke "in the days of Kings Jotham, Ahaz, and Hezekiah of Judah."

He was, in other words, a Judahite seer or prophet, roughly contemporary with the much better known Isaiah.

Although Micah's comments on Judean society strongly parallel those of his presumed contemporary and supplement them to a large degree, there is a pronounced difference in tone between the prophecies of Isaiah and Micah. Micah's is the voice of the countryside, of one who has empirical knowledge of the result of the evil policies that Isaiah, an aristocrat of Jerusalem, could only surmise, however much he wanted to empathize with the suffering of his compatriots. Micah was presumably from the common people, one who felt himself called on in that age of turmoil to speak in the name of Israel's God against evils that were no longer tolerable.

The Times. Although the book of Micah may contain much material that was added to or expanded on that of the original prophetic author, its nucleus goes back to Micah of Moresheth, who, in the latter part of the eighth century BCE, was protesting the internal dissolution of his country and of its religious and national nerve. His prophetic career may have begun about 725 BCE when it had become evident that the northern kingdom of Israel—where prophecy had begun and which had always been the "elder sister" of the kingdom of Judah to the south (Ezek. 23.1–3)—was now doomed to disappear into the outreaches of the voracious Assyrian empire. Judah, by a combination of cynical statecraft, collaborationism, and religiously unacceptable compromise, would still be able to hold off the inevitable for a time; indeed, it outlasted the Assyrians only to become prey to their Neo-Babylonian successors. But this was done by the sacrifice of national and religious integrity, and in the end the result was the same, as Ezekiel (chap. 23) pointed out after the fact.

The Book. The book of Micah, as has already been suggested, begins with the work of an eighth-century BCE prophet whose words have been adapted to changed conditions, added to, and amplified in later generations. This process says nothing against the transmission of the biblical word but rather enhances its integrity. The biblical word, in the mind of those who preserved and developed biblical traditions, was not dead, said for one time, but a living word that could continue to inspire the faith community in which it had been engendered to further insights into the mind of God. Accordingly, the contents of the book of Micah can be outlined as follows:

1.1	A title from a later Judahite editor
1.2–7	A judgment on Samaria: Micah's, but later edited into a universal judgment
1.8–16	Micah's lament over Judah of his day
2.1–5	Micah's particular condemnation of the exploiters
2.6–11	Micah's retort to the "naysayers" of prophecy
2.12–13	Vision of a "new Israel" inspired by Second Isaiah or Ezekiel
3.1–4	Micah's judgment against the rulers of Judah
3.5–8	Against the "prophets of peace" (cf. Jer. 6.14; 8.11)
3.9–12	The end of Jerusalem
4.1–4	The eschatological Zion: a postexilic hymn (= Isa. 2.2–4)
4.5–8	Yahweh and the gods; probably a postexilic fantasy
4.9–11	An exilic or postexilic realization of Judah's fate in the Babylonian period

4.11–5.1   The siege of Jerusalem: Sennacherib's in 701?

5.2–6   The ruler to come; possibly Micah's words

5.7–9   The restoration of the remnant of Jacob; obviously exilic or postexilic

5.10–15   An oracle of judgment, probably Micah's

6.1–8   God's lawsuit against Israel, possibly Micah's

6.9–16   God's judgment on social injustice, especially of the northern kingdom; probably Micah's, at least substantively

7.1–7   Another condemnation of social justice, probably by Micah

7.8–10   Recovery of Zion; some postexilic prophet

7.11–20   Rebuilding of Zion and Zion's prayer; some prophet after 445 BCE.

BRUCE VAWTER, C.M.

MIRIAM. Sister of Moses and Aaron. Miriam is presumably the sister who watches over Moses in the bulrushes in the story in Exodus (2.4, 7–8; see Num. 26.59). She is called a prophet in Exodus 15.20, when she leads the women dancing with tambourines after the victory at the Sea of Reeds (cf. Jephthah's daughter in Judg. 11.34). Then in Exodus 15.21 she is said to sing the first verse of the song just attributed to Moses (15.1–18). Since both Moses and Miriam are connected in the text to this "Song of the Sea," it has been speculated that the song was originally attributed to Miriam (cf. the Song of Hannah in 1 Sam. 2.1–10; the Song of Deborah in Judg. 5:1–30; and the reports of women singing victory songs in 1 Sam. 18:7; 21:11; 29:5; 2 Sam. 1:20). The process by which the name of a dominant figure like Moses could become attached to a piece of poetry and supplant the name of a less common figure like Miriam is more easily understood than the converse.

The other major biblical story about Miriam is her and Aaron's criticism of Moses' leadership in Numbers 12. They complain for two reasons, that Moses has married a "Cushite" woman and that Yahweh has spoken through them as well as through Moses (see Exod. 4.14–16; 15.20; Mic. 6.4). The story in fact serves to affirm Moses' position as leader (vv. 6–9). Yahweh is greatly angered by their complaints and punishes Miriam (but not Aaron, despite v. 11) for speaking against Moses. She is afflicted with a skin disease that turns her skin white. Aaron asks Moses to intercede with Yahweh on her behalf, and when he does she is healed after spending seven days outside the camp (see the reference to this story in Deut. 24.9 and cf. Lev. 13–14). The reference to a father spitting in his daughter's face and the seven-day period of purification (v. 14) is obscure. If Cush in this story is meant to refer to Ethiopia, as it often does in the Bible, then Miriam's white-as-snow skin is an ironic punishment for a complaint that would have included her objection to Moses' taking an African wife. More likely Cush here refers to Midian (see Cushan in Hab. 3.7) and Moses' marriage to the Midianite woman Zipporah (Exod. 2.11–22) is the source of the criticism, although the reference could still also have suggested the dark skin color of Ethiopians in contrast to Miriam's disease.

Miriam died while the Israelites were at Kadesh, and she was buried there (Num. 20.1). She was remembered in Micah 6.4 as one of the leaders of the Exodus along with Moses and Aaron.

JO ANN HACKETT

MOAB. A nation whose affiliation with Israel may have been the closest of all her neighbors. This is indicated by the affinity of the Moabite language and writing tradition to Hebrew; by David's ancestry from the Moabite Ruth and his sending his parents for sanctuary in Moab (1 Sam. 22.3–5); by the legend of Moab's birth through the incestuous union of Lot and his elder daughter (Gen. 19.30–37); and by religious affinities to Yahwism portrayed in the Moabite Stone.

Moab (Map 1:Y5–6) lay along the east side of the Dead Sea. North Moab, including the plains of Moab opposite Jericho (Num. 22.1; 33.48–49), covered an area from just north of the top of the sea to the Arnon 40 km (25 mi) south, which is mostly well-watered tableland, 600–850 mi (2000–2800 ft) above mean sea level; here lay Heshbon, the peaks of Nebo and Pisgah, Medeba, Beth-meon, Ataroth, and Dibon. South ("true") Moab, from the Arnon to the Zered, the boundary with Edom, is tableland 300 m (1000 ft) higher and more marginal agriculturally. A text of Pharaoh Ramesses II (early thirteenth century BCE) designates this region by the name Moab. Topographic survey, which at first seemed to display an occupation gap from roughly 2000 to 1300 BCE, has more recently contributed evidence of settlement throughout the second millennium, even in the south. Probably Moab was first a tribal society, then a monarchy.

Relations between Moab and Israel are complex and difficult to discern from the record—whether enmity or amity. The issue is bound up with whether north Moab was under Moabite control. Thus, Numbers 21 depicts the Amorite king Sihon as having displaced Moab from north of the Arnon and makes Sihon, not Moab, Israel's foe. The Balak/Balaam story in Numbers 22–24, on the other hand, portrays enmity and puts the action in north Moab. Deuteronomic tradition condemns Moab for inhospitality to Israel during the. Trans-jordanian trek (Deut. 23.34; Judg. 11.17), but asserts that Yahweh granted Moab its (southern?) territory, so Israel is not to harass Moab (Deut. 2.9). Judges 3.12–30 pictures enmity, showing Moab in possession of the north with a foothold at Jericho ("city of palms"); Judges 11, on the other hand, implies amity with Moab (11.24–27).

Saul reportedly defeated Moab (1 Sam. 14.47–48), but it is David who subjugated it, militarily and by vassal treaty (2 Sam. 8.2). The next explicit information comes from the Moabite Stone about 830 BCE, where Mesha, king of Moab at Dibon, asserts he liberated north Moab from the control of the Israelite northern kingdom's Omri Dynasty, dispossessing the "men of Gad" during Ahab's reign or more probably at Ahab's death about 850 BCE (2 Kings 1.1; 3.4–8). Mesha's inscription implies that Omri had regained this control; had Moab escaped subjugation sometime between Solomon and Omri? The accounts in 2 Kings 3 (Jehoram of Israel) and 2 Chronicles 20 (Jehoshaphat of Judah) contribute contemporary episodes of conflict with Moab, further suggesting struggle for independence at the end of the Omri dynasty. And 2 Kings 10.32–33 places Hazael of Damascus in north Moab in this period; perhaps Moab gained freedom from Israel only to lose it to Syria.

Moab came under loose Assyrian control, probably through vassal treaty, around 732 BCE. In the mid-seventh century, it functioned as loyal vassal by quelling Arab rebellion against Assyria. Moab appears as Nebuchadrezzar's client (2 Kings 24.2), helping put down Jehoiakim's revolt around 600 BCE. This period of subservience to the great powers is the setting for Amos 2.1–3, Isaiah 15–16, and Jeremiah 48 (cf. Num. 21.27–30), which link Moab

M

to Yahweh's international dominion. These oracles judge Moab, lament over it, and convey to it divine promises. After the Babylonian conquest of the region, Moab disappears from available records, though the Ezra-Nehemiah campaign against mixture with foreigners suggests that Moab still designates a people in the late fourth century BCE (Ezra 9.1–2; Neh. 13.23).

EDWARD F. CAMPBELL

MONOTHEISM. Discussion of monotheism in the ancient world sometimes blurs the distinction between theology and religion. In non-Western settings, religion is a complex of behaviors that mark a culture. Theology, however, involves cohesive ideological speculation to justify behaviors. A single religion can have many competing or complementary theologies.

Scholars have traditionally taken a theological and prescriptive approach to the issue of Israelite monotheism: monotheism is the conviction that only one god exists, and no others. This conviction is, however, difficult to document.

Ancient Near Eastern Background. Egyptian, Mesopotamian, Hittite, Greek, and early Canaanite myths all present developed pantheons. These texts relate how one generation of gods succeeds the next just as humans succeed one another; this succession entails war among the gods. In Mesopotamia, the creation of the universe results from this conflict. Mesopotamian, Hittite, and Canaanite myths relate how the storm god defeats the sea god (in Egypt, the battle is essentially between the Nile and the desert): a god responsible for life-giving water wins control of the cosmos. The focus in all of these myths is the succession of a patriarchal high god's royal son.

These pantheons all have a high god, under whose direction other gods—of the sun, of pestilence, and so forth—act, often independently. The high god is usually the state god. In some cases, the subordinate gods in the state pantheon represent local high gods, of areas in an empire. Thus different states may share essentially identical pantheons but identify different high gods: in Mesopotamia, the Babylonian high god was Marduk; the Assyrian high god was Ashur. Sennacherib had the Babylonian creation epic rewritten to award Marduk's role in it to Ashur.

Yet state myths did not reflect the subjective experience of a worshiper in a god's cult. Mesopotamian literature is filled with pleas to gods and goddesses, such as Ishtar of Arbela, Ishtar of Nineveh, Shamash (the sun god), and Addu (biblical Hadad). In prayer, the god being addressed is the sole object of devotion.

Scholars refer to this phenomenon as effective henotheism, devotion to one god conceding the potency of others. This principle was elevated to state policy in Egypt under Akhnaton (ca. 1350 BCE), the pharaoh who channeled resources into the cult of the solar disk at a cost to competing cults. A similar attempt to impose a god atop a state pantheon, under the sixth-century BCE Babylonian king Nabonidus, exhibits the same characteristics, with statues of all the other gods being brought to Babylon, possibly for the New Year. Nabonidus's attempt, like Akhnaton's, proved abortive.

These failures, however, show that the line between monotheism and polytheism should not be too precisely drawn. Akhnaton and Nabonidus, the two great religious reformers of Near Eastern antiquity, focused the cult on their respective gods. Not dissimilar are the monotheistic traditions of Judaism, Christianity, and Islam: all admit the existence of subordinate divinities—saints, angels, demons, and, in Christianity and Islam, Satan, the eternal antagonist of the high god. But if these traditions are not monotheistic, no religion (as opposed to theology) is. The term monotheism loses its meaning.

Monotheism, Yehezkel Kaufmann observed, postulates multiple deities, subordinated to the one; it tolerates myths of primordial struggle for cosmic supremacy. Two elements distinguish it from polytheism: a conviction that the one controls the pantheon, and the idea of false gods.

Ancient Israel and Its Immediate Neighbors. From the outset, Israelites identified themselves as "the people of YHWH" (Judg. 5.13). The expression implies a societal commitment to a single, national god. Israelite personal names offer confirmation: these include either the name of a god or a divine epithet. Almost uniformly, the god in Israelite personal names is YHWH or an epithet of YHWH, such as "god" 'el), "lord" (*ba'al*), or "(divine) kinsman" ('amm).

This practice resembles that of the Transjordanian nations of Ammon, Moab, and Edom, Israel's nearest neighbors and, in the folklore of Genesis 12–25, closest relations. Conversely, in Canaanite and Phoenician city-states, personal names include the names and epithets of a variety of gods and goddesses. The ethnic nations that emerged in Canaan in the thirteenth–twelfth centuries BCE, unlike the states of Syria and Mesopotamia, are early tied to national gods.

None of these cultures, however, denied the existence of divinities other than the high god. The ninth-century Moabite Stone, though treating the national god, Chemosh, as Israel treated YHWH, nevertheless mentions sacrifice to a subordinate of his. An eighth-century inscription from Deir 'Allā, in the Israelite-Ammonite border area, mentions a pantheon, or group of gods, called Shaddayin. Similarly, many biblical texts, from the twelfth century down to the Babylonian exile, describe the divine court over which YHWH presides as the council of the gods: these report to and suggest strategy to YHWH, praise YHWH, and are assessed by YHWH (Deut. 32.43b [with 4QDeutª]; 1 Kings 22.19–23; Isa. 6; Pss. 29.1–2; 82.1, 6; Job 1.6–2.10). In monarchic theologies, the subordinate gods administered other nations for YHWH (Deut. 32.8–9 [LXX]; Mic. 4.5; 1 Sam. 26.19). But they also received Israelite homage—the sun, moon, and host of heaven, the stars who fought as YHWH's army against Canaan (Deut. 33.2–3; Josh. 5.13–14; cf. 10.12–13; Judg. 5.20; 1 Kings 19.19–23): the host was YHWH's astral army, and YHWH was regularly represented through solar imagery.

The astral gods—the host of heaven—figure prominently in early sources. The meaning of YHWH's name has long been in dispute. However, the name associated with the ark of the covenant, and prevalent throughout the era of the monarchy, is YHWH Seba'ot ("Lord of Hosts"). On the most common interpretation of the name YHWH, this means, "He [who] summons the hosts [of heaven] into being." If so, the full name of Israel's god in the Pentateuch's Yahwistic source (J), YHWH Elohim, means, "He [who] summons the gods into being." And before the revelation of the name YHWH to Moses, the Priestly (P) source calls the high god El Shaddy: originally, this, too, associated YHWH with sky gods, Shaddayin, known from the Deir 'Alia inscription.

The Israelite cult also embraced the ancestors. Israelites invoked the ancestors for aid in matters familial, agricultural, and political. The ancestral spirits could intervene with YHWH, to the benefit of the family, the landholding corporation that inherited its resources from the fathers.

The Emergence of Monotheism. Starting apparently in the ninth century BCE, Israelites began to distinguish YHWH starkly from other gods. It is unknown whether the distinction originated from the opposition between YHWH and foreign high gods or between YHWH and local ancestral gods. Still, the alienation of the local gods from YHWH ensued, as subordinate gods were identified as foreign.

Our first indications of the cleavage come from a ninth-century nativist revolution against the house of Omri, the ruling dynasty of the northern kingdom of Israel. Solomon had earlier constructed a Temple in Jerusalem. This Temple incorporated representations of cherubim (1 Kings 6.23–29) and, judging from later developments, probably of YHWH's asherah, or consort, Ashtoret (Astarte). Opposite the Temple, Solomon also consecrated shrines to YHWH's subordinates—Ashtoret, Milkom, and Chemosh (1 Kings 11.7; 2 Kings 23.13–14). After seceding from Jerusalem under Jeroboam I, the kingdom of Israel had maintained a more conservative separation of state shrines from the capital. Ahab, however, installed a new temple in Samaria (1 Kings 16.32); in the Near East, a temple in the capital signified a divine grant of dynasty. Jehu's revolt, however, destroyed the temple and reaffirmed Jeroboam's cultic policy (2 Kings 10.18–29; cf. Hos. 1.4).

The earliest biblical writer to contrast YHWH with his subordinate deities is Hosea. This eighth-century prophet rejects calling YHWH Israel's "baal" (lord) and claims that attention to the "baals" (YHWH's subordinate gods) deflects attention from the deity responsible for their ministrations (see especially Hos. 2). The alienation of the subordinates (who in the traditional theology administer other nations for YHWH) from YHWH, who administers Israel, permits Hosea to identify pursuit of the "baals" with foreign political alliances. Intellectually, the same alienation was part of a critique of traditional culture leveled by the "classical," that is, the literary, prophets.

In the eighth century, Israel enjoyed a trading network embracing the Assyrian empire in western Asia and Phoenician trade outposts around the Mediterranean. As a bridge on the spice trade route to the south, and as a producer of cash crops such as olives and grapes, Israel underwent incipient industrialization, developing capital reserves. Foreign goods, texts, and practices became increasingly familiar to a growing middle class. In reaction, the elite was impelled to define distinctively Israelite values and culture. Groping for its identity, the elite discovered the gap between the elite theology, in which YHWH was completely sovereign, and popular practice, with its devotions to subordinate deities and ancestors; between theology, in which repentance was increasingly individuated, and ritual repentance, a matter of behavior, not attitude; between theology, in which one worshiped an unseen god, and a cult employing icons. The critique by the literary prophets thus predicated that the symbol or manifestation—the icon, the ritual, the subordinate god—was alien from, and not to be mistaken for, the Reality—the high god, or one's own inner essence.

Ahaz of Judah first implemented this critique, removing plastic imagery from the Temple nave (2 Kings 16.17). In preparation for the Assyrian invasion of 701, his successor Hezekiah concentrated the Judahite population in fortified towns; his ideologians articulated attacks on the high places, the centers of traditional rural worship, and on the ancestral cult, linked to the agricultural

M

Giovanni Francesco Barbieri's *The Eternal Father*

207

areas he planned to abandon to the aggressor (Isa. 28). Assyria then deported most of the population outside of Jerusalem; Hezekiah's spokesmen took this as YHWH's judgment on the rural cult, which they interpreted to be identical with the cult of the northern kingdom (Isa. 1–5)—Samaria had fallen prey to total deportation in 720. Jerusalem's survival, by contrast, represented YHWH's imprimatur on the state cult.

Some scholars hypothesize that Israelite monotheism was husbanded by a small, "Yahweh-alone" party until the time of Hezekiah or even Josiah. However, no text indicates such a doctrine before Josiah's reign, and the chief indices suggest its gradual development rather than some perpetual keeping of a flame. Solomon's high places, for example, survived Hezekiah's reform, although the "Mosaic" snake-icon, Nehushtan, did not (Num. 21. 5–9; 2 Kings 18.4). Child sacrifice continued in the Jerusalem Topheth—an activity directed toward the host of heaven (Jer. 19.13). Personal seals continued to include astronomical imagery, though this was increasingly astral rather than solar as earlier.

In the seventh century, however, Josiah destroyed Solomon's shrines to gods now identified as foreign and dismantled state shrines in the countryside. Josiah's campaign against the ancestral cult included tomb desecration and the exposure of bones for the first time in Israelite history. A term previously reserved for the ancestors, Rephaim, was now applied to the Canaanite aborigines allegedly proscribed by YHWH. Deuteronomy, the legal program of Josiah's court or of a later extension of it, enjoined the worship of YHWH alone. Deuteronomy, Jeremiah, and Zephaniah explicitly identified the host of heaven as foreign, as objects of apostasy. The Priestly source of the Pentateuch rewrote the traditional ancestral lore, suppressing all references to superhuman agencies other than YHWH; it forbids any imagery in the cult—correspondingly, seals are increasingly aniconic.

Sennacherib's deportations and the processes of industrialization and cash cropping had destroyed the effectiveness of the old kinship groups among whom the traditional religion, with its multiple divinities, was rooted. The imposition of state dogma of exclusive loyalty to the state god reflects the state's ambition to deal directly with the individual, bypassing the centers of resistance, the lineages. Thus, Deuteronomy 13.6–11 instructs the Israelite to inform on brothers, children, or wives who worship other gods, such as the host of heaven.

In this period, not in the exile as earlier scholars claimed, the notion of reliance on a single god took root. That idea survived, as a doctrine distinguishing Israel from other, polytheistic nations, through the exile and over the course of the restoration. Some of the elite, such as Second Isaiah, accepted the implications of philosophical monotheism, identifying YHWH as the source of evil as well as good (Isa. 45.7). Yet even in sources that accept the activity of subordinate deities, such as Job 1–2, the concept of exclusive loyalty to the state god had taken hold. Affirmation of the cult of the one god—the ultimate cause of events—could persist despite the assumption that other divinities existed, too. The doctrine of a Trinity, or of angels in heaven, or of a devil, coexisted happily with the idea in Judaism, Christianity, and Islam of an enlightened community distinguished from others by its monotheism.

BARUCH HALPERN

MOSES. As primary leader of the Israelites in their Exodus from Egypt and during their wanderings in the wilderness, and as mediator of the Law, Moses dominates the biblical traditions from Exodus through Deuteronomy. In fact, Exodus-Deuteronomy appears to have been edited as a biography of Moses, reporting his birth at the beginning and his death at the end. Between these events the Bible relates many episodes about his life and work.

Born in secret during the oppression in Egypt as the younger of the two sons of a Levite couple, Amram and Jochebed (Exod. 6.18–20), Moses was hidden away for a time to avoid slaughter at the hands of the Egyptians and then placed in a basket amid the reeds of the Nile. Discovered by a daughter of Pharaoh who had pity on the child, he was spared and, through the intervention of his older sister (Miriam: Exod. 15.20; Num. 26.59), was nursed by his own mother. Raised by Pharaoh's daughter as her son, the child received the name Moses (Hebr. *mōšeh*, understood as a participle of the verb *mōšâ*, "to draw out;" the name actually appears to be a form of the Egyptian verb *mśw*, "to be born," or the noun *mesu*, "child, son," appearing in such names as Thut-mose and Ah-mose; Exod. 2.1–10). When grown up, Moses killed an Egyptian whom he saw beating a Hebrew and, when word of his deed spread, he fled the country to save his life (Exod. 2.11–153). Taking refuge in Midian (2.15b–21), he married Zipporah, the daughter of a Midianite priest who is variously referred to as Reuel (2.18), Jethro (3.1; 4.18; 18.1), or Hobab (Num. 10.29; Judg. 4.11). While in Midian, she bore him two sons, Gershom and Eliezer (Exod. 2.22; 4.20; 18.3–4).

While Moses was tending his father-in-law's flocks near Horeb, the mountain of God, God revealed himself in a burning bush and commissioned him to return to Egypt and, with the help of Aaron, to lead the Hebrews out of the land of oppression (Exod. 3.1–4.17). Moses returned to Egypt (4.18–31), and he and Aaron produced signs and nine plagues to persuade Pharaoh to allow the Hebrews to depart Egypt, either to go on a three-day journey into the wilderness to offer sacrifice to God (3.18; 5.1; 7.16; 8.28; 10.7–11, 24–26) or to leave the land for good (6.10–11). The signs and plagues failed to convince Pharaoh, who repeatedly gave and withdrew his permission to leave (5.1–10.29). With the tenth plague, the slaughter of the firstborn, Pharaoh and his people urged the Hebrews to leave (11.1–12.36).

Moses and the people departed (Exod. 12.37–14.4) only to be pursued by Pharaoh, whose army was drowned in the returning waters of the Red Sea after the waters had parted for the Israelites to cross (14.5–15.21).

During their long stay in the wilderness and on their journey to the Promised Land (Exod. 12.22–Deut. 34.8), Moses endured the people's recurrent murmuring and complaining. He aided in securing good drinking water (Exod. 15.22–26; 17.1–7; see Num. 20.2–11), oversaw the receipt of quails and manna (Exod. 16.1–36; see Num. 11.4–5, 31–35), directed their war with the Amalekites (Exod. 17.8–16), and, at the suggestion of his father-in-law, established judges to hear and adjudicate the people's disputes (18.1–27; see Num. 11.16–30).

At Sinai (Exod. 19), Moses committed the people (19.3–8) to observe the commandments of God (20.1–23.33), communicated to him during a forty-day stay on the mountain (24.18) and then addressed to the people (24.3) and subsequently written down by either Moses (24.4) or God (24.12). He received instructions for constructing the tab-

M

ernacle and its accoutrements (25.1–31.17). The first tablets of the Law presented to Moses (31.18) were smashed by him (32.19) when he returned to the camp to discover that Aaron had supervised the construction of a golden calf around which the people were celebrating (32.1–35). Moses intervened with God not to destroy the people (33.1–22), and God (34.1) or Moses (34.27–28) again wrote the words of the commandments (34.17–26) during a second forty-day period (34.28), which were again proclaimed to the people (34.29–35). Moses then supervised the construction and erection of the tabernacle (35.1–40.38), received further laws and instructions (Lev. 1–7, 11–27), and consecrated the tabernacle and ordained Aaron and his sons as priests (Lev. 8–10).

After staying at Sinai for eleven months (Exod. 19.1; Num. 1.1), a census was taken of the non-Levitical males above the military age of twenty, totaling 603,550 (Num. 1.2–54), the Levites one month and older, totaling 22,000 (3.14–39; see 4.1–49), and the firstborn males one month and older, totaling 22,273 (3.40–43). After receiving further commandments from God (2.1–34; 5.1–6.27; 8.1–26; 19.9–14; 10.1–10), consecrating the Levites (3.5–13; 4.46–49), supervising receipt and employment of the leaders' special offerings (7.1–89), Moses and the people observed the Passover (9.1–8) and departed from Sinai on the twentieth day of the second month of the second year after leaving Egypt (10.11–36).

For the next thirty-nine years, Moses led the people in their journeys (see the itinerary in Num. 33.1–49) in the wilderness. Kadesh (-barnea), an oasis in the northern Sinai desert (Map 2:T2), and its vicinity are the scene of many of the episodes reported in Numbers 11.1–20.21. During this period the people continued their murmuring and complaining (11.1–6; 14.1–4; 20.2–5), were fed with manna and quails (11.4–35), and were supplied with water (20.2–13). Moses was confronted with complaints about his wife (whether Zipporah or not remains uncertain) by Miriam

Michelangelo's *Moses* in San Pietro in Rome, Italy

M

and Aaron (12.1–16) and with a rebellion led by Korah and his associates (16.1–17.13). Spies were sent out to make a reconnaissance of Canaan but returned with a discouraging report about the strength of the inhabitants (13.1–14.38). A belated attempt to invade the region from the south, apparently without Moses' approval, led to disaster (14.39–45). During these episodes, Moses and Aaron received further ordinances from God to be communicated to the people (15.1–41; 18.1–19.22). After the death and burial of Miriam at Kadesh (20.1), Moses sent messengers to the king of Edom to request permission to pass through his country but was refused (20.14–21).

The last phase of Moses' life (thirty-eight years, according to Deut. 2.14) was concerned with the movement of the people into and their conquest of Transjordan. Journeying from Kadesh, they defeated the king of Arad (Num. 20.22; 21.1–3) and came to Mount Hor, where Aaron died

(20.23–29). Leaving Mount Hor, Moses led the people southward to bypass the land of Edom (21.4). When God sent fiery serpents against the people because of their impatience, Moses constructed a bronze serpent as an instrument of healing (21.4–9). The people eventually arrived in the territory north of the land of Moab, where they defeated kings Sihon of the Amorites and Og of Bashan (21.10–35). While the Israelites encamped near the Jordan across from Jericho, King Balak of Moab hired Balaam to curse Israel (22.1–24.25). After a plague ravaged the people because of their worship of the Baal of Peor (25.1–18), Moses ordered a census, which counted 601,730 males above the age of twenty fit for the military (26.1–51). After the census, Moses received instructions from God about dividing the land (26.52–65), about women's inheritance rights (27.1–11; see 36.1–12), the designation of Joshua as his successor (27.12–23), a calendar of sacrifices (28.1–

29.40), and women's vows (30.1–16). A battle against the Midianites provided the occasion for divine instructions about the division of battle spoils (31.1–54). Moses allotted the captured territory in Transjordan to the tribes of Reuben and Gad and half of Manasseh (32.1–42) and transmitted divine instructions about dividing the land west of the Jordan (34.1–29) and setting aside cities for the Levites (35.1–8) and cities of refuge for those guilty of accidental homicide (35.9–34)

On the eve of his death, the first day of the eleventh month of the fortieth year after the Exodus (Deut. 1.3), Moses delivered a series of farewell addresses to the people, expounding again the Law and its requirements for living in the land (1.6–4.40; 5.1–29.1; 29.2–30.20), offering a personal adieu (32.1–6), a song (31.30–32.43), and blessings on the tribes (33.1–29). With Joshua properly commissioned as his successor (31.7–8, 14–15, 23), and having inscribed his song (31.16–29) and written and given directions for the reading and safekeeping of the book of the Law (31.9–13, 24–29), at the command of God (32.48–52; see Num. 17.12–23) Moses went up Mount Nebo, viewed the Promised Land, and died at the age of 120 years, full of life and vigor. He was buried by the Lord, "but no one knows his burial place to this day" (34.1–8). God did not allow Moses to enter the land he viewed, either because of his own failure to provide proper recognition of God (Num. 20.10–13; 27.12–14; Deut. 32.48–52) or because of the sins of the people (Deut. 1.37–38; 3.18–28).

Any critical attempt to assess the historicity of the portrait of Moses presented in Exodus to Deuteronomy must take into account a number of characteristics of this literature and its presentation. First, many of the stories are legendary in character and are built on folktale motifs found in various cultures. The theme of the threatened child who eventually becomes a great figure, for example, was employed from Mesopotamia to Rome and appears in the stories about Sargon the Great, Heracles, Oedipus, Romulus and Remus, Cyrus, and Jesus. Second, Israel's theology located the giving of the Law and the formation of the national life outside the land it occupied and thus considered the wilderness period as its constitutional time. Hence, laws and institutions from diverse times and conditions are located in this formative era. Third, the duplications in the texts and the frequent lack of cohesion in the narratives and of consistency in details indicate that the material is composite and multilayered. Fourth, the lack of external frames of reference makes it impossible to connect any of the events depicted about Moses with the history of other cultures. The Egyptian Pharaoh of the oppression, for example, goes unnamed and no contemporary nonbiblical sources mention Moses. Finally, Moses is depicted as the archetype of several offices. Throughout he is representative not only of the good leader but also of the ideal judge and legal administrator, intercessor, cult founder, and prophet. In all of these he excelled and thus served as the standard by which others were judged.

In biblical literature outside the Pentateuch, Moses is most often mentioned in the phrases "the book of Moses," "the law of Moses," and "the book of the law of Moses," indicating the development of the concept of the Torah as such and of its special authority and Mosaic authorship, themes that will become central for subsequent Jewish tradition. The same implication of the special scriptural authority of the first five books of the Bible, the books of Moses, is found in the New Testament, where there are repeated appeals to what Moses said (Matt. 8.4; 19.7; 22.24; Mark 7.10; John 7.22; Rom. 10.5) as well as to the "law of Moses" and the "book of Moses."

Postbiblical tradition elaborated on Moses' biography from his birth to his death in such texts as the *Testament of Moses* and in haggadic literature. Details of these embellishments are also found in the New Testament in the reference to Jannes and Jambres (2 Tim. 3.8) and in the account of the dispute between Michael and the devil over Moses' body (Jude 9; cf. also Acts 7.22).

These haggadic legends were also known to such Hellenistic Jewish writers as Philo and Josephus, who added to them the Hellenistic concept of the ideal man, so that the details of Moses' life reveal him to be the consummate human being and as such the appropriate founder of the theocratic state. This may be the background for the parallels drawn in the gospel of Matthew between the lives of Moses and Jesus. Yet for Matthew, as for the author of the letter to the Hebrews, Jesus is superior: Moses' presence at the transfiguration confirms Jesus' sonship (Matt. 17.1–8), and that sonship is clearly superior to Moses' status as God's servant (Heb. 3.1–6; cf. Num. 12.7; Deut. 34.5; Josh. 1.2; Ps. 105.26; Mai. 4.4).

The artistic tradition of depicting Moses with horns on his forehead arose from the understanding by some ancient translators of the Hebrew verb *qāran* (Exod. 34.29) as related to the noun *qeren,* "horn;" an alternative is to understand the verb as meaning "to shine" (so NRSV, and most earlier English translations).

JOHN H. HAYES

NAHUM, THE BOOK OF. The three chapters of this book constitute a powerful poem that interprets events surrounding the fall of Nineveh in 612 BCE in terms of the Lord's control of history on behalf of his people.

Nahum means "comfort," a name that stands in contrast with the violent vengeance portrayed in the book. He is identified as "the Elkoshite," but the location of Elkosh is unknown. We have no other information about this prophet.

This is the only prophetic work that is called a "book" in the text (1.1). It is also called an oracle or "burden," a term for a prophecy spoken against a nation under judgment, and a "vision," a description it shares with Isaiah and Obadiah; the latter term probably means a literary presentation of an inspired experience of being in the heavenly court of God, to observe how God deals with nations and people in history. The book contains some of the most powerful poetry in the Bible, a witness to its inspiration in another sense. The prophet-poet who wrote the book looked beyond the facts of Nineveh's destruction to discern and portray God's intentions in it.

The book may be outlined as follows:

I. Yahweh, the avenging God of his people, will destroy Nineveh and bring peace to Judah.
   A. An acrostic poem: the Lord takes vengeance (1.2–8)
   B. The leaders of Nineveh are addressed (1.9–11)
   C. Good news for Judah: no more invaders (1.12–15)
II. Nineveh's enemies are triumphant.
   A. The last battle (2.1–12)
   B. The Lord's curse on Nineveh (2.13–3.6)
   C. A taunting song over the doomed city (3.7–19).

Israel's relation to Assyria and its capital city Nineveh extended over more than a century, when the Assyrian empire was at the height of its power. Nineveh (Map 6:H3) was the most important city in Assyria. Its greatest period came during the last century of the empire (730–612 BCE), which coincides with Israel's contacts with it. Great buildings of that period have been excavated, constructed by the emperors Sennacherib, Esarhaddon, and Ashurbanipal. One palace housed what was at that time the best library in the world. Fortifications included two sets of walls that protected palaces and temples. Ishtar, goddess of love and war, was the city's benefactor. The finest gate was dedicated to her and decorated with her image and symbols, and a magnificent temple housed her statue.

Assyria inherited the crumbling Hittite and Mitanni empires in the upper Mesopotamian valley in the early second millennium. In the eighth century BCE her emperors, Tiglath-pileser III, Sargon II, and Sennacherib, sent armies into Syria, then to Judah, and finally into Egypt. Some of the earliest of the Minor Prophets note these movements and interpret them

as God's judgment on Israel and the nations (see Amos 3.9). Samaria fell to Assyrian forces in 722 BCE (2 Kings 17). Judah and her neighbors were vassals to Assyria during the following century; this authority was enforced by Assyrian arms several times (see 2 Kings 18). But Assyrian power began to weaken in the late seventh century, and Josiah apparently owed his relative freedom of action to this development.

By 614 BCE three powers, Media, Babylon, and Egypt, were prepared to fight for succession to Assyria's empire. Media seized the section east and north of the Euphrates Valley; Babylon seized the south and eventually pushed into Syria; Egypt seized her own territory and extended her control north into Palestine. Babylon laid siege to Nineveh and finally destroyed it in 612 BCE. A small Assyrian army escaped the city and fled toward Haran; it was finally destroyed in 609 BCE.

Nahum's powerful poem portrays the last days of Nineveh. This is seen as good news for Israel, a hope that is short-lived, since Egypt and Babylon turned out to be worse masters than Assyria. But the poem is correct in marking the event as a turning point in history.

There is tension in the Minor Prophets in their views toward Nineveh: repentant and the object of God's care in Jonah, the instrument of God's judgment on Israel and Judah in Amos,

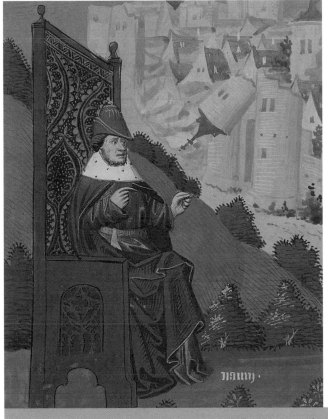

Nahum announcing the destruction of Nineveh

and the symbol of ultimate evil opposed to God in Nahum. A similar tension exists in Isaiah's portrayal of Assyria as the rod of the Lord's anger against Israel in chap. 10 and God's judgment on Nineveh in 30.27–33 and 31.8–9.

In Nahum a historic event is presented as symbolic of the struggle between God and ultimate evil. In a similar way, Isaiah 47 portrays the fall of Babylon to Persian forces. The book of Revelation speaks of Babylon (or Rome) in similar fashion in chaps. 12–13 and 17–18.

JOHN D. W. WATTS

NAMES OF GOD IN THE HEBREW BIBLE. The Bible often refers to God by his proper name, which was probably pronounced Yahweh. In the Hebrew Bible, the consonants *yhwh* are usually to be read as Adonai (*'ădōnāy*), "my Lord," for the sake of reverence, and English versions represent the word by "Lord" or (less often) "God" in capital letters. The Hebrew word is a plural of majesty (with a singular meaning) of *'ădôn*, which is translated "Lord" (e.g., Isa. 1.24; 3.1). The name Yahweh often appears in the phrase "Yahweh of hosts," as the Hebrew is probably to be translated (cf. "Yahweh of Teman" or "of Samaria" in the Kuntillet 'Ajrud inscriptions of ca. 800 BCE), or the longer "Yahweh the God of hosts" (e.g., 2 Sam. 5.10). Some have thought that the hosts, Sabaoth (*ṣĕbā'ôt*), are the armies of Israel (cf. 1 Sam. 17.45), but a reference to these human armies is inappropriate in, for instance, prophetic denunciations of Israel (e.g., Isa. 1.24), and the word probably denotes heavenly or angelic armies. Some maintain that Sabaoth is an epithet in apposition to Yahweh and that it means something like "the Mighty One," but there is no evidence in Hebrew for such a meaning.

The usual Hebrew word for God is Elohim (*'ĕlōhîm*), another plural of majesty with a singular meaning when used of Yahweh. The singular form Eloah (*'ĕlōah*) appears, mainly in the book of Job, but the most common singular noun for God is El (*'ēl*), which has cognates in other Semitic languages and whose Ugaritic counterpart is used both for the chief god and as a general word for any god. The Israelites adopted this common Semitic word (cf. Gen. 33.20: El-Elohe-Israel, "El the God of Israel"), and some of the divine names compounded with El in the Hebrew Bible were probably originally used of non-Israelite deities. In Genesis 14.18–20, 22, we find El Elyon (*'ēl 'elyôn*), "God Most High," whose priest is Melchizedek but who is identified by Abram with Yahweh. The word Elyon is used of Yahweh in other places in the Bible (e.g., Pss. 18.13; 87.5). In the fourth century CE, Philo of Byblos is cited by Eusebius of Caesarea as referring to Elioun, the Most High (Greek *hupsistos*), as a Phoenician god (*Praeparatio Evangelica* 1.10.15). The Aramaic cognate of Elyon is *'lyn* (perhaps *'elyān*), and a god with this name appears alongside El in a treaty of the eighth century BCE from Sefire in Syria.

The element El is found in divine names in Genesis, sometimes in connection with various places, such as Bethel, "the house of God" (cf. 28.19, 22), and we find El-Bethel, "God of Bethel" (35.7; cf. 31.13). Thus, at a place in the desert there is El-roi ("a God of seeing," 16.13), and at Beer-sheba there is El Olam ("the Everlasting God," 21.33; cf. *špš 'lm* in a Ugaritic letter, and *špš 'lm* in a Phoenician text of ca. 700 BCE, both of which mean "the eternal sun" god or goddess). Another name is El Shaddai, usually translated "God Almighty," and the Priestly writer (P) in the Pentateuch maintains that God first made himself known by that name before revealing his name Yahweh (Exod. 6.3; cf. Gen. 17.1; 35.11; 43.14; 48.3). The name is not restricted to P, for it is found in a number of places (Num. 24.4, on the lips of Balaam, a non-Israelite; Ruth 1.20–21; Job 5.17; etc.), and it is part of the names Zurishaddai and Ammishaddai (Num. 1.6, 12). It is perhaps related to an Akkadian word for "mountain."

It is uncertain whether El-berith ("God of the covenant") in Judges 9.46 refers to Yahweh, for this deity seems to be the same as Baal-berith in 8.33; 9.4, and may be a Canaanite god. On the other hand, Baal, which means "lord," was sometimes used of Yahweh in early times without necessarily always identifying him with the Canaanite god Baal. In 1 Chronicles 12.6, there is the personal name Bealiah, "Yah is Baal" (cf. *yhwb'l* on an unpublished seal). Saul and Jonathan, who were worshipers of Yahweh, had sons named, respectively, Esh-baal and Merib-baal (1 Chron. 8.33–34), which were changed by editors to Ish-bosheth and Mephibosheth (2 Sam. 2.8; 9.6; etc.), in which "bosheth" ("shame") was substituted for "Baal." Jerubbaal (Jerubbesheth in 2 Sam. 11.21), Gideon's other name, is probably to be explained similarly, notwithstanding the forced explanation in Judges 6.31–32. David also had a son named Beeliada (*b'lyd'*, 1 Chron. 14.7), probably identical with Eliada in other lists. Hosea 2.16 says that Israel will call God "my husband" (lit. "my man") and no longer "my Baal" (i.e., "my lord," another word for husband), which may imply that some Israelites addressed God in the latter way.

Both God's holiness and his relation to his people are reflected in the phrase "the Holy One of Israel," which is characteristic of the book of Isaiah. Although it is not strictly a name, it is relevant to mention this title here.

Yahweh is frequently described as *melek*, "king" (e.g., Deut. 33.5; Pss. 29.10; 98.6), "a great king over all the earth" (Ps. 47.2; cf. 47.7; 48.2) or "above all gods" (Ps. 95.3), "my" or "our king" (Pss. 5.2; 47.6; 68.24; 74.12), or "the King of glory" (Ps. 24.7–10). He "reigns" or "has become king" (Pss. 47.8; 93.1; 96.10; 97.1; 99.1; Isa. 52.7), and he "will reign forever" (Exod. 15.18). Personal names include Malchiel (Gen. 46.17; Num. 26.45; 1 Chron. 7.31) and Malchiah (Jer. 21.1; 38.1, 6), meaning "El" or "Yah is king." Isaiah sees a vision of "the King, Yahweh of hosts" (6.5).

Various epithets and figures of speech are applied to God, but they cannot all be described as names or titles. In Genesis 15.1, Yahweh says to Abram "I am your shield" (cf. Ps. 84.11), but that does not prove the theory that "the Shield of Abraham" was a title. On the other hand, God is described as "the Fear of Isaac" (Gen. 31.42, 53)—the suggested alternative translation, "the Kinsman of Isaac," lacks sufficient evidence—and as "the Mighty One of Jacob" (Gen. 49.24; etc.); these may be titles reflecting the special relationship of God with particular individuals. His relationship with people is also shown by names containing the element *'āb*, "father," such as Abijah, Abiel, and Abra(ha)m. Yet although God was viewed thus (Jer. 31.9; Mal. 2.10; cf. 1.6), and could be addressed as "my (or our) Father" (Jer. 3.4; Isa. 63.16; 64.8), it is doubtful whether the evidence suffices to justify the claim that "Father" was a title, let alone a name.

J. A. EMERTON

NAZARETH (Map 12:X3). A town in southern Galilee about fifteen miles southwest of the Sea of Galilee and twenty miles from the Mediterranean westward. It was probably located at or near the site of the town by the same name in modern Israel. References to it occur in the Gospels and Acts, and all agree that Jesus was from Nazareth (Mark 1.9; Matt. 4.13; 21.11; Luke 4.16; John 1.45; Acts 10:38).

View of Beit Netofa Valley in Galilee, Israel, including Nazareth

Although not situated on any main commercial roads, Nazareth was not far from them, and it was only several miles from Sepphoris, an important city near the road from Ptolemais to Tiberias. Its secluded position may explain the absence of references to it before Roman times, and this may indicate that it was an insignificant Jewish town (John 1.46). On the other hand, Luke's references (1.26; 2.4, 39) to it as a city rather than a village may indicate that it was not an insignificant place. Distinctions, however, between the two were not great, and they were sometimes used interchangeably; furthermore, Luke's knowledge of Palestine is not always correct.

Located on a hill in the Plain of Esdraelon, it was about 365 m (1200 ft) above sea level. From its heights one could see mountains in three directions and view the Plain of Esdraelon on the south. The moderate climate, sufficient rainfall, and fertile soil were favorable for growing fruits, grains, and vegetables. The water supply of the town itself was restricted to one spring, supplemented by cisterns. If the spring is to be identified with the "Mary's Well" shown to tourists, it is the only shrine of the many in Nazareth that may go back to Jesus' time.

EDWIN D. FREED

NEBUCHADREZZAR. The king of Babylonia (605–562 BCE), frequently named in Jeremiah, Ezekiel, and Daniel, as well as by classical writers. The name is also rendered Nebuchadnezzar, a biblical variant; the form Nebuchadrezzar is closer to the Babylonian Nabû-kudurri-uṣur, "the (god) Nabu has protected the succession." He was renowned as the most distinguished ruler of the Neo-Babylonian (Chaldean) Dynasty founded by his father, Nabopolassar, in 627 BCE, and as the conqueror of Jerusalem who took the Judeans into exile.

Nebuchadrezzar acted as commander in chief for his aging father when in 605 BCE he took Carchemish from the Egyptians and drove them back to their borders, thus freeing Syria and Palestine. According to the Babylonian Chronicle and Josephus, he broke off this campaign in order to return to take the throne of Babylon on hearing of his father's death. He campaigned frequently in the west,

receiving tribute from many rulers and from Tyre, which he subsequently besieged for thirteen years. His vassals included Jehoiakim of Judah who, however, defected in 601, misinterpreting the fierce battle between the Babylonians and Egyptians that year as a victory for the latter. Nebuchadrezzar gained revenge by capturing Jerusalem on 16 March 597, when he set up a new king (Mattaniah/Zedekiah) sympathetic to him. Jehoiachin, whom he called Yaukin, king of Judah, was taken prisoner to Babylon with the Temple vessels and many Judeans (2 Kings 24.10–17). Nebuchadrezzar also fought against Elam (cf. Jer. 49.38) and the Arabs, and was present in the operations that led to the sack of Jerusalem in August 587/586 BCE as a reprisal for Zedekiah's activity as the focus of anti-Babylonian opposition. At that time, more Judeans were taken into exile, as they also were following a later raid, including one on Egypt attested in a fragmentary Babylonian text dated 568–567 BCE (cf. Jer. 43.8–13).

Little is known of the last thirty years of Nebuchadrezzar's rule. The tale of his madness (Dan. 4.23–33) may be a pejorative account of a period in the reign of his successor Nabonidus. Nebuchadrezzar's character may be reflected in his inscriptions, which do not emphasize his military exploits yet reflect his exercise of law, order, and justice as well as stressing moral qualities and religious devotion. He rightly claims to have rebuilt Babylon, its walls, palaces, temples, and defenses as a wonder to which all peoples came with tribute; the famous "hanging gardens" of Babylon are also attributed to him in some traditions. He died during a period that saw the seeds of economic decline resulting from the cost of his enterprises; he was succeeded by his son Amel-Marduk (Evil-Merodach of 2 Kings 25.27).

DONALD J. WISEMAN

NEHEMIAH, THE BOOK OF. It is difficult to determine the precise relationship between the persons of Ezra and Nehemiah. It is understandable that Nehemiah is not mentioned in the memoir of Ezra in Ezra 7–10, because Nehemiah had not yet begun his mission. It is, however, difficult to understand why Ezra is not explicitly referred to in the memoir of Nehemiah, especially after his activities in teaching the

Nehemiah Looks Upon the Ruins of Jerusalem (Neh. 2.11–16) (James Jacques Joseph Tissot)

put down the revolt in Egypt in 456 BCE, was also the satrap of the Trans-Euphrates. Megabyzus had generously promised the captured Egyptian king Inarus and certain Greek generals their release after the war. Artaxerxes, however, listened to his mother, the wife of Xerxes, the former king, and commanded their execution. This was a heavy blow to the pride of Megabyzus, and in 449 he fomented a rebellion against the Persian king, which Artaxerxes was unable to put down. Later, however, Megabyzus stopped the revolt and once again became a loyal subject of the king. It was thus politically expedient for Artaxerxes to send out Nehemiah, obviously one of his loyal officials, to Judah, one of the smaller but important provinces of the satrapy.

The Work of Nehemiah. After Nehemiah arrived in Jerusalem he conducted a secret inspection of the walls of the city. It seems that he tried to hide his true intentions from the people so that news about his plans would not reach neighboring enemies. After the inspection Nehemiah decided to organize the Jews and to rebuild the walls. Nehemiah allotted sections of the walls to various persons and groups of persons to rebuild. Some scholars think the period of fifty-two days too brief to rebuild the walls, but if we keep in mind that a significant part of the wall needed only restoration, this time was not too short for such repairs. It has been pointed out that in similar circumstances the Athenians built a wall around Athens in just a month, and, in the face of an imminent attack on Constantinople by Attila after the wall was destroyed by an earthquake, the Eastern Romans restored it in sixty days.

With the building of the wall two serious problems developed for Nehemiah and the Jews. The first was a well-orchestrated attack of psychological warfare to stop building. This was done by neighboring nations, led by Sanballat I, governor of Samaria, and assisted by Tobiah, probably a Persian official of the Ammonites; somewhat later, these were joined by Geshem (Gashmu), chieftain of the Nabateans or Arabs to the south and southeast of Judah, as well as by the Ashdodites of the old Philistine territory to the west. With Samaritans to the north and Ammonites to the east, Judah was nearly encircled by its enemies. They made use of rumors and threats to discourage Nehemiah and the Jews. But Nehemiah did not hesitate to take strong measures to ensure the safety of the workers on the walls. The last resort for his enemies was to try to divide the Jewish people by infiltrating their ranks with false rumors and to induce prophets to give false prophecies. But Nehemiah saw through all these attempts. In the end, the wall was completed and his enemies conceded that they had failed to achieve their goal.

The second problem was the poverty of the Jews. At that stage Judah had a weak economic infrastructure and the burden of taxes was heavy. The satrap collected taxes for the royal treasury, and both the satrap and his officials from the different provinces of the satrapy had to be paid. Furthermore, the governor and his officials collected taxes for their work. (Nehemiah, however, well aware of his subjects' poverty, did not collect taxes for himself and his officials.) Beyond these expenses, there were the tithes that the Jews were obliged to pay for the maintenance of the service in the

Law, especially as it pertained to intermarriage. Because of the paucity of evidence this problem is hard to solve.

Historical Background. It is generally accepted that Nehemiah came from Susa (Map 6J4) in Persia to rebuild the walls of Jerusalem in 445/444 BCE. As the cupbearer of the Persian king Artaxerxes (probably Artaxerxes I, 465–424 BCE), Nehemiah held a high office of some influence at court. It is also probable that Nehemiah, serving in the presence of the queen, was a eunuch; this may explain why he was unwilling to flee to the Temple of the Lord as protection against his enemies (Neh. 6.10–14). It is clear that Shemaiah tried to lure him to the Temple in order to get him to transgress the stipulation forbidding eunuchs to enter the sanctuary (cf. Deut. 23.1; Lev. 21.17–24). If he had done so, he could have lost his influence with the people and their trust.

After Nehemiah heard of the plight of his people in Jerusalem and that the city was in ruins without a wall of defense against their enemies, he asked the Persian king's permission to go to Jerusalem in order to see what could be done. This was granted; Nehemiah was sent out as a governor of Judah with all the privileges pertaining to the post of governor of a province in the satrapy of Trans-Euphrates. To secure his safety he was granted an escort of soldiers to accompany him; this stands in contrast to the mission of Ezra, in which no such escort was requested. It is, however, noteworthy that the mission of Nehemiah was of a political nature while that of Ezra was religious.

Artaxerxes's friendly gesture to Nehemiah was made just after a serious revolt broke out in the satrapy of the Trans-Euphrates. Megabyzus, the Persian general in Egypt, who

Temple. It is thus not surprising that they had to go into debt and often were forced into debt-slavery in order to meet their obligations. After becoming aware of this problem, Nehemiah canceled all debts.

Nehemiah served for twelve years as governor of Judah and then returned to the royal court in Persia. After a few years, ca. 430 BCE, he went once more to Jerusalem, and was shocked by what he saw. The principles he had laid down during his previous service as governor had been neglected. Nehemiah was so dismayed that he took strong action (Neh. 13). Having discovered that a place was furnished in the Temple for Tobiah the Ammonite by Eliashib the priest, Nehemiah threw the furniture of Tobiah out of the room and commanded that the place be purified. As a result of heavy taxes, the paying of tithes had been neglected; Nehemiah reinstituted the levy. Another problem was the desecration of the Sabbath by foreign traders in Jerusalem; he forbade them to do any business on the Sabbath within or outside the walls of Jerusalem. Finally, Nehemiah vehemently confronted the issue of marriages with foreigners. He even assaulted some of the men and pulled out their hair.

The book of Nehemiah ends abruptly without telling the reader what happened to either Nehemiah or Ezra. Nothing is said of the success of the measures taken against certain Jews described in Nehemiah 13.

Author, Composition, and Sources. As with the book of Ezra, the great majority of modern scholars consider the book of Nehemiah to have been composed by the later Chronicler sometime in the fourth century BCE. The composition of the book of Nehemiah is, however, full of problems. Nehemiah 1.1–7.5 contains part of the memoir of Nehemiah written in the first person; we may accept this as verbatim quotation by the Chronicler. In Nehemiah 7.6–72, we find a list of returnees to Judah which is essentially the same as the list in Ezra 2. Probably these lists came from the same source, but it remains unexplained why the Chronicler should have repeated it. Nehemiah 8–10 is problematic because it likely represents Ezra's memoir. Several scholars have proposed that these chapters are displaced and must be added after Ezra 10 or must be inserted between Ezra 8 and 9. From a modern point of view this is logical, but it is difficult for a modern scholar to determine what motivated the arrangement of material by an ancient compiler. Nehemiah 9 in the Ezra memoir is a hymn of praise and thanksgiving to God for his guidance of Israel through history, a typical addition of the Chronicler; however, the sense of guilt expressed in this hymn is uncharacteristic of the Chronicler.

In Nehemiah 11–13, we have a variety of sources intermixed by the Chronicler and furnished with commentary, and it is difficult to determine what precisely was taken over from Nehemiah's memoir. Among a variety of proposals made by scholars, it seems possible that Nehemiah 11.1–3; 12.31–43 and 13.4–31 are to be regarded as part of the memoir. In Nehemiah 11.1–3, the third person is used for Nehemiah, but in 12.31–43 and 13.4–31 the first person is used. In 12.31–43, we have the description of the dedication of the walls of Jerusalem. In 13.431, the second visit of Nehemiah to Jerusalem is described along with the measures he took to combat certain abuses. It is obvious from the work of the Chronicler in Nehemiah 11–12 that he had a preference for genealogical lists, as we also know from the books of Chronicles. In the list of high priests in 12.10–11 (which supplements that in 1 Chron. 5.27–41), we are brought to a time well after 400 BCE. Some even regard the high priest Jaddua as a contemporary of Alexander the Great

late in the fourth century BCE. One thing, however, is clear: the late Chronicler who did the final editing of this book was active well into the fourth century BCE.

Theology of the Book. Because the book is for the most part derived from Nehemiah's memoir, one can form an excellent idea of his beliefs. The most important feature in the religion of Nehemiah is his sense of a living relationship with God. Despite his high regard for the Law, he did not regard it as the only form of mediation between humans and God. If we accept the authenticity of the prayers of Nehemiah, it becomes evident that he believed in immediate contact with God through prayer. As did other Jews in postexilic times, he believed in the dominant role of the Lord as the God of history: God could move the Persian king to give Nehemiah permission to go to Jerusalem; God determined every step that Nehemiah took after his arrival in Jerusalem. Although the work of Nehemiah was mainly political (see Sir. 49.13), a close relationship between politics and religion was presumed. Nehemiah never doubted that God was on his side and would finally grant him victory over his adversaries.

F. CHARLES FENSHAM

NOAH. The son of Lamech, and the father of Shem, Ham, and Japheth (Gen. 5.28–32), Noah was the hero of the biblical Flood narrative (Gen. 6.9–9.17) and the first vintner (Gen. 9.18–28). After observing the corruption of all creation, God determined to cleanse and purify the earth through a flood (Gen 6.1–7). Noah, however, found favor with God (Gen. 6.8–9), and he, together with his family and the seed of all living creatures, entered the ark and survived the deluge. From them the earth was then repopulated (Gen. 10).

In many respects Noah was a second Adam. The genealogy of Genesis 5 makes his birth the first after the death of the progenitor of humanity. Like Adam, all people are his descendants. God's first command to the primordial pair to "be fruitful, and multiply, and fill the earth" (Gen. 1.28) is echoed in God's first command to Noah and his sons after the Flood (Gen. 9.1).

Other biblical figures in turn look back to Noah and are compared to him. Moses also had to endure a water ordeal (Exod. 2.1–10); in fact, the only other time that the Hebrew word for ark (*tēbâ*) is used in the Bible is for the basket in which Moses was saved (Exod. 2.3, 5). In Christian tradition, Noah is viewed as a precursor of Jesus (Luke 17.26–27), and the waters of the Flood are compared to the waters of baptism (1 Pet. 3.18–22).

Noah has traditionally been viewed as an exemplary righteous person (Ezek. 14.14, 20; Heb. 11.7; 2 Pet. 2.5; and extensive postbiblical Jewish, Christian, and Muslim literature). However, the phrase "righteous in his generation" (Gen. 6.9) has also been interpreted to mean that at any other time Noah's righteousness would not have been viewed as extraordinary (*b. Sanh.* 108a).

The legend of a hero who survives an inundation to repopulate the earth is one found in many cultures. Most closely related to the biblical account are the stories from ancient Mesopotamia. In the Sumerian flood story, the pious king Ziusudra survives two to three attempts, including a flood, to destroy humanity. After his ordeal, he offers a sacrifice to the gods, repopulates the earth, is granted immortality and sent to live in paradisiacal Dilmun. The eleventh tablet of the Gilgamesh Epic relates the story of Gilgamesh's ancestor Utnapishtim, who survived the flood to gain immortality through a capricious act of the god Ea/Enki. Many of the

Statue of Noah and Ark from the façade of Cologne Cathedral, Germany

images and details of the story parallel the biblical account. Contextually closest to the biblical story is the Atrahasis Epic, which places the flood story in the context of a primeval history. In this version Atrahasis, the "exceedingly wise one" (also an epithet of Utnapishtim), survives three attempts to destroy humanity, the last of which is a flood. The great noise of humanity and the earth's overpopulation are given as reasons for the god Enlil's wish to bring destruction. After the flood, a divine compromise is reached on ways to limit the earth's population, an idea specifically rejected in the biblical account (Gen. 9.1).

CARL S. EHRLICH

NUMBERS, THE BOOK OF. The book of Numbers appears in the first major section of literature in the Bible, that section known as Torah or, in its Greek dress, the Pentateuch. The name of the book in English reflects the Greek title, *arithmoi*, and arises from various texts at the beginning of the book that refer to the numbers of people counted in a census of Israel (see 1.2). The title of the book in Jewish tradition, *běmidbar* ("in the wilderness"), appears as a key term in the first verse of the book and locates events about to be described. Indeed, the principal topic in the entire book is Moses' leadership of the people of Israel "in the wilderness" under the direction of God.

Analysis. The book falls into two major sections, 1.1–10.10 and 10.11–36.13. The first section continues the tradition carried in the last part of the book of Exodus and the entire book of Leviticus by reporting items in the legal corpus associated with the gift of the Law at Sinai. The second section picks up the narrative tradition from Exodus 19, a tale that recounts the arrival of Israel at Sinai, by reporting Israel's departure from the holy mountain and the continuation of the wilderness journey. The narrative about the wilderness wanderings does not end with the close of the book of Numbers. Rather, it continues into Deuteronomy, ending with an account of the death of Moses while the people of Israel are poised before the Jordan. Indeed, one must ask whether the narrative does not move beyond the classical definition of Torah or Pentateuch in order to recount traditions about Israel's entry into the land of Canaan in the book of Joshua. In that case, the larger literary context for the book of Numbers would be the Hexateuch.

As a part of the received text of the Bible, the final form of the book of Numbers does not demand interpretation as an independent and distinct unit. It is an intrinsic part of a larger whole. Perhaps the most important point about the position of Numbers in the canonical shape of the Pentateuch/Hexateuch is the juxtaposition of law (Num. 1.1–10.10) and narrative (Num. 10.11–36.13). For the final shape of the book of Numbers, the law carried by the traditions about the events at Sinai cannot be separated from the narrative that declares God's leadership for Israel through the wilderness. Indeed, the legal corpus appears in Numbers and its larger Pentateuchal context simply as a part of the larger theme about Israel's journey in the wilderness. There is a remarkable unity between the book of Numbers and the larger Pentateuchal/Hexateuchal context. But there is a similar mark of unity within the book itself, a unity that binds 1.1–10.10 with 10.11–36.13. Despite its character as legislation that distinguishes it generically from its larger narrative context, the legal section belongs intrinsically with the narrative. It is simply the detail that identifies the importance of Sinai in the larger narrative about events at various sites in the wilderness.

Yet, despite the formal unity in the book of Numbers, some evidence of disunity in the text can nevertheless be detected. Literary analysis of the Pentateuch/Hexateuch has identified at least four strands of narration used in the composition of the text as it now appears. These four sources, identified classically by the labels J, E, D, and P, were used by editors, according to the hypothesis, to construct the present form of the Pentateuchal/Hexateuchal text. Some evidence for such different literary sources appears in Numbers, particularly in the second major section of the book. A clear distinction between the sources J and P emerges, for example, when one considers the character of literary unity in the story about the spies sent by Moses to explore the land that lay before the Israelites (Num. 13–14). On the other hand, little if any evidence for the sources D and E appears in the book of Numbers, nor is there any evidence for J in its first section. The issue of literary unity and the sources focuses on the narrative section in 10.11–36.13. But even at this point, problems posed by an editorial combination of the two sources do not detract from the sense of theological unity in the received text, a unity created by combining the law in the first section with the narrative in the second section. That sense of theological unity resides in the sources as well as in the final edition of the Torah.

The origin of the book of Numbers must be described not only in terms of a literary process of editing that combined the sources J and P but also in terms of a process that brought the traditions as story and law over the generations to the point that produced the written sources. Storytellers must have recited the traditions about Moses or Balaam, Baal Peor or Midian through generations before the written sources appeared.

Literary Genres. The tools of the storyteller's trade appear clearly in the narratives of Numbers. The larger narrative context that connects Numbers with the story about Moses and the people of Israel in the wilderness is a classic example of a heroic saga, an episodic narrative that moves the story of the hero from his birth (Exod. 2) to his death (Deut. 34). The episodes in the saga include tales such as those in Numbers 13–14 and 16 and legends such as those in 12 and 22–24. A tale describes an event that unfolds in the story around the dramatic structure of a plot. A legend describes a person without emphasis on the drama that embroils the person with other people in a series of events. Indeed, a legend emphasizes a virtue in the person's character that can be imitated by subsequent disciples of the hero. But in addition to the tales and legends of the saga, the narrative in the book of Numbers also contains a fable. In 22.21–35, the famous seer, Balaam, stands under judgment for mistreating his donkey, who can see better than he can. The fable typically demolishes overblown images of the great by showing them in their true colors.

It should be clear that the saga embraces not only the narrative episodes, the tales, legends, and the fable, but also the legal units. In 1.1–10.10, legal genres build the structure of the book just as narrative genres in 10.11–36.13 do. Indeed, some narrative genres appear in the legal section (Num. 6. 21–27); and some legal genres appear in the narrative section (Num. 26.1–65).

The legal genres, like the narrative genres, contribute to the process of developing group identity. The first section in the book, for example, is a legal definition of the people, a list of names that appears as the product of a census. The census no doubt allowed the people as a whole to conscript an army in the face of a crisis. But the more significant feature of the list is its definition of structure in the organization of the people. The twelve-tribe unity of the people as a whole lies at the center of the tradition. The unit is important for the history of the tradition about the structure of the people, however, because Levi does not appear as a constitutive part of the whole. But in order to hold the number in the organization of the people at twelve, Ephraim takes over the position of Joseph, his father, and Manasseh, the brother of Ephraim, assumes the empty spot in the organization. Numbers 26 contains a parallel to the census text, another census of the people in the wilderness. Again Levi is not counted as one of the tribes in Israel, no doubt a reflection of the same stage in the history of the tradition that appears in chap. 1. In this case, Joseph remains as one of the formal units in the organization of the people. But the same entry, 26.28, breaks the tribe of Joseph into the two constitutive tribes, Ephraim and Manasseh. And 26.35 introduces the sons of Ephraim as a distinct factor in the tribal list. It is essentially the same tradition as the list in chap. 1. In both cases, the census list defines the structure of the people of Israel and thus contributes to specification of national identity, indeed, of legal structure in that national identity.

The concern for identity in terms of statistics continues in chaps. 3–4. Chap. 5 creates a legal structure for securing family stability. Chap. 6 defines the structure of life for the nazirites. In 6.22–27 the series of ordinances controlling domestic life is broken with a small narrative unit that contains the Aaronic blessing for the whole people. Then, 7.1–10.10 specifies cultic ordinances for the people, a significant qualification for Israelite worship. At the heart of these ordinances are specifications for Passover, 9.1–14, and for moving the camp, 9.15–10.36. The couplet in 10.35–36 reflects a formula for moving the ark in whatever context, doubtlessly an ancient formula, but given the meager role for the ark in these narratives, somewhat out of place.

Significance. The historical significance of the book of Numbers belongs to the larger context that embraces the book, the historical significance of the Pentateuch/Hexateuch. For the larger context and thus for the book of Numbers, value does not reside in historical accuracy or the lack of historical accuracy. It is not possible to determine, using the standards of verification basic to scholarship, whether a prophet named Balaam really confronted the Israelites with a plan to curse them. The value for the book lies more sharply in the ability of the narrator to paint a portrait of Israel struggling with Balaam, a product that captures by its aesthetic quality a significant witness to Israel's identity. Its aesthetic quality, its ability to depict identity not only for the Israelites in the wilderness under Moses' leadership but for all future disciples of Moses, gives the story value. Indeed, that very quality confirms the claim of the story as true. The book of Numbers is historically significant not because it recounts who Moses was and what he did for the children of Israel in the wilderness but rather because it tells the descendants of Israel, or any other disciples of Moses, who they are.

That historical significance merges in the book of Numbers, as it does in the larger Pentateuchal/Hexateuchal context, with distinctive theological significance. Both story and law tell the disciples of Moses that they belong not simply to Moses, but also to God. The overall structure for the narrative derives from an itinerary that shows the movement of Israel from Egypt to the Jordan. But the itinerary documents not only the movement of Israel along the way in the wilderness but also the leadership of God in that movement (see 10.11–13).

The emphasis falls, however, not only on the presence and leadership of God but also on the obedience of the people to that divine leadership. One facet of the tradition remembers Israel in the wilderness as faithful, obedient to God and to Moses (see Jer 2.2; Hos. 2.14–15). The focus of the legends on obedience to God's word (Num. 12.22–24) highlights this facet of the tradition. But in contrast, the narrative in Numbers reports that the people in the wilderness were rebels, rejecting Moses and the God whom he served. The double picture of Israelite response to God and Moses in the wilderness reflects Israel's struggles to understand its identity.

The story does not end with the end of the book of Numbers. The itinerary structure puts the Israelites on the plains of Moab by the Jordan, opposite Jericho. The conclusion combines that ending of the narrative structure for Numbers with the legal dimension: "These are the commandments and ordinances that the Lord commanded through Moses to the Israelites in the plains of Moab by the Jordan at Jericho" (36.13). At the end of Numbers, the reader must ask: "Where do the people go from here? What will they do with the commandments and ordinances?" The book of Numbers necessarily depends not only on the narrative in Deuteronomy but also on the narrative in Joshua to complete the story. The ending calls for recognition of the major literary and theological context as the Hexateuch.

GEORGE W. COATS

OBADIAH, THE BOOK OF. This book of twenty-one verses, the shortest in the Hebrew Bible, is formed of three distinct parts. Vv. 1–4 announce the Lord's decision to destroy Edom because of its pride and its betrayal of Judah. Vv. 15–18 announce the day of the Lord for all nations. And vv. 19–21 proclaim that the Lord's dominion will be demonstrated by the return of dispersed Israelites to live in Canaan.

The title gives us no information about the author except a name; Obadiah means "servant of the Lord." It gives no help in dating the book, though internal references imply that the destruction of Jerusalem of 587/586 BCE had already occurred.

Biblical tradition sees the Edomites as distant relatives of Israel through a common ancestor, Isaac. The Edomites are understood to be the descendants of Esau, as Israelites are descendants of Jacob (Gen. 25.19–26; 36). Already settled in Edom when Moses led the Israelites toward Canaan, they refused the Israelites passage through their territory (Num. 20.14–19). Edom and Judah were rivals for territory and power through the period of the monarchy. Although neither 2 Kings nor 2 Chronicles mentions Edom's participation in the sack of Jerusalem in 587/586 BCE, other books imply their guilt (e.g., Ps. 137.7; Lam. 4.21–22; Isa. 63.1–6; Joel 3.19; Mai. 1.4). All mention of Edom ends during the early part of the fifth century BCE, but no account of its destruction is available.

The book is called a "vision;" the books of Isaiah and Nahum share that description. It apparently describes a literary form that allows the readers to hear God announcing his decisions relating to history. All the forms are highly dramatic and include insights into the happenings of the heavenly court where the Lord reigns.

Obadiah's position among the Minor Prophets is stable in most texts. It is a pivotal book in the ascending scale toward Micah in the center. It is an exponent of the return-from-exile style of eschatology (vv. 19–21), also found in Amos 9, Jeremiah, and Ezekiel. This contrasts with the view in Hosea, Joel, and the books after Micah, in which the future of Israel is seen as being a worshiping people among the empires, hoping for a rebuilt Temple but not expecting a return to political power.

The first part of the book (vv. 1–18) proclaims the Lord's readiness to exact retribution from Edom for wrongs done to Judah, her neighbor.

The last section (vv. 19–21) proclaims the hope that the kingdom of God will be established, that the dispersed people of Israel and Judah will return to their homelands, and that they will have power over their neighbors, especially Edom.

The book should be read in the context of the Minor Prophets and of Isaiah, for Obadiah's views are balanced by Habakkuk and other books from Micah through Malachi. They put much more emphasis on the future Israel's worship of the Lord in Jerusalem than on political power over others.

JOHN D. W. WATTS

ORPHAN. In biblical Israel, as in the ancient Near East in general, the socioeconomic well-being of a community depended primarily on the ability of adult males to provide financially for those around them, to protect them from physical harm, and, in general, to uphold their honor ("name"). Persons without a specific male to fulfill these obligations were at greatest risk in the community; therefore, there are many calls for the protection and proper treatment of the husbandless ("widows") and the fatherless ("orphans"), as well as others at risk in an Israelite community. In the Hebrew Bible, "widows" are mentioned alongside "orphans" in thirty-four of the forty-two occurrences of the latter. This pairing continues into the Apocrypha (e.g., 2 Macc. 3.10), the New Testament (James 1.27), and early church writings (e.g., 1 Clem. 8.4). Other individuals at risk mentioned less frequently with "orphans" are aliens (Deut. 24.17, 20, 21), the weak, the needy, the poor, the destitute (Ps. 82.3–4; Isa. 10.1–2; Zech. 7.9–10), and Levites (Deut. 14.29; 16.11, 14). The greatest concerns of these individuals are that they will be unable to protect the property they have (Job 24.3; Prov. 23.10), unable to support themselves financially (2 Kings 4.1), and unable to maintain the "name" of their deceased husband or father (Deut. 25.5–7; 2 Sam. 14.7).

To provide care for these individuals is to "do justice" to them (Deut. 10.18; 24.17; 27.19; Ps. 10.18). Tragically, the males in a community often shirk this responsibility (Deut. 25.5–10; Ruth 4.6) or even exploit their neighbors and relatives who are at risk (2 Sam. 14.4–11; cf. Judg. 11.1–3). The failure or inability of "orphans" and others at risk to gain support forces them to turn to royal administrators for help (2 Kings 4.13; 8.5; Jer 22.1–3). So, a primary responsibility of Israel's kings is to care for needy persons, like orphans (Ps. 72.14, 12–14). Unfortunately, this responsibility is mentioned most often in prophetic condemnations of the royal bureaucracy for failing to fulfill it (Isa. 1.23; 10.2; Jer. 5.28; Ezek. 22.7). The theological foundation for these condemnations is important to recognize. God is the ultimate example of one who is concerned for the welfare of individuals like orphans (Deut. 10.18; Pss. 10.14, 8; 94–6; 146.9); he is the ultimate "redeemer" for the orphan (Prov. 23.10–11; cf. Ps. 68.6). The king and his officials are watched and criticized more than others because they have been designated as God's overseers of the people, including orphans. The failure of the king and his officials to "do justice" to orphans not only reflects badly on them but also on the God who established them.

In the New Testament, besides the exhortation to "care for orphans and widows in their distress" (James 1.27), the only reference to "orphans" appears in John 14.18 ("I will not leave you orphaned"). The imagery suggests that Jesus' followers, by themselves, would not be able to maintain their "inheritance" from God; but Jesus is saying that he will act as their protector and provider.

TIMOTHY M. WILLIS

PARADISE. Originally a Persian word meaning "park" or "enclosure," paradise first appears in the Septuagint with reference to the garden of Eden (Gen. 2) and became associated with a pristine state of perfection free of suffering. In apocalyptic literature the loss of this original paradise represented the loss of the presence of God in human experience, and therefore redemption was imagined as the recovery of paradise whether it was on earth or in heaven. At the end of the world the righteous would be rewarded by a return to paradise.

Although paradise was initially an earthly garden, New Testament writers lifted it above the evils of this world. Paul says that his visionary flight to the "third heaven" carried him into paradise (2 Cor. 12.1–4), and according to Luke 23.43 Jesus tells the penitent thief that at the moment of death they will be together in paradise. Yet Jesus also is reported to have said that the eschatological paradise described by Isaiah (35.5) was manifested in his ministry (Matt. 11.5) and that the qualities of Eden were revealed in his person (John 4.10–14). Clearly, early Christian writers believed that the traditions of paradise were fulfilled in Jesus and his ministry.

GREGORY SHAW

PASSOVER. This festival, observed on the fourteenth day of the month of Nisan (March/April), commemorates the Exodus of the Hebrews from Egypt. Of the five lists of festivals in the Hebrew Bible (Exod. 23.14–17; 34.18–25; Lev. 23.1–37; Num. 28–29; Deut. 16.1–6), only the last three make reference to Passover (Lev. 23.5; Num. 26.16; Deut. 16.1–8), and all of these associate the celebration with the seven-day festival of unleavened bread, which commences on the fifteenth of the month. Exodus 23.14–17 and 34.18–23 mention only the festival of unleavened bread as an early spring celebration. The narrative in Exodus 12.1–36 provides an explanation of the origin of Passover as well as the features involved in its celebration; this narrative also associates Passover (12.1–14) with the festival of unleavened bread (12.15–20).

According to Exodus 12.1–13, the following were characteristic of Passover. On the tenth day of the month, the animal to be slaughtered was selected and set aside for safekeeping; according to Exodus 12.5, the animal was an unblemished, one-year-old goat or lamb, although Deuteronomy 16.2 includes calves. The animal was slaughtered on the fourteenth day late in the afternoon. Some blood of the animal was smeared on the doorposts and lintels of the houses. The animal was roasted whole (see Exod. 12.46 and Num. 9.12; Deut. 16.7 specifies boiling, which would have required dismemberment). The flesh was eaten, along with unleavened bread and bitter herbs, by members of the household or associated households. The meal was eaten in haste, with the participants dressed for flight. Any uneaten meat, should there be any, was to be burned the next morning.

The eating of unleavened bread at the meal is explained by the haste with which the Israelites had to flee (Exod. 12.34,

39), but no biblical explanation is offered for the consumption of bitter herbs. The daubing of the blood on the doorposts, later assumed to have been part of only the original episode, is described as marking the houses of the Israelites so that God would bypass their homes in the slaughter of the firstborn. (Note the similar substitution of a ram for the firstborn in Gen. 22, and the similar use of a red marker to avoid death in Josh. 2.17–21.)

If people were ritually unclean or away on a journey when Passover was observed in Nisan, they could celebrate the festival in the second month in similar fashion (Num. 9.1–13). Foreigners and thus non-Jews who had settled among the people were allowed to keep the Passover, provided they were circumcised (Exod. 12.48–49; Num. 9.14).

Although Exodus 12 seems to imply that Passover was a home festival and thus could be observed apart from a pilgrimage to a sanctuary, Deuteronomy 16.5–7 requires that the slaughter of the animal and the meal occur at a place (sanctuary) that God would choose. The same pilgrimage requirement seems assumed by Exodus 34.25 and Leviticus 23.4–7.

The Hebrew name of the festival, Pesah, is derived from the verb that means "to protect," "to have compassion," "to pass over," and is used to describe the action of God in the

The Passover, from the Altarpiece of the Last Supper

Exodus narrative (12.13, 23, 27). The English designation "passover" shows the influence of the Vulgate translation.

Most scholars assume that Passover was originally a spring festival, associated with a shepherding culture, that was secondarily related to the Exodus story (note the reference to a festival in Exod. 5.1 before the Exodus). Such a celebration would have been connected with either the annual spring change of pastures or the sacrifice of the firstborn to insure the continued fertility of the flocks (see Exod. 22.29–30) or both. Characteristics pointing to such an origin for the festival in Exodus 12 are the lamb or goat to be slaughtered, cooking by roasting, the time of the year (which coincides with the lambing season and the change of pastures), the absence of priest and altar, the lack of dedicating any part of the edible flesh to God, the family nature of the celebration, and the nocturnal observance at the time of full moon.

The tractate *Pesaḥim* in the Mishnah provides a description of the way that the rabbis (about 200 CE) understood Passover to have been celebrated before the destruction of the Second Temple (70 CE). Many of the features reflected in *Pesaḥim* are thus characteristic of the observance at the time of Jesus, and some have continued in Jewish tradition to the present. The following elements in the celebration are noteworthy.

The people brought their Passover animals to the Temple in the late afternoon and, because of the numbers of worshipers, were admitted to the sanctuary in three separate groups. The worshipers slaughtered their animals and the priests caught the blood and tossed it against the altar. The animals were flayed and cleaned in the Temple courtyard, with the required fat and internal portions being burned on the altar (Lev. 3.3–4). While each group was performing these functions, the Levites sang the Egyptian Hallel psalms (Pss. 113–118) and repeated them if time allowed (*Pesaḥ.* 5.5–10).

The animals were carried from the Temple precincts and cooked for the Passover meal. Cooking was done by roasting so as not to break any bone in the animal (*Pesaḥ.* 7.1,11; see Exod. 12.46; John 19.36).

At the meal, everyone ate at least a portion of the Passover animal. The flesh was eaten along with varied herbs (*Pesaḥ.* 2.6), unleavened bread, a dip (*ḥărōset*) composed of pounded nuts and fruits mixed with vinegar, and four cups of wine. After the second cup, a son asked the father, "Why is this night different from all other nights?" and the father instructed the son on the basis of Deuteronomy 26.5–11. Between the second and third cups, Psalm 113 (or 113–114) was sung. After the fourth cup, the Hallel was concluded. At the conclusion of the meal, the people departed but not to join in revelry (*Pesaḥ.* 10.1–8).

The people sought to celebrate the meal as if they themselves had come out of Egypt—"out of bondage to freedom, from sorrow to gladness, and from mourning to festival day, and from darkness to great light, and from servitude to redemption" (*Pesaḥ.* 10.5).

JOHN H. HAYES

PASTORAL LETTERS, THE. Since the second half of the eighteenth century, the two letters to Timothy and the letter to Titus have been known as the Pastoral Letters. The three are closely related in both content and form and offer advice about the exercise of the pastoral office in the care and oversight of congregations.

Outline.

1 TIMOTHY

   I. Opening (1.1–2)

  II. Body of instructions (1.3–6.21a):

    A. The authority of Paul to give instructions to Timothy in the face of false teachers (1.3–20)

    B. The instructions (2.1–6.21a):

      1. On prayer for all (2.1–7)

      2. On the inner connection between the prayer of men and women and their conduct (2.8–10)

      3. On women who are false teachers (2.9–15)

      4. On bishops (3.1–7)

      5. On deacons (3.8–13)

      6. Interlude: basis of and need for instructions for the household of God in the face of false teachers who deny the goodness of marriage and creation (3.14–4.5)

      7. To Timothy to teach Paul's instructions (4.6–5.2)

      8. On widows (5.3–16)

      9. On elders (5.17–25)

     10. To slaves (6.1–2a)

     11. To Timothy to teach the foregoing instructions in the face of greedy false teachers (6.2b—21a)

 III. Closing (6.21b)

2 TIMOTHY

   I. Opening (1.1–2)

  II. Thanksgiving (1.3–5)

 III. Body of letter: Paul's example, exhortations, and predictions form his last will and testament for Timothy (1.6–4.18):

    A. Paul bequeaths to Timothy the deposit of faith for which he suffers (1.6–18)

    B. Exhortation to Timothy to be prepared to suffer, like Paul, as a teacher (2.1–7)

    C. Example of Paul who draws strength from the gospel as he suffers (2.8–13)

    D. Exhortation to Timothy to teach faithfully in the face of the evil conduct of false teachers (2.14–26)

    E. Prediction that false teachers will abound in the last times (3.1–9)

    F. Example of Paul's life of teaching amid great persecution (3.10–17)

    G. Exhortation to Timothy to teach persistently; prediction that people will give little heed to sound teaching (4.1–5)

    H. Example of Paul, who at death's door trusts in God to save him (4.6–18)

 IV. Final greetings and closing (4.19–22)

TITUS

   I. Opening (1.1–4)

  II. Body of instructions (1.5–3.11):

    A. Instruction to Titus to appoint elders and bishops in Crete who will promote sound teaching in the face of those teaching Jewish myths (1.5–16)

    B. Instructions that accord with sound doctrine (2.1–15):

      1. On older men and women (2.1–3)

      2. On younger women and men (2.4–8)

      3. On slaves (2.9–10)

      4. Theological and christological bases of the instructions (2.11–15)

    C. Additional instructions (3.1–11):

      1. Instruction to live a harmonious, generous, and gracious life with all (3.1–7)

2. Instruction to do good deeds and to avoid idle words (3.8–11)
III. Closing (3.12–15)

Authorship. The authorship of these letters, called pastoral because they deal largely with pastoral or practical matters and grouped together because they address the same issues in a uniform style, is contested. While the Pastoral Letters have a noticeable Pauline character, there are five major areas in which they differ from the indisputedly genuine Pauline letters. First, the vocabulary (e.g., "the saying is sure" [1 Tim. 1.15; 3.1; 4.9; 2 Tim. 2.11; Titus 3.8]) and style vary greatly from those of the letters to the Romans and Corinthians and are closer to those of the apostolic fathers such as Polycarp. Second, the theological concepts (e.g., "the faith") and the stress on public respectability differ markedly from emphases in the undisputed Pauline letters. Third, church order—bishops, elders, widows, deacons—does not correspond to that found in the genuine Pauline letters but is more like that in evidence toward the end of the first century CE. Fourth, the author relies much more heavily on traditions, both creedal and hortatory, than the Paul of the authentic letters; unlike Paul in Galatians, for example, he rarely argues theologically with opponents but merely upbraids them. Finally, the Pastoral Letters do not fit into the career of Paul as detailed in Acts and Romans. The chronology of the Pastoral Letters presupposes that Paul was freed from his imprisonment in Rome, changed his plans to go to Spain, journeyed back to the East on another missionary enterprise, was imprisoned a second time, and was then martyred.

Theories that attempt to account for these differences are as follows. First, accepting the Pastoral Letters as fully authentic, it is felt that Paul was indeed freed from his first imprisonment and returned to the East for further missionary work. 1 Timothy and Titus reflect this mission. Arrested again, Paul was imprisoned, tried, and executed in Rome. 2 Timothy issues from the time of this second imprisonment. Paul's need to establish church order in communities and to counteract false teachers accounts for the different vocabulary of the Pastoral Letters. These last letters date to ca. 65 CE, and because they stem from an aged Paul, they lack the theological acumen of a vibrant and young Paul.

Another theory also presupposes further missionary work by Paul in the East, but it accounts for the high incidence of uncharacteristic Pauline elements in the Pastoral Letters by postulating that Paul employed a secretary to whom he gave greater responsibility in creating these letters ca. 65 CE.

A third theory holds that the Pastoral Letters contain so many un-Pauline words and concepts because they were written by a later author, who, ca. 85 CE, desired to apply the teaching of Paul to new situations in the Pauline missionary territory. This author worked into his letters fragments of genuine Pauline letters, such as 2 Timothy 1.15–18, 4.6–22, and Titus 3.12–14. These authentic fragments account for the personal notes, which a later author presumably would not have invented.

A fourth theory is more radical and maintains that the letters are completely pseudonymous and are in this regard like the contemporary pseudonymous Socratic letters, which are written under Socrates' name and apply his teaching to a later time. In writing three letters, the author was influenced by the trend in evidence in Cicero, Seneca, and Pliny of publishing a collection of letters. Writing ca. 100 CE, the author uses personal notes to add verisimilitude to the letters and to present Paul as an example to be imitated. Thus, for exam-

Statue of St. Paul (Adamo Tadolini, 1838)

ple, the personal note of 2 Timothy 4.13, which depicts the imprisoned Paul asking that the cloak he left behind in Troas be brought to him, adds local color to the letter and also shows how Paul embodies his teaching of contentment with the basic necessities of life (1 Tim. 6.8). The view adopted here is a modification of this fourth position and dates the Pastoral Letters ca. 85 CE.

Purpose. The goal of the Pastoral Letters is to provide instructions on how the household of God should live in Paul's spirit during the post-Pauline era, when the expectation of the Lord's imminent coming has receded and teachers are propounding false doctrine in the apostle's name. In this situation the author writes to two of Paul's most trusted collaborators with a message that is actually addressed to an entire church, be it a long-standing gentile church like that of Ephesus addressed in 1 Timothy or a new Jewish Christian church like that of Crete addressed in Titus. The instructions that are to govern the churches addressed in 1 Timothy and Titus have Paul's apostolic authority behind them (note the imperatives that run throughout the letters, e.g., 1 Tim. 2.1, 8, 12; Titus 2.1, 6; 3.1). By obeying these imperatives, the entire church, but especially its leaders, will inculcate sound teaching in the face of false teachers (1 Tim. 6.1; Titus 2.5). Paul's last will and testament in 2 Timothy requires that the church imitate Paul's example (especially his willingness to suffer for the faith, 1.8; 3.10–11), follow his instructions (4.1–5), hold on faithfully to the deposit of faith (1.13–14), and be guided by his predictions (3.1–10). In doing so, they will be able to combat false teaching (14–19).

It is somewhat difficult to ascertain the exact nature of the false teaching countered in the Pastoral Letters. This is because, unlike Paul, the author rarely argues with the false teachers but is content to hurl stereotyped charges against them, paralleled primarily in popular philosophy. These charges follow a set schema: the false teachers are greedy (1 Tim. 6.5; Titus 1.11), do not practice what they preach (2

Tim. 3.5; Titus 1.16; 3.8–9), are involved in verbal quibbles (1 Tim. 1.4, 6; 4.2; 6.4; 2 Tim. 2.14, 16, 23; Titus 1.10; 3.9), are guilty of many vices (1 Tim. 1.9–10; 2 Tim. 3.2–4), and take advantage of women (2 Tim. 3.6).

Once the stereotypical aspects of the polemic are discounted, the following picture of false teachers emerges. They are Jewish Christians who emphasize the Law (1 Tim. 1.7; Titus 3.9; cf. Titus 1.14), Jewish myths (Titus 1.14; cf. 1 Tim. 1.4; 4.7; 2 Tim. 4.4), and genealogies (1 Tim. 4.3–5). They teach that the resurrection has already occurred (2 Tim. 2.18). Some of the proponents of their doctrine are women (1 Tim. 2.9–15). If this false teaching with its emphasis on speculation and depreciation of the material is to be called gnosticism, then it would be advisable to call it proto-gnosticism, for it cannot be identified with any later known gnostic system or group.

Theology. While the Pastoral Letters were not written by Paul, there is no doubt of their Pauline character. The image of Paul as a prisoner for the faith, known from Philippians and Philemon, is reflected throughout 2 Timothy (1.8, 12; 2.8–13; 3.11–13). The Pauline emphasis on the universality of the gospel (see Rom. 1.5) is prominent (1 Tim. 2.4–7; 3.16; 4–10; 2 Tim. 4.17; Titus 2.11). The Pauline accent of God's fidelity to promise (see Rom. 3.3) finds expression in 2 Tim. 2.13; Titus 1.2. That redemption is through Jesus Christ (see Rom. 3.24–25) is underscored (1 Tim. 2.5–6; 2 Tim. 2.11–12; Titus 2.14). The Pauline hallmark that salvation and "justification are by faith alone and not by works (see Rom. 3.28) echoes in 1 Tim. 1.13–16; 2 Tim. 1.9–10; Titus 3.5–7. The creative theologizing of the Paul of Romans may be past, but the results of that creativity live on in traditions and are actualized by the Pastoral Letters for Pauline churches of the generation after Paul.

In combating the doctrines of the false teachers, the author develops a theology of creation. The theology of the Pastoral Letters fears a benevolent God, who wills life, goodness, and salvation for all men and women (Titus 3.4–7). All that this God has created is good: marriage (1 Tim. 2.15; 4.3), food (1 Tim. 4.3), wine (1 Tim. 5.23), possessions (1 Tim. 6.17–19), the round of humdrum daily human chores (Titus 2.1–10). The instructions that form much of 1 Timothy and Titus demonstrate that this God does not desire that chaos exist in God's world; order in human affairs is willed by the divine creator.

As a corollary of his teaching on creation, the author stresses the human side of "Christ Jesus our Savior" (Titus 1.4). He is also the mediator between God and individual men and women; he is the human being who has given himself up as a ransom for all persons (1 Tim. 2.4–6). Christ Jesus, in the face of the opposition of Pontius Pilate in his earthly life, remained steadfastly obedient to God's will and made the good confession (1 Tim. 6.13). In Titus 2.13–14 we find dynamically juxtaposed the divinity and humanity of Jesus, the great god and savior who died to redeem men and women from all iniquity and to gather them into a people.

Some of the ethical teaching in the Pastoral Letters has been evaluated as a middle-class or bourgeois ethic, which does not challenge the status quo but strives to live by its norms. Thus, for example, the qualities required of a bishop in 1 Timothy 3.1–7 are basically those required of a general by Onosander (died 59 CE). Similarly, the norms of Titus 2.1–10 are largely those of the patriarchal model of the author's society.

The author's world-affirming ethic and desire to conform to society's standards are also evident in his great concern that the conduct of church leaders should be irreproachable in the eyes of the larger public: bishops (1 Tim. 3.7; Titus 1.6, 7), deacons (1 Tim. 3.10), and widows (1 Tim. 5.7, 10). He takes great pains to ensure that the conduct of slaves (1 Tim. 6.1; Titus 2.10) and of young wives (Titus 2.5) should not bring discredit on the word of God or on the sound teaching.

The church order of the Pastoral Letters is not that of Ignatius of Antioch (ca. 110 CE) with his insistence of the monarchical bishop with elders and deacons under him. It reflects rather the somewhat loose structure evident in 1 Clement (ca. 95 CE), in which bishops and elders exist side by side. With their offices of bishop (1 Tim. 3.1–7; Titus 1.7–9), elders (1 Tim. 5.17–22; Titus 1.5–6), deacons, both men (1 Tim. 3.810, 12–13) and women (1 Tim. 3.11), and widows (1 Tim. 5.3–16), the Pastoral Letters reflect the transition period between Paul, who taught that the church was animated with diverse charismata, and Ignatius, who insisted that one individual be in charge of the churches of a distinct area. In the Pastoral Letters the leaders' task, as demonstrated by the instructions to the two representative leaders, Timothy and Titus, is to guard the deposit of faith (2 Tim. 1.14) and to be apt teachers of sound doctrine, capable of refuting false teachers and revilers (1 Tim. 3.3; 5.17; 2 Tim. 4.1–2; Titus 1.9).

ROBERT J. KARRIS, O.F.M.

PAUL. Paul was born at Tarsus in Cilicia (Map 7.F3), at about the beginning of the common era. A member of a Hellenistic Jewish family, which could trace its descent to the tribe of Benjamin (Rom. 11.1; Phil. 3.5), he was given the Hebrew name Saul, as well as the name Paul. Unlike many Jews, he was also a Roman citizen (Acts 16.37; 22.25–28).

As a child, Paul would learn of his Jewish heritage in the local synagogue at Tarsus. He received at least the final stages of his education in Jerusalem, though, under the guidance of Rabbi Gamaliel (Acts 22.3; 26.4). He soon rose to a position of some eminence as a Pharisee, perhaps even becoming a member of the Sanhedrin (Acts 26.5; Phil. 3.5).

When Christianity first came to prominence in Jerusalem, he was strongly opposed to it and was prepared to take personal responsibility for ensuring its extermination (Acts 9.1–2; 1 Cor. 15.9; Gal. 1.13). But while on his way to Damascus in Syria, chasing Jewish Christians who had fled there, he had a remarkable experience that changed the course of his life. Looking back on it twenty years later, he compared it to the appearances of Jesus to the disciples after the Resurrection (1 Cor. 15.1–11); as a result of that encounter, his fervent devotion to biblical faith as understood by the Pharisees was augmented by an unqualified commitment to the gospel.

From this point, his life took a new direction, as he threw himself into missionary work throughout Asia Minor and Greece. He established many churches, and saw himself as God's chosen agent to take the gospel to the gentiles (Gal. 1.15–16, 2.7–8). The New Testament nowhere mentions his death, but reliable traditions depict him as a martyr in Rome, beheaded during the persecution of Nero in the mid 60s CE.

Sources. We have two major sources of information about Paul: his letters and the book of Acts. There has been much debate concerning their relative worth. Paul's own writings must obviously have priority, though it is certainly not easy to reconstruct the story of someone's life on the basis of a miscellaneous and incomplete collection of occasional letters. Acts at least appears to provide a plausible framework, but is not always easy to correlate with what can be deduced from the letters.

Both sources must be treated with some caution, for neither was intended to be a biography. He features prominently in Acts, but the main focus there is on the rapid spread of Christianity from Jerusalem to Rome. The letters are mainly concerned with specific circumstances in the life of various churches, and inevitably reflect more of these than they do of Paul's own life. They contain limited personal details and report very few incidents.

Additionally, Acts and the letters deal with different aspects of Paul's life. Acts shows him as a great missionary pioneer, taking the gospel to far-flung corners of the empire. It therefore reports his initial preaching of the gospel to non-Christians and their reactions to it, but it never mentions the letters! But they were written to Christians, and show how Paul related to those already in the church. For this reason alone it is difficult to draw direct comparisons between the two sources of information.

Yet we have little alternative but to try to combine the two sources. Acts provides the one really useful clue to the chronology of Paul's life. The reference to his encounter with Gallio at Corinth (Acts 18.12–17) dates this incident somewhere between 1 July 51 and 1 July 52, and by judicious deductions from that it is possible to work out a general outline of Paul's life. But there are still problems. There is no agreement on the number and sequence of his early contacts with the Jerusalem Christians (Acts 11–15; Gal. 1–?). There is also doubt over the number of times he was imprisoned, with Paul apparently implying an imprisonment at Ephesus not mentioned in Acts (Rom. 16.7; 1 Cor. 15.32; 2 Cor. 1.8; 11.23).

Background. Tarsus was a typical Hellenistic city, with a cosmopolitan population and a variety of religious options for its people. Its citizens were well known for their interest in philosophy, and Tarsus was home to several prominent Stoics, including Athenodorus, adviser to Augustus. No doubt, Paul had at least a passing acquaintance with their thinking, as well as some knowledge of the various mystery religions and of Greek philosophy in general. He occasionally makes specific reference to Stoic writers (1 Cor. 15.33), and some have thought his letters show influence from Stoic and Cynic debating styles. But it is unlikely that he had a formal education in such subjects. He did, however, enjoy and appreciate life in the Hellenistic cities, and his metaphors demonstrate close knowledge of urban activities (1 Cor. 3.10–15; 4.9; 9.25–27).

Throughout his letters, Paul exhibits a passionate devotion to his Jewish heritage (Rom. 11.1–6; Gal. 1.13–14; Phil. 3.4–6). He was always at pains to demonstrate that his understanding of the gospel was quite consistent with biblical faith, and that Christian believers were spiritual heirs to ancient Israel. Toward the end of his ministry, he invested much time and energy in maintaining good relations between gentile Christians and the church in Jerusalem (2 Cor. 8.1–15; Rom. 15.25–33). It was his insistence that gentile churches give financial aid to the church in Jerusalem that ultimately led to his arrest and transportation to Rome (Acts 21–28).

His thinking also owed a good deal to the beliefs of the original disciples. Admittedly, he could declare himself independent of the Jewish apostles (Gal. 1.11–12, 17), but that was a tactical move in the face of strident opposition. When his presentation of the gospel is compared with other parts of the New Testament, it turns out to have the same basic structure as the preaching of Peter and other leading apostles. Moreover, the practical advice he gave his converts is surprisingly similar to that of other New Testament writers.

St. Paul

The nineteenth-century Tübingen school dismissed this picture as a harmonization produced by the writer of Acts in the interests of the later catholic church. They thought Paul radically different from Jerusalem and Jewish Christianity. More recently, things have turned full circle and some have argued that Paul was actually under the control of the Jewish church, and took his orders from Jerusalem; that too seems unlikely. Nevertheless, Paul was concerned for the unity of Jews and gentiles in the church, and we misunderstand him if we place his life and thinking outside the mainstream of first-generation Christianity.

Missionary Activity. Paul was convinced that on the Damascus road God had commissioned him to take the gospel to the gentiles. Both tactically and theologically he felt it was important that the gospel also be proclaimed to Jews (Acts 13.46–48; Rom. 1.16; 9–11; 1 Cor. 9.2021), and,

P

223

according to Acts, his usual practice was to go first to the local synagogue. Galatians 2.7–9, however, indicates that his activity was apparently directed exclusively to gentiles.

In his travels, Paul took advantage of the fine highway system built by the Romans, and in the course of three extended tours he visited most of the key centers in Greece and Asia Minor. Although he had a physical weakness (2 Cor. 12.7–8), he must have been incredibly tough, judging from the list of hardships he survived (2 Cor. 11. 23–27).

Paul seems to have had a carefully designed strategy for evangelism. He aimed to establish churches in the largest population centers, which he could easily reach on the paved Roman roads. From there, local converts could take the message into more remote towns and villages. This was evidently successful. At least one of his letters (Colossians) was written to a church founded in this way, and later in the first century most of the areas he visited had many flourishing congregations.

Paul's converts were a typical cross section of Roman society. Many Christians were slaves, though the gospel also attracted cultured upperclass Romans. Some were clearly influential people (Rom. 16.23), the kind who would take personal disputes to law courts (1 Cor. 6.1–11) and who could afford to make donations for good causes (2 Cor. 8.1–15; Rom. 15.25–33). Paul's coworkers also enjoyed the typically mobile lifestyle of the upper classes; in the absence of church buildings, the Christian community depended on the generosity of its richer members to provide facilities for corporate worship and hospitality for wandering preachers (Rom. 16.3–16; Philem. 2, 22; 1 Cor. 16.19). At the same time, Paul was certain that the gospel transcended the barriers of race, sex, and class, and insisted on the equality of all believers (Gal. 3.28; 1 Cor. 12.1–31).

The Letters. Literary epistles were common in the Roman world. Though Paul followed the style of the day, in some ways his letters are not literary works. He was essentially a speaker, and his letters contain what he would have said had he been physically present (2 Cor. 1.15–2.4). This no doubt explains his often uneven style. It also highlights some of the problems faced by the modern reader. At least one of Paul's letters (1 Corinthians) was clearly written in answer to previous correspondence from the church at Corinth (1 Cor. 8.1), and most of the others are a response to information that had reached him in one way or another. But of course we only have one side of the correspondence. And we may not even know that as well as we think, for ancient letter writers often entrusted significant parts of their message to the bearer of the letter to deliver orally. At best, therefore, reading Paul's letters is like overhearing one side of a telephone conversation: it is possible to pick up the general drift, but specific details are more elusive.

Not all of Paul's letters are like this. Some think Romans a more considered statement of Paul's thinking. Ephesians seems to have been a circular letter, sent to several churches. And in many letters, Paul shows that his writing can be sophisticated (1 Cor. 13), while his detailed arguments must have been carefully worked out before they were written down (e.g., Rom. 5–8).

Scholars disagree on whether all thirteen letters attributed to Paul are genuine. He regularly used a secretary, and wrote along with associates, so we may expect variations in style. But most doubt that the Pastoral letters come from Paul (1–2 Timothy, Titus), while others have questioned Ephesians, Colossians, and 2 Thessalonians, on a variety of theological, stylistic, and literary grounds.

The letters certainly give us an insight into Paul's character. He was a formidable opponent (Galatians), but he also had a remarkable capacity for deep concern and true friendship (Rom. 16.1–6; 1 Thess. 2.6–9). He had a realistic understanding of human relationships, and was sensitive to those less robust than himself (1 Cor. 7–8). He also had an uninhibited sense of humor (Gal. 5.12).

Theology. Paul did not become a Christian because he was disillusioned with Judaism. He was totally dedicated to biblical faith, and quite certain that it made sense (Gal. 1.14; Phil. 3.6). It was his conversion experience that changed his life and played a major part in the development of his theology.

He discovered that Jesus was no longer dead, but alive—and must be "the Son of God" (Gal. 1.15–16; 2 Cor. 4.6). He realized that the Law was not central to salvation, for on the Damascus road God had burst into his life not because of his obedience to the Law but in spite of it. All he could do was to respond to this demonstration of God's freely given love. As he did so, Paul became aware of a moral and spiritual transformation taking place within him, a process that would ultimately remake him to be like Jesus (2 Cor. 2.18; Gal. 2.19–20).

This challenged his preconceptions, especially his attitude to the Law. How could he reconcile his previous understanding of God's will with his new perspective? He did so most eloquently in the conflict with the judaizers of Galatia, arguing from the Bible itself that the Law had always been intended as merely a temporary word from God (Gal. 3.24), and that faith had always been the true basis of salvation, as far back as the time of Abraham (Gal. 3.6–9). This was why he was prepared to argue with such force that gentile converts did not need to become Jews in order to be proper Christians.

But this was not the only way Paul described his beliefs. Elsewhere he refers to the Christian life as "a new creation" (2 Cor. 5.17), in which men and women have been "rescued from the power of darkness and transferred to the kingdom of God's beloved son" (Col. 1.13–14). The "age to come" was not locked up in the future; it had burst into the present through the life, death, resurrection of Jesus, and the coming of the Holy Spirit.

Paul knew well enough that God's will was not yet fully effective on earth, and he expected a future divine intervention when the power of evil would finally be crushed, and when Jesus would return in glory (1 Cor. 15.20–28; 1 Thess. 4.13–5.11). But he was certain that Christians were already a part of God's new order, and the church was to be an outpost of the kingdom in which God's will might become a reality in the lives of ordinary people. Through the work of God's Spirit, individuals (Gal. 5.22–23), society (Gal. 3.28), and the whole structure of human relationships (1 Cor. 12–14), could be radically transformed, so that in the context of a physically renewed world system (Rom. 8.18–23; Col. 1.15–20), God's people should grow to "the measure of the full stature of Christ" (Eph. 4.14).

JOHN W. DRANE

PENTECOST. The word Pentecost (Greek "fiftieth") appears twice in the Septuagint as one of the designations of the "feast of weeks" (Exod. 34.22; Deut. 16.10;), which comes between Passover and Tabernacles. In the Hellenistic period, the feast also called for renewal of the covenant God made with Noah (Gen. 9.8–17). Later, after the destruction of the Temple in 70 CE, the feast began to lose its agricultural association and became linked with Israel's sacred history by celebrating the giving of the Torah on Sinai. In synagogue worship, it became customary to read the book of Ruth and Exodus 19–20.

Luke gives new significance to the first Pentecost following the resurrection and ascension of Jesus. For Luke (Acts 2) it is the fulfillment of Jesus' promise that his followers would receive power when the Holy Spirit would come upon them (Luke 24.49; Acts 1.5, 8; and see also Acts 2.16–21, quoting Joel 2.28–32).

The narrative is replete with allusions to biblical traditions, including creation and the Flood, the tower of Babel (Gen. 11.1–9), and various theophanies, especially that at Sinai. Luke does not tell us where the followers of Jesus were assembled when the Spirit came, but the subsequent scene seems to be in the Temple court. The Spirit's coming was attended by "a sound like the rush of a violent wind" filling the house where they were gathered, and is marked by the appearance of "tongues, as of fire;" then the followers "were filled with the Holy Spirit and began to speak in other languages" (Acts 2.24). While the reported charge of drunkenness (v. 13) may suggest the kind of ecstatic speech that Paul describes in 1 Corinthians 12–14, Luke understands these "other tongues" as foreign languages and articulate witness. Within Israel, near and distant neighbors are finding their unity in the gospel. For Luke, what happens at Pentecost is a promise of what will happen among all the nations when the gospel will be preached to the gentiles (see Acts 1.8; 10).

For Christianity, Easter as the new Passover and Whitsunday as the new Pentecost became the basis for the liturgical year.

JOHN FREDERICK JANSEN

PERSIA (Map 7:K4–5). The home territory of the ancient Persians was the mainly mountainous terrain east of the head of the Persian Gulf. They called it Parsa (Grk. Persis); it was roughly equivalent to the modern Fars. The first appearance of this name (Parsua) in history, however, on the Black Obelisk of the Assyrian king Shalmaneser III (ca. 843 BCE) and followed eight years later by a mention of twenty-seven chiefs there, indicates a position somewhere in Iranian Kurdistan; but a similar name is recorded somewhere to the southeast a generation later. In 692–691 BCE, the name is cited in an alliance of peoples against Sennacherib, which seems to have been centered in the Zagros further to the southeast.

By about 640 BCE, when a king named Kurash (Cyrus) appears in Assyrian annals, the Persians seem to have been established in Parsa; this ruling family was Achaemenid (descended from a semilegendary ancestor Achaemenes). It has been supposed that there were two Achaemenid royal lines, one (that of Darius) in Parsa, the other (that of Cyrus the Great) in a land called Anshan; but in 1972 it was discovered that Anshan lay in the middle of Parsa. These Persians were Indo-Iranian speakers like the Medes (Darius spoke of himself as Ariya, i.e., Aryan or Iranian). They may perhaps have reached Parsa in stages from beyond the Caucasus; but some at least could have gradually infiltrated by way of northeastern Iran and Carmania. They were subject to the Medes before Cyrus the Great overthrew King Astyages in 550 BCE; according to Herodotus, they had been subject for the best part of a century.

Under Cyrus and his son Cambyses great conquests occurred in rapid succession: the Median empire in 550 BCE, western Asia Minor (the Lydian kingdom of Croesus) about 546 BCE, the Babylonian empire with Elam and the Levant in 539 BCE, and (under Cambyses) Egypt in 525 BCE. Darius I added Sind (Hindush) about 516 BCE. Thus the three great

river lands of the Tigris and Euphrates, the Indus, and (until 402 BCE) the Nile were subject, and the resulting empire was the most extensive that the world had known.

Efficiency in military preparations and fighting skills had given the Medes and Persians a reputation for invincibility. But the failure to subdue the Scythians about 513 BCE and serious reverses in Greece between 492 and (under Xerxes) 480–479 BCE caused a collapse in confidence. After this, the sole successful major expedition in one hundred years was that in which the heroic marshal Megabyxos reconquered the Delta after a revolt (459–454 BCE). The later kings relied largely on Greek mercenaries and even fleets in their military operations in the west, with no great success, however, until the ruthless Artaxerxes III was able to bring his revolting satraps (governors) under control and in 345–343 BCE to reconquer Phoenicia and Egypt. In the east of the empire and the Arabian fringes, however, peace seems to have generally been maintained with little exertion of force.

The system of imperial government set up by Darius I continued with little change until the end of Persian rule. In the Iranian and Anatolian satrapies noble Persian fief-holders kept household brigades and maintained order except in mountain regions where occasional punitive expeditions would be launched. Communication with the imperial chanceries was normally in Aramaic.

In Babylonia and Egypt, a developed administrative system was in existence and was taken over. The kings appointed fiscal overseers in the temples and normally enjoyed the cooperation of the priesthoods. Confiscation after conquest and revolts gave rise to great estates belonging to the king, royal relatives, and leading nobles or court officials. In Babylonia, many fiefs were related to obligations of military ser-

Pentecost, from "Heures a l'Usage de Rome" (Acts 2.1–4)

vice. In what had once been Solomon's kingdom west of the Euphrates, deportation in Assyrian times had resulted in a mixed population with little nationalistic feeling except in Judah and Phoenicia; prompt acquiescence to Persian rule had saved the "people of the land" from confiscations after Cyrus's conquest of Babylon.

The Achaemenids worshiped Zoroaster's god Ahuramazda with his polarization of Justice (or Order) and the Lie; but this did not lead to religious intolerance. The deities Anahita and Mithra were hardly less revered by the Persians, and fire was worshiped as a god. The officiants were Magi. Among gods of the subject peoples the Greek Apollo, the Syrian goddess Alilat, and Yahweh seem to have been specially favored. Thanks to Cyrus and Darius I, the new Temple in Jerusalem was completed (515 BCE); subsequently Nehemiah (445 BCE) and Ezra (either 428 or 398 BCE) were sent there on special missions, and Darius II seems to have yielded to objections from the Jerusalem priesthood about the right of the Jewish garrison at Yeb (Elephantine, in Upper Egypt) to rebuild its temple and also to keep its own special feast of the Passover.

Persian rule thus allowed considerable cultural assimilation and religious syncretism, Babylon above all becoming a cosmopolitan center. Their art was a composite in which different traditions merged. The court style, which (like the Old Persian script) was devised by Darius I, exalted the grandeur of the king in a timeless setting; as seen in the Persepolis friezes it is impressive in its composure.

After the conquest by Alexander the Great (334–323 BCE) the lands of the empire were ruled by Macedonian successor kings, Parthians, and Romans. Persia had no further importance in biblical history.

J. M. COOK

PETER, THE LETTERS OF. *This entry consists of two articles, the first on* 1 Peter *and the second on* 2 Peter.

1 Peter

Content and Structure. After opening greetings (1.1–2) the writer moves to a prayer of thanksgiving for the Christians' hope of salvation (1.3–12). Reborn through the resurrection of Christ (1.3–5) they can await the end in hope (1.6–9), for they know more than the prophets (1.10–12). Consequently, they are summoned to a life of holy endeavor and to the avoidance of sin against one another (1.13–21); all this they can achieve because they have been born of the Word and continue to feed on it (1.22–2.3), are members of a holy people built on Christ, and have roots lying in God's choice of Israel (2.4–10).

Building on this, the writer then details the kind of behavior that should distinguish the readers as God's people (2.11–3.12) and lead unbelievers to glorify him (2.11–12). He outlines the duties of free citizens (2.13–17), slaves (2.1825; Christ should be their example), and wives and husbands (3.1–7), and finally reminds them of their need to hold together and to react gently to outside provocation (3.8–12).

When they suffer, however, it should be because of doing good and not because they have committed some crime (3.13–17). Christ himself, although innocent, had suffered for their salvation; God vindicated him, and they may also expect to be vindicated (3.18–22). They must therefore separate themselves from their former ways of life (4.1–6) and stay together in love, for the end is not far off (4.7–11). They ought not, however, be surprised if, before it arrives, they are persecuted; if persecuted, it must not be as criminals but

as Christians (4.12–19). Finally, leaders of the church are addressed (5.1–5), and all are reminded yet once again to stand firm against outside forces (5.6–11). In 5.12–14, the writer gives the closing greetings.

Although it is structured like other letters of the period, 1 Peter contains little of a personal nature; addressed to Christians in a wide area (1.1), it reads more like an address than a letter. Some scholars have therefore viewed it as a baptismal sermon or as a letter that includes, or was derived from, such a sermon or baptismal liturgy. It is preferable to regard it as a letter of a general nature, directed to readers far distant from the writer, who is unfamiliar with the details of their situation. In writing it, he makes considerable use of existing Christian tradition in the way of creedal (3.18, 21b, 22) and catechetical (2.13–3.7) material, as well as of the Septuagint and the traditions about Jesus.

Recipients. Paul's preaching led to the beginning of the church in the Roman province of Asia (Acts 19.1–20) and in Galatia. It is not known how the churches in the other areas mentioned in 1.1 came into existence. Those addressed in the letter had almost all been converted from Greco-Roman religions (1.14, 18; 4.3) and came from a wide range of social, economic, and educational backgrounds. The churches would not have been large bodies but consisted instead of little knots of believers dispersed over a wide area. They have already been persecuted and expect to be persecuted again; these persecutions, however, were not directed by the state. Those of Nero (64 CE) and Domitian (in the last decade of the first century CE) did not affect the areas to which the letter was addressed; those described by the Roman writer Pliny the Younger as taking place in part of the area are too late (112 CE). The Christians were persecuted rather by members of their own families (3.6), neighbors, and city authorities because of their withdrawal from many common activities and because of their distinctive life-style (2.12, 20; 3.14–17; 4.3–4, 14–16). Their isolation is reflected in the many exhortations to support one another with mutual love (1.22; 2.17; 4.8) and in their feeling that they are exiles (1.1; 2.11). They need to stand firm and not to retaliate against their persecutors (2.21–24; 3.13–17; 4.12–14).

Authorship. Three views have been held. According to the first, the letter was written by the apostle Peter because his name appears on it, it has reminiscences of the teaching of Jesus that he could have provided, and 5.1 may suggest the writer was an eyewitness to the death of Jesus. But the Greek in which the letter is written suggests an educated author rather than a simple fisherman; the Septuagint, to which Peter would not have been accustomed, is used in biblical quotations in the way someone brought up with it would use it; the account of the death of Jesus (2.22–24) is not that of an eyewitness but is drawn from Isaiah 53. So it has been suggested that Silvanus (5.12) acted as secretary to Peter; the general thought in the letter would have been that of Peter, but its actual expression that of Silvanus. Since, however, the main support for Peter's authorship comes from the detail of the letter and not its general thought, this makes difficult the idea of Silvanus as secretary. If he had been secretary, we might expect him to add his own greetings (cf. Rom. 16.22). It has been suggested that he wrote it after the death of Peter to preserve Peter's teaching, but it is hardly likely that he would then have introduced the self-praise of 5.12. Increasingly, therefore, scholars have come to believe that the letter is pseudonymous (writing in the name of another person was not unknown in the ancient world). Disciples of Peter after his death may have continued to expound the special themes of his teaching, believing it should be made known to a wider circle. Each of these theories fits with the belief that the letter was written from Rome (Babylon in 5.13 is probably a code name for Rome) where Peter died.

Date. The letter must have been written prior to 120–130 CE, for by then other writers know it. It shows the influence of Pauline ideas and terms, and this suggests it must be later than 60 CE, for it was about this time that Paul came to Rome. If Peter himself wrote it from Rome, it was also about this time that he arrived there. The sporadic and local nature of the persecutions means they cannot help in determining the date. Their strength together with the areas to which the letter was written, most of which do not appear to have been evangelized early, suggest a period later than the death of Peter, perhaps around 80 CE.

Significant Features. In 2.13–3.7 and 5.2–5, we have an example of a type of instruction in common use among the early Christians (see Eph. 5.22–6.9; Col. 3.18–4.1; 1 Tim. 2.8–15; 5.3–8; 6.1–2; Tit. 2.1–10); a code of duties is provided for various areas of behavior in the household, society in general, and the church. These codes came to the church from the Hellenistic world via Judaism. While the areas for which advice was required did not vary in passing from secular writers to Christian, the advice itself did. It relates necessarily to the situation and period of the letter: 2.13–17 presupposes a nondemocratic government, 2.18–25 the existence of slaves, and 3.1–6 a male-dominated society. In each case, a strong element of subjection is present and a careful attitude toward the non-Christian world is demanded (cf. 2.11–12). Indeed, one of the main themes of the letter concerns the relation of the Christian community to secular society (2.11–12); such a concern is inevitable where a community is being persecuted.

One of the most puzzling passages in the letter is 3.19, and no agreement exists as to its precise meaning. From it and other New Testament passages (Acts 2.27; Rom. 10.7; Eph. 4.9) the phrase in the Apostles' Creed, "descended into hell" was derived. There are many stories in ancient literature, both Greek and Jewish, of visits to the underworld. The "spirits in prison" have been understood as either the unrepentant dead of Noah's time or the fallen angels ("sons of God") of Genesis 6.14. These angels featured largely in contemporary Jewish thought, especially in 1 Enoch, a writing that some Christians regarded highly. It is normally supposed that Christ made the journey mentioned in 3.19 during the period between his crucifixion and resurrection, but it is possible that it is that of his ascension. Whichever it was, on it he preached to "the spirits in prison." This preaching may have been either of judgment or salvation; if the former, it implied that the power of the spirits was finally broken (cf. v. 22); if the latter, there is no indication that they accepted it, repented, and were saved. The reference in 4.6 may or may not deal with the same event. In it, the "dead" are neither the spiritually dead nor the righteous dead of the Hebrew Bible, but either Christians who have already died (the delay in the return of Christ worried many Christians as to the fate of their dead; cf. 1 Thess. 4.13) or all the physically dead who died before Christ could be preached to them.

Although the letter does not contain the word "church," it is penetrated throughout by a strong sense of togetherness. Its recipients are being persecuted. This has estranged them from the society in which they live and forced them to cling closely to one another. To sustain them, the writer reminds them that, even if they seem small in number, they belong to a body whose roots lie in the Bible. He does so by applying to them texts that were originally written in relation to Israel (see especially 2.4–10). In an age when antiquity was revered, this gave them a standing both in their own eyes and in those of outsiders. At the same time they are also reminded that they have been chosen by God to be his people. As such, they are depicted as the stones of his temple with Christ the cornerstone, and they themselves also as priests within the temple offering the sacrifice of holy living. The realization of their new position before him should compensate for any loss of position in the secular world and enable them to withstand the physical and verbal abuse of their neighbors. Certainly they should give no offence to those outside but should be continually seeking to win them to their number by declaring God's wonderful deeds. Even the wife who is abused by her husband because she is a Christian may win him for Christ by her meek and sober behavior (3.1).

The main purpose of the letter, however, is not to encourage the recipients into missionary activity or to teach them the relation of the Christian church to non-Christian society. The letter is not primarily a handbook of Christian ethics, although it contains much on this subject; nor is it a tract on the nature of the atoning death of Christ. Rather, it is written to give its readers hope in a situation that may terrify them because of its hostility. The situation will not continue for long, because Christ will soon return (1.6; 4.7; 5.10). Let them then rejoice even though they suffer (1.8; 4.13), for they have been born anew to a fresh hope (1.3) in God (1.21), which will be fulfilled when Christ returns.

ERNEST BEST

St. Peter

P

2 Peter

2 Peter presents itself as a testament or farewell discourse of the apostle Peter, written in the form of a letter shortly before his death (1.14). Its object is to remind readers of Peter's teaching and to defend it against false teachers, who were casting doubt on the Lord's coming to judgment (the parousia) and advocating ethical libertinism.

Structure. (For the symbols, see below, Genre.)

Address and Greeting (1.1–2)
T^1 Theme: a summary of Peter's message (1.3–11)
T^2 Occasion: Peter's testament (1.12–15)
A^1 First apologetic section (1.16–21)
    Reply to Objection 1: the apostles based their
       preaching of the parousia on myths (1.16–19)
    Reply to Objection 2: biblical prophecies were the
       products of human minds (1.20–21)
T^3 Peter's prediction of false teachers (2.1–3a)
A^2 Second apologetic section (2.3b–10a)
    Reply to Objection 3: divine judgment never hap-
       pens (2.3b—10a)
E^1 Denunciation of the false teachers (2.10b—22)
T^4 Peter's prediction of scoffers (3.1–4) (including
    Objection 4: v. 4)
A^3 Third apologetic section (3.5–10)
    Two replies to Objection 4: that the expectation of
       the parousia is disproved by its delay (3.5–10)
E^2 Exhortation to holy living (3.11–16)
Conclusion (3.17–18)

Genre. 2 Peter is clearly a letter (1.1–2). But it also belongs to the literary genre of "testament," which was well known in Jewish literature of the period. In such testaments a biblical figure, such as Moses or Ezra, knowing that his death is approaching, gives a final message to his people, which typically includes ethical exhortation and prophetic revelations of the future. In 2 Peter, four passages (marked T1-T4 in the analysis) particularly resemble the testament literature and clearly identify the work as Peter's testament. In 1.12–15, a passage full of conventional testament language, Peter describes the occasion for writing as his awareness of approaching death and his desire to provide for his teaching to be remembered after his death. This teaching is summarized in 1.3–11, which is in form a miniature homily, following a pattern used in farewell speeches. There are also two passages of prophecy (2.1–3a; 3.1–4) in which Peter foresees that after his death his message will be challenged by false teachers.

The rest of 2 Peter is structured around the four passages belonging to the testament genre. It includes three apologetic sections (A^1-A^3), which give the work a polemical character and whose aim is to answer the objections the false teachers raise against Peter's teaching. There are four such objections, only the last of which is explicitly stated as such (3.4). In the other three cases, the objection is implied in the author's denial of it (1.16a, 20; 2.3b). Finally, there are two passages (E^1, E^2) that contrast the libertine behavior of the false teachers, denounced in 2.10b-22, with the holy living expected of readers faithful to Peter's teaching (3.11–16).

Author and Date. Testaments were generally pseudepigraphal, attributed to biblical figures long dead, and probably understood as exercises in historical imagination. The use of the genre suggests that 2 Peter is a work written in Peter's name by someone else after his death, though it is possible that the testament genre could have been used by Peter to write his own, real testament. But it should also be noticed how the predictive character of the testament is used in 2

Peter. Nothing in the letter reflects the situation in which Peter is said to be writing; the whole work is addressed to a situation after Peter's death. The predictions of false teachers function as pegs on which is hung the apologetic debate about the validity of Peter's message. Moreover, whereas the testamentary passages speak of the false teachers in the future tense, predicting their rise after Peter's death (2.1–33; 3.1–4; cf. 3.17), the apologetic sections and the denunciation of the false teachers refer to them in the present tense (2–3b-22; 3.5–10, 16b). It is scarcely possible to read 2 Peter without supposing the false teachers to be contemporaries of the author. The alternation of predictive and present-tense references to them is therefore best understood as a deliberate stylistic device to convey the message that these apostolic prophecies are now being fulfilled. In other words, Petrine authorship is a fiction, but one that the author does not feel obliged to maintain throughout his work. In that case, it must be a transparent fiction, a literary convention that the author expected his readers to recognize as such.

For these and other reasons, most modern scholars consider 2 Peter to be pseudepigraphal, though some still defend Petrine authorship. The most cogent additional reasons for denying Peter's authorship are the Hellenistic religious language and ideas, and the evidence for dating the work after Peter's death in the mid-60s CE. Scholars differ widely on the date of 2 Peter, which many consider to be the latest New Testament writing, written well into the second century CE. But the clearest evidence for a postapostolic date is 3.4, which indicates that the first Christian generation has died, and this passage may well suggest that the letter was written at the time when this had only just become true, around 80–90 CE. This was the time when those who had expected the parousia during the lifetime of the apostolic generation would face the problem of the nonfulfillment of that expectation, but there is no evidence that this continued to be felt as a problem in the second century.

The literary relationship between 2 Peter and Jude is another consideration relevant to the date of 2 Peter. There are such close resemblances (especially between Jude 4–13, 16–18 and 2 Peter 2.1–18; 3.1–3) that some kind of literary relationship seems certain. Some scholars have held that Jude is dependent on 2 Peter or that both depend on a common source, but most conclude that 2 Peter has used Jude as a source. Of course, this requires a late date for 2 Peter only if Jude is dated late.

If 2 Peter was written not by Peter, but after his death, why did the author present his work in the form of Peter's testament? Probably because his intention was to defend the apostolic message in the period after the death of the apostles (cf. 3.4) against teachers who held that, in important respects, the teaching of the apostles was now discredited. By writing in Peter's name he claims no authority of his own, except as a faithful mediator of the apostolic message, which he defends against attacks. The form of the letter as an apostolic testament is therefore closely connected with its apologetic purpose as a vindication of the normative authority of the apostolic teaching. That the author chose to write *Peter's* testament is probably best explained if he was a leader of the Roman church, which had counted Peter as the most prestigious of its leaders in the previous generation.

Opponents. The opponents have usually been identified as gnostics, but this identification, as recent scholarship has recognized, is insecure. The only features of their teaching that are clear from our author's refutation of it are eschatological skepticism and moral libertinism. The parousia had

P

been expected during the lifetime of the apostles, but the first generation had passed away and in the opponents' view this proved the early Christian eschatological hope mistaken (3.4, 9a). This attitude seems to have been based on a rationalistic denial of divine intervention in history (cf. 3.4b) as well as on the nonfulfillment of the parousia prophecy. But it was also related to the ethical libertinism of the opponents. Claiming to be emancipating people from fear of divine judgment, they felt free to indulge in sexual immorality and sensual excesses generally (2.2, 10a, 13–14, 18).

There is no basis in 2 Peter itself for supposing that these teachings of the opponents had a gnostic basis. They are more plausibly attributed to the influence of popular Greco-Roman attitudes. The false teachers probably aimed to disencumber Christianity of elements which seemed to them an embarrassment in their larger cultural environment: its apocalyptic eschatology, always alien to Hellenistic thinking and especially embarrassing after the apparent failure of the parousia hope, and its ethical rigorism.

In response to this challenge the author of 2 Peter mounts a defense of the apostolic expectation of judgment and salvation at the parousia and of the motivation for righteous living which this provides. The author argues that the apostles' preaching of the parousia was soundly based on their witnessing of the transfiguration, when God appointed Jesus to be the eschatological judge and ruler (1.16–18), and on divinely inspired prophecies (1.19–21). Scriptural examples prove that divine judgment does happen and prefigure the eschatological judgment (2.3b—10a). As God decreed the destruction of the ancient world in the Flood, so he has decreed the destruction of the present world in the fire of his eschatological judgment (3.5–7, 10). The problem of the delay of the parousia is met by arguments drawn from Jewish tradition: that the delay is long only by human standards, not in the perspective of God's eternity, and should be seen as God's gracious withholding of judgment so that sinners may repent (3.8–9). Throughout his work, the author is concerned that the hope for the vindication and establishment of God's righteousness in the future (cf. 2.9; 3.7, 13) necessarily motivates the attempt to realize that righteousness in Christian lives (3.11, 14).

Theology. The peculiar theological character of 2 Peter lies in its remarkable combination of Hellenistic religious language and Jewish apocalyptic ideas and imagery. For example, the author summarizes Peter's teaching in a passage that, in its ethical and religious terminology, is perhaps the most Hellenistic in the New Testament (1.3–11). On the other hand, he accurately and effectively reproduces Jewish apocalyptic ideas, especially in 3.3–13. This combination of theological styles is to be explained by the author's intention of interpreting and defending the apostolic message in a postapostolic and Hellenistic cultural situation. But this is a delicate task; in the author's view, in his opponents' attempt to adapt Christianity to Hellenistic culture they were compromising essential features of the apostolic message. In order to defend the gospel against this excessive Hellenization, therefore, the author resorts to sources and ideas close to the apocalyptic outlook of early Christianity, including the letter of Jude. The author thus keeps a careful balance between a degree of Hellenization of the gospel message, and a protest, in the name of apocalyptic eschatology, against extreme Hellenization that would dissolve the substance of the message. The letter is a valuable witness to Christianity's difficult transition from a Jewish to a Hellenistic environment, and provides an instructive example of how the message of the gospel was preserved through the process of cultural translation.

RICHARD J. BAUCKHAM

PHILEMON, THE LETTER OF PAUL TO. Philemon was a Christian who lived in the Phrygian town of Colossae (Map 14:E3) in the middle of the first century CE. The chief concern of the brief letter is the fate of Philemon's slave Onesimus. That name meant "useful," and it was frequently given to slaves. It seems that this slave had at first been useful to his master, but had become useless because, having found conditions intolerable, he had fled from Colossae, probably taking with him certain valuables belonging to the owner (v. 11).

The letter speaks of what followed that escape. Making his way to a larger city, Onesimus had been arrested and thrown into prison, where he met Paul. Here the slave was converted (v. 10) and soon made himself useful to Paul. On his release, the new Christian had to decide what to do about the claims of his defrauded master. To return to him was to risk severe punishment, for escape from slavery was a capital offence and Philemon would have every right to select his own penalty. Encouraged by Paul, however, the slave decided to return and set out for Colossae, accompanied by Tychicus (Col. 4.9) and bearing this letter from Paul. Such a decision must have been the result of intense inner struggle; on the one hand, there was the risk of punishment, at the very least the loss of freedom; on the other, the urging of Paul and the authority of his new master, Christ.

On the delivery of the letter, the master must also have faced a difficult decision. There would have been resentment over the violation of his property rights, supported as they were by Roman law and universal custom. Yet the letter was an appeal from an apostle through whom Philemon, as well as his slave, had been converted (v. 19). Paul asked the owner to welcome his slave as a brother, to accept restitution for former losses, and to treat him as if he were Paul himself. As master, Philemon must recognize the supreme authority of his own master, Christ. Even more than forgiveness was at stake, for Paul seems to have asked Philemon not only to free Onesimus but even to send him back to Paul to help in the mission work as a substitute for his onetime owner. Reading between the lines of the letter, we can see that each member of this triangle was taking a risk and making a sacrifice stemming from his allegiance to Christ.

For Paul this was no private matter but a communal concern. By including the greetings of his colleagues, he claimed their support for his request. In addition to Timothy (v.1), he mentioned five fellow workers, including the prisoner Epaphras, to whom the church in Colossae may have owed its origin (Col. 4.12). He also wanted the members of the church in Colossae to become involved (v. 2). To help them understand the issues at stake, Paul probably sent, in the same mail as it were, another letter, the longer Colossians (Col. 4.7, 9), in which he made the radical claim that all social distinctions have been erased among those who belong to Christ (3.11–21).

In this letter, as in all ancient documents, many points remain uncertain. The hometown may have been Laodicea and not Colossae. The location of the prison is uncertain: Rome, or more likely Ephesus. The slaveowner may have been Archippus and not Philemon. Nothing is known of the later history of the major characters, though it is barely possible that the onetime slave later became the bishop in Ephesus (Ignatius, *Eph.* 1.3). What is certain, however, is the radical character of conversion, not only of people but

P

Ruins of the Roman forum at Philippi.

of their attitudes toward their own property, their rights, and their obligations. Brief as it is, the note gives a colorful vignette of life in a congregation in western Asia Minor.

PAUL S. MINEAR

PHILIPPIANS, THE LETTER OF PAUL TO THE.

The Church at Philippi. The letter that bears the title "To the Philippians" was addressed to the church in Philippi, an important city in Macedonia (Map 14:02). The emperor Octavian had made Philippi a Roman colony and gave to its citizens the rights and privileges of those born and living in Rome. According to the account in Acts, the church in Philippi began as follows: Paul, on his second missionary journey, left Asia Minor for Macedonia, came to Philippi, preached the gospel; Lydia, a prominent woman from that area, and a few others became Christians. The church apparently was first housed in Lydia's home (Acts 16.9–40). In spite of its small beginnings, it grew and became an active Christian community, taking an important part in evangelism (Phil. 1.3–8), readily sharing its own material possessions, even out of deep poverty (4.16; cf. 2 Cor. 8.1–5), and generously sending one of its own people to assist Paul in his work and to aid him while he was in prison (2.25–30). Paul visited this church on at least three occasions (Acts 16.12; 2 Cor. 2.13; Acts 20.6).

Author and Date. No writer in ancient times and scarcely any today question that Paul wrote the letter to the Philippians. But from where did he write it, and when? On these questions there is divergence of opinion. Most scholars hold that Paul wrote the letter from Rome; others have suggested Corinth or Ephesus; a good case can also be made for Caesarea. But from wherever Paul wrote, it had to be a place where he was in prison, where there was a Roman praetorium (i.e., emperor's palace, or a provincial governor's official residence; see 1.12, 13), and where there were members of Caesar's household (i.e., the royal entourage at the palace

or at any provincial capital; see 4.22). Hence, Rome (ca. 60 CE) or Caesarea (ca. 58 CE) are the most likely places, since each had a praetorium with its royal staff, and in each Paul is reported to have been jailed.

Integrity. An increasing number of scholars consider Philippians to be not a single letter but several—at least two, possibly three—woven into one. The disjointed nature of the letter as it stands (note the abrupt transition in tone and content between 3.1 and 3.2); Paul's leaving his "thank you" to the end (4.10–20); and Polycarp's reference in his own letter to the Philippians (3.21) to Paul's having written them several letters, are some of the reasons for suggesting that Philippians is a composite made up of different letters, or letter fragments. But the abruptness noted above is hardly an argument against the integrity of Philippians, for it is not inconsistent with the characteristics of private speech, nor with Paul's style (cf. Rom. 16.16–18; 1 Thess. 2.13–16). And though Polycarp mentions that Paul wrote several letters to the Philippians, he apparently knew and used none other than this.

Contents of the Letter. Paul begins his letter with the typical greeting (1.1–2), and continues with thanksgiving to God and prayer for the Philippians' continued growth in love and good works (1.3–11). He makes known to them how the gospel has advanced even while he is in prison (1.12–18), and assures them that he will be released and will return to Philippi (1.19–26). He begs them to live worthily of the gospel in unity, harmony, and generosity without grumbling or complaining, keeping always before themselves Jesus Christ as the supreme model for any moral action (1.27–2.18). He exhorts them further by describing the qualities of Timothy and Epaphroditus, and he promises to send both to Philippi (2.19–30). He warns them against evangelistic Jews or judaizers, whose teaching and practices are contrary to the gospel (3.119), and concludes the letter by making a final appeal for unity (4.1–3), offering suggestions as to how Christians should think and act (4.4–9) and thanking the Philippians for their numerous gifts to him (4.10–20). He closes with salutations (4.21–23).

The Hymn. Philippians 2.6–11 is an exquisite example of an early Christian hymn, used and probably modified by Paul for his purposes here. Its interpretation has long been debated. Differences in interpretation revolve primarily around two Greek words, *harpagmos* (2.6) and *kenoō* (2.7). Some understand the former to mean "a thing to be held on to," and understand Christ as possessing equality with God, but not clinging to it as something he might lose. Others understand it to mean "a snatching after" and see Christ as a second Adam, who unlike the first refused to grasp after being equal with God (see the NEB, and cf. Gen. 3.5). Mere recently, some have shown that *harpagmos* is part of an idiomatic expression referring to an attitude of mind one has toward that which is already possessed. Thus, Christ is seen as not regarding his being equal with God as a condition to be used (NRSV: "exploited") for his own benefit.

The other word, *kenoō*, often translated as "to empty," also means, "to make powerless," "to pour out." Some see this as an act of the human will of Jesus, the last Adam. "He made himself powerless," that is, he deliberately chose the lot of fallen humanity. Others, however, understand this as an act of the will of the preexistent, divine Christ.

The vocabulary and tone of the hymn, as well as the context in which it is placed, argue for the interpretation that sees Jesus Christ as preexistent, divine ("in the form of God"), equal with God, but who nevertheless refused to take advantage of all this for his personal gain. Instead, in that preexistent state, he willed to pour himself out, to serve by becoming human. He considered being equal with God not as an excuse for avoiding service and redemptive suffering but as that which uniquely qualified him for these tasks. Thus, God exalted him and gave him the highest name in heaven and on earth, the name "Lord."

If the hymn is about Christ, it is also about God, making clear the true nature of God. The Christ of the hymn shows by both his attitude and actions that for him to be in the "form of God," to be "equal with God," meant that he must give and spend himself. The hymn, then, makes it clear that God's true nature is not selfishly to seize but openhandedly to give.

Understood in this way the hymn fits perfectly into the context of chap. 2. Whereas the Philippians were acting selfishly, living with a grasping attitude (2.3–4), Christ's attitude and actions were exactly the opposite. So Paul appeals to them to bring their conduct into harmony with the conduct of Christ. Here is a splendid example of Paul's method of encouraging the Christian life by presenting sublime theological truth.

GERALD F. HAWTHORNE

PHILISTINES. A group of Aegean origin, the Philistines were one of the Sea Peoples who ravaged the eastern Mediterranean world subsequent to the collapse of Mycenean civilization at the end of the Late Bronze Age. Attempting to land in Egypt, they were repulsed in a great land and sea battle by Ramesses III (ca. 1190 BCE), after which they settled on the southwestern coastal strip of Canaan (Map 3:W5). There they established a confederation of five city-states, the pentapolis consisting of Ashdod, Ashkelon, and Gaza on the coast, and Ekron and Gath inland (Josh. 13.3; 1 Sam. 7–14). Their expansion inland brought them into conflict with the Israelite tribes (Judg. 3.31; 13–16; 1 Sam. 4–6), who attempted to counter the threat by organizing themselves into a kingdom

(1 Sam. 7–14). Although the Philistines were able to prevail against Saul, the first Israelite king (1 Sam. 31), David, Saul's successor and an erstwhile vassal of Achish, the Philistine king of Gath (1 Sam. 27; 29), decisively defeated them and halted their expansion (2 Sam. 5.17–25; 8.1; 21.15–22; 23.9–17; 1 Chron. 11.12–19; 14.8–17; 18.1; 20.4–8). Over the next few centuries their relations with Israel were for the most part in the form of border skirmishes (1 Kings 15.27; 16.15–17; 2 Chron. 26.6–7; 28.18). In the tenth century Philistia came under loose Egyptian hegemony. As a consequence of the imperialistic ambitions of the Neo-Assyrian empire, the Philistines came under Assyrian rule in 734 BCE. Despite occasional revolts against their overlords, they remained part of the Assyrian imperium, even prospering during the seventh century, until the fall of Assyria (612 BCE). Subsequently caught between Egypt and Babylonia, Philistia was conquered and ravaged by Nebuchadrezzar in 604 BCE. This effectively ended the history of the Philistine people, although their name as handed down through Greek and Latin eventually became a name for the whole of the land they were never able to subdue, namely, Palestine.

Archaeological activity focusing on recovering the material remains of the Philistines has been intense in recent years. Ashdod, Ashkelon, and Ekron (Tel Miqne), as well as smaller sites such as Tel Qasile on the coast and Tel Batash (ancient Timnah) inland, have been or are still being investigated. A picture has emerged of an extremely rich and highly developed civilization, putting a lie to the modern usage of the term "philistine."

CARL S. EHRLICH

PILATE, PONTIUS. Governor of Judea (Luke 3.1) under Tiberius Caesar, he ruled the province 26–36 CE. In addition to details about him occurring in the literary sources discussed below, he is also mentioned in an inscription found at Caesarea in 1961.

The first mention of Pilate in the Gospels concerns "the Galileans whose blood Pilate had mingled with their sacrifices" (Luke 13.1), who were presumably visiting Jerusalem for Passover; this atrocity may explain the enmity (Luke 23.12) between him and Herod Antipas, ruler of Galilee. At the next Passover (3 April 33 CE, rather than 7 April 30 CE?), Pilate was again in Jerusalem to keep order, when the case of Jesus was brought before him for review (Luke 23.1). Only now is he mentioned in the other three Gospels (Matt. 27.2; Mark 15.1; John 18.29); since the last two do not even explain who he was, he must already have been fixed in the apostolic preaching (see Acts 2.23; 3.13; 4.28; 13.28; 1 Tim. 6.13) as a historical anchor.

All four gospel accounts focus on Pilate's question, "Are you the King of the Jews?" In John (18.36) Jesus claims that his kingdom was "not of this world." In Luke (23.2, 5) the Jewish authorities assert that he was a rebel. According to John, Caiaphas, as high priest, had long foreseen the need to act against Jesus in the political interest of the nation (John 11.48–50, 53), but only Pilate could impose the death penalty (18.30–31). Pilate's skepticism about the political charge was neatly turned into a threat to his own status as "Caesar's friend" (John 19.12). Pilate washed his hands before the crowd to make clear where the moral onus lay (Matt. 27.24) and ironically retaliated against the authorities by identifying Jesus on the cross as "King of the Jews" (John 19.19).

The New Testament has Pilate maneuvered against his better judgment into authorizing what Jewish authorities had planned. Within two centuries he could be seen (by Ter-

P

231

tullian) as in effect a Christian, and by the sixth century CE he had become a saint and martyr in the Coptic Church. Some modern analyses have attempted to shift responsibility back onto him: Jesus (or part of his following) was indeed revolutionary; it was a Roman detachment that arrested him (John 18.12); the Sanhedrin was capable of carrying out a death penalty had it needed to and may not even have met formally on this occasion. The momentum of this argument arises partly from the monstrous price exacted in our age for the cry "His blood be on us and on our children," found only in Matthew (27.25) and to be understood in terms of that writer's own perspective as well as first-century politics.

The "procurator" (see Tacitus *Annals* 15.44) of Judea was responsible for the estates of Tiberius Caesar there and for the Roman taxes. The Sanhedrin and other local authorities handled most other administration. In his military capacity, Pilate was also referred to as "prefect," that is, in command of the province, his powers including the supervision of justice. But being only of second (or equestrian) rank, he was subordinate to the senatorial legate of Syria. Pilate's long term implies an understanding with the high priestly dynasty of Annas. He shares their success in keeping the peace, earning the oblique compliment of Tacitus (*Histories* 5.9), "under Tiberius nothing happened." His coinage, unlike Herod's and Caesar's (Matt. 22.20), did not offend the second commandment by carrying a human likeness. He yielded to a suicidal protest by the Jews against the medallions on the military standards even though he had veiled them when brought into Jerusalem (Josephus *War* 2.9.169–74). But when they protested against the expenditure of Temple funds on an aqueduct for the city, he showed no mercy (*War* 2.9.175–77). When similarly brutal tactics were used against the Samaritans in 36 CE, the latter appealed to Vitellius, the legate of Syria, who ordered Pilate to Rome to explain himself (Josephus *Ant.* 18.4.85–97).

Jesus is brought before the people by Pontius Pilate before his crucifixion (Mark 15.6–15).

In 41 CE Philo published a "letter" of Herod Agrippa to Gaius Caesar, successor of Tiberius, denouncing Pilate as "inflexible, stubborn, and cruel" (*Leg.* 299–305) and citing an episode when Tiberius had ordered him to remove from the palace in Jerusalem some shields that offended Jewish scruples. Clearly in the end Pilate lost the support of the Jewish leaders. Their threat to report him to Tiberius (John 19.12) may imply that he was under suspicion as an appointee of Sejanus, the head of government whom Tiberius overturned in Rome in 31 CE. Certainly Philo's tirade would not have been possible if Pilate had been granted an honorable retirement.

EDWIN A. JUDGE

POETRY, BIBLICAL HEBREW. Poetry is the elevated style in which songs, hymns, lamentations, proverbs, wisdom, and prophetic speeches are composed. Biblical poems tend to be of short or medium length, ranging from two to about sixty lines. Longer poems exist, such as Psalm 119, but they are rare, and there is no continuous poem of epic proportion. Unlike most epic traditions, the Bible contains few narrative poems: its major narratives are in prose. Nevertheless, close to one-third of the Hebrew Bible is poetry, distributed in small amounts among the narrative books, in greater amounts in the prophetic books, and predominant in the collections of Psalms, Proverbs, and Lamentations, and in the wisdom books of Job and Ecclesiastes.

Biblical poetry is characterized by a terse, binary form of expression that is eloquent and evocative. The terseness is effected by the juxtaposition of short lines with few specific connectives between them. The connective may be lacking altogether, or may consist of the multipurpose conjunction *wāw*, meaning "and," "but," "or," and so forth. Thus, the exact relationship between lines is often not made explicit. The lines themselves are short, usually three or four words, and their terseness is enhanced by the omission, in many cases, of the definite article, the relative pronoun, and other grammatical particles. Two examples, the first from a narrative poem and the second from a psalm, illustrate the terseness and parataxis of biblical poetry:

> Water he asked:
> Milk she gave:
> In a lordly cup she offered cream.
>
> (Judg. 5.25)
>
> You give to them, they gather:
> You open your hand, they are satisfied well.
>
> (Ps. 104.28)

These two excerpts also illustrate the most prominent feature of biblical poetry, its binary form of expression known as parallelism. Parallelism is the pairing of a line (or part of a line) with one or more lines that are in some way linguistically equivalent. The equivalence is often grammatical—that is, both parts of the parallelism may have the same syntactic structure, as in "Water he asked: Milk she gave." In many cases, however, the grammatical structure is not identical, at least on the surface level. In Judges 5.25, the third line expands and rearranges the syntax of the first two lines. Similarly, in Psalm 104.28 there is partial grammatical equivalence by virtue of the "you-they || you-they" pattern, but the syntax of the lines is, different. Grammar has many facets, and any one of these facets may be brought into play in parallelism.

Another common form of equivalence is semantic equivalence; the meaning of the lines is somehow related:

perhaps synonymous, perhaps reflecting the converse or reverse, or perhaps extending the meaning in any one of a number of ways. Again, equivalence does not imply identity. The second line of a parallelism rarely expresses exactly the same thought as the first; it is more likely to expand or intensify it. The relationship between "they gather" and "they are satisfied well" in Psalm 104.28 is a progression. The relationship between "water he asked" and "milk she gave" in Judges 5.25 is more than a progression—it sets up an opposition, a conflict, between the request and its fulfillment.

Grammatical and/or semantic equivalence account for most parallelisms, but because there are so many equivalent permutations for any given line, the number of potential parallelisms is enormous if not infinite. Although readers/listeners may learn to anticipate a parallelism, they cannot, except in the most formulaic of expressions, predict exactly what the parallelism will be. Each parallelism is cast to fit its context, and the effect of each must be evaluated individually.

There are, however, several general effects that parallelism has. For one thing, it helps to bind together the otherwise paratactic lines, so that the basic structure of the poem is not a single line but rather sets of lines (often called a couplet or a bicolon). Another by-product of parallelism is the rhythm or balance that it creates. Scholars have long sought metric regularity in biblical poetry, but no system—be it syllable counting, stress counting, thought-rhythm, or syntactic constraints—has met with unanimous acceptance. If there is such a metric form, it continues to elude us. It is more likely that the Hebrew poets embraced a looser system—one in which many lines of a poem are more or less the same length and partake of the rhythm of their parallelisms, but without the requirement of precise measurement.

Beyond the level of specific parallel lines it is possible to find a larger structural unit that is often called a strophe or stanza. This is identified by dividing the poem into its major sections, based on contents or on structural or lexical repetitions. Although a longer poem is likely to have more strophes, that is, more subdivisions, the strophe is less well defined than the couplet and seems less basic to the overall poetic structure. The principles whereby couplets are combined into longer segments or entire poems is not well understood, but it is clear that poems have movement and development, and that their lines and couplets cohere as unified compositions. Psalm 104, for example, portrays the creation of the world by means of a description of God's habitat, the sky, and then moves to various natural habitats and the creatures that occupy them. The progression in the poem is obvious even though its strophic divisions may not be.

In addition to their main characteristics, terseness, and parallelism, biblical poems often employ devices such as word repetition, word association, ellipsis, sound play, chiasm (an *A-B B-A* pattern of words, grammatical structures, or lines), inclusio (frame or ring composition), and imagery. Although these devices are not limited to poetry, and are not poetic requirements, they do enhance the poeticality, that is, the sense of elevated style and rhetoric associated with poetry. We draw again on Psalm 104 to illustrate:

> Wrapped in light as (in) a garment:
> Spreading the sky like a curtain. (Ps. 104.2)

Through similes, the first elements of creation, light, and the heavens become the personal effects of God, the glory surrounding and enhancing him. There is also a good deal of assonance in the Hebrew in these two lines, as there is else-

where in the poem. The psalm begins and ends with "Bless the Lord, O my soul," which provides a sense of closure.

The rhetorical impact of biblical poetry is considerable and its aesthetic dimensions manifold. The prophets used it to convince, the wise to instruct, the psalmists to offer praise. In the Bible, language—that is, forms of verbal expression—takes on paramount importance; and it is in poetry that verbal expression reaches its epitome.

ADELE BERLIN

POOR. As the formulaic association of the poor with widows and orphans in ancient Near Eastern literature in general and in the Hebrew Bible in particular shows, poverty was an undesirable condition and not an ascetic discipline to be embraced for a higher goal. Protection and special care for these economically deprived members of society was a responsibility of kings, who demonstrated their power in part by their ability to help those unable to help themselves. This royal responsibility is found in Israel as well, as the interchange between David and Nathan in 2 Samuel 12.1–6 implies and the royal instruction in Proverbs 31.8–9 makes explicit; see also Psalms 72.2, 12–14; Proverbs 29.14.

In premonarchic Israel this obligation was incumbent on the nation as a whole. In some of its earliest legislation, Israel is instructed to ensure that the poor have both a fair hearing in judicial contexts and food from the harvest and sabbatical fallowness (Exod. 23.6, 11; see Lev. 19.10; 23.22), and to lend money to the poor without interest (Exod. 22.25). The prophets repeatedly reminded Israel of these obligations; see Isaiah 10.1–4; 58.7; Amos 2.6–7; 4.1; Ezekiel 18.

What was incumbent on the nation as a whole was also required of the individual. Job's passionate declaration of innocence is a summary of the individual Israelite's moral code; as part of his assertion of complete righteousness, Job details his concern for the poor (Job 29.11–17; 31.16–22; see also Deut. 15.11). This ethical obligation continues to be stressed in the New Testament and in the Qur'ān.

Those who oppressed the poor, then, were the wicked (Ps 37.14; Prov. 14.31), and God was the protector of the poor (Ps. 140.12). He would reward those who gave to the poor (Prov. 19.17) and would ultimately provide for them himself (Isa. 41.17).

All of these texts make it clear that poverty was an unfortunate state. Its origins are explored only in wisdom literature, where it is often attributed to moral shortcomings or at least to a lack of industry, an example of the dominant biblical view that God rewards goodness and punishes wickedness. It must be noted, however, that this point of view is found in literature originating in well-to-do circles, mainly in Proverbs (10.4; 13.18; 14.23; 20.13; 23.21; 29.19).

In the New Testament as well, poverty, especially self-impoverishment, is not an ideal in itself, but rather a condition temporarily assumed for the sake of some higher goal. Paul illustrates this when he speaks of "the generous act of our Lord Jesus Christ, that though he was rich, yet for your sakes he became poor, so that by his poverty you might become rich" (2 Cor. 8.9). The larger context of the verse is the collection for the poor of the church in Jerusalem, an effort to which Paul was committed (see Gal. 2.1–10; 1 Cor. 16.1–4; Rom. 15.25–27); Paul appeals to the Christians of Corinth to imitate the selfless love of Jesus, out of concern for their more needy brothers and sisters. This idea of the "imitation of Christ," also present in Philippians 2.5–8, is made a general ideal in later, monastic Christianity, where

P

poverty is embraced not just or not even primarily for the sake of others but as a means of freedom from material goods that enables one to attain a higher spiritual state in union with Jesus, who in an apparently hyperbolic proverb, said to one who would follow him: "Foxes have holes and birds of the air have nests, but the Son of man has nowhere to lay his head" (Matt. 8.20; Luke 9.58).

The advice of Jesus to the rich young man to "sell all and give to the poor" (Mark 10.21 par.; cf. 10.23–31) must be interpreted in the light of the eschatological urgency felt by early Christians and probably by Jesus himself, as well as the narrative context, despite later abstraction of that command into an ideal of "evangelical poverty." Following earlier biblical descriptions of divine judgment, Jesus is apparently anticipating a reversal of fortune when the kingdom of God appears: the undesirable conditions of the poor, hungry, mourning and persecuted will be altered (Luke 6.20–23; cf. 1 Sam. 2.4–8 and Luke 1.51–53; Isa. 61.1–4 and Luke 4.16–21).

MICHAEL D. COOGAN

PREDESTINATION. The notion of predestination, God's foreknowledge and arrangement of events, has been an important doctrine in certain forms of Christianity, mostly Protestantism, and particularly in forms historically and theologically related to John Calvin, the sixteenth-century reformer from Geneva. In particular this doctrine refers to God's predetermining who is elected and therefore, naturally, who is not. In the ancient world, however, the idea of predestination and foreknowledge had a wider connotation and was common in secular as well as religious writings.

God's providence or forethought was a common feature of ancient Greek writers from the time of Plato (*Timaeus* 30b; 44c) and Xenophon (*Memorabilia* 1.4.6; 4.3.6), and later in the writings of Diogenes Laertius (3.24k) and Plutarch (*Moralia 425f*; 436d). It is therefore not surprising to find that foreknowledge (Grk. *pronoia*) figures prominently in such first-century writers as Josephus and Philo. Josephus claims that it may have been *pronoia* that somehow allowed him to avoid participating in the mass suicide at Jotopata at the outbreak of the Jewish revolt in 67 CE (*War* 3.8.391); while others died or killed each other, Josephus was spared, taken captive by Vespasian, and lived to write his multivolume works *The Jewish War* and *The Antiquities of the Jews*. Philo wrote an entire treatise on *pronoia*. That a person should be able to ascertain God's plan and will or enjoy the predestination of the divine was a claim to one's own influence and position. Such claims were not nearly as fanciful to ancient writers and philosophers as they may seem to many moderns.

In the New Testament the few times this concept is employed it involves trying to figure out how God's actions embodied in Jesus of Nazareth can be understood in the context of and reconciled with God's plans. The writers who took this point up were deeply steeped in the Hellenistic milieu of the cities of Asia Minor and the Greek East. The speculative and philosophical nature of this discussion accords well with the ethos of these eastern urban Greek centers. Thus, the author of 1 Peter says that the elect were chosen by the foreknowledge of God (1.2) and also claims that Jesus was foreknown before the foundation of the world (1.20). Likewise, Acts 2.23, in a speech attributed to Peter, asserts that Jesus was delivered up "by the predestined plan and foreknowledge of God."

Paul utilized this language to articulate what he believed God had done in Jesus of Nazareth and what this means for Jews, gentiles, and current believers in Jesus. To the church in Rome he says God foreknew and predestined those whom he called to become the image of his son (Rom. 8.29). In both Romans 11.2 and Galatians 3.8 Paul tries to reconcile God's predestiny of Israel with the predestiny of believers who are not Jews. This is a difficult argument. He claims finally that God has both chosen and foreordained Israel, and God predestined non-Jews or gentiles to be included in Israel through his selection of Abraham to be a light to the nations. God was able to foresee that the gentiles would be justified by faith through the gospel preached to Abraham beforehand when he said, "All the nations shall be blessed in you" (Gal.3.8, quoting Gen. 12.3).

In the New Testament, then, the rather common Greek notions of foreknowledge and predestiny were used by writers comfortable with the Greek philosophical milieu to reconcile the events that had taken place recently in Jesus of Nazareth with the historic events and promises of Israel's past.

Over the centuries the notion of *pronoia* itself was modified and utilized for a host of theological and social conflicts that the Greek and Jewish writers of the first century CE could not have anticipated and probably would never have imagined.

J. ANDREW OVERMAN

PRIESTS AND HIGH PRIEST. The major cultic persons in Israel. Through the centuries documented in the Bible, priestly duties and activities varied somewhat, but primary in the early period, and always basic, was the idea that a priest is a person attached to the service of God in a sanctuary, God's house. The original concept of the priest as server or minister of God in the sanctuary was analogous to that of a king's minister in the palace. As ministers in a palace set food on the table of an earthly king, early Israelite priests set holy bread on a table before God (1 Sam. 21.4–6), a practice that underlay the provisions for the bread of the presence. As ministers of a king served as intermediaries for citizens wishing to ask the king what course of action to take, or what the king's mind might be, early Israelite priests, using the Urim and Thummim in the ephod, asked God the same sorts of questions for others, including the leaders of the people (Judg. 18.5; 1 Sam. 14.3, 36–42; 22.9–10, 13, 15, 18; 23.9–12; 30.7–8), a practice which evolved into the priestly giving of *tôrâ*, or law, as manifestation of the divine mind. It was as intermediary between God in his holy place and the people outside that a priest communicated God's blessing to the people (Num. 6.22–27; Deut. 10.8; 21.5).

Priests and Sacrifice. In early narratives, including J and E, it was perfectly right for someone who was not a priest to offer a sacrifice on an altar not attached to a sanctuary, without any priestly intervention. When sacrifice was offered at a sanctuary, however, the priests of that sanctuary were involved in it already in the premonarchic period (1 Sam. 2.12–17), and their sacrificial prerogatives increased during the monarchic period. In Deuteronomy 33.10, bringing incense and burnt offerings before God is mentioned among the activities characteristic of priests, but it is in last place. In Ezekiel's prescriptions for priests as they are to function after the exile (Ezek. 44.15–31), their sacrificial activity is in first place (44.15–16), and in Jeremiah 33.18, within a postexilic addition to the book, priests are characterized entirely in terms of sacrificial work. This extension of the sacrificial role of priests can be correlated with an extension of the high degree of holiness proper to the interior of the sanctuary, the place where God's presence was focused, to the open-air altar in the courtyard in front of the sanctuary. The prerogatives of priests to perform all acts inside the house of God was extended to include any act entailing contact with the altar of sacrifice in the courtyard outside. In all of this the fundamental principle remained that the highest degree of holiness among human beings was that of priests, and that only they could rightly enter the spaces whose degree of spatial holiness was the highest.

Priests and the Divine Will. In early texts a priest is characterized not as a person engaged in sacrifice but as one who carries the oracular ephod (1 Sam. 22.18) containing the Urim and Thummim, which were manipulated in order to provide an expression of God's mind or will in answer to a question put to him. In the oldest part of the blessing of Moses for Levi, the Urim and Thummim are still character-istic of a priest (Deut. 33.8), but in 33.10, generally taken as part of a later expansion of the blessing for Levi added toward the middle of the monarchic period, God's ordinances and God's law (Hebr. *tôrâ*) are the primary objects of priestly responsibility, mentioned before incense and burnt offering. The word *tôrâ* may originally have been the word designating the divine response, communicated through a priest with his Urim and Thummim, to a question put to him; the Akkadian word *têrtu*, akin to Hebrew *tôrâ*, signified the response pro-cured in certain types of Mesopotamian divination. If so, Isra-elite *tôrâ* evolved from a simple manifestation of God's will in the form of an answer "Yes" or "No" (through the Urim and Thummim) into a more complex pronouncement expressing the divine will in cultic matters based on such questions as the distinction of the holy from the profane, the pure from the impure (see the *tôrâ* described in Hag. 2.10–14), and in ethical matters too, because of the divine requirement of right behavior on the part of persons approaching what is holy, or, more profoundly, persons divinely expected to be holy (Ps. 15.2, 5; Lev. 19.2). By the end of the monarchic period the meaning of *tôrâ* had been extended to include all divinely sanctioned law, of the types codified in the Pentateuch, and it was then as typically associated with a priest as the word of God was with a prophet (Jer. 18.18). In this expanded sense of "law," sacred because it was an expression of the divine will, *tôrâ*, something in which priests had always been the right-ful experts, became something in which they were compe-tent for deciding questions and settling disputes. Ultimately they became responsible not only for upholding all divine law but also for all casuistry and jurisprudence based on it (Lev. 10.10–11; Deut. 17.8–13; 21.5; Ezek. 44.24). This is not to say that priests became teachers or preachers, unless by that, one has in mind their communicating law and legal decisions to the people. In the postexilic centuries priestly involvement with law weakened in the general consciousness, and priests increasingly came to be associated with sacrifice. The tra-ditional idea of priests as persons making statutes and legal judgments known to the people (i.e., as persons with judicia-ry duties) was alive in the second century BCE (Sir. 45.14–17), but as jurists learned in the law they were by then being sup-planted by the scribes (Sir. 39.1–11). Membership of priests in commissions having judicial duties as well as administrative ones in the Roman period may have been due in large part to their social and political connections.

Historical Evolution of Priesthood. The historical roots of early Israelite priesthood probably lie, culturally, in the cultic systems of the Canaanites and other Northwest Semitic peoples, whose usual word for priest is essentially the same as the Hebrew word. Israelite settlements in Pales-tine had their Yahwist sanctuaries, and throughout the land there continued to be a multitude of such sanctuaries, each

with one or more priests, until the ultimate suppression of all but the Temple in Jerusalem in the reign of Josiah left Jerusalem the only place where anyone could actually func-tion as a priest (2 Kings 23.5, 8–9, 15–20). In the period of the judges and in the early monarchic period one could be a priest without being a member of the tribe of Levi (Judg. 17.5; 1 Sam. 7.1; 2 Sam. 8.18; 20.26; 1 Kings 12.31), and yet a Levite was particularly desirable as a priest (Judg. 1718). If the unnamed ancestor of Eli in 1 Sam. 2.27–28 is Levi, as the context strongly suggests, then the priests of the sanctu-ary of the ark at Shiloh were Levites. Of the personal origins of Zadok, the founding head of the priesthood of Jerusalem (1 Kings 2.35; 4.2), nothing at all is said in the narratives in which he appears, or in any preexilic text. In some scholarly hypotheses concerning his undocumented origins he is held to have been a Levite, in others not.

By the time of Josiah's abolition of all sanctuaries except that of Jerusalem three centuries later, there was no longer any question of anyone's functioning as a priest unless he was a Levite, and the Levitical quality of the Jerusalemite "sons of Zadok" seems at that time not to have been called into ques-tion. Later still, when all priests were considered "sons of Aar-on," the postexilic Chronicler arranged things by presenting Zadok as an aide to an Aaronite commander in David's time (1 Chron. 12.27–29) and by giving Zadok himself an Aaroni-te genealogy (1 Chron. 24.1–6); the purpose of this is clearly that of giving the priests of Jerusalem Aaronite legitimacy, and its historicity is dubious. In any case, while any Levite, according to Deuteronomy, might in principle function as a priest if he were admitted to do so at the sole remaining sanc-tuary, in Ezekiel 40–48 only members of traditionally priestly families of Jerusalem (the "sons of Zadok") are admitted to the exclusively priestly service of the altar; all other Levites are relegated to a lower status with functions of Temple service that, except in 40.45, were not reckoned as priestly. The dis-tinction between priests and subordinated Levites was firmly established in the postexilic restoration, but the fact that in P the priests are not called sons of the clearly Jerusalemite Zadok but "sons of Aaron" may indicate that some members of Levitical families not originally of Jerusalem, but of other cities in the south, were admitted to priesdy service together with the "sons of Zadok" after the exile, as they had perhaps been admitted before the exile, before or after Josiah's reform. All of the cities assigned to the sons of Aaron in the final form of the lists of Levitical cities (Josh. 21.9–19; 1 Chron. 6.54–60) are indeed in the south.

In the actual division of duties between priests and Lev-ites prescribed by P, the priests did everything that entailed contact with the altars and with the offerings after they had contracted holiness (Lev. 1–7; 10.16–20; 16; 17). They were responsible for rites of purification, because of the sacrifices and sacrificial blood involved (Lev. 11–16; Num. 19). In the Persian, Hellenistic, and Roman periods each priest did his Temple service as a member of one of twenty-four divisions (1 Chron. 24.7–19), each division functioning only during a short period of the year (see Luke 1.5, 8). When leadership in matters of piety passed largely to the Pharisees around the second century BCE, priests retained respected and in many cases high social status. Some ordinary priests, in order to make ends meet, engaged in secular occupations, and many lived outside Jerusalem.

The High Priest. Priesthood in Jerusalem in the days of the monarchy had been hierarchically structured, under a head, usually called simply "the priest" (1 Kings 4.2; 2 Kings 11.9–11; 12.8; 16.10–12; 22.12, 14; Isa. 8.2), or, if he needed to be distinguished from the "second priest," he might be called the "chief priest" (2 Kings 25.18). The head of the priesthood of Jerusalem had always held a high place in the kingdom's administrative circles, but after the exile the high priest quickly became the head of the Jewish nation, both civilly and religiously. The presence of a Jewish civil administrator appointed by the Persian imperial government at certain times (ca. 520 BCE, and during the last half of the fifth century) did little to alter the high priest's position as far as the nation itself was concerned. Although Hasmonean rulers of the second and first centuries BCE assumed the title "king," they retained the high priesthood and its title, which was more important within the Jewish community itself. From this time on, the high priests and those close to them, rather worldly in their interests, were of the aristocratic party of the Sadducees. With Herod the Great (37–4 BCE) ruling power in Judah passed completely out of priestly families, life tenure in high priesthood was abolished, and each appointment to the office of high priest was thereafter made by the Herodian ruler or, between 6–41 CE, by the Roman procurator. In the New Testament the plural "the high priests" refers to high priestly families as a group, or at times (e.g., Acts 9.14) to the Sanhedrin or some other group possessing official jurisdiction under the leadership or presidency of the high priest.

In the distribution of ritual responsibilities codified in P, on the basis of degrees of holiness, only the high priest, whose degree of holiness as a person was supreme, could enter the holy of holies, the innermost part of the Temple building and the place whose degree of spatial holiness was the highest, for the rites to be performed there on the annual Day of Atonement (Lev. 16.2–3, 15, 32–34; see Sir. 50.5–21; Heb. 9.6–7).

AELRED CODY, O.S.B

PROMISED LAND. When God called Abraham, one of the things promised was land (Gen. 12.1–2). Though the passage perhaps dates from the tenth century BCE, the promised territory specified in Genesis 15.18 is the land of Canaan from the river of Egypt to the Euphrates River (cf. Deut. 11.24); other boundaries given for the land are more modest. Genesis also records that the promise was subsequently reaffirmed to Abraham's descendants: Isaac (Gen. 26.3), Jacob (Gen. 28.4, 13; 35.11–12), Joseph (Gen. 48.4), and Jacob's other sons (Gen. 50.24).

In biblical narrative, the promise was also renewed in the time of Moses (Exod. 6.5–8). According to Leviticus 25.23, however, the land belonged to God; the Israelites were merely tenants. Deuteronomy represents the land as a gift (Deut. 5.31; 9.6; 11.17; 6.10–11) and describes it in somewhat hyperbolic terms (8.7–9), but continuance on the land was conditional upon obedience to the law. Both Leviticus and Deuteronomy offer the threat of exile and scattering among the nations if the Israelites break the law (Lev. 26.21, 32–33; Deut. 28.63–64) as well as the hope of restoration to the land should they subsequently repent (Lev. 26.42; Deut. 30.1–16). The Pentateuch thus contains different attitudes toward the land, reflecting the historical contexts of its authors, attitudes modeled in part at least on such ancient Near Eastern practices as royal grants of land as rewards to individual subjects.

Joshua began the conquest of Canaan. While some passages indicate complete victory in his time (Josh. 10.40; 11.16–17; 21.43–44) followed by "rest from war" (Josh. 11.23), others make it clear that it was not that quick. When Joshua was an old man, there was still much territory left to seize (Josh. 13.1; Judg. 1.21–36). It was actually David who completed the conquest in the tenth century BCE (2 Sam. 8).

In about 921 BCE, the nation of Israel split into two kingdoms: Israel in the north and Judah in the south. Because of sin, prophets arose to warn the people of judgment. Amos addressed the northerners, threatening them with exile (Amos 5.27; 7.17). Israel, the northern kingdom, fell to Assyria in 721 BCE. Many were taken away to other parts of the Assyrian empire. Jeremiah, in the last days of the kingdom of Judah, predicted exile (Jer. 25.11–12). Judah fell to Babylon in 587 BCE, with the result that many of the leaders were exiled to Babylon. The book of Kings was written in the sixth century BCE to explain the two catastrophes: both kingdoms fell because of idolatry (2 Kgs. 17; 2 Kgs. 21.1–16). Although the prophets pronounced the judgment of land loss, they also looked beyond the disasters to future times of healing and restoration (Amos 9.14–15; Jer. 16.15 = 23.7–8; 24.6; 29.10; 32.41; Ezek. 20.41–42; 34.11–17; 36.24; 37.12–14, 21–22).

During the exile, the Jews longed to return to their land but they learned to maintain their identity without it. While they could not offer animal sacrifice, since that could only be done in Jerusalem, they could preserve their distinctive religion through prayer, Sabbath keeping, circumcision, and observing dietary laws.

In 538 BCE, King Cyrus of Persia, having conquered Babylon a year earlier, allowed the Jews to return and rebuild their Temple in Jerusalem (Ezra 1.1–4; 6.3–5), yet not all the Jews returned. Some became established in Babylon, giving rise to a community that thrived there for centuries. Those in the Dispersion contributed money to support the Temple. Land and sacrifice, now restored, were elevated in importance again, but Israelite religion was not exclusively tied to the land.

In 70 CE, the Temple was destroyed again, this time by the Romans, and the Jews were once more dispersed abroad. They survived this tragedy by maintaining their traditions wherever they went. It would be wrong to say that Judaism is indifferent to the land, however, for the devout Jew prays daily that Jerusalem will be rebuilt speedily, and part of the Passover celebration includes the hope that next year the feast will be eaten in Jerusalem.

In the late nineteenth century, Zionism developed. Largely a secular movement, its goal of the establishment of a homeland for the Jewish people was not primarily to fulfill biblical prophecy but to have a country where Jews could live in security, safe from persecution.

In the New Testament, there is little emphasis on geography, but the imagery of the promised land is symbolically used in the letter to the Hebrews. Abraham is a paradigm for Christians: just as he left his home country by faith, seeking a new one, so Christians should seek the heavenly country or city that God is preparing for them (Heb. 11.8–16).

Hebrews also alludes to the wilderness wandering and the conquest. A whole generation was denied entrance into the land because of rebellion, disobedience, and unbelief (Heb. 3.7–19). The admonition, then, is not to be apostate like them. Hebrews also suggests that Joshua did not really give the people rest (Heb. 4.8–9); rather, God offers rest to those who are obedient and faithful. The author then encourages his audience to enter that rest, which refers not to conquering land and enjoying the ensuing peace, as it did earlier (Josh. 11.23), but rather to trusting in God's works and ceasing from one's own (Heb. 4.9–10).

Nationhood and land are not always spiritualized in the New Testament. Though Paul viewed those Jews who did

Plain of Rephaim from Zion (William Holman Hunt, 1855)

not embrace Jesus as Messiah to be outside of God's favor (Rom. 9–11), he looked forward to a day when the Jewish people as a nation would turn back to God and be forgiven (Rom. 11.26). Jesus also affirmed that the meek would inherit the earth (Matt. 5.5; Ps. 37.11). The book of Revelation tells of a thousand-year period when martyrs of the church would rule with Jesus (Rev. 20). It also predicts the creation of a new heaven and a new earth (Rev. 21.1–4).

Despite this spiritualization of the concept of the promised land, Christians too have on occasion seen themselves as "heirs according to the promise" (Gal. 3.29) in a territorial sense. Both the Boers of South Africa and the Puritan colonizers of New England saw themselves as a new Israel, led by God to a new Canaan, a "providence plantation."

WILLIAM B. NELSON, JR.

PROPHETS. *This entry consists of two articles, the first on prophets in* Ancient Israel, *and the second on the phenomenon of prophecy in* Early Christianity. *For discussion of individual prophets, see the entries under their names or the books that bear their names.*

Ancient Israel

No comprehensive definition of an Israelite prophet is possible. The persons conventionally included in this category appear to have manifested great diversity of character and function. They are referred to by a number of terms that in some texts are used interchangeably, and some of these shed some light on their functions: "seer" implies a recipient of visions, and "man of God" suggests some kind of close relationship with the deity. But the most common designation; *nābîʾ*, usually translated as "prophet," is of uncertain derivation. The prophets of the eighth century BCE seem to have avoided terminological classification altogether.

In general, it may be said that prophets were men or women believed to be recipients through audition, vision, or dream of divine messages that they passed on to others by means of speech or symbolic action. The persons they addressed might be individuals, particular groups of Israelites, the whole nation, or foreign nations. The prophets, then, were divine messengers, as is indicated by the formula, "Thus Yahweh has said," which precedes many of their utterances. Frequently, these messages were unsolicited and were delivered under divine compulsion, though on some occasions a prophet was consulted by persons who inquired whether there was a message from God for them. Several of the prophetic books contain "call narratives" in which the prophets express their conviction that they have received a particular summons to prophesy (Isa. 6; Jer. 1; Ezek. 1.1–3.15; Amos 7.15). Several prophets, notably Jeremiah, recorded their reluctance and even strong resistance to this divine constraint. These call narratives, however, belong to a literary genre (see also Exod. 3.1–12; Judg. 6.11–17), and may not be simply (auto)biographical.

Prophetic activity was not confined to Israel, nor were all prophets prophets of Yahweh. Although the term *nābîʾ* is not found elsewhere in the ancient Near East, activities comparable with those of the Israelite prophets are attested among other Semitic peoples, notably at Mari in the eighteenth century BCE. In Israel an early reference to prophets (1 Sam. 10.5–11) is found in a narrative that associates their activity with the founding of the Israelite kingdom by Saul. For the next four centuries, both in northern Israel and in Judah, prophets are mainly found in close connection with the kings and with political events generally.

It is not possible to give a systematic account of this early prophecy—or indeed of much of the prophetic activity in the ensuing period—because the information available is so diverse. One can only note certain rather disparate scraps of

Detail of the Portico de la Gloria with the Old Testament prophets from the Cathedral of St. James in Spain by (Master Mateo, 1168-1188)

The prophets of the eighth and seventh centuries BCE stood for the same principles as their predecessors. For this period, however, our sources of information are mainly of a different kind. The prophetic books (Isaiah, Jeremiah, Ezekiel, and the books of the twelve "minor" prophets) contain far fewer stories about prophets, and consist mainly of what purport to be records of words spoken by the prophets whose names they bear. The word of God received and transmitted by the prophet now assumes primary importance. It is, however, no easy matter to identify these words and to distinguish them from other material. In their present form, the prophetic books have all become repositories of other and later material, both prophetic and nonprophetic. This additional matter has its own importance and should not be regarded as in any way inferior to the words of the original prophet; but its presence makes it difficult to form a correct notion of his message.

The extent to which the prophecy of the eighth century BCE marks a decisive change in the character of Israelite prophecy is disputed. Two features, however, call for notice: first, the eighth- and seventh-century prophets addressed themselves not only to kings and other individuals and particular groups but also to the whole people; second, they were, as far as our information enables us to judge, the first to prophesy the destruction of the entire nation as a punishment for its sins. This prophecy of national disaster, sometimes presented as avoidable through repentance but sometimes not, was the main feature of the message of the prophets of the eighth century BCE (Hosea, Amos, Isaiah, and Micah) and also of Jeremiah and Ezekiel in the late seventh/early sixth. The latter, however, who survived the destruction of Judah and Jerusalem in 587/586 BCE, also offered hope for the future beyond the disaster. The prophets of the exile and the postexilic period were chiefly concerned with the hope of a restoration of the nation's fortunes and with current problems of the postexilic community.

The prophets were not primarily theologians; but some of them, in their attempt to present their message coherently and persuasively, achieved profound insights into divine and human natures and the relationship between God and his people Israel. (The theological teachings of the individual prophets are described in more detail in the articles on each prophet.)

The prophets whose words have been preserved were only a small and probably unrepresentative minority. Other prophets are frequently mentioned by them, usually unfavorably. It is clear that, especially in the time of Jeremiah, there were two groups of prophets opposed to one another. Jeremiah regarded his opponents, who offered the people a comforting message of national security based on the belief that God would protect them irrespective of their conduct, as false or lying prophets (Jer. 14.13–16). Passages such as this reflect the problem faced by the people when two groups of prophets, each claiming to speak in Yahweh's name, proclaimed diametrically opposite messages. Attempts were made to establish criteria for identifying the genuine prophet (e.g., Jer. 28.8–9; Deut. 13.1–5; 18.15–22), but these were unable to resolve the problem.

information. There was the solitary prophet, liable to appear suddenly to confront the king (1 Kings 18; 21.17–24), in contrast with the groups known as the "sons of the prophets" (NRSV: "company of prophets") who lived in isolated communities under a leader (2 Kings 4.38–41; 6.1–7; see also Amos 7.14); these are in turn to be differentiated from groups of prophets maintained at the royal court (1 Kings 22). Other individuals appear to have been local seers or prophets (the explanatory note in 1 Sam. 9.9 does not throw much light on the distinction) who might be consulted in cases of lost property but might also serve in some local cultic capacity (1 Sam. 9). While in some cases prophetic activity took the form of apparently insane behavior attributed to seizure by the spirit of God (1 Sam. 10.10–13) and prophets could simply be dismissed as "mad" (2 Kings 9.11), others acted as military advisers to the king (1 Kings 22; 2 Kings 3) or confronted kings with their moral or religious misdeeds (1 Kings 18; 21), condemning them in God's name; in some cases, they were even capable of fomenting a coup d'état, deposing one king and choosing and consecrating another (2 Kings 9). As miracle workers, they might make an ax head float (2 Kings 6.6) but might also call down fire from heaven (1 Kings 18.36–39; 2 Kings 1.10) or raise a dead person to life (1 Kings 17.17–24; 2 Kings 4).

Such examples of contrasting behavior and activity could be multiplied from the evidence of the books of Samuel and Kings and, to some extent, from the prophetic books. These stories, which represent popular views of prophets, are to a large extent legendary in character; but they show clearly that Israelite prophecy was a manysided phenomenon. Apart from some accounts of rather trivial miracle-working, however, they have one common characteristic: they represent the true prophet as the agent and defender of Yahweh in opposition both to religious apostasy and syncretism and to the authority of kings when these failed to uphold the cause of Yahweh or flouted his moral demands. This is especially true of the ninth-century prophets Elijah and Elisha.

Prophets who delivered unpalatable messages not only encountered difficulties in gaining acceptance as authentic messengers of Yahweh but were liable to suffer humiliation (Amos 7.1013) and even threats to their lives (Jer. 26; 3640). Yet insofar as they were believed to have an intimate relationship with God they were feared. Even kings were unable to ignore them. On the other hand, it is unlikely that prophets generally enjoyed an official status in either the religious or the political establishment. Recently, attempts have been made to define their role in sociological terms. Whatever results may eventually emerge from this kind of study, it can be safely asserted that the prophets about whom we have any detailed information came from a wide variety of social backgrounds and functioned in a variety of ways.

R. N. WHYBRAY

Early Christianity

Prophecy in the New Testament is the reception and subsequent communication of spontaneous and divinely given revelations; normally, those who were designated "prophets" in early Christianity were specialists in mediating divine revelation rather than those who prophesied occasionally or only once. The exhortation to desire earnestly to prophesy (1 Cor. 14.1) may be best explained as a call to all those who regarded themselves as gifted with inspired utterance (the "spiritual" ones of 14.37) to aspire to prophesy rather than to speak in tongues: none are excluded *a priori* from the gift, but God will not in fact distribute any one gift to all. From what we can deduce about them from Acts and the Letters, as well as from the book of Revelation (a document that self-consciously presents itself as Christian prophecy in written form), prophets might conduct their ministry in one congregation or throughout a region (Acts 15.22, 32), singly or more often in groups (Acts 11.27; 13.1; 21.10–11 cf. Rev. 22.9). In the lists of ministries (1 Cor. 12.28–30; Eph. 4.11) they are mentioned next after apostles; they are associated with teachers in the church at Antioch (Acts 13.1).

In the context of the church meeting (1 Cor. 14.26–33) the ministry of the prophet is spoken of as "revelation," and such an utterance is associated with the Spirit of God (cf. 1 Thess. 5.19). This prophetic speech is not the same as speaking in tongues (see 1 Cor. 14.22–25, 27–29), nor is it the interpretation of tongues; it is some perception of the truth of God intelligibly communicated to the congregation. In Paul's view, it is an abuse of prophecy to pretend to an ecstatic frenzy so that prophets become, so to speak, out of hand; he insists that "the spirits of prophets are subject to the prophets" (1 Cor. 14.32), that is to say, each is in full possession of his or her faculties and is able to restrain the impulse to speak if the interests of order so require.

Most important, prophets were not to be given undiscerning credence. The utterances required "testing" or "evaluation" by other prophets (1 Cor. 14.29); only then were they to be received as the word of the Lord. This testing is not only to distinguish the Spirit's word from the speaker's natural impulses, but also to identify and exclude false prophecy. The most important criterion put forward by Paul for the evaluation of prophetic speech (or indeed for viewpoints expressed through a variety of oral and written forms of communication) was the content of the message, which should agree with the generally accepted beliefs and customs of the Christian community (Rom. 12.6; 1 Cor. 12.3).

The gift of prophecy gradually fell into disuse and, in spite of occasional revivals, into a measure of disrepute because of the continuing presence of false prophecy and the difficul-

ties or uncertainties involved in discerning it. Other factors contributing to the decline of prophecy were the increasing authority of an official ministry in a church becoming more institutionalized, and the tendency to rely more on rational and didactic forms of spiritual utterance; the latter led to the place of prophets being taken by teachers, catechists, scholars, and theologians, whose authority depended not on any revelation directly received but on the exposition of an existing authoritative tradition, especially the Bible.

DAVID HILL

PROVERBS, THE BOOK OF. A teaching compendium for postexilic Judaism, Proverbs is traditionally placed among the "Writings" and considered part of the wisdom literature. It consists in part of short sayings expressing in pithy form insights into human affairs, especially of a social and religious nature. The Hebrew word *(māšāl)* translated "proverb" can mean comparison, and many of the proverbs contain a metaphor or simile. The dates of the material within the book range over a wide period of time; while the final edition was made after the exile, probably in the fifth century BCE, much of the actual contents is earlier and some of it is even premonarchic. The oral origins are often obvious.

Most scholars recognize five separate collections in the book. The first collection (1.1–9.18), labeled "Proverbs of Solomon," is really instruction genre, a series of essays on the nature of wisdom, the meaning of life, and the path to success. Solomon's legendary wisdom (see 1 Kings 3; 4.29–34) resulted in a number of later works being attributed to his authorship; but there is little reason to doubt the essential accuracy of the tradition (see 1 Kings 4.32–33) that he did compose proverbs, just as his father David composed songs. This collection, however, is probably the work of the final editors who placed it at the beginning of their compilation as a statement of intent, and so it probably dates to the fifth century BCE. It presents the ideal of a fully integrated human being, one who is liberally educated and morally stable. Perhaps written for a generation that had become estranged from its cultural and religious roots, it sets out to inculcate human and religious values. To do so it presents wisdom under two guises: parental instruction (aimed at reason) and a personalized Wisdom who appeals directly in her own name (aimed at the emotions). The key to a fruitful integration of the secular and the religious is "fear of the Lord," a sense of the divine that permeates every aspect of life and impregnates the secular. These nine chapters, more theological than the rest, present a highly sophisticated worldview with a high regard for human capacity to achieve fulfillment.

The second collection (10.1–22.16), also attributed to Solomon, is simpler in style than the first and is probably preexilic. It is a gathering of heterogeneous, semi-independent proverbs, maxims, and precepts—really a literature of the schools dealing mainly with moral life and virtue. It suggests how best to live in the world. More secular than chaps. 1–9, it inculcates control of the tongue, social awareness, and respect for the mystery of existence. In the efforts to master life one must recognize that there are limits not just of volition but to human knowledge, which is finite (16.1, 9; 19.14, 21; 21.30). Justice seems to be inspired by a concern for equity rather than religion.

The third collection (22.17–24.22), entitled "the words of the wise," is a compilation of thirty instructions probably modeled on an Egyptian source, the *Instruction of Amenem-ope,* probably to be dated ca. 1000 BCE. Although it

P

has the appearance of a textbook, it warms to an intimate, parental style and may date to the same period as the editorial project itself. After a brief introduction (22.17–21) comes a series of warnings, counsels, and appeals to the reader's moral sense. Integration of the secular and religious, which was evident in chaps. 1–9, appears again. Good graces, culture, and social bearing are not alien to holiness. "Fear of the Lord" is part of education (23.12–18).

The fourth collection (24.23–34), much shorter than, although similar to, the third, bears the title "these also are sayings of the wise;" it represents an addition to the previous collection and may be by the same editor. Certainly the tone remains consistent. Social awareness is its topic. It presents the practical aspects of justice in a legal maxim (24.23b—29) and appends a portrait of one who neglects his social duties (24.30–34).

The fifth collection (25.1–29.27) has a clear attribution: "proverbs of Solomon that the officials of King Hezekiah of Judah copied," which places the collection, if not the composition, of these proverbs in the late eighth or early seventh century BCE. It represents what might be called an editorial program, sophisticated and quite unified. Again there is a concern to integrate secular and religious wisdom. It deals with the structure of society—government administration (25.1–73), social responsibility (27.11–14), and human conduct (28.1–22). To a greater extent than usual God is invoked as arbiter of morality, and the traditional concept of retribution loses its overtly dogmatic tone: the human act itself has its own repercussions.

Four appendices (30.1–31.31) close the book. Although containing older elements, these appear to be a later redactional effort, perhaps intended as a general conclusion. The first (30.19) is an essay on skepticism; the second (30.1033) deals with the mysterious dimensions of life, the inexplicable and therefore the fascinating; the third (31.1–9) is a "manual for rulers" personalized by being put in the form of a queen mother's teaching—moral rather than administrative; and the final appendix (31.10–31) is a carefully drawn portrait of the ideal woman, which leaves us with the question, "Have we arrived at the practical expression of 'Lady Wisdom' presented in chaps. 1–9?"

The book is an ambitious undertaking, offering the reader "wisdom" and opening up to the willing student a world of learning. It shows how to cope with life by organizing the range of human experience so as to evolve practical rules of comportment and to develop balanced judgment, as the editorial introduction makes clear (1.2–7). On this basis of personal and inherited experience and by means of different kinds of literature—sentence, instruction, maxim, proverb— it shows "what really works" and how to achieve success in the business of living a full life. Thus, it is didactic literature in the truest sense of the term. It represents a sage, parent, or teacher, who, out of her or his treasury of experience and knowledge of the mysteries of life, speaks to a pupil in the name of natural or social values and good sense. A frequent formula is "Hear, my child" (1.8; 2.1; 3.1, 11, 21; 4.1, 10; etc.), an indication that the teaching is seldom directly imperative; the hearer reacts on the basis of personal judgment and a personal assessment of the situation. The aim is to urge the individual to think realistically about life; it does so by making the learner personally face up to the problems that besiege humanity: ignorance and poverty (9.7–12; 22.7–8), right and wrong (16.10–15), the need to adapt oneself to life in society (22.1–4), and finally, although somewhat indirectly, the need to accommodate to a mysterious divinity (16.1–19).

Sometimes, indeed, contradictory proverbs are placed side by side (26.4–5) so as to provoke thought: which applies in my situation? The different kinds of literature found here share common aims: the desire to impart knowledge (1.2–7) and to form character (1.8–19), to encourage a learner to achieve maturity. Since the pupil's experience may often differ from that of the parent or teacher, it is essential to learn how to think for oneself to survive. This is suggestive, for the verbal root from which the word "proverb" derives (*māšāl*) has the significance of "dominating something." These proverbs are frequently artistic, and humor is not absent (25.11; 23.2935), but the ultimate function of wisdom, and the dominant intention of the editors, was the mastery of the human environment by the ac quisition of a personal standard of values and an effective "know-how," both of which could be derived from an appreciation of cosmic order and design.

What at first sight appears to be a collection of heterogeneous instructions, proverbs, and wise sayings in fact enjoys a certain coherence, imposed, it is true, by editorial intention, to which is due the powerful educational impact the book made on later generations. As it now stands, it represents a many-faceted ideal of religious humanism, in which many disparate kinds of teaching contribute to one purpose—the formation of a whole person by leading a student on paths of uprightness, intelligence, and conviction to human fulfillment.

DERMOT COX, O.F.M.

PSALMS, THE BOOK OF.

Introduction. The book of Psalms derives its name from the ancient Greek translation, *psalmoi,* which designates instrumental music and, by extension, the words that accompany the music. In Hebrew it is known as "the book of praises." One hundred fifty psalms were numbered consecutively in the Hebrew tradition. The same number is found in the Greek and Latin versions, though there is a variation of usually one digit within Psalms 10–147 (e.g., Ps. 72 is 71 in the Greek). One of the Dead Sea Scrolls and many Greek manuscripts have other psalms as well, especially Psalm 151, which is recognized as canonical by some Orthodox churches. By the Hellenistic period, the psalms were provided with superscriptions indicating authorship ("by" or possibly "concerning" David), musical annotations (e.g., "with stringed instruments"), and even the setting (e.g., Ps. 51, after David's sin with Bathsheba). Titles exist for 116 psalms, but the information contained in most of them is no longer understood (e.g., Ps. 69, "according to Lilies"). Nothing much can be said about the psalms as musical compositions. There are many references to musical accompaniment, and one may infer that the words were sung, but nothing is known about melody or orchestration.

There is evidence of a complicated history behind the present form of the psalter. It seems to be divided into five "books" by the insertion of doxologies: 41.13; 72.18–19; 89.52; 106.48; 150.6 (or perhaps all of Ps. 150). Behind this stand earlier collections: Psalms of David (73 in all), of Asaph (Pss. 73–83), of the Korahites (Pss. 42; 44–49; 84; 85; 87; 88), and so on. The fact that the generic name for God, Hebrew *ʾĕlōhîim,* outnumbers the sacred name (*yhwh,* probably pronounced Yahweh) by about four to one in Psalms 42–83 suggests a separate collection of psalms; hence, this section has been called the "Elohistic psalter." Another sign of earlier compilation is the presence of duplicate psalms (14 = 53; 40.13–20 = 70).

Modern English translations are irregular in verse references. Some follow the Hebrew numbering, while others, such as the New Revised Standard Version (NRSV), follow the tradition of the Authorized Version, which does not count the title as a verse. Hence, there is often a difference of one digit or more between the Hebrew and English references to the verse numbers (thus, NRSV 51.1 = Hebr. 51.3). In this article, the NRSV numbering is followed.

More significant are the differences in rendering that can be found in all translations. At many points, the traditional Masoretic text of the Psalms is corrupt and in need of emendation. Such correction is based on the usual sources, especially the ancient translations. But these are not always trustworthy; the rendering of the tenses in the Septuagint is particularly misleading. In order to restore the supposedly original form of the text, scholars also have recourse to the resources of related Semitic languages, especially for the meanings of words. In modern times, the discovery of Ugaritic language and literature has provided a window on the Hebrew text that has led to improved translation.

Literary Types. Modern scholarship is skeptical about two aspects of the traditional titles: authorship (hence dating) and setting. There is no hard evidence for Davidic authorship of any of the psalms. David's reputation as a musician (1 Sam. 16.23; Amos 6.5) makes it reasonable to associate him with the psalms, but it is not possible to prove authorship. As regards the setting, modern scholarship is much more modest in its claims. The ancients were overspecific. Rather, one can only describe the setting in a very generic way: a lament of an individual or community, a song of praise in the Temple, and so on. In other words, literary classification has replaced the historicizing tendency that the titles display.

Hermann Gunkel (1862–1932) originated the modern literary analysis of the psalter. His conclusions have been modified somewhat by subsequent scholars, but his classification of the psalms remains basic. Many psalms resist easy classification, but the following description is helpful.

Hymns. The hymn, or song of praise, begins on a joyful note in which the psalmist summons self (Pss. 103–104) or a community (Ps. 117) to praise the Lord. Usually two reasons are given, and they constitute the heart of the prayer: God's creative activity and saving intervention is Israel's history. The pattern is: "praise the Lord, because. . . ." As far as creation is concerned, one must be ready for the skilled and imaginative portrayal of the divine creativity, recorded throughout the Bible. One thinks of the majestic description of the effortless activity in Genesis 1, a creation by word, but there is also the picture of the divine potter in Genesis 2.7. Another mode of representation was the battle with chaos, personified in the redoubtable Leviathan (Pss. 74.14; 104.26; cf. Isa. 27.1; Job 3.8; 41.1–34), or Rahab (Ps. 89.9–10; Job 9.13; 26.12–13), or characterized simply as "Sea" (probably to be understood against the background of Baal's conflict with Yamm ["Sea"] in Ugaritic literature; cf. Ps. 74.13). Attention is not limited to the action of God at the beginning; creation is also continuous (Ps. 104). The Israelites obviously were able to relish and savor the creative activity of God.

Another reason for solemn praise is the divine intervention in history on behalf of Israel, especially the Exodus (Pss. 78; 114; cf. Exod. 15.1–18). This sacred history could also be commemorated in such a way as to teach Israel a lesson (Ps. 78) or to move the people to penitence (Ps. 106). This "history" was not antiquarianism. It was re-presented in the liturgy and re-created in the hearts of the people, for whom it also guaranteed a future.

The structure of the song of praise is simple: after the initial invocation, certain themes are developed as the reason for praising the Lord. The psalm often ends on the general note of praise. But certain hymns have received special classification due to their content.

The first of these are the "Songs of Zion" (Pss. 46; 48; 84; 87; 122). They are clearly hymns, but the praise is centered on Jerusalem. They do not view Jerusalem apart from the Lord; the Holy City is preeminently the divine dwelling place among the people, where the divine "name" (Deut. 12.11) or presence is to be found. A frequent theme is the invincibility of Zion (Pss. 46; 48). This attitude can turn out to be a trap for those who place a false confidence in the "city of God" (cf. Jer. 7.1–15; 24.1–10). But Israel saw truly that her greatness was connected with the Lord's presence.

The second type deals with the enthronement of the Lord: "the Lord is king" (or, "has become king"). These psalms (most clearly, 47; 93; 95–99) celebrate the Lord as king, and have as themes the divine creative power as well as the divine domination of history. The kingship of the Lord is not conceived as a recent claim; it is rooted in the past and is re-presented in the liturgical celebration itself.

Thanksgiving psalms. Gunkel regarded these as the prayers offered up after deliverance from distress—a counterpart to the laments (see next paragraph): e.g., Psalms 18; 30; 40; 66; 116; 118; cf. Jonah 2.2–9. They begin like a song of praise and then quickly acknowledge that the Lord is the rescuer. This confession is sometimes expanded into a witness directed to bystanders (see Ps. 30.4–5), who may share in the thanksgiving sacrifice offered by the psalmist. At times there is a flashback, as the psalmist recounts the difficult period before deliverance (Ps. 116.1011). Psalm 100 is entitled a song for thanksgiving, and vv. 4–5 (cf. Jer. 33.11) are found in variant form in Psalms 106.1; 107.1; 118.1; and 136.1.

Laments. The psalms of lament can be considered from an individual or from a collective point of view. Most of

Mercy and Truth are met together, Righteousness and Peace have kissed each other (Ps 85.10) (William Blake, 1818)

P

241

them are psalms of individual lament, and indeed this literary type is the most frequent in the psalter (some forty psalms, e.g., 22; 42–43; 69). The prayer usually begins with a cry for help to the Lord ("my God"), followed by a description of the distress of the psalmist. This can be manifold: sin (Ps. 51), sickness and death (Pss. 6; 38), false accusation (Ps. 7), and especially persecution by enemies (Pss. 38.12–20; 41.5–11). It is paradoxical but true that in most cases one cannot pinpoint the precise reason for the complaint. This is because the imagery is so extravagant; Psalm 22, for example, mentions "bulls of Bashan," dogs, the sword, the lion, and wild oxen. But this can be an advantage for modern readers, who can interpret the vivid language of the psalmist in the light of their own distress. What at first sight seems to be a disadvantage turns out to be profitable, provided the modern reader develops an appreciation for the symbolic language (the abyss, Sheol, the pit, the "waves" and "billows" of the Lord, etc.). Biblical writers are fond of extremes. Death is not a static mystery at the end of one's days; death is parallel to Sheol, the place of the dead, and both are visualized as a power that affects a human being in this life. To the extent that a person experiences nonlife (suffering, etc.)—to that extent one is in Sheol. Hence, the psalmist can express joy over deliverance by saying "You brought me up from Sheol" (Ps. 30.3). There has not been a resuscitation or resurrection; the psalmist has been delivered from the nonlife of suffering and distress.

The grim portrayal of personal agony in the individual lament is lightened by frequent cries for help, and especially by motifs of why the Lord should intervene. Appeals are made to the divine "steadfast love" (Hebr. *ḥesed*), which binds together the Lord and the covenanted Israelite. The psalmist even alleges personal integrity and loyalty (Pss. 17; 26) and also trust (Pss. 13.5; 25.1) as motives to induce the Lord to act.

In almost all the individual laments (Ps. 88 is a significant exception) a certainty is expressed that the Lord has heard the prayer, but the explanation for the change in mood is not obvious. Is it due to the psychological strength of the psalmist's trust? Or could it be that there are two moments here: the before and the after of deliverance, which have been joined together? A promising solution, which has gathered wide support, is to recognize here the liturgical background of the prayer. When one uttered a lament in the Temple, it was followed by an oracle of salvation from one of the Temple personnel, and then the response to this was the proclamation of certainty. There are some hints of oracular assurance in several psalms (12.5; 35.3; 85.8; 91.14–16), but the lament has not retained the oracle as part of its structure.

Gunkel regarded the motif of trust, so frequent in the individual laments, as the seed of another type of psalm, the psalms of confidence (e.g., 4; 11; 16; 23; 62; 131). The motif of trust becomes the heart of the prayer.

National laments would have been characteristic of special days of crisis, such as a drought or military defeat (cf. Joel 1.13–14; 2 Chron. 20.3–12). The community would be summoned to the rites celebrated in the Temple for a day of national mourning. There is no fixed structure, but most of the elements that appear in an individual lament are present here: a cry for help, the challenge of "why?", a description of the distress, and often a vow to praise the Lord (perhaps akin to the motif of certainty). Among these psalms can be included 44, 74, and 79.

Royal psalms. This classification derives from content, not from literary factors. Indeed, many settings and moods are reflected in them: a royal coronation or anniversary (Pss. 2; 72; perhaps 110); a royal thanksgiving (Ps. 18; cf. Ps. 144); prayers before (Ps. 20) and after (Ps. 21) military operations; a royal wedding (Ps. 45), a "mirror of princes" (Ps. 101). In the course of time such psalms would have become "democratized." Although originally featuring the monarch as the main figure, they came to be applied to and used by the average person (e.g., Pss. 28; 61; 63).

Why were the distinctly royal psalms preserved after the fall of Jerusalem in 587/586 BCE? Monarchy disappeared until the short-lived triumphs of Simon Maccabee and the Hasmonean rulers (142–63 BCE). The most reasonable answer is that the royal psalms were reinterpreted, always bearing in mind the promise of 2 Samuel 7 (cf. Pss. 89; 132). The temporary awakening of messianism in the time of Zerubbabel (Hag. 2.2–9, 20–23; Zech. 3.8; 4.8–11; 6.1112), if it met the aspirations of the people, did not receive the approval of the Persian authorities.

The royal psalms are not predictive; in their literal historical meaning they refer to the currently reigning king. Nonetheless, they were perceived as open-ended in Jewish and Christian tradition, and from that point of view can be considered as messianic in the future sense of that word.

Wisdom psalms. Not all would agree that this classification is proper, and there is a wide variation in determining which of the psalms might come under this rubric. The criteria for the classification remain somewhat vague: typical wisdom language (such as "teach" and "fear of the Lord"); acrostic patterns (e.g., Pss. 34; 37); the contrast between the just and the wicked (Ps. 1); the problem of retribution (Pss. 37; 73); a meditative style (Ps. 90). If the literary genre remains difficult to pin down, perhaps it is better to speak of wisdom influence on such psalms as 1; 32; 34; 37; 49; 73.

Liturgies. In a broad sense, most of the psalms can be considered liturgical, but certain poems capture the spirit of a liturgy more obviously, particularly those in which oracles, questions, and litany response are featured. A liturgical format (question and answer) is conspicuous in the gate or entrance liturgies of Psalms 14 and 23 (cf. Isa. 33.14–16; Mic. 6.8). Prophetic oracles appear in Psalms 50; 75; 85. Psalm 136 is virtually a litany, with the repetition of the enduring "steadfast love" in each verse.

Recent Developments. Since the pioneering work of Gunkel, certain refinements in literary classification have been proposed. Sigmund Mowinckel (*The Psalms in Israel's Worship* [1951; Engl, trans. 1967]) went beyond Gunkel's analysis in his emphasis on the liturgical background of the psalter, not merely in its use in the period of the Second Temple but in its origins as well. It seems that most of the psalms were written in the first instance for liturgical performance in the Temple. There is not sufficient evidence for the feast of Yahweh's enthronement, which Mowinckel postulated, and with which he associated about forty psalms. However, the idea of the enthronement of Yahweh certainly dominates many psalms (e.g., 47; 93; 96–99).

Claus Westermann (*Praise and Lament in the Psalms* [1977; Engl, trans. 1981]) proposed to incorporate the traditional thanksgiving psalm into the class of hymns. He regarded such psalms as declarative songs of praise (e.g., Ps. 30), as opposed to descriptive songs of praise (e.g., Ps. 136). Indeed, he regarded the hymn (praise) and lament

P

as the dominant categories of the psalter, and he presented the psalms as a movement from lament to praise.

Walter Brueggemann (*The Message of the Psalms* [1984]) has added another dimension to the interpretation of the psalter. While recognizing the traditional literary types established by Gunkel, he placed a new grid on the classification, based upon the categories of the philosopher Paul Ricoeur. He distinguished between psalms of orientation (all is right with the world; hymns such as Pss. 8; 33; 104), or disorientation (laments such as Pss. 13, 74, 88), and of new orientation (e.g., Pss. 23; 30; 66). These three categories are not univocal, since traces of movement from one stage to another can be found in many psalms. Neither is his approach merely psychological; it helps the reader to see things that may not be seen otherwise, by underscoring the dimension of personal experience.

Importance. These prayers illustrate the theology and worship of the Israelites across the six centuries in which they were composed and collected. No other book in the Bible has this kind of origin and orientation. One learns what kind of God Israel worshiped and both the history and the mystery of the covenanted relationship. At the same time, one learns much about the warmth and dynamism of Israel's faith. An important mix of theology and anthropology is the result.

In both Jewish and Christian tradition, the psalter is one of the most treasured books. It is aptly considered a school of prayer, not simply because it contains prayers that can be appropriated for personal use but because it also teaches one to pray. The familiarity and the frankness of the lament, the enthusiasm of the hymn, the confessional character of the thanksgiving—all these characteristics speak to the human heart before God.

ROLAND E. MURPHY, O. CARM.

PURITY, RITUAL. Throughout the Bible, reference is made to a system of ritual purity that had both social and theological significance for the Israelites. While its specific origins are not known, it can be related to practices in other ancient Near Eastern cultures in which cultic functionaries followed similar regulations, involving, for example, ritual washing and food restrictions. What appears to be unparalleled about the biblical system, however, is its extension beyond the priesthood to the general population.

In addition to cultic activity, texts describing ritual purity focus on food and individual status related to specific events. With regard to priestly behavior, those participating in sacrifice are required to purify themselves beforehand. This purification is achieved through ritual immersion. In Leviticus 11 and Deuteronomy 14, detailed lists are given of animals that are ritually pure and therefore permitted for consumption, and of those that are ritually impure and therefore prohibited. Leviticus and Numbers also contain regulations concerning the purification of individuals, regardless of cultic status, after childbirth, menstruation, ejaculation, disease, and contact with corpses.

While the regulations concerning ritual purity may be clear, their significance has been variously interpreted. The Hebrew words *ṭāhôr* and *ṭāmēʾ* are commonly translated "clean" and "unclean" respectively, renderings which imply associations with dirt or hygiene not present in the original. Additional confusion results from the fact that while in our culture the difference between the human and the divine is often identified with the difference between the material and the spiritual, that was not the case in early Israel. Ritual purity and impurity could be considered spiritual states, yet they are inextricably linked to physical processes. In turn, physical acts such as sacrifice and sprinkling are used to alter relationships with the divine.

Following the lead of anthropologists such as Mary Douglas, many contemporary biblical scholars consider the status of being *ṭāmēʾ* as one of pollution resulting from a disruption of divine order. Thus, animals prohibited for food are those that cross paradigmatic boundaries of sky, earth, and sea. Shellfish, for example, live in the ocean but crawl like land animals. From this perspective, human ritual impurities are connected with disorder since they involve uncontrolled bodily emissions or death.

Another interpretation of biblical notions of ritual purity focuses on impurity as a state of power rather than pollution. Again using anthropological models, this view examines the relationships between human ritual impurity and liminal states, transitions between one status and another or between life and death. In a biblical context, it is argued, these moments are linked to the nature and power of the divine, a power that contains death and destruction as well as life and creation. They are also tied to actions, such as procreation and care for the dead, which are positive and necessary for social order. Thus, rather than being "unclean" or "impure" in a negative sense, the biblical state of ritual impurity is the result of contact with the sacred. This sense of ritual impurity is evident in the later rabbinic definition of canonical (i.e., sacred) texts as those which "render the hands ritually impure." Biblical rituals of purification may have been the result of a belief that direct contact with divine power could be dangerous if sustained too long. This conception of divinity is supported by passages such as Exodus 33.20, where God warns Moses, "You cannot see my face; for no one shall see me and live." Another possibility is that ritual purifications served as a consistent reminder that the power of life and death is not human but divine.

A third interpretation addresses the social implications of the ritual purity system. The sociologist Nancy Jay has pointed out the priestly control involved in purifications and its retribution of reproductive powers from the individual women who exhibit them in menstruation and childbirth to the male (imaged) deity represented by male priests. Food prohibitions can also be interpreted functionally as a means of social separation.

While it may be argued that legislative texts concerning ritual purity are descriptive and relational in their uses of the terms *ṭāhôr* and *ṭāmēʾ*; other biblical writings imply a more polarized viewpoint. Ezekiel, for example, frequently uses *ṭāmēʾ* in contexts that clearly indicate a notion of defilement not only of persons but also of places, an impurity that is rooted in apostasy. Texts such as Lamentations 1.9 associate negative concepts of defilement with female sexuality as exemplified by menstruation. These different perspectives may be due to historical change, since the legislative materials are generally dated to earlier periods than the historical and prophetic texts.

With the destruction of the First and Second Temples, the cultic basis of the system of ritual purity was first disrupted and then destroyed. Remnants of the system were preserved in rabbinic practices such as ritual immersion for conversion or following menstruation, handwashing, and the separation of implements as well as categories of food in keeping kosher. While Christianity rejected the system as a whole, it retained ritual immersion in baptism.

DRORAH O'DONNELL SETEL

QUEEN AND QUEEN MOTHER. Although several Hebrew words are translated "queen," they denote different statuses or types of royal women. The two primary terms are *malkâ* and *gĕbîrâ*. *Malkâ* seems not to have been used, even as a descriptive title, for any Judean or Israelite ruler's wife. Instead, the Bible commonly refers to the "king's wife" or the "king's mother" (1 Kings 1.11; 2.13, 19; Prov. 31.1). *Malkâ* may connote foreignness; the queen of Sheba, Vashti and Esther (wives of the Persian king: Esther 1.9; 2.22), and the abominated queen of heaven are all called *malkâ*. *Gĕbîrâ* seems to refer to the mother of the acknowledged heir to the throne or to the mother of the reigning king, hence "queen mother" (Maacah: 1 Kings 15.13; Jezebel: 2 Kings 10.13; Nehushta: Jer. 13.18). She may also be the chief wife (1 Kings 11.19; 2 Kings 10.13).

In a dynastic succession, heredity is the crucial factor. Almost every accession notice of a Judahite king includes not only his father's but also his mother's name (e.g., 1 Kings 15.2, 10). The queen mother's identity seems to have been relevant in establishing the legitimacy of the new Davidide. The *gĕbîrâ* frequently appears to come from a rich and well-connected Israelite family. It has been suggested that important provincial power groups ("the people of the land") had a vested interest in promoting a local woman to be the king's wife and subsequently pressuring the king to make her the *gĕbîrâ*.

With a power base of sorts behind her, a *gĕbîrâ* would have been able to exert some independent, if informal authority. Underlying Asa's removal of Maacah from being *gĕbîrâ* (1 Kings 15.13) was probably a power struggle between court factions. The formal notice of the demotion suggests its unprecedented nature; it also implies that the *gĕbîrâ* enjoyed not only prestige but tangible privileges.

Several episodes have led scholars to conclude that the queen mother had official status (1 Kings 2.13–25: Bathsheba; 1 Kings 15.13: Maacah; 2 Kings 24.15: Nehushta). But recent studies have pointed out, on the basis of extra-biblical parallels, that the queen mothers involved in these episodes were unusual in having maneuvered their own sons into power even though the son had no legitimate claim to the throne. In such cases the new king owed a debt to his mother that he could scarcely ignore, and the queen mother's power might grow even greater.

Besides marrying women from local families, Israelite kings, like their ancient Near Eastern counterparts, had an eye to advantageous alliances and often chose wives from neighboring royalty. Solomon's foreign wives are proverbial (1 Kings 11.1–8). Jezebel was the daughter of the king of Tyre (1 Kings 16.31), and her daughter Athaliah married Jehoram of Judah (2 Kings 8.18).

Kings' daughters generally receive little mention, although a Hebrew seal inscribed "Maadanah, daughter of the king" has come to light. Michal, Saul's daughter and David's wife (1 Sam. 18.20–27; 19.11–17; 25.44; 2 Sam. 3.1316; 6.16–23) is exceptional, as is Athaliah's enterprising rebel daughter Jehosheba (2 Kings 11.12).

With their status and wealth, wives of rulers throughout the ancient Near East were often able to transcend the otherwise static boundaries determined by gender and society. In Mesopotamia, rulers' wives supervised their own households, administered palace industries, engaged in diplomacy, and participated in religious rituals apart from their husbands. This recalls the experience of the most documented biblical queen, Jezebel. She ran her own religious establishment (1 Kings 18.19) and used her authority to initiate and execute policy (18.4). She sent official messages (19.2; cf. Prov. 9.3), counseled her husband (1 Kings 21.5–7; cf. Esther 4.16–17; 6.14–7.6), and, although 1 Kings 21.8 says that she arranged Naboth's death in Ahab's name, elsewhere the wording may mean that the murder was committed on Jezebel's own authority (21.11, 14–15).

The deposition of Athaliah, the daughter of Ahab, King of Israel (2 Kings 11.14; 2 Chr 23.13).

Occasionally women ruled independently in the ancient Near East. The queen of Sheba, who conducted economic negotiations with Solomon, may have belonged to a dynasty of queens who ruled in North Arabia, and during the Hasmonean period Salome was for a brief time queen of Judea (76–67 BCE). Ancient records, however, tend to look with disfavor on women who ruled in their own name, whether it is the Sumerian "king" KU.BAU (third millennium BCE), the Egyptian Pharaoh Hatshepsut (1486–1468 BCE), or Athaliah of Judah (843–837 BCE), whose six-year reign (2 Kings 11.3) was the only break in the Davidic succession of Judahite kings.

In its attitude toward the historical queens of Israel and Judah, the Bible is either neutral (the royal accession notices), suspiciously laconic (e.g., Bathsheba and the wife of Jeroboam I), or decidedly negative (Maacah, Jezebel, Athaliah). Only Esther, in what is essentially a morale-raising fiction, merits an unequivocally favorable portrayal. From a literary point of view, however, Sarah seems to be a positive paradigm for the *gĕbîrâ*, just as Abraham is a paradigm for David. The narrative's insistence (Gen. 17.19–21; 21.12–13) that Sarah, not Hagar, will bear the son of the promise (cf. Rom. 9.9), is reminiscent of the attention paid to the identity of the king's mother in the royal accession notices. The gospels of Matthew and Luke may reflect this when they stress Mary's role in bearing Jesus, another son of the promise and a future king. The later tradition of Mary as the heavenly queen, however, derives not from biblical but from imperial Roman political vocabulary.

MARY JOAN WINN LEITH

QUR'ĀN AND THE BIBLE, THE. The belief that God speaks through scripture he has inspired is shared by Jews, Christians, and Muslims. In spite of the considerable differences among them, these three monotheistic communities lay claim to a common distinction that links them as "People of the Book." Each community deems itself to be in possession of a written record of God's will, revealed at moments of crisis in history, recorded for the instruction of future generations, and constantly reinterpreted in acts of individual and corporate remembrance. Each community is founded upon a faithful response to the word it has received, using as its model of obedience to the divine call the example of Abraham.

The Qur'ān (Koran) is the holy book of Islam. Muslims believe that it was revealed by God to the prophet Muhammad, through the agency of the angel Gabriel. These revelations came to Muhammad between 610 CE (the year of his call to be the messenger of God) and 632, the year of his death. The Qur'ān consists of 114 sūrahs, or chapters. The length of the complete book is about two-thirds that of the New Testament. The Arabic word *qur'ān* most probably means "that which is to be read aloud." The first sūrah to be revealed to Muhammad starts with the command "Read! [aloud] in the name of your Lord who creates." In the Arabic the opening imperative *iqra'* ("Read!") contains the same consonantal elements that form the word Qur'ān.

The sūrahs are named. Some of the names are familiar to readers of the Bible: "Jonah" (10), "Joseph" (12), "Abraham" (14), "Mary" (19), "The Prophets" (21), "The Resurrection" (75). Others are unfamiliar: "The Cow" (2), "The Pilgrimage" (22), "The Pen" (68), "The Dawn" (89). Others are introduced by combinations of letters, the precise significance of which is unknown. In addition to its name, each sūrah is prefaced by an indication of the place where it was revealed, either Mecca or Medina. The language of the Meccan sūrahs

The Lesson (Rudolphe Ernst)

is appropriate for summoning an unbelieving people to accept Islam as a matter of immediate and urgent decision. At the last day, unbelievers will be given the reward merited by their unbelief, and cast into *jahannam* (Gehenna), which is graphically described. On the other hand, the reward for believers on the day of reckoning will be the afterlife in paradise, a place described with comparable vividness. The Medinan sūrahs are longer, and chiefly concerned with the organization of life in the developing Islamic community.

In 622 CE, Muhammad and his small group of Muslim converts were obliged to leave Mecca because of persecution; this event is called the *hijrah* (hegira). They moved to Yathrib, about 465 km (290 mi) to the northeast. In honor of Muhammad, the place was renamed *madīnat (alnabī)*, "City (of the Prophet)." Medina, the name by which it is still known, is the city in which Muhammad lies buried. The year 622 CE divides the Meccan from the Medinan period in the life of the prophet Muhammad, and is the year from which the Islamic community dates the beginning of a new era, whose dates are sometimes given the designation A.H. (Latin *Anno Hejirae*).

Unlike the Bible, which emerged over a period of centuries as the work of many different (and often unnamed) witnesses to God's redemptive activity, the Qur'ān passed from the oral tradition to its written form in just over a decade after the death of Muhammad. The revelations were passed on by Muhammad orally, and those who listened to him wrote them down on whatever materials were to hand, including dried leaves, sun-bleached animal bones, and stones. This written material was finally brought together during the caliphate of 'Uthmān (644–656 CE), the third "Rightly Guided Caliph" (Arabic *khalīfah*, "successor" of the prophet Muhammad), to form the authoritative written text of the Qur'ān. No additions or deletions have ever been permitted by Muslim authorities, though many textual variations

245

Holy Qur'ān

in the manuscripts have been collected by western scholars. After the first short sūrah, which is a brief exordium of praise to God, who is both creator and guide, and which is sometimes compared to the Lord's Prayer, the other surahs follow each other in an order of decreasing length. The first sūrah to be revealed is numbered 96 in the final sequence.

Both Jews and Christians were present in parts of Arabia prior to the time of Muhammad. In Mecca and in Medina (as well as in his travels north and south over the ancient caravan routes), Muhammad would have come in contact with some of them. But the internal evidence of the Qur'ān provides little evidence to support the view that Muhammad had any direct knowledge of the Jewish and Christian scriptures. According to Islamic tradition he was, in any case, unable to read or write. That such an unlettered man was able to "read" the revelations has always been accepted by Muslims as a special sign of God's favor.

The similarities between the biblical and the Qur'ānic material suggest that, even had there been any direct borrowing from the former to the latter, it was highly selective. Major prophets like Amos and Jeremiah, for example, do not appear in the Qur'ān. And the Qur'ānic interpretation of trinitarian orthodoxy as belief in the Father, the Son, and the Virgin Mary, may owe less to a misunderstanding of the New Testament itself than to a recognition of the role accorded by local Christians to Mary as mother in a special sense.

The use of historical criticism in studying the Qur'ān has been resisted by Muslims. For them, the Qur'ān is the sure guide to right belief, thinking, and action. The guidance it furnishes is complemented by guidance about what constitutes knowledge and about the way knowledge is to be attained. Knowledge consists of that which God has revealed. The path to knowledge is that of submission (*islām*) to the revealed will of God. There are limits to human speculation, precisely because of what God has revealed. Intellect, will, and reason are all to be schooled by the revelation. To study the Qur'ān according to methods developed in a non-Muslim society is not encouraged in Islam. Discussion about whether or not the Qur'ān is "the Word of God" belongs to a different intellectual tradition.

According to Islamic belief, each sacred "Book" was revealed at the appropriate time and place by God, through the agency of human messengers. The message of all scriptural revelation is essentially the same; it could not be otherwise, since God himself is the author. Thus, any differences between the scriptures of the "People of the Book" are to be attributed to human distortion, and not to divine caprice. To Moses and his people was given the *Tawrah* (the Torah); to David and his people was given the *Zabūr* (the book of Psalms); to Jesus and his people God gave the *Injīl* (the gospel); and finally, to Muhammad was revealed the Qur'ān, the restatement of the eternal and unchanging purposes of God, to which all the messengers originally bore witness. Muslims believe that the Qur'ān is God's authoritative final word, with a particular significance for Muhammad's own people, but also a universal message for humankind.

The designation "People of the Book," viewed from outside the Islamic community, is as much a reminder of the differences as of the similarities that exist between Jews, Christians, and Muslims in their understanding of what constitutes scripture. Yet despite this there are still points of contact between the Bible and the Qur'ān, as the references to monotheism and to Abraham, Moses, David, and Jesus indicate. In the Bible and in the Qur'ān, the themes of God's creative and re-creative activity are taken up. The reader is confronted by the one true God, besides whom there is no other. In these different scriptures are revealed the divine will and plan for human-kind, the service required by God of those whom he has created, the way of salvation, and the penalty for self-imposed separation from God.

Other names and incidents are recorded in both the Bible and the Qur'ān. Two examples can be mentioned to provide a start for further reading. The first is the story of Joseph in Genesis 37–50 compared with the story of Yūsuf ("the fairest of stories" in the Qur'ān, sūrah 12). Common to both accounts is Joseph's rise to power and authority in Egypt after being brutally treated by his brothers, his faithfulness to God through periods of suffering, his careful use of the gifts given to him by God, and his reconciliation with his family following their appeal for food in time of famine. In the Qur'ānic account, Joseph finds favor because of his exemplary acceptance of everything that God willed for him, both in times of adversity and in times of success. His submission to the will of God is held up to succeeding generations of Muslims as an example worthy of imitation.

The second example is that of Mary, the mother of Jesus. Sūrah 19, called *Maryam* (Mary), may be compared with Matthew 1.8–2.23 and Luke 1.5–2.51. To anyone familiar with the New Testament passages in which Mary appears, this holds a twofold interest. Qur'ānic account acknowledges the virgin birth of the child Jesus (*'Īsa*). The second is in the Qur'ānic denial of the implications of trinitarian theology. In the Qur'ān, Jesus is a human being, a messenger of God, but still a creature; he is not God incarnate. In associating the creature with the Creator, Christians are, therefore, guilty of the gravest impropriety. The belief of Muslims is expressed in sūrah 4.171: "O People of the Book! Commit no excesses in your religion: nor say of God (Allāh) aught but truth. Christ Jesus, the son of Mary, was (no more than) an Apostle of Allāh, and his (Allāh's) Word, which he bestowed on Mary. And (Jesus was) a spirit proceeding from him (Allāh). So believe in Allāh and his apostles. Say not 'Trinity.' Desist, it will be better for you. For Allāh is one (Allāh). Glory be to him. He is far exalted above having a son. To him belong all things in the heavens and on earth."

EDWARD HULMES

RABBI. A term that arose in the first century CE for those ordained to be authoritative in their study, exposition, and practice of Jewish law. The rabbi could be found expounding the Torah in the synagogue, much as Jesus did (Mark 1.21; 6.2), although the application of the title to him (Matt. 26.25, 49; Mark 9.5; 11.21; etc.) was early and preserved its etymological meaning of "my master" (see John 1.38). The rabbi functioned as an interpreter of Torah and as a judge, most often of the claims of the poor. By the third century, the rabbi was regarded as having magical powers such as the ability to communicate with the dead.

Rabbis generally worked part-time at a trade, as carpenters, cobblers, and the like. Not until the Middle Ages did the rabbinate become a profession. The rabbis were not a separate caste. They mixed with the common folk on a regular basis and usually came from the ranks of ordinary people, as in the case of the most eminent of all rabbis, Akiva. The rabbis believed that all Jews could live a holy life through observance of Torah, and they said that, if all Jews observed just two Sabbaths completely, salvation would come. Thus, common folk played an important part in the rabbinate's scheme. Rabbis could be entrusted with great responsibilities far removed from the world of Torah study in the rabbinical schools. There are instances of rabbis assuming public health responsibilities, including disaster prevention so that buildings would not collapse in a storm, and the rabbi would act to see that no one in his village lacked food to eat. Such was the central role of rabbis in late antiquity.

The earliest literary monument of the rabbis is the Mishnah. Completed around 200 CE, the Mishnah is basically a rambling legal compilation, striking in its ahistorical character as compared with earlier Jewish writings and in its lack of reference to scripture to support its rulings. Nevertheless, it was authoritative and became the basis for the Jerusalem Talmud (ca. 400 CE) and the Babylonian Talmud (ca. 500 CE), which comment on the Mishnah and supply its wants, ideological as well as scriptural (e.g., the Mishnah does not talk of the Messiah).

The rabbis essentially shared the traditions and views of the Pharisees. They embraced an all-knowing, all-wise, just, merciful, and loving God who supervised the lives of individuals and decreed the fates, even while giving room for free will to choose between good and evil. A world to come existed where recompense for the evils of this world could be expected. Both this world and the next revolved around Torah. The religion of the rabbis exalted the holy faith, the holy man, and the pursuit of a holy way of life. A part of that holy existence involved daily prayer, and the roots of the current Jewish prayerbook are to be found in the Mishnah. It was only by pursuing the holy on a daily basis that salvation could be achieved and the Messiah would come.

PHILIP STERN

RACHEL. Rachel, whose name means "ewe," was the younger daughter of Laban (brother of Rebekah) and the wife of Jacob. The account of the meeting and subsequent marriage of Rachel and Jacob is a love story, succinct in its narration. Jacob was charged by his father Isaac to find a wife among his mother's people at Haran in Mesopotamia (Gen. 27.46–28.5). At the end of his journey, he came to a well where shepherds gathered to water their flocks. When he learned that they were from Haran, he asked them if they knew Laban; the shepherds pointed out to Jacob that Laban's daughter Rachel was approaching with her father's

Carrying the Scrolls of the Law (Simeon Solomon, 1867)

sheep. As soon as Jacob saw Rachel, he rolled the stone from the mouth of the well and watered the flock of Laban, his uncle. He kissed Rachel and made himself known to her as a relative. She then returned home and gave her father the news of the arrival of Jacob. Laban went to Jacob, greeted him, and brought him to his house, where he stayed a month helping with the daily chores. At the end of this time, his uncle suggested that even as a relative he should not serve for nothing. When he asked Jacob what his wages should be, Jacob, who loved Rachel, said, "I will serve you seven years for your younger daughter Rachel" (Gen. 29.18); this was agreed upon. At the end of the term, which passed quickly for him because of his love, he asked Laban for her hand in marriage.

A feast was prepared and Jacob received his wife who according to custom was veiled. In the morning he discovered that he had been deceived into accepting Rachel's elder sister, Leah. When he confronted Laban, he was told that in that country the younger daughter was not given in marriage before the elder; disappointed but undaunted, Jacob worked another seven years for Rachel. Needless to say, she was his favorite wife and eventually became the mother of Joseph and Benjamin.

Some time later—after a quarrel between Laban and Jacob, in which Rachel took her husband's part and then stole her father's household gods, the entire clan departed

Jacob meets Rachel (Gen. 29.9–12)

stealthily on the long journey to Canaan (Gen. 31.14–21), where she died at Ephrath giving birth to her younger son Benjamin (Gen. 35.19).

ISOBEL MACKAY METZGER

REBEKAH (in Rom. 9.10, Rebecca). A woman of insight and determination, Rebekah was the daughter of Bethuel (Gen. 24.15) and the sister of Laban the Aramean (25.20). She was brought from Haran to be the wife of Isaac, the son of Abraham, in the following way. After the death of Sarah, Abraham commissioned his oldest servant to find a wife for Isaac from Abraham's kindred. The servant traveled to Haran in Mesopotamia, the city of Abraham's brother, Nahor. On arrival outside the city in the evening about the time when the women usually came to draw water from the well, the servant made the ten camels he had brought with him kneel down nearby. He then prayed that God would guide him in making the right choice of a wife for Isaac. It so happened that Rebekah was the one thus identified. After she had given water to the camels, the servant introduced himself, gave her a gold ring and two bracelets, inquired whose daughter she was, and discovered that she was the daughter of Bethuel, son of Nahor (Abraham's brother). She immediately ran off to tell her mother's household about her encounter at the well. Her brother Laban, on hearing the news, went out to the servant and offered him hospitality. The servant would not accept any food until he had disclosed his mission. On hearing his words, Laban and Bethuel agreed that "the thing comes from the Lord" (Gen. 24.50), so they were willing to have Rebekah go back with the servant to become Isaac's wife.

Isaac and Rebekah were married and became the parents of twin sons, Esau and Jacob (Gen. 25.24), who were later to vie for their father's blessing when he was old and blind (chap. 27). Rebekah favored Jacob and helped him through deceit to win the father's blessing. She died apparently while Jacob was in Mesopotamia and was buried in the cave of Machpelah (Gen. 49.31).

ISOBEL MACKAY METZGER

RED SEA. The traditional translation (beginning with the Septuagint) of the Hebrew expression *yam sûf*, Red Sea is the name of the body of water crossed by the Israelites in their Exodus from Egypt. This translation, followed by later Greek biblical tradition (Jth. 5.13; Wisd. of Sol. 10.18; 1 Macc. 4.9; Acts 736; Heb. 11.29) and the Vulgate, would connect the miracle of the crossing (Exod. 14–15) with either the western (the Gulf of Suez; Map 2:R3–4) or the eastern (the Gulf of Aqaba/Eilat; Map 2:R3–4) branch of the Red Sea. But in Exodus 2.3–5 (and elsewhere in the Bible) *sûf* means "reed," and this is how the Septuagint and Vulgate translate it there; *yam sûf* refers to the eastern branch of the Red Sea in only two other texts (1 Kings 9.26; Jer. 49.21). Most contemporary scholars, and a few modern translations (e.g., NJV), therefore prefer to translate the phrase "Reed Sea" or "Sea of Reeds."

The record of Israel's miraculous crossing is a complex one. According to what has been taken as the more ancient stratum of Exodus 14.21–22, perhaps from J, "The Lord drove the Sea back by a strong east wind all night, and turned the sea into dry land." Another stratum, possibly from P, reads: "Then Moses stretched out his hand over the sea . . . and the waters were divided. The Israelites went into the sea on dry ground, the waters forming a wall for them on their right and on their left," after which the waters enveloped the Egyptians. A third version, perhaps from E (14.24–25), reads, "At the morning watch, the Lord in the pillar of fire and cloud looked down upon the Egyptian army and threw the Egyptian army into panic. He clogged their chariot wheels so they turned with difficulty. The Egyptians said: 'Let us flee from the Israelites, for the Lord is fighting for them against Egypt.'" In the first case we have a natural event, where the miracle lies in the synchronism of natural forces; in the second we deal with a miracle in the absolute sense, so that any explanation is immaterial; in the third we have neither water nor a miracle proper; the Egyptians realize that something is going wrong and withdraw. A variant of the second version is found in chap. 15. Any connection with volcanic or seismic phenomena should therefore be excluded.

The term "Sea of Reeds" or "Reed Sea" seems to mean a marshy area or a large body of water abundant in reeds in the eastern delta. One possible localization of the event, among the many that have been proposed, is Lake Sirbonis (Map 2:R–SI), where, depending on the tides, fresh water and saltwater can be found; another is the swampy region in the vicinity of the "Bitter Lakes" (Map 2:R2). We must remember, however, that we are dealing here, as in the desert wanderings, with mythical data (see Ps. 114.3–6), so with few exceptions, the localities mentioned cannot and perhaps should not be identified.

J. A. SOGGIN

REVELATION, THE BOOK OF.

Content and Structures. The book calls itself an apocalypse (1.1) or revelation, which Jesus gave, for his servants, through his angel to John, but it begins in letter form, "John to the seven churches that are in Asia, grace to you and peace" (1.4), and ends like a Pauline letter with the "grace" (22.21). The risen Christ appears to John on the island of Patmos, off the coast of the Roman province of Asia and orders him to write to the seven churches (chaps. 2 and 3); the messages warn the complacent and the worldly, and encourage the faithful. Summoned up into heaven, John sees God enthroned, holding a sealed scroll no one can open. He hears that the lion of the tribe of Judah has won the right to open it, and he sees standing by the throne a lamb bearing the marks of sacrificial slaughter (chaps. 4 and 5).

The Lamb's opening of the seals unleashes the first of three series of disasters, which represent God's wrath against an idolatrous and impenitent world: seven seals opened (6; 8.1), seven trumpets blown (chaps. 8 and 9), and seven bowls poured out (chap. 16). Symbolic visions in between depict the opposing forces in cosmic war, which comes to a climax in chap. 19: the Lamb and the 144,000 who bear his name and God's seal, over against the seven-headed beast, Satan's emissary (the Antichrist), and those who bear his mark. The beast's city, Babylon, the "great whore," is destroyed, the beast is defeated, Satan is bound, and the saints reign for a thousand years (the millennium) until Satan is released for his final assault (19.11–20.10). Then follows God's judgment of the world, and a new heaven and earth replace the old. The holy city, Jerusalem, the bride, comes down from God, and all earth's splendor is gathered into it.

It is a bewildering kaleidoscope of scenes, punctuated by voices and bursts of heavenly hymnody. Scholars have seen a variety of structural patterns, based on liturgy (Jewish or Christian), or drama (each city had its theater), or astrology or numerology (both staple diet for first-century folk). Each suggestion may contain some truth, but none has won general assent. The clearest structural element is the four series of seven (letters, seals, trumpets, bowls). The background for this structure is the apocalyptic discourse of Jesus on the Mount of Olives (Matt. 24; Mark 13; Luke 21), of which John's apocalypse may be seen as an updating.

Outline.

Chaps. 1–3.	Seven letters warning against deception and lawlessness (cf. Matt. 24.4, 5, 9–12)
Chaps. 4–7.	Seven seals on a heavenly scroll, opened by the Lamb
6	War, famine, plague (Matt. 24.6–8; birthpangs of the new age)
7	God's servants sealed: 144,000
Chaps. 8–14.	Seven trumpets of warning
8–9	Disasters modeled on the plagues of Egypt (Exod. 7–11)
10–11	Counterpoint of witness (the little scroll)
12–13	Victory in heaven, disaster for earth—Antichrist and false prophet (Matt. 24.15–24)
14	The 144,000 over against worshipers of the beast. Judgment
Chaps. 15–22.	Seven bowls of God's final wrath
16	Disasters for the beast's worshipers and city (Exod. 7–11 again)
17–18	Destruction of the whore, Babylon
19–20	Coming of Christ, the millennium, and the last judgment (Matt. 24.27–31)
21	Descent of the bride, New Jerusalem, in counterpoint with the fall of Babylon (17.1 and 21.9)

In the three series of disasters, there is both recapitulation—each covers the same ground—and development. The seals serve as overture, centering on the "beginning of the birthpangs" (Matt. 24.8). The trumpets lead up to the "desolating sacrilege" (Matt. 24.15), Rome and its emperor. The bowls set out their destruction and the "coming of the Son of Man" (Matt. 24.27)—bridegroom and bride over against beast and harlot.

Two further structural points are important for interpreting the book. Enclosing the scenes of destruction are the visions of God, creator and redeemer (chaps. 4 and 5), and of the new creation (chap. 21): the destructions are not simply negative; the rebelliousness of earth is finally overcome. Enclosing all the visions is the epistolary opening and ending: the whole disclosure is a message to Christians of the day in their particular situations. Scattered among the visions are calls for discernment and fidelity (13.9, 10, 18; 14.12; 16.15; 17–9)

This analysis suggests that the aim of John's revelation was to warn the churches against compromise with the religious, social, and economic values of a world heading for self-destruction because of its idolatry and to encourage them in the witness to God and purity of life which alone could defeat the deceptions of Satan and his minions. The letters to the

R

The Last Judgment

churches show that some were sliding into a worldly lifestyle (2.14, 20), while others were asleep (3.2), complacent (3.17), or lacking in love (2.4). There is wholehearted praise only for Smyrna (2.8–11) and Philadelphia (3.7–13), where faithful Christians were suffering on behalf of Christ.

Recipients. At first sight, John is writing to seven particular congregations; many other cities in the Roman province of Asia are known to have had Christians (see Acts 19.10, 26; 1 Cor. 16.19; 2 Cor. 1.8). But seven is the number symbolic of wholeness (see below), and these churches probably represent the whole church. The seven cities were all centers of communication, set on a circular route beginning at Ephesus, the nearest to Patmos. The writer knows the geography and traditions of each city and clearly is acquainted with the circumstances of each church. But the particular warnings and encouragements add up to a message for all the churches (2.23; cf. 22.16), and he claims divine authority for his book (22.18, 19).

What kind of Christians were they? The warnings against Nicolaitans and others who teach Christians to "eat food sacrificed to idols and practice fornication" (2.6, 14–15, 20) remind us of issues at Corinth (1 Cor. 6.12–20; 8; 10.14–30). Later writers connected the Nicolaitans with gnosticism. It looks as if there was an influential movement for compromise with the world, based perhaps on Pauline teaching about Christian freedom and the divine mandate of the state (Rom. 13.1–7) and on gnostic belief in present spiritual salvation to which behavior in the material world is irrelevant. The emphasis on Christ's imminent coming may be directed against an assumption that eternal life is already here, which might have been drawn from the teaching of the Fourth Gospel. Paul, and later the apostle John according to tradition, had both been active at Ephesus. The book seems to be recalling Christians to the apostolic standard; there is perhaps an echo of the decree of the Apostolic Council (Acts 15.28) in the letter to Thyatira (2.24).

Situation and Date. Irenaeus (ca. 180 CE), who came from Asia and had known Polycarp, bishop of Smyrna (ca. 70–150 CE), and others of his generation, dated the book of Revelation toward the end of the reign of Domitian (81–96 CE; cf. *Against the Heresies* 5.30.3, as usually interpreted). The picture of the Antichrist reflects popular belief that Nero, who had stabbed himself in the throat, would return from the dead (13.3, 12, 14), and many scholars see Revelation as a response to the enforcement on Christians of Domitian's demand for worship as "Lord and God." But the evidence that he persecuted the church, as opposed to a few individuals who may or may not have been Christians, dissolves on inspection, and the letters to the churches reveal no state persecution, only Jewish "slander" (2.9; 3.9). The only martyr mentioned is Antipas (2.13–referring to a past event), and the general picture is of affluence and complacency.

On the other hand, Nero's mysterious death evoked immediate rumors that he was still alive, and would return with an army from the east; and the civil wars that followed his death (68–69 CE, the Year of Four Emperors), coinciding with the Jewish War (66–70 CE), seem to lie behind the breakup of the Roman world depicted in chaps. 6–18. Consequently, some scholars date Revelation about 68–70 CE: the intensity of hatred against Rome (17.6; 18.24; 19.2) does at first seem to demand a date close to the fire at Rome (64 CE) and Nero's massacre of Christians (Tacitus *Annals* 15.44). Irenaeus's date is open to question.

There is an apparent clue to the date in the interpretation of the beast's seven heads as emperors, "of whom five have fallen" (17.7–11), but in fact there is no telling which emperor the series starts with, and seven is probably again symbolic. The seven heads represent the empire as a whole, and the beast that "ascends from the bottomless pit" is "an eighth, but belongs to the seven;" it is the quintessence of imperial power, latent now but soon to be revealed in its true colors.

But this is not yet. The present is a time when the beast-like character of the empire is out of sight. In the Roman province of Asia, the Flavian emperors (Vespasian and his sons, Titus and Domitian) were popular, being efficient and generous administrators. Inscriptions hail them as "savior," "benefactor," "son of God," and there was a local zeal for the emperor cult. So Irenaeus's date in fact fits the evidence from the letters well: a time of patriotic enthusiasm, expressed in terms of religious veneration, from which Christians were not holding aloof. There was as yet no state compulsion for ordinary people to take part in the emperor cult, as long as they kept clear of law courts and the taking of oaths. Pliny's letter to the Emperor Trajan (ca. 112 CE; *Letters* 10.96), about people being accused of being Christians in the neighboring province of Bithynia, shows the danger; once accused they had the choice either of cursing Christ, worshiping the gods, and praying to the emperor's statue, or of cruel execution. Trajan agreed but said they should not be sought out. So if Christians did not provoke their neighbors by active witness and by nonparticipation in the ordinary social and patriotic decencies, then they would come to no harm. But in John's view they would be buying temporal safety at the cost of eternal loss (14.9–11). The chief threat to the church was not physical danger, as at Smyrna, but social, economic, and religious temptation. Its chief need was discernment: "let anyone who has an ear listen to what the Spirit is saying to the churches" (2.7, 11; 13.9).

Author and Sources. Irenaeus and most later writers assumed that the author was the John who wrote the Gospel and letters, and that he was the son of Zebedee. But some, like Dionysius of Alexandria (third century), anticipated the majority of modern scholars by questioning this identification because of differences of thought, style, and language. Dionysius relied on hints that there had been two writers named John in Ephesus; and Papias (ca. 140 CE) mentions a John who was an elder, as well as the apostle.

Another possibility is that Revelation is pseudonymous, claiming a great figure of the past as author, like much other apocalyptic literature. There is a later tradition that the apostle John was martyred as his brother James had been (Acts 12.2; cf. Mark 10.39; Matt. 20.23, which may be the source of the tradition); as one of the inner circle, associated as he was with Jesus at the Transfiguration and on the Mount of Olives (Mark 13.3), he would have been a good figurehead for an apocalypse calling Christians to face martyrdom. If it was published ca. 95 CE, its later acceptance as genuine could have given rise to the widely held belief that John lived to a great age in Ephesus.

But the evidence for John's martyrdom is flimsy, and if "John" is a fiction, it is odd that no capital is made out of it; the author is simply "your brother," and mentions the twelve apostles of the Lamb (21.14) without hint that he is one of them. The only status he claims is, by implication, that of prophet (1.3; 22.9). This tells also against genuinely apostolic authorship, but not decisively; and Dionysius's comment concerning differences in thought and style may be due to differences in situation and genre; there are also many marks of Johannine theology and expression. John's language is indeed extraordinary, breaking all sorts of grammatical rules—but not out of incompetence; he can write correct and powerful Greek. He seems to be echoing Hebrew constructions, perhaps to give a biblical feel to the book.

The whole book purports to be what John has seen and heard, but it is clear that his visionary experience has been shaped both by canonical and apocalyptic writings like Enoch and by the Gospels (or the traditions on which they depend)—so much so that some see the book as a scriptural meditation, based perhaps on the Sabbath readings from the Law and the Prophets, which has been cast in visionary form. Probably it is a mixture of genuine experience and literary elaboration. Biblical metaphors and images—dragon, lamb, harlot, bride—come to new life in his imagination. There are allusions to or echoes of practically every book in the Hebrew Bible. Daniel and Ezekiel are particularly formative; Isaiah, Jeremiah, Zechariah, and the Psalms are pervasive influences; so too are the stories of creation and Exodus, and of the return from Babylon and rebuilding of Jerusalem, which Isaiah depicted as a new Exodus and act of creation. Revelation is a rereading of biblical tradition in the light of the death of Jesus, and though no doubt Jewish, the author is also a citizen of the Greco-Roman world and knows its myths and astrology (see, for example, commentaries on 12.1–6).

Unity. Visionary experience and scriptural meditation may indeed be inextricably woven together, but is the book as it stands a unity? At first sight it is full of loose ends, inconsistencies, and repetitions, and many scholars have detected interpolations, revisions, and dislocations of the text. For example, there are two "last battles" (19.9; 20.8), and two visions of the holy city coming down (21.2, 10). "See, I am coming like a thief! . . ." (16.15) seems manifestly out of place in the middle of the vision of the sixth bowl, but at home in the letter to Sardis (3.3). There are obvious glosses, interpreting the heavenly incense as "the prayers of the saints" (5.8), or the bride's fine linen as "the righteous deeds of the saints" (19.8).

But the glosses may come from the author himself. The apocalyptic genre is by nature dreamlike, and thus apparently incoherent; it is best to try to make sense of what we have on its own terms, in the absence of evidence in the manuscripts for disorder.

Symbolism and Interpretation. The symbolism of Revelation is kaleidoscopic and multivalent. One picture melts into another. God's people can appear as a woman (who can be virgin, wife, or mother) or a city, and the great city where the two witnesses are killed is "spiritually called Sodom and Egypt, where also their Lord was crucified" (11.8).

Satan is both God's ancient enemy and has a place in heaven (12.7–9); likewise the sea is both an adornment of heaven (4.6), and the abode of the seven-headed beast, which represents the powers of chaos (13.1). Here is implicit the belief that evil is a corruption of what God has created good, a corruption that he can redeem; if Jerusalem can become the "great city" that murders the Lord and his witnesses, cannot the great city become the holy city? In the final vision, the kings of the earth bring in all the glory of the nations (21.24–26), though they have been slain by the Word of God (19.13, 21). In the new creation, the dualism of this age, the gap between God's will and earth's obedience, has been overcome; there is no more sea (21.1).

Numbers, like places, are also symbolic. There are twelve months, signs of the zodiac, tribes of Israel, apostles of the lamb (21.12–14). There are seven planets, days of the week, colors of the rainbow. These are numbers of wholeness. The slain Lamb has seven horns and seven eyes (5.6); the slain beast, the Antichrist that parodies his death and resurrection, has seven heads (13.1, 3, 14). His number is six, one short of seven. Satan was created the highest of the angels, but the good claiming to be the best is the very devil. His number is intensified as 666 (13.18). Second, the ancients did not have Arabic numerals, but used the letters of the alphabet (A = 1, B = 2, etc.). So by adding up numerical values (gematria) a number could represent a name. Nero Caesar, written in Hebrew letters, adds up to 666; Jesus, in Greek letters, makes 888. He died on the sixth day of the week, and rose on the eighth, the first day of the new age.

John wrote to illuminate his own situation.

Later, when his specific circumstances were forgotten, some took Revelation as a literal prediction of the future; others, in reaction against crude literalism, especially with regard to the millennium, interpreted it allegorically and saw the millennium as the present age of the church. In the twelfth century, Joachim of Fiore drew from Revelation (along with the rest of scripture) an understanding of the whole movement of history; his vision came to be widely influential. At various times, people have seen Revelation as a veiled picture of the subsequent history of the world or of the church, placing themselves at the penultimate moment and identifying beast and harlot with current bogeys, whether emperor or pope, church or sect. But it is now clear that John wrote for a past situation and that to look for literal fulfillments in the events of our day is misguided.

In spite of Alexandrian doubts, Revelation has had a firm place within the New Testament canon; it has had an immense influence on later Christianity. It can be seen as the most unchristian book—the Judas Iscariot of the New Testament, according to D. H. Lawrence (*Apocalypse* [1931])—but, with its echoes of the beginning, the tree of life restored and no more curse (22.2, 3), it is a fitting climax to the whole Bible story.

JOHN SWEET

ROMAN EMPIRE. Later Christian writers looked back to the origin of their faith and saw the work of divine providence in the coincidence of the birth of Jesus and the reign of Augustus, the first Roman emperor. Under Augustus and his successors, the empire stretched from the northwest corner of Europe to Egypt and from Mauritania to the Black Sea. It brought fifty million or more inhabitants under relatively stable rule—an ideal setting for the growth of a new religion.

Rome Before the Emperors. Roman imperial institutions and ideas of citizenship went back to the Republic and Rome's origin as a city-state. According to tradition, the city of Rome (Map 14:62) was founded by Romulus and Remus in 753 BCE at the northern edge of the plain of Latium in central peninsular Italy. Initially, the city-state was ruled by a king with the advice of the Senate, a council of elders from Rome's leading families who served for life. Important decisions, such as declarations of war, were ratified by an assembly of citizen-soldiers. The last king was expelled in 509 BCE, and his function was assumed by a pair of consuls elected annually by the citizen assembly from the body of senators. Later political thinkers interpreted these institutions as a mixed constitution with elements of monarchy (consuls), aristocracy (senate), and democracy (assembly), but in reality the senatorial aristocracy seems to have been most influential in making decisions.

Rome began its expansion in Latium as early as the regal period, but it was not until 338 BCE that Roman hegemony there was secured. From that base Rome came to dominate Italy by 270 BCE and the western Mediterranean following the two great wars against Carthage (264–241 BCE and 218–201 BCE); then the Romans moved quickly to establish hegemony over the whole Mediterranean basin with the defeat of Philip V of Macedonia (197 BCE) and Antiochus III of the Seleucid empire in Syria (189 BCE). Rome dominated from the early second century BCE but annexed these areas as provinces only slowly over the next century and a half. Syria and parts of Asia Minor came under direct Roman rule as a result of Pompey's eastern campaigns in the 60s BCE.

Rome's unparalleled victories yielded vast concentrations of wealth and power in the hands of some citizens. The world empire left the city-state constitution and idea of citizenship outdated. Roman citizenship, a status inherited from citizen parents, had formerly entailed privileges of participation in politics in the city and responsibility for military service. As Roman power spread, though, citizenship was diffused well beyond the city by the establishment of citizen colonies in Italy and abroad and by selective grant to the conquered (first to their Latin neighbors, then to all free Italians). Participation in voting assemblies in the city of Rome was impracticable for most of these new citizens, yet citizenship continued to bestow privileged status, legal rights to marry and make contracts under Roman law, and *provocatio* (protection of a citizen from arbitrary whipping or execution by magistrates through appeal to higher authorities).

The traditional Republican constitution was ultimately inadequate to the tasks of governing a vast empire abroad and of containing political competition at home. In striving with each other to attain the highest honors, senators resorted to escalating violence, culminating in two decades of civil war initiated by Julius Caesar in 49 BCE and finished by his adopted son, Augustus, who established himself as the first emperor.

Roman Imperial Social Structure. Augustus sought to legitimize his new regime by claiming to restore the *Respublica* and incorporating Republican institutions and aristocratic families. He styled himself *princeps* or first citizen, a traditional title for the leader of the Senate that avoided drawing attention to his autocracy. As part of his program of restoration, Augustus reaffirmed the traditional social order and strengthened its hierarchical divisions. It was a hierarchy based on wealth, respectable birth, and citizenship. High rank was marked by special clothing, the best seats at public spectacles, and various legal privileges.

At the top of the hierarchy were six hundred senators, propertied citizens of great wealth (at least one million sesterces or about one thousand times the annual salary of a legionary) who were chosen for the traditional senatorial offices at Rome. Equestrians or knights held second rank; they were citizens of free birth who possessed a census of at least four hundred thousand sesterces. Through the centuries of the empire, they were recruited to serve in the imperial administration in increasing numbers. In addition to this imperial elite, each of the thousands of cities of the empire had its own local aristocracy from which was chosen a governing council consisting of a hundred or so of the town's wealthiest men (many of whom did not have Roman citizenship). These leisured elites became collectively known by the early second century CE as the *honestiores* or "more honorable men," in contrast to the humbler masses or *humiliores*, who constituted more than 90 percent of the population.

Several important distinctions of status divided ordinary working people. There were the citizens, concentrated mainly in Italy in Augustus's day but increasingly scattered throughout the provinces by the settlement of colonies and by imperial grant to favored individuals and communities. Noncitizen free provincials formed a huge amorphous group. The empire encompassed enormous cultural variation between city and countryside, and between regions. If Latin was spoken by the urban elites of the western empire and Greek was the primary tongue in the eastern cities, ordinary provincials continued to speak their native tongues, whether it be Aramaic in Palestine or the Punic language around Carthage. They also continued to worship their own gods, which in some cases were assimilated to the Roman gods. Roman emperors and officials could be sensitive to the cultural diversity: the early governors of Judea tried to avoid affronts to Jewish monotheism, but later ones were less careful. When Florus attempted to take a large sum from the Temple treasury in Jerusalem in 66 CE, he provoked a fierce rebellion that required seven years, the destruction of Jerusalem, and widespread slaughter to suppress.

Beneath the free population in the social hierarchy were slaves. Slavery as an institution was taken for granted; there were no serious abolitionist movements in antiquity. Slaves formed a substantial proportion of the population in Italy (perhaps one-third), where they were heavily involved in all aspects of economic production. In most of the provinces slaves were common only as domestic servants. By law, slaves were property who could be bought or sold, beaten or tortured at the owner's whim. As the attitudes of owners varied, so also did the living conditions of slaves.

Imperial Political and Administrative Structures.
The emperor ruled the peoples of the empire from Rome with the help of men chosen from the elites; with the demise of Republican elections, the popular voice in politics was lost. The capital city had a population of about one million and encompassed extremes of wealth and poverty, lavish public monuments and filthy, cramped apartments. Much of the population, perhaps even a majority, was made up of slaves and freedmen from the eastern Mediterranean, Germany, and elsewhere. Rome was able to grow to be the largest city of pre-industrial Europe because of the privileges of conquest: provincial agriculture was taxed, and part of the grain was sent to Rome to feed the masses. To keep the urban plebs quiet, the emperor also put on various spectacles, including the gladiatorial fights and wild beast hunts, in which some Christians met their end. Despite the food distributions and public entertainment, violence occasionally broke out in the city, prompting emperors to expel foreigners or to find scapegoats. So Claudius expelled the Jews from Rome (see Acts 18.2), and Nero began the official persecution of Christians when he needed scapegoats to blame for the great fire of 64 CE.

Italy was the land of citizens. As such, it was privileged with exemption from the land tax until the late third century CE. No governors were set over Italy; administration was largely left to the municipalities, with important matters referred to imperial officials in Rome.

Beyond Italy lay the Roman *imperium*, including client kings and directly ruled provinces. The Romans were slow to annex areas around the Mediterranean as provinces because they lacked a developed administrative apparatus. It was convenient to leave the governing of some peripheral areas to local kings in return for support of Rome in matters of foreign policy through occasional tribute and troops for Roman wars. Client kings paid heed to the authority of the emperor and the senior governors of nearby provinces. Accounts of the reign of Herod the Great, the best-known client king, illustrate how dependent he was on the continuing goodwill of the emperor and his officials, which he curried by careful attention to their wishes as well as by gifts and bribes. Gradually, as in Palestine, the client kingdoms were added to the list of directly ruled provinces.

The several dozen provinces were administered by governors sent out from Rome. Their two principal concerns were the maintenance of law and order and the collection of taxes. Roman administration can be characterized as general oversight by a handful of imperial officials who relied on local leaders. The major provinces were governed by senators in different capacities. Provinces with legions were administered by imperial legates appointed by the emperor from among those senators he considered most reliable. Syria, with the largest legionary army of the eastern empire, was a province of this type. Major provinces without armies, such as Achaea, where supervised by senatorial proconsuls chosen in the Senate. Judea from 6 CE was one of those lesser provinces administered by equestrians (initially army officers called prefects, then imperial agents with the title of procurator). All governors held broad authority, limited by their responsibility to the emperor, who issued some instructions for administration (*mandata*); equestrian procurators also occasionally received guidance from senatorial governors of neighboring provinces.

Governors were accompanied to their provinces by minimal staffs, including friends and relatives who acted

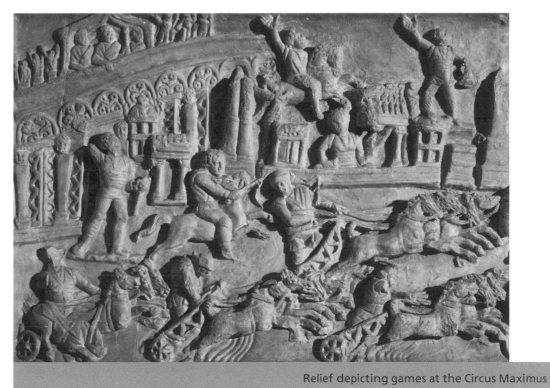

Relief depicting games at the Circus Maximus

as advisory councils. The meager staffs were supplemented by military officers and soldiers acting as major figures of authority in provincial administration (as in Acts 22.23–30; 27.1). In their judicial capacity, governors heard the cases of Roman citizens who were subject to Roman law and also adjudicated some other serious cases. For the most part, noncitizens were subject to local law and custom, and were left to local magistrates (Acts 16.19–23). Roman governors, reluctant to become entangled in squabbles among the natives, were often content to hold local leaders responsible for the preservation of order in their noncitizen communities. This tacit arrangement explains both the worry of Caiaphas that disorder would provoke violent suppression from Rome (John 11.49–50) and the aloofness of the Roman proconsul Gallio when Paul was brought before him (Acts 18.12–17). It also accounts for the slow and sporadic pattern of persecution of the Christians before 250 CE. Roman governors were instructed to punish with death anyone brought before them who persistently admitted to being a Christian, but they were not actively to seek out Christians. As a result, in the province of Africa the first execution on the charge of Christianity did not come until about 180 CE.

Most provincials encountered Roman government over the matter of taxes—taxes on the land, on the people who worked the land, on goods moving across provincial borders, on inheritances, on sales in the market, to name but a few. The Romans did not impose a uniform tax system on conquest, but usually took over local arrangements and contracted out the collection to private agents, the *publicani*, infamous for their rapacious methods of enrichment. Julius Caesar began to phase out these middlemen at the highest levels, but they continued into the Principate to collect indirect taxes, such as custom duties. In order to assess the main land and head taxes, imperial officials occasionally carried out censuses in which provincials were required to register themselves and their property. The imperial legate Quirinius oversaw such a census in Judea in 6 CE, which, on grounds of date and Roman administrative procedures, seems to be impossible to reconcile with the account in Luke 2.1–5.

In Augustus's day, the resources of the Roman empire were sufficient to fulfill the relatively light demands of the state, but they were limited by the agricultural base and the stagnant technology of the economy. Under the Christian emperors of the later empire, increasing demands for money and recruits to support the growing army and bureaucracy were met by more determined resistance. As the "barbarian" tribes pressed ever-harder against the frontiers, the limits left emperors unable to ward off the threats. In 410 CE, the Eternal City was sacked by Alaric and his Visigoths; the last Roman emperor of the west, Romulus Augustulus, was deposed by the German leader Odoacer in 476 CE.

RICHARD P. SALLER

ROMANS, THE LETTER OF PAUL TO THE.

Circumstances of the Letter. Romans, the longest of Paul's letters and the only one in which the apostle does not name a companion or coauthor, is the most carefully worked out statement of his view of the Christian faith. Although Paul had never visited the Christian community in Rome, despite his repeated hope to do so (1.11, 13), and hence cannot have been one of the founders of Christianity in the capital city of the Roman empire, he intended to visit it soon, both to encourage the believers and be encouraged by them (1.12).

Also in Paul's mind as he dictated this letter (16.22) was his plan to carry his mission to the western half of the Mediterranean world, as far as Spain (15.24), after he had delivered a gift of money to the "poor among the saints at Jerusalem" (15.26; cf. Gal. 2.10). Paul probably hoped that the Christians in Rome would underwrite this mission (15.28–29). Acts, however, reports nothing of this mission to Spain, and the danger that Paul feared in Jerusalem from nonbelievers (15.31) in fact materialized in a different way with his arrest there (cf. Acts 21.30).

It is probable that there was more than one Christian community in Rome, since Paul refers to a "house church" (16.5); others may have been in the houses of Prisca and Aquila (16.3; cf. 1 Cor. 16.19 for the house church they sponsored in Corinth), of Aristobulus (16.10), and of Narcissus (16.11). It is also probable that the Christian community there was composed of converted Jews as well as gentiles, despite an earlier order by the Emperor Claudius that all Jews be expelled from Rome (41 or 49 CE). That this also affected Christians is evident from the reference in Acts 18.2 to Prisca and Aquila, who were Jewish Christians. Paul's direct address to Jews (e.g., 2.17), and his concern with their history (e.g., 3.1; 4.1; 9–11), owes more to the content of his own faith and the style of his argument than to actual debates he anticipated with Jews in Rome.

Although Paul had never been to Rome, he knew many Christians who lived there and included greetings to them at the end of his letter (chap. 16). Arguments to the effect that these greetings could not have belonged to the original letter are not persuasive, since mobility within the Roman empire was great, and there were many who migrated to Rome during this period. The extent to which women played a key role within the early church is evident also from the same chapter: for example, Phoebe, a deacon, 16.1; Prisca, 16.3 (cf. 1 Cor. 16.19, Acts 18–2); Mary, 16.6; Junia, an apostle, 16.7–all of whom, as the language indicates, were active in the Christian mission.

Specific information is not available concerning the circumstances surrounding the composition of the letter, such as the place from which it was written or the exact date of its composition. Scholars are not in agreement on a chronology of Paul's life, and the most that can be said is that the letter seems to have been written toward the end of his life. Since it is not known how well Paul was acquainted with the circumstances of Christians in Rome, we are unable to determine whether his ethical discussions in the letter (cf. 14.1–15.13) refer to specific problems, or whether they are the kind of general admonition he thought any group of Christians might read with profit. That the problem was not between Jewish and gentile Christians about dietary matters is clear from the fact that no Jewish dietary laws forbade the general eating of meat (14.2) or the drinking of wine (14.21). The admonitions read like a generalized account of the problem that Paul faced in Corinth (see 1 Cor. 8), and hence they are probably intended, as is the rest of the letter, to be a summary of Christian faith and practice.

Content of the Letter. A more detailed outline of Paul's letter to the Christian communities in Rome is the following:

I. God's lordship and the problem of the past: wrath and grace (1.1–4.22)
    A. Opening (1.1–13)
    B. The gospel and God's wrath (1.14–3.20)
    C. The gospel and God's grace (3.21–4.22)

II. God's lordship and the problem of the present: grace and law (4.23–8.39)
   A. Sin and grace: Adam and Christ (4.23–5.21)
   B. Sin, grace and law (6.1–7.25)
   C. The spirit and the surety of grace (8.1–39)
III. God's lordship and the problem of the future: Israel and God's gracious plan (9.1–11.36)
   A. God's grace and Israel's rejection (9.1–29)
   B. Grace, faith, and the purpose of the law (9.30–10.21)
   C. Israel and her future with God (11.1–36)
IV. God's lordship and the problems of daily living: grace and the structures of life (12.1–16.27)
   A. Grace and the community (12.1–21)
   B. Grace and the state (13.1–7)
   C. Grace and the neighbor (13.8–14)
   D. Grace and unity in the faith (14.1–15.13)
   E. Grace and Paul's plans (15.14–33)
   F. Conclusion (16.1–27)

The central theme of Paul's letter to the Christian communities in Rome is the universal scope of God's redemptive act in Jesus Christ, offered to all who accept it in trust. That redemption, by which God reestablishes his gracious lordship over his rebellious creation, is offered not only to Jews but also to gentiles.

First Section (1.1–4.22). Paul assumes that apart from Christ, all humanity has rebelled against God, the characteristic form of that rebellion being to set something other than God at the center of one's life. Such substitution of some part of creation for the true God, whether self or some other reality, Paul understands as idolatry (1.22–23, 25). Because there was enough evidence from the created universe itself to warn human beings away from idolatry (1.19–20), such rebellion against God is culpable (1.21) and brings wrath (1.18, 24–31). Although gentiles show by their actions that they possess a sense of morality (2.14–16), they will not be saved by being morally pure, since moral purity cannot reconcile them to the God they have rejected. Similarly, though Jews belong to God's chosen people (3.1) and possess the Law (2.17–20), these features will not deliver them from divine wrath brought on by their rejection of God's act of redemption in his Son, Jesus Christ. Hence all people stand in rebellion before God (3.9–18), including those who belong to the chosen people, to whom the Law was given (3.19–20).

In Christ, however, God has come in grace to rebellious humanity, and he offers a remedy as universal as the malady (3.23–24). That remedy is to be received in faith (3.25), a remedy open to all, of whatever origin, since God is the God of all, and he offers a restored relationship to himself through trust in the love he has shown in his Son (3.28–30). In fact, a right relationship with God on the basis of trust is not something new, but was already the case with Abraham (chap. 4). It was Abraham's trust in God that allowed him to stand in a positive relationship to God (4.18–22); that positive relationship is what Paul calls "righteousness." Such righteousness, based on trust, came to Abraham before he was circumcised; hence, faith is open to all, whether uncircumcised, as Abraham was when he first trusted, or circumcised, as Abraham later became (4.9–12, 16).

The record of Abraham's trust in God has, however, more than historical interest; Paul affirms that it also bears directly on his readers (4.23). With that announcement, Paul begins the second major part of his letter.

Second Section (4.23–8.39). Turning his attention to the present, Paul explains what his readers may now experience (5.1–5) as a result of the new opportunity for forgiveness of sin and a restored relationship to God which is offered in Christ (4.24–25). That new relationship is based on God's initiative in opening the way through Christ to righteousness in the present and to salvation in the future (5.6–11). The divine initiative remains necessary in the present, since the present continues to suffer from the inheritance of Adam, namely, the rebellion mentioned earlier (5.12–14): the universality of sharing in Adam's rebellion is demonstrated for Paul by the universal fate of death for all people (5.12). It was from that rebellion and its negative results that Christ has saved human beings (5.15–19).

Where does God's law fit into all this? Paul raises that question (5.20–21) and then considers it in the next two chapters. Discussing the relationship of law, sin, and grace in every possible combination (6.1: sin and grace; 6.15: law and grace; 7.7: law and sin), Paul argues that baptism into Christ's death breaks the power of sin (6.1–11), and hence Christians are now free not to sin (6.12–14). Paul next argues that everyone, whether Christian or not, is under the power of some force, whether of sin or of grace (6.16–23), and that only God's grace releases a person from the power of sin through the death of Christ (7.1–17). Third, Paul argues that the close relationship of sin and law shows that those under the Law are incapable of extricating themselves from it (7.7–23). Only Christ is able to do that (7.24), as Paul had already stated in 6.1–14.

A mosaic featuring St Paul displayed over the chapel of the Basilica of St. Paul Outside-the-Walls.

The section 7.13–23 is thus Paul's reflection on the past, namely what life under the Mosaic law looks like from a Christian perspective; 8.1–39, on the other hand, is his reflection on the present, namely what life under Christ and freed from law looks like from a Christian perspective. Thus, a life restored under the gracious lordship of God through Christ is a life wherein the enmity between God and human beings is at an end (8.1–11), and where they, restored to the family of God (8.12–17), may look beyond present deprivation (8.18–25) to the presence of God's Spirit with them (8.26–27). Life in such a situation is safe from any hazard (8.28–39).

Third Section, 9.1–11.36. One problem remains, however, and that is the rejection by the chosen people, the Jews, of God's plan for their redemption in Jesus Christ. Since God had promised them blessing through Abraham, does not their rejection of the fulfillment of that promise in Christ mean that God's promise, and thus his word, has failed (9.6)? Paul answers this question by pointing out that since God has always worked with a remnant in Israel, it should not be surprising that he continues to do so in the case of the small minority in Israel who believe in Christ (9.1–29). Furthermore, by putting the Law ahead of Christ as an expression of God's will, the Jews have continued to resist trust in God as the way of salvation (9.20–10.4).

Yet such trust, not limited by birth, as was the Law, is God's chosen way of the redemption of sinners (10.5–13), a way that has been proclaimed to Jews as well as gentiles (10.14–21). Despite the Jews' rejection, however, God has not rejected the Jews (11.1–10), nor will the rejection of Christ by the Jews be final. Rather, that rejection is part of God's merciful plan: by rejecting Christ, the Jews have created the opportunity for gentiles to hear the proclamation of salvation. When that proclamation has been completed, the Jews will also finally accept trust in God through Christ (11.11–16). Using the analogy of grafting branches into an olive tree (11.17–24), Paul makes the point that the hardened attitude of Jews toward Christ is not the final word; in the end, they too will share in God's gracious lordship established through trust in Christ (11.25–31). All of this is part of God's merciful plan (11.32), knowledge of which calls forth praise to God, who works in such strange yet gracious ways (11.33–36).

Fourth Section, 12.1–16.27. Having ended the third section with hymnic praise to the God whose gracious ways with sinful humanity are mysterious and past finding out, Paul gives attention to the ways in which God's gracious lordship, established through trust in Christ, relates to the structures of everyday life. Showing successively how that gracious lordship impinges on life in the community (12.1–21), in the state (13.1–7), and on one's relationship with one's neighbor (13.8–14), Paul then considers how Christians should deal with differences among themselves (14.1–15.13). Taking as his example the distinction between the "weak" (those who have scruples about eating meat, 15.2, or observing the Sabbath, 15.5–6, or drinking wine, 15.14) and the "strong" (those who regard such scruples as unnecessary), Paul affirms that the personal preferences of the strong are to be laid aside lest the weak be offended, and thus be lost to the Christian community (14.15; 15.1).

In the final verses, Paul outlines his travel plans (15.14–33) and sends greetings (16.1–16, 21–23) along with final exhortations (16.17–20) and a benediction (16.25–27).

Influence. Because of the range and depth of theological topics discussed in it, the letter to the Romans has played a key role at critical junctures in the history of Christianity.

Amid the crumbling institutions of a Roman empire which had embraced the church, Augustine learned from Romans a view of human nature and of the state that could survive the demise of civilization. Amid the pomp of a church grown self-important, Luther and Calvin found in this letter, particularly its treatment of justification by faith alone, a way to construct a worshiping community that allowed God's gracious lordship to be more clearly expressed. In a period of naive identification of cultural progress with God's will, Karl Barth heard in Romans the divine "no" to any attempt to equate human accomplishment with divine grace. Paul's acknowledgement of the continuing validity of God's special relationship to the Jews (e.g., 3.1–2; 11.29) stands in the way of any Christian exaltation over the modern heirs of ancient Israel. To those who pay careful heed, Romans continues to be an important guide for all who seek to make sense of their lives in the midst of historical change and cultural conflict.

PAUL J. ACHTEMEIER

RUTH, THE BOOK OF. Ruth is a gripping short story, incorporating folkloric features that make for ease of appreciation as common human experience, as well as distinctive cultural features commending Israel's theology and ethics. Ruth stands eighth, between Judges and 1 Samuel, in the canon of the Bible familiar to Christians, but first among the five small festival scrolls (megillot) of the Hebrew canon, usually right after Proverbs. Ruth is the festal reading for Shavu ot (Pentecost) in Jewish tradition.

The book begins with a background scenario of a Bethlehemite family, two parents and their two sons, sojourning in Moab because of famine back home. The sons marry Moabites. Father and two sons die, leaving three widows, Naomi, Orpah, and Ruth. Naomi, choosing to return home, urges her daughters-in-law to remain in Moab. Orpah does so, but Ruth cleaves to Naomi. Naomi, lamenting bitterly, arrives in Bethlehem with Ruth accompanying her; she sees little prospect of fullness of life. Scene two (chap. 2) has Ruth initiate efforts to support herself and Naomi by gleaning at the harvest, where she chances upon the field of Boaz, a worthy Bethlehemite. Boaz notices her, at first makes minimal provision, then moves to progressively greater care for this woman who has displayed such loyalty to her family.

In scene three (chap. 3), Naomi, encouraged by the success of Ruth's first steps, directs her how to move things from a temporary to a longterm resolution: marriage and offspring for Ruth, redeemer care for Naomi. Ruth forces the matter with Boaz in a provocative scene at the threshing-floor, only to learn that the redeemer responsibility falls first upon a person other than Boaz. In the final scene (4.1–17), while Ruth and Naomi wait, Boaz maneuvers this other person to yield his role at a public forum in the town gate. The way is clear for Boaz to marry Ruth, provide an heir to Ruth's first husband, and provide a redeemer for Naomi. The redeemer is Obed, David's grandfather—this information is the striking climax of a chorus by the Bethlehem townspeople celebrating first Boaz, then Ruth and Naomi. The story closes (4.18–20) with a genealogy connecting David through Obed and Boaz to Perez, Judah's offspring (Gen. 38).

Scholarly efforts to reconstruct earlier stages in the development of the story or to identify additions to the original have yielded little insight into its meaning; even the conclusion that the genealogy at the end (cf. 1 Chron. 2.5–15) is an appendix is now regularly challenged, and interpreters study the book as a carefully crafted whole.

Almost two-thirds of the story is conveyed in conversation, a characteristic of biblical storytelling artistry. Both conversation and narration include captivating literary devices. For example, on the road back to Bethlehem, the hesitation of Orpah and Ruth, the combined urging and complaint of Naomi, and the commitment of Ruth are all handled with superb pacing and beautiful language. Guide words such as "return" in scene one and "glean" in scene two bind episodes internally. Key words in pairs are used to link scene to scene and connect the posing of plot problems to their resolutions (e.g., "lads" Naomi has lost in 1.5 with the "lad" Naomi gains in 4.16; Yahweh's "wings" of care in 2.12 with Boaz's "wings" of marital commitment in 3.9). The storyteller is sparing in detail, providing only the essentials and sometimes leaving gaps: we are taken by surprise in 4.3 by a field that Naomi can sell, and are not told whether Boaz and Naomi ever meet.

Emphasizing these literary characteristics follows the trend of current scholarship on Ruth, and it means playing down questions of historicity on the one hand or of the book's role as polemic on the other. In the past, Ruth was often seen as composed in the fourth century BCE to oppose the Ezra-Nehemiah effort to dissolve mixed marriages. Instead, interpretation now focuses on Ruth as historical fiction, serving as an edifying and entertaining encounter with typical events in a typical town. Clearly, care for those in danger of being left on society's margins is a crucial concern—in the Ruth story typified by two widows, one a foreigner. Structures exist to meet this concern: the gleaning provision (cf. Lev. 19.9–10; Deut. 24.19–22); marriage to one's husband's relative (Ruth 2.12–13; 4.5); redeeming, which involves responsibility for property recovery and care of persons; responsibilities devolving upon members of a wider circle designated by Hebrew words translated "kinsman" in 2.1 and 3.2. The story brings all these customs to bear, assuming that the audience knows how they worked. Among these, the particular practice called levirate marriage (Deut. 25.5–10; Gen. 38) *may* pertain; alternatively, Ruth 1.12–13 and 4.5 may point to some allied custom otherwise unattested in the Bible. What the story does portray clearly is the interplay of agents of care and recipients of care within society: in turn, the three principal characters both give and receive. Orpah and the potential redeemer in 4.3–6 are ready to give *some* help; the drama lies with the greater risk and commitment required of Ruth and Boaz to bring good out of bad, a theme expressed in the key concept *hesed*, "kindness," in 1.8; 2.20; and 3.10.

Theology is muted in Ruth. The book participates in an exploration of divine providence also seen in the Joseph cycle (Gen. 37–50), in 2 Samuel 9–20, and in Job. Only Ruth 1.6, 4.13, and probably 2.20 assert divine intervention, but the greetings and blessings and outcries of the characters keep deity present. The sharp outcry against God by Naomi in 1.20–21 sounds the prominent biblical theme of lament.

The climax, which comes with the note about David in 4.17, suggests that blessing of Israel's royal line is an issue here. The blessing speeches in 4.13–17 are comparable to other Near Eastern royal blessings. If the David theme is intrinsic to the book—this was often debated in the

Ruth meeting Boaz while working in his fields (Ruth 2.4–13)

past—then it provides the historical datum that David had a Moabite ancestor. The book is quite probably part of a cycle of stories about David's ancestry, which would include Genesis 38 and other episodes now lost—for instance, about Perez and Zefah prepared for by Genesis 38.27–30, and about Obed prepared for by Ruth 4.16–17.

To decide about the date and audience of Ruth is difficult. Linguistic criteria and judgments about its place in the development of thought, invoked in the past as pointers to a late date, have lost their cogency. A date anywhere in the time of the Judean monarchy is plausible. The audience was probably village people and the storyteller a professional bard, quite possibly a wise woman (cf. 2 Sam. 14.1–20). Alternatively, the story may be a self-conscious imitation of a folktale, written at the royal court.

The universal appeal and the plausible presentation of typical Israelite life mask precise time and place, and release the story of Ruth for the pleasure and edification of all. The Targumic tradition and rabbinic commentary build the relation between Naomi and Ruth into a paradigm for the education of a proselyte. They celebrate the portrayal of "kindness" and probe the institutions of levirate, shoe transfer (4.6–8), and redemption. Down the centuries, more modern literary allusions give us Dante's "gleanermaid, meek ancestress" of David, Bunyan's "Mercy," Milton's chooser of the better part, Keats's recipient of the nightingale's solace "amid the alien corn," and Goethe's accolade: the most beautiful "little whole" of the Hebrew Bible.

EDWARD F. CAMPBELL

SABBATH (Hebr. *šabbāt*). The last day of the week; the only day bearing a name, the others being merely numbered. It is considered the absolute day of rest without exceptions. Its observance is probably very old but is attested only since the eighth century BCE (Amos 8.5; Hos. 2.13; Isa. 1.13, 2 Kings 4.23). An earlier date is suggested by Israelite legal traditions (Exod. 23.12; 34.21); the references in the Ten Commandments (Exod. 20.8–11; Deut. 5.12–15) may not be older than Deuteronomy itself.

The etymology of *šabbāt* is uncertain. A relation to the verb *šbt*, to which it has naturally been connected (see Gen. 2.2–3; Exod. 20.11), is questionable, since *šbt* is never attested in the intensive form or in connection with the practice of resting from work, while its meaning is "coming/bringing to an end." A connection with the Akkadian *šab/pattu*, the day of the full moon, falling on the fifteenth of the lunar month, or with the seventh, fourteenth, twenty-first, and twenty-eighth days should probably be rejected, as they are unpropitious days, the opposite of what the Sabbath seems to be. Nevertheless, the former connection is so obvious etymologically that one should ask whether the abstention from work on such a day does not lead, eventually, to the Israelite concept of rest. Sometimes the Sabbath is connected with the feast of the new moon (Amos 8.5; Hos. 2.13; Isa. 1.13); what this means we do not know.

The origins of the Sabbath are also obscure. Biblical tradition (but in late texts) attributes it to Moses; this, however, cannot be verified and, since the practice presupposes a relatively advanced agricultural society, is improbable. In preexilic times its observance cannot have been very strict; 2 Kings 11.5–9 tells us, without any criticism, of the arrest and execution on the Sabbath of the Queen Mother Athali-ah, who had been usurping the kingship, something inconceivable in later times.

By postexilic times keeping the Sabbath had become one of the distinctive practices of observant Jews. During this period detailed regulations developed so as to make its observance absolute, a tendency already evident in the explanations in the Ten Commandments. The Sabbath was also a socioeconomic institution and meant feeding humans and animals although they were not working, besides losing profit; thus attempts were made to circumvent the law, and these needed to be countered. In Maccabean times, the problem of fighting on the Sabbath arose (1 Macc. 2.32–38; 2 Macc. 6.11), the faithful preferring to be killed rather than desecrate the Sabbath.

In the New Testament and in rabbinic Judaism we hear echoes of the debates that developed around the observance of Sabbath until finally a criterion was proposed: "Every case of danger of life allows for the suspension of the Sabbath" (*Yoma* 8.6). According to Rabbi Akiba, one should not desecrate the Sabbath for things that can be done the day before or the day after, but no desecration exists when such a possibility is not offered. Therefore a midwife can function and should be helped on the Sabbath. Rabbinic teaching differs from the New Testament in that healing in the New Testament is considered to fall under the principle of "danger of life," a point that later rabbinic teaching did not accept. The rabbis concluded: "Sabbath has been given to you; you have not been given to the Sabbath" (*Mekilta* to Exod. 31.13; cf. Mark 2.27). Some sectarians thought otherwise; so at Qumran on the Sabbath one was not supposed to help an animal when it was giving birth or involved in an accident.

New Testament discussions about the Sabbath seem therefore to be inner-Jewish discussions. By the end of the first century CE, the first day of the week was celebrated as the day of the Lord, to which Christian observance of the Sabbath was transferred (see Rev 1.10; also Acts 20.7; 1 Cor. 16.2). Some Christian groups, notably the Seventh-day Adventists, following biblical legislation exactly, observe the seventh day of the week, the original (and continuing) Jewish Sabbath.

J. A. SOGGIN

SACRIFICE. The offering of some commodity to God, generally making use of the services of a cultic official, a priest. In the Bible, the various kinds of sacrifices are presented most systematically in Leviticus 1–7 (cf. Num. 15). The different sacrifices cited there can be classified in several ways. Most prominent are those utilizing clean animals (cattle, sheep, goats, doves, pigeons). All such animal sacrifices have a number of

A Hassidic family gathers round the Sabbath table in Jerusalem, 2006.

Samson and Delilah and the destruction of the Temple (Judg. 16.23–30)

features in common: killing/dismemberment of the victim, burning of at least some part of it (the fat in particular) on the altar, application of the blood to the altar by the priest in some manner (sprinkling or smearing).

The burnt offering or holocaust is particularly distinctive (Lev. 1.3–17; 6.8–13). As the latter name implies, a complete consumption of the victim's remains (except for the skin, which was given to the priest: Lev. 7.8) by fire was involved here. The rite opened with the offerer's laying his hand on the victim's head (Lev. 1.4a); this gesture of self-identification signifies that, through the beast, he is offering himself to God. The intended purpose of the holocaust was to effect atonement with Yahweh for the offerer (Lev. 1.4b).

Another major animal sacrifice is the peace offering (NRSV: "offering of well-being;" the differently translated Hebrew word is šelĕmîm), described in Leviticus 3.1–17; 7.11–36. In this instance, the designation employed points to the ritual's aim, that is, to (re-)establish "peace," fellowship between the divine and human parties. In line with this end, the victim's remains are divided between God (for whom the fat is burned on the altar), the assisting priest, and the offerer's household. The peace offering can further be specified, in accordance with the motive prompting it, as a thanksgiving, votive, or freewill offering. In the first instance, the victim's flesh must be consumed on the day of the sacrifice itself (Lev. 7.15); in the latter two, the time allotted for this extends through the following day (Lev. 7.16).

Two further animal sacrifices are the sin offering and the guilt offering (Lev. 4.1–6.7; 6.25–7.10). The Bible does not clearly distinguish these in terms of either their ritual or the situations that necessitate them (see Lev. 7.17). Both are designed to effect atonement in cases of a nondeliberate offense (e.g., bodily discharges, contact with the unclean), and in both it is only the victim's fat that is burned on the altar. The sin offering is, however, the more public of the two, being offered on the major feasts of the year (Num. 28–29), while the guilt offering functions as part of a process of reparation undertaken by an individual (Lev. 5.16; 6.4).

The Bible also prescribes various nonbloody sacrifices; these utilize cereals (Lev. 2.1–15), frankincense, and wine. Of these, the last must accompany other sacrifices, whereas the first two may be offered separately. Finally, biblical narratives evidence familiarity with the practice of human sacrifice (see, e.g., Gen. 22; Judg. 10.30–40; 1 Kings 16.34; 2 Kings 3.27); this, however, is strongly condemned in the laws of the Pentateuch (e.g., Lev. 18.14).

Taken as a whole, the Hebrew Bible manifests a certain ambivalence regarding sacrifice. In the Pentateuch, it is solemnly enjoined as a positive divine requirement, while other passages seem to articulate God's rejection of the practice as a whole (e.g., Amos 5.21–27; Isa. 1.10–20; Ps. 51.16–17). The latter formulations are best seen as hyperbolic reminders of the truth that cultic sacrifice is pleasing to God only when offered by one whose whole life is lived in accordance with God's will.

In the New Testament, particularly in Hebrews, the death of Jesus is described as a sacrifice that definitively secures for the whole of humanity the effects (atonement, fellowship with God) that older sacrifices brought about only temporarily (Heb. 9.23–28). Likewise in the New Testament, the notion of a spiritual sacrifice comes to the fore (Rom. 12.1; 15.16; Phil. 2.17; 4.18; 1 Pet. 2.5). In this conception, every action of a Christian's life has the capacity, when performed in faith, to be an offering acceptable to God.

CHRISTOPHER T. BEGG

SAMSON. Samson (whose name is derived from the word for "sun") was the twelfth and last judge of Israel (Judg. 13–

16) before civil war threatened to tear the tribes apart (Judg. 17–21). He harassed the Philistines in the border country between his native Dan, Judah, and Philistia. Besides killing thousands of Philistines, Samson ripped a lion apart with his bare hands (14.5–6) and told a riddle about it (14.14), loved two women who betrayed him for very different reasons (14.15–17; 16.5–6), burned Philistine crops (15.4–5), visited a Philistine prostitute and carried off the city gates of Gaza on the same night (16.1–3), was blinded and enslaved by the Philistines (16.21), and caused his own death by toppling the pillars of the Philistines' temple upon himself and his foes (16.28–30).

With his powerful libido, Samson resembles other judges who fell outside the behavioral norms of Israelite society (left-handed Ehud, the woman Deborah, young Gideon, the bastard Jephthah). Unlike other judges, however, Samson was neither an adjudicator nor (despite Judg. 13–5) a "deliverer" of his people. Personal vengeance was the motive for his single-handed forays against the Philistines. Samson's obliviousness to the requirements of his Nazirite status (Judg. 14.8–9, 10; 15.15) suggests that it is not original to the Samson legend, although it is important in the literary framework of the biblical narrative.

The Samson story reflects an early stage of actual Philistine-Israelite confrontations, but it is rooted in Danite folktales and perhaps Philistine story traditions. It resembles tales of intertribal relations told in other areas where neighboring groups borrow story lines from each other. The Philistines were related to Homer's Mycenaean Greeks, and the Samson saga has motifs in common with Greek and other Indo-European literatures. Samson also resembles Gilgamesh, as well as tricksters like Jacob.

Josephus is typical of early Jewish and Christian interpreters in his verdict that Samson's heroic death transcended the sins of his life (Ant. 5.8.317). Samson's questionable morality could even be glossed over (Heb. 11.32), or, as later for Milton in *Samson Agonistes*, superseded by his heroic death.

Judges 13–16 is one of the most artfully composed tales in the Bible. It is framed by a prediction of Samson's birth to his barren mother (Judg. 13; cf. Gen. 17.15–19; 18; 1 Sam. 1) and his spectacular death (Judg. 16.22–30), episodes that mirror each other (e.g., in the obtuseness of both Manoah and the Philistines, and the rituals for Yahweh and Dagon). There is an exuberance of wordplay, including etiologies (15.17, 19), riddling couplets (14.12–14, 18), and ring compositions (especially Judges 13). One finds foreshadowing (13.7), crisp characterizations (Samson, his mother and father), and clever inversions from episode to episode (compare the restraining of Samson by the men of Judah and by Delilah). Most of all, the narrative presents a subtle study of deception and betrayal, by humans and by God, for good and for ill.

MARY JOAN WINN LEITH

SAMUEL, THE BOOKS OF.

Title. The two books are in reality one (cf. Kings, Chronicles): in the Hebrew text, they run continuously, with the counting of words and sections characteristic of the Hebrew tradition coming only at the end. The division into two appears first in the Greek translation (the Septuagint) and then in the Latin Vulgate: from there it came to be used in other translations, and by the sixteenth century also in printed Hebrew Bibles. The traditional title "Samuel" reflects the fact that he dominates much of the material, particularly in the establishing of the monarchy; hence he came to be seen as the author. The Greek and Latin texts use titles that cover

also the following books of Kings—thus either "four books of kingdoms" or "four books of kings." Since these four books together cover the whole period of the monarchy, these latter titles are really more appropriate.

Contents. Briefly the contents are:

1 Samuel 1–15:	Samuel and Saul
1 Samuel 16–31:	Saul and David
2 Samuel 1–8:	David's rise to power
2 Samuel 9–20:	David's reign
2 Samuel 21–24:	narratives, psalms, and lists.

Such an outline does not show the complex interweaving of themes which the books reveal, and for a proper understanding we also need to consider both what precedes and follows, as well as the subdivisions and interlinkages within the books themselves.

What precedes in the Hebrew text is the book of Judges. (Ruth in that text stands in the third section of the canon, as one of the Five Scrolls, with Song of Solomon, Ecclesiastes, Lamentations, and Esther.) The sequence in this form is clearly right for the narratives: Eli the priest at Shiloh, who appears in the first four chapters, is depicted so as to fit into the series of "judges," his activity rounded off at his death (4.18) with the statement that "he had judged Israel forty years." In addition, the refrain in Judges 17–21, "in those days there was no king in Israel; all the people did what was right in their own eyes" (17.6; 18.1; 19.1; 21.25), may be seen as an appropriate preface to the establishment of the monarchy. The order in the English text places Ruth after Judges: this derives from the Greek and Latin versions and is also intelligible—not only is the book of Ruth set "in the days when the judges ruled" (1.1), but it has its climax in the birth of a son to Ruth who was to be the grandfather of David. The story of Ruth prepares for the appearance of David as king.

There is no break between Samuel and Kings; the story of David does not end, as we might have expected, at the end of 2 Samuel; it continues into 1 Kings 1–2. A commonly held view is that the group of chapters from 2 Samuel 9 to 1 Kings 2—ignoring for the moment 2 Samuel 21–24—forms a continuous unit, often called the "Succession Story" or the "Court History of David" (see below).

The recognition of continuity into 1 Kings and of the link back to Judges, itself continuous with Joshua, points to the understanding of the whole group of books from Joshua to Kings. They form a "history" from the conquest of Canaan to the fall of Judah. Because of many links of language and thought with the book of Deuteronomy, which precedes them, they are often termed the Deuteronomic (or Deuteronomistic) history, though it is evident that the differences between the books, in particular in their style of presenting the narratives, raise many questions about the nature of this whole compilation.

Nevertheless, whatever the processes involved, we are invited to read the books as a sequence, and at many points later parts of the story can only be fully understood by reference back to earlier, as well as back to the presentation of Israel and its laws offered by Deuteronomy.

A closer look at the material within the main sections as set out above shows many different kinds of writing now woven together. The proper understanding of the books involves the recognition of these different elements and a discussion of their possible origin and significance, but also an appreciation of the overall presentation, its patterns and its functions. The date of the books of Samuel can only be

S

determined within this broader framework: its final shaping must belong at the earliest in the sixth century BCE.

The Text of the Books of Samuel. The detailed problems of the Hebrew text and its relationship to alternative forms, attested by the early Greek translation and by the fragmentary manuscripts from Qumran, are a matter for a full commentary. There are passages where the evidence points to the existence of more than one recension, and, as may be seen from the brief notes in NRSV and from similar notes in other modern translations, there are many instances of small variations between the alternative texts. For example, the last verses of 1 Samuel 1 differ considerably in the Greek, and the psalm in 1 Samuel 2.1–10 is there followed by the addition of a passage found also in Jeremiah 9.23–24, expounding the ideas of knowledge of God and of divine justice. In addition, some parts of the Samuel text—the death of Saul and sections of the David story—are to be found in a different form and arrangement in 1 Chronicles, and the psalm in 2 Samuel 22 appears also as Psalm 18. Textual questions arise in all such duplicate texts.

Sources. As mentioned above, various types of material are found in the final form of the books of Samuel. The psalm in 2 Samuel 22 may be set alongside that in 1 Samuel 2.1–10; the latter does not appear in the book of Psalms, but it is clearly a psalm, used in the narrative to draw out the significance of the birth of Samuel in relation to the establishment of the monarchy. (The hymn in Luke 2.46–55 is closely related to this poem.) 2 Samuel 22 is immediately followed by another short poetic passage (2 Sam. 23.1–7), which depicts David as prophetic spokesman, though it also has considerable links with psalms relating Davidic kingship to the rule of God.

Two poems of a quite different kind, laments over the dead, appear in 2 Samuel 1.19–27 and 3.33–34. These seem likely to be early: the first is cited from the Book of Jashar, the second has a gnomic quality. Some material in the books is of archival character: the family and officials of Saul are noted in 1 Samuel 14.49–51; the family of David in 2 Samuel 3.2–5 and 5.13–16, distinguishing his kingship in Hebron from that in Jerusalem; and David's officials in two slightly variant forms in 2 Samuel 8.15–18 and 20.23–26. The genealogical material is paralleled in the much more elaborate lists in 1 Chronicles; the lists of officials (cf. also 1 Kings 4.1–6 and 7–20) function as markers at the end of narrative sections. Lists of David's warriors, found in 2 Samuel 21.15–22 and 23.8–39, appear also, and in part more fully, in 1 Chronicles 21.4–8 and 11.10–47.

The major part of the two books consists of narratives. These are grouped around the main characters or associated with particular themes. Thus, 1 Samuel 1–4 are associated with Eli, head of the priestly house at Shiloh and linked to a first defeat by the Philistines and the loss of the ark of God: in part they are more concerned with the appearance of Samuel and the interweaving of the downfall of Eli's priesthood with the anticipation of a new and lasting priesthood alongside a royal house (2.27–36, also 3.10–18). The ark theme of 1 Samuel 4 continues in 5–6, and reappears in 2 Samuel 6: this has led to the supposition of an "ark source," though it may be doubted whether such a source existed independently of other material. Various stories, clearly not all of one piece, have gathered around the figure of Samuel: he is depicted as a prophet (so, for example, in 1 Sam. 2; 9–12), a judge (so 1 Sam. 7.15–8.3), and a military leader (1 Sam. 7.3–14). As a prophet, he continues to appear in the narratives, or in some measure to overshadow them, not only through to his death

Shimei at the feet of David, who saved his life (2 Sam. 19.16–23)

(1 Sam. 25.1) but beyond it, in his appearance to pronounce doom on Saul in 1 Samuel 29. Saul, as also his son Jonathan, appears in heroic stories such as 1 Samuel 11 and 13–15. They appear as foils to David in 1 Samuel 16–31, in stories gathered more closely around the figure of David as the true king increasingly recognized as designated to replace Saul, who had been divinely chosen but then divinely rejected. With the death of Saul, told in two forms in 1 Samuel 31 and 2 Samuel 1, the way is clear for David to establish his kingship, over the south at Hebron, over the north with the death of Saul's feeble son Ishbaal (Ishbosheth), and with victories over the Philistines and the surrounding lands (2 Sam. 5 and 6). The stories of his reign in 2 Samuel 9–20; 21; 24 reveal further aspects of his achievements and his weaknesses, in effect brought to a conclusion when the succession of Solomon is defined in 1 Kings 1–2.

The two stories in 2 Samuel 21 and 24 are concerned with the consequences of religious disobedience (cf. also 1 Sam. 13 and 15): 2 Samuel 21.1–14 records a failure by Saul which had dire repercussions rectified by David; 2 Samuel 24 a failure by David resulting both in disaster and in the establishment of a new holy place.

The variety in style and level of the many stories suggests various origins. If we may judge from what is told of other heroic figures, both biblical and nonbiblical, it is likely that some are popular legends now attracted to a particular figure. Some may be early; others are evidently late, at least in their present form (so, for example, the Samuel war story in 1 Sam. 7). How much of actual history they contain is debated; precision of detail, such as is to be found in the intimate accounts of the life of David and his court, for example in 2 Samuel 12 and 13, are often thought to have eyewitness character. But this is deceptive; a good storyteller will provide the details that makes a story vivid, whether or not it is closely linked to actual events.

A Literary Work. Various theories have been propounded to account for the present shape of the books of Samuel

S

and to describe their literary evolution. Older views saw the possibility of parallel sources combined; the stories of the establishment of the monarchy in 1 Samuel 9–12, showing both favorable and unfavorable attitudes, seem to point clearly in that direction. But there is little evidence of continuous sources; alternative traditions have been brought together (so, for example, 1 Sam. 24 and 26: David's sparing of Saul's life; and 1 Sam. 31 and 2 Sam. 1: the death of Saul). Attempting harmonization in such cases is not satisfactory. An attempt has also been made to discover blocks of material, such as the Samuel birth narratives, the ark narratives, the story of David's rise to power, the Succession Story or Court History of David. It is difficult to determine where such blocks begin and end, and to understand the function of such blocks before they were incorporated into the final work. 2 Samuel 9–20 with 1 Kings 1–2, most often recently designated the "succession story" and the one most widely accepted as an ancient source, presents substantial problems; those who have studied it most closely do not agree on its function: Is it a pro-Solomon apology or a virulent anti-Solomon polemic? Is it virtually the work of an eyewitness (with candidates for authorship from the entourage of David) or a later reflective compilation? Did it originally stand in the work, or, bearing in mind that most of it is absent in 1–2 Chronicles, was it a late insertion? It may be proper to recognize that this, sometimes hailed as the earliest piece of real historical writing in the Bible and on occasion used as evidence for a supposed period of Davidic-Solomonic enlightenment, is perhaps more a construction of modern scholarship than an actual ancient independent work.

More recently, there has been a tendency to think rather in terms of a great wealth of stories, naturally attached to that period in which monarchy came to be instituted and looking to the almost legendary characters of David and Solomon, which have been worked over to produce a now vivid literary work, highly structured and skillfully woven together, to be read as one: the unevennesses and discrepancies that exist, which a modern reader notes, reveal both something of the diversity of origin and also much of a literary technique not concerned with historical evaluation but with meaning and impact.

Discerning larger patterns in the arrangement and handling of the material has led to illuminating insights: the stories of David, for example, have been thought to be so ordered as to depict him as first under divine blessing and protection and then under a divine curse (cf. also the changing picture of Saul in 1 Sam.); but not everything fits so easily into a single pattern. Structuralist approaches, though sometimes so elaborate as to be unconvincing, have nevertheless pointed to the literary skill of the work: the narrator anticipates, provides occasional resumes, offers comment on the meaning of events (so for example in 1 Sam. 12 and 2 Sam. 7), and, sometimes explicitly but more often implicitly, points to the significance of what is being told. The comments are often religiously based, and in some measure linked to the thought of Deuteronomy; more clearly, they show the attempt of a compiler concerned to understand the contemporary situation in which the community now exists by relating the story of the past. Some clues (so, for example, in 1 Sam. 4–6) may point to the sixth-century BCE period of Babylonian conquest and exile for leading members of the Judean state; the victory of the captive God of the ark in a foreign land (that of the Philistines in the story) suggests hope for a defeated people, deprived of political and religious leadership and institutions: their God might

be thought defeated and captive, but in reality he mocks his powerless opponents. Such an interpretation would also fit with the overall impression of the Deuteronomic history, which reflects on Israel's failures but has a climax at the end of 2 Kings in the release of the captive Davidic king, suggesting some hope of restored life.

At first sight there is a certain miscellaneous quality about the various elements in 2 Samuel 21–24, but they should not be seen merely as an "appendix": there is a similar collection in Judges 17–21. A closely knit structure is evident in 2 Samuel: two narratives (21.1–14 and 24) enclose two lists and brief anecdotes of heroes (21.15–22 and 23.8–39), which in their turn enclose two psalms (22 and 23.1–7). The first narrative finally resolves the problem of the royal family of Saul; the first hero list provides a link passage associated with the Philistine wars, which brought the downfall of Saul and the triumph of David (cf. 1 Sam. 17–18 and 31; 2 Sam. 1; 5). The first psalm is associated by its heading with the deliverance of David from "all his enemies . . . and from Saul" (22.1). The second psalm depicts the kingship of David and points to a final kingdom; its military theme is drawn out in the hero lists and stories of 23.8–39. The second narrative in chap. 24 draws together the theme of David's failures and that of his establishment of kingdom and Temple—for though the Temple is not here mentioned, the placing of this narrative as a lead-in to the succession of Solomon is clearly designed to imply what later (1 Chron. 22.1) was regarded as established fact.

History and Interpretation. In the light of the comments already made, it is clear that questions about the actual history of the period with which it deals are difficult to answer. Estimates vary greatly. There are those who would claim that much of the material lies very close to the events, and therefore believe that reasonably firm statements can be made about events and characters. Some would see particular sections or narratives as authentic in this sense, and others, such as 1 Samuel 7, as late inventions. Other commentators, while recognizing the presence of stories based on ancient traditions, would doubt the possibility of a historical reconstruction. The work presents considerable chronological difficulties. Eli belongs within the judge style of presentation, with his forty year period of rule; Samuel is similarly described, but without any figure given (cf. 1 Sam. 12.1–2; 25.1). The reign of Saul is problematic, since clearly the "two years" of 1 Samuel 13.1 is an error. David (like Solomon) again has forty years; the division of the reign into seven years in Hebron and thirty-three in Jerusalem does not suggest good chronological information. Problems arise when the attempt is made to order events alluded to or described: the stories of 2 Samuel 9–20, together with those of 21 and 24, do not make up a satisfactory sequence. Unlike the material of 1 Kings 15 to 2 Kings 25, there is no overall archival framework into which the individual sections are fitted. Numerous stories could derive from popular legend, now applied to particular figures. The story of Absalom's rebellion looks like history, but is in many respects more stylized than real.

The view taken by an individual reader or by a historian will often depend on the degree to which some measure of harmonization is undertaken. But it may be doubted whether such historical uncertainty is a serious disadvantage in reading the books. What appears to be more important, for writer and reader alike, is the overall picture. We may observe the development and interpretation of a number of interrelated themes. Within the whole story, from the conquest of Canaan to the fall of Judah, changes clearly took

S

place in the life of Israel: the shift from tribal life with local leaders to national life under the monarchy; the question of true king-ship arose; the one shrine was established, Jerusalem; a true priestly line emerged, to stand alongside the royal dynasty—a theme that was to become vital during the period of the exile and to result in various claims and counterclaims in the postexilic community.

All these issues are dominant in the books of Samuel. Ostensibly, the story is one of the past. But in reality, its final shaping has drawn together themes that serve not simply to describe what was believed about the past; claims are being made about the present, to depict for a community that has its own questions and uncertainties the meaning of that age which had brought into being the major institutions of the monarchical period and to invite a revaluation of these institutions in a later time of change.

PETER R. ACKROYD

SARAH. The wife of Abraham and mother of Isaac. Before Genesis 17.15 she is called Sarai; the two forms of the name are linguistic variants, both meaning "princess." The book of Genesis describes her as a beautiful woman (12.11, 14), a theme elaborated by later tradition, especially the *Genesis Apocryphon* from Qumran. According to the biblical narrator, Abraham was so conscious of her beauty that before they entered Egypt at the time of a severe famine in their own land, he begged her not to reveal to the Egyptians that she was his wife but rather his sister, lest he be killed. Indeed, as it turned out, the Egyptians thought her so beautiful that she was taken into Pharaoh's house to be his wife (Gen. 12.15), and for her sake Abraham prospered. In time, however, after great plagues had afflicted Pharaoh and his household (Gen. 12.17; cf. Exod. 7–12), the true identity of Sarah was revealed to Pharaoh, who ordered Abraham to be gone with his wife and all his possessions. A variant of this story is found in Genesis 20.1–14 (cf. also Gen. 26.6–11).

During their years of wandering, Sarah was childless, and so God's promise that she would be the ancestor of nations (Gen. 17.16) was unfulfilled. Accordingly she persuaded Abraham to take her Egyptian slave, Hagar, as his wife. He did so, and she bore him Ishmael. At the age of ninety, however, Sarah bore Isaac, thus fulfilling the divine promise. Sarah lived to be 127 years old, died in the land of Canaan, and was buried at Machpelah (Gen. 23.1–20).

In Isaiah 51.2 Sarah is referred to as the great mother of the nation; in the New Testament she is held up as an example of a wife's proper respect for her husband (1 Pet. 3.6). Paul uses the account of the birth of a son to Sarah by divine promise to develop an allegory of the new covenant in Christ and the heavenly Jerusalem (Gal. 4.22–31).

ISOBEL MACKAY METZGER

SATAN. The name of the archenemy of God and the personification of evil, particularly in Christian tradition. The name may derive from a Semitic root *śṭn*, but the primitive meaning is still debated, the most popular suggestions being "to be remote" and "to obstruct." Some alternative roots include *śwṭ* (cf. Hebr. "to rove") and *śyṭ* (cf. Arabic "to burn," especially of food).

In the Hebrew Bible *śāṭān* could refer to any human being who played the role of an accuser or enemy (1 Sam. 29.4; 2 Sam. 19.22; 1 Kings 5.4; 1 Kings 11.14). In Numbers 22.32 *śāṭān* refers to a divine messenger who was sent to obstruct Balaam's rash journey.

Job 1–2, Zechariah 3, and 1 Chronicles 21.1 have been central in past efforts to chart an evolution of the concept of *śāṭān* that culminates in a single archenemy of God. However, such evolutionary views have not gained general acceptance because *śāṭān* in these passages does not necessarily refer to a single archenemy of God and because the relative dating of the texts remains problematic. In Job 1–2, the *śāṭān* seems to be a legitimate member of God's council. In Zechariah 3.1–7 *śāṭān* may refer to a member of God's council who objected to the appointment of Joshua as chief priest. The mention of *śāṭān* without the definite article in 1 Chronicles 21.1 has led some scholars to interpret it as a proper name, but one could also interpret it as "an adversary" or "an accuser" acting on God's behalf.

Most scholars agree that in the writings of the third/second centuries BCE are the first examples of a character who is the archenemy of Yahweh and humankind. Nonetheless, the flexibility of the tradition is still apparent in the variety of figures who, although not necessarily identical with each other, are each apparently regarded as the principal archenemy of God and humankind in Second Temple literature. Such figures include Mastemah (Jubilees 10.8), Semyaz (1 Enoch 6.3), and Belial at Qumran (Zadokite Document 4.13). Still undetermined is the extent to which the concept of the Hebrew *śāṭān* was influenced by Persian dualism, which posited the existence of two primal and independent personifications of good and evil.

Although it shares with contemporaneous Jewish literature many of its ideas about demonology, the New Testament is probably more responsible for standardizing "Satan" (Greek *satanas*) as the name for the archenemy of God in

The archangel Michael defeating Satan

David playing the harp before Saul (1 Sam. 16.23)

Western culture. However, the devil (the usual translation of "Satan" in the Septuagint), Beel-zebul ("the prince of demons," Matt. 12.24), "the tempter" (Matt. 4.3), Beliar (2 Cor. 6.15), "the evil one" (1 John 5.18), and Apollyon (Rev. 9.11) are other names for Satan in the New Testament. Lucifer, a name for Satan popularized in the Middle Ages, derives ultimately from the merging of the New Testament tradition of the fall of Satan from heaven (Luke 10.18) with an originally separate biblical tradition concerning the Morning Star (cf. Isa. 14.12).

According to the New Testament, Satan and his demons may enter human beings in order to incite evil deeds (Luke 22.3) and to cause illness (Matt. 15.22; Luke 11.14). Satan can imitate "an angel of light" (2 Cor. 11.14), has command of the air (Eph. 2.2), and accuses the faithful day and night before God (Rev. 12.10). Jude 9 mentions the struggle between Satan and the archangel Michael for the body of Moses. Revelation 20.2, among other texts, equates "the Devil and Satan" with "the dragon," thus reflecting the merging of ancient myths concerning gigantic primordial beasts that wreak havoc on God's creation with the traditions concerning Satan. Satan's destiny is to be cast into a lake of fire (Rev. 20.10–15).

In 563 CE the Council of Braga helped to define the official Christian view of Satan that, in contrast to dualism, denied his independent origin and his creation of the material universe. As J. B. Russell (*Lucifer: The Devil in the Middle Ages*, 1984) notes, writers and theologians of the medieval period popularized many of the characteristics of Satan that remain standard today and that have roots in, among other sources, Greek, Roman, and Teutonic mythology. Although the Enlightenment produced explanations of evil that do not refer to a mythological being, the imagery and concept of Satan continues to thrive within many religious traditions.

HECTOR IGNACIO AVALOS

SAUL. The first king of Israel, who ruled ca. 1020–1000 BCE. His story is part of the larger account, in the books of Samuel, of how Israel became a nation-state. Saul is one of the few biblical characters of whom the term "tragic" has often been used. Glimpsing this dimension, D. H. Lawrence in his play *David* has Saul say of himself, "I am a man given over to trouble and tossed between two winds."

His story begins in 1 Samuel 8 with the elders of Israel asking Samuel, priestly prophet and judge, to appoint a king to judge (govern) them "like all the nations." For the people, the theocratic rule that Samuel delegates to his corrupt sons portends disaster. Only a generation earlier such corruption in the house of Eli had incurred Yahweh's anger and brought Israel defeat. For the deity, however, the request spells yet again the people's failure to see Yahweh's sovereignty and providential care. To an equally affronted Samuel, Yahweh observes that it is "not you they have rejected, but me they have rejected from being king over them" (1 Sam. 8.7). Yet, surprisingly, Yahweh decrees that the prophet obey the people and appoint for them a king. And so it transpires, much against Samuel's better judgment, which he expresses in mighty counterblasts against both king and people (1 Sam. 8; 12). Thus, the kingship is grounded in conflict between deity, prophet, and people.

Saul (whose name means "asked for"), the handsome son of a wealthy Benjaminite, is Yahweh's "designate" (Hebr. *nāgîd*; NRSV: "ruler"). He goes looking for his father's livestock and finds kingship instead (1 Sam. 9–10).

Saul is made king before Yahweh at the cult center in Gilgal, and in Gilgal his kingship begins to unravel (1 Sam. 13). Pressed to act decisively when a great host of Philistines threatens his fearful and deserting army, he refuses to wait for Samuel beyond a time previously appointed by the prophet (10.8), and he offers a sacrifice. Samuel, as though waiting in the wings, immediately appears and, ignoring the king's explanation, condemns him outright. Saul, asserts the prophet, has not kept Yahweh's commandment, and his kingdom will not continue. Yahweh has sought out another "designate," a man aligned with the divinity's own intention ("heart").

Commentators have long debated the reason for the condemnation. Other texts in Samuel and Kings make it unlikely that it is simply a matter of cultic law, involving the king's intrusion upon a priestly or prophetic office (cf. 1 Sam. 14.33–35; 1 Kings 3.3). Rather, the immediate cause appears to be Saul's breaking of Samuel's ambiguous instruction to wait—as interpreted by Samuel. But lying behind Samuel's readiness to condemn lurks perhaps a more pertinent reason rooted in the origins of Saul's kingship. Saul, asked for by the people, represents rejection for both prophet and deity. For the sake of theocracy this king must, in turn, be rejected.

In Gilgal comes final rejection (1 Sam. 15). Returning from a campaign against the Amalekites with the captured king, Agag, and the best of the livestock, Saul once again meets a vehement Samuel. Why, demands the prophet, has Saul not done as instructed and "devoted [by destruction]" to Yahweh all living things? Saul responds that he has done what he was commanded to do, and that the animals have been brought to Gilgal for sacrifice. The issue turns on the difference between "devotion" and "sacrifice." Samuel, however, ignores Saul's explanation and invokes Yahweh's judgment upon him. Before such unrelenting opposition Saul acquiesces and asks pardon. But spurning him, Samuel declares that he is rejected as king—Yahweh has chosen "a neighbor" who is "better" than he. The reader soon learns that this man is David, son of Jesse (1 Sam. 16).

The remainder of the king's story is played out against this backdrop. Saul knows that the deity has rejected him, but he does not know his successor's identity. Yahweh, soon to be so eloquent for David (see 1 Sam. 23.6–14; 30.7–8), remains silent before Saul. That silence produces the irony of the young David being introduced into Saul's court in order to make him well. It also feeds the king's growing suspicion and jealousy of the successful and admired young captain (1 Sam. 17–18). Yet, as if that corrosive silence were not enough, the deity provokes Saul directly: an "evil spirit from God" goads him to violence (1 Sam. 18.10–11) and disrupts his son Jonathan's attempt at reconciliation (1 Sam. 19.1–11).

David's fortune is Saul's fate: whatever Saul attempts to turn against David rebounds against Saul. Using as bait his own daughter, Michal, Saul seeks to entice David into a suicide mission; instead, he gains two hundred Philistine foreskins and loses his daughter, who will herself later betray her father to save the husband she loves (1 Sam. 18–19); her subsequent story is poignant (1 Sam. 25.44, 2 Sam. 3; 6). Likewise, Saul's savage revenge upon the priests of Nob for having helped the fleeing David only displaces into the fugitive's hand the oracular ephod (1 Sam. 21–22).

Both Jonathan with goodwill and Saul with resentment come to see David's succession as inevitable (1 Sam. 20.12–17, 30–33; 23.16–18; 24.16–22; 26.25). Saul, moreover, spared twice by his elusive rival (1 Sam. 24, 26), confesses publicly the superior justice of David's actions. King and competitor each forswear all hostile intent toward the other, but they keep their distance and go their own way (26.25). As David works for the Philistines and accumulates power (1 Sam. 27–29), Saul faces them in battle (chap. 28). He seeks again a word from the silent Yahweh and, in desperation, has a medium conjure up the spirit of Samuel. The word he receives is a reiteration of rejection, but with one addition: on the next day he and his sons will die. So it happens that as David carries off booty from the Amalekites (1 Sam. 30), Saul and his sons fall to the Philistines on Mount Gilboa among the slain men of Israel (1 Sam. 31).

The king asked for by the people has failed: the way is now open for the king offered by Yahweh. Yet the people's king never forfeits their loyalty. The book ends with a moving epilogue. The inhabitants of Jabesh-gilead, delivered by Saul as his reign began, now risk their lives to close his reign with dignity. Retrieving his body from the walls of Philistine Beth-shan, they claim him as their own and honor him with burial in Jabesh. David, too, pays his own homage in a poem of beauty and irony (2 Sam. 1.17–27), a poem perhaps more beautiful than honest.

DAVID M. GUNN

SHECHEM. A major Canaanite and Israelite city in the hill country of Ephraim (Map 1:X4), Shechem first appears in the historical record as an enemy of Egypt in an execration text and on a stele of the nineteenth century BCE. During the Amarna period (fourteenth century), Shechem, under its ruler, Labayu, and his sons, asserted itself against the other Canaanite city-states and, hence, against the weakening Egyptian hegemony in Canaan.

Shechem appears prominently in the ancestral narratives. Abraham had a theophany near Shechem and built an altar there (Gen. 12.6–7), as did Jacob (Gen. 33.18–20). In Genesis 34, Simeon and Levi kill the inhabitants of Shechem and plunder it in retaliation for the rape of their sister Dinah by Shechem, son of Hamor (cf. Gen. 49.5–7). Joseph's body was brought back from Egypt and buried at Shechem (Josh. 24.32; see also the somewhat erroneous Acts 7.16), and Joshua's great covenant renewal ceremony took place there (Josh. 24). The first abortive Israelite attempt at kingship under Abimelech was centered at Shechem, but Abimelech exacted a terrible revenge in the city after a mutual falling

out (Judg. 9). It was to Shechem that Jeroboam I went to be crowned first king of Israel (1 Kings 12.1), and it served as his first capital (1 Kings 12.25).

Shechem has been located at the site of Tell Balatah, guarding the pass between Mount Ebal to the north and Mount Gerezim to the south, near modern Nablus. After earlier village occupation of the site in the Chalcolithic period, a large and well-fortified urban center developed at Shechem in the Middle Bronze Age (ca. 1850–1550 BCE). Of particular interest are the temples found at the site, including one designated the "fortress temple" because of its massive walls. After a violent destruction at the end of the Middle Bronze Age, presumably by one of the early pharaohs of Dynasty XVIII, Shechem lay uninhabited for close to a century. Completely rebuilt, probably with Egyptian consent, the city prospered during the first part of the Late Bronze Age, only to suffer destruction at the hands of Labayu's enemies, whether Egyptian or Canaanite or both. The subsequent Late Bronze Age city was not as prosperous, yet it managed to survive into the early Iron Age, when it probably passed peacefully into Israelite hands. The destruction of Shechem in the late twelfth century is generally attributed to Abimelech. Shechem recovered to some extent during the following centuries, becoming a town of some importance, until it was once again destroyed, this time by the Assyrians in their campaign of conquest of the northern kingdom Israel (724–722 BCE). The habitation of Shechem remained poor and sparse throughout the remainder of the Iron Age and the first part of the Persian period. During the Hellenistic period (as of ca. 330 BCE) Shechem regained some of its ancient importance and glory as the Samaritan rival of Jerusalem. The city was finally destroyed in 107 BCE by the Hasmonean John Hyrcanus.

CARL S. EHRLICH

SIMON PETER. The son of Jonah (Matt. 16.17) or John (John 1.42); originally he was known as Simon (or Simeon, Acts 15.12). According to the Gospels, Jesus gave him the name Peter, the Greek translation of an Aramaic word "Cepha(s)" meaning "stone, rock" (Mark 3.16; Matt. 16.18; John 1.42). He and his brother Andrew were fishermen (Mark 1.16) of the poorer class, since apparently they did not own a boat. He was among the first disciples whom Jesus called (Mark 1.17; John 1.40–42). Married (Mark 1.29–31), his wife later traveled with him on some of his missionary journeys (1 Cor. 9.5).

An apostle and one of the twelve (Mark 3.14–19), he was prominent among them, belonging to a small inner group (Mark 5.37; 9.2; 13.3; 14.33). He often acted as their spokesperson (Mark 8.29; 11.21; 14.29), especially in acknowledging Jesus as the Messiah, though he did not understand Jesus would have to suffer (Mark 8.27–33). On several other occasions, he is presented in a poor light (Matt. 14.28–31; Mark 9.5–6; 14.29–31), particularly in the gospel of Mark and especially in his denial of Jesus (Mark 14.66–72). We should, however, remember that the purpose of the Gospels is to inform us about Jesus, not to give a biography of Peter. Peter's failures serve to highlight Jesus' courage and compassion.

After the resurrection, Peter was the first male disciple to see the risen Jesus (Luke 24.34; 1 Cor. 15.5), and he quickly took a leading position in the young church (Acts 1–12, 15; Gal. 1.18–19; 2.1–10). According to Luke, he preached (Acts 2.14–36; 3.12–26; etc.), healed the sick (Acts 3.1–10; 9.32–42), went as envoy from Jerusalem to oversee the work

St. Catherine's Monastery, below the traditional Mount Sinai, Egypt

of other missionaries (Acts 8.14–25), and suffered for his faith (Acts 4.13–22; 5.17–41; 12.1–11). Guided by a vision, he was the first to preach to and convert gentiles (Acts 10.1–11.18), and he supported Paul on this matter in the council of Acts 15. Paul's own account of Peter's position in the controversy differs somewhat; in Galatians we are told that on a visit to Antioch, Peter refused to have full fellowship with gentile Christians (Gal. 2.11–14). At either the council of Acts 15 or another (Gal. 2.1–10), Paul was allotted the gentiles as his missionary concern and Peter the Jews. After this Peter disappears from the New Testament story. James, the brother of Jesus, apparently became the sole leader of the Jerusalem church, and Peter went traveling (1 Cor. 9.5). He may have visited Corinth and/or the areas mentioned in 1 Peter 1.1 and came to Rome shortly before his death. Extrabiblical tradition says that he was martyred when Nero persecuted the Christians there (64 CE). Yet later tradition claims that St. Peter's in Rome was built over his burial place.

The meaning of Jesus' words to Peter in Matthew 16.17–19 have been disputed. Is the rock Peter himself, his confession, or Peter as confessor? Is the power of the keys that of ecclesiastical discipline or of admitting to the church through preaching? Is binding and loosing the determination of what is correct and orthodox or the power to excommunicate? Is this power restricted to Peter alone or given to the whole church (Matt. 18.18)? Were the words of 16.17–19 spoken by the incarnate Jesus, the risen Jesus (cf. John 21.15–19), or did they come into being later to represent the position Peter actually attained?

Two of the writings of the New Testament are attributed to him. Early tradition associates him with the gospel of Mark. Some later apocryphal writings were written in his name, a gospel of Peter and at least two apocalypses. There was also an Acts of Peter. Their appearance indicates his importance for the second-century church. In the first century, there was a group that strongly supported him (1 Cor. 1.12; 3.22; 9.5).

ERNEST BEST

SINAI (Map 2:S–T2–4). A triangular peninsula, bordered on the north by the Mediterranean Sea, on the west by the Gulf of Suez and the Suez Canal, and on the east by the Gulf of Aqaba/Eilat. Moving from the coastland south, the terrain gradually rises to the Ijma Plateau, near the center of the peninsula. The region south of the plateau becomes mountainous before the terrain descends to a narrow coastland between the mountains and the gulfs. From the fourth millennium BCE the mountains have been mined for copper, which was exported to both Egypt and Canaan.

It is generally assumed that somewhere on this peninsula is Mount Sinai, the mountain from which Moses reputedly delivered the Ten Commandments to the Israelites, but evidence is scant for determining which of the many mountains was called Mount Sinai during the time of the wilderness wanderings. Since Sinai is the wilderness nearest Egypt, this seems the most likely place for Mount Sinai (Num. 33.8–10; Deut. 1.1; Josephus, *Apion* 2.2.25), But there are problems. The mountain from which Moses received the commandments is sometimes called Sinai (generally in J and P) and sometimes Horeb (E and D). It is also labeled "the mountain of God" (Exod. 3.1; 4.27; etc.) and simply "the mountain." It is not certain whether these were different names for the same place or different mountains. Some have thought it was initially Horeb but was renamed Sinai after the peninsula, but no one knows when the peninsula was named "Sinai;" neither Josephus nor Paul (Gal. 4.25) calls it by that name.

One of the ways scholars have tried to identify Mount Sinai has been to conjecture the route the Israelites traveled on their way to Canaan. Since the most direct route from Egypt follows the Mediterranean coastline, some have assumed that the Israelites took this route, and that one of the nearby mountains in the northern lowland or southern Canaan was Mount Sinai, but archaeological remains show that the Egyptians had this well-traveled route fortified (and see Exod. 13.17); consequently, refugees probably avoided such confrontation. It is more likely that they turned south (see Num. 33.8–10). Since they reportedly lived in this wilderness for about forty years, they may not have planned originally to settle in Canaan.

The most popular candidate for Mount Sinai is Jebel Musa ("the mountain of Moses"; Map 2:84) near Saint Catherine's Monastery. This identification was apparently first made by Byzantine monks in the fourth century CE, and there is no evidence to show that they had any local data that are not known today for choosing the site. Most of the modern sites are named after plants, trees, and topographical features, and they provide no clues to ancient Israelite history. Other possible sites include several mountains in northwestern Arabia, and Mount Karkom in Machtesh Ramon just west of the Arabah; the latter conjecture, made in 1985, was based on art and architecture found on and around Karkom, but it depends on a date for the Exodus in the third millennium BCE.

When Byzantine monks settled in Sinai (300–600 CE) they were able to dig wells, make terraces and direct rainfall, and raise gardens and orchards in valleys. The Emperor Justinian had a church constructed and a monastery fortified (527 CE); this was later called Saint Catherine's Convent. Within an area of two square miles is the Byzantine identification of the site of the burning bush, the place where Moses struck the rock, the mountain where God spoke to Moses, and the hill where Aaron made the golden calf. The monks apparently found an isolated location in this historic peninsula where they could survive. They then identified biblical sites with places in their immediate surroundings.

GEORGE WESLEY BUCHANAN

SODOM AND GOMORRAH. Two cities, legendary for their incorrigible wickedness (Gen. 13.13) and for their ultimate annihilation by God in a cataclysm of "brimstone and fire" (Gen. 19.24–25). In the story of Abraham's war against the kings of the east (Gen. 14), Sodom and Gomorrah are numbered among the "five cities" in the "Valley of Siddim," along with Admah, Zeboiim, and Zoar. Abraham's nephew Lot sojourned for a time in Sodom but fled at divine instigation before the city's final devastation (Gen. 19.15–22). Passages mentioning Sodom and Gomorrah generally agree in locating them along the southern shore of the Dead Sea, but so far no archaeological evidence for their existence has been found there. Suppositions that their remains may yet be discovered beneath the shallow waters of the southern Dead Sea are unlikely ever to be proved. Early Bronze Age (third millennium BCE) settlements and cemeteries at Bab edh-Dhra and Numeira on the southeastern edge of the Dead Sea do, however, provide evidence for very early pre-Israelite occupation in the region. The presence of these ruins, abandoned long before the advent of the Israelites in Canaan, may have given rise much later to local legends that their destruction resulted from divine wrath. At a subsequent stage these legends may have become attached to stories of the wanderings of Abraham and Lot in Canaan.

Whatever the origin of these legends, Sodom and Gomorrah become powerful symbols of human wickedness and divine retribution. Sodom and Gomorrah together (or more frequently, Sodom alone) are held up as archetypes of sinfulness, justly deserving and finally receiving God's punishment. This theme is prominent in prophetic writings (Isa. 1.9; Jer. 23.14; Ezek. 16.44–58; Amos 4.11) and in the New Testament (Matt. 10.15; Luke 10.12; Rom. 9.29; 2 Pet. 2.6; Rev. 11.8).

JOSEPH A. GREENE

SOLOMON. The son of David and Bathsheba, Solomon ruled over Israel ca. 962–922 BCE. His exploits are detailed in 1 Kings 1–11 and 1 Chronicles 28–2 Chronicles 9. Supported by Bathsheba, Nathan, and Benaiah, he came to power in a coup d'état that sidetracked his older brothers Adonijah and Joab. His reign was marked by prosperity and prestige, grandiose building projects, and a cultural transformation.

The prosperity is portrayed in the fulsome description given in 1 Kings 4.20–28 and 10.14–29, in the marriage with Pharaoh's daughter (and there was a considerable harem; 1 Kings 11.3), in the international role indicated by his dealings with Hiram of Tyre (1 Kings 9.26–28; 10.11–12) and the visit of the Queen of Sheba (1 Kings 10.1–10), as well as the extensive international trade (a fleet at Eziongeber, 1 Kings 9.26; "Tarshish" ships, 10.22; trading in horses and chariots, 10.26–29).

Lot and his Daughters leaving Sodom (Gen. 19.29–30)

Solomon's building program consisted principally in the Temple as well as the palace complex (the palace, the "House of the Forest of Lebanon"—a kind of armory—and even a palace for his Egyptian wife). In addition, he built up a corps of chariots and cavalry that functioned out of chariot cities in the realm (1 Kings 10.26). Such opulence was sustained by a revision of the administrative areas in the kingdom (1 Kings 4.7–19), which led to increased revenue for the crown, as well as to a weakening of the old tribal ties and to further assimilation of the Canaanite population. All this was obtained at a price, as is suggested by Solomon's having to cede land to Hiram of Tyre (1 Kings 9.10–14; but contrast 2 Chron. 8.2) and by the *corvée*. Despite 1 Kings 9.20–22, it appears that Israelites as well as Canaanites were involved in forced labor, and this became a major complaint against Solomon (5.13–14; cf. 4.6; 12.18).

The cultural transformation of the population must have been considerable, though it is largely a matter of historical inference. But political centralization won out over the old tribalization; a new wealthy class emerged, and cleavage between rich and poor increased. This aspect of Solomon's reign is not reflected in the tradition. Rather, his reign is acclaimed, and his personal wisdom is underlined. His wisdom is compared to that of the Egyptians (4.29–34), and is illustrated by the famous incident of the two prostitutes (3.16–28). Hence he has come down in the tradition as the wise man par excellence, to whom several works were eventually attributed: Psalms 72 and 127, the book of Proverbs, the Song of Solomon, and Ecclesiastes within the Hebrew Bible; Wisdom of Solomon among the apocrypha; Psalms and Odes among the pseudepigrapha. Scholars have inferred that such compositions as the Yahwist history (J) probably date to the Solomonic period.

The theological judgment passed upon Solomon is mixed. The name Jedidiah (beloved of Yah or the Lord) was given him by the prophet Nathan ("the Lord loved him," 2 Sam. 12.24–25). The description of his sincerity and simplicity is highlighted in the sacrifice at Gibeon (1 Kings 3). He asks for a "listening heart" (1 Kings 3.9; NRSV: "understanding mind") whereby to rule the people, and the Lord assures him of this as well as of riches and glory. On the other hand, the typical Deuteronomic judgment on royalty is also passed upon Solomon (1 Kings 11), and notice is taken of the "adversaries" whom the Lord raised up: Hadad the Edomite, Rezon of Damascus, and especially Jeroboam, who was to lead the rebellion against Rehoboam, Solomon's son.

Nothing is known of "the Book of the Acts of Solomon" (1 Kings 11.41), which might have cast a fuller light on the reign of the fabled monarch. But the immediate dissolution of the united monarchy in the lifetime of his son is surely suggestive of the inadequacies of Solomon's reign (1 Kings 12.14).

ROLAND E. MURPHY, O. CARM.

SONG OF SOLOMON. The Song of Solomon follows the book of Ruth in the Hebrew Bible and Ecclesiastes in the Septuagint. Also called the Song of Songs (i.e., the most excellent song) and the Canticle (of Canticles), it was divided in the Middle Ages arbitrarily into eight chapters, which do not correspond to significant units of content. This brief composition of fewer than two hundred poetic verses has always been an enigma, and little agreement exists concerning such questions as origin, date of composition, structure, and unity.

Authorship and Date. The attribution "to Solomon" affixed to the Song is an editorial superscription that links this poetry to Israel's famous poet and sage rather than a declaration of authorship. No hint of actual author or authors appears in the text. The intense style of poetry belongs to the genre of love lyrics found in ancient Egyptian collections. Lush, extravagant imagery appealing to the senses of smell, taste, and touch, detailed descriptions of the human body, male and female, and highly stylized terms of endearment like dove, sister, and king link the Song to other ancient Near Eastern cultures.

The Song of Solomon displays striking metaphors from a variety of flora and fauna, some twenty-five species of plants and ten of animals, mentioned not as a display of learning but for the images they invoke. It also exploits the evocative power of place names like Lebanon, home of fragrant cedars (3.9), Gilead, famous for its balm (4.1), snow-covered Amana (4.8), and Tirzah, ancient capital of the northern kingdom of Israel (6.4).

Nothing in the Song itself proves its date of composition. It seems to be made up of lyrics that came down in oral tradition long before they were gathered into their canonical form. The appealing subject matter and vivid imagery, like the woman being compared to a mare that throws the war stallions of the pharaoh's chariots into disorder (1.9), explain why these lyrics were preserved in the schools of the Temple of Jerusalem. They proved to be a useful teaching tool. Boldness of imagery, repetitions, and variations on erotic themes point to frequent recital before they were edited in the final form, possibly between 450–400 BCE. This date is plausible because of widespread scribal activity at that time, because the syntax exhibits Aramaic constructions, and because the Persian loan word for paradise is found in 4.13.

After the destruction of the Second Temple in 70 CE, the Song of Solomon was incorporated into the Jewish canon over the objections of some rabbis, who found its subject matter unsuitable for Israel's sacred literature. Once it became part of the official scriptures, commentators both Jewish and Christian attempted to interpret it in religious terms. Eventually it was recited as part of the services for the final day of the Passover celebration.

Structure and Nature. Commentators are divided concerning the structure of the Song of Solomon. Three approaches persist: that it is a literary unity; that it is a systematic organization of love poems; and that it is a random collection of lyrics. Some find as many as eighty distinct units. The literal sense of the verses describes movements of passion and affection between a man and a woman, who is called "my darling" (Hebr. *ra'y tî;* NRSV: "my love") nine times, a term never found elsewhere in the Bible. Poetic features like chiasm, inclusion, historical allusions, refrains, and thematic repetition provide a basis for the variety of theories about the Song's structure. Both Jewish and Christian exegetes have found deeper meaning in its verses. Medieval qabbalists proposed a sacred code as key to its interpretation.

The theories about the nature of the Song can be divided into five headings.

Allegorical. The Aramaic translations called Targums preserve traditions that read the Song as an allegory of the Lord's love for Israel. On this basis allusions to events in Israel's history are found throughout. Christian mystical tradition as early as Origen took a similar approach. His commentary, part of which is extant in Latin translation,

S

interprets the Song as celebrating Christ's love for his church or for the believing soul. The most famous medieval example of the allegorical method of reading the Song is the eighty-six homilies of Bernard of Clairvaux, covering only the first two chapters.

Dramatic. A few ancient Greek manuscripts assign sections of the lyrics to specific speakers. Following that tradition, some exegetes read the Song as describing a shepherd's courtship of the Shulammite maid (6.13). They often introduce Solomon as rival suitor. They disagree about how to assign the dramatis personae and where to place the climaxes. They usually find from five to eight scenes. The dramatic theory was especially popular in the nineteenth century.

Literal-historical. By far the most common interpretation of the Song of Solomon is that it is a collection of lyrics celebrating human love. This approach, based on affinities with ancient Near Eastern love poetry, seeks to do justice to the plastic language and sensuous imagery that reveal vivid imagination and artistic skill. As lyric poetry the Song employs language that functions simultaneously on a literal and a symbolic level. The garden and vineyard are places of nurture, whether for plants or for sexual capacity. The pasture is a place for feeding the shepherd's flock and for nourishing human intimacy. Eating applies to both physical and sexual satisfaction. Such flexibility of language is the stuff of masterpieces that attract readers of every generation.

Some scholars suggest that the Song was a collection of songs assembled as a repertoire for wedding celebrations. The vivid portrayal of the body of the woman (4.1–7; 6.4–7; 71.0) and of the man (5.10–16) resemble Arabic *wasfs* sung at weddings. This genre includes vivid metaphors: hair falling like descending flocks of mountain goats; teeth sparkling like newly shorn goats; cheeks glistening like the inside of a pomegranate covered by a thin veil. Stylized royal imagery explains the designation of the lover as king.

Other scholars search for the origin of these lyrics in dream fantasy, because the woman speaks of having a dream in 5.2, and possibly in 3.1–4. Such an origin could account for the stream-of-consciousness succession of events from city streets to wine cellars to country landscapes to remote deserts and mountain tops inhabited by hostile animals.

Other students of the Song of Solomon feel that the nature of these lyrics does not point to a specific point of origin. Rather, they share the universal language of love poetry with such commonplace themes as the excitement of seeking and finding or the terror of seeking and not finding the loved one. Their appeals to such a wide range of smells and shapes and colors are ways of portraying the universal presence of love. The scribe who finally brought these lyrics together proclaims love to be "strong as death" (8.6), so powerful that even floods cannot drown it. That comment encouraged efforts to find deeper meaning in the Song.

Cultic or ritualistic. The mention of death as well as unusual situations pictured have led some commentators to see the Song as originating in an ancient ritual, possibly a sacred marriage or fertility rite or in ceremonies to ward off death. They find cultic origins for the elaborate procession of 3.6–11 and the phrase "house of my mother" (3.4; 8.2).

Parabolic or typological. Some commentators have made ingenious efforts to tie these lyrics, which never mention God, closer to his saving plan. They read the Song of Solomon in terms of certain topics of Israelite theology, like the covenant relationship between Yahweh and Israel, which was compared to marriage in the prophetic tradition. This interpretation finds a variety of second-level meanings in the imagery: for example, the man signifies the Lord and the woman Israel; their coming together portrays the restoration of intimacy lost in the garden of Eden; the woman's spontaneity recalls original innocence.

Significance. The Song of Solomon embodies a surplus of meaning in its artistic unfolding of lyrics that portray a poetic genius and emotional warmth of universal impact and appeal. Its unusual vocabulary (almost fifty words appear nowhere else in the Bible) adds excitement to the swift pace and evocative scenes. A minority of critics read it as containing some kind of narrative or thematic unity reflected in repetitions like "caresses sweeter than wine" (1.2 and 4.10) and the refrain in 2.7; 3.5; 5.8; 8.4. But most modern editors present it as a collection of related lyrics loosely united, composed not to teach but to touch, to please, and to delight. The power of its beauty is its celebration of and appeal to love.

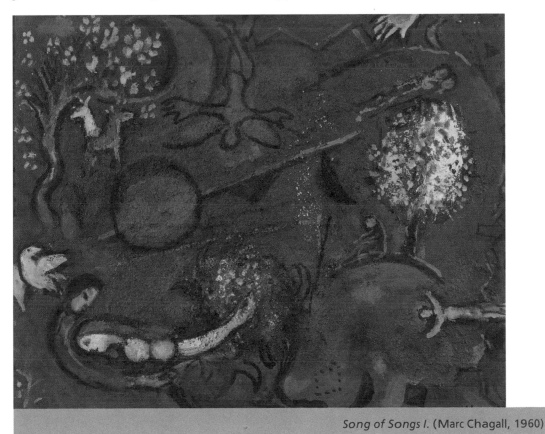

Song of Songs I. (Marc Chagall, 1960)

S

Son of God (Viktor Vasnetsov, 1885–1886)

No apparent order governs the flow of its verse, except perhaps the final verses that point to the reflective bent of the sage inviting readers to resonate to the power of love. The New Testament contains no reference to the Song.

JAMES M. REESE, O.S.F.S.

SON OF GOD. The Hebrew *ben* and Aramaic *bar,* "son," designate not only a male descendant but also a relationship to a community, a country, a species (e.g., animals), etc. "Son of God" can thus mean both a mythological figure of divine origin, a being belonging to the divine sphere (such as an angel), or a human being having a special relationship to a god. In antiquity, son of god was used predicatively of kings begotten by a god (in Egypt) or endowed with divine power (in Mesopotamia). In the Roman period, it also was used in the East as a title for the emperor.

In the Hebrew Bible, sons of God occur in Genesis 6.1–4, where they marry human women and became fathers of the giants (KJV) or Nephilim (NRSV); in Job 1.6; 2.1 (NRSV: "heavenly beings"), where they make up the court of God; and also in Deuteronomy 32.8 (NRSV: "gods"); Psalms 29.1 and 89.6 (NRSV: "heavenly beings"); cf. Psalm 82.6 "sons of the Most High" (NRSV: "children of the Most High"). Elsewhere, the designation son of God is used especially of the king. Thus, in the primary passage of the Israelite ideology of divine kingship, it is said of Solomon, "I will be his father, and he will be my son" (2 Sam. 7.14; cf. 1 Chron. 17.13). Neither in 2 Samuel 7.12–14 nor in Psalm 89.26–29 does the designation son of God express anything more than a special relationship; there is no question of deification. This also applies to Psalm 2.7, where God says to the king, "You are my son; today I have begotten you"; "today" rules out a mythological interpretation. The title son of God indicates that the king has his kingdom from God, and the saying belongs to the coronation day or its anniversary.

This manner of speaking of God as a father and the correlative usage, son or sons of God, has also been extended to cover the people of God. In Exodus 4.22 and Jeremiah 31.9, God calls Israel his firstborn son; in Exodus 4.23 and Hosea 11.1 his "son." Correspondingly, in Deuteronomy 32.6, 18 and Jeremiah 3.4, God is called the people's "father," and in Deuteronomy 14.1; 32.5, 19 the Israelites appear as "sons" (and "daughters") of God. Finally, the plural form may designate a special group, like the pious (Ps. 73.15) or the priests (Mal. 1.6).

In postbiblical literature, "son of God" designates either the pious (Sir. 4.10) or the suffering righteous (Wisd. of Sol. 2.18; cf. 2.13, 16; 5.5; cf. also Psalms of Solomon 13.9), while the plural denotes the elect people (Wisd. of Sol. 9.7; 12.19, 21; Psalms of Solomon 17.27). Obviously, son of God was not a common messianic title in Judaism before Roman times. Passages like 2 Esd. 7.28–29; 13.32, 37, 52; 14.9, which speak of "my son [the Messiah]," and 1 Enoch 105.2, do not alter this, since both are influenced by the "servant of the Lord" in Second Isaiah. Messianic usage of the expression outside the New Testament from this period does occur in the Dead Sea Scrolls, as in a fragment of a Daniel Apocryphon from Qumran (4Qps-Dan A[a]) and in 4Q246, another fragment, which has a close parallel in Luke 1.32, 35. But the fact that the title was used for the king makes it understandable that it could also be applied to the Messiah.

In the New Testament, Son of God (and its abbreviated form, "the Son") is a title often used in christological confessions. From the beginning it seems to have been used in connection with the belief in the resurrection and exaltation of Jesus. The confessional fragment in Romans 1.3–4 speaks of the gospel "concerning his Son, who was descended from David according to the flesh and was declared to be Son of God with power according to the spirit of holiness by resurrection from the dead." The originally exchangeable expressions Son of David and Son of God are here conferred on the earthly Jesus and the risen Lord, it being presupposed that before his death Jesus was Messiah-designate, and that the resurrection implied a new position (cf. Acts 2.36). The authors of Acts 13.33 and Hebrews 1.5; 5.5 also quote Psalm 2.7 in this connection. Yet it is still possible to speak of a special "Son of God" Christology insofar as the designation expresses Jesus' unique relationship to God. From an early stage, this belief included the idea of a preexistence and the sending of Jesus to the world (cf. Gal. 4.4 and also Phil. 2.6–11; John 1.1). The tide seems to have attracted to it ideas connected with wisdom as well.

In the synoptic Gospels, we may observe how the title Son of God has penetrated into the traditions about the life of Jesus. In Mark, it is used only by God and the demons (cf. 1.11; 9.7; 3.11; 5.7); the one time it is used by a human (15.39), the past-tense ("was") suggests a distinction between the confession of the centurion to the deceased Jesus, and later on, to the risen Lord. In Matthew, we also find it in the confessions of the disciples (14.33; 16.16; cf. also 26.63), in the story of the temptation (4.3, 6), and the story of the mocking at the cross (27.43; cf also Matt. 11.27). In Luke, it is mostly found in traditional material; the idea of a virgin birth probably does not belong here. In John, the Son of God, together with the title the Son, plays a central role in depicting Jesus as being one with the Father (e.g., 3.35–36 and 1.18; 10.30).

The origin of the title seems, in the first place, to be Jesus' unique addressing God as father (see especially Mark 14.36, where the Aramaic *abba* is preserved), and second, its connection with kingship ideology in view of the conviction that

S

Jesus was the anticipated son of David. Yet characteristically in the New Testament it stands beside the usage of the phrase sons of God, referring to those whom Jesus has brought to salvation (Rom. 8.14–21; 9.8, 26; Gal. 3.26; Matt. 5.9, 45; John 1.12; 1 John 3.1). In the apostolic fathers, the designation describes the divine nature of Jesus as apart from his human nature (e.g., Ignatius, *Ephesians* 20.2; *Epistle of Barnabas* 12.10, where it corresponds to son of man).

To summarize the evidence in the New Testament, it might be said that the title Son of God primarily expresses Jesus' unique relation to God, while the Lord, the christological title preferred by Paul (see 1 Cor. 12.3; Phil. 2.11), emphasizes his position in the church and in the world.

MOGENS MÜLLER

SON OF MAN. The self-designation most often used by Jesus in the Gospels. It occurs seventy-two times in the synoptics; two passages (Matt. 18.11; Luke 9.56) are, however, textually uncertain, and if parallels are not counted, the number of different Son of man sayings is forty-three. To these may be added thirteen in the Fourth Gospel. John 12.34, like Luke 24.7, is only an apparent exception to the rule that the expression is always uttered by Jesus himself, the only genuine exception being Acts 7.56. Apart from John 5.27, the designation in all these passages is literally "the son of the man." In the New Testament the undetermined form, "a son of man," is found in Hebrews 2.6 (quoting Ps. 8.5) and in Revelation 1.13 (the exalted Christ) and 14.14 (an angel).

The Son of man sayings in the synoptics fall into two groups, those about the Son of man's mission and his fate on earth (e.g., Mark 2.10 par.; 2.28 par.; 10.45 Par) together with the passion predictions (Mark 8.31 par.; 9.31 par.; 10.33 Par) and those concerning the position and role of the risen and exalted Son of man and his parousia (e.g., Mark 8.3 par.; 13.26 par.; 14.62 par.). All Son of man sayings are christologically significant. Nevertheless, in the synoptics there are many passages without the expression where textually and linguistically there could be no objection to it (e.g., Mark 2.17 par.), and such passages sometimes have synoptic parallels containing the expression (e.g., Luke 22.27; cf. Mark 10.45 and Matt. 20.28). In the synoptics, there seems to be an increasing monopolization of the expression in sayings of Jesus about his mission, his fate, and his position beyond the resurrection. In the Fourth Gospel the situation is different: here Son of man sayings compete with the "I am" sayings and the self-designation "the Son." The distinction in usage is always significant; "Son of man" is always used in major statements.

Being central in the Gospel tradition, then, it is no wonder that Son of man is one of the most debated expressions in the New Testament. Its seemingly enigmatic character can be measured by the endless attempts to find an acceptable solution as to its meaning, and despite tendencies apparent in more recent research, it is not accurate to speak of a growing consensus. It is possible, however, to distinguish between two main views: (1) The expression was current and, under certain circumstances, understandable as a messianic title at the time of Jesus. (2) Such usage must be excluded on linguistic grounds alone. There is also the question whether the expression as it now stands in the Gospels is to be understood as a messianic title or not. And in the case of the former, are we to presume a development in meaning from Jesus to the Gospel tradition?

The New Testament itself does not give us the slightest hint as to the meaning of the expression, and there is no evidence for the double-determined form ("the Son of the man") before it appears in the New Testament. In the Greek of the Septuagint it appears only in the undetermined form, which, similar to the Hebrew original *ben 'ādām,* conveys a generic meaning synonymous with "man," that is, human being (Ps. 8.5; Ezek. 2.1; Dan. 8.17). In the Hebrew Bible, the expression occurs 108 times, 93 of which are in Ezekiel as God's way of addressing the prophet. The Aramaic equivalent, *bar 'ĕnāš,* occurs only once, in Daniel 7.13, which speaks of "one like a (son of) man." This saying has had a decisive impact on the understanding of Son of man in the New Testament, and it is quoted or alluded to many times (see Mark 13.26 par.; 14.62 par.; but also Rev. 1.7, which does not actually mention any son of man). The imagery of Daniel 7.13–14 may be the foundation of the Son of man sayings relating to the status of the exalted Christ.

Now, "one like a man" in Daniel 7.13 is by no means a messianic figure, but a symbol of the victorious Israel, the kingdom of the saints of the Most High, which succeeded the four world empires (Dan. 7.18, 22, 25, 27). Thus, when we find in 1 Enoch 46–71 and 4 Ezra 13 similar imageries of a son of man or simply a man, these cannot be independent witnesses of a special concept, but uses of the imagery of Daniel to describe a messianic figure. The comprehensive attempt earlier this century to verify the existence of a special son of man conception, sometimes assumed to be a variant of the ancient Near Eastern myth of the primeval man, universal and transcendent in its outlook (in contrast to the nationalistic and earthly expectation of a Davidic messiah), has obviously failed.

Another question is whether the expression in the Gospels and Acts 7.56 is to be understood as a title. With the exception of Matthew 16.13 and John 9.35, this is possible. On the other hand, the title never occurs in confessions (e.g., Jesus is

First apparition of the Son of Man between the seven churches of Asia and the seven stars. (Rev. 1.12–16) (Apocalypse of St. John de Lovao, 12th. century)

the Son of man), nor is it used predicatively (Jesus, the Son of man). The determined form must not be taken as a reference to the expression "like a son of man" in Daniel 7.13.

There is, however, yet another possibility. Granted that the Greek form of the expression originates in Aramaic, it may be explained as a direct extension of the idiomatic use of the expression *bar 'ĕnāš*. It is now almost universally agreed that at Jesus' time this expression was in general usage in Galilean Aramaic both as a noun (meaning "a human being") and as a substitute for the indefinite pronoun and as a periphrasis for "I," the actual meaning depending on the context. The double entendre may express a generalization, meaning "one," "a human," or it may be a self-reference provoked by awe, modesty, or humility, in accord with the content of the actual saying. In that case, the double entendre is deceptive, a near parallel being Paul's way of speaking of himself in 2 Corinthians 12.2–3. It is possible to understand the Gospel Son of man sayings in accordance with this Aramaic idiom. But the double entendre has been done away with by the Greek rendering with its awkward literalness ("the son of the man"), which substitutes an explicit indication of the identity of the subject speaking. This does not mean, however, that the expression has become a title. In the Gospels it is, at the same time, Jesus' periphrasis for "I" and a way to emphasize who is speaking. In other words, it is not the expression "son of man" that tells us who Jesus is, but on the contrary, it is Jesus who tells us who the Son of man is.

It is thus reasonable to suppose that the usage of the expression in the Gospels originates in the way in which Jesus spoke of himself. The question of the genuineness of the individual Son of man sayings must therefore depend on their content: are they understandable in the mouth of the historical Jesus or not? Naturally, the answer will depend upon the individual interpreter's idea of what Jesus believed and preached about himself, and what may be referred to the early community. It seems probable that the sayings about the risen and exalted Son of man and his parousia, depending on Daniel 7.13–14 for their imagery, were created in the process of interpreting the faith in the resurrection of Jesus, and that they were shaped in analogy to other sayings of Jesus about himself. As indicated by 1 Thessalonians 4.15–17, this interpretation is early and reflects the same tradition expressed later in Mark 13.26 and especially Matthew 24.30–31.

The uncomplicated way in which the expression is used in the Gospels indicates an early foothold in the Greek gospel tradition, which is confirmed by its occurrence also in the Fourth Gospel. In this gospel, one can perceive a beginning of reflection upon its wording, which transcends the purely idiomatic meaning it had in Aramaic (see especially John 5.27). In the apostolic fathers, it is understood as a statement of Christ's human nature and corresponds to the title Son of God (see Ignatius *Ephesians* 20.2; cf. Epistle of Barnabas 12.10). Later, it is seen as a reference to the figure in Daniel 7.13 and is read as a messianic prophecy (Justin, *Apology* I.51). Not until the nineteenth century do we find an attempt to see a specific conception behind the expression.

MOGENS MÜLLER

SONS OF GOD. The sons of God (or children of God; Hebr. *Bĕnê 'ĕlōhîm*, and variants) are divine members of God's heavenly assembly. They are depicted in many roles: praising God at the dawn of creation (Job 38.7); praising God in heaven (Ps 29.1); meeting in the heavenly assembly before God (Job 1.6, 2.1; cf. Pss. 82.1, 6; 89.6–8); representing the foreign nations (Deut. 32.8, following a text from Qumran and the LXX); and, most curiously, marrying and having offspring with human women (Gen. 6.1–4). Other terms, such as seraphim, angels (i.e., "messengers"), and hosts of heaven also refer to these members of God's heavenly assembly (see 1 Kgs. 22.19; Isa. 6; Ezek. 13.25). The sons of God are also identified with the stars in heaven (Job 38.7; cf. Judg. 5.20). The title "sons/children of God" is familiar from Ugaritic mythology, in which the gods collectively are called the "children of El (literally, God)" (*bn 'il*). One of El's titles is "Father of the Children of God," indicating that the term refers to the gods as his physical offspring, with Asherah (called "Creatress of the Gods") as their mother. The sons/children of God are also found in Phoenician and Ammonite inscriptions, referring to the pantheon of subordinate deities, indicating that the term was widespread in West Semitic religions. Beginning in the seventh and sixth centuries BCE, several Israelite writers (especially Jeremiah, the Deuteronomist, and Second Isaiah) explicitly rejected the notion that there were gods other than Yahweh, and depicted the "hosts of heaven" as a foreign intrusion in Israelite monotheism.

RONALD S. HENDEL

STEPHEN. The first Christian martyr, Stephen appears only in Acts. He is first mentioned as one of the seven appointed to ensure equitable distribution of food between "Hebrews" and "Hellenists" (Acts 6.1–6). The seven were probably leaders of the Hellenistic group in the Jerusalem church.

Paradise. (Jacopo Robusti Tintoretto, 1577)

According to Acts 6, in an explicit literary parallel to Luke's story of Jesus, Stephen was charged with blasphemy and summoned to defend himself before the supreme Sanhedrin (Acts 6.8–15).

His defense (Acts 7.2–53) is a detailed exposition of the teaching that had provoked the charges against him. The speech may be regarded as a manifesto of early Hellenistic Christianity or at least of one phase of it. It does not represent Luke's point of view: for most of Luke's narrative, his appraisal of the Temple is much more positive than Stephen's. Quoting the scriptures in support of his position, Stephen argues that to speak of the Temple as an institution to be destroyed or superseded was not to commit blasphemy, because God is independent of any building. It was commonly held by many early Christians that in Christ the Temple order had given way to something better, but Stephen's assertion that the Temple was a mistake from the beginning is without parallel in the New Testament. The position nearest to it is in the. letter to the Hebrews, but its author simply ignores the Temple and bases his exposition of the high-priestly ministry of Christ on the biblical account of the wilderness tabernacle.

Stephen was apparently found guilty of blasphemy and sentenced to death. His execution took the form of a judicial stoning, carried out in accordance with the Law (Lev. 24.15–16). Those who bore witness against him had the duty of throwing the first stones (see Deut 17.7); on this occasion "a young man named Saul" guarded their cloaks as they did so, and thus Paul makes his first appearance.

Analogies have been found to Stephen's position among the Samaritans, the Qumran community, and the Ebionites. These groups, for various reasons, expressed a negative attitude to the Jerusalem Temple and its ceremonial. But Stephen's critique is distinctive; not only is it rooted in the preexilic prophets but it has a new basis in the Christ event. The radical Hellenistic theology represented by his speech survived particularly in Alexandrian Christianity, where its best-known expression is the letter of Barnabas (late first/ early second century CE).

Stephen's impeachment and execution are said to have precipitated a persecution of the Jerusalem church, especially its Hellenistic members, who were forced to leave Jerusalem and Judea. But they preached the gospel wherever they went. Stephen's fellow-almoner Philip preached it in Samaria; others, unnamed, preached it to the Greeks of Antioch. Stephen's blood proved to be the seed of gentile Christianity.

F. F. BRUCE

SYNAGOGUE. The emergence of the synagogue constituted a revolutionary development in the history of Judaism. The synagogue represented not only a wholly new concept of religious observance but also a new form of communal institution. With the synagogue the nature of official worship shifted dramatically, with prayer, study, and exhortation replacing sacrifice as the way to serve God. Officiating on behalf of the community was no longer confined to a small coterie of priests but was open to all. Ceremonies were conducted in full view of the participants, with the masses of people no longer being relegated to outer courtyards, as was the case in the Jerusalem Temple. Moreover, the synagogue was a universal institution and not confined to any one specific locale.

Despite its importance in Jewish history, the origins of the synagogue and its early development are shrouded in mystery. Only during and after the first century CE does liter-

St. Stephen, from the Altarpiece of Pierre Rup

ary and archaeological evidence appear for Palestine. As for the Roman Diaspora, references before then are practically nonexistent (and what does exist refers to the Diaspora). Synagogue inscriptions from third- and second-century BCE Egypt have been preserved, as have remains of a Delos synagogue building dating from the first century BCE.

Owing to the paucity of sources, opinions have varied widely as to when, where, and why the synagogue developed. Theories have ranged from the late First Temple period (eighth-seventh century BCE), through the exilic (sixth century) and postexilic (fifth century) eras, and down to the late Persian (fourth century) and Hellenistic times (third or second century). Most scholars have assumed a midway position, one that posits the emergence of the synagogue closely following the destruction of the First Temple in 587/586 BCE, either during the Babylonian exile or soon after, when the Jews returned to Judea during the era of restoration.

Over the centuries the synagogue became a fully developed communal institution and apparently the central one in most communities. It served as a place for study, sacred meals, court proceedings, depositing communal funds, and political and social meetings, as a hostel, and as a residence for certain synagogue officials. Of central importance, of course, were the religious services. At first these consisted pri-

273

marily of the Torah-reading ceremony and its accompanying activities: translation of the Torah into the vernacular, be it Aramaic (Targums) or Greek, the *haftarah* or a selected reading from the prophets, and a sermon. The sources from the Second Temple period—Josephus, Philo, rabbinic writings, and the Theodotus inscription—point to this centrality. The existence of regular communal prayers at this time is unclear. While prayer appears to have been an integral part of the religious service in the Diaspora, its presence in Palestinian synagogue settings before 70 CE is unattested. Only after this date are we on firm ground in assuming the importance and centrality of public prayer in all synagogue settings.

These two components of the religious service—Torah reading and prayer—were characterized in antiquity by their fluidity no less than their uniformity. While Torah reading was accepted as normative on Sabbaths and holidays and later on Mondays and Thursdays as well, the division into weekly portions varied considerably. In Palestine, the Torah was read over a three- or three-and-a-half-year period with a plethora of local traditions on the precise divisions of the weekly portions (141, 154, 161, 167, and 175). Moreover, the practice in Babylonian communities living in late Roman and Byzantine Palestine only added to this diversity: They concluded the Torah reading in one year. How widespread the custom was of translating the Torah portion into the vernacular is unknown, but the use of Greek in addition to Aramaic cannot be denied. The place of the sermon in the synagogue service was likewise diverse. The content, of course, might have varied considerably from one of an expository nature to one of ethical, political, halakhic, or even eschatological dimensions. When sermons were delivered on the Sabbath (Friday evening, Saturday morning, or Saturday afternoon), or when during the service (before or after the Torah reading), might differ widely from one congregation to another.

The diversity is found also with regard to prayer. Undoubtedly by the post-70 era the two main foci of the prayer service had crystallized. The Shema prayer (Deut. 6.4–9) with its accompanying paragraphs (Deut. 11.13–21; Num. 15.37–41) had been adopted from Temple practice and was now supplemented by three blessings, each focusing on a central theme, respectively—creation, revelation, and redemption. Together this unit provided the central ideational portion of the prayer experience and was recited in the synagogue twice daily, during the morning and evening services. The second focus of the prayer service was the Shemoneh Esreh (literally, "eighteen" blessings, although a nineteenth was added some time in late antiquity) or the Amidah (standing prayer). When precisely this prayer came into usage is unknown, but by the second century CE it held a central position. Recited three times daily, no special prayer service, be it on the Sabbath, Holiday, or High Holiday, was complete without it. The Amidah consisted of three parts: the first three benedictions were in praise of God, the last three were expressions of thanks, while the middle section changed each day. On a weekday, twelve (later thirteen) petionary blessings were recited; on Sabbaths and holidays this section expressed the unique message of that particular day. During the early centuries CE prayers were added to the morning service, such as prayers of supplication, morning blessings, psalms of praise, and others.

During the Byzantine period, the recitation of liturgical poems—*pîyyûṭîm*—was added to the service, particularly those for the Sabbath and holidays. When and from where the *pîyyûṭ* developed has been a subject of scholarly debate. Some claim it evolved from earlier midrashim, prayers, or songs recited in the Temple and synagogue, others see it as the adoption and adaptation of liturgical poems recited in Byzantine churches, and still others as a protest against organized, fixed prayers. Whatever the explanation, the *pîyyûṭ* made its appearance in fourth- and fifth-century Palestine, and today we know of at least twenty poets who functioned in the pre-Muslim era. These *pîyyûṭîm* were recited during the morning service, either in addition to or in place of the fixed liturgy.

Archaeological remains of the ancient synagogue abound. In Palestine alone, traces of over a hundred structures have been identified, and in the Diaspora some fifteen. The latter stretch from Dura Europos on the Euphrates River in the east, to Tunisia on the North African coast in the west. The overwhelming majority of synagogue remains in Palestine are located in the Galilee and Golan regions; others are to be found in Beth-shean, coastal areas, and Judea. Architecturally, these synagogues can be divided into three types. The Galilean type, characterized by a monumental and richly decorated facade, was oriented towards Jerusalem, often with three entrances. Fine ashlar masonry of either limestone or basalt was characteristic of these buildings, and their rectangular interiors were simple, with two or three colonnades dividing the hall into a central nave with two or three aisles. Entablatures, pilasters, and friezes typical of Roman art of late antiquity decorated the buildings, along with molded stucco and painted plaster. With but few exceptions, no permanent shrines for the Torah scrolls have been found.

The second type of synagogue modelled itself after the basilical plan used extensively in Byzantine churches, and was modest on the exterior, reserving its splendor for the interior. In contrast to the Galilean type with its splendid entrance on the facade facing Jerusalem, the entrance in the basilica type shifted to the wall opposite the direction of prayer. A round or square apse was set in the wall facing Jerusalem in which the Torah ark rested on a raised platform (*bîmâ*). Only two rows of columns lined the elongated character of the prayer hall. Most notable in the basilica type of synagogue was its richly decorated mosaic floor, often in clear imitation of regnant Byzantine patterns and not infrequently with unique Jewish symbols, such as a menorah, Torah ark, lulav, ethrog, and shofar. Such symbols were practically nonexistent in buildings of the Galilean type. Finally, a third type of building which appears in but a few locales of Palestine and the Diaspora is the broadhouse synagogue. The uniqueness of these buildings is that their focus of worship, either an apse, *bîmâ,* or shrine—which is located along the long wall of the synagogue. These buildings share features common to the other types in most other respects.

Aside from the Jewish symbols mentioned above, Jewish figural art is represented in only a few synagogues: the Aqedah (Genesis 22) at Beth Alpha, Noah at Gerasa, David at Gaza, and Daniel at Na'aran and Susiya. Of an entirely different order is the third-century CE synagogue of Dura Europos, whose walls are covered from floor to ceiling with decorated panels. These panels depict scenes from the Bible, using Greek and Persian artistic motifs and incorporating a significant amount of *midrash* (rabbinic or otherwise) in their interpretations and representations. One of the most striking examples of synagogue art, at Hammath Tiberias and elsewhere, represents Helios, the zodiac signs, and the four seasons. Interpretations of these motifs vary considerably. The first reaction was to interpret them as the gift of the emperor or as an expression of some fringe group in Judaism. With the discovery, however, of such pavements all over Israel, it became clear that this was a popular and accepted form of

S

artistic expression. Among the interpretations proposed of the zodiac motif are: it was simply a decorative motif; it reflects the importance of the Jewish calendar; it represents the power of God in creating the world each day; it stands for the Divine himself; it reflects belief in angels, especially Helios, who was well known within certain Jewish circles of the period. Of these several explanations, none has won general acceptance.

Owing to the centrality of the synagogue as the primary Jewish communal institution and to the extensive remains that have survived, the study of this institution is of paramount importance for those wishing to gain as complete a picture of ancient Judaism as possible. Patterns of Jewish settlements, the diversity of religious practices, the influence of surrounding cultures, Jewish artistic expression, Jewish prosography, titles and professions among synagogue donors are areas well attested in synagogue remains.

LEE LEVINE

SYRIA (Map 6:G4). Syria is a geographical area bounded by the Euphrates River on the east, Palestine on the south, and the Mediterranean Sea on the west. It has been assumed that the name Syria derived from Tyre, which was the port of entry for Romans, Greeks, and others who explored or expanded eastward. Syria's major centers were Damascus, Antioch on the Orontes, and the region of the two rivers, the Tigris and the Euphrates.

In the Hebrew Bible, David extends his kingdom up to Damascus in Syria (2 Sam. 8.6; 1 Chron. 18.6). Syria, generally called Aram, is clearly a foreign country, but close enough to go in and out of, know quite a lot about, and seriously compete with, both religiously and economically. Syrian gods are criticized (Judg. 10.6; Isa. 7.1), and there are wars with numerous Syrian kings and cities.

The region was captured by Tiglath-pileser III in the eighth century BCE, conquered by Alexander the Great, and later became a center for the Seleucid dynasty that ultimately provoked the Maccabean revolt in Palestine in 165 BCE. Roman writers could frequently lump Palestine and Syria together without distinction under the name Coele-Syria. Pompey and leaders after him, including Herod the Great, used Damascus as a center for military and bureaucratic expansion. It was from Damascus that Pompey launched his pacification of Palestine in 66 BCE in the wake of the Hasmonean civil war. Both cities were among the leading cultural, religious, and economic centers of the entire Roman empire.

Syria is rarely mentioned by name in the New Testament. On several occasions, Syria is referred to as proof that Jesus' fame is spreading (e.g., Matt. 4.24); in Acts, Syria is mentioned in the context of the spread of Christianity.

There were numerous and sizable Jewish communities in Syria. The Jews of Antioch are singled out by Josephus as a vibrant community who were constantly attracting gentiles to their religious ceremonies (*War* 7.3.43–45). In the fourth century CE, the sermons delivered by John Chrysostom against the Jews make it clear that the Jewish community in Antioch was still large, popular, and a threat to Christians like Chrysostom.

Similarly Syria and its larger cities became centers for early Christianity. The early second-century writer Ignatius of Antioch emerged as an important figure in the early church, as did Chrysostom, and many early Christian texts, including some of the Gospels, have been associated with Syria.

Syria in history and today remains an intriguing if enigmatic country and culture, which represents and joins city and village, east and west, Jew, Christian, and Muslim. It has played a pivotal role in the development and definition of Jewish and Christian belief and identity.

J. ANDREW OVERMAN

S

T

TABERNACLE. The portable sanctuary constructed by Moses at Sinai and primarily associated with the people's wilderness wandering. Various expressions are used in referring to this sanctuary—"tent," "tent of meeting," "tabernacle," "tabernacle of the testimony [NRSV: covenant]." Conceived as a movable shrine, the tabernacle was constructed so that it could be assembled, dismantled, and reassembled as the people moved from one place to another.

The account of the construction of the tabernacle is found in the book of Exodus: in chaps. 25–31, God provides instructions to Moses for its construction, and chaps. 35–40 report how these were carried out. Included in these texts are directions for the construction of the cultic furniture used in conjunction with the tabernacle. These include the ark (25.10–22; 37.19), table of showbread (25.23–30; 37.10–16), the lampstand or menorah (25.31–40; 37.17–24), the altar of burnt offering (27.1–8; 38.1–7), the altar of incense (30.1–10; 37.1–10), and the bronze basin (30.17–21; 38.8). In addition, directions are given for preparing priestly garments (28.1–43; 39.1–31), for ordaining Aaron and his sons as priests (29.1–46; see Lev. 8), for collecting the sanctuary tax (30.11–16), for mixing the anointing oil and incense (30.22–38; 37.29), and for other matters associated with the ritual of the tabernacle.

The tabernacle and its furnishings were made of materials and with labor contributed voluntarily by members of the community (25.2–7; 35.4–36.7) under the supervision of Bezalel of the tribe of Judah and Oholiab of the tribe of Dan (31.1–11; 35.30–36.1). The tabernacle complex was rectangular in shape, measuring 100 by 50 cubits (27.9–18). The exact dimensions expressed in modern equivalents are uncertain, since the length of the ancient cubit (the distance from the point of the elbow to the end of the middle finger) remains in doubt; estimates range from 45 to 52 cm (17.5 to 20.4 in). The approximate dimensions of the sanctuary were 32 by 23 m (105 by 75 ft). The complex was oriented so that the short sides faced east and west with a 20-cubit entrance on the east protected by the embroidered screen (26.36–37; 27.16).

The tabernacle was divided into three distinct zones of increasing holiness: the courtyard, the holy place, and the holy of holies. The courtyard was divisible into two 50-cubit squares. The eastern square contained the altar of burnt offering where sacrifices and offerings were burned ($5 \times 5 \times 3$ cubits), located at its center, and the basin, to the west of the altar, which held water for the priests to wash their hands and feet before officiating. The western square contained the tent of meeting or tabernacle proper. This was a separate enclosure measuring $30 \times 30 \times 10$ cubits subdivided into the holy place ($20 \times 10 \times 10$ cubits) and the holy of holies ($10 \times 10 \times 10$ cubits).

Located within the holy place were the table of showbread ($2 \times 1 \times 1.5$ cubits) situated on the north side; the menorah on the south side, and the altar of incense or holden altar ($1 \times 1 \times 2$ cubits) located between the table and lampstand immediately in front of the veil to the holy of holies. Every Sabbath twelve freshly baked loaves were placed on the table, arranged in two rows (Lev. 24.5–9; Exod. 25.30). The lamps on the menorah were lit each evening by the high priest and allowed to burn all night (Lev. 24.1–4). Every morning and evening, at the time when the lamps of the menorah were tended, the high priest burned incense on the golden altar (Exod. 30.7–9).

The holy of holies, separated from the holy place by an embroidered curtain (Exod. 26.31–33), housed only the ark ($2.5 \times 1.5 \times 1.5$ cubits) containing the "testimony" (25.21; 40.20), assumed to be the tablets of the Law. A special lid or "mercy seat" covered the top of the ark and was ornamented with two cherubim whose outspread wings overarched the cover and touched one another (25.17–20; 26.34; 37.6–9). The covering of the ark was the place where God promised to meet and communicate with the representative of the community (25.22). Only the high priest was to enter the holy of holies (30.10; Lev. 16.2, 29–34).

The entire courtyard of the enclosure with its perimeter of 300 cubits, with the exception of the entryway, was surrounded by hangings of twisted linen, 5 cubits high, hung on upright posts placed at intervals of 5 cubits (Exod. 27.9–19). The inner rectangle, the tabernacle proper, was enclosed, except on the eastern end, by forty-eight wooden frames (Exod. 26.15–29; 36.20–34). The assembled frames were overlaid first by a covering of sheets of linen (26.1–6) and then by a covering of goats' hair curtains (26.7–13), which was overlaid by a covering of tanned ram skins (26.14).

Gradations of holiness are reflected in the layout, building materials, and use of the tabernacle enclosure. The less holy area, the outer courtyard, was open to the laity, and the metal associated with its construction was bronze. Only priests and Levites were admitted to the holy place in which the items were overlaid with gold (except for the menorah, which was of pure gold). The contents of the holy of holies were gold plated outside and inside (the ark) or else were of pure gold (the mercy seat). The sacredness of the entire precinct is evident from the command that the priests and Levites should camp between the tabernacle and the tents of the tribes on their journeys in the wilderness (Num. 1.53; 2.1–34).

The tabernacle was the place where God was present among his people (Exod. 25.8), where he met with them and communicated with them (25.22; 29.43–46). The symmetry and wholeness of the tabernacle (see 26.6, 11; 36.13, 18) were reflective of the unity and perfection of God and of the divine relationship to creation. Note the association of the construction of the tabernacle with the Sabbath (31.12–17; 35.1–3) and the presence of six formulas of divine address to Moses dividing the material into six units (25.1; 30.11, 17, 22, 34; 31.1), thus paralleling the six days in the account of creation in Genesis 1.12.3.

Questions have been raised about whether an edifice as elaborate as the tabernacle existed in the wilderness. Scholars have pointed to a number of difficulties. Could the Israelites, newly out of slavery in Egypt, have possessed the necessary artistic skills to produce such a structure when later Solomon had to hire the Phoenicians to build the Jerusalem Temple (1 Kings 5.1–6)? Would they have had sufficient precious metals, gems, and fabrics to make the cultic furniture and priestly garments? (Estimates indicate the need for at least 1,000 kg [1 ton] of gold, 3,000 kg [3 tons] of silver, and 2,500 kg [2.5 tons] of bronze.) Could such a massive and heavy structure have been dismantled and reassembled with any practicability? Why is there no mention of carrying the tabernacle across the Jordan in the account of the entry into the Promised Land (Josh. 3) and such infrequent reference to the structure in the narratives after the entry (see Josh. 18.1; 1 Sam. 2.22; 1 Kings 8.4; 2 Chron. 1.3)? How is the tabernacle, situated in the center of the tribal camp and guarded by thousands of Levites, related to the wilderness tent that was pitched outside the camp, guarded by a single individual, and used to communicate with the deity (Exod. 33.7–11)? Such questions have led to the theory that the tabernacle was an idealized version of the Jerusalem Temple projected back into the wilderness and that the portable shrine was much simpler.

In support of the historicity of the tabernacle or at least some modified version of it, scholars have pointed to the use of portable shrines among other cultures, especially Arab Bedouin cultures, to the fact that Egyptian armies camped encircling the sacred tent and artifacts associated with the Pharaoh, and to the "despoiling of the Egyptians" as a source of the wealth required for the tabernacle (see Gen. 15.13–14; Exod. 11.2; 12.35–36; Ps. 105.37).

JOHN H. HAYES

TEMPLE. A building or place symbolizing the presence of a deity or deities, intended for the purpose of worship. In the Bible, "temple" usually refers to the Temple erected by Solomon or the Temple of Zerubbabel that was enlarged and refurbished by Herod.

Terminology. Hebrew *hêkāl* comes from Akkadian *ekallu*, which in turn is derived from Sumerian *É.GAL*, "great house." The term is generic, and can apply to the house of a god (a temple) or to the house of a king (a palace). It is used of Ahab's palace (1 Kings 21.1) and that of the king of Babylon (2 Kings 20.18). As Israel's king, Yahweh dwelt in a palace, seated on a throne (Isa. 6.1). The word is also used of the house of Yahweh at Shiloh (1 Sam. 1.9; 3.3); of Solomon's Temple (2 Chron. 3.17); of the Second Temple, built by Zerubbabel (Zech. 8.9); of the Temple of Ezekiel's vision (Ezek. 40–48); and of God's heavenly dwelling place (Ps. 11.4).

Hebrew *bayit*, "house," by itself, is used very often of the Temple, or in combination, "house of God" (1 Chron. 9.11), and especially "house of Yahweh" (1 Kings 6–8). This word was also used of the tent of worship (Judg. 18.31), of a local shrine (1 Chron. 9.23), and of temples of other gods (Judg. 9.4; 1 Sam. 5.5). The term "house," referring to the Temple at Jerusalem, is a broader term, including the nave (strictly speaking, the *hêkāl*) and the inner sanctuary (the holy of holies). The Temple mount is

known as "the mountain of the Lord's house" (Isa. 2.2) or even "the mountain of the house" (Jer. 26.18; Mic. 3.12).

Greek *hieron*, "sanctuary, temple," in the New Testament is used once of the temple of Artemis (Acts 19.27), but otherwise of the Temple at Jerusalem. The term includes the whole Temple complex. Unfortunately, both this and the next term *(naos)* are translated "temple," which leads to confusion. Jesus, who was not a priest, could not enter the "temple" *(naos),* nor could the money changers (Matt. 21.12), nor could Paul (Acts 21.26). The word used in each instance is *hieron,* which might be more accurately translated "temple mount."

Greek *naos,* "temple," is used in the New Testament of Herod's Temple, that is, the sanctuary itself and not the entire Temple area (Matt. 27.51; Luke 1.21; John 2.20), and of the heavenly sanctuary (Rev. 11.19; 14.17; but there is no temple in the New Jerusalem, for the Lord God himself is the temple, Rev. 21.22). The word is also used of sanctuaries of other gods (Acts 17.24; 19.24, translated "shrines"; *hieron* is used in 19.27). Used figuratively, *naos* refers to the human body (John 2.21; 1 Cor. 3.16–17; 6.19) and to the church (Eph. 2.21).

Greek *oikos,* "house" (referring to the Temple), except for Luke 11.51 and Hebrews 10.21, occurs only in quotations in the New Testament of passages in the Hebrew Bible where *bayit* is used.

Solomon's Temple. The tabernacle had served as the center of worship from the time of Moses to David (2 Sam. 6.17; 7.6). David wanted to build a more permanent struc-

View of the Temple of Artemis illuminated at dusk.

ture, but the Lord forbade it (1 Chron. 22.7–8). David set about collecting materials and making plans for the building to be built by his son, Solomon (2 Sam. 7.13; 1 Chron. 22.2–5; 28.11–19).

The Temple was located on the eastern hill, north of the city of David, where the Dome of the Rock is located today. At that time the Temple mount was considerably smaller, Solomon having enlarged it somewhat (Josephus, *War*, 5.5.185) and Herod having enlarged it still more to the present size of the platform known as Haram esh-Sharif. This is "the threshing floor of Araunah the Jebusite" (2 Sam. 24.18), "Mount Moriah" (2 Chron. 3.1), and probably the Zion of the Psalms and the prophets (Pss. 110.2; 128.5; 134.3; Isa. 2.3; Joel 3.16 [MT 4.16]; Amos 1.2; Zech. 8.3) although the term belonged to the city of David (1 Kings 8.1).

The general plan of the Temple was similar to that given for the tabernacle: rectangular, with a porch or vestibule (*úlām*, 1 Kings 6.3) facing east, a nave (*hêkāl*), and an inner sanctuary (*děbîr*, 6.5) or holy of holies (8.6). The dimensions were double those of the tabernacle: 60 cubits by 20 (1 cubit = 0.5 m [19.7 in]), but triple its height (30 cubits). The building was of hewn stone, dressed at the quarry (1 Kings 6.7). The porch was 10 cubits deep (1 Kings 6.3) and 120 cubits high (2 Chron. 3.4)—a numeral that may have suffered textual corruption. Two columns, Jachin and Boaz, made of hollow bronze, 35 or 40 cubits high, stood at each side of the entrance (2 Chron. 3.15–17). The inner walls of the *hêkāl* were lined with cedar brought from Lebanon (1 Kings 5.6–10; 6.15–16), and the entire structure was lined with gold (v. 22). The holy of holies was overlaid with "pure" gold (v. 20). The skilled work was done by Tyrian artisans supplied by King Hiram (5.1) and under the supervision of a person also named Hiram (7.13) or Huram-Abi (2 Chron. 2.13).

The holiest place contained the ark of the covenant (1 Kings 6.19) and two winged figures (cherubim) of olive wood overlaid with gold (v. 23) that stretched from wall to wall. Doors of olive wood, covered with gold, separated the holy of holies from the nave (v. 31), and similar doors separated the nave from the porch (v. 33). The nave contained the golden altar (7.48, to distinguish it from the bronze altar in the courtyard) made of cedar (6.20) or the "altar of incense" (1 Chron. 28.18), which stood before the holy of holies; the golden table for the bread of the Presence ("showbread"); the golden lampstands and other items (1 Kings 6.48–50).

The building was surrounded by two courts, the inner one constructed of three courses of stone and one of cedar beams (v. 36; also called the court of the priests, 2 Chron. 4.9), and the great court (1 Kings 7.9), which probably also enclosed the royal buildings. The size of the inner court is not given, but if it was double the size of the court of the tabernacle, it would have been 200 by 100 cubits. The inner court contained the bronze altar (2 Chron. 4.1) where sacrifices were offered, the ten bronze basins on ten stands, five on each side of the house, and the great sea (the molten or bronze sea) on the southeast corner of the house. The bronze work was cast in the Jordan valley (1 Kings 7.46), the most impressive being the great sea, 10 cubits in diameter and 5 cubits high, with a capacity of 2,000 baths (approximately 40,000 liters [10,000 gal]). The water was used for supplying the lavers for washing the parts of the sacrificial victims and for the priests' ablutions (2 Chron. 4.6).

The First Temple, having been plundered several times, was finally destroyed by Nebuchadrezzar in 587/586 BCE (2 Kings 25.8–17; Jer. 52.12–23).

Ezekiel's Temple. The Temple in Ezekiel 40–48 is presented as a vision, and so the details may be assumed to be symbolic rather than material. The plan in general follows closely that of Solomon's Temple, although it is markedly symmetrical. Some of the description is more detailed than that given in Kings or Chronicles, and such details as the plan and dimensions of the gates (Ezek. 40.6–16) have been indirectly confirmed by archaeological discoveries at Gezer, Hazor, and Megiddo.

Zerubbabel's Temple. When the Jews returned from exile (538 BCE) there was an effort to rebuild the Temple (2 Chron. 36.23; Ezra 1.1–4). The work was begun (Ezra 3) but languished until 520, when as a result of the encouragement of Haggai and Zechariah, it was resumed and the Temple was finished on the third day of Adar in the sixth year of Darius (12 March 515; Ezra 6.15). It was comparable in size to Solomon's Temple (6.3) and probably also in its ground plan, with the holy of holies and the sanctuary with the golden altar, table lampstand, and other furnishings (1 Macc. 1.22; 4.48–51). It was surrounded by an inner court with the altar of burnt offering and an outer court. According to Josephus, reporting Hecateus, the outer court was approximately 150 by 45 m (500 by 150 ft), and the altar of unhewn stones was 20 cubits square and 10 cubits in height (*Ag. Ap.* 1.198). According to the Talmud (*Yoma* 21b), five things were missing from the Second Temple: the ark, the sacred fire, the *shekinah*, the holy spirit, and the Urim and Thummim.

Herod's Temple. Herod did not tear down the Second Temple—that would surely have instigated a revolt, as Herod recognized (Josephus, *Ant.* 15.11.387). He rebuilt and refurbished it by preparing materials for parts, using priests as carpenters and masons in the sacred areas, and doing the work by sections. The building was made new without ever destroying the old and without interrupting the sacred offerings and sacrifices. Begun in Herod's twentieth year (20 BCE), it was finished in a year and a half (*Ant.* 15.11.420).

Work on the Temple platform may have begun in Herod's fifteenth year (Josephus, *War* 1.21.401), and it continued until ca. 64 CE (*Ant.* 20.9.219). The Kidron valley was partially filled, shifting its bed eastward; likewise the central (Tyropoeon) valley was partially filled, shifting it several hundred feet to the west. Using huge ashlars ("Herodian" stones, ca. 1 m [40 in] high, 1–3 m [3 to 10 ft] long [one measures 12 m (39 ft) in length!], and 4 m [13 ft] wide), the western, southern, and eastern walls were built, and the Temple mount was extended to a width of 280 m (915 ft) across the southern end, 310 m (1,017 ft) across the northern, and approximately 450 m (1,500 ft) north to south. At the southeastern corner, the wall rose 48 m (158 ft) above the Kidron valley. A stoa or portico was built along all four sides, with marble columns 25 cubits high, and ceiled with cedar panels; the royal stoa at the south had four rows of columns, the others had double rows of columns. The stoa along the eastern side was attributed by Josephus (*Ant.* 20.9.221) to Solomon (see John 10.23; Acts 3.11; 5.12).

The Temple itself (Map 9) was surrounded by a wall or balustrade, 3 cubits high, separating the holy place from the court of the gentiles. It was 322 cubits east to west by 135 cubits north to south, raised by 14 and 5 steps (all steps were 1/2 cubit). The holy place was not in the center of the

Temple mount, but more to the north and west. On the surrounding wall were warnings, some in Greek, others in Latin, forbidding the entry of any gentile under penalty of death; two of these have been found. Ten cubits inside the balustrade a wall of 25 cubits high surrounded the sacred area, with seven gates: three each on the north and south sides, one on the east (*Mid.* 1.4).

Within this holy place, there were increasingly sacred areas: the court of the women at the east, the court of the Israelites (i.e., males only), the court of the priests, then the Temple (*naos*). This area was separated from the Women's Court, being 15 steps higher, and could be entered through the Nicanor Gate. The Temple was still higher by another 12 steps; it consisted of the porch (100 by 100 cubits, 11 cubits wide), the nave (40 by 20 cubits) containing the table of the Presence, the lampstand or menorah (taken to Rome by Titus and portrayed on the Arch of Titus), and the altar of incense, and behind that the holy of holies (20 by 20 cubits), which was empty except for a sacred stone. Built into the wall around the Temple were rooms or chambers, increasing the size of the Temple by 70 to 100 cubits. To the east and south of the Temple was the altar, 32 cubits square, and north of the altar the place of slaughtering.

Only the priests could enter the Temple, and only the high priest could enter the holy of holies, and that only on the Day of Atonement (*m. Kelim* 1.9; cf. Heb. 9.25). The priests were divided into twenty-four "courses," each course serving twice a year for a week (see Luke 1.8). A veil of Babylonian tapestry hung in the opening to the nave (*War* 5.5.212); a second veil separated the nave from the holy of holies (219). It would seem that it was the outer veil that was torn at the time of the death of Jesus (Mark 15.38), since the inner veil would not be seen by bystanders.

There were eight gates leading into the Temple mount: one on the north, four on the west, two on the south, and one on the east (*Ant.* 15.11.410); the Mishnah says five [*Mid.* 1.3], naming only one on the west). Along the western wall was the deep central valley, with a paved walk that continued around the southern end of the Temple. A great staircase led up to the triple Huldah gate, and next to the stairs was a structure containing a large number of immersion pools for ceremonial cleansing (Hebr. *miqwā'ôt*). The worshiper, after his or her purification, entered the right of the two double gates and passed through a tunnel leading upward into the Temple area. A second entrance could be made by a large staircase that led to the royal stoa ("Robinson's Arch" marks this entrance), but no purification was available here. Leading from the western hill to the Temple mount was a bridge ("Wilson's Arch" marks this). Details of the other entrances are not clear; they were possibly located where Barclay's and Warren's Gates are now. The Tadi Gate was in the northern wall; possibly the sacrificial animals were brought in by this entrance, since it was near the Sheep Pool and Market. The Susa gate in the eastern wall was used only by the high priest and priests in connection with the ceremony of burning the red cow at a location on the Mount of olives from which the high priest could look directly into the entrance of the sanctuary.

Destruction of the Temple. There is a full account of the capture of Jerusalem in *War* 5–6, according to which Titus commissioned Josephus to urge the Jews to surrender in order to spare the Temple, but to no avail. The Antonia was razed to the ground in August 70 CE, and the continual sacrifice ceased to be offered. Josephus made a second appeal. Titus then decided to destroy the Temple. This occurred on the tenth day of the fifth month (Ab; according to Jewish tradition, the ninth of Ab), the same day on which the First Temple had been burned by the

Model of Herod's Temple in Jerusalem.

king of Babylon. Josephus portrays the Romans as trying to extinguish the fire that had been started by the insurgents. Widespread plundering, murder, and finally the burning of all structures on the Temple mount ended the history of the Temple.

WILLIAM SANFORD LASOR

TEN COMMANDMENTS. Also called the Decalogue ("the ten words"; see Exod. 34.28), the Ten Commandments comprise a short list of religious and ethical demands laid by the Deity on the people of ancient Israel and are of continuing authority for the religious Jewish community and the Christian community. They appear in two places in the Bible (Exod. 20.1–17 and Deut. 5.6–21) and are alluded to or quoted in part in several places in the Hebrew Bible and in the New Testament. The commandments prohibit the worship of any God other than Israel's God, held to be the true God of the other nations as well. They rule out the making of images of the Deity in any plastic form; the misuse of the divine Name and the power associated with it; and they require observance of the Sabbath day and the honoring of one's parents (especially in view are the elderly parents of adults, not the parents of young children). They also prohibit murder, adultery, stealing, false testimony (not primarily the telling of untruths in general), and the coveting of the life and goods of others.

The enumeration of the commandments varies among the religious communities. Worshiping other Gods and making images of the Deity are placed together in a number of religious communities (Jewish, Roman Catholic, Lutheran), while Reformed and Orthodox Christian communities treat these as the first two commandments. For the Jewish community, the first commandment is "I am the LORD your God who brought you out of the land of Egypt, out of the house of bondage," while the ninth and tenth commandments for Roman Catholic and Lutheran communions are the two prohibitions of coveting: the household (commandment 9) and the remainder of the list in Exod. 20.17 (commandment 10). The contents of the Ten Commandments are, however, the same for all of the religious communities, despite the differences in their enumeration. The differences between the contents of Exodus 20 and Deuteronomy 5 are quite small, reflecting changes over time in the way in which the commandments were understood and applied.

The commandments are of enormous value and influence—on the community of Israel, within the Christian community, and throughout the entire world today. The commandments fall into four groups. The first three, the commandments demanding the worship of God alone, against image-making, and against the use of God's name to do harm, are commandments stressing God's exclusive claim over the lives of the people. God will brook no rivalry; as Israel's savior, God demands a commitment that preserves the people from divided loyalties, protects them from supposing that anything in the whole of creation could adequately represent the Deity, the Creator of all, and also protects persons from the religious community's misuse of divine power to serve its own ends.

The next two commandments, calling for observing every seventh day as a day of rest and for honoring parents even when they might no longer be of significant economic value within the community, are special institutions for the protection of basic realities in society—human need for rest from labor as well as for labor and the preservation of human dignity against any kind of exploitation.

The next three commandments focus especially on the life of the individual or the family in the larger community. They insist on the sanctity of human life, the sanctity of marriage and of sexual life, and the necessity to maintain a community in which the extension of the self into one's property is recognized and respected.

The last two commandments are more social and public, calling for speaking the truth before the courts or the community's elders and for living a life not distorted or corrupted by the lust for other persons' goods or lives.

Moses is identified as the great lawgiver in ancient Israel. The Ten Commandments are understood by the community to have been handed down from God through Moses. It is clear, however, that the legal materials of the Hebrew Bible have developed over centuries, reflected changes in religious understanding and practice, and incorporated those changed perspectives into the legal heritage assigned to Moses and to Moses' God.

The substance of the Ten Commandments probably does originate in the work and discernments of Moses. The unique understanding of idolatry reflected in the Ten Commandments, and the requirement that one day in seven be characterized by an absolute break with the other days—by cessation from normal pursuits for a full day—these are without precedent in the ancient Near Eastern world. Other commandments are not unique, but this tenfold collection of short, primarily negative, statements is unique. It stems from a person of extraordinary religious discernment—and Moses was such a person.

The Ten Commandments probably had a place in family life, as a means by which the young were introduced to the

Moses with the Ten Commandments.

T

fundamental requirements of the covenant between God and people. They also had a place in public religious life and in the great festivals when the bond between people and God was regularly reaffirmed and confirmed.

The Ten Commandments were of great value as summations of the demands of God, easily remembered by reference to the ten fingers of the hand. As negative statements, they helped shape the community's recognition of those kinds of conduct that simply ruined life in community and so could not be allowed. They were not intended to be legalistic in character or in effect; they were to ward off conduct from the community that could be its ruin. Positive law must develop in association with these pithy, negatively put demands. Rather than such "dos and don'ts" encouraging oppressive control of a society by its leaders, they are a summons to a life freed to enjoy existence in community.

WALTER HARRELSON

THESSALONIANS, THE LETTERS OF PAUL TO THE. The New Testament includes two letters ascribed to Paul and addressed to the church at Thessalonica in Macedonia (Map 14:D2).

The first follows the normal pattern of Pauline letters in beginning with a formal greeting (1.1), followed by a report of how Paul remembers the church in his prayers; he thanks God for the positive response of its members to his initial preaching of the gospel (1.2–10). He then discusses this work in the town, claiming that he and his companions acted uprightly and lovingly (2.1–12). He returns to the topic of the church's warm response despite disincentives caused by those opposed to the spread of the gospel (2.13–16); his defense of his own conduct may be a reply to slanders current in the town. The continuation of opposition to the church since his departure had worried him so much that he had wished to go back to see how things were; finding this impossible for reasons that he does not divulge, beyond saying that "Satan blocked our way" (2.18), he sent Timothy as his representative, and the latter has now returned full of enthusiasm for the healthy state of the church (2.17–3.13). In the remainder of the letter, Paul gives the church the kind of teaching and practical advice that he would have liked to share with them in person. He encourages the believers to live holy lives—with special reference to the avoidance of sexual immorality—and to continue to grow in love (4.1–12). He gives instruction to comfort Christians who are fearful about the fate of those of their number who had died and assures them that, when the Lord returns, the resurrection of the dead will take place, so that those who "fell asleep" (NRSV: "died") will come with Christ and be united with those still alive. Believers need not worry when this will take place; if they are truly "awake," they will not be taken by surprise (4.13–5.11). Finally, Paul commends brotherly love and encourages the use of spiritual gifts (5.12–24), closing the letter with personal greetings (5.25–28).

The second letter follows the same pattern. The opening greeting (1.1–2) is followed by a prayer report, which also functions as encouragement and teaching: the church is still suffering from opposition, but is bearing it steadfastly, and Paul assures the believers that God will judge those who oppose them and will prepare the church to share in his glory when Christ comes (1.3–12). The center of the letter is teaching about the return of Christ, directed against people who were claiming Paul's authority for asserting that the day of the Lord had begun and that the return of Christ could be expected immediately. Paul replies by stating that a period of Satanic opposition to God on an unparalleled scale must first happen, and then Christ will come to bring it to an end; meanwhile, the church must hold firm (2.1–17). The final part of the letter is exhortation: the church is asked to pray for Paul, and attention is drawn to some Christians who had abandoned their daily work and were living off the generosity of their good-natured friends. Paul condemns this idleness and the consequent nuisance of the idlers strongly (3.1–16). There is a brief closing greeting (3.17–18).

Thessalonica was one of the towns in Macedonia that was visited by Paul, Silas, and Timothy during the second of the missionary tours described by Luke in Acts 16–18. It was in fact the capital of the Roman province, an important commercial center situated on the major highway, the Via Egnatia. Not surprisingly, its population included Jews (Acts 17.1, 5). Paul and his companions spent a brief time here after leaving Philippi, but sufficiently long to gain a number of converts from Jewish and Greek attenders at the synagogue and so to establish a church. According to Luke, Jewish opposition forced the missionaries to leave precipitately. They moved into Achaia and worked briefly at Athens and then for a longer period at Corinth. It was during this period that Timothy paid the visit mentioned in 1 Thessalonians 3.1–6, and that Paul wrote the first letter, doubtless from Corinth.

The history of the church between its foundation and the composition of the letter is known only from allusions in the letter. The picture that emerges is of a church free from groups opposed to Paul, and developing in faith and love. Certainly, Paul was worried about whether the church could stand up to attacks from outside, but this concern arose more from the recent foundation of the congregation than because of any inherent defects.

The major point where Paul felt the need to give instructions was the future advent (or parousia) of the Lord Jesus. It is unlikely that there were any false teachings; it appears rather that the Thessalonian Christians had not fully understood Paul's teaching about the parousia and the resurrection of the dead. The second coming of the Lord played a prominent part in Paul's preaching, for he refers to it with remarkable frequency in the letter (1.10; 2.19; 3.13; 4.13–5.11; 5.23). Otherwise, the letter reflects the typical characteristics of Paul's thought, including the distinctive use of the phrase "in Christ" to characterize the nature of the Christian life.

There is no doubt that Paul was the author of this letter. Theories that it is a forgery need not be taken seriously. Some scholars have argued that the letter has a peculiar shape, and attempt to explain it as a combination of two or more documents or as a document that had been subjected to interpolations, but these theories are more ingenious than convincing.

The second letter raises problems to which there are no generally agreed answers. Its language and content are sufficiently similar to those of 1 Thessalonians to indicate that, if authentic, it was probably written not long after the first letter. Yet it lacks concrete references to the situation of the readers or of the writer. From chap. 1, it appears that attack from outside must have worsened. The pungency of Paul's language may also suggest that he himself was the object of particular attack from people outside the church (see 3.2).

The situation behind chap. 2 is difficult to reconstruct. There must have been a group in the church who believed that they were living in the very last days. They appear to have been encouraged in this view by some statement that was alleged to have come from Paul himself. Paul, however, stopped short of affirming that the end had actually arrived, and he referred to other events that must happen before the return of the Lord. There is no unanimity as to what Paul envisaged by the apostasy and the man of lawlessness, or what he meant by the force that was at present restraining the lawless one from appearing (2 Thess. 2.9). The language used has a mythological character and may reflect apocalyptic literature in which a heavenly force restrains the powers of evil. But whether Paul used this language to refer to specific persons or beings is not certain. One view is that Paul saw the Roman emperor and/or empire as embodying the forces of law and order that restrained the forces of chaos from taking over. Another view, perhaps more persuasive, sees God himself or the preaching of the gospel as the force holding back the full impact of the forces of evil. Paul wrote allusively, even for his first readers, and therefore it is not surprising that we are at a loss to know precisely what he had in mind.

In the final part of the letter we find evidence that some members of the church were living in idleness at others' expense. Although no explicit connection is made, it is hard not to believe that the apocalyptic excitement reflected in chap. 2 contributed to this situation. It called forth strong censure from Paul, who firmly believed that Christians should work for their living. Apparently, discipline in the church consisted of exclusion from the privileges of fellowship.

These comments on 2 Thessalonians have been made in terms of the ostensible historical context of the document as a genuine letter from Paul to the church at Thessalonica. In this view, we must assume that in the period after the writing of 1 Thessalonians a kind of apocalyptic fervor, whose origins can be detected in the earlier letter, developed in the church. Paul does not deal with it in terms of castigating a group of opponents, as in other letters; rather, he writes to believers who may have been misled by a misinterpretation of his teaching.

Such a situation appears to be quite plausible. Yet it does not appear so to some commentators, for whom there is sharp contrast between the nearness of the parousia in 1 Thessalonians and its delay in 2 Thessalonians. This alerts them to other odd features in the latter, such as the lack of personal, concrete allusions, the peculiar repetition of phraseology from 1 Thessalonians, and some differences in language and thought. In the judgment of numerous scholars these differences are incompatible with the traditional understanding of the letter as authentically Pauline. Attempts to solve the problem by arguing that the letters were written in reverse chronological order or that they are compositions of fragments originally written in a different order have not commanded assent. So it is argued that 2 Thessalonians is a later composition by another writer who wished to use Paul's name to correct his teaching or false inferences from it, perhaps even to claim that this letter alone was authentic (cf. 3.17) and that 1 Thessalonians was to be rejected. A solution of this kind can be defended by concentrating on the unusual features of 2 Thessalonians. Its major weakness, however, is the lack of a convincing and plausible reconstruction of the circumstances in which such a letter could have been composed—and directed to Thessalonica in particular. The letter, for example, appears to assume that the Temple in Jerusalem is still standing (2.4). The language refuting the claim that the day of the Lord had already arrived is so cryptic that it is hard to envisage a later writer expressing himself in this fashion if he wanted to persuade his readers. The brazenness of the hypothetical author in writing 2 Thessalonians 3.17 is also remarkable. Although it must be granted that there are some oddities in

An engraving of a view of Salonica (ancient Thessalonica), Greece

the language, structure, and thought of the letter, the difficulties in considering it pseudonymous are greater.

I. HOWARD MARSHALL

TORAH. One of the basic concepts of biblical religion and rabbinic literature. The meaning of "torah" (Hebr. *tora*) is "instruction, teaching." "Torah" is often rendered "law," as consistently in the Septuagint, although Greek *nomos* had broader meaning than simply "law." This rendering has been deplored, but it has validity. For example, Exodus 12.49 reads, "There shall be one torah for the native and for the resident alien." Clearly the translator must render "torah" here as "law." "Law" is an extension of the basic meaning of "torah," for divine instruction assumes the force of law. In Leviticus and Numbers particularly, the individual divine laws are referred to as "torahs" (Hebr. *torot).* Underlying the biblical concept of Torah is another concept, one of these being a way of God that had to be followed, a concept that finds its fullest expression in the prophets and in the Psalms.

If the divinity is the promulgator of Torah as law, Torah in its broadest sense may be promulgated by kings, priests, wise men, and even wise women (Prov. 1.8; 6.20). Most significant historically is the promulgation of Torah through Moses, an idea found already in the Pentateuch, as in Deuteronomy 4.44: "This is the torah that Moses set before the Israelites." The tractate of the Mishnah known as "the Ethics of the Fathers" *(Pirqe 'Abot)* begins with the statement "Moses received the Torah at Mount Sinai," one of the fundamental precepts of rabbinic Judaism. Not only were the Ten Commandments given at Sinai, but, as we shall see, the Torah in a wider sense.

The development of the concept of Torah proceeded as follows: (1) the promulgation of individual divinely directed *tōrōt;* (2) the Torah of the divinely inspired figure of Moses; (3) a definite idea of Torah as the book of the Torah, which by the days of Ezra and Nehemiah meant the Pentateuch in an early form; (4) in the rabbinic period, the Torah as Pentateuch, in a form not unlike the Pentateuch of the present day. Rabbinic usage of the term was quite broad. It could refer to the five books of Moses or to the totality of divine revelation. It included two basic types of materials: legal (halakhic) and literary (aggadic), with the latter including everything from stories to poetry to nonlegal interpretation of biblical texts and more. The rabbis extended Torah to include another dichotomy: the written Torah and the oral Torah, the latter consisting of traditions that were transmitted orally until they were given written expression in the Mishnah, the basis of the Talmud (cf. the "Temple Scroll" from Qumran, which may have functioned as an additional book of Torah). Both Torahs were considered to have descended from heaven; there was even a rabbinic tradition that the Torah preexisted creation, and another that through it God effected creation (cf. Sir. 24.1–23; Prov. 9.22–31). Rabbinic Judaism stressed the joy of fulfilling the Torah's commandments; Torah observance ensured salvation. It is difficult to overstate the importance of Torah in early Judaism, an emphasis that has continued to the present.

In biblical tradition, the role of the king in relation to Torah is specified in Deuteronomy 17.18: "When he [the king] is seated on his royal throne, he shall have written for himself a copy of this torah on a book before the levitical priests." No king of Israel or Judah is known to have followed this law, with the partial exception of Josiah, who read the book without actually having it written out (2 Kings 23.3). The king's role in relation to Torah is hinted

Page from the Mishneh Torah, systematic code of Jewish law written by Maimonides (1135–1204) in 1180. The words at the top are "How I love your Torah; it is my meditation all day long" (Ps. 119.97).

at in the lament of Lamentations 2.9: "Her king and her princes are among the nations; there is no torah." Priests as well are upholders of God's Torah and its interpreters as part of their everyday functions (Jer. 18.18; Hag. 2.11–13). The prophets too were greatly concerned with Torah, especially when the people failed to follow the divine way (Isa. 1.10; 5.24; Jer. 2.8; 9.12). Malachi 4.4 is the only prophetic reference to the Torah of Moses, showing that the early conception of Torah as direct divine teaching had precedence for the prophets over the concept of the Mosaic Torah.

The earliest Christian attitudes toward Torah were ambivalent. One view is found in Jesus' saying in Matthew 5.17: "Do not think that I have come to abolish the law or the prophets; I have come not to abolish but to fulfill. For truly I tell you, until heaven and earth pass away, not one letter, not one stroke of a letter, will pass from the law until all is accomplished." But this clear-cut and positive view is not that of the entire New Testament. Paul, though expressing the belief that the law may be fulfilled through love (Rom. 13.8–10), also asserts that "a person is justified not by the works of the law but through faith in Jesus Christ" (Gal. 2.16) and that "the power of sin is the law" (1 Cor. 15.56). With these radical doctrines, Paul was able to sever the Judaic umbilical cord and to set Christianity on its present track.

PHILIP STERN

TRIBES OF ISRAEL. The Hebrew Bible in its final form takes it for granted that the Israelite people is descended from the twelve sons of Jacob, each being the ancestor of the tribe named after him (1 Kings 18.31). This tradition

Manasseh (697–642 BCE) Amon (642–640 BCE) and Josiah (640-609 BCE) (engraving)

the books of Joshua and Judges preserve traditions of the early history of some of the tribes during and after their settlement in Canaan. Some of these passages (especially Judg. 1) suggest that the tribes, rather than conquering and settling the entire country as a united people (the impression given by the book of Joshua in its present form), possessed no military or political unity at the time of the settlement, but were independent units each making its way into the country, in some cases encountering opposition from the local population.

There can be little doubt that the concept of Israel as a close-knit family of twelve tribes acting in concert before, during, and after the settlement in Canaan is an elaboration of a later period. Although the tribes probably entered the country from outside, they did so for the most part in a piecemeal way, over a long period of time; the people of Israel was in fact constituted for the first time on Canaanite soil. Indeed, some of the tribes, such as Ephraim and Judah, appear to have acquired their names after their arrival in Canaan.

Little is known of the lives of the tribes after their arrival in Canaan, and of the process by which they may have moved toward some kind of national consciousness before the institution of the monarchy; scholarly opinions differ widely. Two groups, Judah (which seems to have been composed of several originally distinct elements) in the south, and the "house of Joseph" (which at some point constituted two distinct tribes, Ephraim and Manasseh) in the central highlands, seem to have been especially prominent. Less is known of the history of the other tribes further north and to the east of the Jordan, with the exception of Dan, which moved, probably under Philistine pressure, from its original territory to the extreme north of the country (Judg. 18; compare chaps. 13–16). The tribe of Levi is an enigma. According to some traditions (Num. 1.47–54; Deut. 10.8–9; 18.1–2; 33.8–11; Josh. 13.14, 33) it was distinguished from all other tribes in that it was given no territorial rights but had special sacerdotal functions that entitled it to material support from the other tribes, among whom its members moved. In other passages (Gen. 34.25–31 and 49.5–7), however, it is portrayed as being on the same footing as the other tribes.

It is important to realize that the word "tribe" does not necessarily suggest a nomadic or seminomadic existence or origin: in the ancient Near East and elsewhere, it frequently denotes a territorial group of settled agricultural or even urban people who claim a common ancestry. Moreover, despite the impression given by many passages in the Bible, the tribe was not the basic social or economic unit in Israel in either premonarchic or later times; the basic units were the family and the village, which were bound together by local agricultural and other common concerns. The larger

has persisted into later times. The book of Genesis records the births of Jacob's twelve sons (chaps. 29–35), and then provides a list of them arranged under the names of their mothers: Reuben, Simeon, Levi, Judah, Issachar, and Zebulun were the sons of Leah; Joseph and Benjamin the sons of Rachel; Dan and Naphtali the sons of Jacob's concubine Bilhah; Gad and Asher the sons of his concubine Zilpah (35.22–26). After Joseph, in Egypt, brought his family from Canaan (Gen. 46–47), the twelve brothers and their families continued to reside in Egypt and there increased in numbers, becoming the people of Israel, literally the "sons of Israel" (Exod. 1.1–7), Jacob's name having been changed by God to Israel (Gen. 32.28; 35.10). This united people, after many vicissitudes, took possession of the land of Canaan and established their home there, with each tribe assigned its own territory (Josh. 13–19; Map 3).

The Bible is, however, not consistent with regard to either the number or the names of the tribes. In the numerous tribal lists found in the various books of the Bible, the number varies from eleven to thirteen. These variations are mainly due to the appearance in some lists of the two sons of Joseph, Ephraim and Manasseh (Gen. 48.8–20) as separate tribes, and to the omission of Simeon or Levi from others. In the Song of Deborah (Judg. 5), which is not necessarily a complete roll call of the tribes, Judah and Gad are missing, while Machir, the son of Manasseh (Josh. 17.1) appears to take the place of his "father." The variations are presumed to reflect fluctuations in the constitution and history of the tribes and their relative size and importance.

Very little is known of the early history of the tribes. The "blessing of Jacob" (Gen. 49) and the "blessing of Moses" (Deut. 33) contain some very ancient, but also very cryptic, allusions to early tribal events and characteristics, but these passages have also undergone later expansions and editing, especially in the blessing of Judah (Gen. 49.8–12), which is a "prophecy" of the kingdom of David, and that of Joseph (Deut. 33.13–17), which reflects the special prominence at some time of the tribes of Ephraim and Manasseh. Parts of body, the tribe, was a much looser unit whose main function was apparently, in the period before the monarchy, to provide a militia in times of danger. With the advent of the monarchy, the tribes lost this function and were henceforth little more than a means of genealogical identification. The division of the kingdom after the death of Solomon was a political rather than a tribal matter.

R. N. WHYBRAY

TRINITY. Because the Trinity is such an important part of later Christian doctrine, it is striking that the term does not appear in the New Testament. Likewise, the developed concept of three coequal partners in the Godhead found in later creedal formulations cannot be clearly detected within the confines of the canon.

Later believers systematized the diverse references to God, Jesus, and the Spirit found in the New Testament in order to fight against heretical tendencies of how the three are related. Elaboration on the concept of a Trinity also serves to defend the church against charges of di- or tritheism. Since the Christians have come to worship Jesus as a god (Pliny, *Epistles* 96.7), how can they claim to be continuing the monotheistic tradition of the God of Israel? Various answers are suggested, debated, and rejected as heretical, but the idea of a Trinity—one God subsisting in three persons and one substance—ultimately prevails.

While the New Testament writers say a great deal about God, Jesus, and the Spirit of each, no New Testament writer expounds on the relationship among the three in the detail that later Christian writers do.

The earliest New Testament evidence for a tripartite formula comes in 2 Corinthians 13.13, where Paul wishes that "the grace of the Lord Jesus, the love of God, and the communion of the Holy Spirit" be with the people of Corinth. It is possible that this three-part formula derives from later liturgical usage and was added to the text of 2 Corinthians as it was copied. In support of the authenticity of the passage, however, it must be said that the phrasing is much closer to Paul's understandings of God, Jesus, and the Holy Spirit than to a more fully developed concept of the Trinity. Jesus, referred to not as Son but as Lord and Christ, is mentioned first and is connected with the central Pauline theme of grace. God is referred to as a source of love, not as father, and the Spirit promotes sharing within the community. The word "holy" does not appear before "spirit" in the earliest manuscript evidence for this passage.

A more familiar formulation is found in Matthew 28.19, where Jesus commands the disciples to go out and baptize "in the name of the Father and of the Son and of the Holy Spirit." The phrasing probably reflects baptismal practice in churches at Matthew's time or later if the line is interpolated. Elsewhere Matthew records a special connection between God the Father and Jesus the Son (e.g., 11.27), but he falls short of claiming that Jesus is equal with God (cf. 24.36).

It is John's gospel that suggests the idea of equality between Jesus and God ("I and the Father are one;" 10.30). The Gospel starts with the affirmation that in the beginning Jesus as Word "was with God and . . . was God" (1.1), and ends (chap. 21 is most likely a later addition) with Thomas's confession of faith to Jesus, "My Lord and my God!" (20.28). The Fourth Gospel also elaborates on the role of the Holy Spirit as the Paraclete sent to be an advocate for the believers (John 14.15–26).

For the community of John's gospel, these passages provide assurance of the presence and power of God both in the ministry of Jesus and in the ongoing life of the community. Beyond this immediate context, however, such references raise the question of how Father, Son, and Spirit can be distinct and yet the same. This issue is debated over the following centuries and is only resolved by agreement and exclusion during the christological disputes and creedal councils of the fourth century and beyond.

While there are other New Testament texts where God, Jesus, and the Spirit are referred to in the same passage (e.g., Jude 20–21), it is important to avoid reading the Trinity into places where it does not appear. An example is 1 Peter

The Holy Trinity in the high altar of the Compania de Jesus church in Quito. The building of the church started in 1605, and it took 160 years to be finished.

Baptism of Christ, surrounded by Twelve Apostles

1.1–2, in which the salutation is addressed to those who have been chosen "according to the foreknowledge of God the Father in holiness of spirit." This reference may be to the holiness of spirit of the believers, but translators consistently take it as the Holy Spirit in order to complete the assumed trinitarian character of the verse: "who have been chosen and destined by God the Father and sanctified by the Spirit" (**NRSV**). This translation not only imposes later trinitarian perspectives on the text but also diminishes the important use of the spirit of human beings elsewhere in 1 Peter (e.g., 3.4, 19).

DANIEL N. SCHOWALTER

TWELVE, THE. "The twelve" is an expression employed by all the Gospel writers, and once by Paul (1 Cor. 15.5), to denote an inner, more intimate circle of followers of Jesus. They are listed by name in Matthew 10.2–4, Mark 3.1619, Luke 6.14–16, and Acts 1.13, and although these lists do not always agree in either the names or their order, the reader is always told that Jesus chose twelve disciples in particular. While these twelve are disciples, they are further distinguished by the designation "the twelve." This is especially the case in Acts 6.1–2, where the disciples and the twelve are juxtaposed; the latter are clearly the authorities in the story. As readers, we know who the twelve are, including Judas Iscariot—a point stressed by all the authors, and we see that they are the recipients of special instruction, have certain expectations from Jesus, and bear the burden of gathering the community of his followers together after the upheaval of the crucifixion and resurrection.

Whether the names and the widespread agreement among the Gospel writers about the number twelve are historical facts is difficult to say. Did Jesus really call twelve followers initially who then called others? This is possible. Did Jesus consciously act as if he were establishing the new Israel by selecting twelve representatives? The symbolic significance of the number twelve is difficult to miss. But there are others in the story who are just as close or closer to him than the twelve, such as some women and others who are called disciples. The twelve do get special teaching; perhaps Jesus was training leaders to carry on in his stead. In Mark, however, the twelve hardly understand anything; the special teaching apparently does not pay off. The roles of the disciples and the twelve are so important in the stories, and they have received so much attention from both the authors and the interpreters, that what actually transpired historically is impossible to retrieve. Matthew himself, for example, uses the terms disciple, apostle, and the twelve interchangeably in chap. 10, as if these were all equivalent or the distinctions were needless.

The symbolism of the number twelve was certainly clear to the authors, and it has not been lost on subsequent interpreters. A program of the renewal if not the reconstitution of Israel by the Jesus movement is strongly suggested by the number itself, as well as the collection of twelve baskets at the multiplication of the loaves and fishes (Matt. 14.20 par; John 6.13), the portrayal of the disciples sitting on twelve thrones judging Israel (Matt. 19.28; cf. Luke 22.30), and the repeated use of the number twelve in the book of Revelation (7.5–8; 12.1; 21.12–14; 21.21; 22.2). The usurpation of Israel's symbols and heroic figures along with Israel's scriptures and myths, and in particular use of the potent symbol twelve, points in this direction for early Christianity. Ultimately, however, the church claimed through Melito, Justin, and others to be a "third race" and not the renewed Israel the number twelve suggested.

J. ANDREW OVERMAN

VIRGIN BIRTH OF CHRIST. As a major tenet of Roman Catholic teaching and a foundation for fundamentalist belief, the virgin birth remains an essential doctrine for many Christians. Since the advent of modern historical criticism, however, others have been skeptical about the virgin birth. Ultimately, the issue will be decided by a person's faith stance and view of scripture.

Belief in the virgin birth of Christ is based on the stories of Jesus' birth found in the gospels of Matthew and Luke. In Luke 1.5–38, shortly after Elizabeth miraculously conceives in her old age, the angel Gabriel appears to Mary who is specifically described as a virgin (Grk. *parthenos*). He tells Mary that she will conceive and bear a son who will inherit the throne of David. Mary, surprised by this news, asks "How can this be, since I do not know a man?" Gabriel reassures her that she will be impregnated by the Holy Spirit and cites as proof the fact that Elizabeth is now with child. There is no confusion possible in Luke's account. The author wants it to be clear that this is a miraculous impregnation of a woman who had not had sexual relations. The detailed nature of this dialogue between Mary and Gabriel suggests that the author of Luke was responding to specific questions about the virgin birth of Christ. Luke also alludes to the virgin birth in his genealogy of Jesus when he says that Jesus was "the son (as was supposed) of Joseph" (Luke 3.23).

Matthew 1.18–25 takes the tradition about Jesus' miraculous conception and develops it in a slightly different way. The angel, who is not named, appears not to Mary but to Joseph, who has discovered that Mary is pregnant. Although Joseph plans to break off his engagement, the angel commands him to go through with the marriage since the child is from the Holy Spirit. As in Luke, Matthew wishes to make it clear that Mary and Joseph had not had sexual relations prior to this announcement (1.18). In fact, the author stresses that Joseph "did not know her until she had borne a son" (Matt. 1.25).

The author of Matthew often attempts to prove that Jesus is the Messiah by showing how the details of his life fulfill the Hebrew scriptures. In this case, Matthew presents a passage from Isaiah 7 in which the prophet is speaking to Ahaz, king of Judah. Ahaz faces attack from the forces of Syria and Israel (734 BCE), and so he is contemplating an alliance with the king of Assyria. God makes it clear to Ahaz that such an alliance should not take place. Isaiah declares that the Lord will provide a sign that will make known the Lord's will in spite of Ahaz's recalcitrance. A young woman who is pregnant will bear a son, and before that child is old enough to tell the difference between good and evil, the powers that threaten Judah will be defeated. Ahaz refuses to believe the sign and sends tribute to the Assyrian king who destroys Damascus and kills the king of Syria (2 Kings 16.9). The other threatening force, Israel, is conquered by Assyria twelve years after the occasion of this sign at about the time that the child mentioned in the sign would have reached the age of maturity.

Isaiah's intent in discussing this child is clearly to set a time frame for the destruction of Israel. There is nothing miraculous about the mother or the conception process. The Hebrew word used, *'almâ*, means simply "young woman," without any implication of virginity. The Greek word *parthenos* used to translate *'almâ* can mean either a young woman or a virgin. Matthew used a Greek Bible, so he naturally reinterpreted Isaiah 7:14 as a prophecy referring to the virgin birth of Jesus. For the evangelist, Isaiah's original meaning was superseded by the identification of Jesus as Immanuel (Grk. *Emmanouēl*).

One of the most frequently raised objections to the virgin birth is that, with the exception of Matthew and Luke, New Testament authors do not make explicit mention of it. Other alleged references are at best vague allusions (Mark 6.3; John 1.13–14; 6.42). Such an argument from silence cannot be determinative, but it is an important consideration for people who see the virgin birth as a feature created within the early traditions about Jesus rather than a historical occurrence.

Those who doubt the historicity of the virgin birth argue that it was created by the early church as a way of honoring the coming of Jesus as the Son of God or of explaining the idea of God becoming flesh. Miraculous human birth stories are common in biblical tradition, going back to Abraham and Sarah (Gen. 17.15–19, 18.9–15, 21.1–7), and numerous references to deities impregnating women are found within the Greco-Roman tradition. The mother of Heracles, for instance, was said to have been impregnated by Zeus (Diodorus Siculus, 4.9,1–10).

Affirmation of the virgin birth by the apostolic father Ignatius (*Smyrneans* 1) confirms that the concept was an early and strongly held belief. As Christian doctrine developed, the virgin birth became a preeminent statement of faith and the ultimate test of belief in biblical inerrancy. It was also expanded in several directions. The veneration of Mary is related to the virgin birth, as is the tradition that Mary was ever virgin. Belief in this latter concept requires that the brothers and sisters of Jesus mentioned in the New Testament must have been stepbrothers and stepsisters or cousins. Mary's virginity also becomes an important factor in ascetic Christianity and in the promotion of a life of celibacy.

DANIEL N. SCHOWALTER

WIDOWS. The term "widow," the usual translation of Hebrew 'almānâ and Greek *chēra*, has a more specific meaning in the biblical texts than the English word conveys. The woman designated by these terms was not merely someone whose husband had died; she lived outside of the normal social structure in which every female lived under the authority of some male; she was responsible to and for herself.

The structure of ancient society was kinship-based and patriarchal. Marriage within this society represented a contract made between two families rather than between two individuals. When a woman married, she passed from the authority of her father's household to the authority of her husband's household. When her husband died, her status was determined in relation to the surviving members of his household.

Biblical law provided for a woman of childbearing age whose husband had died without male issue. By means of a levirate marriage (Deut. 25.5–10) the dead man's wife was given to a relative of the husband's family in order that a child be produced to inherit the dead husband's estate. This practice not only provided for inheritance rights but also secured the well-being of the woman. However, a man could legally refuse to carry out this obligation. For example, concern for the diminution of his own inheritance might prompt the

Jesus and the widow, the lesson of which is to be rich in good works and ready to give (Mark 12.41–44)

dead husband's relative to forgo a levirate marriage. The stories of Tamar, Judah's daughter-in-law who was temporarily an 'almānâ, and Ruth illustrate the implementation of levirate marriage (Gen. 38; Ruth).

While the Hebrew Bible identifies certain women as 'almānôt (plural of 'almānâ; 1 Kings 7.14; 11.26; 17) and specifies their distinctive clothing (Gen 38.19; 2 Sam. 14.5), its depiction of them is sketchy. Laws from ancient Mesopotamia provide some details. In the Middle Assyrian Laws, the *almattu* (cognate with 'almānâ) emerges as a woman whose husband and father-in-law were deceased, and who had no son capable of providing for her. A woman in this state was issued a document verifying her new status, and henceforth could act on her own. Presumably, the document gave her access to a society that normally excluded women from the public sphere.

There is evidence that the biblical 'almānâ may have been similar to the Mesopotamian *almattu*. That she was a woman living beyond male authority is illustrated by the law regarding women's vows (Num. 30.1–15): while the validity of a vow made by a woman depended ordinarily upon the approval of either her father or her husband, the validity of an 'almānâ's vow stood on its own (Num. 30.10).

The 'almānâ's independence from male authority was at the same time a sign of her precarious social position. In more than half of its occurrences, the 'almānâ is linked with the orphan or with the orphan and the client. Existing outside of the normal social structure, these three groups were susceptible to oppression, injustice, and exploitation. Because the 'almānâ had no male protector, Yahweh was pictured as her primary defender and every Israelite was supposed to treat her justly. The Bible legislates the protection and support of the 'almānâ and exhorts against oppressing her. Prophetic texts claim that the welfare of the defenseless 'almānâ, orphan, and alien was the measure by which Yahweh determined the moral fiber of his people. The vulnerability and isolation of the 'almānâ suggested a metaphorical use of the term, and prophetic texts (Isa. 47.8–9; 54.4; Jer. 51.5; Lam. 1.1) describe a vulnerable city (Babylon, Jerusalem) or land (Israel, Judah) as an 'almānâ.

The vulnerable and unconventional social position of the 'almānâ is also evident in laws regulating the priesthood. The affiliation of a priest with such a woman was a source of concern. While Leviticus 21.14 implicitly permits a priest to marry an 'almānâ but forbids a high priest from doing so, in Ezekiel 44.22 no priest is allowed to marry an 'almānâ unless her husband had been a priest. Other legislation (Lev. 22.13) permits a priest's daughter who is an 'almānâ to eat at his table.

From the mention of the widow (Grk. *chēra*) in the Gospels (Mark 12.40, 42–44 par.; Luke 7.12; 18.3–5), it is evident that the Hebrew 'almānâ's precarious and threatened existence persisted into the first century CE. Early Christianity singled out widows as recipients of social welfare,

W

establishing an organized means of caring for this group of women. In the Jerusalem church, a food distribution program is specified (Acts 6.1). 1 Timothy 5 mentions an official list of widows with eligibility requirements that included age and certain religious and moral behavior in addition to the absence of a responsible family member.

PAULA S. HIEBERT

WOMEN. *This entry on the roles and status of women consists of four articles:*

An Overview
Ancient Near East and Israel
Second Temple Period
Early Christianity

The introductory article is an overview of the status of women in biblical times, and the remaining articles are more detailed discussions of women in the Ancient Near East and Israel, *in Judaism of the* Second Temple Period, *and in* Early Christianity. *Related discussion is found in entries on individual women named in the Bible.*

An Overview

Before the Babylonian exile in 587/586 BCE, women in Israel enjoyed a status and freedom comparable to that of men. Israel lived in a patriarchal world, but her society was always informed by a faith that gave equality to women in the eyes of God. Thus, the woman is understood in the tenth-century BCE story of Genesis 2.18 as the necessary complement of the man and as his helper in a relationship of mutual companionship (cf. Mal. 2.14) and assistance, just as male and female both are necessary to the image of God in the sixth-century BCE account of Genesis 1.27. The subordination of women to men is considered to be the result of human sin (Gen. 3), and the subsequent practice of polygamy (Gen. 4.19) is a manifestation of the spread of sin.

Women are found serving as prophets (Exod. 15.20; 2 Kings 22.14–20), judges (Judg. 4–5), and queens (1 Kings 19; 2 Kings 11) in preexilic Israel. They are never excluded from the worship of God (Deut. 16.13 14; 1 Sam. 1–2). They are sometimes honored as models of wisdom (2 Sam. 14; 20.16–22). The honor of mothers ranks with that of fathers in Israel's basic law, the Ten Commandments (Exod. 20.12; Deut. 5.16). The family rights of wives and mothers are protected by law (Gen. 16.5–6; 38). The woman who engages in profitable commercial enterprises, who teaches with wisdom, and who serves the community through deeds of charity is honored as an ideal (Prov. 31.10–31).

Though single females lived under the authority of their fathers in Israel, love and choice in marriage were known (Gen. 24.57, 67; 29.20), and the woman was never considered a piece of property to be bartered. Sexual love was celebrated as a gift of God (Gen. 2.23; Song of Solomon), and the marital relationship was so prized that it could serve as a metaphor of the love between God and his covenant people (Jer. 2.2; Hos. 2.14–20)—an impossibility if marriage had been a repressive relationship for the woman.

Those preexilic stories in the Bible that exhibit cruelty toward women and treat them as objects of degradation reflect the environment in which Israel lived and are intended as protests against it (Gen. 19.8; Judg. 11; 19.22–30).

When Israel was carried into Babylonian exile, her priests in exile determined that they would draw up a plan for Israel's life that would ensure that she would never again be judged by God. They therefore collected together and wrote priestly legislation that would ensure Israel's ritual

Mosaic of the Woman of Samaria (John 4.7) in Sicily, Italy

and social purity. At the same time, they emphasized the importance of circumcision as a sign of the covenant (Gen. 17). This emphasis brought sexuality into the realm of the cult and related females to the covenant community only through their males. The blood of the sacrifice on the altar became the means of atonement for sin (Lev. 10.17–18; 16; 17.10–11), and blood outside of the cult became ritually unclean (Gen. 9.4). Thus, women were excluded from the cult during their menstruation (Lev. 15.19–31) and childbirth (Lev. 12.2–5). Indeed, they were increasingly segregated in worship and society. They had access to the holy only through their males. A woman's court was added to the Temple to distance them from the sanctuary. Their vows to God were no longer considered as valuable as those of males (Num. 27.1–8), and a husband could annul the vow of his wife (Num. 30.1–5). In the Second Temple period, women were excluded from testifying in a court trial; they were not to be seen in public or to speak with strangers, and outside their homes they were to be doubly veiled. They could not even teach or be taught the Torah in their homes a far cry from that time when Huldah the prophet interpreted Deuteronomy for King Josiah (2 Kings 22.14–20)—and they were not to be educated. They had become second-class Jews, excluded from the worship and teaching of God, with status scarcely above that of slaves.

The actions of Jesus of Nazareth toward women were therefore revolutionary. He did not hesitate to engage even unclean foreign women in public conversation (John 4.27). He ignored all strictures of ritual impurity (Mark 5.25–34, 35–43). He himself taught women (Luke 10.38–42), gave them an equal rank with men as daughters of Abraham (Luke 13.10–17), openly ministered to them as "children of wisdom" (Luke 7.35–50), and afforded them the highest respect as persons (Matt. 5.28). Women belonged to the inner circle of the disciples (Luke 8.1–3), and they are attested as the first witnesses of the resurrection (Luke 24.1–11; John 20.18). The Fourth Gospel begins and ends with the testimony of a woman to the Christ (John 4.29; 20.18).

Women therefore played a leading role in earliest Christianity, being baptized and receiving the Spirit (Acts 2.17; 5.14; 8.12; 16.15), doing acts of charity (9.36), suffering imprisonment for their faith (8.3; 9.1–2), and serving as ministers of the church (Rom. 16.1–7). They were allowed to preach and to pray in worship (1 Cor. 11.5), as well as to prophesy (Acts 21.8–9) and to teach (18.25–26). Their equal status in Christ was strongly affirmed by Paul, who considered the ancient subordination of women in Genesis 3.16 to have been overcome by Christ (Gal. 3.27–28). When Paul was faced with the misuse of Christian freedom in his churches, however, he could revert to his Pharisaic background to silence both contentious men and women in his congregations (1 Cor. 14.28, 33–36).

As Christianity spread through the Roman world of the late first and early second centuries CE, it faced the necessity of consolidating its doctrine and regularizing its polity, over against judaizers and gnostics. Unfortunately, in an alien environment, the church bought these developments at the price of the freedom of females. Because some women fell prey to gnostic teachings, they were forbidden leadership in some churches, on the basis of rabbinic interpretations of the scriptures (1 Tim. 2.11–15; 2 Tim. 3.6–9; Tit. 2.1–10). Patriarchal patterns of marriage reasserted themselves (1 Pet. 3.1–6; Col. 3.18), though these were often tempered by a high view of marriage and of the mutual subjection of both husband and wife to Christ (Eph. 5.21–33). Most importantly, political power struggles for control of ecclesiastical districts (cf. 3 John) led to the formation of a male hierarchy in the church that often continues to this day, in opposition to the witness of much of the Bible.

ELIZABETH ACHTEMEIER

Ancient Near East and Israel

The images of women in the Bible were shaped by literary genres and colored by historical circumstances and political ideologies. Furthermore, over the last two and a half millennia the Bible has accumulated additional resonances from the religious traditions that take it as a foundation. In essence, however, the Bible is an ancient Near Eastern document and can best be studied and understood in that context.

Women and the Family. Family and family ties determined the status and fate of women as well as men. An Israelite man or woman's formal name customarily included the name of the father (2 Sam. 20.1; 21.8); alternatively, a woman might be referred to as "PN (personal name) the wife of PN" (Judg. 4.4). Children were subject to their father (but see Deut. 21.18–21; Exod. 21.15) until the parents arranged for their marriage (e.g., Isaac in Gen. 24; Rachel and Leah in Gen. 29). Nevertheless, love poetry from Mesopotamia, Egypt, and Israel (the Song of Solomon) implies that children may have had some influence on their parents' selection. At her marriage the Israelite bride moved to her husband's household (Gen. 24) and was thenceforth subject to him.

The strains in a society so rooted in the family are occasionally apparent in the Bible. The outrages against Hagar (Gen. 16; 21), Dinah (Gen. 34), and the two Tamars (Gen. 38; 1 Kings 13) arise partly out of the sexual dynamics of the family. A childless widow had little autonomy and was supposed to return to her father's house (Lev. 22.13; but

cf. Ruth 1.8). Widows with sons, divorced women (Num. 30.9), and prostitutes (Josh. 6.22) were probably less dependent on male authority, but if they were poor, their lives could become precarious in the absence of a related male protector (Ruth 1.4–6).

The Bible reflects Israel's double standard in its attitude toward male and female sexuality. Virginity was required of the bride but not of the groom (Deut. 22.13–21); by contrast, in Babylon before the sixth century BCE the bride's virginity was not an important part of marriage agreements. Husbands were free to visit prostitutes even as they enjoyed exclusive rights to their wives' sexuality. In Israel adultery with a married woman meant death for both offenders (Lev. 20.10; Exod. 20.14; Deut. 22.22), but a man who raped an unbetrothed virgin was simply compelled to marry her (Deut. 22.28–29; Exod. 22.16–17; cf. 2 Sam. 13.15–16). Deuteronomy 24.1–4 implies that only men initiated divorces (cf. Jer. 3.8; Isa. 50.1). In only one book of the Bible, the Song of Solomon, are male and female sexuality described in an equally positive manner.

The limitations placed on ancient Near Eastern women can be regarded in part as a function of patrilineal systems that try to keep children and property within the family, rather than as an example of low female status. Families usually traced their genealogies through the male line, with sons inheriting the bulk of the father's property. The biblical term for the family household, "the father's house" (Exod. 6.14; Num. 1.2), reflects the priority of the paternal family line. A wife suspected of infidelity thus threatened more than just the husband's honor; the identity of her children could no longer be securely tied to the husband and his lineage.

When there were no sons, daughters could play a role in preserving the integrity of the family property. At Nuzi in eastern Assyria and at Emar in Syria, a father without sons could declare his daughter legally a son and heir. Similarly, Numbers 36 provides for the daughters of Zelophehad to inherit their father's estate (cf. Job 42.15), but with the qualification that they must marry within their father's clan. The fact that the patriarchs were related to their spouses may be a reflex of these sorts of concerns.

It is not surprising that most biblical references to women concern mothers. Whereas Abraham's servant enumerates his master's greatness in terms of property (Gen. 24.35), Sarah's prominence comes from being potentially, then actually, Isaac's mother. Rachel (Gen. 29.31–30.24; 35.16–20) and Hannah (1 Sam. 1) suffer for their apparent sterility. The only stipulation in the Ten Commandments that treats women and men equally is the command to honor both father and mother (Exod. 20.12; Deut. 5.16; cf. Lev. 20.9; Prov. 30.17).

The Bible's focus on male-dominated institutions and values ignores the details of a woman's everyday life in the home. Although the Bible portrays men and women preparing food (Gen. 18.6–7; Gen. 27), it is assumed that women did the cooking for their families. Mothers provided the primary care and nurture for children until they were weaned at about three years old (1 Sam. 1.22, 24). From Proverbs 1.8 and 31.1 and by ethnographic analogy, it appears that mothers were also responsible for the socialization and much of the moral education of their small children (Prov. 6.20).

Mothers are particularly prominent in one of the most familiar biblical stories, that of the miraculous birth of a son to a sterile mother. Despite its primary focus on God and the child, the genre is careful to mark the mother as special. For example, Pharaoh, the most powerful man in the world, cannot resist Sarah's beauty (Gen. 12.12–20; cf. the similar stories of Rachel, Gen. 29.10–30; 31.19, 34–37; Samson's mother, Judg. 13.1–20; and Hannah, 1 Sam. 1.9–2.10). This theme reappears in the Gospel accounts of Elizabeth (Luke 1) and of Mary (Luke 1.26–56; Matt. 1.18–25), whose virginity, rather than sterility, serves to imply that Jesus' birth is the most miraculous of all.

Social Patterns and Female Power. By combining ethnography and archaeology, scholars are reassessing the nature of the premonarchic Israelite community (1200–1000 BCE) and of women's roles in this period. The pattern of complex households in small villages was probably a response to the labor needs generated by early Israel's agrarian environment. Micah's household (Judg. 17–18), with living units occupied by Micah, his mother, his sons (and perhaps their wives), a hired priest, and servants, mirrors the archaeological evidence. Because each household member made a crucial contribution to the household, there was greater scope for women to exercise informal authority (Gen. 25.28; 27.5–17, 42–46; 28.4, 6–7; 1 Sam. 1.22–28; 2 Sam. 25; 2 Kings 4.8–10; 8.8). Indeed, the Bible accepts as normative the phenomenon of wives counseling and influencing their husbands (e.g., Eve; Samson's mother; Abigail; the Shunammite woman; Job's wife).

Samuel is reported to have predicted in the late eleventh century BCE that kingship would break up the rural family and disrupt old patterns of formal and informal family authority (1 Sam. 8.11–13). And, in fact, small freeholds did give way to landed estates (1 Sam. 8.14; 1 Kings 21; Isa. 5.8), although Israel's economy remained agriculturally based, and rural women probably influenced their families more than their urban counterparts. Urban male-dominated royal, military, economic, and religious institutions took the lead in shaping Israelite culture and defining its norms and values. The Bible is rooted in these institutions; this explains why so much of Israelite women's lives, experiences, and values have remained hidden and inaccessible.

Women's Legal Status. Cuneiform tablets show that wealthy Mesopotamian wives and widows throughout history made business contracts and appeared in court as plaintiffs, defendants, and witnesses. They borrowed and lent money, and bought and sold property. Almost always, however, the woman is acting in concert with or on behalf of her husband or another male family member. In Egypt, women from different social strata engaged in litigation and owned houses and fields, which they seem to have been able to bequeath as they liked (but usually within the family).

Israelite seals and seal impressions with women's names provide important evidence that in Israel, as in Mesopotamia and Egypt, women had the right to sign documents, a fact that the Bible never hints at. Relatively egalitarian ideals underlie the old laws of Exodus 21.26–32, where a value is placed on an injury irrespective of the sex of the injured party. But casuistic laws that begin "If a man . . ." usually refer to the man with the Hebrew word ʾîš ("a male") rather than with the generic ʾādām ("human being"). When an occasional law clearly applies to both men and women, ʾiššâ ("woman") may be added (Lev. 13.38; Num. 6.2). Apodictic laws are declared in second person masculine verb forms and may implicitly exclude women, as do many collective social terms. For example, in Exodus 19.14 Moses returns to "the people," who in the next verse are ordered to stay away from women (cf. 2 Sam. 5.1; 19.15; 1 Kings 12.1; 2 Kings 21.24).

Ruth in the Fields (Ruth 2.1–3)

Women's Activities Outside the Home. Besides being wives, concubines, and mothers, the Bible shows women working in the fields (Ruth 2.21–23), fetching water (Gen. 24.11, 15), and tending flocks (Gen. 29.9, Exod. 2.16, 21). They were midwives (Gen. 35.17; Exod. 1.15) and nurses (Ruth 4.16; 1 Kings 1.2, 4). Royal establishments employed women as perfumers, bakers, cooks (1 Sam. 8.13), and singers (2 Sam. 19.35). Although only men are mentioned as potters in the Bible, ethnographic analogies suggest that women were skilled in this important craft, and in weaving as well. There are references to enslaved women, some of whom would have been debt-slaves (Deut. 15.12) or war captives (Deut. 20.14). Prostitutes were tolerated but, as in Mesopotamia, they were relegated to the margins of society (Deut. 23.17 outlaws only prostitutes associated with non-Yahwistic cults).

Wives of rulers, queens, and women of the nobility were able to act with a relative degree of autonomy (1 Kings 21.1–16). The queen of Sheba, who may have belonged to a dynasty of Arabian queens, negotiated with King Solomon (1 Kings 10). Biblical accession formulas in 1 and 2 Kings are careful to note the name of each new Judahite king's mother (e.g., 1 Kings 15.2, 10), and the queen mother may have had quasiofficial status.

Women's Religious Practice and Experience. All biblical evidence for women's religious experience has been filtered through male eyes; thus much remains hidden. The description of the ideal wife (Prov. 31.10–31), for example, mentions her wise advice, but is mute about religious activity. Men and women incurred temporary ritual impurity, and thus exclusion from the cult, for genital emissions (Lev. 12.2–5; 15.1–33), but menstruation especially penalized women. A woman after the birth of a son was impure for seven days, but for fourteen after a daughter's birth (Lev. 12.2–5).

Biblical laws obliged only men to attend the three primary pilgrimage feasts (Exod. 23.17; 34.23; Deut. 16.16), but women such as Hannah clearly participated as well. During the festival she prays and makes a vow (1 Sam. 1–13, 27), and when Samuel is born she praises God with a song of thanksgiving (1 Sam. 2.1–10; cf. Exod. 15.20–21). The detailed legislation regarding women's vows (Num. 30) suggests that this was a significant form of female piety. The personal piety of several women appears in accounts of wives or widows consulting or helping prophets (1 Kings 14.1–6; 17.8–16; 2 Kings 4.1–37). The motif in the Gospels of women appealing to and following Jesus (e.g., Mark 7.24–30; John. 11.1–44) derives in part from these stories.

Monotheistic Israel differed from Mesopotamia and Egypt, where women served many deities as priestesses and even as high priestesses. The Israelite priesthood consisted of men who inherited the office from their fathers. Some women in Israel, called *qĕdēšôt* (formerly translated as "sacred prostitutes") were apparently consecrated to non-Yahwistic cults (Hos. 4.14; Deut. 23.19–20), but their function is unclear. Women served in some unexplained capacity at the tent shrine (Exod. 38.8; 1 Sam. 2.22), and after the exile the Temple employed female singers (Ezra 2.65; Neh. 7.67.).

What Israelite women did at the pilgrim feasts and how their worship differed from that of men is unclear, but it is an instructive question. Recognizing that gender differentiation—in tandem with the preconceptions of the observer—plays a role in determining what is considered "religious," scholars are beginning to reassess the ancient forms of women's piety. For example, Hannah stays home from the feast to nurse Samuel (1 Sam. 1.22), which might suggest that women's spirituality was contingent upon and secondary to men's. Is she temporarily cutting herself off from God, or were there compensatory home-centered rituals?

Besides the preparation of the corpse (cf. Mark 16.1; Luke 23.55–24.1) and funerary lamentations (Jer. 9.17), Israelite women no doubt participated in additional rituals related to the lifecycle. One suspects that midwives performed birth rituals (Gen. 35.17). The tradition of mourning for Jephthah's daughter (Judg. 11.37–40) may have been a rite of passage for adolescent girls. Zipporah performs a marriage-related circumcision (Exod. 4.24–26). The prophets Deborah (Judg. 4.4) and Huldah (2 Kings 22.14) were married women; perhaps they should be compared to postmenopausal women in other societies who become religious practitioners.

Miriam (Exod. 15.20), Deborah (Judg. 4.4), Huldah (2 Kings 22.14), and Noadiah (Neh. 6.14) are called prophets (see also Ezek. 13.17; Joel 2.28). Deborah's and Huldah's prophecy seems to differ in no way from male prophecy. Contemporaneously with Huldah (seventh century BCE), the Assyrians were very interested in and influenced by prophecy; texts mention female prophets, many of whom apparently operated independently of any temple cult.

Power struggles among priestly families may underlie the account in Numbers 12 of Miriam's and Aaron's revolt. Micah 6.4 is mute on the subject of any wrongdoing, and equally commends Miriam, Moses, and Aaron as deliverers. Miriam's very presence in the account of the Exodus (Exod. 15.20—21) and wilderness wanderings, complete with death notice in Numbers 20.1, suggests that she was an important cultic leader in Israelite memory.

Certain practices that the Bible considers abhorrent may at times have constituted mainstream Israelite religious activity. Significant female participation may be sought in lost, hidden, or forbidden categories of worship. The Bible condemns Saul for consulting Samuel's ghost through the

female medium at Endor (1 Sam. 28), and disapproves of what seems to be a cult of the dead (Isa. 65.4); yet recent research has shown that the cult of dead ancestors was important to many Israelites. In the two biblical episodes involving teraphim (household gods related to the cult of dead ancestors), the persons handling them are women (Gen. 31.19; 1 Sam. 19.13).

The numerous female clay figurines (often called Asherah figurines) found in Israelite domestic and tomb contexts must have had a religious function, perhaps related to a mother-goddess cult. Evidence from Kuntillet Ajrud in the Sinai and elsewhere, in combination with reassessments of the biblical text, suggests that many Israelites during the monarchy worshiped the Canaanite goddess Asherah, possibly even as a consort of Yahweh.

It is worth noting two exceptions to the Bible's tendency to treat women as lesser members of the religious congregation; both mark the inauguration in Jerusalem of a new religious era. When David installs the ark in Jerusalem, women and men share in the ritual meal (2 Sam.6.9), and when Ezra conducts his public reading of the Torah (Neh. 8.2–3), the text stresses that his audience consists of understanding men and women. Reminiscent of the latter passage is Genesis 1's assumption of the equal status of male and female (v. 27); the gender-inclusiveness of this text (generally dated to the exilic period) may reflect the importance of women among the exiles in maintaining the cohesion of family, community, and religion in the absence of maledominated institutions such as the kingship and the Temple priesthood, which could no longer be regarded as keepers of the national identity.

Female Symbolism. Women play an important role in the Bible's symbolic repertory. One of the most striking and influential metaphors in the Bible is the personification of Wisdom as a woman (Prov. 1; 8; 9). Jeremiah 31.15 describes war-ravaged Israel as a mother, Rachel, weeping for her dead children. In a familiar biblical metaphor, God too becomes a parent who feels exasperation but also compassion—literally "womb-feeling" (Hos. 2.23; Jer. 31.20)—for the child Israel. Israel, Jerusalem, and even foreign nations and cities may be personified as daughters (see Isa. 1.8; 23.12; Lamentations). Marriage becomes a central metaphor to describe the past and future intimacy of God the husband and Israel the wife (e.g., Hos. 2.14–20; Ezek. 16.1–4; Jer. 2.2), who all too often turns into an adulteress ("playing the harlot") with other gods (Hos. 2; Jer. 3.610; Ezek 16.15). Political considerations help to explain the function of some women in the Bible. Abishag is actually a symbolic pawn, first of the northern tribes (1 Kings 1.3), then of Adonijah (1 Kings 2.17). The story of Rahab (Josh. 2; 6.22–25) and the presence of women in genealogies (1 Chron. 1–9; cf. Matt. 1.1–16) served to imply that the descendants of these women belonged to kinship groups considered subordinate by more dominant Israelite tribes.

Biblical laws against a man lying "with a male as with a woman" (Lev. 18.22) and against crossdressing (Deut. 22.5) suggest that the borders between male and female realms are not to be crossed. Women are not warriors; thus it is ultimate humiliation for Sisera and Abimelech to die at the hands of a woman (cf. Judith). Jeremiah's oracle against Babylon even threatens Babylonian mercenaries with becoming women (Jer. 50.37). At the same time, in the deliberately shocking imagery that characterizes prophetic discourse, Jeremiah epitomizes the newness of the era when

W

Jerusalem will be restored by suggesting some sort of gender reversal (Jer. 31.22).

Negative Views of Women. Women in the Bible are generally less important than men and subject to male authority, but paradoxically women are also very powerful in one respect, their seductive persuasiveness. The Bible singles out foreign women as dangerous, liable to lead their partners away from exclusive Yahwism (Deut. 7.1–4; 23.17–18; Num. 25; 1 Kings 11.16; Ezek. 8.14–15; Ezra 9.2–10.44; Neh. 13.23–27). The Bible condemns Phoenician Jezebel for persuading Ahab to neglect the Israelite covenant with Yahweh (1 Kings 16.31–33; 21). Canaanite Rahab (Josh. 2.9–11) and Ruth the Moabite are exceptions as good foreign women who take Yahweh as their God. The opposite phenomenon—Israelite women led to apostasy by foreign men—is addressed only metaphorically, when Israel is personified as a adulterous wife who has been unfaithful to her husband, Yahweh (Hos. 1–3; Ezek. 16).

The prophets denounce vain and selfish women (Isa. 3.16–23; Amos 4.1), and Proverbs scorns contentious and headstrong women (Prov. 21.19; 27.15; 11.22). The "strange" woman of Proverbs 1–9, a combination of every possible negative female type (an adulteress, a cult-related prostitute, a goddess, a foreign woman), is a literary creation who functions rhetorically as the exact opposite of a positive female figure, Lady Wisdom.

The Bible's negative assessment of several women may arise from an unspoken political or rhetorical subtext (e.g., Michal, Jezebel, Athaliah, Gomer). Potiphar's wife (Gen. 39.6–21) and Delilah (Judg. 16.4–21) are bad women indeed, but folklorists recognize that these "evil" women play a crucial role in propelling the central character toward hero status, a story pattern repeated in countless folktales.

Genesis never refers to a woman as the cause of the human condition. The earliest biblical reference to this concept occurs in Sirach 25.24 (early second century BCE). It is a doctrine, like the related ones of original sin and Satan, that developed during the Second Temple Period (ca. 500 BCE – 70 CE), to be taken up in turn by early Christianity (1 Tim. 2.12–14; cf. Rom. 5.12).

Social Reality and Narrative Patterns. Investigators of women's history view with interest the intersection between religious symbols and narrative patterns on the one hand and social reality on the other. The fact that Ishtar or Hathor is an authoritative female deity does not mean that real-life women could achieve comparable power in Egyptian or Mesopotamian society.

Nevertheless, in actual society and in literature, women who function on the upper or lower margins of normative society—queens, wealthy widows, priestesses, prostitutes—may transcend otherwise static boundaries determined by gender. As high priestess of the Sumerian moon god, the princess Enheduanna (twenty-third century BCE) composed hymns which may have provided a model for later hymnists. The prostitute Rahab negotiates successfully for the common good of her family and Israel (Josh. 2; 6). In the Gilgamesh Epic, the prostitute Shamhat is pivotal in bringing Enkidu from bestiality to civilization; her role may usefully be compared to that of Eve in Genesis 3. Anthropologists have observed that this mediating quality is often a distinctive aspect of femaleness.

A recurrent pattern in biblical stories about women is their use of indirection, even subterfuge, to achieve divinely sanctioned ends (e.g., Rebekah, Gen. 27; Tamar, Gen. 38; Shiphrah and Puah, Exod. 1.15–21; Esther). By seemingly devious actions which invert or overthrow established but restrictive social hierarchies, women often bring about a new order of life and freedom.

MARY JOAN WINN LEITH

Second Temple Period

Interest in the role and status of women in Second Temple Judaism (and generally in Judaism and Christianity) has increased exponentially in the past twenty-five years. As research has progressed, however, the difficulty of reclaiming women's voices from a largely silent patriarchal textual tradition has been acknowledged. The major groups of texts of the Second Temple period are androcentric in focus, written by male authors for a male audience, and they mention women only rarely and usually in peripheral contexts. A second body of evidence that can be utilized in the search for women's lives is archaeological, the material remains of society both in Palestine and in the Diaspora. But material remains are generally silent as to the gender of their owners, and so are subject to the potentially biased interpretation of the excavator. These limitations make the recovery of women's lives from the Second Temple period fraught with difficulty.

Women's Daily Lives. The beginning of the Second Temple period was the era of Persian domination of the ancient Near East (538–332 BCE). During this time Jewish settlement was concentrated in Babylon, Judea, and to a more limited extent in Egypt. Judea in this period was poor, with a rural, agrarian economy. Extended families (the "father's house") worked their own fields and were self-reliant in most matters of daily existence. Both women's and men's work was essential to the survival of the family unit. Women's tasks included agricultural labor, food processing, textile manufacture, and child care (women would often have ten or more pregnancies to insure that a minimum number of children survived to adulthood). Because of the interdependent nature of the family unit, gender roles were not sharply defined except for biological function.

As Greek culture spread over the ancient Near East, especially in the Hellenistic period (332–ca. 200 BCE), the mingling of the two worlds produced the unique blend of culture called Hellenism. Hellenism created a more urban, mobile society, and also saw the rise of an extensive Diaspora community, particularly in Alexandria in Egypt and in Asia Minor. Urban life brought with it smaller families and specialized economic roles, so that women's roles became more circumscribed. While men performed their tasks in the public sphere, women became more confined to the home, limited to their maternal and housekeeping roles (this is primarily true for upper- and middle-class women). Spinning and weaving continued to be women's work. Upperclass women evidently could and did play active roles in the Greco-Roman Jewish Diaspora, but for the vast majority of women such occasions were limited. Educational opportunities expanded for women in this period, but a good part of the population remained illiterate. The visual arts reveal a new interest in the eroticism of women. So women as women are both more visible, in art and literature, and less visible, being more and more confined to the home. This created a tension in Hellenistic society's view of women, reflected in Jewish literature of the period.

Women in Postexilic Biblical Literature. The group of canonical works from the Persian period is small, and few of those are concerned with women; notable exceptions are

Judith with the head of Holfernes (Jth. 13.6–16)

May the Lord do thus and so to me, and more as well, if even death parts me from you!" (1.16–17).

The Song of Solomon (of uncertain date, but with final redaction in the Second Temple period) is the only book in the Bible partly written in a woman's voice. It is a series of love songs that are frankly erotic in character, celebrating the sexual life between an unnamed woman and a man, with the woman acting as a free agent, pursuing her lover, initiating their encounters, and glorying in their physical love. Conspicuously absent are the usual biblical roles for women, those of wife and mother. The couple functions as equals in their erotic union, resulting in an unusual and compelling portrayal of the woman.

Women in the Apocrypha. The Apocrypha are writings considered canonical by the Roman Catholic and Eastern Orthodox churches, but not by Judaism and the Protestant churches. Like the Hebrew Bible, the Apocrypha comprise various types of literature, and also like the Hebrew Bible, they are androcentric, mentioning women only occasionally, when their lives impinge on the activities of men. Two important portraits of women are found in the Additions to Esther and the book of Judith.

The Additions to Esther are six major blocks of material added to the Hebrew book of Esther, along with minor changes in the text, when it was translated into Greek, probably in 78 BCE. The Additions attempt to remedy problems perceived in the Hebrew book: the lack of mention of God and Esther's non-Jewish lifestyle. The changes make Esther a pious but passive girl, relying on God instead of herself, so that God becomes the true hero of the story. Esther's beauty is emphasized and her brains and skill downplayed. The changes may have rendered Esther more palatable as a heroine to a Hellenistic audience accustomed to passive romantic heroines. This, then, is an example of conscious downgrading of the role of a woman.

The book of Judith, probably composed in the second century BCE, presents an unambiguous female hero. In this fictitious narrative, Judith (whose name is a feminine form of the word for "Jew"), a beautiful, wealthy, and pious widow, leaves her quiet existence to save her town of Bethulia from the besieging Assyrians. She does this by pretending to desert to the enemy and then seducing the Assyrian general Holofernes; when he is drunk, she cuts off his head and returns to Bethulia in triumph. Thus "one Hebrew woman has brought disgrace on the house of King Nebuchadnezzar" (14.18). However, this behavior by a woman is acceptable only in national emergencies; after the Assyrians are defeated, Judith returns to her quiet existence, remaining a widow until her death. Women's power is expressed in Judith, but only within the confines of patriarchy.

Women in the Pseudepigrapha. Similarly ambivalent attitudes toward women also exists in the eclectic collection of Jewish writings known as the Pseudepigrapha. The Conversion of Asenath and The Testaments of the Twelve Patriarchs are two examples of the wide variety of portraits of women in this literature.

The Conversion of Asenath was written to answer the question of how Joseph, the quintessential man of God, could have married an Egyptian, "Asenath daughter of Potiphera, priest of On" (Gen. 41.45). According to the story, Joseph does indeed refuse to marry Asenath at first, because she is an idol worshipper. But Asenath, who the text emphasizes is a virgin, is so stricken by Joseph's refusal that she repents and converts to the worship of Joseph's God. The bulk of the story is the account of Asenath's conversion.

the books of Esther, Ruth, and the Song of Solomon, all of which contain positive portrayals of women.

The book of Esther, written in the late Persian-early Hellenistic period, is a fictional account of events leading up to the Jewish festival of Purim. Set in the eastern Diaspora, the book describes how a young Jewish girl named Esther became the consort of the Persian king and saved her people from destruction by her resourcefulness and courage. Notorious for its lack of interest in religious matters (it never mentions God, although the author clearly believes in a divine providence at work in human affairs), the book focuses on the Jews as an ethnic group and on Esther as a human heroine who saves her people by her own actions and thus as a role model for Jews in the Diaspora.

The date of the book of Ruth is disputed, but sometime in the fifth century BCE is reasonable, understanding the book as a response to the postexilic decrees by Ezra and Nehemiah against intermarriage. The main character is Ruth the Moabite, who accompanies her Israelite mother-in-law Naomi back to Judea after the death of their husbands, and eventually, through her own praiseworthy actions, becomes the ancestress of king David. The book concerns itself with the mundane things of life: food, marriage, offspring, and particularly the covenantloyalty of one (foreign) woman for another. Ruth becomes the paradigm of loyalty for all women and men, and her attachment to Naomi resembles the marriage vow: "Where you go, I will go; where you lodge, I will lodge; your people shall be my people, and your God my God. Where you die, I will die—there will I be buried.

She retires to her chamber, puts on mourning garments, and laments and fasts for seven days. On the eighth day she repents of her idolatry and confesses to God. In response an archangel appears to her, declares that her repentance has been accepted, and gives her a mysterious honeycomb to eat. Her marriage to Joseph follows, and she lives (basically) happily ever after. Asenath is the prototype for all future proselytes, an important role for a woman. However, once again her prominence is within the context of patriarchy, for the purpose of her conversion is to enable her to marry Joseph.

The Testaments of the Twelve Patriarchs are part of the genre of pseudepigraphical literature known as testaments, which are the deathbed words of prominent figures from Israel's past, in this case the eponymous ancestors of the twelve tribes. Each testament is concerned with particular virtues or vices, which the patriarch instructs his offspring to practice or ignore. The theme of chastity enjoys special prominence in the Testaments. Therefore in the Testaments women exist chiefly as temptations for pious men, their lewdness often coupled with drunkenness as an aid to fornication. For example, Judah, telling of his intercourse with his daughter-in-law Tamar, says, "Since I was drunk with wine, I did not recognize her and her beauty enticed me because of her manner of tricking herself out" (12.3; *The Old Testament Pseudepigrapha* [ed. James H. Charlesworth, Doubleday, 1983] 1, 798). Reuben, while discussing his sin with his father's concubine Bilhah, says, "Do not devote your attention to a woman's looks, nor live with a woman who is already married, nor become involved in affairs with women" (3.1; ibid., 783). In the Testaments, women exist only as objects to trip up heedless men.

All of the above examples are from literature that in some way features women prominently. But we know almost nothing about the communities that produced this literature and their relation to one another. With classical sources, we are on firmer ground, for we know more about the authors and their audiences.

Women in the Classical Sources. Josephus and Philo are the main sources for Jewish thought about women in classical literature. Josephus, who wrote in Rome under the patronage of the Flavian emperors after the First Jewish Revolt (66–70 CE), wrote several works, including *The Antiquities of the Jews,* which is essentially a rewriting of the biblical text for apologetic purposes. In attempting to present Jews and Judaism in a favorable light to his Greco-Roman audience, Josephus makes many changes in the presentation of biblical narratives, including their portrayals of women. One example will suffice. When Josephus rewrites the story of Esther, he has before him both the Hebrew and the Septuagint versions of the book. He chooses to retain most of the changes introduced by the latter, heightening the erotic aspect even more, and downplaying Esther's active role in the story. Thus, the Jewish people are saved, but mainly because Esther is beautiful and the king desires her sexually, not because of her intelligence and resourcefulness.

Philo, a first-century CE Alexandrian Jew with an extensive knowledge of Greek philosophy and literature, undertakes an allegorical interpretation of the biblical text that is a fusion of Jewish thought and Greek philosophy. Therefore, the women and men in the biblical stories become symbols for higher philosophical realities. In the process the women are completely denigrated. Philo draws his dichotomy of male/female from Pythagorean and Aristotelian schemes. Man is *nous* or "mind," the higher intellectual capacity; woman, on the other hand, is *aisthēsis* or "sense-impression," the lower form of perception. Man *(nous)* is immortal, in the image of God, while woman is mortal, closely connected with *soma,* "body." Since the goal of *nous* is to be free of the troubles of the body, woman is automatically placed in the category of undesirable and wrong. Philo's are the most systematically misogynist of all the writings we have surveyed.

Conclusion. A pattern has emerged in this survey. The earlier literature, stemming from a period when gender roles were more egalitarian and both men and women had essential economic and social roles to play, allows women greater freedom of action and a louder voice (Esther, Ruth, Song of Solomon). The later literature, influenced by Hellenistic culture with its more restricted view of women's roles, allows women to act only in relation to men, or in situations of crisis (Asenath, Judith). Finally, in literature written by men on whom the influence of Greek thought is clear, women are more thoroughly denigrated and swept from the stage of an all-male world (Josephus, Philo).

Sidnie Ann White

Early Christianity

Information on early Christian women is found in the New Testament, writings of the early church fathers, apocryphal and gnostic literature, and archaeological finds such as inscriptions and papyri. In recent years, these sources, historically overlooked for data on women, have been exploited by scholars, resulting in dozens of important secondary works. While the evidence must be treated carefully by the historian and theologian, it furnishes proof that data on the women of antiquity do exist; in fact, the study of women in the New Testament and early church constitutes one of the liveliest and most fruitful areas of biblical scholarship today.

The Greco-Roman and Jewish Heritage. Like Christians in general, women in the early church were products of the wider culture. In general, women were dependent both financially and legally on the men in their lives—fathers, husbands, uncles, brothers, and sons. Women generally married while still teenagers, bore one or more children, and died young (the average life expectancy was thirty-four years), often in childbirth. If a girl survived childhood (i.e., was not exposed), and a woman survived childbirth, she might live a long life and bury her husband: women were the primary caretakers of the graves of family members, including those of in-laws. It was also women who passed on the household (usually the men's) religious practices such as ancestor worship to their descendants.

Except in the most outlying rural areas, women were not isolated from each other or from other men. Middle- and upper-class women living in villas or in urban areas often functioned as chief household managers, especially when their husbands were absent for long periods of time on commerce or at war. While there is considerable evidence for independent and wealthy women, most women lived in slavery, near poverty, or middle-class stability; therefore, most worked for wages for their own economic survival and that of their families, even if they were married to a merchant or freedman. In some cases, women may have been secluded in their homes, but for the most part they moved freely in many spheres of the Greco-Roman world—the agora, baths, businesses, and religious associations.

With regard to religious background, some early Christian women were Jewish, since Christianity was a sect of Judaism for a time. Other women converted from Greco-Roman cults, while still others, often in the same family or neighborhood, remained non-Christian. This coexistence of adherents of different religions systems was often peaceful but could lead to conflict, often over the issue of appropriate roles of women in the various groups.

Evidence from both Jewish and Greco-Roman circles shows that women held leadership roles in these groups. In Judaism, archaeological and other evidence demonstrates that some women in the first few centuries CE held positions such as head of a synagogue *(archisynagōgis)*, leader *(archēgissa)*, elder *(presbytis)*, "mother of the synagogue" *(mater synagogae)*, and priest *(hiereia)*. The exact functions of these women are difficult to ascertain, but they were probably equivalent to the functions of men bearing parallel titles. The evidence further demonstrates that women were integrated into regular services, not segregated in "women's galleries" or separate rooms, and that some were major financial contributors to local synagogues.

Similarly, women held leadership roles in many, if not most, of the myriad Greco-Roman cults that allowed women members. Some of their functions included priest, musician, stolist, prophet, torchbearer, dancer, and mourner. Outside of religion, women worked as midwives, lawyers, merchants, artists, teachers, physicians, prostitutes, and laborers and professionals of all sorts.

Women in positions of authority in religion and society did not constitute a majority: the culture was still patriarchal, that is, controlled primarily by men. However, the fact that women did play some leadership roles in both Judaism and the larger society became significant for the growth of Christianity: women who were drawn to it undoubtedly would have expected to be active participants in the new cult if not leaders. Their presence had a definite effect on the development of the canon, the emerging role of the priest and bishop, as well as liturgy, theology, and battles with heresy and gnosticism.

Women in the Early Christian Movement. The New Testament and early church fathers provide preliminary data on women. The earliest evidence, from Paul's letters, suggests that women functioned as dynamic leaders of the movement (Phil. 4.2–3; Rom. 16), deacons (Rom. 16.1–2), apostles (Rom. 16.7), and missionaries (1 Cor. 16.19; Rom. 16.3–4). The Gospels relate that Jesus had women followers as well as men (Mark 15.40–41; Matt. 27.55; Luke 8.1–3) and treated women as equals (cf. John 4.9, 27; Luke 10.38–42); it was also women who were the first to bear witness to his resurrection. The Acts of the Apostles mention the four daughters of Philip who prophesied (21.9); Lydia from Thyatira, a merchant and the head of her household (16.14–15); the missionary couple, Priscilla and Aquila (chap. 18); house-church leaders (12.12); and prominent converts (17.4, 12).

Thus, in pre-Pauline and Pauline Christian communities, women appear to have functioned almost identically to men. In fact, it is possible that more women than men were house-church leaders, hosting vital prayer meetings that became the kernel of the movement. At least one woman deacon, Phoebe, is recorded in the New Testament (Rom. 16.1–2), and she functioned as an official teacher and missionary in the church of Cenchreae. Euodia and Syntyche from Philippi (Phil. 4.2–3) were prominent leaders of that community, and Junia served the church at Rome as an apostle (Rom. 16.7). The most prominent woman in the New Testament is Prisca/Priscilla, who worked alongside her husband and was probably the more renowned of the pair (1 Cor. 16.19; Rom. 16.3–4; Acts 18). The women Mary, Tryphaena, Tryphosa, and Persis in Romans 16 are described as having labored *(kopian)* for the Lord, the same term Paul used to describe his own evangeliz-

ing and teaching activities. (See Elizabeth Schüssler Fiorenza, *In Memory of Her,* New York, 1983.)

Celibacy became a major life-style choice for both men and women early in the Christian movement, and by the third and fourth centuries men and women were living in houses and monasteries (a term that includes convents) segregated by gender. Renunciation by men was not deemed problematic, but the popularity of female celibacy led to fears that women's independence would undermine the very fabric of home and society. Early attestations of this popularity and the subsequent social tensions it created are found in many of the apocryphal Acts of the second and third centuries, including the Acts of Paul and Thecla, the Acts of Andrew, the Acts of Peter, and the Acts of Thoma. In the stories of these Acts, celibacy was idealized, and many women were portrayed as heroines for breaking off engagements and leaving husbands and traditional home situations for the sake of the gospel. While many of the stories in the Acts may be fictitious, they probably originated in oral form in circles of independent women and reflect actual people, events, and trends.

Other threats to the survival of the young church in the eyes of male leaders included the leadership of independent women in gnostic and heretical groups. Two prophets, Priscilla and Maximilla, were prominent in the Montanist sect of the second century, and women in those groups may have baptized and celebrated the Eucharist (Cyprian, *Ep.* 75[74].10; Epiphanius, *Haer.* 49.2). Some gnostic sects also allowed women to serve as priests and to baptize (Hippolytus, *Haer.* 6.35; Irenaeus, *Haer.* 1.13.1–2; Epiphanius, *Haer.* 42.4; Tertullian, *Praescr.* 41). Bishop Atto of Vercelli (ca. 885–961) wrote in several tracts that women were ordained just like men in the ancient church, were leaders of communities, were called elders (*presbyterae*), and fulfilled the duties of preaching, directing, and teaching.

Female celibacy and other acts of independence led male leaders to disseminate countertreatises in which they prescribed strict behavior for all women and attempted to bring the entire Christian movement more in line with the overall culture's ideal of the patriarchal family and household. The New Testament "household codes" (Eph. 5.21–6.9; Col. 3.18–25; 1 Peter 2.18–3.7), written by followers of Paul, not Paul himself, clearly urged women's subordination to men. The so-called Pastoral letters (1 and 2 Timothy and Titus) are also early works accepted into the New Testament canon. 1 Timothy 2.11—12 forbade women from speaking in church, and Titus 1.7–9 assumed that only men would be bishops.

Retrenchment and Later Trends. The church fathers of the second through fourth centuries, being among those who agitated against women's independence, decreed that women could only minister to other women as deacons or be enrolled as virgins or widows. Women deacons as described in third- and fourth-century documents were at least fifty or sixty years of age, ministered to sick and poor women, were present at interviews of women with (male) bishops, priests, or deacons, and instructed women catechumens. Before the decline of adult baptism, women deacons assisted at the baptisms of women, probably their most important role. Women deacons may have been the only women admitted into ministry in the orthodox church by the laying-on of hands by the bishop. In the earliest church, however, female deacons may have functioned much more similarly to male deacons, since the sources are not always clear.

Widows and virgins, while not ordained, had recognized status and privileges in the early church. However, there

W

were restrictions placed on them. Widows in New Testament times had to be at least sixty years of age and married only once; younger widows were expected to remarry. The references to virgins in the New Testament are more vague (Acts 21.9; 1 Cor. 7.1, 8, 25–38), but the order seems to be closely linked to that of widows.

Meanwhile, the male leaders reserved for themselves the right to serve the whole church in the more important and powerful roles such as elder (*presbyteros*) and bishop (*episkopos*) and adhered to the ideal of the monarchical episcopate: the high reverence due the bishop and the subordination of others to that office. Bishops in these fathers' minds could, of course, only be fellow men, and the directives they set down toward women could be stringent.

Polycarp, bishop of Smyrna, writing to the Philippians around 110 CE, attempted to limit women's behavior by clearly delineating their roles as virgins, widows, and ever-faithful wives. Ignatius of Antioch urged Polycarp to be the "protector" of widows and exhorted women to be "altogether contented with their husbands" (*Ep. Polycarp* 4,5). Libanius (314–95) complained that women distract men from their religious duties (*Ep.* 1057). Canons from the Council of Gangra in 340 declare anathema women who wear male attire, who leave their husbands, and who cut off their hair, a sign of their subjection.

Tertullian, perhaps the most misogynist of all the early fathers, wrote four lengthy treatises dealing with women: *On the Apparel of Women* (ca. 202), *On the Veiling of Virgins* (ca. 204), *To His Wife* (ca. 207), and *On Monogamy* (ca. 208). In *On the Apparel of Women* 1.1, he described women as "the gateway of the devil" and blamed them for leading men astray through their sexual wiles. In chap. 9 of *On the Veiling of Women,* he wrote, "It is not permitted to a woman to speak in the church; but neither is it permitted her to teach, nor to baptize, nor to offer, nor to claim to herself a lot in any manly function, not to say in any sacerdotal office." To Tertullian's way of thinking, the ideal woman was a totally subservient being, completely regulated by strict rules governing every facet of her life—a far cry from the autonomous woman of many of the nascent Christian communities.

One early church leader who was more positive toward women in some ways was Jerome (342–420). In a number of letters between him and the many women of his social circle, Jerome appears as a sort of mentor and father figure to upper-class women who had chosen the celibate life-style. One of his Roman disciples, Paula, founded a monastery near Bethlehem.

However, even some of Jerome's saintly women were admired for leading lives that followed strict rules of behavior, rules not generally applied to men. Fabiola, a young Christian woman from Rome, divorced her husband because he was a sinner; this was applauded by other Christians. However, these same Christians, including Jerome, condemned her for subsequently remarrying: "She did not know that the rigor of the gospel takes away from women all pretext for remarriage, so long as their former husbands are alive." When she finally realized her "mistake," she publicly confessed and was restored to communion. Then, being wealthy, she sold her property and, with the money, founded a hospital to nurse the poor and sick (*Ep.* 77).

Monasticism became increasingly important for women in the face of these restrictions and the eradication of heretical and gnostic groups that had promoted women's independence. A number of women besides Paula, mostly from the upper strata of society, founded or cofounded all-women houses, communities, and nunneries where young women learned to read, write, paint, and draw. Such houses, like those of men, followed rules of order and were self-supporting and devoted to prayer and good works. At first the houses were independent of local church authorities, but over time they were brought under the jurisdiction of the bishop.

While female monasteries may have been centers of opportunity primarily for members of the upper classes, thereby restricting most other women to marriage in patriarchal households or to lives as virgins and widows dependent on men, these communities nevertheless made important contributions to the entire church that have historically been overlooked. While the evidence is meager, especially compared with evidence from all-male enclaves, it suggests that all-women groups produced high-quality illuminated manuscripts; wove many of the tapestries that adorned the great basilicas, as well as the ornate robes worn by clergy; crafted at least some of the silver Communion ware and jewelry used in the liturgy; and contributed to sketch books that served imperial architects as blueprints for exquisite mosaics that decorated many basilicas. Also, women in some communities taught men reading, writing, and drawing; dispensed wisdom to male leaders; and became renowned as leaders of centers of learning.

Significantly, despite attempts by the hierarchy through the ages to conceal the evidence, there is attestation for women priests into the Byzantine era. An epistle of Pope Gelasius I (492–96) to bishops in Italy and Sicily mentions in annoyance that women were officiating at the sacred altars and taking part in ecclesiastical affairs imputed only to men. An inscription from Bruttium dating to the end of the fifth century mentions the presbytera Leta (*Corpus incriptionum latinarum* 10.8079), and another from Salona in Dalmatia (425 CE) mentions the presbytera Flavia Vitalia. While these attestations are rare, they confirm that women functioned sacerdotally—and that male bishops occasionally ordained them.

VALERIE ABRAHAMSEN

W

ZECHARIAH, THE BOOK OF.

Chaps. 1–8. The first eight chapters of the book contain the teaching of Zechariah in a series of eight visions of the night (1.7–6.15) together with accompanying oracles. These are sandwiched between accounts of his preaching in 1.1–6 and chaps. 7–8. Like Haggai, Zechariah is said to have prophesied in the second year of Darius the Persian (520 BCE), but his ministry extended to the fourth year (518 BCE). Like Haggai, therefore, he is addressing and seeking to encourage the postexilic community in Judah in all their frustrations and difficulties.

Several visions and oracles assure the people of God's imminent action on their behalf. While the first vision, that of the horsemen (1.8–13), shows that nothing can yet be seen to be happening (v. 11), the oracle brings assurance that God is deeply concerned for the welfare of Jerusalem, which he is about to "choose" again and to which he will come to resume his dwelling. He will punish the nations that have destroyed the city and taken its citizens into exile, the theme also of the second vision of the "horns" and "smiths" (1.18–20). The third (2.1–5) takes up Second Isaiah's picture of the unlimited size of the restored city (Isa. 49.19–21) and assures them that God's glory (his

Zechariah from the Sistine Chapel

presence) will be in the city (cf. Ezek. 43.1–5; Hag. 2.9). God will protect them as he did when he led the Israelites in the wilderness by a pillar of fire (Exod. 13.21). The oracle that follows (2.6–13) calls on the exiles to return, for Yahweh is about to dwell in the city to which not only Jews, but all nations, will come. The fourth vision (3.1–10) shows the cleansing of Joshua, the high priest (called Jeshua in Ezra and Nehemiah), a sign that God is now determined to forgive and cleanse the community. The fifth (4.1–14) suggests a joint leadership of Zerubbabel as civil governor and Joshua, and contains a promise that Zerubbabel will complete the rebuilding of the Temple, but also a warning that he must do so only in complete reliance on God's spirit (vv. 6–10a). The two visions in chap. 5 announce the cleansing of the restored community, while a final vision (6.1–8), echoing the first, pictures horsemen and chariots patrolling the earth, reporting that God's spirit is now at rest in the north country (traditionally the direction from which Israel's enemies have come in judgment from God; see Jer. 1.14). Now, however, this is the peace, not of inaction, as in the first vision, but of the resolution of the people's problems by God's saving actions. The passage 6.9–15, along with 3.6–10, seems to describe a situation in which the priestly line has assumed preeminence, while messianic hope now attaches to an unnamed and future figure called the Branch (see Isa. 11.1)

The surrounding oracles contain warnings against repeating the sins of preexilic generations who ignored the teaching of the prophets (1.1–6; 7.7–14; 8.14–17). They reinforce the promises of the visions of an imminent new age by assuring questioners (7.1–3) that all mourning fasts for the fall of Jerusalem are about to be replaced by joyful festivals of celebration (8.18–19).

The fact that 1.1–6 and chaps. 7–8 contain echoes of some of the "sermons" in the books of Chronicles (e.g., 2 Chron. 30.6–9) may suggest that the teaching of Zechariah was handed down by preaching and teaching personnel of the postexilic Temple. This is strengthened by the presence of teaching on such subjects as true fasting (7.4–6), found elsewhere in postexilic literature (e.g., Isa. 58). Again, oracles of Zechariah are taken up and expounded afresh in 8.1–8 (cf. 1.14, 16), while 8.9–13 appears to be exposition of Haggai 2.15–19. The universalist tone in Zechariah's teaching (2.11) is strongly and splendidly renewed in 8.20–23.

Zechariah, like Haggai, was thus remembered as a prophet who encouraged the immediate postexilic community by assuring them of God's imminent action in terms that echoed the preaching of Ezekiel and Second Isaiah and took up themes of the preexilic Zion/David theology expressed in many psalms. His picture of a joint messiahship of civil and religious leaders was to reappear in the teaching of the Qumran community. The form of the teaching in a series of visions is reminiscent of one test of a true prophet in some of the earlier literature, namely, that he had been admitted to the council of heaven (Jer. 23.18). The stronger sense here, however, that what is happening on earth is a projection of what is happening in heaven, has suggested to some that in Zechariah 1–8 we have an early hint of apocalyptic.

Chaps. 9–14. In Zechariah 9–14 no mention is made of the building of the Temple that now is standing, nor of the time of Darius I, while there is a reference to "Yawan" (literally, Ionia; NRSV: "Greece") in 9.13. There is nothing corresponding to the visions of chaps. 1–8 or to the ethical teaching of 1.1–6 and chaps. 7–8. For these reasons most scholars assign these chapters to a later time and another hand or hands. Broad thematic features are, however, common to both parts of the book, such as a strongly Zion-centered interest, God's cleansing of the community in preparation for his final act of salvation, a marked universalism, dependance on earlier prophecy, and a concern for a true and proper leadership as one sign of the new age. These suggest that the later parts of the book came from circles that maintained the traditions of Zechariah's teaching.

Many attempts have been made to date these chapters by the supposed historical allusions found in them, but these attempts have yielded such widely differing results that we must question their validity. It is more likely that we have here exposition of earlier prophetic themes in general terms in which particular countries, personalities, and events are now seen as typical or symbolic of the clash of the forces of evil with God's universal kingship. By such means earlier prophecies are related to the writer's own time and their relevance for people of later generations demonstrated.

The material is broadly of two kinds: eschatological passages that look forward to the triumph of God over evil and controversy passages in which strong attacks are made on those who are seen as false leaders of the community, in the manner of some earlier prophetic books.

Chap. 9 speaks of the advance of an enemy, echoing oracles of Amos and Ezekiel (vv. 1–7). God, however, defends Jerusalem, to which her king comes in triumph bringing peace among all nations (vv. 9–10), words later quoted in the New Testament and used of the triumphal entry of Jesus into Jerusalem (Matt. 21.1–9 par.) Vv. 11–17 speak of God's ultimate victory, taking up earlier prophetic themes and the imagery of the enthronement psalms, a note continued in 10.3b-12.

Chaps. 12–14 introduce new themes. In 12.1–13.6 the nations have gathered to attack Jerusalem. Yahweh, however, intervenes to defeat them and delivers both Judah and Jerusalem, this resulting in an act of divine cleansing and renewal of the whole community. Chap. 14 paints an even more cosmic picture, with God himself gathering the nations who come to lay siege to Jerusalem. Only after half the population has been exiled does God come to the aid of his stricken city (vv. 2–3). He appears on the Mount of Olives; the mountain is connected to the city by a great earthquake so that Yahweh once more enters Jerusalem (vv. 4–5). Thereafter all nature is renewed, and God is acclaimed as universal king (v. 9). Jerusalem becomes the highest point in the land (vv. 10–11; cf. Isa. 2.2); all who oppose God's rule are defeated (vv. 12–15) and all nations come to worship him in Jerusalem (vv. 16–21). Because the eschatology of chaps. 12–14 tends more toward that of apocalyptic and because the heading "Oracle" is found,

not only at 9.1 but again at 12.1, some scholars hold that these chapters are later than chaps. 9–11. Since, however, the same degree of dependence on earlier prophecy is found in each section and controversy passages occur in both, they may be more closely connected than some have thought.

The controversy passages (10.1–33; 11.13; 11.4–17; 13.7–9) express increasingly severe condemnation of false shepherds, presumably the priestly leaders of the community at some point, or points, in the postexilic period.

So much is obscure in these chapters that interpretation of them can be only tentative. The view that they came from a sharply eschatological party that found itself increasingly at odds with the official priesthood and Temple, and so looked for a more and more radical intervention of God, would account for much that is here. If that were so, it would mean that some of the factors that later gave rise to the Qumran community were already being felt by those from whom chaps. 9–14 came, perhaps in the third century BCE.

REX MASON

ZEPHANIAH, THE BOOK OF. The ninth book of the Minor Prophets proclaims the coming day of the Lord, with its judgment on Israel and the nations, to be the best hope for salvation.

The prophet's name means "Yah(weh) protects;" in an earlier form it may have been a confession, "Zaphon is Yahweh," Zaphon being the deified Canaanite mountain who is thus identified with Israel's Yahweh. The superscription goes to unusual lengths in giving the prophet's ancestry, which is traced back to Hezekiah, the great Judean king.

The prophecy is dated to the reign of King Josiah (640–609 BCE), who was responsible for major reforms in Judah's worship (2 Kings 22–23; 2 Chron. 34–35). Josiah was the "son of Ammon," who was murdered by revolutionaries (2 Kings 21.23). But a group called "the people of the land" rose up to quell the revolution and put his son Josiah on the throne. This group supported Josiah in his reforms and Jeremiah in his preaching. Zephaniah seems to be very close to their goals and aims.

Zephaniah fought against foreign influences and against the worship of other gods. His message is close to that of the great eighth-century prophets, especially Isaiah. He taught that pride was the major sin of humankind, and that it leads to rebellion against divine authority. He understood God's judgment to be universal. Hope for him lay beyond the great day of judgment. The book serves as a bridge between the eighth-century prophets of judgment such as Hosea and Amos, and the prophets after the exile, such as Haggai and Zechariah, who proclaimed a coming salvation of God.

The book is composed as a dramatic dialogue between Yahweh and someone else, possibly the prophet. Each of the seven parts of the book includes a speech by Yahweh and one by the prophet, except the last, which has only Yahweh's speech.

1. Yahweh's speech (1.2–6) announces a total judgment over all creation. People have stopped serving the Lord and worship other gods. The prophet calls for silence (1.7) and puts a name on the judgment: "the day of the Lord."

2. Yahweh's anger still is hot (1.8–13) as he condemns everyone in Israel, from the rulers to the skeptics. Then the prophet develops his picture of the day of the Lord (1.14–16), verses that serve as the starting point for the medieval hymn *Dies irae*.

3. Yahweh's third speech is more calm (1.17) but still insists that sin will make the people become "dust" and "dung." The prophet's speech is longer (1.18–2.7). He introduces two new themes: that there is a possible way to escape the judgment, and that other nations are to be condemned. The "humble of the land" (2.3) may escape the devastation.

4. Yahweh fills out the prophet's message (2.8–10) by announcing judgment on Ammon and Moab for their pride and promising that the surviving remnant of Israel will plunder their enemies. The prophet continues by noting that the nations are judged because of their idols (2.11). This pair of speeches is a kind of pause in the action.

5. Yahweh speaks out to include Ethiopia in the judgment (2.12). His dialogue partner compares Israel with Assyria (2.13–3.5), which will be completely devastated; Israel is also wicked and will be destroyed.

6. Yahweh's speech begins to resolve the problem (3.6–13). After judgment and destruction comes God's mercy. All the nations are offered the opportunity to "call on the name of the Lord and serve him with one accord" (3.9). Then the Lord will purify their speech; he will remove Israel's shame and forgive her sin (3.13). The prophet calls on Israel to rejoice in God's presence (3.14–17).

7. Yahweh's final speech (3.18–20) summarizes the salvation that he promises Israel, dealing with her oppressors, saving those who are lame, and restoring those in the dispersion.

The book has developed a plot that seems to promise only doom for all creation, including Israel. Such a fate is thoroughly deserved. Then a slight hope is raised for some to survive when specifically identified peoples are marked for the judgment; some hope for the "humble of the land" is disclosed. Finally the Lord's mercy offers a way of escape for the nations and for Israel.

Zephaniah makes a strong contribution to the understanding of the day of the Lord. In the Minor Prophets, this day is understood as a decisive turning point in which the Lord's judgment falls upon Israel and the nations for

Illuminated initial "v" which begins the Latin translation of the book of Zephaniah

their idolatry and pride. The events that lead up to Jerusalem's final destruction in 587/586 BCE are clearly in mind. Zephaniah shows that this terrible moment can bring the opportunity for a new beginning, for both Israel and the nations. The true opportunity is for those who are "humble and lowly" (3.12). The book opens the door to the messages that the following three books of the collection will bring. In Haggai and Zechariah, God leads in rebuilding the Temple a full century after Zephaniah's time, and the final chapters of Zechariah as well as Malachi look to the opportunities and responsibilities of the people of God in the postexilic age.

JOHN D. W. WATTS

ZION. A name of Jerusalem (Map 9). The etymology of the Hebrew term is unknown. Perhaps the earliest reference to Zion is the account in 2 Samuel 5 of David's conquest of Jerusalem, then under the control of, the Jebusites; v. 7 speaks of "the stronghold of Zion." This and other texts, as well as recent archaeological research, suggest that Zion was limited originally to the Jebusite fortress located on the crest of a hill at the southeast corner of Jerusalem, also called the Ophel (2 Chron. 27.3; etc.). After his victory, David renamed the stronghold "the city of David" (2 Sam. 5.9). With its physical features and the presence of the fresh-water spring of Gihon nearby, the site was of strategic importance. The city of Jerusalem soon expanded north along the eastern ridge to include what became the Temple mount, but even then the name Zion could be restricted to the city of David to the south. According to 1 Kings 8.1, at the dedication of the Temple Solomon had the ark of the covenant brought up to the Temple from "the city of David, which is Zion."

Later, poetry recalled that it was David who had found the ark and brought it to Zion, the place Yahweh desired for "his habitation" (Ps. 132.13). Already in early texts from the book of Psalms, however, Zion refers not to David's city but preeminently to Yahweh's dwelling place, Yahweh's "holy hill" (Ps. 2.6). This extension of the term is probably connected with the transfer of the ark from the city of David to the Temple newly constructed by Solomon. The ark represented the footstool of Yahweh's royal throne, and the Temple enshrining it symbolized the presence of Yahweh as king. In this way the term Zion lost its originally precise geographic designation and came to refer to the Temple area and even to the entire city of Jerusalem (Ps. 76.1–2). In later times the name Zion was erroneously restricted to the western hill, still called Mount Zion, but this was uninhabited until the eighth century BCE. But what it lost in geographic precision Zion more than regained in the rich symbolism associated with it.

That symbolism centered on Zion as the dwelling place of Yahweh as king. Since it was viewed as the site of Yahweh's throne, Zion was portrayed as a lofty peak extending into heaven, the point at which heaven and earth meet. Thus, Psalm 48.1–2 depicts Zion as Yahweh's holy mountain "on the heights of Zaphon" (NRSV: "in the far north"). Zaphon was the mountain home of the Canaanite god Baal, and imagery from Canaanite religion is applied to Zion in Psalm 48 and elsewhere. True to its original designation of "stronghold," but especially because Yahweh reigned there as king, Zion was also a symbol of security. Yahweh was Zion's defender against the threats of kings and nations (e.g., Pss. 46; 48; 76). For that reason Zion was also portrayed as the place of refuge, especially for the poor (Isa 14.32; cf. Ps. 9).

Z

The Old City of Jerusalem from the East, with the Muslim shrine the Dome of the Rock on the right, on the ancient Temple Mount.

All of this seems to have given rise to a notion of Zion's inviolability, as reflected in Micah 3.9–12 and Jeremiah 7.1–15. According to these prophets, the people of Jerusalem believed the city's security against Assyrian and Babylonian threats to be guaranteed. The book of Isaiah accepts the notion of Zion's inviolability (8.9–10, 16; 17.12–14) but distinguishes between the security promised to Zion and the destruction with which Yahweh threatens Jerusalem (1.21–26; 29.1–8). Zion will endure even beyond Jerusalem's destruction.

After Jerusalem and the Temple were destroyed in 587/586 BCE, hope for the future was often expressed in terms of the restoration of Zion (Isa. 51.1–6); because of this hope, the modern Zionist movement took the ancient designation as its own. In some texts from the exilic and postexilic periods, Zion/Jerusalem is addressed in royal language common to the Near East (Isa. 45.14–17; 49.22–23; 60.4–7); in others, Zion is portrayed as a mother (Isa. 66.7–11). Occasionally, Zion is identified with the community itself: "saying to Zion, 'You are my people'" (Isa. 51.16). 2 Esdras speaks of Zion in referring to the heavenly Jerusalem that would ultimately replace the earthly one (13.36; cf. Rev. 21.1–17). In Hebrews 12.22, Zion refers to the "new covenant" of Jesus. In all of these diverse ways, Zion is the "city of God" (Ps. 87.3).

BEN C. OLLENBURGER

Z

ACKNOWLEDGMENTS FOR OXFORD EDITION

The *Companion* has seen a long developmental process, and we wish to thank contributors for their ongoing support of the project. We are most grateful, of course, for their expert contributions, which are the essence of the volume; their names are listed after this introduction.

The advisory editors have been extraordinarily helpful in assuring that the *Companion* maintains its balanced perspective, proportion, and scope. Jo Ann Hackett, Barbara Geller Nathanson, William Propp, and Philip Sellew have been generous with their advice and time in suggesting contributors, reviewing the list of entries and individual articles, and a variety of other tasks.

Many people at Oxford University Press have been indispensable in the development and completion of the *Companion*. Invaluable support and wise counsel were provided by Linda Halvorson Morse and Claude Conyers. Stephen Chasteen and Ann Toback were project editors; their coordination of authors, editors, editorial board, copy editors, and production was characterized by skill and tact. We are

also grateful to Mark Cummings, Nancy Davis, Liza Ewell, and Donald Kraus for their continuing assistance.

We especially thank Ted Byfield and Eric C. Banks for their meticulous copyediting, Vida Petronis for her diligent proofreading, and Paul Kobelski and Maurya Horgan for their detailed indexing, all of which resulted in a more consistent and accessible book.

Thanks are due to Johanna Froelich, a graduate student at Princeton University, who translated into English a number of articles written in German. Thanks are also due to Shawn Anglim, Anne Brock, Ah Seng Choo; Andrew Gilman, Julia Weaver, and Karen-Marie Yust, students at Harvard Divinity School, and Elsa Stanger, who typed the original manuscript onto disk, and to Gene McAfee, who directed that process as well as typing a great deal himself.

Bruce M. Metzger and Michael D. Coogan
August 1993

DIRECTORY OF CONTRIBUTORS FOR OXFORD EDITION

VALERIE ABRAHAMSEN, *Waltham, Massachusetts*

ELIZABETH ACHTEMEIER, *Adjunct Professor of Bible and Homiletics, Union Theological Seminary, Richmond, Virginia*

PAUL J. ACHTEMEIER, *The Herbert Worth and Annie H. Jackson Professor of Biblical Interpretation, Union Theological Seminary, Richmond, Virginia*

SUSAN ACKERMAN, *Assistant Professor of Religion, Dartmouth College, Hanover, New Hampshire*

PETER R. ACKROYD, *Samuel Davidson Professor of Old Testament Studies, Emeritus, King's College, University of London, England*

PHILIP S. ALEXANDER, *Nathan Laski Professor of Post-Biblical Jewish Literature, University of Manchester, England*

FRANCIS I. ANDERSEN, *Professor of Old Testament, New College for Advanced Christian Studies, Berkeley, California*

BERNHARD W. ANDERSON, *Adjunct Professor of Old Testament Theology, Boston University, Massachusetts*

HECTOR IGNACIO AVALOS, *Carolina Postdoctoral Fellow, Departments of Religious Studies and Anthropology, University of North Carolina at Chapel Hill*

E. BADIAN, *John Moors Cabot Professor of History, Harvard University, Cambridge, Massachusetts*

KENNETH E. BAILEY, *Research Professor of Middle Eastern New Testament Studies, The Ecumenical Institute, Jerusalem, Israel*

PHILIP L. BARLOW, *Assistant Professor of Theological Studies, Hanover College, Indiana*

WILLIAM H. BARNES, *Associate Professor of Biblical Studies, Southeastern College of the Assemblies of God, Lakeland, Florida*

JAMES BARR, *Professor of Hebrew Bible, Vanderbilt University, Nashville, Tennessee; Regius Professor of Hebrew, Emeritus, University of Oxford, England*

MARKUS K. BARTH, *Professor of New Testament, Emeritus, Universitat Basel, Switzerland*

JOHN R. BARTLETT, *Principal, Church of Ireland Theological College, Dublin; Fellow, Emeritus, Trinity College, Dublin, Ireland*

JOHN BARTON, *Oriel and Laing Professor of the Interpretation of Holy Scripture, University of Oxford, England*

JUDITH R. BASKIN, *Chair, Department of Judaic Studies, State University of New York at Albany*

RICHARD J. BAUCKHAM, *Professor of New Testament Studies, University of St. Andrews, Scotland*

WILLIAM A. BEARDSLEE, *Charles Howard Candler Professor of Religion, Emeritus, Emory University, Atlanta, Georgia*

ROGER T. BECKWITH, *Warden of Latimer House, Oxford, England*

CHRISTOPHER T. BEGG, *Assistant Professor of Theology, Catholic University of America, Washington, D.C.*

ROBERT A. BENNETT, JR., *Professor of Old Testament, Episcopal Divinity School, Cambridge, Massachusetts*

G. E. BENTLEY, JR., *Professor of English, University of Toronto, Ontario, Canada*

JERRY H. BENTLEY, *Professor of History, University of Hawai'i at Manoa*

ADELE BERLIN, *Professor of Hebrew, University of Maryland at College Park*

ERNEST BEST, *Professor of Divinity and Biblical Criticism, Emeritus, University of Glasgow, Scotland*

OTTO BETZ, *Professor and Lecturer of New Testament and Jewish Studies, Retired, Eberhard-Karls-Universitat, Tubingen, Germany*

PHYLLIS A. BIRD, *Associate Professor of Old Testament Interpretation, Garrett Evangelical Theological Seminary, Evanston, Illinois*

M. H. BLACK, *Fellow, Clare Hall, University of Cambridge; former Publisher of Cambridge University Press, England*

MATTHEW BLACK, *Professor of Biblical Criticism, Emeritus, University of St. Andrews, Scotland*

ROBERT G. BRATCHER, *Translation Consultant, United Bible Societies, New York, New York*

PAUL L. BREMER, *Professor of Biblical Studies, Reformed Bible College, Grand Rapids, Michigan*

JOHN A. BRINKMAN, *Charles H. Swift Distinguished Service Professor of Mesopotamian History, University of Chicago, Illinois*

S. P. BROCK, *Reader in Syriac Studies, University of Oxford, England*

BERNADETTE J. BROOTEN, *Kraft-Hiatt Chair of Christian Studies, Near Eastern and Judaic Studies Department, Brandeis University, Waltham, Massachusetts*

F. F. BRUCE, *Rylands Professor of Biblical Criticism and Exegesis, University of Manchester, England, deceased*

GEORGE WESLEY BUCHANAN, *Professor of New Testament, Emeritus, Wesley Theological Seminary, Washington, D.C.*

DAVID G. BURKE, *Director, Translations Department, American Bible Society, New York, New York*

EDWARD F. CAMPBELL, *Francis A. McGaw Professor of Old Testament, McCormick Theological Seminary, Chicago, Illinois*

BRUCE D. CHILTON, *Barnard Iddings Bell Professor of Religion, Bard College, Annandale-on-Hudson, New York*

RONALD E. CLEMENTS, *Samuel Davidson Professor of Old Testament Studies, King's College, University of London, England*

RICHARD J. CLIFFORD, *Professor of Old Testament, Weston School of Theology, Cambridge, Massachusetts*

DAVID J. A. CLINES, *Professor of Biblical Studies, University of Sheffield, England*

GEORGE W. COATS, *Professor of Old Testament, Retired, Lexington Theological Seminary, Kentucky*

AELRED CODY, O.S.B., *General Editor, Catholic Biblical Quarterly, St. Meinrad Archabbey, Indiana*

DONALD COGGAN, *Archbishop of Canterbury, England, 1974-1980*

RICHARD COGGINS, *Senior Lecturer in Old Testament Studies, King's College, University of London, England*

H. J. BERNARD COMBRINK, *Professor of New Testament, University of Stellenbosch, South Africa*

EDGAR W. CONRAD, *Reader in Studies in Religion, University of Queensland, Australia*

DEMETRIOS J. CONSTANTELOS, *Charles Cooper Townsend Sr. Distinguished Professor of History and Religious Studies, Richard Stockton State College of New Jersey, Pomona*

MICHAEL D. COOGAN, *Professor of Religious Studies, Stonehill College, North Easton, Massachusetts*

J. M. COOK, *Professor of Ancient History and Classical Archaeology, Emeritus, University of Bristol, England*

JAMES I. COOK, *Anton Biemolt Professor of New Testament, Western Theological Seminary, Holland, Michigan*

ROBIN C. COVER, *Dallas, Texas*

DERMOT COX, O.F.M., *Professor of Old Testament Exegesis, Universita Gregoriana, Rome, Italy*

JAMES L. CRENSHAW, *Professor of Old Testament, Duke University, Durham, North Carolina*

PETER H. DAVIDS, *Scholar in Residence, Langley Vineyard Christian Fellowship, British Columbia, Canada*

ROBERT DAVIDSON, *Professor of Old Testament Language and Literature, Emeritus, University of Glasgow, Scotland*

JOËL DELOBEL, *Professor of New Testament Textual Criticism and Exegesis, Katholieke Universiteit, Leuven, Belgium*

ROBERT C. DENTAN, *Professor of Old Testament Emeritus, General Theological Seminary, New York, New York*

J. DUNCAN M. DERRETT, *Professor of Oriental Laws, Emeritus, University of London, England*

ALEXANDER A. DI LELLA, O.F.M., *Professor of Biblical Studies, Catholic University of America, Washington, D.C.*

T. KEITH DIX, *Assistant Professor, Department of Classical Studies, University of North Carolina at Greensboro*

JOHN W. DRANE, *Director, Center for the Study of Christianity and Contemporary Society, University of Stirling, Scotland*

JOHN I DURHAM, *Pastor, Greenwich Baptist Church, Connecticut*

JAMES M. EFIRD, *Professor of Biblical Interpretation, Duke University, Durham, North Carolina*

CARL S. EHRLICH, *Professor, Hochschule für jüdische Studien, Heidelberg, Germany*

BARRY L. EICHLER, *Associate Professor of Assyriology, University of Pennsylvania, Philadelphia*

J. A. EMERTON, *Regius Professor of Hebrew, and Fellow, St. John's College, University of Cambridge, England*

DAVID EWERT, *President, Mennonite Brethren Bible College, Winnipeg, Manitoba, Canada*

GILLIAN FEELEY-HARNIK, *Professor of Anthropology, The Johns Hopkins University, Baltimore, Maryland*

F. CHARLES FENSHAM, *Professor of Semitic Languages and Cultures, Emeritus, University of Stellenbosch, South Africa*

JOSEPH A. FITZMYER, S.J., *Professor of Biblical Studies, Emeritus, Catholic University of America, Washington, D.C.*

DANIEL E. FLEMING, *Assistant Professor, New York University, New York*

PAULA FREDRIKSEN, *Professor, Department of Religion, Boston University, Massachusetts*

EDWIN D. FREED, *Professor of Biblical Literature and Religion, Emeritus, Gettysburg College, Pennsylvania*

ERNEST S. FRERICHS, *Professor of Judaic Studies, Brown University, Providence, Rhode Island*

SEÁN FREYNE, *Professor of Theology, Trinity College, Dublin, Ireland*

STEVEN FRIESEN, *Fellow, Program on Cultural Studies, East-West Center, Honolulu, Hawai'i*

KARLFRIED FROEHLICH, *Benjamin B. Warfield Professor of Ecclesiastical History, Emeritus, Princeton Theological Seminary, New Jersey*

REGINALD H. FULLER, *Professor Emeritus, Virginia Theological Seminary, Alexandria, Virginia*

RUSSELL FULLER, *Assistant Professor of Theological and Religious Studies, University of San Diego, California*

FRANCIS T. GIGNAC, S.J., *Professor of Biblical Greek, Catholic University of America, Washington, D.C.*

THOMAS FRANCIS GLASSON, *Lecturer in New Testament Studies, Retired, University of London, England*

ANDRÉ L. GODDU, *Director, Program in the History and Philosophy of Science, Stonehill College, North Easton, Massachusetts*

EDWIN M. GOOD, *Professor of Religious Studies, Emeritus, Stanford University, California*

CYRUS H. GORDON, *Joseph and Esther Foster Professor of Mediterranean Studies, Emeritus, Brandeis University, Waltham, Massachusetts; Director, Center for Ebla Research, New York University, New York*

ROBERT P. GORDON, *Lecturer in Old Testament, University of Cambridge, England*

PROSPER GRECH, O.S.A., *Professor of New Testament Exegesis, Augustinianum, Rome; Lecturer in Hermeneutics, Pontificio Instituto Biblico, Rome, Italy*

JOSEPH A. GREENE, *Curator of Publications, Semitic Museum, Harvard University, Cambridge, Massachusetts*

ROBERT A. GUELICH, *Professor of Theology, Fuller Theological Seminary, Pasadena, California, deceased*

DAVID M. GUNN, *Professor of Old Testament, Columbia Theological Seminary, Decatur, Georgia*

JO ANN HACKETT, *Professor, Department of Near Eastern Languages and Civilizations, Harvard University, Cambridge, Massachusetts*

WILLIAM W. HALLO, *The William M. Laffan Professor of Assyriology and Babylonian Literature, and Curator, Babylonian Collection, Yale University, New Haven, Connecticut*

BARUCH HALPERN, *Professor of History, Pennsylvania State University, University Park*

RAYMOND HAMMER, *Professor of Theology, Emeritus, Rikkyō University, Tokyo, Japan; former Director, Bible Reading Fellowship, London, England*

PHILIP C. HAMMOND, *Professor of Anthropology, University of Utah, Salt Lake City*

ANTHONY TYRRELL HANSON, *Professor of Theology, Emeritus, University of Hull, England, deceased*

DOUGLAS R. A. HARE, *William F. Orr Professor of New Testament, Pittsburgh Theological Seminary, Pennyslvania*

WALTER HARRELSON, *Distinguished Professor of Hebrew Bible, Emeritus, Vanderbilt University, Nashville, Tennessee*

GERALD F. HAWTHORNE, *Professor of Greek, Wheaton College, Illinois*

DAVID M. HAY, *Professor, Department of Religion and Philosophy, Coe College, Cedar Repids, Iowa*

JOHN H. HAYES, *Professor of Old Testament, Candler School of Theology, Emory University, Atlanta, Georgia*

PETER D. HEINEGG, *Professor of English, Union College, Schenectady, New York*

RONALD S. HENDEL, *Associate Professor, Department of Religious Studies, Southern Methodist University, Dallas, Texas*

GEORGE S. HENDRY, *Professor of Systematic Theology, Emeritus, Princeton Theological Seminary, New Jersey*

PAULA S. HIEBERT, *Visiting Instructor, Department of Theology, Boston College, Massachusetts*

THEODORE HIEBERT, *Associate Professor of Hebrew Bible/Old Testament, Harvard Divinity School, Cambridge, Massachusetts*

DAVID HILL, *Reader in Biblical Studies, Retired, University of Sheffield, England*

DELBERT R. HILLERS, *W. W. Spence Professor of Semitic Languages, The Johns Hopkins University, Baltimore, Maryland*

HAROLD W. HOEHNER, *Chairman and Professor of New Testament Studies, and Director, Th.D. Studies, Dallas Theological Seminary, Texas*

CARL R. HOLLADAY, *Professor, Candler School of Theology, Emory University, Atlanta, Georgia*

LATON E. HOLMGREN, *General Secretary, Retired, American Bible Society, New York, New York*

MORNA D. HOOKER, *Lady Margaret Professor of Divinity, University of Cambridge, England*

LESLIE J. HOPPE, O.F.M., *Professor of Old Testament, Catholic Theological Union, Chicago, Illinois*

J. L. HOULDEN, *Professor of Theology, King's College, University of London, England*

J. KEIR HOWARD, *Diocese of Wellington Institute of Theology, New Zealand*

PHILIP EDGCUMBE HUGHES, *Visiting Professor, Westminster Theological Seminary, Philadelphia, Pennsylvania, deceased*

EDWARD HULMES, *Spalding Professorial Fellow, World Religions, Department of Theology, University of Durham, England*

ALAN JACOBS, *Associate Professor of English, Wheaton College, Illinois*

JOHN FREDERICK JANSEN, *Professor of New Testament, Emeritus, Austin Presbyterian Theological Seminary, Texas, deceased*

DAVID LYLE JEFFREY, *Professor of English Language and Litrature, University of Ottawa, Ontario, Canada*

JOSEPH JENSEN, O.S.B., *Executive Secretary, Catholic University of America, Washington, D.C.*

SHERMAN ELBRIDGE JOHNSON, *Dean and Professor of New Testament, Emeritus, The Church Divinity School of the Pacific, Berkeley, California, deceased*

JAKOB JÓNSSON, *Reykjavik, Iceland, deceased*

EDWIN A. JUDGE, *Macquarie University, Australia*

ROBERT J. KARRIS, O.F.M., *Rome, Italy*

HOWARD CLARK KEE, *Aurelio Professor of Biblical Studies, Emeritus, Boston University, Massachusetts; Senior Research Fellow, Religious Studies, University of Pennsylvania, Philadelphia*

JACK DEAN KINGSBURY, *Aubrey Lee Brooks Professor of Biblical Theology, Union Theological Seminary, Richmond, Virginia*

DOUGLAS A. KNIGHT, *Professor of Hebrew Bible, Vanderbilt University, Nashville, Tennessee*

GEORGE A. F. KNIGHT, *Professor of Old Testament Studies and Semitic Languages, Emeritus, and former Principal, Pacific Theological College, Fiji*

GARY N. KNOPPERS, *Assistant Professor of Religious Studies, Pennsylvania State University, University Park*

DONALD KRAUS, *Senior Editor, Oxford University Press, New York, New York*

WILLIAM SANFORD LASOR, *Professor, Fuller Theological Seminary, Pasadena, California, deceased*

SOPHIE LAWS, *Fellow, Religion and History, Regent's College, London, England*

A. R. C. LEANEY, *Professor of Christian Theology, Emeritus, Nottingham University, England*

MARY JOAN WINN LEITH, *Lecturer, Department of Literature, Massachusetts Institute of Technology, Cambridge*

AMY-JILL LEVINE, *Professor, Department of Religion, Swarthmore College, Pennsylvania*

BARUCH A. LEVINE, *Professor of Hebrew and Judaic Studies, New York University, New York*

LEE LEVINE, *Professor of Jewish History and Archaeology, The Hebrew University of Jerusalem; Dean and Director, The Seminary of Judaic Studies, Jerusalem, Israel*

THEODORE J. LEWIS, *Associate Professor of Hebrew Bible and Semitic Languages, University of Georgia, Athens*

I-JIN LOH, *Coordinator of Asia Opportunity Program and Translation Consultant, United Bible Societies, Asia Pacific Region, Taipei, Taiwan*

JOHANNES P. LOUW, *Professor of Greek, University of Pretoria, South Africa*

FRANCIS LYALL, *Dean of Faculty and Professor of Public Law, University of Aberdeen, Scotland*

ABRAHAM J. MALHERBE, *Buckingham Professor of New Testament Criticism and Interpretation, Yale Divinity School, New Haven, Connecticut*

GIORA MANOR, *Editor, Israel Dance Quarterly; Adviser, Israel Dance Library, Jerusalem, Israel*

STEPHEN A. MARINI, *Professor of Religion, Wellesley College, Massachusetts*

I. HOWARD MARSHALL, *Professor of New Testament Exegesis, University of Aberdeen, Scotland*

RALPH P. MARTIN, *Professor of Biblical Studies, University of Sheffield, England*

REX MASON, *University Lecturer in Old Testament and Hebrew, University of Oxford, England*

ULRICH W. MAUSER, *Helen H. P. Manson Professor of New Testament Literature and Exegesis, Princeton Theological Seminary, New Jersey*

GENE MCAFEE, *Harvard Divinity School, Cambridge, Massachusetts*

P. KYLE MCCARTER, JR., *William Foxwell Albright Professor of Biblical and Ancient Near Eastern Studies, The Johns Hopkins University, Baltimore, Maryland*

PATRICK E. MCGOVERN, *Research Scientist, Archaeoceramics and Archaeochemistry, University Museum, University of Pennsylvania, Philadelphia*

WILLIAM MCKANE, *Professor of Hebrew and Oriental Languages, Emeritus, University of St. Andrews, Scotland*

STEVEN L. MCKENZIE, *Associate Professor of Old Testament, Rhodes College, Memphis, Tennessee*

PAULA M. MCNUTT, *Assistant Professor of Religious Studies, Canisius College, Buffalo, New York*

SAMUEL A. MEIER, *Associate Professor of Hebrew and Comparative Semitics, Ohio State University, Columbus*

WILLIAM W. MEISSNER, S.J., *University Professor of Psychoanalysis, Boston College; Training and Supervising Analyst, Boston Psychoanalytic Institute, Massachusetts*

BRUCE M. METZGER, *George L. Collord Professor of New Testament Language and Literature, Emeritus, Princeton Theological Seminary, New Jersey*

ISOBEL MACKAY METZGER, *Princeton, New Jersey*

CAROL L. MEYERS, *Professor of Biblical Studies and Archaeology, Duke University, Durham, North Carolina*

ERIC M. MEYERS, *Professor of Bible and Judaic Studies, Duke University, Durham, North Carolina*

ALAN MILLARD, *Rankin Professor of Hebrew and Ancient Semitic Languages, University of Liverpool, England*

J. MAXWELL MILLER, *Professor of Old Testament Studies, Emory University, Atlanta, Georgia*

PAUL S. MINEAR, *Winkley Professor of Biblical Theology, Emeritus, Yale University, New Haven, Connecticut*

CAREY A. MOORE, *Amanda Rupert Strong Professor of Religion, Gettysburg College, Pennsylvania*

LEON MORRIS, *Former Principal, Ridley College, Melbourne, Australia*

PAUL G. MOSCA, *Professor, Department of Religious Studies, University of British Columbia, Vancouver, Canada*

LUCETTA MOWRY, *Professor Emerita, Department of Religion, Wellesley College, Massachusetts*

JOHN MUDDIMAN, *Fellow, New Testament Studies, Mansfield College, University of Oxford, England*

ROLAND E. MURPHY, O. CARM., *George Washington Ivey Professor of Biblical Studies, Emeritus, Duke University, Durham, North Carolina*

JEROME MURPHY-O'CONNOR, O.P., *Professor of New Testament, École Biblique de Jerusalem, Israel*

MOGENS MÜLLER, *Professor of New Testament Exegesis, Københavns Universitet, Denmark*

BARBARA GELLER NATHANSON, *Professor, Department of Religion, Wellesley College, Massachusetts*

FRANS NEIRYNCK, *Professor of New Testament, Katholieke Universiteit, Leuven, Belgium*

WILLIAM B. NELSON, JR., *Professor, Department of Religious Studies, Westmont College, Santa Barbara, California*

JACOB NEUSNER, *Distinguished Research Professor of Religious Studies, University of South Florida, Tampa*

EUGENE A. NIDA, *Translations Consultant, American Bible Society, New York, New York*

MARK A. NOLL, *Professor of History, Wheaton College, Illinois*

ROBERT NORTH, S.J., *Editor, Elenchus of Biblica; Professor of Archaeology, Emeritus, Pontificio Istituto Biblico, Rome, Italy*

PETER T. O'BRIEN, *Vice Principal and Head, New Testament Department, Moore Theological College, Newton, Australia*

BEN C. OLLENBURGER, *Professor of Religious Studies, Association of Mennonite Seminaries, Elkhart, Indiana*

DENNIS T. OLSON, *Assistant Professor of Old Testament, Princeton Theological Seminary, New Jersey*

RICHARD E. OSTER, JR., *Professor of New Testament, Harding University Graduate School of Religion, Memphis, Tennessee*

J. ANDREW OVERMAN, *Professor, Department of Religion and Classics, University of Rochester, New York*

JOSEPH PATHRAPANKAL, C M.I., *Professor of New Testament and Theology, Dharmaran College, Bangalore, India*

WAYNE T. PITARD, *Associate Professor, Program for Study of Religion, University of Illinois at Urbana-Champaign*

JAMES H. PLATT, *Denver, Colorado*

J. MARTIN PLUMLEY, *Sir Herbert Thompson Professor of Egyptology, Emeritus, University of Cambridge, England*

J. R. PORTER, *Professor of Theology, Emeritus, University of Exeter, England*

SCOTT F. PRELLER, *Christian Science Practitioner, Andover, Massachusetts*

WILLIAM H. PROPP, *Associate Professor of Near Eastern Languages and History, University of California at San Diego*

JAMES M. REESE, O.S.F.S., *Professor, Department of Theology, St. John's University, Jamaica, New York, deceased*

BO REICKE, *Universität Basel, Switzerland, deceased*

ERROLL F. RHODES, *Editorial and Non-English Manager, Department of Translations and Scripture Resources, American Bible Society, New York, New York*

JOHN RICHES, *Professor of Divinity and Biblical Criticism, University of Glasgow, Scotland*

HARALD RIESENFELD *Professor of Biblical Exegesis, Emeritus, Uppsala Universitet, Sweden*

GUY ROGERS, *Associate Professor of Greek, Latin, and History, Wellesley College, Massachusetts*

J. W. ROGERSON, *Professor and Head, Department of Biblical Studies, University of Sheffield, England*

DAVID T. RUNIA, *C.J. de Vogel Professor Extraordinarily in Ancient Philosophy, Rijksuniversiteit Utrecht, the Netherlands*

D. S. RUSSELL, *Baptist Union of Great Britain, Bristol*

LELAND RYKEN, *Professor of English, Wheaton College, Illinois*

BRUCE E. RYSKAMP, *Corporate Vice President, Zondervan Corporation, Grand Rapids, Michigan*

LEOPOLD SABOURIN, *S.J., Professor of Sacred Scripture, Emeritus, Pontificio Istituto Orientale, Rome, Italy*

DENIS BAIN SADDINGTON, *Professor of Roman History and Archaeology, University of the Witwatersrand, South Africa*

KATHARINE DOOB SAKENFBLD, *William Albright Eisenberger Professor of Old Testament Literature, Princeton Theological Seminary, New Jersey*

RICHARD P. SALLER, *Professor of History and Classics, University of Chicago, Illinois*

JAMES A. SANDERS, *Professor of Biblical Studies, School of Theology at Claremont, California*

NAHUM M. SARNA, *Dora Golding Professor of Biblical Studies, Emeritus, Brandeis University, Waltham, Massachusetts; General Editor, Jewish Publication Society Torah Commentary*

JOHN F. A. SAWYER, *Professor, Department of Religious Studies, University of Newcastle upon Tyne, England*

DANIEL N. SCHOWALTER, *Associate Professor, Department of Religion, Carthage College, Kenosha, Wisconsin*

EILEEN SCHULLER, *Professor, Department of Religious Studies, McMaster University, Hamilton, Ontario, Canada*

PHILIP SELLEW, *Associate Professor, Department of Classical and Near Eastern Studies, University of Minnesota, Minneapolis*

C. L. SEOW, *Associate Professor of Old Testament, Princeton Theological Seminary, New Jersey*

DRORAH O'DONNELL SETEL, *Seattle, Washington*

GREGORY SHAW, *Professor, Department of Religious Studies, Stonehill College, North Easton, Massachusetts*

MICHAL SHEKEL, *Rabbi, Jewish Center of Sussex County, New Jersey*

DANIEL J. SIMUNDSON, *Professor of Old Testament, and Dean of Academic Affairs, Luther Northwestern Theological Seminary, St. Paul, Minnesota*

STEPHEN S. SMALLEY, *Dean of Chester Cathedral, England*

J. A. SOGGIN, *Professor of Hebrew Language and Literature, Universitá di Roma, Italy*

WALTER F. SPECHT, *Chair, Department of Religion, Retired, Loma Linda University, California.*

HENDRIK C. SPYKERBOER, *Professor of Old Testament Studies, Trinity Theological College, Brisbane, Australia*

LYNN STANLEY, *Manufacturing Controller, Oxford University Press, New York, New York*

ROBERT H. STEIN, *Professor of New Testament, Bethel Theological Seminary, St. Paul, Minnesota*

KRISTER STENDAHL, *Professor of Christian Studies, Brandeis University, Waltham, Massachusetts*

PHILIP STERN, *White Plains, New York*

ROBERT STOOPS, *Associate Professor, Department of Liberal Studies, Western Washington University, Bellingham*

G. M. STYLER, *Fellow, Corpus Christi College, and University Lecturer in Divinity, retired, University of Cambridge, England*

JOHN N. SUGGIT, *Professor Emeritus, Rhodes University, Grahamstown, South Africa*

WILLARD M. SWARTLEY, *Professor of New Testament, Associated Mennonite Biblical Seminaries, Elkhart, Indiana*

JOHN SWEET, *University Lecturer in Divinity, University of Cambridge, England*

SARAH J. TANZER, *Professor, McCormick Theological Seminary, Chicago, Illinois*

RON TAPPY, *Assistant Professor of Archaeology and Literature of Ancient Israel, Westmont College, Santa Barbara, California*

ANTHONY C. THISELTON, *Professor of Christian Theology, and Head, Department of Christian Theology, University of Nottingham, England*

DEREK J., TIDBALL, *Secretary for Mission and Evangelism, Baptist Union of Great Britain, Marcham, England*

PATRICK A. TILLER, *Visiting Lecturer on Greek, Harvard Divinity School, Cambridge, Massachusetts*

JOHN TINSLEY, *Professor of Theology, University of Leeds, 1962-1976; Bishop of Bristol, 1976–1985, England, deceased*

ANDRIE B. DU TOIT, *Professor of New Testament, University of Pretoria, South Africa*

EMANUEL TOV, *Hebrew University, Jerusalem, Israel*

W. SIBLEY TOWNER, *The Reverend Archibald McFadyen Professor of Biblical Interpretation, Union Theological Seminary, Richmond, Virginia*

STEPHEN H. TRAVIS, *Vice-Principal and Lecturer in New Testament, St. John's College, Nottingham, England*

ALLISON A. TRITES, *John Payzant Distinguished Professor of Biblical Studies, Acadia University, Wolfville, Nova Scotia, Canada*

ETIENNE TROCMÉ, *Professor of New Testament, Université des Sciences Humaines de Strasbourg, France*

GENE M. TUCKER, *Professor of Old Testament, Candler School of Theology, Emory University, Atlanta, Georgia*

DAVID H. VAN DAALEN, *Minister, United Reformed Church, Huntingdon, England*

GERRIT E. VAN DER MERWE, *General Secretary, Emeritus, Bible Society of South Africa, Cape Town*

BRUCE VAWTER, *C.M., DePaul University, Illinois, deceased*

ALLEN D. VERHEY, *Director, Institute of Religion, Texas Medical Center, Houston, Texas*

BEN ZION WACHOLDER, *Solomon B. Freehof Professor of Jewish Law and Practice; Hebrew Union College, Cincinnati, Ohio*

GEOFFREY WAINWRIGHT, *Robert E. Cushman Professor of Christian Theology, Duke University, Durham, North Carolina*

JOHN D. W. WATTS, *Donald L. Williams Professor of Old Testament, Southern Baptist Theological Seminary, Louisville, Kentucky*

GORDON J. WENHAM, *Senior Lecturer in Religious Studies, Cheltenham and Gloucester College of Higher Education, England*

CLAUS WESTERMANN, *Professor Emeritus, Universität Heidelberg, Germany*

RICHARD E. WHITAKER, *Information Research Specialist, Speer Library, Princeton Theological Seminary, New Jersey*

JOHN L. WHITE, *Professor of New Testament and Christian Origins, Loyola University of Chicago, Illinois*

SIDNIE ANN WHITE, *Assistant Professor of Religion, Albright College, Reading, Pennyslvania*

R. N. WHYBRAY, *Professor of Hebrew and Old Testament Studies, Emeritus, University of Hull, England*

TIMOTHY M. WILLIS, *Professor, Religion Division, Pepperdine University, Malibu, California*

ROBERT MCL. WILSON, *Professor of Biblical Criticism, Emeritus, University of St. Andrews, Scotland*

VINCENT L. WIMBUSH, *Professor of New Testament and Christian Origins, Union Theological Seminary, New York, New York*

WALTER WINK, *Professor of Biblical Interpretation, Auburn Theological Seminary, New York*

DONALD J. WISEMAN, *Professor of Assyriology, Emeritus, University of London, England*

DAVID F. WRIGHT, *Senior Lecturer in Ecclesiastical History, and former Dean of Faculty of Divinity, University of Edinburgh, Scotland*

EDWIN M. YAMAUCHI, *Professor of History, Miami University, Oxford, Ohio*

JOHN ZIESLER, *Reader in Theology, University of Bristol, England*

BIBLIOGRAPHY

To assist readers, the editors have prepared this bibliography of some important and useful books about the Bible available in English.

Critical Introductions. These provide summaries of modern scholarly research on the formation of the Bible from the smallest literary units to the final canonical arrangement, as well as a bibliographic starting point.

CHILDS, BREVARD S. *Introduction to the Old Testament as Scripture.* Philadelphia: Fortress, 1979.

CHILDS, BREVARD S. *The New Testament as Canon: An Introduction.* Philadelphia: Fortress, 1985.

COLLINS, RAYMOND F. *Introduction to the New Testament.* Garden City, N.Y.: Doubleday, 1983.

HAYES, JOHN H. *An Introduction to Old Testament Study.* Nashville, Tenn.: Abingdon, 1979.

KOESTER, HELMUT. *Introduction to the New Testament,* vol. 2: *History and Literature of Early Christianity.* Philadelphia: Fortress, 1982.

KAÜMMEL, WERNER G. *Introduction to the New Testament,* Rev. ed. Nashville, Tenn.: Abingdon, 1975.

Popular Introductions. These are frequently used as text in undergraduate courses, and provide readable surveys of the development of the Bible and of the history of the biblical world.

ALTER, ROBERT, AND FRANK KERMODE. *The Literary Guide to the Bible.* Cambridge, Mass.: Belknap, 1987.

ANDERSON, BERNARD W. *Understanding the Old Testament.* 4th ed. Englewood Cliffs, N.J.: Prentice-Hall, 1985.

BARR, DAVID L. *New Testament Story: An Introduction.* Belmont, Calif.: Wadsworth, 1987.

COURT, JOHN M. AND KATHLEEN M. COURT. *The New Testament World.* Englewood Cliffs, N.J.: Prentice-Hall, 1990.

CRENSHAW, JAMES L. *Old Testament Story and Faith: A Literary and Theological Introduction.* Peabody, Mass.: Hendrickson, 1992 (repr. of 1986 ed.).

FREED, EDWIN D. *The New Testament: A Critical Introduction.* 2d ed. Belmont, Calif.: Wadsworth, 1991.

GOTTWALD, NORMAN K. *The Hebrew Bible: A Socio-Literary Introduction.* Philadelphia: Fortress, 1985.

HARRINGTON, DANIEL J. *Interpreting the New Testament: A Practical Guide.* Wilmington, Dela.: Michael Glazier, 1979.

HARRIS, STEPHEN L. *The New Testament: A Student's Introduction.* Mountain View, Calif.: Mayfield, 1988.

JOHNSON, LUKE T. *The Writing of the New Testament: An Interpretation.* Philadelphia: Fortress, 1986.

KEE, HOWARD C. *Understanding the New Testament.* 5th ed. Englewood Cliffs, N.J.: Prentice-Hall, 1993.

METZGER, BRUCE M. *The New Testament: Its Background, Growth, and Content.* 2nd. ed. enlarged. Nashville, Tenn.: Abingdon, 1983.

PERRIN, NORMAN, AND DENNIS C. DULING. *The New Testament: An Introduction.* 2d ed. New York: Hartcourt Brace Jovanovich, 1982.

RENDTORFF, ROLF. *The Old Testament: An Introduction.* Philadelphia: Fortress, 1986.

ROGERSON, JOHN W., AND PHILIP DAVIES. *The Old Testament World.* Englewood Cliffs, N.J.: Prentice-Hall, 1989.

SANDMEL, SAMUEL. *The Hebrew Scriptures: An Introduction to their Literature and Religious Ideas.* New York: Oxford University, 1978.

History

BICKERMAN, ELIAS J. *The Jews in the Greek Age.* Cambridge, Mass.: Harvard University, 1988.

BRIGHT, JOHN. *A History of Israel.* 3d ed. Philadelphia: Westminster, 1971.

COHEN, SHAYE J. D. *From the Maccabees to the Mishnah.* Philadelphia: Westminster, 1987.

EDWARDS, I. E. S., ED. *The Cambridge Ancient History.* 3d ed. Cambridge University, 1970–.

HERRMANN, SIEGFRIED. *A History of Israel in Old Testament Times* 2 ed. Philadelphia: Fortress, 1981.

JAGERSMA, HENK. *A History of Israel in the Old Testament Period.* Philadelphia: Trinity, 1983.

_____. *A History of Israel from Alexander the Great to Bar Kochba.* PHILADELPHIA: FORTRESS, 1986.

KOESTER, HELMUT. *Introduction to the New Testament,* vol. 1: *History, Culture, and Religion of the Hellenistic Age.* Philadelphia: Fortress, 1982.

MILLER, J. MAXWELL, AND JOHN H. HAYES. *A History of Ancient Israel and Judah.* Philadelphia: Westminster, 1986.

SAFRAI, SHMUEL, AND MENAHEM STERN, EDS. *The Jewish People in the First Century: Historical, Geography, Political History, Social, Cultural and Religious Life and Institutions* 2 vols. Philadelphia: Fortress, 1974, 1976.

SCHÜRER, EMIL. *The History of the Jewish People in the Age of Jesus Christ.* 4 vols. Rev. and ed. by Geza Vermes and Fergus Millar. Edinburgh: T. and T. Clark, 1973-87.

SHANKS, HERSHEL, ED. *Ancient Israel: A Short History from Abraham to the Roman Destruction of the Temple.* Washington, D.C.: Biblical Archaeology Society, 1988.

———, ED. *Christianity and Rabbinic Judaism: A Parallel History of Their Origins and Early Development.* Washington, D.C.: Biblical Archaeology Society, 1992.

SOGGIN, J. ALBERTO. *A History of Ancient Israel from the Beginnings to the Bar Kochba Revolt, A.D. 755.* Philadelphia: Westminster, 1985.

DE VAUX, ROLAND. *The Early History of Israel.* Philadelphia: Westminster, 1978.

Nonbiblical Texts. These standard anthologies and surveys provide introductions to the literatures of the ancient Near Eastern and Greco-Roman neighbors of ancient Israel and earliest Christianity, as well as to early Jewish and early Christian writings not included in the canon.

BARRETT, C. K., ED. *The New Testament Background: Selected Documents.* Rev. ed. San Francisco: Harper and Row, 1989

CAMERON, RON, ED. *The Other Gospels: Non-Canonical Gospel Texts.* Philadelphia: Westminster, 1982.

CHARLESWORTH, JAMES H., ED. *The Old Testament Pseudepigrapha.* 2 vols. Garden City, N.Y.: Doubleday, 1983, 1985.

COOGAN, MICHAEL D. *Stories from Ancient Canaan.* Philadelphia: Westminster, 1978.

MILLER, ROBERT J., ED. *The Complete Gospels: Annotated Scholars Version,* Sonoma, Calif.: Polebridge, 1992.

NICKELSBURG, GEORGE W. E. *Jewish Literature between the Bible and the Mishnah: A Historical and Literary Introduction.* Philadelphia: Fortress, 1981.

PRITCHARD, JAMES B., ED. *Ancient Near Eastern Texts Relating to the Old Testament [ANET]; The Ancient Near East in Pictures Relating to the Old Testament [ANEP].* Princeton: Princeton University, rev. ed., 1969. (There is an abridged version of both: *The Ancient Near East: An Anthology of Texts and Pictures [ANETP],* 2 vols., 1958, 1975.)

ROBINSON, JAMES M., ED. *The Nag Hammadi Library.* Rev. ed. San Francisco: HarperCollins, 1988

SCHNEEMELCHER, WILHELM, ED. *New Testament Apocrypha.* Ed. Robert McL. Wilson. 2 vols. Nashville: Westminster/John Knox, 1991 (1965).

SPARKS, H. F. D., ED. *The Apocryphal Old Testament.* Oxford: Clarendon, 1984.

STONE, MICHAEL E., ED. *Jewish Writings of the Second Temple Period: Apocrypha, Pseudepigrapha, Qumran, Sectarian Writings, Philo, Josephus.* Philadelphia: Fortress, 1984.

VERMES, GEZA. *The Dead Sea Scrolls in English.* 3d ed. Sheffield, Eng.: JSOT Press, 1987.

Archaeology

AHARONI, YOHANAN. *The Archaeology of the Land of Israel.* Philadelphia: Westminster, 1982.

BEN-TOR, AMNON, ED. *The Archaeology of Ancient Israel.* New Haven: Yale University, 1991.

KENYON, KATHLEEN M. *The Bible and Recent Archaeology.* Rev. ed. by P. R. S. Moorey. Atlanta: John Knox, 1987.

MAZAR, AMIHAI. *Archaeology of the Land of the Bible: 10,000– 586 B.C.E.* New York: Doubleday, 1990.

STERN, EPHRAIM, ED. *The New Encyclopedia of Archaeological Excavations in the Holy Land.* New York: Simon and Schuster, 1993.

STILLWELL, RICHARD ET AL., EDS. *The Princeton Encyclopedia of Classical Sites.* Princeton: Princeton University, 1976.

WILKINSON, JOHN. *The Jerusalem Jesus Knew: An Archaeological Guide to the Gospels.* New York: Thomas Nelson, 1983.

Geography

AHARONI, YOHANAN. *The Land of the Bible: A Historical Geography.* Rev. ed. Philadelphia: Westminster, 1979.

AHARONI, YOHANAN, AND MICHAEL AVI-YONAH. *The Macmillan Bible Atlas.* 3d ed. New York: Macmillan, 1992.

BALY, DENIS. *The Geography of the Bible.* Rev. ed. New York: Harper and Row, 1974.

MAY, HERBERT G. *Oxford Bible Atlas.* 3rd ed. rev. by John Day, New York: Oxford University, 1984.

ORNI, EPHRAIM, AND E. EPHRAT. *Geography of Israel.* 4th ed. Jerusalem: Israel Universities, 1980.

PRITCHARD, JAMES B. *The Harper Atlas of the Bible.* New York: Harper and Row, 1987.

Religion and Society. All of the following are major contributions to the study of Israelite, early Jewish, and early Christian religion, literature, and culture. While the discussion is frequently technical, they will repay serious reading.

CROSS, FRANK MOORE. *Canaanite Myth and Hebrew Epic: Essays in the History of the Religion of Israel.* Cambridge, Mass.: Harvard University, 1973.

KAUFMANN, YEHEZKEL. *The Religion of Israel from Its Beginnings to the Babylonian Exile.* Chicago: University of Chicago, i960.

KRAEMER, ROSS SHEPARD. *Her Share of the Blessings: Women's Religions among Pagans, Jews, and Christians in the Greco-Roman World.* New York: Oxford University, 1992.

KRAUS, HANS-JOACHIM. *Worship in Israel: A Cultic History of the Old Testament.* Richmond, Va.: John Knox, 1966.

NOTH, MARTIN. *A History of Pentateuchal Traditions.* Trans. Bernhard W. Anderson. Englewood Cliffs, N.J.: Prentice-Hall, 1972.

SANDMEL, SAMUEL. *Judaism and Christian Beginnings.* New York: Oxford University, 1978.

SEGAL, ALAN F. *Rebecca's Children: Judaism and Christianity in the Roman World.* Cambridge, Mass.: Harvard University, 1986.

SCHIFFMAN, LAWRENCE H. *From Text to Tradition: A History of Second Temple and Rabbinic Judaism.* Hoboken, N.J.: Ktav, 1991.

STAMBAUGH, JOHN E., AND DAVID L. BALCH. *The New Testament in Its Social Environment.* Philadelphia: Westminster, 1986.

DE VAUX, ROLAND. *Ancient Israel: Its Life and Institutions.* New York: McGraw-Hill, 1965.

WEBER, MAX. *Ancient Judaism.* New York: Free Press, 1952.

Biblical Theology

BOTTERWECK, G.JOHANNES, AND HELMER RINGGREN, EDS. *Theological Dictionary of the New Testament.* Grand Rapids, Mich.: Eerdmans, 1977–.

BULTMANN, RUDOLF. *Theology of the New Testament.* New York: Scribner's, 1955.

CONZELMANN, HANS. *An Outline of the Theology of the New Testament.* New York: Harper and Row, 1969.

EICHRODT, WALTHER. *Theology of the Old Testament.* 2 vols. Philadelphia: Westminster, 1961–1967.

FREDRICKSEN, PAULA. *From Jesus to Christ: The Origins of New Testament Images of Jesus.* New Haven: Yale University, 1988.

FULLER, REGINALD H. *The Foundations of New Testament Christology.* New York: Scribner's, 1965.

HANSON, PAUL D. *The People Called: The Growth of Community in the Bible.* San Francisco: Harper and Row, 1986.

KITTEL, GERHARD, AND GERHARD FRIEDRICH, EDS. *Theological Dictionary of the New Testament.* Grand Rapids, Mich.: Eerdmans, 1985.

LEVENSON, JON D. *The Hebrew Bible, the Old Testament, and Historical Criticism.* Louisville, Ky.: Westminster/John Knox, 1993.

VON RAD, GERHARD. *Old Testament Theology.* 2 vols. New York: Harper and Row, 1962–1965.

WRIGHT, G. ERNEST. *God Who Acts: Biblical Theology as Recital.* Chicago, Ill.: Regnery, 1952.

Methodology. A series of useful "Guides to Biblical Scholarship" is published by Fortress Press (Minneapolis). More detailed surveys are found in three volumes on "The Bible and Its Modern Interpreters," published by the Society of Biblical Literature and Scholars Press (Atlanta); they are:

KNIGHT, DOUGLAS A., AND GENE M. TUCKER, EDS. *The Hebrew Bible and Its Modern Interpreters.* 1985.

KRAFT, ROBERT A., AND GEORGE W. E. NICKELSBURG, EDS. *Early Judaism and Its Modern Interpreters.* 1986.

EPP, ELDON JAY, AND GEORGE W. MACRAE, EDS. *The New Testament and Its Modern Interpreters.* 1989.

Textual Criticism

ALAND, KURT, AND BARBARA ALAND. *The Text of the New Testament: An Introduction to the Critical Editions and to the Theory and Practice of Modern Textual Criticism.* 2d ed. Grand Rapids, Mich.: Eerdmans, 1989.

METZGER, BRUCE M. *The Text of the New Testament: Its Transmission, Corruption, and Restoration.* 3d ed. New York: Oxford University, 1992.

TOV, EMANUEL. *Textual Criticism of the Hebrew Bible.* Minneapolis: Fortress, 1992.

History of Interpretation. In addition to articles in *ABD* and *IDB* and *IDPSup* (see next heading), good starting points are:

BAIRD, WILLIAM. *History of New Testament Research,* vol. 1: *From Deism to Tübingen.* Minneapolis: Fortress, 1992.

COGGINS, R. J., AND J. L. HOULDEN. *A Dictionary of Biblical Interpretation.* Philadelphia: Trinity, 1990.

GREENSLADE, S. L., ET AL. *The Cambridge History of the Bible.* 3 vols. Cambridge University, 1963–1970.

KÜMMEL, WERNER GEORG. *The New Testament: The History of the Investigation of Its Problems.* Nashville: Abingdon, 1972.

KUGEL, JAMES L., AND ROWAN A. GREER. *Early Biblical Interpretation.* Philadelphia: Westminster, 1986.

MORGAN, ROBERT, AND JOHN BARTON. *Biblical Interpretation.* New York: Oxford University, 1988.

NEILL, STEPHEN, AND N. T. WRIGHT. *The Interpretation of the New Testament, 1861–1986.* 2d ed. New York: Oxford University, 1988.

ORLINSKY, HARRY M., AND ROBERT G. BRATCHER. *A History of Bible Translation and the North American Contribution.* Atlanta: Scholars, 1991.

Reference

Encyclopedic Dictionaries. Of the many Bible dictionaries available, these are some of the better and most recent. All provide extensive bibliography for further reading.

ACHTEMEIER, PAUL J., ED. *Harper's Bible Dictionary.* San Francisco: Harper & Row, 1985.

BUTTRICK, GEORGE A., ED. *The Interpreter's Dictionary of the Bible [IDB],* 4 vols., with *Supplementary Volume [IDBSup]* (ed. K. Crim). Nashville: Abingdon, 1963, 1976.

FREEDMAN, DAVID NOEL ET AL., *The Anchor Bible Dictionary [ABD].* New York: Doubleday, 1992.

MILLS, WATSON E., ED. *Mercer Dictionary of the Bible.* Macon, Ga.: Mercer University, 1990.

MYERS, ALLEN C., ED. *Eerdmans Bible Dictionary.* Grand Rapids, Mich.: William B. Eerdman, 1987.

Concise Commentaries

ANDERSON, BERNHARD W., ED. *The Book of the Bible.* 2 vols. New York: Scribner's, 1989.

BROWN, RAYMOND E., *et al,* EDS. *The New Jerome Biblical Commentary.* Englewood Cliffs, N.J.: Prentice Hall, 1990.

LAYMON, CHARLES M., ED. *The Interpreter's One Volume Commentary on the Bible.* Nashville: Abingdon, 1971.

MAYS, JAMES L., ED. *Harper's Bible Commentary.* San Francisco: Harper and Row, 1988.

NEWSOM, CAROL A., AND SHARON H. RINGE, EDS. *The Women's Bible Commentary.* Louisville: Westminster/John Knox, 1992.

Other Useful Reference Works. These more general encyclopedias have a large number of articles on the Bible and related topics.

ELIADE, MIRCEA ET AL. EDS. *The Encyclopedia of Religion.* New York: Macmillan, 1987. ROTH CECIL, ED. *Encyclopaedia Judaica.* New York: Macmillan, 1972.

Bibliographies

FITZMYER, JOSEPH A. *An Introductory Bibliography for the Study of Scripture.* 3d ed. Rome: Pontifical Biblical Institute, 1990.

HARRINGTON, DANIEL J. *The New Testament: A Bibliography.* Wilmington, Dela.: Michael Glazier, 1985.

STUART, DOUGLAS. *Old Testament Exegesis: A Primer for Students and Pastors.* 2d ed. Philadelphia: Westminster, 1984.

ZANNONI, ARTHUR E. *The Old Testament: A Bibliography.* Collegeville, Minn.: Liturgical, 1992.

INDEX

A

Aaron, 1, 5, 11, 24, 100–101, 183–184, 194, 204–205, 209, 292

Abel, 7, 122

Abimelech, 167

Abraham, 1–2, 7, 10, 18, 22, 32, 40, 50, 80, 86, 88, 93, 97, 104–106, 115, 118, 125, 134, 147, 155, 199–200, 234, 236, 245–246, 248, 255–256, 263–267, 287

Acts of John, 21

Acts of Peter, 21

Acts of the Apostles, 2–6, 10, 13, 21, 23, 30, 32–35, 43, 46–47, 51, 57, 65, 89, 94–95, 98, 100, 106, 109–110, 114, 123, 139–141, 146, 186–189, 191–195, 204, 210, 222–227, 230, 234, 239, 250–254, 258, 265–266, 272–273, 278–279, 286, 290, 296

Adam, 7, 34, 39, 41, 67, 79, 89, 215, 255

Aeneid, 22

Afterlife, 6–8

Agriculture, 8–9

Agrippa I, 108–109, 123

Agrippa II, 109

Ahab, 143, 161, 170–173, 206, 244

Ahasuerus, 77

Alexander III ("The Great"), 9–10, 146, 215, 226

Alien, 10

Altars, 10–11

Amenhotep IV, 69

Ammon, 11–12, 68, 167, 206, 214, 299–300

Amos, The Book of, 8–9, 12–13, 119, 204, 206, 211, 218, 233, 236–241, 258–259

Andrew, 13, 22, 202

Angels, 13–14, 241

Animal Life in the Jewish Tradition, 16

Animals, 14–15, 220, 243, 258

Antichrist, 16

Antiochus IV, 17, 53–54, 92, 130

Antipas, 108

Apocalyptic Literature, 16–19

Apocrypha, 19–22, 218

Aqedah, 22–23

Arabia, 8–9, 21, 23, 118, 214, 226, 245, 267, 277, 291

Archelaus, 108

Ark, 23–24, 84, 216, 276

Armageddon, 24–25, 284

Artaxerxes, 86–87, 92

Artaxerxes III, 226

Asa, 161

Ashur-uballit I, 25

Ashurnasirpal II, 25

Asia, 25–26, 153, 207, 223–226, 230, 249, 251, 294

Assurnasirpal II, 26

Assyria, 12, 25–28, 41, 50, 62, 68–70, 90, 112–113, 116–121, 154, 173–174, 178, 204–208, 211–212, 226, 231, 236, 265, 287, 290, 294, 300–301

B

Baal, 27, 62, 71, 79, 143, 172, 183, 209, 212

Babel, Tower of, 27–28, 225

Babylon, 16, 21, 26–29, 52, 61–64, 68, 92, 103, 115–120, 125–126, 158, 161, 174, 177–178, 188, 204, 206, 211–213, 226, 231, 236, 247, 262, 273, 280, 289–290, 293, 301

Baptism, 29–30

Bar Kochba, 132

Barabbas, 30, 51

Barak, 166, 167

Barbieri, Giovanni Francesco, 207

Barnabas, 4, 93

Bathsheba, 240, 244–245, 267

Behemoth, 30

Bethlehem, 30, 36, 100, 193

Bible, 5–10, 15, 17–25, 29–33, 40–41, 54, 63, 68–69, 74, 78, 82, 84, 98–104, 110–113, 117, 120, 122, 156, 176–181, 194, 210–211, 232–233, 245, 248, 252, 258–260, 269, 275, 280, 285, 290–293

Bishop, 32, 195, 250, 296–297

Blake, William, 58

Boaz, 257

Book of Esther, 20

Book of Visions, 13

Book of Woes, 13

Bowles, Kim, 162

Brothers and Sisters of Jesus, 32

Burial Customs, 32–33

C

Caesar, Julius, 107

Caiaphas, 34

Cain and Abel, 34–35, 118, 122

Caligula, 108

Calvin, John, 71

Cambyses, 225

Capernaum, 35

Christian, 8, 14, 19, 21, 30–32, 35, 42–43, 47–49, 65, 69, 75, 83, 93, 114, 133–134, 150–151, 162, 164, 166, 181, 183, 187–188, 194–195, 197–200, 203, 206, 219, 222–230, 234, 237–239, 242–246, 249–256, 259–260, 263, 266, 273, 275, 280–287, 290, 293, 295–297

Christianity and the Rights of Animals, 15

Christmas, 35–36

Chronicles, The Books of, 10, 12, 20, 23–24, 27, 29, 31–32, 36–39, 56, 71, 87, 105, 118, 179, 185, 202, 212, 215, 231, 235–236, 242, 263, 267, 277–278

Chronology, 39–43

Church, 32, 36, 43–46, 73, 134, 182, 200, 222, 232, 251, 266, 273, 284, 289

Circumcision, 44–45

The City of God, 189

Cleopatra, 78, 107

Colossians, The Letter of Paul to the, 30, 45–46, 74, 227, 230

Corinthians, The Letters of Paul to the, 30, 46–49, 65, 78, 111, 114, 125, 128, 138–139, 179, 181–182, 187, 219, 223, 225, 239, 250, 255, 258, 266, 272, 283, 290, 296

Covenant, 49–50, 82, 90–91, 178–179

Crucifixion, 50–51, 141, 198, 202

Cyrus, 51, 225–226, 236

D

Da Vinci, Leonardo, 135

Damascus Covenant, 59

Daniel, The Book of, 14, 16, 17, 19, 21, 29, 51–54, 57, 102, 114, 145, 203, 213, 272

Darius, 87, 226

David, 6, 11, 24, 27, 30–31, 37–38, 50, 54–57, 68, 86, 106, 112, 118–121, 131, 155, 159–161, 170–175, 182, 188, 200, 203–205, 212, 233, 240–241, 244, 246, 257, 260–267, 270, 275, 278, 284, 287, 298, 300

Day of Atonement, 57, 118, 141–142, 184

Day of Judgment, 57–58

Deacon, 58–59

Dead Sea Scrolls, 18, 52, 53, 59–60, 149, 162, 164, 240, 270

Deborah, 60, 166–167, 205, 260, 292

Delilah, 259–260, 293

Deuteronomy, The Book of, 7, 10, 13, 15, 24, 50, 52, 55, 60–64, 68, 78, 80, 90, 100, 102, 104, 114, 140, 156–158, 168–171, 175, 178, 188, 203–210, 214, 217–220, 225, 233–236, 239, 257–258, 266, 272–274, 280, 283–284, 288–293

Diaspora Jews, 162

Dinah, 64
Disciple, 64
Divine Comedy, 22, 144

E

Easter, 65, 200, 225
Ecclesiastes, The Book of, 7, 65–67
Eden, The Garden of, 5, 67, 89
Edom, 67–68, 122, 218
Egypt, 6, 9, 15, 25–26, 33, 40–41, 63,
    67–70, 78–81, 84, 90, 97–98, 102, 107,
    116–117, 119–120, 157, 165, 174, 182,
    194, 199, 206, 211, 214, 217, 220, 226,
    231, 240, 245, 248–249, 265–268,
    277, 283–284, 291, 294
Elder, 70–71
Eliezer, 115
Elijah, 6, 12, 71, 170–173, 194, 201
Elisha, 12, 71–72
Enoch, 6, 41
Ephesians, The Letter of Paul to the,
    72–75, 142, 227, 239, 264, 290, 296
Esarhaddon, 26, 28
Esau, 75, 97, 115, 248
Esther, The Book of, 38, 53, 75–78, 92,
    182, 244–245, 294–295
Eve, 34, 67, 78–79, 89, 291, 293
The Exodus, 6, 10, 41, 78–82, 157, 174,
    194, 210, 220, 248
Exodus, The Book of, 11, 15, 23–24, 44,
    61, 64–65, 70, 78–84, 88, 90, 98, 100,
    102, 105–106, 153, 174, 177–178, 181,
    183–184, 187–188, 194, 202–205,
    208–210, 215, 217, 219–220, 225, 233,
    237, 243, 249, 258, 263, 266, 276–277,
    280, 284, 290, 292
Ezekiel, The Book of, 1, 14, 16–17, 29, 52,
    67, 78, 84–86, 102, 104, 110, 115, 133,
    145, 153, 203–204, 215, 218, 233–238,
    272, 277–278, 292–293, 298
Ezra, The Book of, 18–20, 29, 38–39,
    50–51, 58, 86–87, 146, 154, 182, 193,
    206, 213, 215, 226, 283, 293–294

F

Faith, 88–89
The Fall, 89
Fear and Trembling, 23
Feast of Booths, 8
Feast of Weeks, 8
Feasts and Festivals, 89–92
First Revolt, 132
The Flood, 92, 215, 225, 229

G

Galatians, The Letter of Paul to the, 88,
    93–95, 104, 111, 119, 125, 133, 142,
    179, 186, 223–224, 234, 237, 254,
    265–267, 283, 290
Galilee, Sea of, 95, 100, 155, 198

Gamaliel II, 150
Genesis, The Book of, 1–2, 5, 10–11, 14,
    23, 27–28, 31, 33–34, 40, 44, 49–52,
    55, 64, 67, 69, 75–76, 80, 83, 86, 92,
    95–98, 102, 105–106, 110, 114–115,
    118–120, 122, 129, 143, 155, 159, 183,
    188, 204–205, 212, 215–216, 225, 227,
    234, 245, 248, 257, 259, 263, 265,
    275, 277, 284, 287–291
Gentile, 98–99, 179, 224
Geography of Palestine, 99–100
Gideon, 167, 174
Golden Calf, 100–101
Golden Rule, 101
Goliath, 54–55
Gomorrah, 154
Gratus, Valerius, 34
Graven Image, 102
Gutenberg Bible, 74
Gutenberg, Johannes, 74

H

Habakkuk, The Book of, 103–104
Hagar, 2, 104, 118, 245, 263
Haggai, The Book of, 104–105, 193, 204,
    235, 242, 298
Hallelujah, 105
Ham, 5
Haman, 76–77
Hanun, 11
Hazael, 11
Hebrew Bible, 38–39, 41, 52–53, 57, 60,
    75, 78, 80, 86, 88, 105–106, 111, 118–
    119, 125, 136–137, 144, 146, 151, 169,
    170, 176–178, 181–184, 194, 203, 212,
    218–219, 227, 232, 233, 251, 257–260,
    268, 270, 275, 278, 283, 288, 294
Hebrews, 6, 57, 104–106, 109, 128, 133,
    140, 142, 194, 210, 215, 235, 237, 248,
    259–260, 270, 278, 301
Herod, 2, 42, 106–107, 123, 130, 133,
    137, 162, 201, 203, 231–232, 253, 275,
    278–279
Herodian Dynasty, 106–109
Hezekiah, 6
Holocaust, 109
Holy Spirit, 30, 74, 110–111, 135, 197,
    198, 224, 225, 285–287
Home, Thomas Hartwell, 32
Homer, 260
Hope, 111–112
Hosea, The Book of, 27, 80, 90, 110–113,
    118, 122, 188, 217, 238, 258, 292
Human Person, 113–114
Hyrcanus, John, 163

I

Ignatius of Antioch, 32, 44
Iliad, 144
Immortality, 6–8

Irenaeus, 250–251
Iron Age, 11, 12, 120
Isaac, 2, 22, 75, 97, 115, 122, 155, 248,
    263
Isaiah, The Book of, 6, 10, 14–17, 22–23,
    28–29, 33, 57–58, 67–68, 75, 80, 90,
    97, 104–105, 113–118, 122, 127–128,
    132, 140, 147, 155, 159, 183, 188,
    203–204, 208, 211–212, 218–219, 233,
    237–238, 242, 248, 258–259, 263,
    275, 283, 288–301
Ishmael, 118, 263
Israel, History of, 1, 4, 6, 9–15, 20, 24,
    28, 33, 55, 61, 63, 70–74, 86, 89, 101,
    113, 114, 116–121, 128, 143, 146,
    155–161, 167–168, 174, 178, 200–204,
    209, 211, 218, 225, 233, 236–238,
    241, 243, 249, 256, 260–267, 280,
    283–289, 292, 300

J

Jacob, 2, 64, 75, 83, 97, 115, 118, 122,
    155, 183, 188, 193, 248, 265, 283
James, 22, 32, 71,122–125, 202, 218, 266
James, The Letter of, 123–125
Jephthah, 167
Jeremiah, The Book of, 9 10, 16, 19,
    21, 24, 29, 33, 68, 70, 84, 98, 100,
    105–106, 125–128, 132, 155, 159,
    176–177, 212, 217–218, 235–244, 248,
    283, 288, 292, 298, 301
Jeroboam II, 12, 112, 121, 153
Jerome, 20, 77, 297
Jerusalem, 1–3, 11, 16, 24, 26, 29–30, 33,
    35, 38, 40, 44, 47–49, 53, 64, 67–70,
    81, 84, 86–89, 93, 106, 113–118, 126–
    134, 137, 146, 149, 159, 162–165, 170,
    172, 176, 179, 189–190, 195, 198–204,
    207–208, 213–215, 218, 222–226, 232,
    235–238, 241–242, 247, 263 268,
    273, 277–280, 289, 299–301
Jesus, 2–8, 13–16, 21, 29–32, 36, 42, 44,
    51, 57–58, 64, 88, 101, 108–111, 114,
    123–124, 133, 135–143, 148–149, 152,
    162–163, 185–187, 194–195, 198, 219,
    224–225, 232, 245–246, 251, 259,
    270, 272, 285, 296
Jesus Christ, 30, 46, 72, 73, 78, 94,
    138–139, 188, 189, 190, 191, 192, 195,
    200, 201, 203, 222, 225, 226, 227,
    228, 229, 231, 234, 246, 249, 250,
    255, 256, 263, 272, 273, 281, 283,
    285, 286, 287, 290
Jew, 14, 19–22, 31, 35, 44, 46, 56, 63, 72,
    74–78, 87, 102, 106, 143, 162, 164,
    176, 214–215, 224, 232, 234, 236,
    245–247, 253, 256, 266, 278, 295
Jezebel, 143–144, 171, 244–245, 293
Job, Book of, 15, 30, 144–146, 207, 212,
    233, 263, 272–273
Joel, Book of, 15, 146, 218, 242
John, 147, 187, 202, 249–252

John the Baptist, 13, 29, 41–42, 64, 107–108, 135–136, 146–149, 189, 201

John, The Gospel According to, 13–15, 30, 33, 35–36, 43, 50, 64–65, 71, 75, 89, 110–111, 121, 136, 138, 140, 148–151, 165, 198, 210, 218–219, 231–232, 247, 251, 254, 264–266, 279, 286–287, 296

John, The Letters of, 151–153, 199, 213

Jonah, The Book of, 76, 104, 106, 153–154, 265

Jordan River, 11–12, 119, 136, 154–155, 159, 209–210

Joseph, 36, 53, 76, 97, 98, 123, 135, 198, 200, 217, 265, 294

Joseph (Husband of Mary), 155

Joseph (Son of Jacob), 155–156

Josephus, 34, 79, 95, 164, 202, 210, 232, 234, 260, 267, 278–280, 295

Joshua, The Book of, 2, 11, 24, 44, 78, 156–159, 194, 204, 207, 210, 231, 236–237, 265, 284

Josiah, 61, 208, 299

Judah, The Kingdom of, 6, 30, 63–64, 68, 84, 86, 89, 103, 112–113, 116, 119–121, 125–126, 143–146, 159–162, 170, 175, 179, 182, 215, 218, 236, 238, 240, 245, 257, 260, 262, 276, 283–284, 288

Judaisms of the First Century, 162–165

Judas Iscariot, 16, 165–166, 202, 252, 286

Jude, The Letter of, 14, 165–166, 210, 228

Judges, The Book of, 10, 14, 23, 27, 30, 60, 110, 166–169, 174, 204–205, 233, 236–237, 259–260, 265, 273, 275, 284, 290, 292

Judith, 20–21, 294

K

Kierkegaard, Søren, 23

Kingdom of God, 169–170

Kings, The Books of, 2, 11, 14–15, 23–24, 27–29, 36, 55–56, 62, 70–72, 80, 84, 90–91, 99, 101, 110, 116–119, 121, 126, 137, 143, 146, 153, 159, 160–161, 170–175, 179, 182–183, 203, 206–208, 211, 213, 218, 231, 235–239, 244, 258–268, 272, 277–278, 288, 291–293

Kingship, 173–175

Klimt, Gustav, 79

L

Laertius, Diogenes, 234

Lamentations of Jeremiah, 176–177, 218, 288

Langton, Stephen, 31

Law, 73, 76, 87, 94, 101, 104, 125, 163, 174, 177–179, 181, 190, 194, 208–210, 215, 222, 236, 247, 256, 273, 277, 283, 288, 291–292

Law and the Bible, 180–181

Lawrence, D. H., 252

Leah, 64, 183

Letter-Writing in Antiquity, 181–183

Levi, 183, 217, 235, 283–284

Leviathan, 30, 183

Leviticus, The Book of, 7, 10, 14–15, 57, 90, 106, 109, 178, 181–185, 188, 203, 205, 209, 235, 257, 259, 277, 291

Lord's Prayer, 137, 185–186, 246

Lord's Supper, 47, 140–142, 186–188

Love, 188–189

Luke, The Gospel According to, 3–4, 9, 14, 16, 21, 29–30, 35–36, 42–43, 50, 64–65, 71, 105, 108, 110, 121, 123, 135–142, 147–148, 155, 169–170, 179, 186–192, 198–199, 204, 213, 215, 219, 225, 231– 236, 249, 264–265, 279, 286–288, 296

M

Magi, 192

Malachi, 194

Malachi, The Book of, 192–194

Manasseh, 61

Manna, 194

Manual of Discipline, 59

Mark, The Gospel According to, 13, 16, 19, 29–32, 35, 43, 50–51, 57, 64, 70–71, 89, 108–109, 114, 123, 135–141, 147, 155, 165, 169–170, 179, 181, 186, 191, 194–197, 210, 231–234, 247, 249, 251, 265, 272, 287–288, 296

Mary, 36, 135, 155, 191, 245, 287, 291

Mary Magdalene, 197-198

Mary, Mother of Jesus, 78, 198–199

Masoretic Text (MT), 60

Matthew, The Gospel According to, 10, 13–16, 29–36, 42–44, 57, 64–65, 75, 80, 88–89, 101, 108, 110, 114, 123, 135–142, 146–147, 155, 169–170, 179–181, 185–187, 193, 198–202, 210, 219, 231–232, 234, 237, 247, 249, 251, 264–266, 272, 275, 283, 285–287, 296, 299

Menorah, 203

Messiah, 19, 74, 118, 139, 148, 162, 187, 191–192, 195–197, 200, 203–204, 237, 247, 287

Methuselah, 204

Micah, The Book of, 30, 105, 110, 113, 116, 204–205,, 238, 242, 291, 301

Miriam, 1, 205, 209, 292

Moab, 68, 100, 116, 120, 167, 205–206, 217, 256, 300

Monarchy, 173–175

Monotheism, 206–208, 292

Moses, 1–2, 11, 18, 23, 39–40, 61–63, 70, 78–84, 88, 105, 118–119, 153, 156, 159, 177–179, 183, 194, 204–205, 208–210, 215, 217, 235, 243, 246, 249, 258–266–267, 276, 280, 283, 292

Muhammad, 245–246

N

Naboth, 172

Nahum, The Book of, 211

Names of God in the Hebrew Bible, 212

Naomi, 256–257

Nathan, 55

Nazareth, 32, 36, 64, 135, 179, 198, 212–213, 234, 272, 289

Nebuchadrezzar, 12, 28–29, 52, 68, 103, 130, 191, 213, 231, 294

Necromancy, 7

Nehemiah, The Book of, 38–39, 91, 100, 146, 193, 206, 213–215, 226, 283, 292, 293–294

Nero, 42, 109, 223, 226, 250–253, 266

Noah, 5, 11, 23–24, 27, 52, 92, 109, 145, 215–216, 225, 227, 275

Numbers, The Book of, 10, 15, 24, 27, 29, 69, 80, 90–91, 109–110, 153, 159, 177–178, 184, 188, 193–194, 204–205, 208–212, 216–220, 236, 263, 266, 277, 284, 288, 291, 293

O

Obadiah, The Book of, 218

Octavian, 230

Odyssey, 22

Orphan, 218

Osiris, 70

P

Palestine, Geography of, 99–101

Paradise, 219

Paradise Lost, 144

Passover, 8–9, 30, 63, 65, 70, 79–81, 90, 131, 138, 142, 187, 217, 219–220, 225, 231

The Pastoral Letters, 32, 59, 220–222

Paul, 2–4, 8, 22, 30, 46, 48, 73–74, 88, 93, 104, 109, 114, 118, 125, 142, 166, 179, 186, 188, 190, 192, 219–224, 234, 237, 239, 250, 254–256, 263, 267, 272, 281–282, 285, 290, 296

Pauline letters, 189–190, 221

Paulus, Sergius, 4

Pentecost, 23, 224-225

Persia, 225–226

Peter, The Letters of, 4, 22, 24, 30, 32, 64, 142, 195, 202, 215, 224–229, 234, 259, 265–266, 286, 296

Pharaoh Akhnaton, 6

Philemon, The Letter of Paul to, 224, 229–230

Philip the Tetrarch, 108

Philippians, The Letter of Paul to the, 58, 59, 230–231, 234

Philistines, 168, 174, 231, 260–261, 262, 265

Phinehas, 5

Pilate, Pontius, 4, 30, 51, 131, 191, 231–232

Pliny the Younger, 226

Poetry, Biblical Hebrew, 232–233

Polycarp, 250

Poor, 233–234

Predestination, 234

Priests and High Priest, 234–236

Promised Land, 210, 236–237

Prophets, 237–239

Proverbs, The Book of, 15, 140, 146, 218, 233–234, 239–240, 244, 283

Psalms, The Book of, 2, 6, 10, 14, 20, 29, 32, 56, 129, 139, 183, 186, 188, 194, 220, 233, 235, 237, 240–243, 259, 268, 272, 300

Ptolemy, 78

Purity, Ritual, 243

Q

Queen and Queen Mother, 244–245

Queen of Sheba, 5

Quirinius, 42

Qur'an, 23, 233

The Qur'an and the Bible, 245–246

R

Rabbi, 163, 222, 246, 258

Rachel, 31, 97, 188, 248, 290, 292

Ramesses II, 70, 79

Ramesses III, 231

Raphael, 20

Rebekah, 75, 115, 122, 248

Red Sea, 69, 79, 80, 209, 248–249

Revelation, The Book of, 14–19, 29, 67, 102, 183, 237, 249–252, 258, 264, 286

Roman Empire, 7, 9, 17, 32, 50, 68, 81, 94, 108–109, 131–132, 138, 163, 180, 191, 195, 197, 201, 224, 226, 230, 232, 236, 249–254, 256, 275, 282

Romans, The Letter of Paul to the, 59, 71, 73–75, 88, 111, 114–115, 139–142, 147, 179, 186, 210, 222, 224, 227, 234, 237, 239, 245, 248, 250, 254–256, 259, 283, 296

Rosh Hashanah, 57, 90–91

Ruth, The Book of, 30, 76, 154, 157, 188, 212, 218, 256–257, 288–295

S

Sabbath, 163–164, 184, 215, 258, 274

Sacrifice, 258–259

Salome, 107, 245

Samson, 168, 259–260, 290

Samuel, The Books of, 7, 10–11, 24, 30–33, 54–57, 90, 104, 106, 110, 117, 120, 143, 159–160, 168–169, 174–175, 182, 188, 203, 205, 207, 212, 218, 231, 234–235, 238, 241, 244, 257, 260–265, 268, 277, 290–291, 300

Sarah, 50, 80, 104, 245, 248, 263, 287, 290

Sargon II, 26

Satan, 35, 136, 197, 249, 251, 263–264, 281

Saul, 7, 11, 27, 30, 37, 39, 55–56, 119–120, 159, 174, 221–222, 231, 244, 261–262, 264–265

Sennedjem, 102

Seth, 39

Shalmaneser II, 26

Shalmaneser III, 225

Shalmaneser V, 26

Shamshi-Adad I, 25

Shechem, 265

Sheshbazzar, 86–87

Simei, 261

Simon Peter, 13, 21, 48, 64, 93, 265–266

Sinai, 100, 128, 177, 184, 209, 225, 266–267, 283

Six Day War, 133

Sodom, 2, 97, 154

Sodom and Gomorrah, 267

Solomon, 7, 11, 20–21, 24, 40, 55, 66, 79, 91, 105, 119–121, 129, 160, 171–172, 175, 207–208, 226, 239–240, 244–245, 267–268, 277–279, 291

Son of God, 270–271

Son of Man, 271–272

Song of Solomon, 6, 8–9, 260, 268–270, 294–295

Sons of God, 272–273

Stephanus, Robert, 31

Stephen, 3–4, 273

Suleiman I, 133

Synagoguc, 46, 247, 273–275

Syria, 9, 22–26, 41, 69, 71 72, 93, 107, 120, 130, 161, 211, 226, 232, 252, 275, 287, 290

T

Tabernacle, 225, 276–277

Talmud, 177, 202, 247

Temple, 15–16, 24, 38, 41, 48, 57, 61, 65, 69–70, 79, 86, 89, 91, 104–109, 114, 117–118, 126, 129–134, 138, 146–147, 162–165, 170, 175, 179, 193–198, 201–203, 207–208, 214–215, 218, 220, 225–226, 235, 242, 247, 259, 267–268, 273, 277–280, 289, 292–293, 298–301

Ten Commandments, 24, 61, 63, 82, 84, 178, 266, 280–283

Thessalonians, The Letters of Paul to the, 16, 114, 140, 179, 225, 272, 281–283

Tiglath-pileser I, 25

Tiglath-pileser III, 26, 121

Tiglathpileser III, 12

Timothy, 47, 78, 220–222, 296

Titus, 48–49

Tomb of Absalom, 32

Torah, 87, 90, 121, 157, 165, 174, 177, 179, 184, 188, 210, 216, 225, 246, 247, 273–274, 283, 292

Tribes of Israel, 283–285

Trinity, 140, 189, 246, 285–286

The Twelve, 286

U

Ussher, James, 41

V

Virgin Birth of Christ, 199, 287

Virgin Mary, 246

W

Wailing Wall, 132

Widows, 288

Women

activities outside the home, 291

ancient Near East and Israel, 290

and early Christianity, 295–297

and female symbolism, 292

and Second Temple Period, 293

classical sources and, 295

daily lives of, 293–294

in postexilic biblical literature, 294

in the Apocrypha, 294

legal status and, 291

negative views of, 292–293

Pseudepigrapha and, 294–295

religious practice and experience, 291–292

social patterns and female power, 291

social reality and narrative patterns, 293

X

Xenophon, 234

Xerxes, 9, 75, 225

Y

Yahweh, 34, 55–56, 68, 71, 79–86, 100–102, 105, 112–113, 125, 143–144, 156–157, 168, 172, 184, 205–206, 211–212, 226, 237–242, 257–260, 263–265, 277, 288, 292–293, 298–301

Yom Kippur, 56–57, 91

Z

Zadok, 235

Zebedee, 95

Zechariah, The Book of, 10, 17, 91, 105, 154–155, 176, 203, 218, 242, 263, 277, 298–299

Zephaniah, The Book of, 6, 57, 129, 188, 299–300

Zerubbabel, 87, 104, 298

Zion, 6, 49, 105, 116, 203, 236–237, 241, 278, 298–301

THE NEW OXFORD
BIBLE MAPS

Map 1   The Land of Canaan: Abraham to Moses

Map 2   The Exodus

Map 3   Isreal in Canaan: Joshua to Samuel and Saul

Map 4   The United Monarchy

Map 5   The Kingdoms of Isreal and Judah

Map 6   The Near East in the time of the Assyrian Empire

Map 7   The Near East in the time of the Persian Empire

Map 8   Central Palestine in Old Testament times

Map 9   Jerusalem in Old and New Testament times

Map 10   Palestine in Persian-Hellenistic times

Map 11   The Near East in the Hellenistic Period:
         Ptolomaic & Seleucid Empires

Map 12   Palestine under the Herods

Map 13   North and Centrral Palestine at the time of the
         Ministry of Christ

Map 14   The background of the New Testament:
         Rome and the East (including Paul's Journeys)

Index to Maps

MAP 1

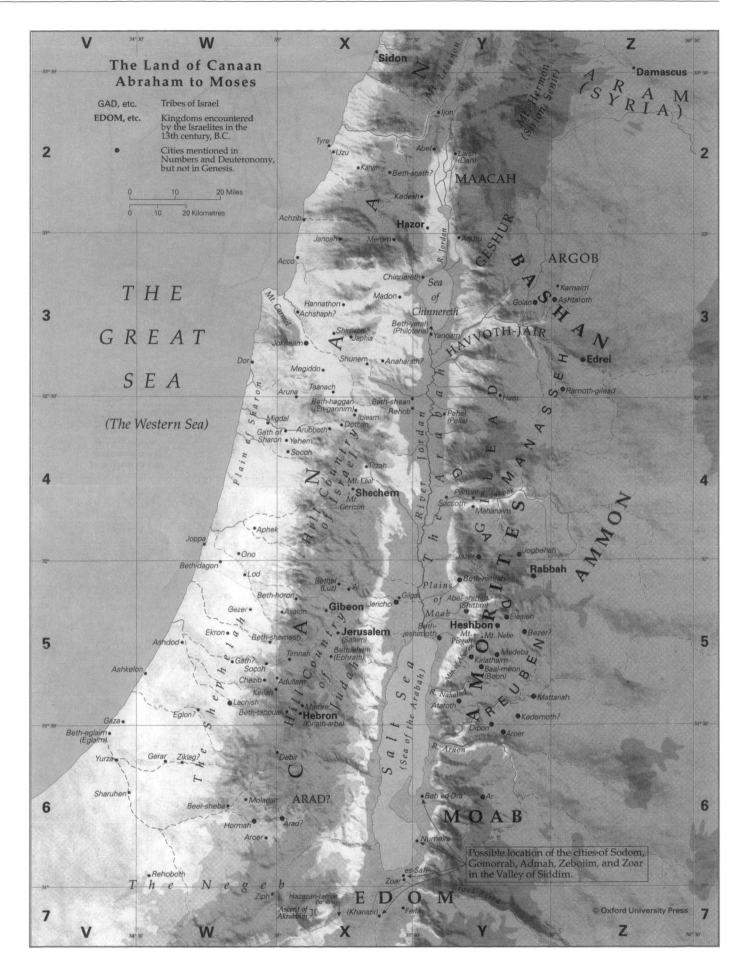

The Land of Canaan
Abraham to Moses

GAD, etc.   Tribes of Israel

EDOM, etc.   Kingdoms encountered
             by the Israelites in the
             13th century, B.C.

•   Cities mentioned in
             Numbers and Deuteronomy,
             but not in Genesis.

0   10   20 Miles

0   10   20 Kilometres

THE

GREAT

SEA

(The Western Sea)

Possible location of the cities of Sodom, Gomorrah, Admah, Zeboiim, and Zoar in the Valley of Siddim.

© Oxford University Press

315

MAP 2

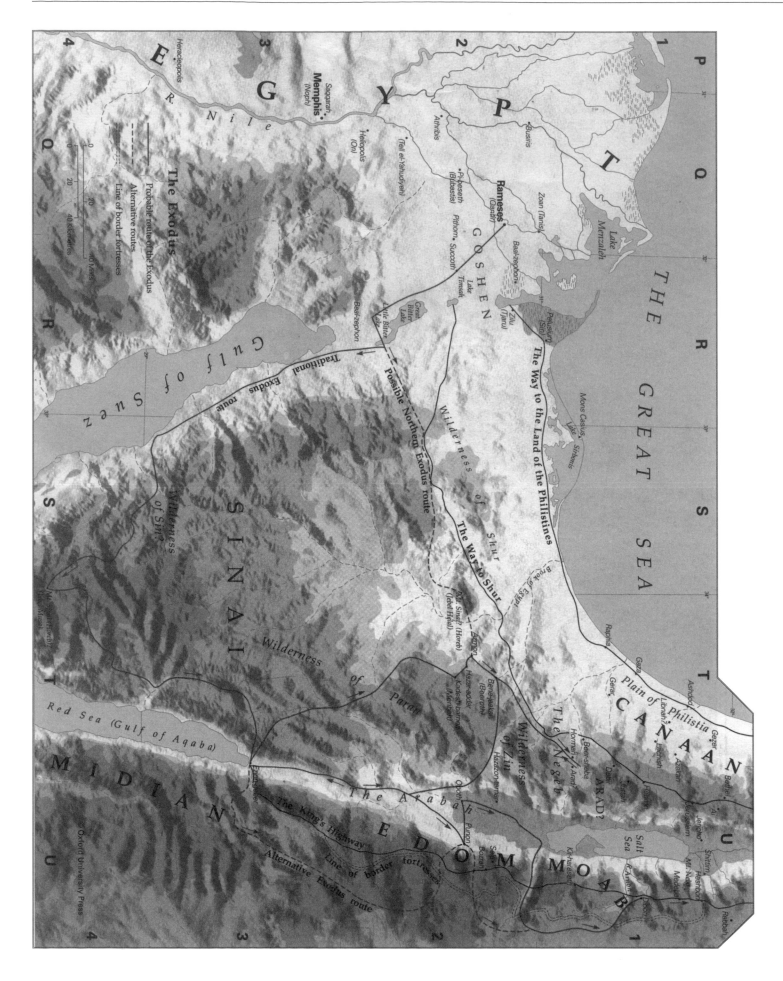

The Exodus

Probable route of the Exodus
Alternative routes
Line of border fortresses

MAP 3

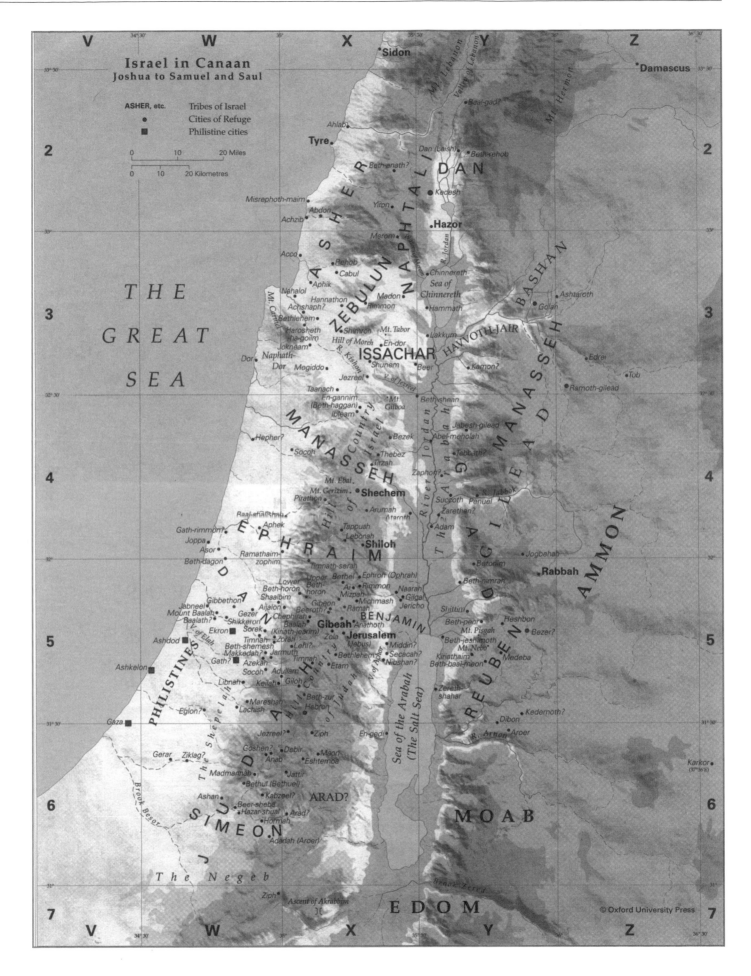

Israel in Canaan
Joshua to Samuel and Saul

ASHER, etc.　Tribes of Israel
● Cities of Refuge
■ Philistine cities

0　　10　　20 Miles

0　　10　　20 Kilometres

THE

GREAT

SEA

Sidon

• Damascus

Baal-gad?

Ahlab?

Tyre

Beth-anath?　Dan (Laish)　• Beth-rehob

Mt. Hermon

Misrephoth-maim　Yiron　• Kedesh

DAN

Achzib　Abdon

Merom

Hazor

Acco

Rehob

Cabul

Aphik　Chinnereth

Sea of

Chinnereth　Ashtaroth

Nahalol　Hannathon　Madon

Hammath

BASHAN

Achshaph?　Rimmon　• Golan

Bethlehem

Shimron　Mt. Tabor

Harosheth-　Hill of Moreh　En-dor

ha-goiim

Jokneam　Beer

Edrei

ISSACHAR

Dor　Naphath-　Shunem

Dor　Megiddo　Jezreel

V. of Jezreel

Taanach

Kamon?

Ramoth-gilead

Tob

Beth-shean

En-gannim

(Beth-haggan)

Ibleam

Mt.

Gilboa

Jabesh-gilead

Abel-meholah

Hepher?

Bezek

Socoh

Thebez

Zabbath?

Tirzah

MANASSEH

Zaphon?

Mt. Ebal

Adam

Mt. Gerizim　**Shechem**

Pirathon

Succoth　Penuel

Zarethan?

GILEAD

Baal-shalishah

Arumah

Aphek　Tappuah　Ataroth

Gath-rimmon?

Lebonah

Joppa

Shiloh

Asor

Ramathaim-

Beth-dagon　zophim

Jogbehah

EPHRAIM

Timnath-serah

Batonim

Upper　Bethel

Lower　Beth-

Beth-horon　horon

Ephron (Ophrah)

Rabbah

Beth-nimrah

Gibbethon

Shaalbim

Ai　Rimmon

Jabneel

Aijalon　Gibeon　Mizpah　Michmash

Naarah

Mount Baalah

Gezer

Beeroth?　Ramah　Gilgal

Jericho

AMMON

Shikkeron

Chephirah　Jericho

Baalath　(Kiriath-jearim)

Shittim

Ekron

Sorek

Gibeah

Anathoth

Beth-peor

Heshbon

Timnah

Zorah

Jerusalem

Mt. Pisgah

Ashdod

Beth-shemesh　Lehi?　(Jebus)　Middin?

Beth-jeshimoth

Bezer?

Makkedah?　Jarmuth

Bethlehem

Secacah?

Mt. Nebo

Azekah

Timnah

Nibshan?

Kiriathaim

Gath?

Etam

V. of Achor

Beth-baal-meon

Medeba

Socoh　Adullam

Libnah　Keilah　Giloh

Zereth-

Mareshah　Beth-zur

shahar

Eglon?　Lachish　Hebron

Dibon

Kedemoth?

Gaza

Jezreel

Ziph

En-gedi

Aroer

Goshen?　Debir

Gerar　Ziklag?　Anab　Maon

Eshtemoa

Madmannah　Jattir

Karkor

(37°36'E)

Bethul (Bethuel)

Ashan

Kabzeel?　**ARAD?**

Beer-sheba

Hazar-shual　Arad?

Hormah

SIMEON

MOAB

Adadah (Aroer)

The Negeb

Ziph

Ascent of Akrabbim

E D O M

© Oxford University Press

THE

GREAT

SEA

Sea of the Arabah

(The Salt Sea)

PHILISTINES

Ashkelon

Brook Besor

The Shephelah

ZEBULUN

NAPHTALI

HAVVOTH-JAIR

Hill of the Country Israel

MANASSEH

REUBEN

BENJAMIN

D A N

A S H E R

MAP 4

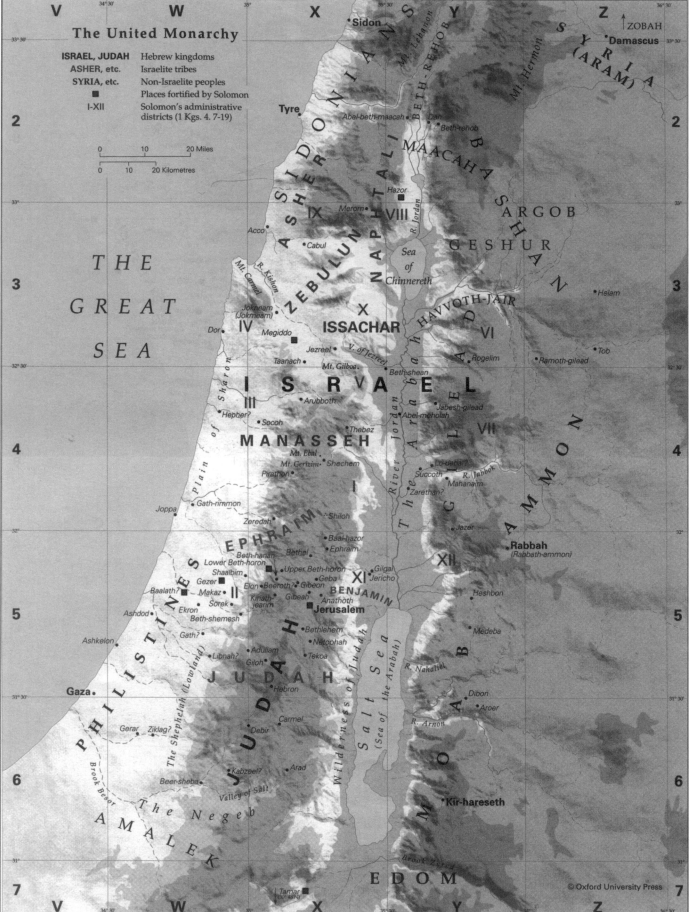

The United Monarchy

ISRAEL, JUDAH   Hebrew kingdoms
ASHER, etc.   Israelite tribes
SYRIA, etc.   Non-Israelite peoples
■   Places fortified by Solomon
I–XII   Solomon's administrative
        districts (1 Kgs. 4. 7-19)

0   10   20 Miles
0   10   20 Kilometres

THE

GREAT

SEA

Sidon

Tyre

SIDONIANS

ASHER

ZEBULUN

NAPHTALI

Abel-beth-maacah

BETH-REHOB

Dan

Beth-rehob

MAACAH

SYRIA
(ARAM)

ZOBAH

Damascus

Mt. Lebanon

Mt. Hermon

Hazor

Merom

Acco

Cabul

IX

VIII

ARGOB

GESHUR

Sea
of
Chinnereth

Helam

X

HAVVOTH-JAIR

Jokneam
(Jokmeam)

Mt. Carmel

R. Kishon

Dor

IV

Megiddo

ISSACHAR

VI

Tob

Jezreel

Taanach

Mt. Gilboa

V. of Jezreel

Beth-shean

Rogelim

Ramoth-gilead

GILEAD

ISRAEL

III

Hepher?

Socoh

Arubboth

Thebez

Abel-meholah

Jabesh-gilead

VII

AMMON

MANASSEH

Mt. Ebal

Mt. Gerizim

Shechem

Lo-debar?

Pirathon

I

Succoth

Mahanaim

R. Jabbok

Zarethan?

Joppa

Gath-rimmon

Zeredah

Shiloh

Jazer

Baal-hazor

Bethel

Ephraim

EPHRAIM

Beth-hanan

Lower Beth-horon

Upper Beth-horon

Geba

Rabbah
(Rabbath-ammon)

XII

Shaalbim

Gezer

Elon

Beeroth?

Gibeon

Gilgal

Jericho

XI

Makaz

II

Kiriath-
jearim

Gibeah

BENJAMIN

Anathoth

Baalath?

Heshbon

Ekron

Sorek

Jerusalem

Ashdod

Beth-shemesh

Bethlehem

Medeba

Ashkelon

Gath?

Netophah

MOAB

Libnah?

Adullam

Tekoa

Giloh

Gaza

PHILISTINES

JUDAH

Hebron

R. Nahaliel

Dibon

Aroer

Carmel

Gerar

Ziklag?

Debir

R. Arnon

The Shephelah (Lowland)

Wilderness of Judah

Salt Sea
(Sea of the Arabah)

Kabzeel?

Arad

Kir-hareseth

Beer-sheba

Valley of Salt

Brook Besor

The Negeb

A M A L E K

Brook Zered

EDOM

Tamar
(??)

River Jordan

The Arabah

Plain of Sharon

© Oxford University Press

MAP 5

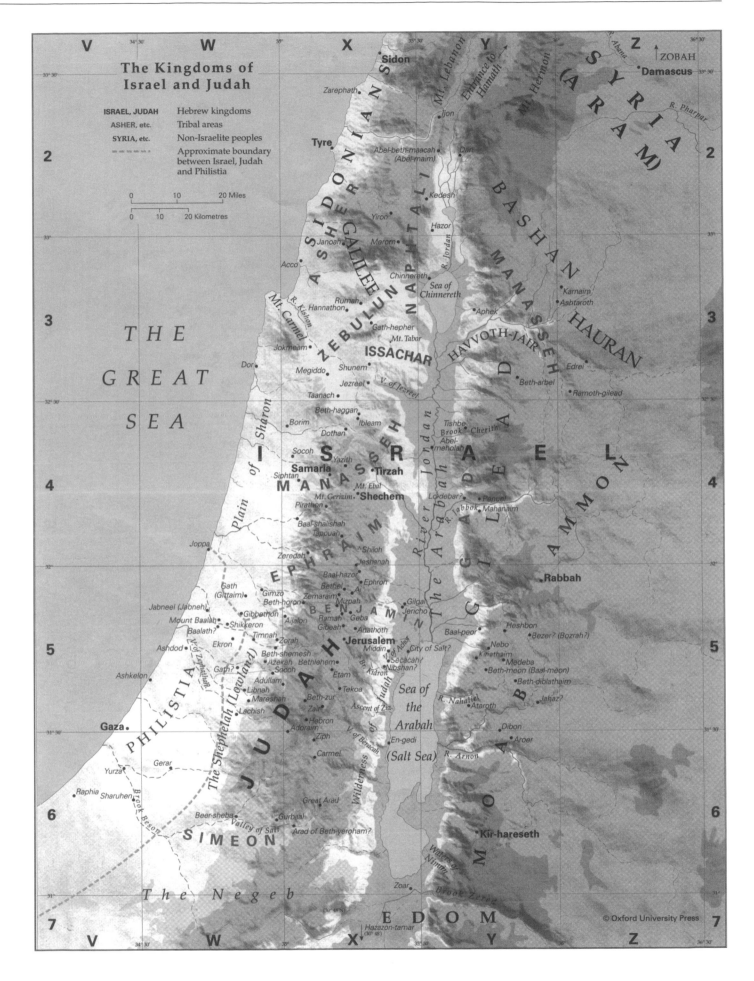

The Kingdoms of Israel and Judah

ISRAEL, JUDAH   Hebrew kingdoms
ASHER, etc.   Tribal areas
SYRIA, etc.   Non-Israelite peoples
   Approximate boundary between Israel, Judah and Philistia

0   10   20 Miles
0   10   20 Kilometres

© Oxford University Press

319

MAP 6

The Near East
in the time of the
Assyrian Empire

Approximate extent of Assyrian domination
in the latter part of the 8th. century.
(Later under Esarhaddon (681-669), Assyria conquered Egypt)

© Oxford University Press

MAP 7

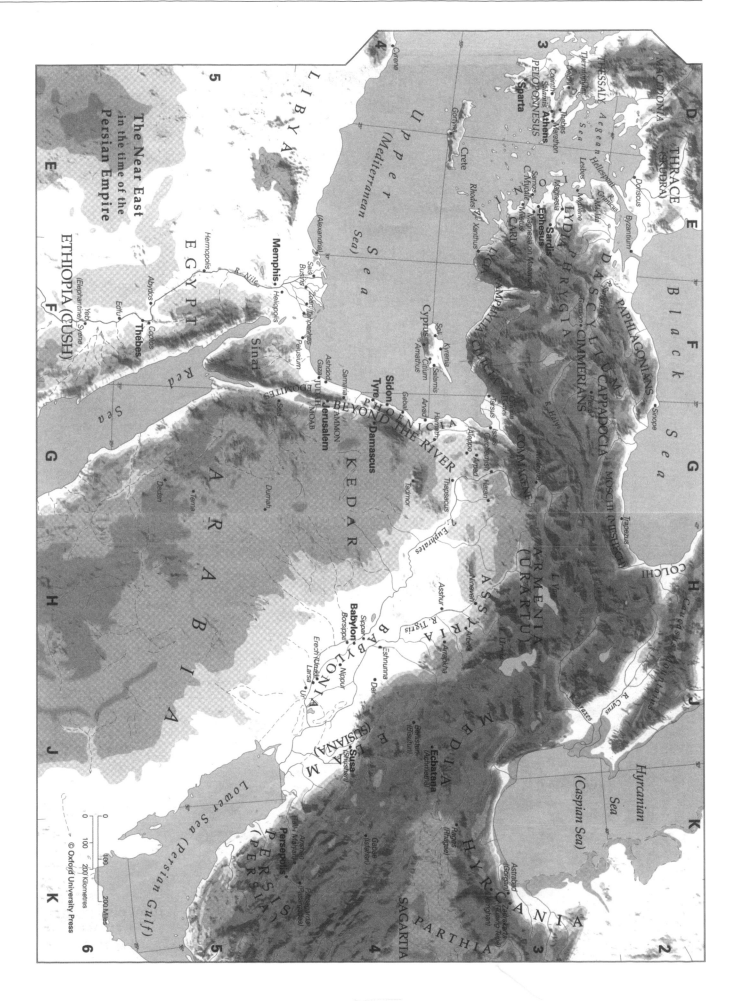

The Near East
in the time of the
Persian Empire

© Oxford University Press

MAP 8

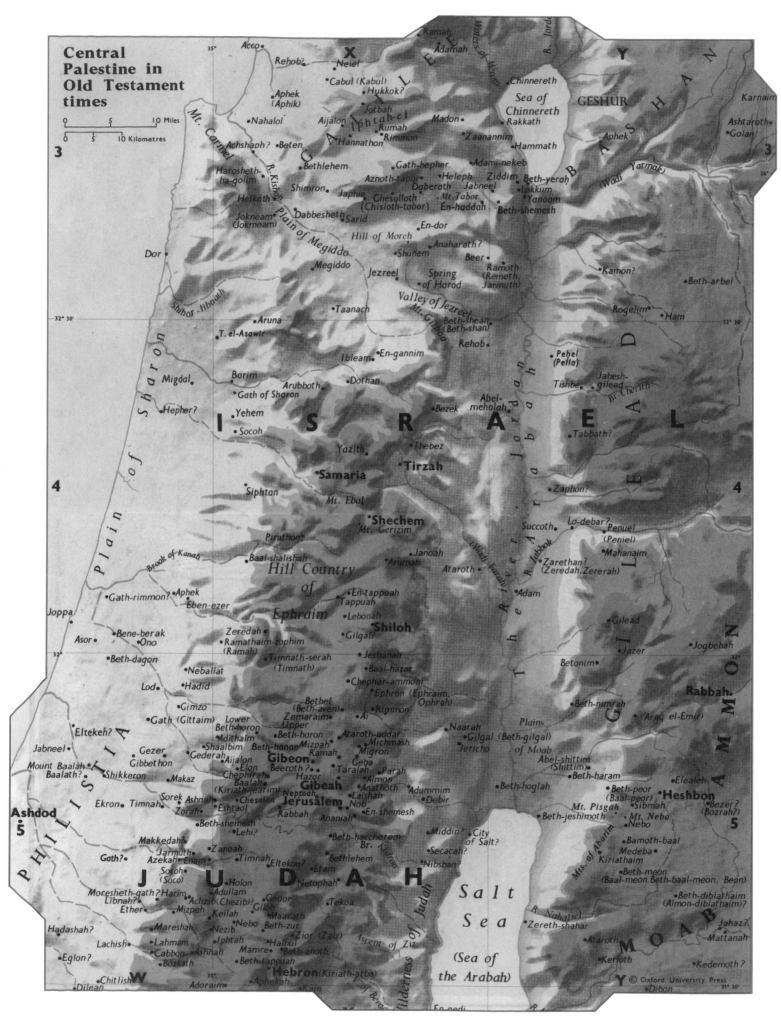

Central Palestine in Old Testament times

0   5   10 Miles
0   5   10 Kilometres

MAP 9

Jerusalem in Old Testament times

Medieval and Turkish Jerusalem

Approximate lines of City Walls:
of original Zion (2 Sam 5:7)
extended under the Kings
(by Maccabees, 2nd Cent. B.C.?)
extended after the Exile
Eastern wall of Nehemiah's city
Modern roads

Original Rock Contours are shown.

Hinnom Valley

(?Topheth)

En-rogel Spring

Pre-exilic Judean tombs

SILOAM

Kidron Valley

Mount of Olives

UPPER CITY

?MISHNA (SECOND QUARTER)

Tombs

Central (Cheesemakers) Valley

Wall of Zion

CITY OF DAVID (LOWER CITY)

OPHEL

Old Pool

Lower Pool

Gate

Conduit

Old Conduit

Gihon Spring

Manasseh's Wall

Solomon's Wall

Wall Herod (Antonia)

Solomon's Wall

Tower of Hananel

TEMPLE
□ ALTAR

? PALACE

Post-exilic Jewish tombs

© Oxford University Press

0   300 Yards
0   300 Metres

The lines of the southern walls of the city after the Exile are uncertain.

Jerusalem in New Testament times

Medieval and Turkish Jerusalem

Approximate lines of City Walls:
under Herod the Great
added by Agrippa I
Wall of Aelia
Modern roads

Original Rock Contours are shown.

OUTWORK OF UNCERTAIN ORIGIN

Tomb of Helena Princess of Adiabene

Hinnom Valley

Essene Gate G

Bethlehem

Family Tomb of Herod

Pool

Aqueduct

Tyropoeon Valley

Herodian Street

Pool of Siloam

Solomon's Pool

Conduit

Gihon Spring

Kidron Valley

TEMPLE

Court of Gentiles

Emmaus

Psephinus

ROYAL PALACE

Praetorium

Golgotha ?

BEZETHA

ANTONIA TOWER

Pool of Bethzatha (Bethesda)

Damascus Gate

ROYAL CAVERNS

Pinnacle of Temple

Ophla

Portico

Solomon's Portico

Tombs

Fuller's Tower

Gethsemane

Pool

B = Bridge
C. of I. = Court of Israel
C. of P. = Court of Priests
C. of W. = Court of Women
G = Gate
Gc = Gate of Coponius = Barclay's
Gd = Double (Huldah) Gate

© Oxford University

0   300 Yards
0   300 Metres

MAP 10

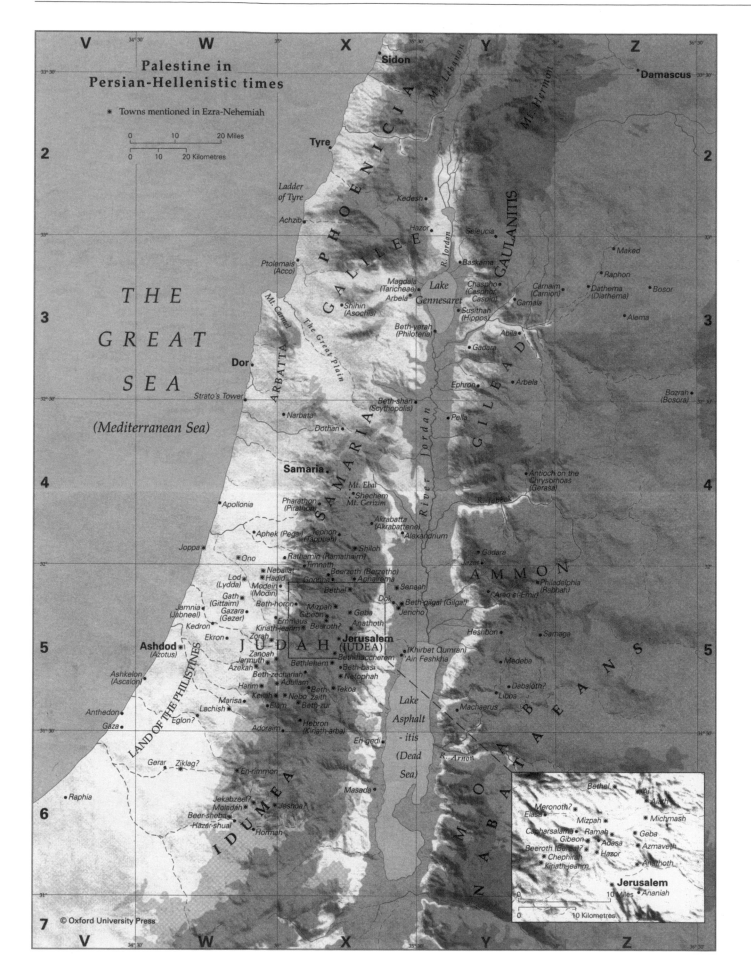

Palestine in Persian-Hellenistic times

• Towns mentioned in Ezra-Nehemiah

0   10   20 Miles
0   10   20 Kilometres

Sidon

Damascus

PHOENICIA

Tyre

Ladder
of Tyre

Achzib

Kedesh

Mt. Lebanon

Mt. Hermon

Hazor

Seleucia

GAULANITIS

Maked

Ptolemais
(Acco)

Magdala
(Taricheae)
Arbela

Lake
Gennesaret

Shihin
(Asochis)

Beth-yerah
(Philoteria)

Baskama

Chaspho
(Casphor)
Casphon

Carnaim
(Carnion)

Raphon

Dathema
(Diathema)

Bosor

Susithan
(Hippos)

Gamala

Alema

Mt. Carmel

GALILEE

Abila

Gadara

Dor

THE
GREAT
SEA

ARBATTA

The Great Plain

Strato's Tower

Beth-shan
(Scythopolis)

Ephron

Arbela

River Jordan

Bozrah
(Bosora)

(Mediterranean Sea)

Narbata

Dothan

Pella

GILEAD

Samaria.

SAMARIA

Mt. Ebal
Shechem
Mt. Gerizim

Antioch on the
Chrysorhoas
(Gerasa)

R. Jabbok

Apollonia

Pharathon
(Pirathon)

Akrabatta
(Akrabattene)

Alexandrium

Aphek (Pegai)

Tephon
(Tappuah)

Shiloh

Gadara

AMMON

Joppa

Ono

Rathamin (Ramathaim)

Jazer

Philadelphia
(Rabbah)

Timnath

Neballat

Beezeth (Berzetho)

Aphairema

('Araq el-Emir)

Lod
(Lydda)

Hadid

Gophna

Sanaah

Modein
(Modin)

Bethel

Dok

Beth-gilgal (Gilgal)

Gath
(Gittaim)

Beth-horon

Mizpah

Gibeon

Gibeon

Gibeon

Jericho

Jamnia
(Jabneel)

Gazara
(Gezer)

Emmaus

Beeroth?

Gebe

Anathoth

Heshbon

Samaga

Kedron

Kiriath-jearim

Jerusalem
(JUDEA)

(Khirbet Qumran)

Ekron

Zorah

Zanoah

Bethhaccherem

'Ain Feshkha

Medeba

Ashdod
(Azotus)

JUDAH

Bethlehem

Beth-basi

Jarmuth

Azekah

Beth-zechariah

Adullam

Beth-
zaith

Netophah

Dabaloth?

Ashkelon
(Ascalon)

Harim

Keilah

Nebo

Tekoa

Libba

Machaerus

Marisa

Elam

Beth-zur

Anthedon

Lachish

Eglon?

Adoraim

Hebron
(Kiriath-arba)

En-gedi

Lake
Asphalt
- itis
(Dead
Sea)

R. Arnon

Gaza

LAND OF THE PHILISTINES

Gerar

Ziklag?

En-rimmon

Masada

NABATAEANS

Raphia

Jekabzeel?

Moladah

Jeshua?

Beer-sheba

Hazar-shual

Hormah

IDUMEA

MOAB

Jerusalem inset

Bethel

Meronoth?

Elasa

Mizpah

Michmash

Capharsalama

Ramah

Gibeon

Geba

Beeroth (Beroth?)

Adasa

Azmaveth

Chephirah

Hazor

Kiriath-jearim

Anathoth

Jerusalem

Ananiah

0   10 Miles
0   10 Kilometres

© Oxford University Press

MAP 11

**The Near East
in the
Hellenistic Period**
Ptolemaic & Seleucid Empires

0   100   200 Kilometres

0   100   200 Miles

© Oxford University Press

D E

THRACE

MACEDONIA

AETOLIA

THESSALY

ACHAEA

Athens

Corinth   Thebes

Pella

Thessalonica

Philippi

Olynthus

Sesta

Byzantium

Dascylium

Nicaea   Calchedon

Heraclea

Sinope

Black Sea

PAPHLAGONIA

PONTUS

Ancyra

Pteria

Trapezus

GALATIA

PHRYGIA

CAPPADOCIA

COMMAGENE

ARMENIA

Carchemish

Aegean Sea

Lysimachia

Ilium (Troy)

R. Granicus

R. Hermus

Mytilene

Pergamum

Cyme

Sardis

IONIA

Ephesus

Samos

R. Maeander

Miletus   Didyma

CARIA   Magnesia

LYCIA   Priene

Halicarnassus

Xanthus

Phaselis

Patara

LYCIA

PISIDIA

CILICIA

Sagalassus

Tarsus

Issus

Alexandria

Nisibis

R. Euphrates

Dura-Europus

Thapsacus

Palmyra

Cydonia

Gortyna

Knossos

Crete

Delos

Rhodes

Mediterranean Sea

Cyprus

Paphos

Citium   Salamis

Marathus

Laodicea

Tripolis

Byblus

Berytus

Sidon   Coele

Tyre   Syria

Antioch

Seleucia

Alexandria

Aleppo

Emesa

Antioch (Gerasa)

Damascus

Philadelphia

Jerusalem

Ptolemais

Dora

Samaria

Azotus

Gaza

Raphia

Petra

Pelusium

Sais

Bubastis

Heliopolis

Arsinoe

Memphis

Crocodilopolis

Alexandria

EGYPT

PTOLE-MAIC

EMPIRE

CYRENAICA

Cyrene

Paraetonium

Oasis of
Ammon
(Siwa)

Hermopolis

Lycopolis

Ptolemais

Nag Hammadi

R. Nile

Thebes

Syene

Red Sea

NABATAEANS

A R A B I A

Persian Gulf

SYRIA

SELEUCID

EMPIRE

MESOPOTAMIA

Babylon

BABYLONIA

Seleucia

Ctesiphon

Nippur

Uruk

R. Tigris

Gaugamela

Arbela

Ecbatana

MEDIA

SUSIANA

Susa

PERSIS

Persepolis

Pasargadae

PARTHIA

HYRCANIA

Hyrcanian Sea

Rhagae (Rhagae)

Gabae

Astrabad
(Gorgan)

Zadracarta

Hecatompylos

R. Araxes

R. Cyrus

L. Van

F G H J K L

3 4 5 6 2

MAP 12

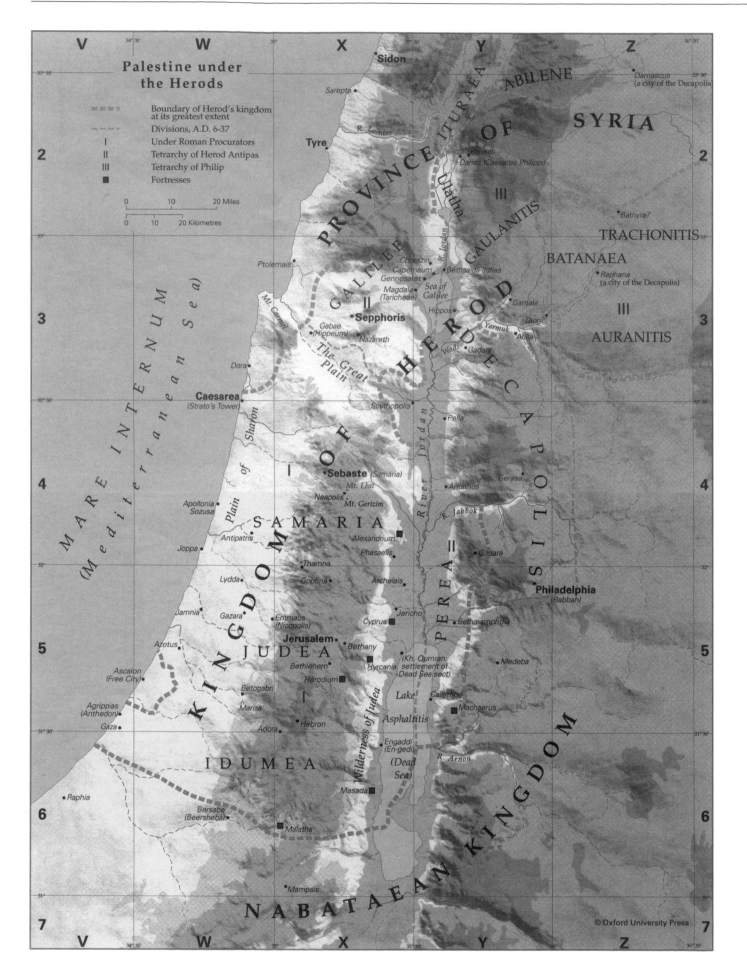

Palestine under the Herods

Boundary of Herod's kingdom at its greatest extent

Divisions, A.D. 6-37

I   Under Roman Procurators

II   Tetrarchy of Herod Antipas

III   Tetrarchy of Philip

■   Fortresses

0   10   20 Miles

0   10   20 Kilometres

Sidon

Sarepta

Tyre

R. Leontes

Ptolemais

PROVINCE

ITURAEA

ABILENE

Damascus
(a city of the Decapolis)

OF

SYRIA

Ulatha

Panias
Danos (Caesarea Philippi)

Bathyra?

TRACHONITIS

GALILEE

Chorazin
Capernaum
Gennesaret
Magdala
(Taricheae)
Sea of
Galilee

Bethsaida-Julias

Hippos

GAULANITIS

Gamala

Dion

BATANAEA

Raphana
(a city of the Decapolis)

III

Sepphoris

Gabae
(Hippeum)

Nazareth

Yarmuk

Abila

III

AURANITIS

The Great Plain

Wadi

Gadara

Mt. Carmel

Dora

Caesarea
(Strato's Tower)

Scythopolis

River Jordan

Pella

HEROD

D E C A P O L I S

Sharon

Plain of

Apollonia
Sozusa

Joppa

Antipatris

SAMARIA

Sebaste (Samaria)

Mt. Ebal

Neapolis
Mt. Gerizim

Amathus

Gerasa

OF

R. Jabbok

MARE INTERNUM

(Mediterranean Sea)

I

Alexandrium ■

Phasaelis

Gadara

KINGDOM

Thamna

Gophna

Archelais

II

PEREA

Lydda

Jamnia

Gazara

Emmaus
(Nicopolis)

Cyprus ■

Jericho

Betharamphtha

Philadelphia
(Rabbah)

Azotus

Jerusalem

Bethany

JUDEA

Bethlehem

Ascalon
(Free City)

Herodium ■

Hyrcania ■

(Kh. Qumran:
settlement of
Dead Sea sect)

Medeba

Agrippias
(Anthedon)

Betogabri

Marisa

I

Callirrhoe

Machaerus ■

Gaza

Adora

Hebron

Lake

Asphaltitis

IDUMEA

Engaddi
(En-gedi)

R. Arnon

*(Dead
Sea)*

Raphia

Masada ■

KINGDOM

Bersabe
(Beersheba)

Malatha

Wilderness of Judea

Mampsis

N A B A T A E A N   *K I N G D O M*

© Oxford University Press

326

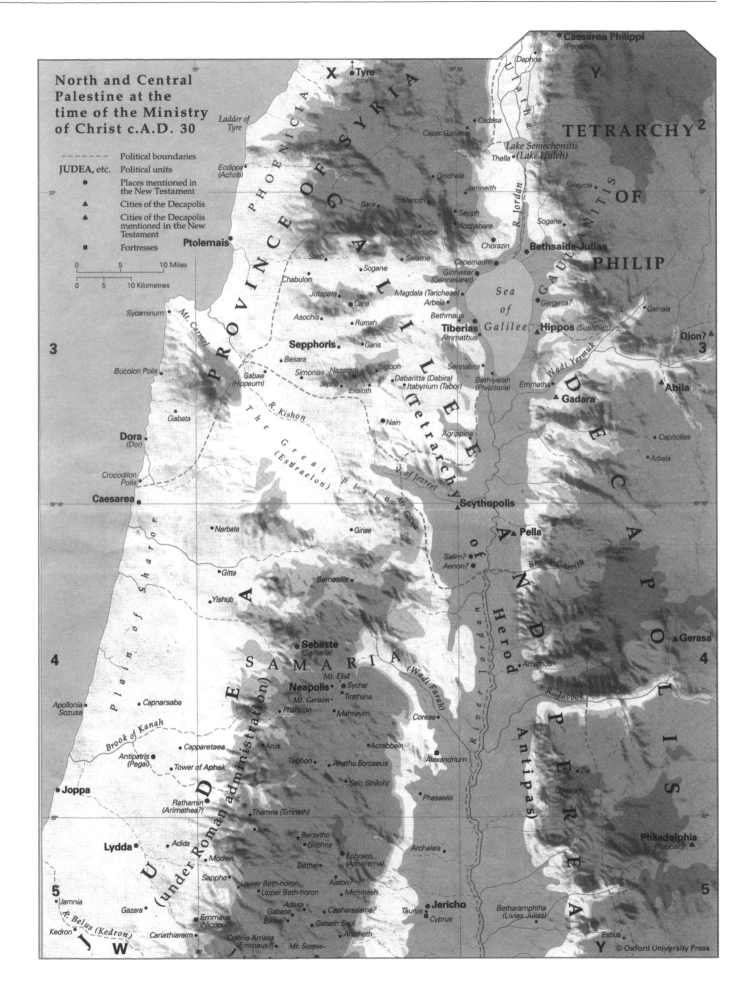

MAP 13

North and Central
Palestine at the
time of the Ministry
of Christ c.A.D. 30

— — — Political boundaries
JUDEA, etc. Political units
• Places mentioned in
the New Testament
▲ Cities of the Decapolis
▲ Cities of the Decapolis
mentioned in the New
Testament
■ Fortresses

0   5   10 Miles
0   5   10 Kilometres

PROVINCE OF SYRIA

PHOENICIA

PROVINCE OF GALILEE (Tetrarchy of Herod Antipas)

Tyre
Ladder of Tyre
Ecdippa (Achzib)
Ptolemais
Sycaminum
Mt. Carmel
Bucolon Polis
Gabata
Dora (Dor)
Crocodilon Polis
Caesarea

Cadasa
Capar Ganaea
Gischala
Baca
Meroth
Bersabe
Saab
Chabulon
Jotapata
Cana
Asochis
Rumah
Sepphoris
Besara
Simonias
Gabae (Hippeum)
Japha
Exaloth
R. Kishon
The Great Plain (Esdraelon)

Lake Semechonitis (Lake Huleh)
Thella
Jamneith
Sepph
Aochabare
Chorazin
Capernaum
Ginnesar (Gennesaret)
Magdala (Tarichaeae)
Arbela
Bethmaus
Tiberias
Ammathus
Garis
Nazareth
Sigoph
Dabaritta (Dabira)
Itabyrium (Tabor)
Nain
Agrippina

Selame
Sogane

Caesarea Philippi (Paneas)
Daphne
TETRARCHY²
Seleucia
Sogane
Bethsaida-Julias
PHILIP
Sea of Galilee
Gergesa?
Gamala
Hippos (Susithah)
Bethyerah (Philoteria)
Emmatha
Gadara
Wadi Yarmuk
Dion?
Abila
Capitolias
Arbela

DECAPOLIS

Narbata
Ginae
Scythopolis
Pella
Salim?
Aenon?
Brook Cherith
River Jordan
Amathus
Gerasa

SAMARIA
Gitta
Bemeselis
Yishub
Sebaste (Samaria)
Mt. Ebal
Neapolis
Mt. Gerizim
Sychar
Tirathana
Pharaton
Mahnayim
Coreae
(Wadi Farah)

JUDEA (under Roman administration)
Apollonia Sozusa
Capnarsaba
Brook of Kanah
Antipatris (Pegai)
Capparetaea
Tower of Aphek
Arus
Tephon
Anathu Borcaeus
Acrabbein
Selo (Shiloh)
Alexandrium
Phasaelis
Joppa
Rathamin (Arimathea?)
Thamna (Timnath)
Ilion
Berzetho
Gophna
Ephraim (Aphairema)
Archelais
Lydda
Adida
Modein
Bethel
Sappho
Lower Beth-horon
Upper Beth-horon
Aialon?
Michmash
Jamnia
Gazara
Adasa
Gabeon
Beroa?
Capharsalama?
Gabath Saul
Taurus
Jericho
Cyprus
Emmaus (Nicopolis)
Cariathiarim
Kedron
R. Belus (Kedron)
Colonia Amasa (Emmaus?)
Mt. Scopus
Anathoth
Betharamphtha (Livias Julias)
Zia
Philadelphia (Rabbah)
Esbus
PEREA
Herod Antipas

© Oxford University Press